William Cunningham Glen

The general consolidated and other orders of the Poor Law Commissioners and the Poor Law Board

William Cunningham Glen

The general consolidated and other orders of the Poor Law Commissioners and the Poor Law Board

ISBN/EAN: 9783742869234

Manufactured in Europe, USA, Canada, Australia, Japa

Cover: Foto ©Suzi / pixelio.de

Manufactured and distributed by brebook publishing software (www.brebook.com)

William Cunningham Glen

The general consolidated and other orders of the Poor Law Commissioners and the Poor Law Board

THE GENERAL CONSOLIDATED

AND OTHER

ORDERS

OF

The Poor Law Commissioners

AND

The Poor Law Board;

WITH EXPLANATORY NOTES ELUCIDATING THE ORDERS, TABLES OF STATUTES, CASES, AND INDEX TO THE ORDERS AND NOTES.

BY

W. CUNNINGHAM GLEN,

BARRISTER-AT-LAW.

SIXTH EDITION.

LONDON:
BUTTERWORTHS, 7, FLEET STREET,
Law Publishers to the Queen's Most Excellent Majesty.
KNIGHT & CO., 90, FLEET STREET,
Publishers by Authority to the Poor Law Board.
1868.

PREFACE.

The Poor Law Commissioners, in their Report on the further amendment of the Poor Law (published in the year 1839), with reference to the Statute Law relating to the relief of the Poor, observed:—It is convenient that some competent authority should expound the intentions of the Legislature to the public, by distributing the Provisions of Acts of Parliament into smaller portions, arranged according to the subject-matter, and by accompanying them with such interpretations and references as may tend to elucidate their meaning. No law can be obeyed which is not effectually promulgated; and the most effectual mode of promulgating a law is to put it in a form comprehensible by the majority of the persons to whom it is addressed, and to make its general Provisions as detailed and specific as possible. They added:—that they had reason to think that the departures from the law, which were frequent under the old system of administration, were not exclusively owing to the want of efficient superintendence, but arose in part from an ignorance of the law.

This Work aims at supplying, in respect of the Poor Law Orders, the interpretations and references in elucidation of their meaning which the Poor Law Commissioners appear to have had in view with reference to the Statute Law.

It contains the whole of the General Orders of the Poor Law Commissioners and Poor Law Board which have been issued down to the time of publication, and which are now in force; and also references to the Special Orders on the same subjects as those to which the General Orders relate.

I have in this Edition revised the notes to the several Orders as published in the former Editions; and I have again greatly extended them.

The Work, it will be seen, therefore, is not only greatly enlarged, but is also printed on a larger page than the former Editions. It has gone through five editions, and the continuance of the demand for it furnishes the best proof that I have successfully embodied, in a convenient and useful form, the information necessary for obtaining a clear perception and understanding of the Orders and Regulations of the Poor Law Commissioners and the Poor Law Board.

This Work, and my Edition of the Poor Law Statutes, which was so flatteringly referred to in the House of Commons by the Right Honourable C. P. Villiers, when President of the Poor Law Board, and recently by Mr. Sclater-Booth, M.P., the late Parliamentary Secretary to the Poor Law Board, comprise the whole Law in relation to the Management and Relief of the Poor.

In the preparation of the present Edition, I have again been ably assisted by Mr. Algernon C. Bauke, of the Poor Law Board; and I am indebted to him for having undertaken the laborious task of checking the dates of the Special Orders referred to in the Work, and superintending the progress of it through the Press, as well as perfecting the Index.

W. C. G.

5, ELM COURT, TEMPLE,
  24th June, 1868.

CONTENTS.

	PAGE
Introduction	xvii
Consolidated Order, Unions (24th July, 1847)	1
Consolidated Order, Parishes (8th December, 1847)	214
Election Expenses Order, Unions (24th July, 1847)	219
Election Expenses Order, Parishes (8th December, 1847)	224
Notice to Guardians Elected, Order (22nd March, 1852)	227
Election of Guardians Amendment Order (14th January, 1867)	231
Election of Guardians Amendment Order, Parishes (1st February, 1867)	238
Election Amendment Order (21st February, 1868)	240
Form of Order for Division of Parish into Wards for Election of Guardians	248
Form of Order for a fresh Election of a Guardian	254
Form of Relief Committees Order	257
Form of District Relief Committees Order	261
Consolidated Order, Amendment Order (26th February, 1866)	264
Order relating to Guardian's Order upon Treasurer (7th April, 1857)	279
Workhouse Dietaries General Order (16th February, 1848)	284
Form of Special Dietary Order	287

Contents.

	PAGE
Metropolitan Casual Poor Dietary Order (3rd March, 1866) . .	293
Insane Persons and Strayed Children Order (3rd December, 1841)	296
Religious Instruction Order (23rd August, 1859)	299
Collector of the Guardians Order (7th October, 1865)	303
Collectors of Guardians Order (27th November, 1866)	312
Appointment of Assistant Officers Order (19th August, 1867) . .	314
Form of Pay Clerk of the Poor Order	319
Medical Appointments Order (25th May, 1857)	328
Medical Officers Qualification Order, Unions (10th December, 1859)	334
Medical Officers Qualification Order, Parishes (27th January, 1860)	339
Medical Officers Qualification Order, Incorporations and Local Act Places (9th February, 1860)	339
Duties of Workhouse Medical Officers Order (4th April, 1868) . .	340
Vaccination Contract Order, Unions (15th February, 1868) . . .	345
Vaccination Contract Order, Parishes (7th March, 1868)	350
Out-door Relief Prohibitory Order (21st December, 1844) . . .	356
Out-door Relief Regulation Order (14th December, 1852) . . .	381
Form of Supplemental Out-door Labour Test Order	393
Duties of Overseers Order (22nd April, 1842)	401
Form of Collector of Poor Rates Order	407
Order relating to Collectors of Poor Rates (15th November, 1867)	413
Apprenticeship Order (29th January, 1845)	418
Taxation of Bills of Costs Order (21st November, 1844)	430
General Order for Accounts (14th January, 1867)	433
General Suspensory Order (17th January, 1868)	544
List of Mr. Glen's Works	546
Index	549

TABLE OF STATUTES.

Statute	PAGE
43 Eliz. c. 2	392, 429, 484
—— s. 1	117
—— 7	272, 529
17 Geo. 2, c. 3, s. 2	409
—— c. 38, s. 1	409
—— 12	6
20 Geo. 2, c. 19, s. 4	40
25 Geo. 2, c. 36, s. 5	432
18 Geo. 3, c. 47	40
30 Geo. 3, c. 49, s. 1	107
41 Geo. 3, c. 23, s. 9	267
44 Geo. 3, c. 88, s. 2	56
52 Geo. 3, c. 146, s. 7	175
—— 11	175
54 Geo. 3, c. 170, s. 7	85, 98, 164
—— 11	495
55 Geo. 3, c. 137	35, 90
—— s. 2	84, 105
—— 5	98, 105
—— 6	35
—— c. 194	119
56 Geo. 3, c. 129	85
—— c. 139, s. 1	42
—— 9	46, 49
59 Geo. 3, c. 69, s. 6	142, 438
59 Geo. 3, c. 12, s. 7	57, 144, 195, 306
—— 12	485
5 Geo. 4, c. 83, s. 3	75, 273
—— 4	273
6 Geo. 4, c. 133	119
1 Wm. 4, c. 45, s. 27	3
2 & 3 Wm. 4, c. 75	169
3 & 4 Wm. 4, c. 90	409
4 & 5 Wm. 4, c. 76, s. 15	97, 109, 161
—— 19	92, 93, 95, 299
—— 22	114
—— 23	108
—— 24	447
—— 26	69, 197
—— 27	61, 402
—— 28	394
—— 38	6, 23, 60, 108, 113, 117, 232
4 & 5 Wm. 4, c. 76, s. 40	2, 3
—— 42	97, 109
—— 43	107
—— 45	77, 78
—— 46	109, 122, 134
—— 47	149
—— 48	15, 112, 134
—— 49	36, 38
—— 51	35
—— 52	356
—— 54	185, 359, 401, 402, 463
—— 58	371, 446
—— 59	153, 371
—— 61	43
—— 62	446
—— 77	117
—— 86	38, 55, 56, 132, 149, 281
—— 93	88, 98, 101, 164
—— 91-94	68, 105
—— 97	478
—— 98	270
—— 104	271
—— 109	278
5 & 6 Wm. 4, c. 69, s. 3	140
6 & 7 Wm. 4, c. 85, s. 3	186
—— c. 86, s. 29	197, 446
—— c. 96, s. 5	409
7 Wm 4 & 1 Vict. c. 22, ss. 25, 27	446
2 & 3 Vict. c. 84, s. 1	270, 271
5 & 6 Vict. c. 35, s. 154	142
—— c. 57, s. 5	75, 85, 164
—— 7	27, 261
—— 9	11
—— 10	19
—— 11	19, 254
—— 13	15
—— 14	117, 187
—— c. 109, s. 6	139, 162, 182
6 Vict. c. 18, s. 4	8
—— 16	169
—— 17	179

Table of Statutes.

Statute	Page
6 & 7 Vict. c. 73, s. 31	432
—— 37	432
7 & 8 Vict. c. 101	16
—— s. 12	40, 43
—— 15	2, 3, 4, 5, 19, 404
—— 16	2, 3
—— 17	20, 21
—— 19	2, 4, 248
—— 25	363, 366, 369
—— 26	367, 386
—— 29	446
—— 31	167, 168, 169, 187, 197, 360
—— 32	22, 148, 271, 444, 448, 478
—— 33	437, 465, 472, 473, 474, 456
—— 35	476
—— 36	476
—— 39	274, 431, 432
—— 43	93
—— 51	368
—— 56	167
—— 59	76, 273
—— 61	57, 144, 409, 444
—— 63	270
—— 68	274
—— 74	93, 94
—— c. 126, s. 48	158
8 Vict. c. 10, s. 18	26
—— c. 17, s. 19	26
8 & 9 Vict. c. 117	162
—— s. 2	273
9 & 10 Vict. c. 66	197
—— s. 2	366
—— 4	151, 366
—— 6	189
—— 7	63, 64
10 & 11 Vict. c. 109, s. 23	70, 72
—— 24	106
—— 25	15
11 & 12 Vict. c. 43, s. 11	273
—— c. 91, s. 1, 2	267
—— 5	475
—— 7	473
—— 8	474
—— c. 110, s. 2	128, 129
—— 8	40
—— 10	63, 68, 372
12 & 13 Vict. c. 103, s. 7	269, 271
—— 12	31
—— 14	368
—— 16	63, 65, 68, 169, 372
12 & 13 Vict. c. 103, s. 19	24, 113
—— 21	195
13 & 14 Vict. c. 57	142, 442
—— s. 7	435, 438, 441
—— c. 99	6, 403
—— c. 101, s. 6	162, 182
14 & 15 Vict. c. 105, s. 2	20
—— 3	14, 21
—— 6	86, 368
—— 9	270, 271
—— 13	63
15 & 16 Vict. c. 81	447
—— s. 33	409
16 & 17 Vict. c. 59, s. 13	56
—— c. 90	166
—— c. 96, s. 28	79
—— 29	79
—— c. 97, s. 37	80
—— 64	146
—— 65	79, 80
—— 66	156, 160
—— 67	78, 70, 159, 166
—— 72	78
—— 77–80	463
—— 79	151, 159
—— 107	273
17 & 18 Vict. c. 104, s. 141–144	49, 50
—— c. 120, s. 16	373
18 & 19 Vict. c. 84	29, 86
—— s. 1	368
—— c. 79, s. 2	167
—— c. 91	373
—— c. 120	26
—— c. 122, s. 80	59
19 Vict. c. 15, s. 8	372
—— 8, 9	362, 372
20 Vict. c. 19	194, 404
20 & 21 Vict. c. 81, s. 6	167
21 Vict. c. 20	56
21 & 22 Vict. c. 89, s. 24	233
—— c. 90	158
—— s. 27	119
—— 33	119
—— 34	129
—— 36	119
—— 37	129
—— c. 96	196
—— c. 101, s. 2	151
22 Vict. c. 21, s. 1	119, 129
—— 2	119
—— c. 35	8
22 & 23 Vict. c. 49, s. 1	32, 39, 54
—— 6	269

Table of Statutes.

xiii

Statute	PAGE
23 Vict. c. 7, s. 3	119, 129
—— 4	119
24 & 25 Vict. c. 55, s. 6	273, 446
—— 7	273
—— 9	268
—— 10	268, 269
—— c. 76	182, 273
—— c. 97, ss. 5, 11, 12, 39	90
—— c. 125, s. 2	438
25 Vict. c. 43, s. 1	368
—— c. 103	139, 440
—— s. 2	21
—— 4	21
—— 8	21
—— 11	110
—— 28	435, 484
—— 30	268
—— c. 111, s. 8	64, 65
—— 19	78, 159
—— 20	77, 158, 166
—— 21	160
—— 31, 32, 33	78
—— 34	79
—— 37	80
—— 38	158
—— c. 113	182, 273
—— s. 4	63
26 & 27 Vict. c. 69	273
—— c. xciii.	211
—— c. 110, s. 2	65
27 & 28 Vict. c. 39	139, 440
—— s. 1	485
—— ss. 1, 2	274
—— s. 11	435, 484
—— c. 42	123, 447
—— c. 69	182
—— c. 116	61
28 Vict. c. 34	61
—— s. 2	61
28 & 29 Vict. c. 78, s. 6	190

Statute	PAGE
28 & 29 Vict. c. 79	50
—— s. 1	197
—— 9	273
—— 10	167
—— 11	266
—— 12	268, 269
29 & 30 Vict. c. 90, s. 38	88
—— c. 110, s. 5	270
—— c. 113, ss. 1, 2	123, 447
—— s. 4	371
—— 9	446
—— 14	29, 86, 290, 368
—— 15	75, 164, 394
—— 16	86, 368
—— 18	4, 194, 241, 249, 317, 390, 404
—— c. 118, s. 14	59
—— 17	86
30 Vict. c. 6, s. 6	61
—— s. 76	123
30 & 31 Vict. c. 84	197, 446
—— s. 6	160
—— 7	348
—— 11	184
—— c. 102, s. 7	6, 484
—— c. 106, s. 4	6
—— 5	4, 19
—— 6	11
—— ss. 7, 8	5, 19, 404
—— s. 9	5
—— 10	3, 19
—— 11	2, 3
—— 12	15
—— 13	106
—— 18	447
—— ss. 18, 19, 20	123
—— s. 21	31, 368
—— 23	67, 70, 79, 88, 158
—— 30	314

TABLE OF CASES.

	PAGE
Aston, Ex parte	15
Attorney-General v. Shillibeer	274, 481
Attorney-General v. Wilkinson	268
Attwood v. Mannings	280
Baker, App., Lock, Resp.	465
Barber v. Waite	35
Barber, In re	431, 432
Bennett v. Brumfitt	478
Bishop v. Helps	8
Black v. Ottoman Bank	133
Broughton v. Broughton	274
Carter v. Filliter	271
City of London Union v. Acocks	268
Claridge v. Evelyn	117
Clark v. Cuckfield	36
Darley v. Reg.	15
Downton, Ex parte the Overseers of	63
Duignan v. Walker	43
Eastern Counties Railway and Overseers of Moulton, Re	193
Elliott v. Martin	36
Eynsham, Ex parte	113
Faulkner v. Elger	26
Galloway v. Corporation of London	274
Greenhow v. Parker	36
Haigh v. North Bierley Union	36, 156
Hale v. City of London Union	268
Henderson v. Australian R. M. S. Co.	36
Hull v. Petch	38
Lake v. Butler	43
Lichfield Union v. Greene	132
Mellish, Ex parte	124
Metcalfe, Ex parte	220
Merrick v. Wakley	161

	PAGE
Molineaux, Ex parte	134
Molyneux v. Bagshaw	111, 122
Moss v. St. Michael, Lichfield	4
Newberry, In re	95
Newbold v. Coltman	270
North, In re	95
Orr v. Union Bank of Scotland	56
Paine v. Strand Union	36
Powell, App., Bradley, Resp.	3
Race, Re Alice	303
Rawlins v. West Derby	8
Reeve v. Yeates	273
Reg. v. Bangor	270
—— v. Braintree Guardians	110
—— v. Buchanan	274
—— v. Birmingham	363
—— v. Carey	143
—— v. Carpenter	15
—— v. City of London Union	475
—— v. Clarke	363
—— v. Collings	112
—— v. Combs	363
—— v. Denbighshire JJ.	437
—— v. Durham	402
—— v. Eaton	438
—— v. Ficst	168
—— v. Greenaway	143
—— v. Griffiths	15, 113
—— v. Grimshaw	114
—— v. Hampton	6, 15
—— v. Howes	89
—— v. Hunt	431
—— v. Hurstbourne Tarrant	270
—— v. Moah	112
—— v. Napton	431
—— v. Parkinson	8
—— v. Poor Law Commissioners	8
—— v. St. Luke, Chelsea	93
—— v. St. Mary, Bermondsey	43

	PAGE		PAGE
Reg. v. St. Marylebone	6	Sanders v. St. Neots	36
—— v. St. Nicholas, Nottingham	46	Saunders v. Owen	114
—— v. Saffron Walden	43	Scadding v. Lorant	436
—— v. Salop JJ.	26	Sellen v. Norman	154
—— v. Sharman	112	Skinner v. Buckee	35
—— v. Shepherd	32	Slater v. Hodgson	438
—— v. Slowstone	8	Smith v. Dimes	432
—— v. Smith	154	Steavenson v. Oliver	119
—— v. Spitalfields	113	Stokes v. Grissell	43
—— v. Stewart	169	Sutton v. Plumridge	150
—— v. Totnes	61, 402		
—— v. Vann	32, 360, 372	Tawney's Case	267
—— v. Westbury-on-Severn	8	Toms v. Wilson	193
—— v. West Riding JJ.	26		
—— v. Wigan	147	Waddington v. The City of London Union	267
—— v. ——, a child	87		
Rex v. Dursley	267	Walker v. Great Western Railway Company	36
—— v. Goodcheap	267		
—— v. Ramsden	15	West v. Andrews	35
—— v. Saunders	154	Wills v. Smith	154
—— v. Vantandillo	87	Wycombe v. Eton	54, 145
—— v. Warren	153		
—— v. Wavell	267	Young v. Grote	56

INTRODUCTION.

In order to a better understanding of the Poor Law General Orders contained in this volume, all of which have the authority of Acts of Parliament, and are as binding as Acts of Parliament upon the persons affected by them, the following concise statement of their provisions is prefixed:—

The Orders first in importance are the General Orders of the 24th July and 8th December 1847, which consolidate the General Orders which had been separately issued were each distinct subject.

The first subject with which these Orders deal is the election of Guardians of the Poor. This subject is further dealt with by the Orders of the 22nd March, 1852, 14th Jan. 1867, and 21st Jan. 1868, which were rendered necessary by the course of legislation subsequent to the year 1847.

Separate General Orders, also dated the 24th July and 8th Dec. 1847, further deal with the subject of elections by providing for the payment of the necessary expenses. The matter of these Orders is now, however, embodied in the Consolidated Orders issued separately to Unions and single Parishes subsequent to the General Consolidated Orders.

The other Orders referred to under the subject of Elections are Orders for the division of Parishes into Wards, for the election of Guardians, and for fresh elections of

Guardians. These Orders, however, are not General Orders, but are issued as occasion requires.

The Consolidated Orders next regulate the meetings and procedure of Boards of Guardians. This is further regulated by Orders for the division of Boards of Guardians into Relief Committees, and the establishment of District Relief Committees when the Union extends over a large area. These latter Orders are also special Orders issued as occasion requires.

After the meetings and procedure of Boards of Guardians the Consolidated Orders regulate the mode of entering into contracts by Boards of Guardians. They regulate the mode of apprenticing pauper children, of obtaining medical relief by permanent paupers, and the relief of non-settled and non-resident poor.

The next subject dealt with is the mode in which the Guardians are to obtain contributions from the parishes towards their funds, and the manner in which they are to make their payments. The Consolidated Orders in these two latter respects have been amended by the Orders dated respectively 7th April, 1857, and 26th Feb. 1866, which were necessary in consequence of the passing of the Union Chargeability Act, and the frauds which were sometimes committed by the misappropriation of the Guardian's cheques drawn upon their treasurer made payable to Bearer. Such cheques are now to be made payable "to order," so that cash cannot be obtained for them except upon indorsement by the persons in whose favour they are drawn.

After providing for the custody of bonds of security given by paid Officers, the Consolidated Orders provide for the government of the Workhouse. They regulate the admission, classification, discipline, diet, and the punishment of paupers for misbehaviour in the Workhouse. The diet of the paupers is further regulated in certain Unions by the General Order of 16th Feb. 1848; and a form of Special

Dietary Order is also given in the work, as well as the forms in which amended Dietary Tables are submitted for the sanction of the Poor Law Board.

In the Metropolis the Poor Law Board have fixed, by a General Order dated 3rd March, 1866, a uniform dietary to be observed in all Workhouses with regard to casual poor persons relieved therein.

There is also another General Order affecting the Metropolis only, which makes provision for giving publicity to the fact of unknown insane persons and strayed children having been received into the Workhouse of any Union or Parish in the Metropolis.

As affecting Workhouse management, the General Order of 23rd August, 1859, provides for the keeping a "Creed Register" in Workhouses, in which is to be entered the religious persuasion of orphan children under the age of fourteen years, who shall be in any Workhouse, and for the religious instruction of such orphans in the particular religious persuasion to which they belong.

The Consolidated Orders then provide for the appointment of Workhouse Visiting Committees, for repairs and alterations in and for the government of the Workhouse by the Guardians.

The Orders then lay down regulations to be observed in the appointment, qualification, remuneration, security for the faithful discharge of their duties, the continuation in office, suspension, and the personal discharge of the duties of the several officers of the Guardians.

Further provision is made with regard to the qualification of Medical Officers by the General Orders of 25th May 1857, and 10th December 1859; and the Order of 4th April, 1868, prescribes additional duties to be performed by Workhouse Medical Officers.

The Order of 26th Feb. 1866, already referred to, further regulates the duties of Clerks to the Boards of Guardians.

In addition to the Union Officers to be appointed under the Consolidated Orders, the General Orders of 7th Oct. 1865, and 27th Nov. 1866, provide for the appointment of collectors of moneys due to the Guardians, and regulate the mode of appointment of such collectors, their qualification for office and duties, etc.

The next subject which the Consolidated Orders regulate is the duties of the various Officers of the Guardians appointed under them; which duties the Orders regulate with minute detail. Lastly, the Orders provide for the receipt and payment of money by Officers of the Guardians, and explains the terms used in them. The Schedules prescribe various Forms to be used in regard to the several matters which the Orders regulate, and contain the names of the Unions and single Parishes to which the Orders have been issued.

The Consolidated Order issued to Parishes under separate Boards of Guardians is almost identical with that issued to Unions, and is therefore not given *in extenso* in this work. The names of the Parishes in which it is in force are, however, set forth.

The next Order in the series is the Vaccination Contract Order addressed to Boards of Guardians. This Order was rendered necessary by the passing of 30 & 31 Vict. c. 84, which repealed all the former statutes relating to public vaccination, and made new provisions on the subject. As necessarily appendant to this Order, the Regulations issued by the Privy Council on the subject of vaccination, have been inserted.

The next class of Orders are those which regulate the administration of out-door relief by Boards of Guardians.

The General Prohibitory Order of 21st Dec. 1844, prohibits out-door relief to every able-bodied person, male or female, save and except in eight excepted classes of cases. It also prohibits the Guardians from giving relief to any person who does not reside in the Union, save and except in eight excepted cases also. It regulates relief to wives in certain cases, and prohibits the payment of the rent of the house or lodging of any pauper out of the poor-rates. It provides, however, for cases in which, owing to special circumstances, the Guardians may have departed from any of its provisions, and regulates the administration of relief by way of loan.

The Out-door Relief Regulation Order applies to a much smaller number of Unions than the Prohibitory Order. Instead of wholly prohibiting out-door relief to able-bodied persons, it requires that one-half at least of the relief allowed to such persons shall be given in articles of food or fuel, or other articles of absolute necessity. It requires that out-door relief, when allowed to indigent poor persons, shall be given or administered weekly, or at such more frequent periods as the Guardians may deem expedient.

By Article 3 the Order declares it unlawful for the Guardians or their officers to establish any applicant for relief in trade or business; to redeem from pawn for any such applicant any tools, implements, or other articles; to purchase or give to such applicant any tools, implements, or other articles, except articles of clothing or bedding, where urgently needed; or food or fuel, or other articles of absolute necessity; to pay directly or indirectly the expense of the conveyance of any poor person, unless conveyed under lawful authority, except in the excepted cases mentioned in the Article; to give money to the applicant for the purpose of effecting any of the prohibited objects; to pay wholly or in part the rent of the house or lodging of any pauper, or to apply relief in payment thereof, either directly or indirectly. In like manner, as in the Prohibitory Order, this Order prohibits the Guardians from giving relief to any person who does not reside in their Union, save and except in six excepted cases; and it declares that no relief shall be given to any able-bodied male person while he is employed for wages or other hire or remuneration, by any person. The Order, then, provides that every able-bodied male person, if relieved out of the Workhouse, shall be set to work by the Guardians, and be kept employed under their direction and superintendence so long as he continues to receive relief. The Order provides, however, in this respect for exceptional cases; and also for relief by way of loan; and provides for cases in which, owing to special circumstances, the Guardians may have departed from any of its provisions.

The next Order relating to out-door relief is the Supplemental Out-door Labour Test Order. This Order is not a General Order, but is issued, where circumstances require its issue, to the Unions named in the Schedule to the General Prohibitory Order of 21st December, 1844. It is supplemental to that Order. It requires that where able-bodied male paupers receive out-door relief with the approbation of the Poor Law Board, such relief shall be given, half at least, in food, clothing, and other articles of necessity, and that no such pauper shall receive relief from the Guardians or any of their officers, or any Overseer, while he is employed for wages, or other hire or remuneration by any person, but that every such pauper so relieved shall be set to work by the Guardians.

The General Orders next in the series relate to Parishes, and not to Unions.

The Order of 22nd April, 1842, prescribes the duties of Overseers with regard to the administration of relief under 4 & 5 Wm. IV. c. 76, s. 54, in cases of "sudden and urgent necessity," and in pursuance of Orders of Justices under s. 27 of the same statute; and also with regard to the election of Guardians; with reference to the poor-rate and the payment of Guardian's Contribution Orders. Next follows a Form of Order issued by the Poor Law Commissioners and Poor Law Board for the appointment of a Collector of Poor-rates under the 7 & 8 Vict. c. 101, s. 62; and lastly, a General Order of the Poor Law Board providing for additional remuneration to Collectors of Poor-rates in Parliamentary Boroughs, in consideration of the increased duties they have to discharge in the collection of the poor-rates in consequence of the provision in the Representation of the People Act, 1867, with regard to the Small Tenements Rating Acts.

The last Order but one applies to Unions as well as to Parishes, and was issued in pursuance of the provision in the 7 & 8 Vict. c. 101, s. 39, with regard to the taxation of bills of costs by Clerks of the Peace, and fixes the allowance to be made for the taxation of bills of costs due to any solicitor or attorney in respect of business performed on behalf of any Parish or Union.

The last General Order in the series is that relating to the keeping of accounts by Overseers, Collectors, and Guardians of the Poor and their officers, and to the audit of such accounts. It prescribes the forms in which the accounts are to be kept, and the manner of keeping, examining, closing, and auditing them. This Order was issued on the 14th Jan. 1867, in consequence of the change of the law with regard to the mode of charging the cost of relief to the Unions instead of to the Parishes to which the paupers belonged, or in which they were settled, and in compliance with the direction to the Poor Law Board in the 11th Section of the Union Chargeability Act, 1865.

THE CONSOLIDATED ORDER.
(24 July, 1847.)

To the **Guardians of the Poor** *of the several* **Unions** *named in the Schedule hereunto annexed;*

> *To the Churchwardens and Overseers of the several Parishes and Places comprised within the said Unions;*
>
> *To the Clerk or Clerks to the Justices of the Petty Sessions held for the Division or Divisions in which the Parishes and Places comprised within the said Unions are situate;*
>
> *And to all others whom it may concern.*

WE, the Poor Law Commissioners, in pursuance of the authorities vested in us by an Act passed in the fifth year of the reign of his late Majesty King William the Fourth, intituled "*An Act for the Amendment and better Administration of the Laws relating to the Poor in England and Wales,*" and by all other Acts amending the same, do hereby rescind every Order, whether General or Special, heretofore issued by the Poor Law Commissioners to the Unions named in the Schedule hereunto annexed, which relates to the several subjects herein provided for, except so far as the same may have related to the apprenticeship of any poor person not yet completed, or may have required or authorized the appointment of any officer, or the giving of any

B

security, or the making of any contract not yet executed, or the making of any orders by the Guardians for contributions and payments not yet obeyed, or may have defined the salaries of any officers, or have prescribed the districts within which the duties of any officer shall be performed, or may have provided for the class of paupers or their number to be received into any particular Workhouse, or may have provided for the election of Guardians in any case where such election shall not have been completed when this Order shall come into force, and except the Order regulating the mode of election of Guardians, bearing date the 6th day of March, 1846, and addressed to the Guardians of the Poor of the Nottingham Union (*a*).

And We do hereby Order, Direct, and Declare, with respect to each of the said Unions, as follows:—

ELECTION OF GUARDIANS (*b*).

Article 1.—The Overseers of every Parish in the Union shall, before the 26th day of March in every year, distinguish in the rate-book the name of every ratepayer in their parish who has been rated to the relief of the poor for the whole year immediately preceding the said day, and has paid the poor-rates made and assessed upon him for the period of one whole year, except those which have been made or become due within the six months immediately preceding the said day (*c*).

(*a*) The Order of 6th March, 1846, divides the parish of St. Mary, Nottingham, into five wards, for the purposes of the election of Guardians (see *post*, p. 248), and provides for all future elections of Guardians for the several Parishes in the Union. The election Amendment Orders of 14th January, 1867, and 21st February, 1868, *post*, pp. 231, 240, do not apply to the Nottingham Union.

(*b*) With reference to the division of parishes into wards, under the 7 & 8 Vict. c. 101, s. 19, for the purposes of the election of Guardians, see the form of order, in such case, *post*, p. 248.

(*c*) By the 4 & 5 Wm. IV. c. 76, s. 40, 7 & 8 Vict. c. 101, ss. 15, 16, and 30 & 31 Vict. c. 106, s. 11, the following are the qualifications required to entitle a person to vote at an election of Guardians:—

1. In the character of ratepayer,—no person shall be deemed a rate-

payer, or be entitled to vote, or do any other act, matter, or thing as such, under the provisions of the Act, unless he shall have been rated to the relief of the poor for the whole year immediately preceding his so voting or otherwise acting as such ratepayer, and shall have paid the parochial rates and assessments made and assessed upon him for the period of one whole year, as well as those due from him at the time of so voting or acting, except such as shall have been made or become due within six months immediately preceding such voting or acting. (4 & 5 Wm. IV. c. 76, s. 40.) Such parochial rates and assessments shall be deemed to extend only to rates made for the relief of the poor (7 & 8 Vict. c. 101, s. 16), but where Money has been collected in any parish by an assessment under the name and as and for a poor-rate, the same shall be deemed to be a rate made for the relief of the poor within the meaning of 4 & 5 Wm. IV. c. 76, s. 40, and 7 & 8 Vict. c. 101, s. 16, notwithstanding any defect in the form of such assessment. (30 & 31 Vict. c. 106, s. 11.)

Where any corporation aggregate, joint stock, or other company, commissioners, or public trustees shall be rated, any officer of such corporation, company, commissioners, or public trustees from time to time appointed by the governing body thereof whose name shall be sent in writing to the overseers before the 1st March in any year, to be entered in the rate book under the name of such corporation, etc., shall be entitled to vote in respect of the property assessed as if he were assessed in his own name for the same; and in the case of a parish divided into wards, shall vote in that ward where the principal office of the corporation, etc., shall be situated, if any, or otherwise in that ward where the greatest part of the property assessed shall be situated. (30 & 31 Vict. c. 106, s. 10.)

Minors cannot vote at an election of Guardians, but it is apparently not necessary that the voter should have been of full age the whole time that he was rated and paid rates. To entitle a person to be registered under the Reform Act, 2 Wm. IV. c. 45, s. 27, in respect of the occupation of a house, etc., it is not necessary that he should have been of "full age" during the whole of the prescribed period of occupation. (Powell App., Bradley, Resp., 18 C. B. N. s. 65.)

2. In the character of owner,—no owner of property shall be entitled to vote as such, either in person or proxy, during the year following the 25th March in any year unless before the first day of February next preceding such 25th day of March he had given the statement required by the 4 & 5 Wm. IV. c. 76, s. 40 (as to which, see *post*, p. 16), signed by him, nor unless such statement contain a description of the nature of the interest or estate he may have in such property, and a statement of the amount of all rent-service (if any) which he may receive or pay in respect thereof, and of the persons from whom he may receive or to whom he may pay such rent-service. (7 & 8 Vict. c. 101, s. 15). Corporations, etc., will vote as owners by their officer. (4 & 5 Wm. IV. c. 76, s. 40.)

3. In the character of proxy,—no person shall be entitled to vote as proxy until fourteen days after he have made his claim so to vote in the manner required by the 4 & 5 Wm. IV. c. 76, s. 40, but no owner shall vote by proxy at the election of a guardian for any parish or ward

Art. 2.—The Clerk shall at every future annual election of Guardians perform the duties hereby imposed upon him, and all other duties suitable to his office which it may be requisite for him to perform in conducting and completing such election; and in case the office of clerk shall be vacant at the time when any duty relative to such election is imposed on the Clerk by this Order, or in case the Clerk, from illness or other sufficient cause, shall be unable to discharge such duties, the Guardians shall appoint some person to perform such of the said duties as then remain to be performed, and the person so appointed shall perform such duties (*a*).

Art. 3.—The Guardians shall, before or during every such election, appoint a competent number of persons to assist the Clerk in conducting and completing the election in conformity with this Order; but if the Guardians do not make such appointment within the requisite time, the

---

therein if at the time of such election he shall be residing within the said parish (30 & 31 Vict. c. 106, s. 5.) The word *parish* is defined by 29 & 30 Vict. c. 113, s. 18, but the definition there given does not apply to a "ward" into which a parish may be divided for the purposes of the election of guardians; see, however, the last clause of 7 & 8 Vict. c. 101, s. 19, and the form of Order, *post*, p. 248, for the division of a parish into wards.

The following is the scale of voting, for both owners and ratepayers:—

If the property in respect of which the person is entitled to vote be assessed upon a rateable value of less than £50, he shall have *one vote*.

If it amount to £50, and be less than £100, *two votes*.

If it amount to £100, and be less than £150, *three votes*.

If it amount to £150, and be less than £200, *four votes*.

If it amount to £200, and be less than £250, *five votes*.

If it amount to or exceed £250, *six votes*. (7 & 8 Vict. c. 101, s. 15).

See also 33 O. C. March 44, p. 58, and 24 O. C. (N.S.) 60, on this subject.

As regards the separate votes of partners in a firm, it was held, in *Moss* v. *St. Michael, Lichfield*, 7 M. & G. 72, with reference to the Parliamentary franchise, that a partner in a firm who was not actually rated was not qualified, though he occupied the premises jointly with his partner, and paid the rates.

(*a*) With regard to the officers who are to conduct the election, see Art. 202, No. 13, as to the Clerk, and Art. 215, No. 15, as to the Relieving Officers.

Clerk shall take such measures for securing the necessary assistance as he may deem advisable.

Art. 4.—The persons appointed under Article 3 shall obey all the directions relative to the conduct of the election which may be given by the Clerk for the execution of this Order.

Art. 5.—The Overseers of every Parish in the Union, and every Officer having the custody of the poor-rate books of any such Parish, shall attend the Clerk at such times as he shall require their attendance, until the completion of the election of Guardians, and shall, if required by him, produce to him such rate-books, and the registers of owners and proxies, together with the statements of owners, and appointments and statements of proxies, and all books and papers relating to such rates in their possession or power (*b*).

Provided that, where any register of owners shall have been prepared in any Parish containing a population exceeding two thousand persons, it shall not be necessary to produce the statements of owners.

Art. 6 (*c*).—The Clerk shall prepare and sign a notice, which may be in the Form marked (A.) hereunto annexed (*d*) and which shall contain the following particulars:—

1st. The number of Guardians to be elected for each Parish in the Union.

2nd. The qualification of Guardians (*e*).

(*b*) See 7 & 8 Vict. c. 101, s. 15, as to the annual scrutiny of the register of owners claiming to vote, and also 30 & 31 Vict. c. 106, ss. 7, 8. See also 56 O. C. (N.S.) 76, as to the duty of the Overseers on receiving such claims. The Returning Officer at the election of Guardians shall, in all parishes in which a revision can take place, be concluded by the entries in the register, whether such register has or has not been revised (30 & 31 Vict. c. 106, s. 9.)

(*c*) The provision in Article 6 does not apply to the sending the nominations, as Article 8 provides that they shall be sent *after*, not *on* the 14th March. See the form of notice in the Order of 21st February, 1868, *post*, p. 240.

(*d*) The form of notice prescribed by this Order has been rescinded by the Order of the 14th of January, 1867, Article 1, and again by the Order of 21st February, 1868, *post*, p. 240, and a new form of notice prescribed.

(*e*) The qualification required for the office of Guardian is the being

3rd. The persons by whom, and the places where, the Nomination Papers in respect of each Parish are to be received, and the last day on which they are to be sent (*a*).

4th. The mode of voting in case of a contest, and the days on which the Voting Papers will be delivered and collected (*b*).

---

rated to the poor-rate of some parish or parishes in the Union at such an amount as shall have been fixed by the Poor Law Commissioners in the particular Union, but not so as to require a qualification exceeding the annual rental of £40. (4 & 5 Wm. IV. c. 76, s. 38.) But now the qualification of a Guardian shall be determined with reference to the annual rateable value of the property in respect of which his qualification is claimed. (30 & 31 Vict. c. 106, s. 4, and Order of 21st February, 1868, *post*, p. 240.) If a Guardian ceases to be rated in respect of property of the required value, he becomes disqualified for the Office of Guardian, and it makes no difference in this respect, whether it is as occupier or as owner that he ceases to be rated.

A rating under the 17 Geo. II. c. 38, s. 12, will suffice. (See *Reg.* v. *St. Marylebone*, 14 J. P. 559, in which it was held that such a rating was sufficient to acquire a settlement.) So also an owner rated under the the Small Tenements Rating Act, 13 & 14 Vict. c. 99, whatever may be the value of any premises in his own occupation. In the case of *Reg.* v. *Hampton* (13 L. T. N. s. 431; 12 Jur. N. s. 587; 29 J. P. 757), the Court decided that under the terms of a proviso in the West Bromwich Local Act (13 & 14 Vict. c. IV.) the occupiers of the small tenements whose landlords were assessed and paid the rates were entitled to vote as ratepayers in the election of the Guardians for the parish. They gave no decision as to the effect of the statute 13 & 14 Vict. c. 99, the general "Small Tenements Rating Act," as no question arose upon it. (Circular P. L. B. 2nd April, 1866.) As regards the rating of Small Tenements in Parliamentary Boroughs, see now the 30 & 31 Vict. c. 102, s. 7, in Glen and Lovesy's Representation of the People Act, 1867.

(*a*) A place for the reception of nomination papers need not necessarily be appointed in every parish. It will suffice if some place be specifically appointed for the several parishes; but there ought to be a convenient number of places appointed.

(*b*) In the consolidated orders now issued (*i. e.* to Unions declared since 1847) by the Poor Law Board, the following additional clause is required to be inserted in this notice in this place:—

"The day on which voting papers may be received if there should be a default of delivery, and the day on which voting papers may be delivered to the Clerk if there should be a default in the collection;" but provision in regard to both of these matters is now made in the order of 14th of January, 1867, *post*, in respect of all Unions.

5th. The time and place for the examination and casting up of the votes.

And the Clerk shall cause such notice to be published on or before the 15th (*c*) day of March, in the following manner:—

1st. A printed copy of such notice shall be affixed on the principal external gate or door of every Workhouse in the Union, and shall from time to time be renewed, if necessary, until the Ninth day of April.

2nd. Printed copies of such notice shall likewise be affixed on such places in each of the Parishes of the Union as are ordinarily made use of for affixing thereon notices of parochial business (*d*).

Provided that whenever the day appointed in this Order for the performance of any act relating to or connected with the Election of Guardians shall be a Sunday or Good Friday, such act shall be performed on the day next following, and each subsequent proceeding shall be postponed one day.

Art 7.—Any person entitled to vote in any Parish may nominate for the office of Guardian thereof, himself, or any other person or number of persons (not exceeding the number of Guardians to be elected for such Parish), provided that the person or persons so nominated be legally qualified to be elected for that office (*e*).

(*c*) If the 15th of March should happen to fall on a Sunday, the 16th of March will be the last day for giving the notice.

(*d*) This Article confers no authority for publishing notices as to the election in the newspapers, and therefore any expenditure thereby incurred cannot legally be paid out of the poor-rates.

(*e*) A nomination paper once sent in to the clerk, or to the person appointed to receive it, cannot be withdrawn; and a person having once nominated the full number of persons he is entitled to nominate, *i. e.* the number to be elected as Guardians for the particular parish, cannot by a subsequent document nominate other persons; for his power to nominate is exhausted by the first nomination, and he cannot afterwards stultify his act any more than he can withdraw his nomination. There is nothing in the order to prevent any person from nominating different candidates in separate papers, provided that he does not nominate, in the whole, a greater number than there are Guardians to

Art. 8.—Every nomination shall be in writing in the Form marked (B.) hereunto annexed, and be signed by one person only, as the party nominating, and shall be sent after the *Fourteenth* and on or before the *Twenty-sixth* (a) day of March, to the clerk, or to such person or persons as may have been appointed to receive the same; and the Clerk or such person or persons shall, on the receipt thereof, mark thereon the date of its receipt, and also a number according to the order of its receipt; provided that no nomination sent before the Fifteenth or after the said Twenty-sixth day of March shall be valid (b).

Art. 9.—If the number of the persons nominated for the office of Guardian for any Parish shall be the same as or

---

be elected for the parish. Under the 22 Vict. c. 35, it has been held that the nominator of a candidate for election as Town Councillor must himself be a burgess of the ward for which the candidate is nominated. (*Reg.* v. *Parkinson*, 3 L. R. Q. B. 11; 17 L. T. N. s. 169; 37 L. J. Q. B. 52.) Where, therefore, a parish has been divided into wards for the election of Guardians, it would appear that the nominator must be qualified to vote in the particular ward for which he nominates a Guardian.

(a) See *Reg.* v. *Westbury-on-Severn*, 4 El. & Bl. 314, and 18 J. P. 758; S. C. nom. *Reg.* v. *Poor Law Commissioners*, 1 Jur. (N. s.) 251, as to the 26th falling on a Sunday, with reference to the proviso to Article 6. In that case the 26th of March fell on a Sunday, and a nomination paper dated the 25th was delivered to the Clerk on the 26th, which the Clerk rejected. The Court held, that the paper was delivered in due time, and might be treated as a delivery on the Monday following. See also *Rawlins* v. *West Derby*, 15 L. J. R. (N. s.), C. P. 70, in which it was held, that a notice under 6 Vict. c. 18, s. 4, might legally be given on a Sunday when the 20th of June fell on that day. A mere error in the date of the nomination paper will not invalidate it, if in other respects there be no objection to it, as to form or time of delivery. If a nomination paper be posted on the 26th, and does not reach the Returning Officer's hands till the 27th, though delivered according to the ordinary course of the Post, it will be too late. (See *Reg.* v. *Slowstone*, 21 L. J. M. C. 145, and *Bishop* v. *Helps*, 2 C. B. 45.)

Further, with reference to this article, see the Circular of the Poor Law Board, dated 27th of February, 1857, regarding the change of days when any one of the appointed days falls upon a Sunday or Good Friday. See also the table on the next page.

(b) See Art. 3, of the General Order of 14th of January, 1867, *post*, p. 232, as to the hours at which nomination papers are to be delivered. See also Articles 4 and 5 of the same order as to the publication of the names of the persons nominated as Guardians.

The following Table has been computed showing the days for each of the proceedings connected with the Elections of Guardians in each of the years 1869 to 1875:—

		1869.	1870.	1871.	1872.	1873.	1874.	1875.
Art. 6.	Last day for Publication of Notice of Election	15 Mar.	15 Mar.	15 Mar.	15 Mar.	15 Mar.	16 Mar.	15 Mar.
,, 8.	First day for sending in Nomination Papers	15 ,,	15 ,,	15 ,,	15 ,,	15 ,,	16 ,,	15 ,,
,, 8.	Last day for sending in Nomination Papers	27 ,,	26 ,,	27 ,,	26 ,,	26 ,,	27 ,,	27 ,,
,, 11.	Day for delivery of Voting Papers	6 Apr.	5 Apr.	6 Apr.	5 Apr.	5 Apr.	6 Apr.	6 Apr.
,, 17.	Day for collection of Voting Papers	8 ,,	7 ,,	8 ,,	8 ,,	7 ,,	8 ,,	8 ,,
,, 19.	Last day on which application may be made for Voting Papers	8 ,,	7 ,,	8 ,,	8 ,,	7 ,,	8 ,,	8 ,,
,, 20.	Day on which Voting Papers may be delivered to Returning Officer, if not duly collected on day appointed	9 ,,	8 ,,	9 ,,	9 ,,	8 ,,	9 ,,	9 ,,
,, 21.	Day on which Votes are to be cast up	10 ,,	9 ,,	11 ,,	10 ,,	9 ,,	10 ,,	10 ,,

less than the number of Guardians to be elected for such Parish, such persons, if duly qualified, shall be deemed to be the elected Guardians for such Parish for the ensuing year, and shall be certified as such by the Clerk under his hand as hereinafter provided in Article 22.

Art. 10.—But if the number of the duly qualified persons nominated for the office of Guardian for any Parish shall exceed the number of Guardians to be elected therein, the Clerk shall cause Voting Papers in the Form marked (C.) hereunto annexed (*a*) to be prepared and filled up, and shall insert therein the names of all the persons nominated, in the order in which the Nomination Papers were received, but it shall not be necessary to insert more than once the name of any person nominated (*b*).

Art. 11.—The Clerk shall on the *Fifth* day of April cause *one* of such Voting Papers to be delivered by the persons appointed for that purpose, to the address in such Parish of each ratepayer, owner, and proxy qualified to vote therein (*c*).

Art. 12.—If the Clerk consider that any person nominated is not duly qualified to be a Guardian, he shall state in the Voting Paper the fact that such person has been nominated, but that he considers such person not to be duly qualified.

Art. 13.—If any person put in nomination for the office of Guardian in any Parish shall tender to the Officer con-

---

(*a*) The form of voting paper prescribed by this order has been rescinded by the General Order of the 14th of January, 1867, Art 1, *post*, p. 231, and a new form of voting paper prescribed.

(*b*) See Article 4 of the General Order of 14th of January, 1867, *post*, as to the publication of the names of the candidates and their nominators. If there should be more than one nomination of the same person as Guardian, the names of all the nominations should appear in the voting papers, as there is no authority in the order for excluding any of them. The same voting paper cannot be issued to two or more persons entitled to vote in respect of the same tenement; to each of them a separate and distinct voting paper must be issued.

(*c*) See Article 6 of the General Order of 14th of January, 1867, *post*, p. 233, as to agents of the candidates accompanying the deliverers of the voting papers.

ducting the election his refusal, in writing, to serve such office, and if in consequence of such refusal the number of persons nominated for the office of Guardian for such Parish shall be the same as or less than the number of Guardians to be elected for such Parish, all or so many of the remaining Candidates as shall be duly qualified shall be deemed to be the Elected Guardians for such Parish for the ensuing year, and shall be certified as such by the Clerk under his hand, as hereinafter provided in Art. 22 (*d*).

Art. 14.—Each Voter shall write his initials in the Voting Paper delivered to him against the name or names of the person or persons (not exceeding the number of Guardians to be elected in the Parish) for whom he intends to vote, and shall sign such Voting Paper; and when any person votes as a proxy, he shall in like manner write his own initials and sign his own name, and state also, in writing, the name of the person for whom he is proxy (*e*).

(*d*) See the 5 & 6 Vict. c. 57, s. 9, which enacts, that if any person put in nomination for the office of Guardian tender to the officer conducting the election of Guardians, his refusal, in writing, to serve such office, the election of Guardians, so far as regards such person, shall be no further proceeded with. In pursuance of this provision, the refusal need not be personally tendered to the officer conducting the election. If it be in writing, and be sent so as to reach the officer in proper time, the section would be complied with; and it seems that it cannot be tendered after the voting papers have been collected, as the election is then complete, though the result may not be ascertained till afterwards. It is, moreover, not competent for a person to recall or withdraw his refusal to serve, or to prevent its legal effect in staying further proceedings in regard to the election.

(*e*) As regards voting in wards when a parish has been divided into wards, it is enacted by 30 & 31 Vict. c. 106, s. 6, that no person in any election of Guardians entitled to vote shall give in the whole of the wards into which a parish may be divided a greater number of votes than he would have been entitled to have given if the parish had not been divided into wards, nor in any one ward a greater number of votes than he is entitled to in respect of property in that ward; but any such ratepayer or owner may, by notice in writing signed by him, and delivered to the Overseers of the parish before the day appointed for the annual nomination of candidates, elect in what ward or wards he will vote for the ensuing year, and determine what proportion of votes, having regard to the property situated therein, he will give in any one or more such wards. If he do not give such notice, his vote shall only be taken for

Art. 15.—Provided that, if any Voter cannot write, he shall affix his mark at the foot of the Voting Paper in the presence of a witness, who shall attest the affixing thereof, and shall write the name of the Voter against such mark, as well as the initials of such Voter, against the name of every Candidate for whom the Voter intends to vote.

Art. 16.—If the initials of the Voter be written against the names of more persons than are to be elected Guardians for the Parish, or if the Voter do not sign or affix his mark to the Voting Paper, or if his mark be not duly attested, or his name be not duly written by the witness, or if a proxy do not sign his own name, and state in writing the name of the person for whom he is proxy, such Voter shall be omitted in the calculation of votes.

Art. 17.—The Clerk shall cause the Voting Papers to be collected on the *Seventh* day of April, by the persons appointed or employed for that purpose, in such manner as he shall direct (*a*).

Art. 18.—No Voting Paper shall be received or admitted, unless the same have been delivered at the address in each Parish of the Voter, and collected by the persons appointed or employed for that purpose, except as is provided in Article 19 (*b*).

Art. 19.—Provided that every person qualified to vote, who shall not on the *Fifth* day of April have received a Voting Paper, shall, on application before the *Eighth* day

---

the ward in which he resides, or, if he do not reside within the parish, for that ward in which the greater part of such property according to its annual rateable value shall be situated; provided that no person shall be qualified to nominate a Guardian for any ward in which he is not qualified to vote.

(*a*) See Art. 6 of the General Order of 14th of January, 1867, *post*, p. 233, as to agents of the candidates accompanying the collectors of the voting papers; and also Art. 7, as to the provision of collecting boxes or bags; and the duty of the returning officer with respect to the same.

(*b*) The collection of the voting papers at or from any other place than the residence or address of the particular voter is not an authorized proceeding under this article, nor is it in accordance with the terms of the voting papers.

of April to the Clerk at his office, be entitled to receive a Voting Paper, and to fill up the same in the presence of the Clerk, and then and there to deliver the same to him (c).

Art. 20.—Provided also, that in case any Voting Paper duly delivered shall not have been collected, through the default of the Clerk, or the persons appointed or employed for that purpose, the Voter in person may deliver the same to the Clerk before twelve o'clock at noon on the *Eighth* day of April (d).

Art. 21.—The Clerk shall, on the *Ninth* day of April, and on as many days immediately succeeding as may be necessary, attend at the Board Room of the Guardians of the Union, and ascertain the validity of the votes, by an examination of the rate-books, and the registers of owners and proxies, and such other documents as he may think necessary, and by examining such persons as he may see fit; and he shall cast up such of the votes as he shall find to be valid, and to have been duly given, collected, or received, and ascertain the number of such votes for each Candidate (e).

Art. 22.—The Candidates, to the number of Guardians

(c) Note that the application for the voting paper must, under this article, be made to the Clerk *before* the 8th of April. An application on the 8th would be too late.

(d) If in any year the 8th day of April should fall upon a Sunday, the proper day for delivering the voting paper to the Clerk will be Monday, the 9th of April; and in that case Tuesday, the 10th of April, will be the day for the examination and computation of the votes under Article 21. See the Circular of the Poor Law Board, dated 28th of February, 1855, and the Table, *ante*, p. 9.

(e) See Article 8 of the General Order of 14th of January, 1867, *post*, p. 234, as to the presence of the candidates at the casting up of the votes; and the duty of the returning officer with regard to the votes. If the 9th day of April should be the day of meeting of the Board of Guardians, and in consequence thereof it be impracticable for the Clerk to ascertain the votes on that day, he should, nevertheless, open the proceedings on that day, pursuant to the notice, and then adjourn to the next day. He should, however, take care that the proceedings are commenced in due form on the 9th, and are duly adjourned; and it would be well that he should give notice beforehand of the intended adjournment. (3 O. C. 105.)

to be elected for the Parish, who being duly qualified, shall have obtained the greatest number of votes shall be deemed to be the elected Guardians for the Parish, and shall be certified as such by the Clerk under his hand.

Art. 23.—The Clerk, when he shall have ascertained that any Candidate is duly elected as Guardian, shall notify the fact of his having been so elected, by delivering or sending, or causing to be delivered or sent, to him a notice in the form (D.) hereunto annexed.

Art. 24.—The Clerk shall make a list containing the names of the Candidates, together with (in case of a contest) the number of votes given for each, and the names of the elected Guardians, in the Form marked (E.) hereunto annexed, and shall sign and certify the same, and shall deliver such list, together with all the Nomination and Voting Papers which he shall have received, to the Guardians of the Union, at their next meeting, who shall preserve the same for a period of not less than two years (*a*).

(*a*) See Article 9 of the General Order of the 14th of January, 1867, *post*, p. 234, as to the inspection of the voting papers after they have been delivered to the Guardians.

If there be any evidence of malpractice to justify an information under the 14 & 15 Vict. c. 105, s. 3, the production of the papers before the Justices can then be compelled by the ordinary process of a subpœna. That Act provides that if any person, pending or after the election of any Guardian or Guardians, shall wilfully, fraudulently, and with intent to affect the result of such election, commit any of the acts following :—
fabricate, in whole or in part, alter, deface, destroy, abstract, or purloin any nomination or voting paper used therein ; or personate any person entitled to vote at such election ; or falsely assume to act in the name or on the behalf of any person so entitled to vote ; or interrupt the distribution or collection of the voting papers ; or distribute or collect the same under a false pretence of being lawfully authorized to do so ;—every such person so offending shall for every such offence be liable, on conviction thereof before any two Justices, to be imprisoned in the common gaol or house of correction for any period not exceeding three months, with or without hard labour. With reference to this enactment, it may be observed that in grants and conveyances of lands, and bargains and sales of goods, etc., "fraud" means deceit to the damage of another person, which may be either by suppression of the truth or suggestion of falsehood. Therefore a conviction under this statute would

Art. 25.—The Clerk shall cause copies of such lists to be
printed, and shall deliver or send, or cause to be delivered

---

not be a fraud within the meaning of the 4 & 5 Wm. IV. c. 76, s. 48,
disqualifying for office.

The 10 & 11 Vict. c. 109, s. 25, enacts that in no proceedings shall it
be lawful to question the qualification or validity of the election of any
person as a Guardian after the end of twelve months next following the
election, or the time when the alleged disqualification or want of qualification of the person against whom such proceedings shall be directed
shall have arisen ; and 5 & 6 Vict. c. 57, s. 13, enacts, that no defect in the
qualification or election of any person acting as a Guardian at a Board
of Guardians, the majority of persons assembled at which shall be entitled to act as Guardians, shall be deemed to vitiate or make void any
proceedings of such Board in which he may have taken part. The Court
of Queen's Bench at one time refused to issue a writ of *Quo warranto*
to try the title of a Guardian of the poor. (*Ex parte Aston*, 6 A. & E.
784. Sc. *nom Reg.* v. *Carpenter*, 1 Nev. & P. 773. See also *R.* v.
Ramsden, 3 A. & E. 456.) But this was before *Darley* v. *Reg.*, in the
House of Lords, 12 CL & F. 349, *Reg.* v. *Griffiths*, 17 Q. B. 164, and
Reg. v. *Hampton*, 6 B. & S. 923. But it is enacted by sect. 8 of the
same statute, that in case any question shall arise as to the right of any
person to act as an elective Guardian, it shall be lawful for the Poor Law
Board, *if they shall see fit*, to inquire into the circumstances of the case,
and to issue such order or orders therein under their hands and seal as
they may deem requisite for determining that question. The object of
this provision is to prevent litigation by providing a means whereby the
question raised can be settled without expense to the parties. The
Board have a discretion whether or not they will entertain the question ;
and they would decline to do so when the parties do not intend to acquiesce in their judgment, if it should be adverse to them. In such a
case the Board recommend them to apply for a *quo warranto* at once,
as in *Reg.* v. *Hampton*, 6 B. & S. 923 ; 13 L. T. (N. s.) 431 ; 12 Jur.
(N. s.) 583, in which the Court of Queen's Bench held that *quo warranto*
will lie in respect of the office of Guardian of the Poor, per Cockburn,
C. J., the exercise of the jurisdiction given to the Poor Law Commissioners to inquire is discretionary with them. But even if they had
thought fit to exercise their jurisdiction, there is nothing to take away
the jurisdiction of this Court ; and as this is a matter which ought to be
tried according to the usual and well-known course of legal procedure,
it is one rather for the exercise of the jurisdiction of this Court than for
the Board of Commissioners sitting in private.

When any question as to the election of a Guardian is decided by
the Poor Law Board, and according to their decision, the election in the
parish for which he shall have been returned is declared to have been
null, the Guardian elected at any election in the previous year shall not
be entitled to serve as such Guardian for the remainder of the current
year, but the Poor Law Board shall issue an order for a fresh election.
(30 & 31 Vict. c. 106, s. 12.)

or sent, one or more of such copies to the Overseers of each Parish (a).

Art. 26.—The Overseers shall affix, or cause to be affixed, copies of such list, at the usual places for affixing in each Parish notices of parochial business.

Art. 27 (b).—In case of the decease, necessary absence, refusal, or disqualification to act, during the proceedings of the election, of the Clerk or any other person appointed or employed to act in respect of such election, the delivery of the Nominations, Voting Papers, or other documents to the successor of the Clerk or person so dying, absenting himself, refusing or disqualified to act, shall, notwithstanding the terms of any notice issued, be as valid and effectual as if they had been delivered to such Clerk or person.

(a) When an election of a Guardian takes place under a special order of the Poor Law Board, it is not necessary to send a return of the Guardian or Guardians elected under that order to any other than the particular parish interested.

(b) The Commissioners have not set out in any Order now in force Forms for the Statement of Owners of Property, for the Appointment of Proxies, the Statements of Proxies, and the register of those Statements and Appointments; they have, however, reconsidered those formerly prepared with reference to the alterations made by the Statute, 7 & 8 Vict. c. 101, and have stated that Forms to the following effect might be safely used :—

A.

Owner's Statement.

To the Churchwardens and Overseers of the Poor of the Parish of —— in the County of ——

This —— day of —— 18—.

I, the undersigned, claim to be entitled to vote, according to the provisions of the statutes of the fifth year of the reign of King William the Fourth, and the eighth year of the reign of her present Majesty, relating to the Administration of the Laws for the Relief of the Poor (4 & 5 Wm. IV. c. 76, and 7 & 8 Vict. c. 101), as Owner of the Property hereinafter described, which is situated in the Parish of ——, that is to say.*

I do also state that the interest or estate which I have in such property, and the amount of all the rent-service which I receive or pay in respect thereof, and the names of the persons from whom I receive or to

* Here insert a clear Statement of the Property, as House, Building, House and —— Acres of Land.

whom I pay such rent-service, are set forth in the Form hereunder written.

Description of Property (a)	In respect of which I have an Estate or Interest of (b)	And in respect of which I receive in Rent-service the sum of (c)	From (d)	And in respect of which I pay in Rent-service the sum of (e)	To (f)
		£. s. d.		£. s. d.	

———— Signature of Claimant.
———— Address of Claimant.

B.
Appointment of Proxy.

To the Churchwardens and Overseers of the Poor of the Parish of ———— in the County of ————.

This ———— day of ———— 18——.

I, the undersigned, being Owner of the Property hereinafter described, which is situated in the Parish of ————, do hereby appoint ————, of ————, to vote as my Proxy in all cases wherein he may lawfully do so, under the provisions of the Statutes of the fifth year of the reign of his late Majesty King William the Fourth, and the eighth year of the reign of her present Majesty, relating to the Administration of the Laws for the Relief of the Poor. And I do hereby state, that the Description of the said Property is as follows; viz. (g).

———— Signature of Owner.
———— Address of Owner.

C.
Proxy's Statement.

To the Churchwardens and Overseers of the Poor of the Parish of ———— in the County of ————.

This ———— day of ———— 18——.

I, the undersigned, having been appointed by ————, of ————, Owner of the Property hereinafter described, which is situated in the Parish of

(a) Describe the property by its Name, Situation, or the name of the Occupier, or any other designation by which it may be identified.
(b) Describe the Estate or Interest, as *an estate in fee simple*, *a freehold*, *a term of —— years*, and also whether it is held by the Claimant solely, or jointly with others.
(c) If the Property is let by the Owner, insert the amount of rent received from each tenant.
(d) Insert Name of Tenant or Tenants.
(e) If the Owner is a Lessee paying rent, insert the amount of all the rent he pays.
(f) Insert the name of the Lessor.
(g) Describe the Property by its Name, Situation, or the Name of the Occupier, or any other Designation by which it may be identified. It is not necessary here to set out the description of the estate or interest of the Owner, nor the statement of the amount of rent received or paid by him.

——, to vote as his Proxy, under the provisions of the Statutes of the fifth year of the reign of his late Majesty King William the Fourth, and of the eighth year of the reign of her present Majesty, relating to the Administration of the Laws for the Relief of the Poor, do hereby give you Notice, that I am entitled to vote as such Proxy. I herewith transmit to you (a) —— the writing under the hand of the said —— appointing me such proxy.

The following is a Description of the Property in respect of which the said —— is entitled to vote as Owner, and in respect of which I am entitled to vote as his Proxy; viz. (b). —— Signature of Proxy.
—— Address of Proxy.

The adoption of these Forms is not compulsory upon any Owner or Proxy, and, consequently, any Forms which may contain in substance the information therein set forth, which appears to be what is required by the Statutes, will be fully available for the purposes of the Election.

The Form of Register of Owners and Proxies is directed by the General Order as to the duties of Overseers, bearing date the 22nd of April, 1842.—*Instr. Letter*, 1845.

The following memorandum was issued by the Poor Law Commissioners on the 31st December, 1844, with the view of conveying information in reference to the alteration in the law affecting the votes of Owners and Proxies, by the Act 7 & 8 Vict. c. 101, which requires that—

1. Every Owner, in order to be entitled to vote either as Owner or by Proxy, at the Election of Guardians, should, *before the 1st day of February*, have given to the Overseers a statement of his name and address, together with a description of the property in the parish for which he claims to vote. Such description must show the nature of the interest or estate he may have in such property; it must also show the amount of rent-service (if any) which he may receive or pay in respect of such property; and the names of the persons from whom he may receive, or to whom he may pay, such rent.

2. If this has been done, the Owner may vote himself, or he may vote by proxy; but if he vote by proxy, the proxy must, fourteen days at least before he votes, send to the Overseers the original, or an attested, copy of his appointment as proxy; together with a statement of the Owner's name and address, and the property in respect of which he claims to vote as proxy.

3. On or before *the 5th of February*, the Overseers of Parishes containing a population exceeding 2000, according to the last Census, are to prepare a registry of the names and addresses of the Owners and Proxies who have given the statement, or made the claim above referred to, before the 1st of the month.

4. This registry is to be open to the inspection of all persons any time between *the 5th and 10th of February;* and any Owner or Proxy who has given in his statement, or made his claim to vote, or any ratepayer, may object to the vote of an Owner, by delivering, before *the*

(a) If the appointment itself be not sent, insert the words *as attested copy of*.
(b) Describe the Property by its Name, Situation, or the Name of the Occupier, or any other Designation by which it may be identified. It is not necessary here to set out the description of the estate or interest of the Owner, nor the statement of the amount of rent received or paid by him.

15*th of February*, a notice, in writing, of the grounds of his objection to the Clerk of the Guardians; and also at the address of the person objected to.

5. On or before *the 20th of February*, the Clerk is to provide for the revision of the list, so far as regards Owners objected to, which will be revised on some day between *the 24th of February* and *1st of March*. Any objection to be held valid must be supported by the person objecting at the time of revision.

Further, with reference to voting by proxy, see 30 & 31 Vict. c. 106, s. 5, *ante* p. 4; and as regards the revision of the register of Owners, see 7 & 8 Vict. c. 101, s. 15, and 30 & 31 Vict. c. 106, ss. 7–10.

It may be useful to notice here the provisions contained in ss. 10 & 11 of the 5 & 6 Vict. c. 57, with regard to Guardians. The eleventh section enables the Poor Law Board to accept the resignation of any person elected as a Guardian, tendered for any cause that they may deem reasonable. The following form is applicable in such case:—

I, ——, of ——, being an elected Guardian for the —— of ——, in the —— Union, in the County of ——, do hereby for the following cause (*here state the cause*) tender my resignation of the said office of Guardian of the said —— for the acceptance of the Poor Law Board. As witness my hand this —— day of ——, 18—.

——, *Witness*.   *Signature*. ——

By the 10th section it is enacted, that in every case in which no person shall be elected for the office of Guardian in any parish at any annual election of Guardians, the persons elected for the previous year may continue to act as Guardians until the next annual election. It is not compulsory upon a Guardian so to act, and the enactment does not enable Guardians to continue to act for more than *two* years after their election. If there be two Guardians or more to a parish, and one only is elected, neither of the old Guardians can act without a fresh election. If a Guardian should decline to act as such for the second year, before the Poor Law Board issue an order for a fresh election for the parish, it is necessary that the Guardian declining to act should sign a statement in the following form, declaratory of his intention not to continue to act as Guardian:—

To the Guardians of the Poor of the —— Union, in the County of ——.

I, ——, of ——, do hereby declare that I was elected for the office of Guardian in the (*parish* or *township*) of ——, in the County of ——, at the annual election of Guardians, in the month of ——, in the year 18—, and, having been informed that no person has been elected at the election of Guardians for the present year in the said (*parish* or *township*), I do declare that it is not my intention to act hereafter as a Guardian for the same.   Signed, this —— day of ——, 18—.
—— *Witness*.

If there should be an entire failure to elect Guardians for a parish, an order for a fresh election cannot be issued by the Poor Law Board until it is seen whether the old Guardians will continue to act.

If a Guardian loses the qualification upon which he was elected, he

MEETINGS OF THE GUARDIANS (a).

Art. 28.—The Guardians shall upon the day of the week, and at the time of day, and at the place already appointed for holding the ordinary meetings, hold an ordinary meeting once at the least in every week or fortnight for the execution of their duties; and may, when they think fit, change the period, time, and place of such ordinary meeting, with the consent of the Commissioners previously obtained (b).

Art. 29.—The Guardians shall at the first meeting after the Fifteenth day of April, elect out of the whole number of Guardians a Chairman and a Vice-Chairman, who, provided they be Guardians at the time, shall continue respectively to act as such Chairman and Vice-Chairman for the Year next ensuing (c).

---

should at once cease to act as such; no resignation in that case is necessary, indeed, as he would not be a Guardian at all, he would have no office to resign.

(a) With respect to the division of Boards of Guardians into committees for the purposes of relief, and the appointment of district committees, see the respective orders, *post*.

(b) In every case of a change of meeting, whether as regards the day or period, *i.e.* from weekly to fortnightly, the consent of the Poor Law Board to the change must be obtained.

(c) Art. 31 provides for the case of a vacancy in the office of Chairman or Vice-Chairman. In some of the orders issued subsequent to 1847, this article has been slightly varied. Note, that these appointments must be made at the first meeting *after* the 15th April. See 14 & 15 Vict. c. 105, s. 2, as to the continuance in office of the old Board of Guardians until the 15th April inclusive, in each year; which, however, does not apply to Guardians elected for parishes in which relief to the poor is administered under a separate Board of Guardians. By 7 & 8 Vict. c. 101, s. 17, however, in such a parish the Guardians of the preceding year shall continue in office for the period of forty days, or until the election of Guardians for the succeeding year has taken place. If the day of ordinary meeting fall on the 15th day of April, the old Guardians will meet on that day, and the new on the next day of meeting thereafter. The ordinary practice is for the Chairman of the Guardians of the past year (if he be still entitled to act as Guardian) to take the chair at the commencement of the first meeting of the new Board of Guardians after the 15th April. If he then be re-elected Chairman, he will retain the chair; or, in the event of any other Guardian being appointed to the office, he will resign the chair to such Guardian, or to the Vice-Chairman who may be elected, if he be then present. If the day of the first meeting after the 15th April should fall on Good Friday, some of the new Guardians should attend on Good Friday and adjourn the meeting.

With reference to the 14 & 15 Vict. c. 105, s. 2, the Poor Law Board, in their circular of 30th September, 1851, "say that it removes a doubt " which has frequently arisen in respect of unions or parishes divided into " wards for the election of Guardians. In some parishes or wards there " may be no contest, and the election of Guardians for such parishes or " wards may be completed on the last day of nomination; whereas in " others the election may be contested, and protracted for a considerable " time. It has been doubted who are to constitute the Board of Guar- " dians during the interval; namely, whether the whole of the Guardians " of the last year, or those whose election is completed, together with " the Guardians of the last year for the parishes where the election is " not complete.

" This section provides that the Guardians who are elected for the " several parishes in a union, or for the several wards in any parish, shall " continue to act as such until the 15th day of April inclusive in each " year; and after that day every Guardian newly elected for any such " parish or ward shall act as such Guardian for the ensuing year.

" If on this day the election shall not have been concluded in respect " of any parish or ward, the provision in the 7 & 8 Vict. c. 101, s. 17, " will, as the Board presume, come into operation, and the Guardian " of the previous year will continue to be entitled to act for the period " of forty days after the 25th of March, or until his successor has been " elected."

At the first meeting after the annual election, the Guardians must also appoint from among themselves any number, not less than six nor more than twelve, to be a Committee, consisting partly of *ex officio* and partly of elected Guardians, to be called the Assessment Committee of the Union, for the investigation and supervision of the valuation lists of the several parishes in the Union (25 & 26 Vict. c. 103, s. 2). The Committee should be appointed at the first meeting after the 15th April, and not at any meeting of the Guardians prior to that date, even though at the time the annual election of Guardians may have been completed. By 25 & 26 Vict. c. 103, s. 8, " any Guardian of the Union may be present at any meeting of the Committee, but shall not be entitled to take part in the proceedings thereof." This, however, does not confer a right to a Guardian who is not a member of the Committee to be present at the deliberations of the Committee upon any particular matter; for the Committee can lawfully, if they think fit during any of their meetings, clear the room of all persons but members of the Committee whilst they are deliberating on the decision to be given in any case which has been heard before them. When the Committee have heard the whole of any case, they may either retire from the room to deliberate and return to it when their deliberations are concluded, or clear the room and close it during their deliberations, and re-open it afterwards for the admission of other persons. If the Guardians fail to make the appointment at such meeting, a special order of the Poor Law Board must be issued before the appointment can be made (s. 4). (See Fry's Union Assess- ment Committee Act, 1862.) The provision of s. 8 of the Union As- sessment Committee Act, 1862, which required the first meeting of the

Art. 30.—The Guardians at any time may elect two Vice-Chairmen, and if such Vice-Chairmen be appointed at the same time, the Guardians shall determine their precedence; according to which precedence one of the said Vice-Chairmen shall thenceforth preside and act as in the case when only one Vice-Chairman is elected (a).

Art. 31.—If a Chairman or a Vice-Chairman cease to be a Guardian, or refuse, or become incapable, to act as Chairman or Vice-Chairman, before the expiration of the term of office, the Guardians shall, within one month after the occurrence of the vacancy, refusal, or incapacity, elect some other Guardian to be Chairman or Vice-Chairman, as the case may be (b).

Art. 32.—Whereas no act of any meeting of the Guardians will be valid unless three Guardians be present and concur therein; if three Guardians be not present at any meeting, the Clerk shall make an entry of that fact in the minute-book, and the time for holding such meeting shall

---

Committee to be held at the Board Room on a day to be fixed by the Guardians, only applied to the Committee when first appointed, and not to the Committees appointed in subsequent years.

As regards the appointment of Managers of the Metropolitan Asylum District and the Metropolitan Sick Asylum Districts, see Art. 6 of the Order of 15th May, 1867, and Art. 5 of the Order of 15th January, 1868, constituting the Kensington Sick Asylum District. The Guardians of Unions in School Districts are to elect members whose term of office may have expired, to represent them at the Board of Management on one of the two ordinary meetings before the 25th March.

(a) As to the selection of the Vice-Chairman entitled to vote in the election of a District Auditor when there are two Vice-Chairmen, see 7 & 8 Vict. c. 101, s. 32. If two Vice-Chairmen be elected at *different* times, the one who was first elected will have the precedency. It is only when the election of both is simultaneous that the Guardians must determine their precedence. If a vacancy should occur in the office of Vice-Chairman (where there are two), the remaining Vice-Chairman will be entitled to precedence over the Vice-Chairman subsequently elected to fill the vacant office.

(b) This article is directing only as to time. The Article does not require that notice of the election should be given, but it is generally desirable that notice should be given. It is not necessary that the Vice-Chairman should resign his office to enable him to be elected Chairman; his acceptance of the latter office would vacate that of Vice-Chairman. It does not seem that the Article is imperative that a vacancy occurring in one of two Vice-Chairmen shall be supplied.

be deemed to have expired as soon as the said entry shall have been made. But one hour at least shall be allowed to elapse from the time fixed for the commencement of the meeting, before such entry shall be made (c).

Art. 33.—If three or four or more Guardians be present at any ordinary meeting, such three, or the majority of such four or more Guardians, may adjourn the same to the day of the next ordinary meeting, or to some other day previous to the next ordinary meeting.

Art. 34.—An extraordinary meeting of the Guardians may be summoned to be held at any time, upon the requisition of any two Guardians, addressed to the Clerk. Every such requisition shall be made in writing, in the Form (F.) hereunto annexed, and no business other than the business specified in the said requisition shall be transacted at such extraordinary meeting.

Art. 35.—Notice of every change in the period, time, or place of holding any meeting, and notice of the adjournment of any meeting, and notice of every extraordinary meeting, shall be given in writing to every Guardian. Every such notice shall be respectively in the Forms (G.), (H.), and (I.) hereunto annexed, and shall be given or sent by the Clerk to every Guardian, or left at his place of abode two days, if practicable, before the day appointed for the meeting to which it relates.

(c) The 4 & 5 Wm. IV. c. 76, s. 38, provides that, "except where otherwise ordered by the Poor Law Commissioners, and also except for the purpose of consenting to the dissolution or alteration of any Union, or any addition thereto, or to the formation of any Union for the purposes of settlement or rating,—no *ex officio* or other Guardian of any such Board as aforesaid [*i. e.* Board of Guardians], shall have power to act in virtue of such office except as a member, and at a meeting of such Board." And further, that "No act of any such meeting [*i. e.* of a Board of Guardians] shall be valid unless three members shall be present and concur therein." Therefore if the meeting consist of only three Guardians, no act can be done by it if the Guardians are not unanimous. It may here be added, that it is illegal to pay any Guardian of the Poor out of any parish rate or fund for attending to the discharge of his duty as Guardian. Neither can they be lawfully repaid any expenses which they may personally incur in attending the meetings of the Guardians, but see *post*, p. 31.

Art. 36.—If any case of emergency arise, requiring that a meeting of the Guardians should immediately take place, they, or any three of them, may meet at the ordinary place of meeting, and take such case into consideration, and may make an order thereon.

Proceedings of the Guardians.

Art. 37.—At every meeting the Chairman, or in his absence a Vice-Chairman, shall preside; but if at the commencement of any meeting the Chairman and Vice-Chairman or Vice-Chairmen be absent, the Guardians present shall elect one of themselves to preside at such meeting as Chairman thereof, until the Chairman or a Vice-Chairman take the chair (*a*).

Art. 38.—Every question at any meeting consisting of more than three Guardians shall be determined by a majority of the votes of the Guardians present thereat, and voting on the question; and when there shall be an equal number of votes on any question, such question shall be deemed to have been lost (*b*).

(*a*) The Guardian elected as presiding chairman will sign the minutes of the last ordinary and of any other meeting, if they are read whilst he is in the chair. (See Art. 41 (firstly), and note (*a*), p. 28.) The Chairman can of course, like any other Guardian, move a resolution for adoption by the Guardians, or propose an amendment to or second a resolution brought forward by some other Guardian. It may be added, that if the regular Chairman of the Guardians be present at any meeting, it is incumbent upon him to fill the chair so long as he is present; and that he cannot vacate it, and act as an ordinary member of the Board of Guardians at the meeting. So if the Vice-Chairman takes the chair in the absence of the Chairman, he may, if he think fit so to do, continue in the chair, though the Chairman may come to the meeting after the chair has been occupied by the Vice-Chairman.

(*b*) In the Consolidated Orders issued to Unions, formed since 1847, this article stops at the word "question." The 12 & 13 Vict. c. 103, s. 19, has since enacted that, "in the case of an equality of votes upon any question at a meeting of the Guardians of any Union or Parish, the presiding Chairman at such meeting shall have a second or casting vote." The presiding Chairman is entitled to have his vote on any question recorded in the same manner as the vote of any other Guardian present at the meeting; and if the votes are then found to be equal, he will be entitled to give a second or casting vote. If the Chairman has not already voted, and the votes are found to be equal, he may give his casting vote; and it is immaterial whether he has previously voted or not. If, however, before voting at all the Chairman declare the numbers, he cannot afterwards give a vote making them equal, and then a casting vote deciding the question. See 9 O. C. 184. Further upon this subject see note to Art. 155, *post*. The votes are taken by a show of hands, and the result declared by the Chairman after counting them; and it would seem, therefore, that a scrutiny of the votes then given cannot be made unless the result is called in question at the time, and the Chairman then acquiesces in the correctness of it. In taking the votes of the Guardians, the Poor Law Board think that the following should be the course of proceeding:—When the question is put to the meeting, the Chairman should take the votes of the Guardians present by a show of hands, and then declare the motion to be adopted or rejected, as the case may be. The Board think that if any Guardian disputes the correctness of the Chairman's decision, he is entitled to claim to have the names of the Guardians called over, and each Guardian's vote taken down by the Clerk with the view of counting them, and thus of testing the accuracy of that decision; if the result of that counting should be to reverse the Chairman's decision, the Board think that the question must be determined by the counting of the votes consequent upon the taking down of the names; but that any Guardian will be entitled to claim the vote of any Guardian who has held up his hand upon one side of the question to be counted on that side, even though, on calling the names, he may have given his vote the other way. This is in conformity with the practice of the House of Commons, where the rules are the result of long experience and are of recognized utility. (56 O. C. (N. S.) 78.) There are no legal authorities which bind the Chairman to the adoption of any particular course with regard to the manner in which amendments to an original motion shall be put to the meeting. The most convenient course appears to be for the Chairman to allow of only one amendment to be moved at the same time to an original motion; and if it be lost, then to allow other amendments to be moved in succession, until all the amendments are disposed of. If they are all rejected, the original motion should then be put; but if an amendment be carried, it should then be put as an original motion, upon which an amendment may be again moved.

After a division of the Board of Guardians on any motion duly proposed and seconded, the number of Guardians who voted for and against the motion should be recorded on the minutes; but it is not necessary that the names of the Guardians who voted should be entered on the minutes. The Chairman, if he intends to vote on the question before the Board of Guardians, should give his vote immediately after he has counted the votes of the other Guardians, and before he declares the numbers voting on each side from the chair. If he then finds that the votes are equal, he should give a second or casting vote. If, however, he should declare the numbers voting before he gives any vote himself, the Poor Law Board have stated that they think that in such case the Chairman's votes are not entitled to count. (44 O. C. (N. S.) 184.)

The following is a later decision of the Poor Law Board bearing on this point:—The Clerk of Croydon Union stated that a resolution was

Art. 39.—No resolution agreed to or adopted by the Guardians shall be rescinded or altered by them, unless some Guardian shall have given to the Board seven days' notice of a motion to rescind or alter such resolution, which notice shall be forthwith entered on the Minutes by the Clerk (*a*). Provided always, that this regulation shall not extend to any resolution which immediately concerns the

---

carried by six votes to five; but the Guardians doubted the correctness of this mode of stating the result of the voting, and wished to receive the opinion of the Poor Law Board. Before the Chairman's vote was given, the number of votes for and against the motion was equal; and as the Chairman did not give a second vote, the Clerk considered that the Chairman's vote could not be properly called a casting vote. In reply, the Board stated that they thought the Clerk correct. A casting vote, they said, may signify one of two things, either the single vote of a person who only votes in the case of an equality, or the double vote of a person who first votes with the rest, and then upon an equality creates a majority by giving a second vote. In the present instance the vote given by the Chairman in his capacity of Guardian was a casting vote in the former of these senses, as it turned an equality of votes into a majority. (57 O. C. (N. s.) 84.)

As to voting by ballot, see *Faulkner* v. *Elger*, 4 B. & C. 455, in which the objection taken was, that it presents an insurmountable difficulty to a scrutiny, because no person can tell for whom a particular individual voted. As a general rule, it is desirable that the votes of the Guardians should be given openly, and not in any secret mode. See, however, 8 Vict. c. 16, s. 18, and *ib.* c. 17, s. 19, and 18 & 19 Vict. c. 120, in which the Legislature have acknowledged vote by ballot. The Guardians are not restrained by this order from so voting if they think fit to do so.

If a motion intended to be submitted to the Guardians be illegal in its nature if carried, or if an illegal amendment to a legal motion be made, the Chairman is not bound to submit either to the vote. (3 O. C. 38)

Further with regard to the votes of the Guardians, see note to Article 155, *post*. It may here be stated, as the question has been asked, that a Guardian must discharge the duties of his office in person, and that it is not competent for him to appoint a deputy to act for him, or to vote for him by proxy, on any question at a meeting of the Guardians.

(*a*) Thus if a notice to rescind a resolution be given at a meeting of the Guardians held on a Monday, the day for bringing the motion on for discussion will be the following Monday, as seven days' notice means one day inclusive and the other exclusive. (See *Reg.* v. *JJ. of West Riding*, 4 B. & A. 685, and *Reg.* v. *JJ. of Salop*, 8 A. & E. 173.) Any other notices of motion need not be entered on the minutes by the Clerk, unless a special direction be given by the Guardians in that behalf. (See note to Art. 155.)

allowance of relief to any person, or the punishment of any pauper, or to any resolution which the Commissioners may request the Guardians to reconsider or amend, or to any question of emergency (*b*).

Art. 40.—The Guardians may, from time to time (as occasion may require), appoint a Committee to consider and report on any special subject, and such Committee may meet at such times and places as to them may seem convenient; but no act or decision of any such Committee shall of itself be deemed to be the act of the Guardians (*c*).

Art. 41.—At every ordinary meeting of the Guardians the business shall, as far as may be convenient, be conducted in the following order (*d*):—

Firstly.—The minutes of the last ordinary meeting, and

(*b*) In some Unions it is the practice of the Clerk to send to the whole of the Guardians notice of any special business intended to be brought before the Board at a future meeting. Though it may be expedient to send such notices when it is considered desirable to have a full attendance of the Guardians during the discussion of the particular business, the practice will be found, as a general rule, to operate prejudicially to the interest of the Union, for it is found that the Guardians are generally less diligent in attending the Board when they know that only the ordinary relief business is to be transacted. The Clerk, therefore, should not send any such notices except when required to do so by the regulations in force.

(*c*) The Guardians may, however, by a resolution adopting any report which may be made to them by a committee, constitute the recommendations in such report an act or decision of the Guardians. It must be understood that a committee appointed under this Article is to be composed of a selected number of Guardians, and not of the whole Board. As regards the appointment of district committees for the purposes of relief, see the 5 & 6 Vict. c. 57, s. 7. Under this Article a Settlement and Poor Removal Committee may be appointed, but the Committee must be careful in such case not to exercise any of the functions of the Board of Guardians in regard to the proceedings for obtaining orders of removal.

(*d*) The order of business indicated by this Article is not obligatory on the Guardians, but it will in general be found convenient.—*Instr. Letter*, 1842. See also 44 O. C. (N. s.) 184.

It may be here stated that strangers have no right to be present at the meetings of the Guardians; the Guardians may, however, if they think fit, permit any person to be present at their meetings. On a stranger being directed to withdraw, he must do so forthwith; and if he refuse, the Guardians may use necessary force to remove him, and to that end may call in the aid of a police officer.

of any other meeting which may have been held since such ordinary meeting, shall be read to the Guardians ; and, in order that such minutes may be recognized as a record of the acts of the Guardians at their last meeting, they shall be signed by the Chairman presiding at the meeting at which such minutes are read, and an entry of the same having been so read shall be made in the minutes of the day when read (*a*).

Secondly.—The Guardians shall dispose of such business as may arise out of the minutes so read, and shall give the necessary directions thereon.

Thirdly.—They shall proceed to give the necessary directions respecting all applications for relief made since the last ordinary meeting, and also respecting the amount and nature of relief to be given and continued to the paupers then in the receipt of relief, until the next ordinary meeting, or for such other time as such relief may be deemed to be necessary (*b*).

(*a*) The minutes are intended to be a true record of the proceedings of the Board, and the confirmation of the minutes by the succeeding Boards will merely authenticate the accuracy of the record, without affecting the acts of the previous meeting, which in general require no subsequent confirmation.—*Instr. Letter.*

The minutes should always be copied into the fair minute-book in the intervals between the meetings of the Guardians, and be ready to be laid before the Board at the following meeting for the purpose of being read, and afterwards signed by the presiding Chairman of that meeting.

As already observed, the reading over the minutes of the proceedings of the Guardians at the succeeding meeting, and their signature by the Chairman, are only intended to authenticate the entry as being a faithful record of what took place at the meeting to which they relate.

Art. 41 requires that the minutes shall be read; and though it is competent for any Guardian at the reading of them to call in question the correctness of the entry, he cannot raise again any discussion upon points determined in the resolutions as entered on the minutes.

(*b*) The fundamental principle with respect to the legal relief of the poor is, that the condition of the pauper ought to be, on the whole, less eligible than that of the independent labourer. The equity and expediency of this principle are equally obvious. Unless the condition of the pauper is on the whole less eligible than that of the independent labourer, the law destroys the strongest motives to good conduct, steady industry, providence, and frugality among the labouring classes, and induces persons, by idleness or imposture, to throw themselves upon the poor-rates for support. But if the independent labourer sees that a recurrence to the poor-rates will, while it protects him against destitution, place him in a less eligible position than that which he can attain to by his own industry, he is left to the undisturbed influence of all those motives which prompt mankind to exertion, forethought, and self-denial. On the other hand, the pauper has no just ground for complaint, if, at the same time that his physical wants are amply provided for, his condition should be less eligible than that of the poorest class of those who contribute to his support.—*Report of Poor Law Commissioners on Amendment of the Poor Laws,* p. 45.

On the subject of relief generally :—The function of the Guardians is to relieve destitution actually existing, and not to expend the money of the ratepayers in preventing a person from becoming destitute; that is to say, they can only expend the poor-rates in supplying the destitute persons with actual necessaries, such as food, clothing, or lodging, or the means of procuring food, clothing, or lodging temporarily, if the destitute person cannot be immediately received into the Workhouse. Expenditure incurred for the purpose of setting a poor person up in trade, in purchasing tools or implements of trade for him, or replacing a horse or cow that may have died, redeeming goods from pledge, or purchasing goods seized for rent, replacing goods or furniture destroyed by fire, or for purposes of a like or similar nature, is illegal; and, if incurred, must be disallowed by the auditor. So also, if the expenditure be incurred in the education out of the Workhouse of an adult person, or in procuring an adult person to be taught a trade, such person not having whilst a minor been apprenticed in the manner directed by Articles 52–69, *post*.

As regards the relief of persons who are in the receipt of charitable contributions, it may be observed that if the fact comes to the knowledge of the Guardians in the case of an application to them for relief, they are bound to act upon it, and either wholly to refuse relief or to give such an amount only as, with the other assistance the applicant receives, will be sufficient to relieve his or her actual necessities.

The 18 & 19 Vict. c. 34, enables the Guardians to provide for the education of children in the receipt of outdoor relief. The Poor Law Board think that payments for school fees under that Act would be better made by the Guardians direct to the school than through the Relieving Officer. See also the 25 & 26 Vict. c. 43, which enables the Guardians to provide for the education and maintenance of pauper children in certified schools or institutions established for the instruction of blind, deaf, dumb, lame, deformed, or idiotic persons. The Act, however, does not apply to any certified Reformatory School.

By 29 & 30 Vict. c. 113, s. 14, if the parent, step-parent, nearest adult relative, or next of kin of any child not belonging to the Established Church, relieved in a workhouse or in a district school, or in case there should be no parent, step-parent, nearest adult relative, or next of kin, then the god-parent of such child make application to the said Board in such behalf, the Board may, if they think fit, order that such child shall be sent to some school established for the reception, maintenance, and education of children of the religion to which such child shall be proved to belong, and duly certified by the Poor Law

Board under the 25 & 26 Vict. c. 43; and the Guardians of the Union or parish to which such child shall be chargeable shall, according to the terms of such order, cause the child to be conveyed to such school, and pay the costs and charges of the maintenance, lodging, clothing, and education of the said child therein, and all the provisions of the said Statute shall thenceforth apply to the said child.

Applications to the Poor Law Board to send children to schools under the above enactment should be made in the following form:—

I, the undersigned, being the (set forth what degree of relationship exists, or in default of relationship, state what god-parent, strike out from "and" to "kin" inclusive), and nearest adult relative, or next of kin of ——, a child aged —— years, not belonging to the Established Church, but to the (insert religion) now relieved [in the workhouse of the —— Union [or] in the workhouse of the Parish of —— in the county of —— [or] in the —— District School in the county of ——]. Apply to the Poor Law Board to order that such child shall, if they think fit, be sent to the School established at —— for the reception, maintenance, and education of children of the religion to which such child belongs, and which school has been duly certified by the Poor Law Board under the Statute of the 25 and 26 Vict. c. 43.

I offer the accompanying documents and testimonials in proof of my being such (set forth what degree of relationship exists, or in default of relationship what godparent), of the said child, and that such child belongs to the said (insert religion) religion.

Signed this day of —— at ——.
In the Parish of ——, in the County of ——.

A. B. (*Description*.)

If the applicant cannot write, he must make a mark; and this mark must be attested by a witness, who must, also, sign his name and give his description and place of abode.

As regards the relief of persons possessed of house or other property, who may be in circumstances of destitution so as to require relief:— such persons may be unable, from some cause or other, to convert their property into money, or where they may be taking measures to do so, the sale may not have been completed. Such cases ought to be dealt with according to the actual circumstances of the applicant at the time, and the relief given or withheld accordingly. The Guardians may in such cases require the applicant to sell his property, and apply the proceeds, as far as they will go, in the support of himself and his family before the poor-rates are permanently drawn upon for his maintenance; or they may give the relief on loan, to be afterwards recovered from the applicant. See also note to Art. 88.

It may be stated, further, that the Guardians would not be legally justified in paying out of the poor-rate the subscriptions of poor persons to friendly societies, when such persons become unable to provide for the payment thereof out of their own resources.

If the application be for temporary relief only, the Guardians will order it to be given for such short period as they may consider the exi-

Fourthly.—They shall hear and consider any application for relief which may be then made, and determine thereon (a).

---

gencies of the applicant require. If, on the other hand, the applicant be likely to remain permanently chargeable, they will extend the period for which they order it to be given; but under no circumstances should the relief be ordered for a longer period than six months. By limiting the relief to six months, the Relieving Officer will have to report the cases to the Guardians at least once in every half-year in his Application and Report Book; upon which occasion, and indeed whenever he reports an application for relief, he must enter in the book the full particulars of the case, and thus place before the Guardians on each Boardday the particulars of all the cases they will have to decide on that day.

In ordering relief, the Guardians should specify what relief is to be given in each case, and the time for which it is to be allowed. If, before the expiration of the specified period, a continuance of the relief should not be necessary, the Relieving Officer should report the circumstance to the Guardians, and take their directions accordingly.

The Guardians may provide for the reception, maintenance, and instruction of any adult pauper, being blind or deaf and dumb, in any hospital or institution established for the reception of persons suffering under such infirmities, and may pay the charges incurred in the conveyance of such pauper to and from the same, as well as those incurred in his maintenance, support, and instruction therein. (30 & 31 Vict. c. 106, s. 21.)

The giving of relief in a case where the applicants are really destitute should not be delayed pending inquiry into any other matters. The primary duty is to relieve actual destitution existing in the Union, and the duty of the Guardians in deciding as to the relief of any person within the Union is to look simply at the question of destitution. When doubt arises as to the removability of a pauper, the question may be submitted to the Poor Law Board in the manner for which the 12 & 13 Vict. c. 106, s. 12, provides. A convenient form of statement, settled by Mr. Fry, in which the question may be submitted, can be procured from Messrs. Knight and Co., Publishers, Fleet Street, London.

(a) With respect to the administration of relief to the able-bodied, see the provisions of the general relief orders, post. It may be here stated that the Guardians cannot by a general direction authorize the Workhouse Master to give provisions to paupers waiting at the Workhouse for the decision of the Board upon their cases. If paupers so waiting are actually in need of immediate temporary relief, the Guardians can direct the relieving Officer to apply such temporary relief as may be necessary, until a decision has been come to in respect of the case. It should also be stated that the Guardians cannot lawfully direct the Master of the Workhouse to provide them with refreshments from the Workhouse stores when attending meetings of the Board of Guardians; see 56 O. C. (N. S.) 80, in which the Poor Law Board stated that they had occasion to consider this question with reference to a disallowance made

Fifthly.—They shall read the report of the state of the Workhouse or Workhouses, examine all books and accounts relative to the relief of the paupers of the Union, and give all needful directions concerning the management and discipline of the said Workhouse or Workhouses, and the providing of furniture and stores and other articles (*a*).

---

by an auditor of sums charged for the supply of refreshments to the Guardians when attending the meetings of the Board. "The Board are not able to find any legal authority to support such a charge. It appears to them that members of the Board of Guardians cannot be legally provided, at the cost of the poor-rate, with refreshments while engaged in the discharge of their duty at the Board, any more than they can be remunerated for the loss of time which they bestow upon the duties of their office, or the cost of their conveyance to attend the meetings of the Board; and as the expenditure is not in itself lawful, the Board are not aware of any order or resolution which they could issue to give validity to the practice. See also 3 O. C. p. 85, as to providing provender for the horses of the Guardians at the cost of the poor-rates.

The regulation (fourthly) does not absolutely require that the Guardians should hear personally the applications of the paupers, but nevertheless the Guardians should admit the paupers and allow them to be heard before the Board whenever any pauper may desire it.

With regard to the liability of persons to obtain relief or assistance for those of their household, *Reg.* v. *Shepherd*, 31 L. J. (N. s.) M. C. 102, may be referred to. It was there held that the mother of a girl of eighteen years of age was not liable to be convicted of manslaughter because she did not procure the assistance of a midwife for her daughter in her confinement, who usually supported herself by her own labour. In 1 Russell on Crimes, 493, 3rd edition, it is said that it is by no means clear that a woman who, without means of providing food for her children, neglects to apply to the Relieving Officer, and allow them to die for want of food, is not guilty of manslaughter; but Erle, C. J., in the above case, said that he should have been much surprised if any one had been convicted of felony for not applying to a Relieving Officer. See also *Reg.* v. *Vann*, 5 Cox, C. C., 379; 21 L. J. (N. s.) M. C. 39, on the same subject, which, however, had reference to burial.

(*a*) The Poor Law Board in a circular dated 28th March, 1864, state that the applications made to them by Boards of Guardians for their orders (under 22 & 23 Vict. c. 49, s. 1) to extend the time for the payments of claims, disclose to the Board the existence of much laxity in respect of the ordering of goods for the workhouse, and the performance of small repairs to it, or to the furniture in it.

They find that the orders are very frequently given without directions from the Board of Guardians, and the bills are frequently presented for payment without the previous knowledge of the Guardians

Sixthly.—They shall examine the Treasurer's account, and shall, when necessary, make orders on the Overseers or other proper authorities of the several Parishes in the Union, for providing such sums as may be lawfully required by the Guardians on account of the respective Parishes (*b*).

Seventhly.—They shall transact any such business as may not fall within any of the above classes (*c*).

Art. 42.—When the Guardians have allowed relief in the Workhouse to any applicant, a written or printed order for his admission therein, signed by the Clerk, shall be forthwith delivered to the applicant, or to any person on his behalf (*d*).

---

as to the orders for the work, or supplies which form the subject matter of such claims.

The Board add that if the regulations in Art. 41 (fifthly) *ante*, Art. 208, No. 24, and Art. 209, *post*, and Art. 16, No. 2, of the accounts order, *post*, are duly observed, the irregularities to which they have referred cannot occur, and they request the Guardians to bring them under the notice of their officers, and to impress upon them the necessity of their being strictly attended to for the future.

The Board say, that if applications be made to them for their order to extend the time for the payment of such claims, when the same has been accidentally delayed, they desire to be furnished with the invoices for the goods supplied, or work done, extracted from the Order Check Book, or with extracts from the minutes of the Guardians, containing the directions for ordering the same to be supplied or executed, as the case may be.

(*b*) With respect to the Treasurer's balance, see Articles 202, No. 7, and 203, Nos. 3 and 4; and the Order of 26th of February, 1866, *post*, as to the contribution orders of the Guardians upon the Overseers. As regards the examination of the books, referred to in this and preceding sections, no precise directions can be set out for the discharge of this duty. When the books are before the Guardians, they will, in general, be able to determine for themselves whether any defect or irregularity exists in the mode of keeping them, and whether they are in accordance with the regulations. An examination of this nature tends to make the officers careful in the discharge of this portion of their duty, and the Guardians informed of the working of the law, in regard to the administration of relief, and also as to their financial condition.

(*c*) As to Boards of Guardians petitioning Parliament on subjects connected with their duties, see 56 O. C. (N. S.) 79.

(*d*) The order of admission should be filled up by the Clerk, and if the applicant be present at the Board, it should be given to him (or her); if not present, it may be given to the person who makes the application

Art. 43 (a).—When the Guardians have allowed out-door relief, in money or kind, to any applicant, the particulars of such relief shall be entered, by the proper Relieving Officer, in a ticket according to Form (K.) hereunto annexed, and such ticket shall be delivered by him to the applicant, or to some person on his behalf.

CONTRACTS OF THE GUARDIANS.

Art. 44.—All contracts to be entered into on behalf of the Union relating to the maintenance, clothing, lodging, employment, or relief of the poor, or for any other purpose relating to or connected with the general management of the poor, shall be made and entered into by the Guardians (b).

---

on his behalf. If neither the applicant nor his or her representative be present, the Relieving Officer may be required by the Board of Guardians to deliver the order. The Relieving Officer is empowered by Article 215, No. 6, *post*, to give an order of admission to the workhouse in any case of sudden or urgent necessity, but no one but the Clerk can sign the order of admission when relief in the workhouse is given in pursuance of an order of the Board of Guardians. The order should embrace the whole family of the applicant, if they are residing together, and are all destitute. But see note to Art. 88, on this subject.

(a) It is desirable that a pauper to whom the Guardians have ordered relief should be accurately informed, not only of the nature and amount of the relief, but of the period for which that relief is to be allowed. As regards the Relieving Officer, the insertion of the period seems a proper proceeding to prevent error or misconception on his part.

In those cases in which permanent relief is thought necessary, it is advisable that the order for the relief should be made for "6 months" or "26 weeks," or any shorter period which the Guardians may think proper, and should be so entered in the Application and Report Book. The cases would then, as a matter of course, be regularly brought again before the Guardians at the end of the time for which the relief was granted. A definite period may be inserted in the ticket in cases where there is no reasonable ground to suppose that the circumstances of the pauper will soon undergo any material alteration. In other cases the requirement of this article will be satisfied if the ticket be made conditional, and the time for which the relief is ordered be indefinitely expressed. Thus, the column might be filled up, "until further reported by the Relieving Officer," "whilst reported by the Medical Officer as being unable to work," etc.

With respect to the powers of the Relieving Officer to discontinue or vary, upon his own authority, the amount of relief ordered by the Guardians in any case, see note to Article 215, No. 10.

When the Relieving Officer shall, in any special case, have departed from the order of the Guardians, the Guardians, when the report of his having so done is made to them, should either cancel the ticket or give a fresh one with an increased or diminished amount of relief, or they may make the period for which the relief is ordered conditional instead of specific.

(*b*) The Guardians should bear in mind that the 55 Geo. III. c. 137, and 4 & 5 Wm. IV. c. 76, s. 51, impose heavy penalties on persons having the management of the poor if concerned in contracts for the supply of goods for the use of such poor. These enactments extend to any person who, either in his own name or in the name of any other person or persons, provides for his own profit any goods, materials, or provisions for the use of any workhouse, or who may be concerned, directly or indirectly, in furnishing the same. Consequently, if the Guardians were to enter into a contract for the supply of goods with the partner of one of their number, the case would come within the statute, and the Guardian, whose partner supplied the goods, would be liable to the penalties enforced by the statute. But if the goods are supplied by the Guardian without profit to himself, *Skinner* v. *Buckee*, 3 B. & C. 6, would seem to decide that he would not incur any penalties. See also *Barber* v. *Waite*, 1 A. & E. 514, on the same point.

Where a Master of a Workhouse bought provisions for the use of the poor in the workhouse from one of the Guardians of the parish, it was held that the Guardian who supplied the goods was liable to the penalty of £100, imposed by the 55 Geo. III. c. 137, s. 6. (*West* v. *Andrews*, 5 B. & Ald. 328.)

The prohibition would not extend to a Guardian who is a member of a joint-stock company supplying the goods, but it would to a Guardian who is a member of an ordinary partnership firm which supplies goods for the relief of the poor; nor perhaps would the prohibition apply to a Guardian who only supplies "work and labour," but it is obviously very objectionable that the Guardians should employ one of themselves to do work for the Union, and they should therefore avoid such an arrangement.

There appears to be nothing illegal in an individual Guardian purchasing goods or old stores belonging to the Union, though his doing so might, on principle, be considered objectionable. Neither is a Guardian incapacitated from acting as the attorney of the Board of Guardians, or from transacting any professional business for any of the parishes in the Union; nor is he liable to penalties for being concerned in a contract to supply *work* and *labour* in repairs to the workhouse.

With reference to members of Boards of Guardians being concerned in contracts for the supply of goods to the Union, the Commissioners, in their Official Circular, No. 10, have stated that they are of opinion, that a Guardian, in supplying a contractor with milk consumed in the workhouse, would be liable to the penalties imposed by the 55 Geo. III. c. 137, for being concerned *indirectly* in furnishing a supply of provisions for the use of the workhouse.

A Guardian of the poor knowingly supplying goods for any workhouse for profit, upon the verbal order of the Master of the Workhouse, renders himself liable to the penalty imposed by the 55 Geo. III. c. 137, s. 6, as extended by 4 & 5 Wm. IV. c. 76, s. 51, although the Master

D 2

Art. 45.—The Guardians shall require tenders to be made in some sealed paper for the supply of all provisions, fuel, clothing, furniture, or other goods or materials, the consumption of which may be estimated, one month with another, to exceed ten pounds per month, and of all provisions, fuel, clothing, furniture, or other goods or materials, the cost of which may be reasonably estimated to exceed fifty pounds in a single sum, and shall purchase the same upon contracts to be entered into after the receipt of such tenders (*a*).

Art. 46.—Any work or repairs to be executed in the

was not expressly authorized by the Guardians to make the purchase, as required by the orders of the Poor Law Commissioners. (*Greenhow v. Parker*, 31 L. J. (N. s.) Ex. 4; 6 H. & N. 882.)

Concerning the validity of contracts made by or on behalf of any parish or Union, not in conformity with the regulations of the Commissioners, see 4 & 5 Wm. IV. c. 76, s. 49.

(*a*) Arts. 45–49 require the Guardians to purchase goods, etc., upon tender. The Commissioners are aware that the system of purchase by tender is sometimes productive of inconvenience, and that goods may occasionally be obtained on more advantageous terms without a recourse to this method. They believe, however, that on the whole it affords the best security to the public; and the practice of the administrative bodies which make the largest purchases of goods (viz. the Military and Naval Departments) strongly confirms them in this conclusion. Art. 49 allows of an exception being made in extraordinary cases, with the consent of the Commissioners.—*Instr. Letter*, April, 1842. The Guardians by these Articles are not bound to accept the lowest tenders given in, nor in the event of there being only one person tendering for the supply of a particular kind of goods are they bound to accept his tender. Moreover, they are not bound to accept any tender that may be sent in if they are not satisfied that it would be advantageous to the Union to do so, but may advertise again; or they may enter into a special contract, with the sanction of the Poor Law Board, under Art. 49. (See 3 O. C. 148.) With regard to the breach of a contract by a bread contractor, and the power of the Guardians to reject the supplies, see *Elliott v. Martin*, 2 Mee. & W. 13.

As to contracts of the Guardians not under seal, see *Paine v. Guardians of the Strand Union*, 15 L. J. R. (N. s.) M. C. 89; *Haigh v. North Bierley*, 31 L. T. 213; 5 Jur. (N. s.) 511; 4 E. B. & E. 873; 28 L. J. (N. s.) Q. B. 62; *Sanders v. St. Neots*, 8 Q. B. 810; *Clark v. Cuckfield*, 21 L. J. Q. B. 349.

In the case of a trading company it has been held, that where a contract is essential to the purposes and objects of the company, it may be enforced against them, although it be not under seal. (*Henderson v. Australian Royal Mail Steam Navigation Company*, 24 L. J. R. (N. s.) Q. B. 322. See also per Martin, B., in *Walker v. Great Western Railway Company*, 2 L. R. Exch. 229.)

Workhouse, or the premises connected with the Workhouse, or any fixtures to be put up therein, which may respectively be reasonably estimated to exceed the cost of fifty pounds in one sum, shall be contracted for by the Guardians, on sealed tenders, in the manner prescribed in Articles 45 and 47.

Art. 47.—Notice of the nature and conditions of the contract to be entered into, of the estimated amount of the articles required, of the last day on which tenders will be received, and the day on which the tenders will be opened, shall be given in some newspaper circulating in the Union, not less than ten days previous to the last day on which such tenders are to be received; and no tender shall be opened by the Clerk, or any Guardian, or other person, prior to the day specified in such notice, or otherwise than at a meeting of the said Guardians (*b*).

Art. 48.—When any tender is accepted, the party making the tender shall, in pursuance of these regulations, enter into a contract, in writing, with the Guardians, containing the terms, conditions, and stipulations mutually agreed

---

(*b*) The purpose of inserting Union advertisements in newspapers is to obtain the utmost publicity for them, and the Commissioners have stated, that they consider that the advertisements ought to be inserted in the newspaper which circulates the most widely among the class of persons who are likely to make the desired tenders, or to whom the advertisements may be in other respects addressed, and that the choice of a newspaper ought to be determined by these considerations, without any reference to the opinions, either on the administration of the Poor Law, or any other subject which may have been expressed in the newspapers.—*Off. Cir.* vol. ii. p. 238. If, after advertising, no tender be received, the Guardians should advertise again or contract with the former contractor, or any other respectable person, on the best terms they can make. (See note to Art. 45, *ante*.)

It will be observed that this Article is imperative in requiring the notices to be published in a newspaper. Of course, in addition to this, the Guardians, if they think fit, may cause printed placards to be posted throughout the Union, inviting tenders for the supply of goods for the Union ; but if the latter course only were to be had recourse to, sufficient publicity would not be given, and tradesmen at a distance would consequently be precluded from tendering, and the Union in many cases be charged higher for articles supplied by resident tradesmen than would be charged if the articles were supplied by large dealers at a distance.

upon, and whenever the Guardians deem it advisable, the party contracting shall find one or more surety or sureties, who shall enter into a bond conditioned for the due performance of the contract, or shall otherwise secure the same (a).

Art. 49.—Provided always, that if, from the peculiar nature of any provisions, fuel, clothing, furniture, goods, materials, or fixtures to be supplied, or of any work or repairs to be executed, it shall appear to the Guardians desirable that a specific person or persons be employed to supply or execute the same, without requiring sealed tenders as hereinbefore directed, it shall be lawful for such Guardians, with

---

(a) These contracts and bonds, as well as any mortgage, instrument, or any assignment thereof, in pursuance of the rules, etc., of the Poor Law Board, are exempt from stamp duty. (See 4 & 5 Wm. IV. c. 76, s. 86.)

It may also be stated here, that a contract entered into by the Guardians, which is not in conformity with the foregoing regulations, is not in itself void, but only voidable if the Poor Law Board shall so direct. (See 4 & 5 Wm. IV. c. 76, s. 49.)

Every receipt which is given by a Board of Guardians for the payment of money is liable to stamp duty, unless it be such a receipt as is directed to be given or taken by the 4 & 5 Wm. IV. c. 76, or by any order or regulation of the Poor Law Commissioners or of the Poor Law Board.

The acceptance of tenders is not sufficient; for in the absence of a written contract under seal, the Guardians would have no redress against the person tendering. The proper course is for the Guardians to have the contracts ready when the tenders are opened, and to require the persons tendering to attend and execute them, and the Guardians should then cause the Union seal to be affixed. Further on this point, see *Hull v. Petch*, 10 Exch. Rep. 610. The following are the facts of that case: The Guardians of Hull, acting under a local Act with a view to obtaining tenders for meat, etc., for the use of the workhouse, issued an advertisement stating that they would receive tenders for the supply of the Workhouse with meat for three months—that sealed tenders were to be sent to the clerk of the Corporation, and that *all contractors would have to sign a written contract after acceptance of the tender*. The defendant having given in a tender which was accepted by the Guardians, on being informed of the acceptance immediately afterwards wrote to the Guardians to say that he declined to supply them with meat; and it was held that as a written contract was to be executed, the acceptance of the tender did not form a binding contract so as to render the defendant liable for refusing to supply the Workhouse with meat in accordance with his tender.

the consent of the Commissioners first obtained, to enter into a contract with the said person or persons, and to require such sureties and securities as are specified in Art. 48.

Art. 50.—Every contract to be hereafter made by any Guardian shall contain a stipulation requiring the contractor to send in his bill, or account of the sum due to him for goods or work, on or before some day to be named in the contract (*b*).

Art. 51.—The Guardians shall fix some day or days, not being more than twenty-one days after the end of each quarter, for the attendance of contractors and tradesmen, or their authorized agents, and the Clerk shall notify such day to every contractor or tradesman to whom money may be due, or to his agent, or he shall, under the direction of the Guardians, cause the same to be advertised in some newspaper (*c*).

(*b*) With reference to the Payment of Debts Act, 22 & 23 Vict. c. 49, s. 1, it will be convenient if the day of payment for the goods supplied is made to fall within a given short period after Michaelmas Day and Lady Day respectively. The debts, in such case, would not accrue until after those days, and more time would consequently be given for the payment of the contractors than would be the case if the debts accrued within the half-year when the goods were supplied.

(*c*) The intention of the rule is, that the Guardians shall require the attendance of the contractors before the Board on a fixed day in each quarter, to receive payment of their bills for goods supplied to the Union during the previous quarter. See also Art. 220 as to the transmission of money (or cheques) by the Clerk to the persons for whom such money (or cheques) is intended. Article 51 is confined in its terms to contractors and tradesmen; but the Guardians can require their officers to attend to receive their salaries without reference to this regulation.

It will be borne in mind that under the 22 & 23 Vict. c. 49, s. 1, any debt which may be lawfully incurred by or become due from the Guardians, shall be paid within the half-year in which the same shall have been incurred or become due, or within three months after the expiration of such half-year, but not afterwards; the commencement of such half-year to be reckoned from the time when the last half-year's account shall or ought to have been closed, provided that the Poor Law Board, by their order, may, if they see fit, extend the time within which such payment shall be made for a period not exceeding twelve months from the date of such debt. Further, with regard to this statute, see note to Art. 41 (fifthly), *ante*, p. 32.

APPRENTICESHIP OF PAUPER CHILDREN.

Parties (*a*).

Art. 52.—No child under the age of nine years, and no child (other than a deaf and dumb child) who cannot read and write his own name, shall be bound apprentice by the Guardians (*b*).

(*a*) The Guardians are not restricted by the statute or by the regulations contained in this order from binding, as apprentices, children who are not actually in the receipt of relief, or whose parents may not be in the receipt of relief as paupers at the time of the binding. Such children as may ordinarily be considered "poor children" are within the scope of the provisions respecting the apprenticeship of pauper children. But the Poor Law Commissioners, in the circular letter accompanying the original apprenticeship order, stated that apprenticeship is a species of relief, and consequently can only be given subject to the regulations which may exist in any particular Union or Parish with regard to relief in such Union or Parish generally. Therefore if the proposed apprentice be the child of an able-bodied person, the sanction of the Poor Law Board to the relief should be obtained under Art. 6 of the Order of December 21, 1844, *post*, or of 14 Dec., 1852, *post*, accordingly as the order may apply to the particular Union. Under the 7 & 8 Vict. c. 101, s. 12, and 11 & 12 Vict. c. 110, s. 8, the Guardians can bind pauper children who are chargeable to the common fund as apprentices, and charge the expenses to that fund. It may here be observed that the 20 Geo. II. c. 19, s. 4, enables the Justices to discharge an apprentice bound by the Guardians under these regulations, without the consent of the Guardians to the discharge being obtained.

The object in framing these regulations has been to secure a careful attention on the part of the Guardians who are to bind out the children to the fitness and propriety of the step which is to affect permanently the future condition of these children, and a due performance afterwards by the masters of the duties which appear naturally to result from the relation of master and apprentice. The Commissioners added, however, that they by no means desired to express any opinion as to the propriety of the Guardians extending the practice of parish apprenticeship, and that they did not wish the Guardians in those parts of the country where the system had not been generally pursued, to infer that they entertained any desire to promote its introduction in consequence of having issued the order to which the circular had reference.—*Instr. Letter*, 1 January, 1845.

(*b*) If the child be taught to read and write his or her own name only, it is considered that it will suffice under this Article. The word child, as used in this Article, may include a person who is eighteen years of age; but the indenture will not, according to the 18 Geo. III. c. 47, be obligatory upon the apprentice after attaining the age of twenty-one years.

Art. 53.—No child shall be so bound to a person who is not a housekeeper, or assessed to the poor-rate in his own name (*c*).

Or who is a journeyman, or a person not carrying on trade or business on his own account;

Or who is under the age of twenty-one;

Or who is a married woman.

The Premium (*d*).

Art. 54.—No premium, other than clothing for the apprentice, shall be given upon the binding of any person above the age of sixteen years, unless such person be maimed, deformed, or suffering from some permanent bodily infirmity, such as may render him unfit for certain trades or sorts of work.

Art. 55.—Where any premium is given, it shall in part consist of clothes supplied to the apprentice at the commencement of the binding, and in part of money, one moiety whereof shall be paid to the master at the binding, and the residue at the termination of the first year of the binding.

Term.

Art. 56.—No apprentice shall be bound by the Guardians for more than eight years.

Consent.

Art. 57.—No person above fourteen years of age shall be so bound without his consent.

And no child under the age of sixteen years shall be so bound without the consent of the father of such child; or if the father be dead, or be disqualified to give such

---

(*c*) It will apparently suffice if the proposed master be a housekeeper without being a ratepayer, and *vice versâ*.

(*d*) Clothing given to a pauper on his being apprenticed must be regarded in the same light as relief; and the premium and cost of such clothing, if supplied by the Relieving Officer, should be entered accord-

consent, as hereinafter provided, or if such child be a bastard, without the consent of the mother, if living, of such child.

Provided, that where such parent (*a*) is transported beyond the seas, or is in custody of the law, having been convicted of some felony, or for the space of six calendar months before the time of executing the indenture has deserted such child, or for such space of time has been in the service of her Majesty, or of the East India Company, in any place out of the United Kingdom, such parent, if the father, shall be deemed to be disqualified as hereinbefore stated; and if it be the mother, no such consent shall be required.

PLACE OF SERVICE.

Art. 58.—No child shall be bound to a master whose place of business, whereat the child is to work and live, is distant more than thirty miles from the place in which the child is residing at the time of the proposed binding, or at the time of his being sent on trial to such master;

Unless in any particular case the Commissioners shall, on application to them, otherwise permit (*b*).

---

ingly in his Outdoor relief List. If the master of the workhouse supplies the clothing and any premium which he may pay under the directions of the Guardians, should be entered by him in his Receipt and Expenditure Book. On the other hand, if the Guardians themselves order payment to be made to the master of the apprentice directly, they should make an order upon their Treasurer for the amount, to be dealt with in the usual way.

(*a*) If the parent or surviving parent be lunatic, the apprenticeship may take place without his or her consent, provided that all the other regulations with regard to apprenticeship contained in the order are duly observed.

(*b*) It should be remembered also that by 56 Geo. III. c. 139, s. 1, no child shall be bound apprentice to any person or persons residing or having an establishment in trade, at which it is intended such child shall be employed, out of the same county, at a greater distance than forty miles from the parish or place to which such child shall belong, unless such child shall belong to some parish or place which shall be more than forty miles from the city of London, in which case the Justices may make a special order for that purpose. The distance will be

PRELIMINARIES OF THE BINDING (c).

Art. 59.—If the child whom it is proposed to bind apprentice be in the Workhouse, and under the age of fourteen years, the Guardians shall require a certificate in writing from the Medical Officer of the Workhouse as to the fitness in regard to bodily health and strength of such child to be bound apprentice to the proposed trade, and shall also ascertain from the Master of the Workhouse the capacity of the child for such binding in other respects.

Art. 60.—If the child be not in the Workhouse, but in the Union by the Guardians of which it is proposed that he

---

measured, not by the nearest practicable road, but by a straight line from point to point on the horizontal plain, "as the crow flies." (*Lake* v. *Butler*, 24 L. J. R. (N. s.) Q. B. 273; *Stokes* v. *Grissell*, 23 L. J. R. (N. s.) C. P. 141; *Reg.* v. *Saffron Walden*, 9 Q. B. 76; 15 L. J. R. (N. s.) M. C. 115; *Duignan* v. *Walker*, 5 Jur. (N. s.) 976.)

(c) With regard to the allowance of indentures of apprenticeship by justices, the Poor Law Board, in answer to an inquiry, have stated that the 7 & 8 Vict. c. 101, s. 12, expressly provides that " it shall be lawful for the Guardians of such Union or Parish respectively to bind any such poor child to be an apprentice, and in such case the indentures of apprenticeship shall be executed by the said Guardians, and shall not need to be allowed, assented to, or executed by any justice or justices of the peace :" consequently, it is not required that the indenture should be allowed by the justices of either county. The Board, moreover, consider that since the passing of the 7 & 8 Vict. c. 101, s. 12, and the issuing by the Poor Law Commissioners, under the authority of that provision, of the orders and regulations on the subject of parish apprenticeship, it is not necessary that the justices should certify, in accordance with the 4 & 5 Wm. IV. c. 76, s. 61, upon an indenture entered into by a Board of Guardians appointed under that Act, that the rules and regulations have been conformed to in the binding. The 7 & 8 Vict. c. 101, s. 12, in the case of a binding by the Guardians, expressly dispenses with the assent or allowance of justices; and it therefore seems, on a careful examination of the provisions bearing on the subject, that it is only in a case where such assent or allowance would still be required, that it is necessary that the justices should certify as to the fact of the rules of the Commissioners having been conformed to in the binding. The 4 & 5 Wm. IV. c. 76, s. 61, provides that the certificate "in question is to be in addition to such assent, consent, order, or allowance of justices." (56 O. C. p. 65.)

It has been held, with reference to this article, that the regulations it contains are directory, and that the omission to comply with them (if established) would not affect the validity of the indenture. (*Reg.* v. *St. Mary, Bermondsey*, 2 E. & B. 809; 23 L. J. R. (N. s.) M. C. 1.)

shall be bound, the Relieving Officer of the district in which the child is residing shall examine into the circumstances of the case, the condition of the child, and of his parents, if any, and the residence of the proposed master, the nature of his trade, the number of other apprentices, if any, then bound to him, and generally as to the fitness of the particular binding, and shall report the result of his inquiry to the Guardians.

Art. 61.—If in any case within Article 60 the Guardians think proper to proceed with the binding, they shall, when the child is under the age of fourteen years, direct the Relieving Officer to take the child to the Medical Officer of the district, to be examined as to his fitness in respect of bodily health and strength for the proposed trade or business; and such Medical Officer shall certify in writing according to his judgment in the matter, which certificate shall be produced by the said Relieving Officer to the next meeting of the Guardians.

Art. 62.—If the child be not residing within the Union, the Guardians who propose to bind him shall not proceed to do so unless they receive such a report as is required in Article 60 from the Relieving Officer of the district in which such child is residing, and a certificate from some medical man practising in the neighbourhood of the child's residence to the effect required in Article 61.

Art. 63.—When it is proposed to give a premium other than clothing upon the binding of any person above the age of sixteen years, the Guardians shall require a certificate in writing from some medical practitioner, certifying that the person is maimed, deformed, or disabled, to the extent specified in such Article (a), and shall cause a copy of such certificate to be entered on their minutes before they proceed to execute the indenture.

Art. 64.—When such certificate, as is required by Articles, 59, 61, 62, and 63, is received, or in case, from the age of the child, no such certificate is required, the Guar-

---

(a) See Article 54.

dians shall direct that the child and the proposed master, or some person on his behalf, and, in case the child be under the age of sixteen, that the parent or person in whose custody such child shall be then living, attend some meeting of the Board to be then appointed.

Art. 65.—At such meeting, if such parties appear, the Guardians shall examine into the circumstances of the case; and if, after making all due inquiries, and hearing the objections (if any be made) on the part of the relatives or friends of such child, they deem it proper that the binding be effected, they may forthwith cause the indenture to be prepared, and, if the master be present, to be executed; but if he be not present, they shall cause the same to be transmitted to him for execution; and when executed by him, and returned to the Guardians, the same shall be executed by the latter, and shall be signed by the child, as provided in Article 67.

Art. 66.—If the proposed master reside out of the Union, but in some other Union or Parish under a Board of Guardians, whether formed under the provisions of the first recited Act, or of the Act of the twenty-second year of the reign of King George the Third, intituled "*An Act for the better Relief and Employment of the Poor*," or of any local Act, the Guardians shall, before proceeding to effect the binding, communicate in writing the proposal to the Guardians of such other Union or Parish, and request to be informed whether such binding is open to any objection; and if no objection be reported by such Guardians within the space of one calendar month, or if the objection does not appear to the Guardians proposing to bind the child to be sufficient to prevent the binding, the same may be proceeded with; and when the indenture shall have been executed, the Clerk to the Guardians who executed the same shall send notice thereof in writing to the Guardians of the Union or Parish wherein the said apprentice is to reside (*b*).

(*b*) The object of the notice in this Article is not to raise any question of settlement, because no objection by the Guardians of the Union

INDENTURE (a).

Art. 67.—The indenture shall be executed in duplicate, by the master and the Guardians, and shall not be valid unless signed by the proposed apprentice with his name, or, if deaf and dumb, with his mark, in the presence of the said Guardians; and the consent of the parent, where requisite, shall be testified by such parent signing with his name or mark, to be properly attested, at the foot of the said indenture; and where such consent is dispensed with under Article 57, the cause of such dispensation shall be stated at the foot of the indenture by the Clerk.

Art. 68.—The name of the place or places at which the apprentice is to work and live shall be inserted in the indenture.

Art. 69.—One part of such indenture, when executed, shall be kept by the Guardians; the other shall be delivered to the master.

DUTIES OF THE MASTER OF A PAUPER APPRENTICE.

Art. 70.—And We do hereby prescribe the duties of the master to whom such poor child may be apprenticed, and the terms and conditions to be inserted in the said indenture, to be as follows:—

No. 1. The master shall teach the child the trade, business, or employment set forth in the indenture, unless

---

in which the master resides would affect it, but to enable the Guardians of that Union to communicate any fact which may be in their knowledge regarding the proposed master or otherwise which may induce them to consider the binding calculated to be detrimental to the future welfare of the apprentice.

(a) If the indenture be cancelled for any cause, the consent of the Justices, under the 56 Geo. III. c. 139, s. 9, must be obtained; it is, however, open to some doubt whether the power of the Justices to cancel an indenture of apprenticeship extends to cases where the premium is over £5.

Apparently it is not necessary that the apprentice should seal as well as sign the indenture. This Article only requires that the indenture shall be signed by the apprentice; and according to *Rex* v. *St. Nicholas, Nottingham*, 2 T. R. 726, it was not requisite that the apprentice should have executed the indenture of apprenticeship to constitute a valid binding.

the Guardians authorize the substitution of another trade, business, or employment.

No. 2. He shall maintain the said child with proper food and nourishment.

No. 3. He shall provide a proper lodging for the said child.

No. 4. He shall supply the said child with proper clothing during the term of the binding, together with the necessary provision of linen.

No. 5. He shall, in case the said child be affected with any disease or sickness, or meet with any accident, procure, at his own cost, adequate medical or surgical assistance, from some duly qualified medical man, for such child.

No. 6. He shall, once at least on every Sunday, cause the child to attend some place of divine worship, if there be any such within a reasonable distance, according to the religious persuasion in which the child has been brought up, so, however, that no child shall be required by the master to attend any place of worship to which his parents or surviving parent may object, nor, when he shall be above the age of sixteen, any place to which he may himself object.

No. 7. Where such parents or parent or next of kin desire it, he shall allow the said child to attend any Sunday or other school, which shall be situated within the same parish, or within two miles' distance from his residence, on every Sunday ; and, if there be no such school which such child can attend, he shall, at some reasonable hour on every Sunday, allow any minister of the religious persuasion of the child to have access to such child for the purpose of imparting religious instruction.

No. 8. Where the apprentice continues bound after the age of seventeen years, the master shall, in every case, where the Guardians require him so to do, pay to such apprentice, for and in respect of every week that he duly and properly serves the said master, as a remuneration, a sum to be inserted in the indenture, or to be agreed upon by the Guardians and the said master when that time arrives, or, if they cannot agree, to be settled by some person to be then chosen by the said master and such Guardians, and, until such sum be agreed upon or settled, not less than one-fourth of the amount then commonly paid as wages to journeymen in the said trade, business, or employment.

No. 9. The master shall, himself or by his agent, produce the apprentice to the Guardians by whom such apprentice was bound at their ordinary meeting next preceding the end of the first year of the binding, and before the receipt of the remainder of the premium, if any be due, and shall in like manner produce the said apprentice at some one of their ordinary meetings, to be held at or about the middle of the term, and whenever afterwards required to do so by the said Guardians: Provided, that if the apprentice reside out of the Union by the Guardians whereof he was bound, the apprentice shall be produced, as hereinbefore directed, to the Guardians of the Union or Parish, as described in Article 66, in which the apprentice may be residing.

No. 10. The master shall not cause the said apprentice to work or live more than ten miles from the place or places mentioned in the indenture, according to Articles 68, without the leave of the Guardians so binding him, to be given under their common seal: Provided, that such Guardians may in such licence so to be given under their common seal, by express words to that effect, if they think fit, authorize the master, at any time during the residue of the term of the apprenticeship, to change the place of the abode or service of the apprentice, without any further application to them or their successors.

Art. 71.—These duties of the master set forth in Article 70 shall be enforced by covenants and conditions to be inserted in the indenture to be executed by him.

Art. 72.—The master shall also covenant, under a penalty to be specified in the covenant, not to assign or cancel the indenture, without the consent of the Guardians, under their common seal, previously obtained, and to pay to the said Guardians all costs and expenses that they may incur in consequence of the said apprentice not being supplied with medical or surgical assistance by the master, in case the same shall be at any time requisite (*a*).

Art. 73.—The indenture shall be made subject to the following provisoes:—

No. 1. That if the master take the benefit of any Act for the relief of insolvent debtors or be discharged under any such Act, such indenture shall forthwith become of no further force or effect.

No. 2. That if, on a conviction for a breach of any one of the aforesaid covenants and conditions before a Justice of the Peace, the Guardians who may be parties to the said indenture declare by a resolution that the indenture is determined, and transmit a copy of such resolution, under the hand of their Clerk, by the post or otherwise, to the said master, such indenture shall, except in respect of all rights and liabilities then accrued, forthwith become of no further force or effect.

Art. 74.—Nothing contained in this Order shall apply to the apprenticing of poor children to the sea service (*b*).

(*a*) The master of the apprentice is the proper person to assign the indenture, but the Guardians must give their consent under the terms of the covenant in the indenture required by this Article. The Justices must also give their consent under 56 Geo. III. c. 139, s. 9.

(*b*) The following are the provisions of the Merchant Shipping Act, 1854 (17 & 18 Vict. c. 104), with respect to apprenticeship to the sea service:—

Sect. 141. All shipping masters appointed under this Act shall, if applied to for the purpose, give to any Board of Guardians, Overseers, or other persons desirous of apprenticing boys to the sea service, and to masters and owners of ships requiring apprentices, such assistance as is in their power for facilitating the making of such apprenticeships, and may receive from persons availing themselves of such assistance such fees as may be determined in that behalf by the Board of Trade, with

MODE OF OBTAINING MEDICAL RELIEF BY PERMANENT PAUPERS.

Art. 75.—The Guardians shall, once at least in every year, cause to be prepared by the Clerk or Relieving Officers, a list of all such aged and infirm persons, and persons permanently sick or disabled as may be actually receiving relief from such Guardians, and residing within the

---

the concurrence, so far as relates to pauper apprentices in England, of the Poor Law Board in England.

Sect. 142. In the case of every boy bound apprentice to the sea service by any Guardians or Overseers of the Poor, or other persons having the authority of Guardians of the Poor, the indentures shall be executed by the boy and the person to whom he is bound, in the presence of, and shall be attested by, two Justices of the Peace, who shall ascertain that the boy has consented to be bound, and has attained the age of twelve years, and is of sufficient health and strength, and that the master to whom the boy is to be bound is a proper person for the purpose.

Sect. 143. All indentures of apprenticeship to the sea service shall be exempt from stamp duty, and all such indentures shall be in duplicate.

Sect. 144. Subject to the provisions hereinbefore contained, all apprenticeships to the sea service made by any Guardians or Overseers of the Poor, or persons having the authority of Guardians of the Poor, shall, if made in Great Britain, be made in the same manner and be subject to the same laws and regulations as other apprentices made by the same persons.

The above provision in s. 144 overrules the provisions of the 56 Geo. III. c. 139 as regards the apprenticeship of pauper boys from parishes in the metropolis to the sea service.

The passing of the 28 & 29 Vict. c. 79 rendered necessary the revision of the forms issued by the Board of Trade for the apprenticeship by Guardians of poor boys to the sea service. These forms have accordingly been revised, and their Lordships have issued a circular on the subject to the superintendents of mercantile marine officers in England and Wales, dated August, 1866. The circular is in the following terms:— Consequently on the coming into operation of the Union Chargeability Act (28 & 29 Vict. c. 79), the Form H, hitherto used for "Parish Apprentices' Indentures" throughout the United Kingdom, will no longer be applicable to most parishes. The new Forms H 1, H 2, and H 3, for "Union" and "Parish Apprentices' Indentures" (England and Wales) of which copies are sent herewith, have been settled by the Poor Law Board and the Board of Trade to meet the requirements of the new law. They will be printed on parchment and paper, and can be obtained by the superintendent upon application in the ordinary manner, on the order forms, wherein the new forms must be entered in until the amended forms are issued. The circumstances under which the forms are to be used are stated on each of them.

district of each Medical Officer of the Union, and shall from time to time furnish to each District Medical Officer a copy of the list aforesaid.

Art. 76.—Every person whose name is inserted in such list shall receive a ticket in the Form (L.) hereunto annexed, and shall be entitled, on the exhibition of such ticket to the Medical Officer of his district, to obtain such advice, attendance, and medicines, as his case may require, in the same manner as if he had received an order from the Guardians; and such ticket shall remain in force for the time specified therein, unless such person shall cease to be in the receipt of relief before the expiration of such time (*a*).

RELIEF OF NON-SETTLED AND NON-RESIDENT POOR (*b*).

Art. 77.—If any Board of Guardians undertake to administer relief allowed to a non-settled pauper living within the Union for which they act, on behalf of the Officers, or of the Board of Guardians, of the Parish or Union in which such pauper is deemed to be settled, every such undertak-

---

(*a*) Arts. 75 and 76 are intended to facilitate the obtaining of attendance and medicines by the permanent paupers; a class whose destitution is acknowledged, and which necessarily includes the most helpless portion of the community.—*Instr. Letter.*

In the administration of medical relief to the sick poor, the objects to be kept in view are:—1. To provide medical aid for all persons who are really destitute; 2. To prevent medical relief from generating or encouraging pauperism; and with this view to withdraw from the labouring classes, as well as from the administrators of relief, and the medical officers, all motives for applying for or administering medical relief, unless where the circumstances render it absolutely necessary.

To entitle the person to medical relief under Article 76, his or her name must be actually on the list, and not merely the name of the head of the family (3 O. C. 14); and the Medical Officer ought not to discontinue his visits so long as the Guardians give a ticket entitling the pauper to permanent medical relief, as the Medical Officer's attendance is thereby required for the case while the ticket remains in force. (39 O. C. (N. S.) 106).

(*b*) Non-settled poor are those who have no settlement in the Union in which they are resident and are relieved; non-resident poor are those who are residing in another Union than the Union the Guardians of which give the relief and in which the paupers are settled.

ing shall be made in conformity with the rules and regulations of the Commissioners in force at the time (*a*).

Art. 78.—No money shall be transmitted to any Guardians or to any officer of a Parish or Union, to be applied to the relief of any non-resident pauper, except in conformity with the provisions of this Order (*b*).

(*a*) Arts. 77–80 neither permit nor forbid the allowance of non-resident relief in any case in which such relief is not now permitted, or is not now forbidden; nor do they prevent the Guardians from transmitting relief to a poor person who is non-resident, in cases where the same may lawfully be given, through any private channel or means other than the officers of another Union or Parish, however objectionable such a course may be. (See the Minute of the Commissioners on the relief of persons non-resident within their Union, dated 26th January, 1841, Appendix No. A., 7th Annual Report, p. 106). All that these Articles do is to require that, when the agency of another Board of Guardians is employed, certain rules shall be adhered to. Whether the Board of Guardians allowing the non-resident relief choose to employ that agency is a matter for their own consideration, and whether the Board of Guardians of the Union where the pauper resides choose to act in the capacity of agents, and direct their officers to administer the relief, is again a matter of choice. If two boards do so agree to act together, these regulations must be observed, since no contract in opposition to them could be enforced by one party against the other, and the officers of the respective Unions are of course bound to act in conformity with law.—*Instr. Letter*, 21st December, 1844.

The provisions of the Order in regard to the administration of non-resident relief are compulsory so far as they go, and it does not depend on the choice of a Board of Guardians to adopt them or not; but they do not profess to direct that one Board shall undertake to be the agents of another Board whether they like to do so or not. It is also quite within the legal discretion of the Guardians to decide whether or not they will continue to allow non-resident relief to paupers belonging to the Union, or whether or not they will continue the agents of other Boards of Guardians, for the purpose of administering non-resident relief allowed to the paupers of such other Unions. If in any case in which non-resident relief may lawfully be granted, the Guardians of the Union where the pauper resides decline to administer non-resident relief for the Guardians of other Unions, some respectable agent in the parish where the pauper resides should be found to undertake to administer the relief weekly; and the Guardians on whose account it is given should repay the relief to the agent at the end of each quarter, by an order on the Union Treasurer or by some other means. Moreover, it should be borne in mind, that the regulation contemplates that the Guardians should give a special undertaking to relieve in the case of each pauper; and that it does not enable them to give a general authority to their Relieving Officers to relieve for other Unions when applied to.

(*b*) It will be seen by this Article that the officers of the Guardians are in effect prohibited from acting as the agents of any Board other than that whose officers they are. The inconveniences which have arisen from Relieving Officers so acting form the principal reasons on account of which the Commissioners thought it expedient to make this regulation. They state that they have found that Relieving Officers were apparently placed in an anomalous position, receiving orders as it were from more than one Board of Guardians, and often being liable in two ways for the relief of the same pauper; that is to say, in their capacity of agent to some distant Board, and in their position as Relieving Officers of their own district in which that pauper resides. For reasons in some measure similar to those which apply to the Relieving Officers, and for others of a more general character, the prohibition is extended to any officer of a Union or Parish. It is always to be remembered that no undertaking to give relief to a pauper residing at a distance has any legal effect in lessening the obligation cast by the law on the Guardians and Officers of the spot where the pauper dwells or becomes destitute. The Board of Guardians at a distance may incur a moral responsibility by promising to provide for the case, and may transmit from time to time the means of subsistence; but if by neglect or error or peculation, those means fail, or owing to any change of circumstances become insufficient, it is on the authorities at the place where the pauper is that the weight of legal responsibility will fall. A voluntary act on the part of one person or one body does not remove the positive legal duty already cast on another. Much of the ambiguity on this head will cease when the regulations in Articles 77-80 are acted upon, since the Relieving Officer can only act as the officer and agent of his own Board, though some misapprehension is inseparable from any system of non-resident relief. A further advantage contemplated is the removal of those opportunities for fraud and for wilful detention of money thus entrusted to a distant officer which have so often acted as a temptation and a snare to persons who would otherwise have preserved an honest and trustworthy character. And as the money thus misapplied does not come into the officer's hands in the capacity of officer of the Parish or Union in which he acts, but as a private agent for distant Boards and for Overseers of other Parishes in general, in case of peculation, such money could not be recovered from his sureties, since they were answerable for him only in the capacity of Relieving Officer. Another benefit will be the avoiding of errors and misstatements of a statistical nature, which occur in consequence of the same persons and the same relief being charged in the accounts of two Unions. The Commissioners feel satisfied that these regulations will ensure a better understanding of the duties and responsibilities connected with the relief of non-resident poor, that they will act as a powerful obstacle to peculation and fraud, and that they will prevent error in the returns of expenditure and the enumeration of paupers, which are otherwise unavoidable. The relief of non-resident and non-settled poor administered under this order will, of course, become the subject of correspondence between the Boards of Guardians of the Unions where they are relieved and where they reside, and this correspondence will be conducted by the Clerks of the Unions concerned. Wherever non-resident relief is now given, either the ordinary correspondence with reference to these cases is conducted by the Clerk, or

Art. 79.—No money shall be paid on account of any non-resident pauper to the Guardians or to the Officer of any Union or Parish in which the relief is administered by a Board of Guardians, except in one of the three following ways :—

No. 1. By post-office order payable to the Treasurer of the Union or Parish to the account of which the money is to be paid, or to the banker of such Treasurer.

No. 2. By cheque or order payable to the Treasurer of such Parish or Union, or to his order.

No. 3. By cheque payable to bearer (where the same may lawfully be drawn), and crossed as payable through the Treasurer of such Parish or Union, or his banker, or through the agent of such Treasurer or banker; and every such cheque shall be so crossed by the Clerk before it is signed by the presiding Chairman.

Art. 80.—Every account for relief duly administered to non-resident poor shall be discharged by the Guardians, within two calendar months from the receipt of such account, by the transmission of the amount due, in one of the modes prescribed in Art. 79 (*a*).

---

difficulties arise from time to time which produce long and tedious disputes, by letter, leading probably to appeal to the Commissioners, and terminating in no satisfactory result, the matter devolving upon the Clerk in the more advanced stages, and when complicated by previous misunderstandings.—*Instr. Letter*, 21st December, 1844.

(*a*) See Article 202, No. 9, as to the duty of the Clerk to make up and transmit these accounts at the end of each quarter; and as to the liability of the Guardians of the Union on whose behalf the relief is granted, if that duty be neglected, see the case of *Wycombe* v. *Eton*, 1 H. & N. 687; 26 L. J. (N. S.) M. C. 97, in which it was held that an action cannot be maintained by the Guardians in respect of relief afforded to the non-resident poor of another Union, unless the accounts of such relief have been transmitted quarterly in conformity with this regulation, notwithstanding that the relief was duly ordered and never countermanded. That case leaves it doubtful whether an action could be maintained against the Guardians, even if the accounts had been duly transmitted. Unless the account is sent in by the Clerk in conformity with the regulation in Article 202, No. 9, and it be not settled within the time allowed by 22 & 23 Vict. c. 49, s. 1, the time for payment cannot be extended by the Poor Law Board, as the claim will not have become legally due from the Guardians.

ORDERS FOR CONTRIBUTIONS AND PAYMENTS.

Art. 81.—(*This Article is rescinded by the order of the Poor Law Board of the 26th February, 1866, post. See now Art. 1 of that order.*)

Art. 82.—(*This Article is rescinded by the order of the Poor Law Board of the 26th February, 1866, post. See now Art. 2 of that order.*)

Art. 83.—Every such order shall be made according to the Form (M.) hereunto annexed (*b*). It shall be signed by the presiding Chairman of the meeting, and two other Guardians present thereat, and shall be countersigned by the Clerk (*c*).

Art. 84.—The Guardians shall pay every sum greater than Five Pounds by an order (*d*), which shall be drawn upon the Treasurer of the Union, and shall be signed by the presiding Chairman and two other Guardians at a meeting, and shall be countersigned by the Clerk (*e*).

It may be here stated that, according to the opinion of the Commissioners of Inland Revenue, letters acknowledging the receipt of cheques in repayment of non-resident relief, when such relief amounts to £2 and upwards, are within the exemption from stamp duty contained in the 4 & 5 Wm. IV. c. 76, s. 86. They say that the 4 & 5 Will. IV. c. 76, s. 86, should be construed liberally, and that though acknowledgments of money in respect of non-settled relief are not mentioned *eo nomine* in the Act or in the consolidated order; yet as they are a direct and necessary consequence of the cheques, orders, or payments required by that order, they must be considered "instruments made in pursuance of the Act," and as such exempt from stamp duty.

(*b*) See the order of the Poor Law Board of 26th February, 1866, *post*, which prescribes a new form of contribution order.

(*c*) In Unions which contain a large number of Parishes, one original order may be made to be served upon the most responsible of the Overseers, and printed copies of it may then be served upon the others. The copies to be kept by the Clerk may also be printed. As to the service of these orders on the Overseers, see Article 4, No. 2, of the General Order of the Poor Law Board of 7th October, 1865, *post*.

(*d*) The consolidated order issued to Unions formed since 1847 prescribes in this Article the form of order upon the Treasurer, and it is similar to the form prescribed by the order of 7th April, 1857, *post*.

(*e*) See Articles 219 and 220 as to the transmission of the Guardians' cheques to the persons in whose favour they are drawn, and Art. 202, No. 6, as to the counter-signature of the order by the Clerk; see also 56 O. C. (N. S.) 72.

Art. 85.—The Guardians shall examine at their Board, or shall cause to be examined by some Committee or Guar-

---

As regards the liability of the Treasurer for paying forged cheques or orders, see *Young* v. *Grote*, 4 Bing. 253, and *Orr* v. *Union Bank of Scotland*, 24 L. J. 1.

It appears from the Circular of the 4th January, 1854, that the Poor Law Board, with reference to the 16 & 17 Vict. c. 59, deemed it advisable to submit to the Commissioners of Inland Revenue, under section 13 of that Act, an order drawn and issued by the Guardians of a Union upon their Treasurer, who was not a banker, in favour of a creditor. The Board informed the Commissioners that the order was drawn and executed in conformity with the 84th Art. of the General Consolidated Order, and suggested that the 86th sect. of the 4 & 5 Wm. IV. c. 76, was therefore applicable, and rendered it exempt from the stamp duty which is chargeable upon a draft or order for the payment of a sum of money payable to the bearer on demand; and those Commissioners acquainted the Board that they considered that the draft is an instrument made in pursuance of the Poor Law Amendment Act, and therefore exempt from stamp duty. This decision applies equally to the statute 21 Vict. c. 20, imposing a stamp duty upon drafts drawn upon bankers. The Poor Law Board have since (7 April, 1857) issued a General Order (*post*), requiring that cheques drawn by Guardians shall in all cases be made payable "to order" instead of "to bearer." (See also 56 O. C. (N. S.) 72.)

Orders for the payment of money drawn by the Guardians on their Treasurer in the form prescribed by this order are exempt from stamp duty, whether drawn upon a banker or other person; and the distance between the drawer and the person on whom the order is drawn, makes no difference as to that exemption—neither is it material whether the document passes through other hands than those of the person to whose order it is drawn.

It may be stated here, in reference to the amount of the Guardians' orders, that by the 48 Geo. III. c. 88, s. 2, which is still in force, all notes, bills, drafts, or undertakings, negotiable or transferable for money, or any orders, notes, or undertakings, negotiable or transferable for goods, specifying the value in money, cannot be made for less than 20s., for the Act declares all such to be void. Therefore, all bills or notes made payable to bearer or order for sums not amounting to 20s. are void in law. The Act however does not apply to drafts made payable to a particular person, and not negotiable. Drafts or orders so drawn by a Board of Guardians, that is made payable to the payee and not to him or order, would be liable to the penny stamp duty, as they would not be in conformity with the order of the Poor Law Board of the 7th April, 1857.

The order does not apply to a cheque drawn for a sum under £5; and therefore an order drawn upon the Treasurer for a sum under that amount would not be exempt from stamp duty. (See 58 O. C. (N. S.) 100.) When the Guardians have numerous payments to make, of sums less than £5, the most convenient course is to draw a cheque payable to the order of their Clerk, and for that officer to obtain cash for it and make the payments on behalf of the Guardians.

dian authorized by them for the purpose, every bill exceeding in amount one pound (except the salaries of officers) brought against the Union; and when any such bill has been allowed by the Board, or by such Committee or Guardian, a note of the allowance thereof shall be made on the face of the bill before the amount is paid (*a*).

CUSTODY OF BONDS.

Art. 86.—The Guardians shall provide for the safe custody of all bonds given in pursuance of the Regulations of the Commissioners, so always that no bond given by any person shall remain in the custody of such person himself.

Art. 87.—The Guardians shall, at the audit next after the Twenty-fifth day of March in every year, cause every person having the custody of bonds given by any officer of the Union to produce such bonds to the Auditor for his inspection (*b*).

(*a*) All bills should be examined with the invoices and contracts under which the goods were supplied, or work done, and the several items must be cast up in order that the correctness of the totals may be ascertained and certified.

(*b*) See Articles 184–186, as to the security of the officers. As to the report of the Auditor on those securities, see Art. 51 of the Order for Accounts, *post*, which applies to the bonds of all Union officers, Collectors and Assistant-Overseers, Vestry Clerks, and other officers required to give security.

By Art. 202, No. 2, it is made the duty of the Clerk to the Guardians to produce the bonds to the Auditor for his inspection. If the Clerk shall have given a bond, it should be deposited with the Treasurer of the Union, who is required by Art. 203, No. 5, to produce it to the Auditor. As to the securities of Assistant-Overseers and Collectors, see 7 & 8 Vict. c. 101, s. 61, which requires that every Collector or Assistant-Overseer appointed under the 59 Geo. III. c. 12, s. 7, or under an order of the Poor Law Commissioners or Poor Law Board, shall be bound to give to the Board of Guardians of the Parish or Union sufficient security for the due performance of his duties. Such bond is exempt from stamp duty; and every bond given in pursuance of the 59 Geo. III. c. 12, s. 7, or 7 & 8 Vict. c. 101, s. 61, shall, if the Guardians shall see fit, be put in suit by the Board of Guardians of the Union in which the Parish or District for which the officer acted or has acted may be situated, notwithstanding that it may have been originally given to the Overseers or to any other person. The provision in the latter Act so far supersedes the 59 Geo. III. c. 12, s. 7, that if security be given to the Guardians

GOVERNMENT OF THE WORKHOUSE (a).

ADMISSION OF PAUPERS.

Art. 88.—Every pauper who shall be admitted into the Workhouse, either upon his first or any subsequent admission, shall be admitted in some one of the following modes only; that is to say:—

---

it is not necessary that additional security should be given to the Churchwardens and Overseers. The latter provision, however, does not repeal the former. The expense of preparing Assistant-Overseers' bonds should be defrayed by the persons who give them, and not out of the poor-rates. The preparation of such bonds does not come within the Clerk's duties in Art. 202, No. 4, as to which see the note thereon, *post*, unless he is directed by the Guardians to prepare the bond when given to them.

(*a*) The Workhouse principle is thus enunciated by the Poor Law Commissioners in their Report on the Amendment of the Poor Law:—

"By means of the Workhouse and its regulations, it is in the power of the Guardians to place the condition of the pauper accurately at its level—to provide for all his wants effectually—and yet so as to make the relief thus afforded desirable to those only who are *bonâ-fide* in need of it. This principle of the Workhouse system is very well understood as respects the able-bodied labourers, and the benefits which arise from its application are admitted and appreciated. If the condition of the inmates of a Workhouse were to be so regulated as to invite the aged and infirm of the labouring classes to take refuge in it, it would immediately be useless as a test between indigence and indolence or fraud; it would no longer operate as an inducement to the young and healthy to provide support for their later years, or as a stimulus to them, whilst they have the means, to support their aged parents and relatives. The frugality and forethought of a young labourer would be useless if he foresaw the certainty of a better asylum for his old age than he could possibly provide by his own exertions; and the industrious efforts of a son to provide a maintenance for his parents in his own dwelling would be thrown away, and would cease to be called forth, if the Almshouse of the district offered a refuge for their declining years, in which they might obtain comforts and indulgences which even the most successful of the labouring classes cannot always obtain by their own exertions."

The Poor Law Commissioners say:—"If the rules we have issued for workhouses be examined, they will be found to consist of two classes of regulations:—1. Those which are necessary for the maintenance of good order in any building in which considerable numbers of persons of both sexes and of different ages reside. 2. Those which are necessary, not for that purpose, but in order that these establishments may not be almshouses, but workhouses in the proper meaning of the term, and may produce the results which the Legislature intended. By far the greater part of the regulations belong to the first of these classes."

By a written or printed order of the Board of Guardians, signed by their Clerk, according to Art. 42.

By a provisional written or printed order, signed by a Relieving Officer or an Overseer.

By the Master of the Workhouse (or, during his absence or inability to act, by the Matron), without any order, in any case of sudden or urgent necessity.

Provided that the Master may admit any pauper delivered at the Workhouse under an order of removal to a Parish in the Union (b).

(b) By the Industrial Schools Act, 1866, 29 & 30 Vict. c. 118, s. 14, two justices or a magistrate while inquiry is being made respecting a child, or respecting a school to which he may be sent, may, by order signed by them or him, order the child to be taken to the Workhouse of the Union or Parish in which he is found or resident, and to be detained therein at the cost of the Union or Parish for any time not exceeding seven days, or until an order is sooner made for his discharge, or for his being sent to a certified Industrial School; and the Guardians of the Union or Parish to whom the order is addressed are empowered and required to detain him accordingly.

Any child apparently under fourteen years of age—
1. That is found begging or receiving alms (whether actually or under the pretext of selling or offering for sale anything) or being in any street or public place for the purpose of begging or receiving alms;
2. That is found wandering and not having any home or settled place of abode, or proper guardianship, or visible means of subsistence;
3. That is found destitute, either being an orphan or having a surviving parent who is undergoing penal servitude or imprisonment.
4. That frequents the company of reputed thieves, may be sent to a certified Industrial School, 29 & 30 Vict. c. 118, s. 14. (See the second volume of Glen's 'Poor Law Statutes,' p. 327.)

As to sending refractory children from the Workhouse to such schools, see post, p. 86.)

By the Metropolitan Buildings Act, 18 & 19 Vict. c. 122, s. 80, justices may cause the inmates to be removed from dangerous structures " by a constable or other peace officer, and if they have no other abode, he may require them to be received into the Workhouse established for the reception of the poor of the place in which such structure is situate." The Act, however, only applies to Unions and Parishes within the district of the Metropolis, as defined by the Act.

Under Article 88 an order for the admission of a pauper into the Workhouse can be given by the Board of Guardians, absolutely; and provisionally, by a Relieving Officer, or an Overseer, including a Churchwarden, who is an Overseer by virtue of his office. If, however, a pauper resides in another Union, and application be made to the Guardians of a Union in some parish of which he is settled, those Guardians, though they may grant non-resident relief to the pauper, if the case comes within any of the exceptions to the out-door relief Regulation Orders, cannot grant an order for the admission of the pauper to the Workhouse of the Union in which he is settled, until the pauper actually comes within the Union. Moreover, the Master, or, in case of his absence or inability to act, the Matron, is empowered to admit any pauper without an order, in any case of sudden or urgent necessity; and by Art. 208, No. 1, and Art. 210, No. 1, it is made the duty of the Master or Matron to admit into the Workhouse every person who applies at the Workhouse for relief under such circumstances. If the Master and Matron should be both absent from the Workhouse, or incapable of performing their duties at the same time, it is by Art. 214, No. 3, the duty of the porter to admit and place in the receiving ward any person who may apply at the Workhouse for relief under similar circumstances. The Commissioners do not contemplate that the Master, Matron, and Porter, should simultaneously be absent from the Workhouse, or incapable of performing their duties; and therefore they have made no provision for this contingency. In order to prevent the occurrence of error, the Commissioners have thought it right to point out that an order for admission into the Workhouse cannot be given by any person in any of the following capacities; namely, as (1), a Guardian not acting as a member of the Board, 4 & 5 Wm. IV. c. 76, s. 38; (2), a Justice of the Peace; (3), a ratepayer of the Parish or Union. Any one, however, may bring under the notice of the Master a person in circumstances of sudden or urgent necessity; and the Master is bound, by the Article above-cited, to admit every person applying for relief at the Workhouse under such circumstances. Moreover, in Unions or Parishes where the Commissioners have sanctioned regulations respecting mendicity, vagrant mendicants are directed to the Workhouse by a ticket containing the recommendation of a ratepayer of the Union or Parish. It will likewise be, in general, the duty of the Master of a Workhouse situate within the Metropolitan district to admit into the Workhouse any person who may be brought thither by a policeman, as having been found abroad in a state of destitution. The duty of the Master to admit into the Workhouse under these circumstances, rests on the supposition that the fact of the applicant's being brought by a policeman is *primâ facie* evidence of urgent want, and implies that he has committed no such offence within the cognizance of the officers of that force, as would authorize his detention in custody. It follows from this, that drunken persons, or persons who can be proved to have committed an act of vagrancy, are not within the class of cases properly entitled to admission under these circumstances; but the Masters of Workhouses will always do wisely to admit in the first instance, and afterwards to make an official representation of the conduct of any police constable of whom they may have cause to complain. It is to be observed, generally, with respect to all persons who may apply for admission into the Workhouse under circumstances of urgent necessity, that their destitution, coupled with the fact of their being within the Union or Parish, entitles them to relief; and that their title to relief is altogether independent of their settlement (if they have one), which is a matter for subsequent inquiry, and only renders them liable to removal in consequence of their becoming chargeable. On the duty of the officers to give immediate relief, without preliminary inquiry into settlement, see the letters of the Commissioners, Fourth Ann. Report, App. A., No. 2, and Fifth Ann. Report, App. A., No. 10, in which they stated that "what they were most anxious to have made known is, that the relief of actual destitution, in cases of emergency, should always precede the investigation of any question as to its cause, or as to the liability of other parties than the Parish to contribute to it;" and on the nature of settlement as affecting the right to relief, see the Minute of the Commissioners on Non-Resident Relief, 7th Annual Report, p. 106.—*Instr. Letter*, 5th February, 1842.

As regards the relief of houseless poor in the Metropolis, reference should be made to the 27 & 28 Vict. c. 116, 28 Vict. c. 34, and 30 Vict. c. 6, s. 6, to the Minute of Mr. Villiers, President of the Poor Law Board, dated December 23, 1863, on the destitute houseless poor in the Metropolis, and to the circulars of the Poor Law Board, dated respectively August 4 and October 26, 1864, August 30 and November 30, 1865, and January 20, 27, 30 and 31, 1866, respectively, which will be found in their Annual Report.

In the Circular of the 27th January, 1866, the Poor Law Board state that pursuant to the provisions of 28 Vict. c. 34, s. 2, they have made arrangements with the Commissioner of Metropolitan Police for the inspection, by the officers of police, of the wards and other places of reception provided under that Act for the Metropolitan houseless poor, and request that the police officers authorized to undertake this duty may be allowed the requisite facilities for entering and inspecting the wards, and obtaining such information as may enable them to make their reports on the subject to the Poor Law Board, as required by the Act.

Amongst others to whom the Commissioners refer as not having authority to give an order for admission to the Workhouse, is a justice of the peace. The case of *Reg.* v. *Totnes*, 7 Q. B. 690, points out the steps to be taken by a justice before he makes any order for relief under the 4 & 5 Wm. IV. c. 76, s. 27. If, however, a person in distress applies to a justice, and the justice comes to the conclusion that such person is destitute, he may properly give him a written recommendation to the Master of the Workhouse, or to the Relieving Officer, that he be relieved, and the officer would incur a grave responsibility if he refuse to act upon such a recommendation. The Poor Law Board would in that event, upon a complaint being made to them, require the officer to give a satisfactory explanation to justify his conduct.

Generally, with respect to the admission and discharge of paupers, it is to be observed, that they should be admitted and discharged on Sundays and holidays the same as on other days, but not during the performance of Divine Service; the Master must also admit those who present a proper order, or who apply without one under urgent circumstances, at any time of night, but he is not in general bound to discharge a pauper in the night-time. The Master has no authority to discharge a pauper from the Workhouse against the pauper's wish, without directions from the Board of Guardians, nor has the Relieving Officer or Clerk to the Guardians such a power. Overseers are only authorized to give relief in cases of "sudden and urgent necessity;" the giving of an order for the Workhouse amounts to relief, but such order is only operative until the next meeting of the Guardians. The Guardians, or in their absence, the Master, must determine what applicants are paupers, *i. e.* actually destitute. Although, under this Article, the Master is relieved from the consequences of improperly admitting persons who are not paupers when they produce an order from an Overseer, he is not precluded from exercising his judgment as to the fact of the applicant being a pauper. The Guardians cannot withdraw the power of the Overseers to give provisional orders for the admission of paupers into the Workhouse, nor will the refusal of the Relieving Officer to give an order prevent the Overseers from doing so, but the latter will be bound to establish that the case was one of sudden and urgent necessity. The order is termed "provisional," because it is valid only for the interval from the time it is given to the next ordinary meeting of the Guardians, when the admission of the pauper by such an order (see Art. 90) is brought before them for their decision on the propriety of the pauper remaining in the Workhouse or not. An Assistant-Overseer to whom the giving of relief is assigned as one of his duties, or whose appointment authorizes him to perform such of the duties as pertain to an Overseer of the Poor, has power to give orders for the admission of paupers in like manner as Overseers.

The remarks made above in reference to the discretionary power of the Master as to the orders of the Overseers, will apply also to orders given by the Relieving Officers.

It sometimes happens that a person presents himself alone at the Workhouse with an order for the admission of himself, his wife and children. In such a case, the order being distributive, it is the duty of the Master to admit the applicant, as he is not bound to require him to bring the rest of his family with him; who may either be not destitute, or may be living with friends, or be otherwise provided for. But see Article 1 of the General Prohibitory Order as to the relief of able-bodied persons.

Again, if a person alleged to be destitute be brought to the Workhouse, whether by the police or by any other persons, without an order of admission, the Master must examine into the circumstances of the case, and if he find that the destitution exists, and that there is urgent necessity in the case, it is his duty to admit the destitute person into the Workhouse, and report the case to the Guardians at their next meeting, and then take their directions upon it. If, on the other hand, the Master should not be satisfied that the person brought to him is really destitute, he should refuse to admit him; but in so acting he should exercise great caution, and be fully satisfied that the case is not a proper one for admission to the Workhouse. Sometimes persons in charge of the police as offenders are taken to the Workhouse; but ordinarily such cases ought not to be admitted, as it is the duty of the police, and not of the Poor Law authorities, to provide for the safe custody of such persons. Paupers who are committed to prison for offences in the Workhouse cannot be readmitted to the Workhouse after their discharge from prison without a fresh order, unless the case of the applicant be urgent, when the Master may readmit the pauper provisionally.

If a poor person labouring under an infectious disease presents a provisional order for admission, he should be placed in the ward appropriated for the reception of such cases; and if there be no means of separating the pauper so affected from the other inmates, the Master should immediately send for the Relieving Officer, who will in such a case be responsible for providing some temporary accommodation for the pauper.

If on searching the pauper, money is found on him sufficient for his present maintenance, the Master is not bound to keep him in the house, if the person can on leaving procure food and shelter; but all such cases should be forthwith reported to the Board of Guardians. The Guardians are empowered to discontinue or refuse all relief to a person possessed of property or means available for his independent support; but in such case the question for their consideration will be, is the property in the possession of the applicant practically available for his immediate support? The possession of a watch, articles of jewellery, a horse and cart, a cow, etc., will raise a question as to whether the applicant is, strictly speaking, actually destitute of the means of support. If, however, relief be refused on this ground, the Guardians should be satisfied that the applicant has at the time a reasonable opportunity of raising money on the property in his possession; further on this point, see note (*b*) to Art. 41, p. 30, and the provisions in the 11 & 12 Vict. c. 110, s. 10, and 12 & 13 Vict. c. 103, s. 16.

The proviso to Article 88 is intended to meet the provision in the 9 & 10 Vict. c. 66, s. 7, " that delivering of any pauper under any warrant of removal directed to the Overseers of any Parish, at the Workhouse of such Parish, or of any Union to which such Parish belongs, to any Officer of such Workhouse, shall be deemed the delivery of such pauper to the Overseers of such Parish." English paupers removed from Scotland to England under an order of the Sheriff or two Justices, are required by the 25 & 26 Vict. c. 113, s. 4, to be delivered at the Workhouse of the place to which the removal is to take place, or of the Union or Parish containing the port or place nearest to the place mentioned in the warrant as the place of the pauper's ultimate destination. By sect. 5 of the same Act, the Master of the Workhouse of the Union or Parish in England to which the warrant is addressed shall be bound to receive delivery of the poor person named in such warrant, under a penalty of £10 for each case of refusal, which may be recovered by the person applying for the warrant by an action in any County Court in England, or other competent Court having jurisdiction in the place where such master is resident at the time when such action is brought. (See the Statute in the second volume of Glen's ' Poor Law Statutes.') The case of *Ex parte the Overseers of Downton*, 27 L. J. R. (N. S.) M. C. 281, shows that the Master of the Workhouse may be indicted if he refuse to receive at the Workhouse a pauper brought to him under an order of Justices. The order of removal should be kept by the Master of the Workhouse, unless the Overseers desire that it be given up to them.

Section 13 of 14 & 15 Vict. c. 105, authorizes the officers who are empowered by the 9 & 10 Vict. c. 66, s. 7, to deliver a pauper under an order of removal at the Workhouse of the Parish or Union to which such pauper is to be removed, at the same time to deliver a written statement of the charges for the maintenance of the pauper to the officer of the Workhouse, which delivery is to be deemed to be a delivery of such statement to the Overseers of the Parish, and a sufficient demand in any proceedings for the recovery of such charges.

The Poor Law Commissioners, in their Circular of the 17th of September, 1846, advised the Guardians to give directions to the officers of the Workhouse, especially the Master and the Porter, that when a pauper should be brought to the Workhouse with a warrant of removal under the 9 & 10 Vict. c. 66, s. 7, they should take the earliest opportunity of communicating the fact of his delivery at the Workhouse to the Overseers to whom the warrant was addressed; and the Poor Law Board, in their Circular of 30th September, 1851, recommend the Guardians to give similar directions with reference to this statement of charges, and it is the more important that this should be done, as the Overseers upon service of such a statement become immediately liable to proceedings for the discharge of the amount.

The remarks in the two immediately preceding paragraphs must now, however, be read with reference to the provisions of the Union Chargeability Act, 1865, under which paupers are to be removed under orders obtained by the Guardians, and not by the Overseers.

The 25 & 26 Vict. c. 111, s. 8, provides for the reception and treatment in Workhouses of chronic cases of lunacy. The section empowers the Visitors of any Asylum, and the Guardians of any Parish or Union within the district for which the asylum has been provided, if they shall see fit, to make arrangements, subject to the approval of the Commissioners in Lunacy and the President of the Poor Law Board, for the reception and care of a limited number of chronic lunatics in the Workhouse of such Parish or Union, to be selected by the Superintendent of the Asylum, and certified by him to be fit and proper so to be removed. The Poor Law Board, with reference to this provision, in their Circular of the 15th of December, 1862, say that they are at present not aware of any Workhouse in which any such arrangements could conveniently be made; but they will be ready to consider any proposals on the subject when the Visitors and the Board of Guardians of any Union shall find it convenient or practicable to act upon this clause.

The following are the arrangements sanctioned by the Commissioners in Lunacy in November, 1863, with regard to the removal of chronic lunatics from Asylums to Workhouses under the 25 & 26 Vict. c. 111, s. 8:—

1. The arrangements authorized are, in the opinion of the Board, intended to meet the deficiency of accommodation in Asylums, and to enable Visitors, in special cases, to make provision for the immediate reception into the Asylums of all recent and probably curable cases. The Legislature clearly did not contemplate the reception into Workhouses generally of the chronic patients referred to, and the constitution thereby of a number of small lunatic establishments; but the selection by the Visitors of one or more Workhouses in which adequate accommodation, care, and attendance can be ensured. Consequently all applications for the approval of the Commissioners must originate with Visitors of Asylums; and no such application received directly from a Board of Guardians can be entertained.

Art. 89.—No pauper shall be admitted under any written or printed order as mentioned in Art. 88, if the same bear date more than six days before the pauper presents it at the Workhouse (a).

Art. 90.—If a pauper be admitted otherwise than by an

---

2. Proper rules and regulations, modified according to circumstances, will be required to be prepared and approved. In the meantime the Board consider and determine that the following conditions are (amongst others) indispensable, and will, in all cases, be insisted on, viz. :—

(1.) Separate wards properly constructed, arranged, and furnished for the patients of the respective sexes. The dormitories to be distinct from the day-rooms, and the former to afford cubical space per patient, of 500 feet, and the latter 400. Single bed-rooms to contain at least 600 cubic feet.

(2.) A liberal dietary analogous to that of the Asylums.

(3.) Ample means of out-door exercise and recreation.

(4.) Due medical visitation.

(5.) Properly qualified paid attendants.

(6.) Medical and other registers; records similar to those in use in licensed houses.

The Law Officers of the Crown have advised the Commissioners in Lunacy that the 25 & 26 Vict. c. 111, s. 8, as regards the removal of chronic lunatics from an Asylum to a Workhouse, is confined to the cases of pauper lunatics of the Union or Parish to which the Workhouse belongs. But now, by 26 & 27 Vict. c. 110, s. 2, it is declared, that the words "chronic lunatics" in the 25 & 26 Vict. c. 111, s. 8, include chronic lunatics chargeable to other Parishes or Unions, as well as chronic lunatics chargeable to the Parish or Union into the Workhouse of which they are proposed to be received.

As regards the disposal of a deceased pauper's furniture, the Poor Law Board say that the personal representative of the deceased is entitled to the property which belonged to him; although the person who defrayed the expenses of burying the body would have a legal claim to be reimbursed out of the produce of the property. If the body of the deceased was buried at the cost of the Union, the Guardians can reimburse themselves out of such property under the provision contained in the 12 & 13 Vict. c. 103, s. 16. See 57 O. C. (N. S.) p. 89.

The Guardians cannot detain, or authorize the Master of the Workhouse to detain and open letters addressed to paupers in the Workhouse which contain money. But when the money has come into the possession of the pauper, they may take and appropriate it in repayment of his relief, under the 12 & 13 Vict. c. 103, s. 16; and for that purpose it is thought the Guardians may employ force if the pauper refuses to give up the money voluntarily. See 3 O. C. 160, which, however, was prior to the above-mentioned statute.

(a) It is considered that the Guardians may, if they think fit so to do, limit the order to the day on which it bears date, there being nothing in this Article to preclude them from so doing.

order of the Board of Guardians, the admission of such pauper shall be brought before the Board of Guardians at their next ordinary meeting, who shall decide on the propriety of the pauper's continuing in the Workhouse or otherwise, and make an order accordingly (*a*).

Art. 91.—As soon as the pauper is admitted, he shall be placed in some room to be appropriated to the reception of paupers on admission, and shall then be examined by the Medical Officer.

Art. 92.—If the Medical Officer, upon such examination, pronounce the pauper to be labouring under any disease of body or mind, the pauper shall be placed in the sick ward, or in such other ward as the Medical Officer shall direct (*b*).

(*a*) It is certain that the Board of Guardians possess the power of discharging from the Workhouse, and refusing all other relief to any pauper, whom they may consider capable of supporting himself. The Commissioners, however, believe that, if the Workhouse be properly regulated, persons who are not really destitute will, in general, be unwilling to remain in it. They, therefore, think that the power of discharging from the Workhouse should be exercised with the utmost caution; and in general only in cases where a pauper can be proceeded against criminally, under the Vagrant Act, for neglecting to maintain himself or his family.—*Instr. Letter*, 5th February, 1842.

The Guardians can, in the exercise of their discretion, order the discharge from the Workhouse of any poor person whom they may think able to maintain himself; but, beyond the offer of shelter in the Workhouse, it does not seem to fall within the scope of either the Guardians' powers or duties to provide residences for the poor, or to supply them with the means of purchasing furniture or work-tools; these not being articles required for the relief of actual destitution. When work, which a pauper can readily accept, is offered at adequate wages, the Board think that it would be proper, in most cases, for the Guardians to direct the discharge of the pauper to whom the employment is offered, after due notice of their intention to do so. But if it is admitted that the man cannot procure a house, either in his own parish or elsewhere, the Board would not advise that he be ejected from the Workhouse against his will, so long as such inability to procure shelter for himself and family exists. (7 O. C. 199.)

(*b*) It will be the duty of the Guardians and the Master to see that the receiving wards are kept in proper order, and that no unnecessary delay in the examination of the paupers in the receiving wards occurs on the part of the Medical Officer. A preliminary examination of the paupers by the Medical Officers is necessary, in order to prevent the introduction of contagious or infectious diseases into the Work-

Art. 93 (c).—If the Medical Officer pronounce the pauper to be free from any such disease, the pauper shall be placed in the part of the Workhouse assigned to the class to which he may belong.

Art. 94.—No pauper shall be detained in a receiving ward for a longer time than is necessary for carrying into effect the regulations in Arts. 91, 92, and 93, if there be room in the proper ward for his reception.

Art. 95.—Before being removed from the receiving ward, the pauper shall be thoroughly cleansed, and shall be clothed in a workhouse dress, and the clothes which he wore at the time of his admission shall be purified and deposited in a place appropriated for that purpose, with the pauper's name affixed thereto. Such clothes shall be restored to the pauper when he leaves the Workhouse (d).

Art. 96.—Every pauper shall, upon his admission into the Workhouse, be searched by or under the inspection of the proper officer, and all articles prohibited by any Act of Parliament, or by this Order, which may be found upon his person, shall be taken from him, and, so far as may be proper, restored to him at his departure from the Workhouse (e).

---

house. If the pauper, on inspection, should be found to labour under a contagious or infectious disease, he must not, on that account, be refused admission into the Workhouse, but he should, after being inspected, be placed in the ward appropriated for the reception of persons afflicted with contagious or infectious disorders, and proper precaution should be taken to prevent the spread of the disease amongst the other inmates. But see note to Art. 88, p. 63. It may here be remarked that the law does not admit of the Medical Officer or of the Guardians resorting to compulsion to examine into the state of a sick pauper, when such pauper (being of sound mind) refuses to permit an examination of his or her person to be made. But see 30 & 31 Vict. c. 106, s. 22, as to the detention of sick paupers in a workhouse, *post*, p. 87.

(c) With respect to the classification of the paupers, see Article 98.

(d) Paupers admitted into the Workhouse are, under this Article, to be clothed in a dress furnished by the Guardians, and their own clothes are to be kept, and restored to them upon their quitting the Workhouse. Under Article 97, an exception is made for vagrants, as they usually remain in the Workhouse only a short time. See also Article 110, as to the description of clothing to be worn by the paupers.

(e) Reference may here be made to the 11 & 12 Vict. c. 110, s. 10,

Art. 97.—Provided always, that the regulations respecting the admission, clothing, and searching of paupers shall not apply to any casual poor wayfarer, unless the Guardians shall so direct, or unless he is compelled to remain in the Workhouse from illness or other sufficient cause, in which case he shall be admitted regularly as an inmate (*a*).

CLASSIFICATION OF THE PAUPERS.

Art. 98.—The paupers, so far as the Workhouse admits thereof, shall be classed as follows :—

Class 1. Men infirm through age or any other cause.

Class 2. Able-bodied men, and youths above the age of fifteen years.

Class 3. Boys above the age of seven years, and under that of fifteen.

---

and the 12 & 13 Vict. c. 103, s. 16, with respect to searching poor persons, professing to be destitute wanderers or wayfarers, on their admission to the Workhouse, and the appropriation by the Guardians of certain property of paupers. This Article does not interfere with those statutes in any way. The search will naturally be made at the time when the pauper's clothes are changed under Article 95. The adult male paupers ought to be searched by the Porter; the female paupers and the children by the Matron, or by some female servant under her direction. (See Art. 210. No. 2, and Art. 214, No. 5.) The right to search under 11 & 12 Vict. c. 110, s. 10, arises upon the application for relief; and the officer, when having once commenced it, is entitled to complete it, notwithstanding that the pauper may afterwards decline to receive the relief for which he has applied. It would seem that under the authority conferred by the statute so much force as is absolutely necessary may be employed in making the search. The following are examples of prohibited articles :—1. Spirituous or fermented liquors. (4 & 5 Wm. IV. c. 76, ss. 91-94.) 2. Articles of food not allowed by the dietary. (Art. 107.) 3. Letters or printed papers having an improper tendency. (Art. 119.) 4. Cards or dice. (Art. 120.) 5. Matches or highly-combustible articles. (Art. 121.) The Guardians are not empowered to direct the hair of any adult pauper to be cut off under ordinary circumstances; but only in some extraordinary case, where such a proceeding may be necessary for the protection of the health of the inmates of the house. (*Instr. Letter*, February, 1842.) In no case will they be justified in forcibly cutting off the hair of adult female paupers of sane mind. The children's hair may be cut whenever it is proper or necessary to do so.

(*a*) In that case he must be treated in all respects in the same manner as the other inmates of the class to which he may belong.

Class 4. Women infirm through age or any other cause.
Class 5. Able-bodied women, and girls above the age of fifteen years.
Class 6. Girls above the age of seven years, and under that of fifteen.
Class 7. Children under seven years of age.

To each class shall be assigned that ward or separate building and yard which may be best fitted for the reception of such class, and each class of paupers shall remain therein, without communication with those of any other class (*b*).

(*b*) Section 26 of the 4 & 5 Wm. IV. c. 76, after enabling the Commissioners to unite Parishes for the administration of the laws for the relief of the poor, and declaring that upon such Union the Workhouse or Workhouses of such Parishes shall be for their common use, proceeds to enact that "the said Commissioners may issue such rules, orders, and regulations as they shall deem expedient for the classification of such of the poor of such united Parishes in such Workhouse or Workhouses as may be relieved in any such Workhouse." In order to enforce the observance of decency and good order, it is necessary that the inmates of a Workhouse should be separated into certain classes. In no well-managed institution of this sort, in this or any other country, are males and females, the old and the young, the healthy and the sick, indiscriminately mixed together. The classes of paupers prescribed by the Commissioners are indicated in Article 98. The Commissioners believe that every well-regulated Workhouse should contain the means of dividing the inmates into at least as many classes as are indicated in this Article. It is to be observed that, although the Guardians are required to divide the paupers into the seven classes specified in this Article, they are permitted to subdivide any one or more of these classes in any manner which may be advisable, and which the internal arrangements of the Workhouse may permit. For example, it is very desirable that females of dissolute and disorderly habits should be separated from those of a better character; inasmuch as it is the duty of the Guardians to take all reasonable care that the morals of persons admitted into the house be not corrupted by intercourse with inmates of this description. On this point, see Art. 99, proviso 2. (*Instr. Letter.*) Reference may be made to 3 O. C. 94, as to the mode of dealing with women of bad character, who make a practice of frequently discharging themselves from the Workhouse for immoral purposes.

With regard to the treatment of the mothers of illegitimate children in Workhouses, the following extract from the Official Circular, 55 (N. S.), 64, is here inserted:—The Guardians of a Union having recommended that the mothers of illegitimate children should rise half an hour earlier, and go to bed one hour later than the other inmates, and that these portions of time should be employed in picking oakum, or some other industrial occupation, the Poor Law Board, in reply, stated that, "so long as the inmates of the Workhouse conform themselves to the prescribed rules and regulations, the law does not recognize any distinction amongst them founded upon their antecedent conduct; and the Board cannot therefore sanction a particular treatment in respect of a peculiar class of inmates, which is intended to operate as a punishment for offences committed previous to their entrance into the Workhouse. The Board concur with the Guardians in considering it highly desirable to observe the strictest classification as regards the mothers of illegitimate children, and they cannot be too careful not to employ them in the kitchen or in domestic work generally, in which the younger and more innocent inmates of the house are engaged. It is within the discretion of the Guardians to select any reasonable industrial occupation for the women in question; but the Board cannot, for the reasons which they have stated, sanction any difference in their treatment, in respect either to the hours of their rising or retiring to rest, their dress, or their diet."

It sometimes happens that mothers of illegitimate children affiliated upon the putative fathers make a practice of discharging themselves and their children from the Workhouse, and receiving the amount due under the orders, which they spend, and then apply for readmission in a state of destitution. In such cases, if they be really destitute, an order for their readmission should not be denied; but, when admitted, the regulations in Articles 88 to 96, *ante*, should on each occasion be observed, and the performance of a proper task of work exacted from them while in the house.

Any measures which appear likely to rescue abandoned women from a profligate life, and to hold out to them a prospect of earning an honourable livelihood when they leave the Workhouse, are not only desirable, but are highly to be commended. It has been suggested that with this view the mothers of illegitimate children when in the Workhouse, who are of sufficient capacity and ability, should be trained under the direction of the Medical Officer as sick nurses, and to attend upon women in their confinement. This it is competent for the Guardians to direct to be done under Article 112, which provides that the paupers of the several classes shall be kept employed according to their capacity and ability. Further with regard to nursing in Workhouses, see note to Art. 213, *post*.

It may be further remarked upon this Article that it is the duty of the Master, under the direction of the Medical Officer, to separate from the other inmates any pauper patient labouring under any infectious or contagious disease, for the purpose of preventing the disease from spreading; and in case of necessity, he would be authorized in confining the patient in a separate apartment or sick ward, and preventing all intercourse between him and the other inmates. On this point, see 30 & 31 Vict. c. 106, s. 22, *post*, p. 87.

The exceptions to the regulation that paupers of different classes shall not communicate with one another are stated in the several provisoes of Art. 99. As to Classes 1 and 4, see Art. 99, proviso 3, and the provision contained in the Act 10 & 11 Vict. c. 100, s. 23, which enacts, that when any two persons, being husband and wife, both of

Art. 99.—Provided,—

Firstly. That the Guardians shall from time to time, after consulting the Medical Officer, make such arrangements as they may deem necessary with regard to persons labouring under any disease of body or mind (*a*).

Secondly. The Guardians shall, so far as circumstances will permit, further subdivide any of the classes enumerated in Article 98, with reference to the moral character or behaviour, or the previous habits of the inmates, or to such other grounds as may seem expedient (*b*).

Thirdly. That nothing in this order shall compel the Guardians to separate any married couple, being both paupers of the first and fourth classes respectively, provided the Guardians shall set apart for the exclusive use of every such couple a sleeping apartment separate from that of the other paupers (*c*).

---

whom shall be above the age of sixty years, shall be received into any Workhouse, such two persons shall not be compelled to live separate and apart from each other in such Workhouse. In pursuance of this provision, separate apartments should be provided for married couples, but each separate couple is not entitled to a separate living or day room, as well as separate sleeping room. A distinct living room may, however, be provided for the exclusive use of this class of paupers at the times when they are not engaged in such work as they may be employed upon during the usual working hours.

(*a*) As to the detention of dangerous lunatics in the Workhouse, see Art. 101, and 30 & 31 Vict. c. 106, s. 22, *post*, p. 87. With regard to fever cases in the Metropolitan Unions and Parishes, they will be dealt with in future under the " Metropolitan Poor Act, 1867," 30 Vict. c. 6; see Glen's edition of that Act.

(*b*) This provision enables the Guardians to place persons of bad character in classes by themselves, so that they may not contaminate the virtuous and well-conducted inmates of the house. See remarks on the subject in note to Article 98.

(*c*) The regulation of the Commissioners, in consequence of which a husband and his wife are separated during their residence in the Workhouse, has been by many persons considered objectionable. A regulation of this sort is required by the internal arrangements of a Workhouse, and for the reasons stated in the Commissioners' First Annual Report, pp. 32–36, and in their Report on the Further Amendment of the Law, p. 52, they have thought it necessary to retain this regulation in the Order now issued. In order that all married couples should live

Art. 99.—Fourthly. That any paupers of the fifth and sixth classes may be employed constantly or occasionally in any of the female sick wards, or in the care of infants, or as assistants in the household work; and the Master and Matron shall make such arrangements as may enable the paupers of the fifth and sixth classes to be employed in the household work, without communication with the paupers of the second and third classes.

Fifthly. That any pauper of the fourth class, whom the Master may deem fit to perform any of the duties of a nurse or assistant to the Matron, may be so employed in the sick wards, or those of the fourth, fifth, sixth, or seventh classes; and any pauper of the first class, who may by the Master be deemed fit, may be placed in the ward of the third class, to aid in the management, and superintend the behaviour of the paupers of such class, or may be employed in the male sick ward (a).

---

together in a Workhouse, in a manner consistent with decency and propriety, it would be necessary not only that the internal arrangements and discipline of Workhouses should be altogether altered, but that their size and cost should be greatly increased.—*Instr. Letter.*

Aged married couples (whose residence in the Workhouse is likely to be of longer duration than that of able-bodied persons) the Guardians may, under this proviso, place in a separate sleeping apartment. See 10 & 11 Vict. c. 109, s. 23, as to the separation of married couples above sixty years of age, and note to Article 98. Moreover, the Guardians can allow out-door relief to any aged couple whom it may be inexpedient from any cause to retain in the Workhouse.

(a) Proviso 4 permits able-bodied women and girls above the age of seven years to be employed as nurses, or to give assistance in the household work out of their own wards. Proviso 5 permits infirm women to be employed similarly as nurses or assistants to the Matron, and infirm men to be employed as superintendents of the boys. With respect to the use of pauper servants, the Commissioners remark that they require the strictest superintendence on the part of the Master and the other officers. The employment of paupers in offices of trust in the Workhouse is inexpedient, inasmuch as it tends to impair the discipline of the house. In offices of mere labour, which can be performed under trustworthy superintendence, paupers may be useful. In such case they should in general receive only the common fare and clothing. Where

Art. 99.—Sixthly. That the Guardians, for a special reason to be entered on their minutes, may place any boy or girl between the ages of ten and sixteen years in a male or female ward respectively, different from that to which he or she properly belongs, unless the Commissioners shall otherwise direct (*b*).

Seventhly. That the paupers of the seventh class may be placed in such of the wards appropriated to the female paupers as shall be deemed expedient, and the mothers of such paupers shall be permitted to have access to them at all reasonable times (*c*).

Eighthly. That the Master (subject to any directions given or regulations made by the Guardians) shall allow the father or mother of any child in the same Workhouse, who may be desirous of seeing such child, to have an interview with such child at some one time in each day, in a room in the said Workhouse to be appointed for that purpose. And the Guardians shall make arrangements for permitting the members of the

---

responsibility is involved, paid servants should be engaged. If a pauper be competent to superintend or teach any kind of work, the Commissioners have no doubt of the right of the Guardians to require him to do so. The expediency of compelling any pauper inmate of a Workhouse to teach a trade which he is unwilling to teach, is, however, very doubtful. Tuition under the influence of compulsion would probably be of little value to the children receiving it.—*Instr. Letter*, February, 1842.

(*b*) Workhouses in or near populous towns commonly contain boys and girls between the ages of ten and sixteen, whom it is more expedient to class with the adult men and women than with the other boys and girls. This proviso enables the Guardians to depart, in cases of this description, from the classification prescribed by Art. 98.—*Instr. Letter*, February, 1842.

(*c*) This proviso permits children under the age of seven years to be placed in the wards of the female paupers, and also permits the mothers to have access to their children at all reasonable times. The Commissioners remark upon this proviso, that so long as any mother is suckling her child, she ought to have access to it at all times, except when she is at work, and that the child ought not even then to be completely beyond the mother's reach.—*Ib*. So long as a mother and her infant child remain in the Workhouse, the Guardians can exercise their own judgment as to the custody and care of the child under this proviso.

same family who may be in different Workhouses of the Union to have occasional interviews with each other, at such times and in such manner as may best suit the discipline of the several Workhouses (*a*).

Art. 99.—Ninthly. That casual poor wayfarers admitted by the Master or Matron shall be kept in a separate ward of the Workhouse, and shall be dieted and set to work in such manner and under such regulations as the Guardians, by any resolution now in force or to be made hereafter, may direct (*b*).

(*a*) This proviso contains regulations for the daily interviews of parents and children who may be in the same Workhouse, and for the occasional interviews of members of the same family who may be in different Workhouses.—*Instr. Letter*, February, 1842. Respecting visits to paupers in the Workhouse by persons not being inmates of the Workhouse, see Art. 118, and note. By Art. 208, No. 14, it is the Master's duty to apprise the nearest relation in the Workhouse of the sickness of any pauper; and by Art. 208, No. 16, it is his duty to give immediate information of the death of any pauper in the Workhouse to the nearest relations of the deceased, who may be known to him, and who may reside within a reasonable distance.—*Instr. Letter*, February, 1842.

(*b*) With respect to the relief of vagrants, see the Minute of the Poor Law Board of 4th August, 1848, 1st Annual Report, p. 29, and as regards the Metropolis, *ante*, p. 61. Whenever any vagrants or mendicants are received into the Workhouse, they ought, unless their stay exceeds a single night, to be kept entirely separate from the other inmates. This is a precaution necessary for preventing the introduction of infectious or contagious diseases in the Workhouse. An allowance of bread or potatoes should be given to each person so received at night. The bedding provided for vagrants should be sufficient for warmth, but may be inferior in quality and character to that used for the other inmates of the house. Except in severe weather it is not desirable to allow a fire in the vagrant ward. Wet clothes may be dried and returned to the wearer on the next day, he being accommodated in the meantime with old clothes from the Workhouse Store reserved for this purpose. No smoking or card-playing should be permitted in the vagrant ward. The Medical Officer should be called in to visit any vagrant alleging that he is sick, and immediate attention should be paid to his wants (*Instr. Letter*, February, 1842); and if the sickness assume a serious character, the vagrant should be removed to the Workhouse infirmary. (See Art. 97.) It is in the discretion of the Guardians, with a view to the orderly conduct of the Workhouse, to limit the hours during which vagrants shall be admitted, and they are not bound to provide lodgings which shall be open all night to trampers and that class of mendicants and wanderers who habitually resort to the rates for support. Emergent cases must, however, be admitted at all hours. The 5 & 6 Vict. c. 57,

s. 5, empowers the Guardians to prescribe a task of work to be done by any person relieved in any Workhouse, in return for the relief and lodging afforded to such person. This is done by the Guardians passing a resolution in the following form, and transmitting a copy of it to the Poor Law Board, who signify their consent under seal:—

Ordered:—By the Guardians of the —— Union, at a Meeting of the Board, held this —— day of ——, one thousand eight hundred and sixty ——.

That the Master of the Workhouse of the —— Union do set every adult person not suffering under any temporary or permanent infirmity of body being an occasional poor person who shall be relieved in the said Workhouse, in return for the food and lodging afforded to such person, to perform the following task of work, that is to say:—

Males;—

Females;—

Provided that no such person shall be detained against his or her will for the performance of such task of work, for any time exceeding four hours from the hour of breakfast, on the morning next after admission.

And provided also that such amount of work shall not be required from any person to whose age, strength, and capacity it shall appear not to be suited.

Signed ——, *Clerk to the Guardians.*

The Guardians are not empowered to detain any person against his will for the performance of the task of work for any time exceeding four hours from the hour of breakfast in the morning succeeding the admission of such person into the Workhouse; and if any person, while in the Workhouse, refuse or neglect to perform such task of work suited to his age, strength, and capacity, or wilfully destroy or injure his own clothes, or damage any of the property of the Board of Guardians, he may be taken before Justices and punished as an idle and disorderly person, within the meaning of the 5 Geo. IV. c. 83, s. 3.

The task of work prescribed should be specific in its nature, *i. e.* it should be so fixed that it can be increased in respect to *quantity*, and not in respect to time. It must not, however, be a greater task than can reasonably be expected to be performed in the space of four hours.

The refusal of the vagrant to take the breakfast offered him in the morning does not exonerate him from the liability to perform the task of work in return for the food and lodging afforded him on the previous night. The task should not, however, be exacted in any case in which it is not suited to the age, strength, and capacity of the individual.

By 29 & 30 Vict. c. 113, s. 15, when the Guardians of any Union or Parish shall prescribe a task of work to be performed by any poor person, to whom, or to whose wife, if he be liable to maintain such wife, or child, whether legitimate or illegitimate, under the age of sixteen, relief shall have been lawfully granted by such Guardians out of the Workhouse, such task being suited to the age, sex, strength, and capacity of such person, and being of a nature and description of which the Poor Law Board shall have previously approved, and such person shall refuse or wilfully neglect to perform such task, or shall wilfully destroy or

Art. 100.—The Guardians shall not admit into the Workhouse, or any ward of the same, or retain therein, a larger number or a different class of paupers than that heretofore or hereafter from time to time to be fixed by the Commissioners; and in case such number shall at any time be exceeded, the fact of such excess shall be forthwith reported to the Commissioners by the Clerk (*a*).

---

damage any of the tools, materials, or other property belonging to the Guardians, he shall be deemed to be an idle and disorderly person within the meaning of the 5 Geo. IV. c. 83, and shall be liable to be prosecuted and punished in the manner therein provided in respect of idle and disorderly persons; and the 7 & 8 Vict. c. 101, s. 59, shall apply to any such prosecution.

(*a*) This Article is intended to prevent the reception into any Workhouse of a large number of inmates than it is capable of containing, consistently with their health and comfort. When the number of the inmates shall have reached the maximum approved by the Poor Law Board, the Guardians will inform the Board of the fact, and will cease to make any fresh admissions until the number shall have been diminished. If the order prohibiting outdoor relief to the able-bodied is in force in the Union, the Guardians will be enabled to make exceptions to its provisions under Art. 6, and to report such exceptions to the Commissioners.—*Instr. Letter*, February, 1842.

Should the Guardians at any time make alterations or additions to their Workhouse, so as to render it capable of containing a larger number, they should report to the Poor Law Board the number which they consider the house, with the increased accommodation afforded, can accommodate, with a view to obtaining their consent to the extension of the number.

In former editions of this work it was stated that it was considered that each inmate of a Workhouse should, upon an average, have allotted to him 300 cubic feet of space, in rooms occupied by day or night, and 500 cubic feet when the room is occupied both by day and night, as a sick or infirm ward.

In the opinion of the Committee appointed by Mr. Gathorne Hardy, the late President of the Poor Law Board, to 'consider the requisite amount of space and other matters in relation to Workhouses and Workhouse Infirmaries,' there should be allotted to each sick inmate (including surgical, venereal, itch, and other cutaneous cases) in the Metropolitan Workhouses a space of not less than 850 cubic feet on an average; and in those cases where the height of the ward is more than 12 feet, such additional height should not be taken into account in calculating the cubic space of 850 feet; and there should be allowed a clear space of six feet across each bed, and no bed should be placed on the middle of the floor.

The Committee are also of opinion that where a day-room is provided for chronic and infirm cases an average of 500 cubic feet for each bed

Art. 101 (b).—No pauper of unsound mind, who may be dangerous, or who may have been reported as such by the Medical Officer, or who may require habitual or frequent restraint, shall be detained in the Workhouse for any period exceeding fourteen days, and the Guardians shall cause the proper steps to be taken for the removal of every such pauper to some asylum or licensed house as soon as may be practicable.

---

will suffice, and in lying-in wards 1200 cubic feet on the average should be provided.

The Committee recommend no increase in the minimum space of 300 cubic feet for each bed in wards occupied by night only by healthy adults and children.

As regards ventilation, the Committee suggest watchful and constant attention to ventilation; to its easiest, cheapest, and most effective methods, and to the means of adapting them to the various forms and dimensions of existing rooms. They say, whatever methods are adopted should be rigidly enforced by some resident officer, or frequent inspection; that they should be made secure against the intermeddling of the pauper inmates, and servants of the house, and that they should avoid the ingress of strong currents of cold air, or, at least, the incidence of such currents upon the bodies of the inmates.

In the sick wards, and in rooms of the aged and infirm, the Committee say that the temperature during the night ought not to be allowed to fall much below the day average, and that the arrangement should be under the control of the Medical Officer.

The Committee avoid expressing any opinion on the provision of nurses for the sick in Workhouses, but refer to a paper (annexed to their report) supplied to them by Miss Nightingale.

(b) Section 45 of the 4 & 5 Wm. IV. c. 76, enacts that "nothing in this Act contained shall authorize the detention in any Workhouse of any dangerous lunatic, insane person, or idiot, for any longer period than fourteen days; and every person wilfully detaining in any Workhouse any such lunatic, insane person, or idiot, for more than fourteen days, shall be deemed guilty of a misdemeanour." The words "dangerous lunatic, insane person, or idiot," in this clause, are to be read "dangerous lunatic, dangerous insane person, or dangerous idiot," according to the opinion of the Law Officers of the Crown given to the Poor Law Commissioners.

Further, with regard to the detention of dangerous lunatics in Workhouses, see 25 & 26 Vict. c. 111, s. 20, which prohibits the detention in a Workhouse of any lunatic, or alleged lunatic, beyond the period of fourteen days, unless in the opinion of the Medical Officer such person is a proper person to be kept in a Workhouse, and the accommodation therein is sufficient for his reception; and any person detained in a Workhouse in contravention of this section (that is without such opinion, or where the accommodation is insufficient), shall be deemed to be a proper person to be sent to an asylum, within the meaning of 16 & 17 Vict. c. 97, s. 67.

The section also declares that the Medical Officer shall, for all the purposes of that Act, be deemed to have knowledge that a pauper resident within his district is a lunatic, and a proper person to be sent to an asylum, and that it shall be his duty to act accordingly, and further to sign such certificate as is contained in Schedule F., No. 3, to the above statute, 16 & 17 Vict. c. 97.

Inasmuch as there are not in a Workhouse the proper conveniences for the detention of dangerous lunatics, it is desirable that any dangerous lunatic who may be temporarily deposited in one should not be detained there during a longer time than is necessary for taking the steps preparatory to his removal to a county lunatic asylum or licensed house, under the 16 & 17 Vict. c. 97, s. 67, and 25 & 26 Vict. c. 111, s. 19.

The 31st section of the 25 & 26 Vict. c. 111, gives power to two or more Commissioners in Lunacy, where, upon their visitation of any Workhouse, it appears to them that any lunatic, or alleged lunatic, therein is not a proper person to be kept in a Workhouse, to direct by an order under their hands such lunatic to be received into an asylum, and their order is to have the same effect as that of a Justice, under the 16 & 17 Vict. c. 97, s. 67.

An appeal to the Secretary of State for the Home Department against such order is given to the Guardians, and his order shall be binding on all parties concerned.

By the 32nd section a similar power is given to such Commissioners to visit any pauper lunatic not in the Workhouse, and after the same examination as is required to be made by a Justice, to direct such lunatic to be received into an asylum.

According to section 33 their order may authorize the admission into any asylum other than that of the county or borough in which the parish is situate from which the lunatic is sent, and into any registered hospital or licensed house, under the same circumstances, and subject to the same conditions as are provided for in statute 16 & 17 Vict. c. 97, s. 72.

From the express prohibition of the detention of dangerous persons of unsound mind in a Workhouse, contained in the 4 & 5 Wm. IV. c. 76, s. 45, coupled with the prevalent practice of keeping insane persons in Workhouses before the passing of that Act, it may be inferred that persons of unsound mind, not being dangerous, may be legally kept in a Workhouse. It must, however, be remembered that, with lunatics, the first object ought to be their cure, by means of a proper medical treatment. This can only be obtained in a well-regulated asylum; and therefore the detention of a curable lunatic in a workhouse is highly objectionable, on the score both of humanity and economy. The Commissioners, indeed, believe that most of the persons of unsound mind detained in Workhouses are incurable, harmless idiots. But although the detention of persons of this description in a Workhouse does not appear to be liable to objection on the ground of illegality or of defective medical treatment, they nevertheless think that the practice is often attended with serious inconveniences, and they are desirous of impressing upon the Guardians the necessity of the utmost caution and vigilance in the management of any persons of this class who may be in the Workhouse.—*Instr. Letter*, February, 1842.

Under 30 & 31 Vict. c. 106, s. 22, a poor person suffering from mental disease may, on the report of the Medical Officer that such person is not in a proper state to leave the Workhouse without danger to himself or others, be detained in the Workhouse. See *post*, p. 87.

The Guardians should inform themselves, through the Medical Officer of the Workhouse, and through the Medical Officers in whose districts paupers of unsound mind reside, whether the cases of any of them present a reasonable prospect of cure if submitted to the treatment of an asylum. All such cases should at once be sent to some asylum where they may receive the full benefit of medical care and professional superintendence. It is most important to bear in mind the fact, that the more recent a case of insanity is, the greater is the chance of cure, and therefore humanity and sound policy equally demand that persons so situated should receive the best professional aid at as early a stage as possible of their malady.

With reference to the 16 & 17 Vict. c. 97, s. 67, it is necessary to add that it is the duty of the Relieving Officer immediately on an order being made by the Justices for the reception of a lunatic in the Workhouse into a Lunatic Asylum, to take the necessary steps for the removal of the lunatic, notwithstanding the provision in Article 101 of the Consolidated Order. The notice of the Medical Officer, under the above-mentioned section, should be given to the Relieving Officer of the district in which the Workhouse is situated.

Reference may also be made to the provisions of the Lunacy Acts with regard to the visits of the Commissioners in Lunacy to Workhouses, and the visitation of lunatics in asylums. With regard to the former, it is enacted by 16 & 17 Vict. c. 96, s. 28, that any one or more of the Commissioners in Lunacy may, on such day or days, and at such hours in the day, and for such length of time as he or they shall think fit, visit all such Parish and Union Workhouses in which there shall be, or be alleged to be, any lunatic, as the Commissioners shall, by any resolution or resolutions of the Board, direct, and shall inquire whether the provisions of the law as to lunatics in such Parish or Union have been carried out, and also as to the dietary, accommodation, and treatment of the lunatics in such Workhouse, and shall report in writing thereon to the Poor Law Board.

By sect. 29 the Commissioners in Lunacy are also empowered, for any special reason, to appoint any competent person to visit and report upon lunatics in Workhouses.

By the 16 & 17 Vict. c. 97, s. 65, any physician, surgeon, or apothecary to be appointed by the Guardians, and also the Guardians of any Union or Parish, and the Overseers of any Parish, may, whenever they see fit, between the hours of eight in the morning and six in the evening, visit and examine any or every pauper lunatic, chargeable to the Union or Parish, confined in any asylum, registered hospital, or licensed house. But the Medical Officer of the asylum has power to refuse to allow such visit, if he should be of opinion that the visit would be injurious to the lunatic.

Sect. 34 of the 25 & 26 Vict. c. 111, requires the superintendent of every asylum, once at the least in each half-year, to transmit to the

DISCIPLINE AND DIET OF THE PAUPERS (a).

Art. 102.—All the paupers in the Workhouse, except the sick and insane, and the paupers of the first, fourth, and seventh classes, shall rise, be set to work, leave off work, and go to bed at the times mentioned in the Form (N.) hereunto an-

Guardians of every Union and Parish a statement of the condition of every pauper lunatic chargeable to such Union or Parish. This return will enable the Guardians to determine whether they should exercise the power given to them by the statute 16 & 17 Vict. c. 97, s. 65, of sending a physician or other medical practitioner, or a committee of themselves, to visit and examine any or all the pauper lunatics chargeable to the Union in the asylum. In the event of a committee being sent, the Poor Law Board, in their circular of 15th December, 1862, recommend that only a limited number should be appointed for the purpose, so that there be no unnecessary expense incurred in the visit. Considerable discussion has arisen between the Guardians and the auditors in several Unions, where the latter have objected to the number of Guardians sent on such visits and the amount of the expenses incurred in their visits. The Board think that, as a general rule, a Committee of three, or at the most five, Guardians would be sufficient for the purposes of the contemplated examination.

The attention of the Guardians is particularly directed to sect. 37, which requires the Visiting Committee of every Union and every Parish under a Board of Guardians, once at the least in each quarter of a year, to enter in a book, to be provided and kept by the Master of the Workhouse, such observations as they may think fit to make respecting the dietary, accommodation, and treatment of the lunatics, or alleged lunatics, for the time being in the Workhouse, and further requires that the book containing the observations made in pursuance of this section by the Visiting Guardians shall be laid by the Master before the Commissioners on their next visit. The Commissioners in Lunacy are of opinion that in framing the above section the Legislature were desirous of securing a periodical and full investigation by the Guardians of the mental and bodily condition of all the pauper lunatics detained by them in the Workhouse, and that therefore the word "treatment" should be considered not only as having reference to the medical care of the patients, but as affecting their moral and general treatment also, and would include inquiries as to the provision made for their exercise, occupation, and amusement, and the state of their persons, clothing, and bedding, and to the conduct and efficiency of the attendants, whether paid or otherwise, who may be appointed to take care of them.

Further with regard to the Law of Lunacy, see Fry's 'Lunacy Acts,' published by Knight & Co.

(a) The several times specified in Form (N.) annexed to the Order can be altered by the Guardians, with the consent of the Commissioners; but if no such alteration should be made, the time specified in the Form must be observed in the Workhouse.—*Instr. Letter*, February, 1842.

As to the employment of the paupers, see Article 112, and 54 O. C. p. 31.

nexed, and shall be allowed such intervals for their meals as are therein stated, and these several times shall be notified by the ringing of the bell; provided always that the Guardians may, with the consent of the Commissioners, make such alterations in any of the said times or intervals as the Guardians may think fit.

Art. 103.—Half an hour after the bell shall have been rung for rising, the names of the paupers shall be called over by the Master and Matron respectively, in the several wards provided for the second, third, fifth, and sixth classes, when every pauper, belonging to the respective wards, shall be present, and shall answer to his name, and be inspected by the Master and Matron respectively, provided that the paupers of the third and sixth class may be called over and inspected by the Schoolmaster and Schoolmistress (*b*).

Art. 104.—The meals shall be taken by all the paupers, except the sick, the children, persons of unsound mind, casual poor wayfarers, women suckling their children, and the paupers of the first and fourth classes, in the dining-hall or day-room, and in no other place whatever, and during the time of meals order and decorum shall be maintained (*c*).

Art. 105.—No pauper of the second, third, fifth, or sixth classes shall go to, or remain in, his sleeping-room, either in the time hereby appointed for work, or in the intervals al-

(*b*) It is desirable that the Master and Matron should every day call over the name of every pauper belonging to the classes enumerated, in order that they may not only be certified of the pauper's presence in the Workhouse, but also that every pauper of these classes may every day be necessarily brought under their attention.—*Instr. Letter*, February, 1842.

(*c*) With the exceptions specified in this Article, all the paupers ought to consume their meals in the dining-hall or day-room. With respect to the sick, the children, and persons of unsound mind, it is often necessary that they should eat their meals in their bedrooms. It may be here observed that the Officers of the Workhouse, in order to save themselves trouble, sometimes give out at once all the bread which each pauper is to consume during the day. This practice leads to waste and irregularity, and ought not, in general, to be permitted by the Guardians. All articles of food which the paupers may not consume in the dining-hall during the meal will be removed by the Officers; and no pauper will be allowed to carry away any food from the dining-hall. It may be added, that no pauper ought to be allowed to secrete articles of

lowed for meals, except by permission of the Master or Matron.

Art. 106.—The Master and Matron shall (subject to the directions of the Guardians) fix the hours of rising and going to bed, for the paupers of the first, fourth, and seventh classes, and determine the occupation and employment of which they may be capable; and the meals for such paupers shall be provided at such times and in such manner as the Guardians may from time to time direct (*a*).

Art. 107.—The paupers shall be dieted with the food and in the manner set forth in the Dietary Table which may be prescribed for the use of the Workhouse, and no pauper shall have or consume any liquor, or any food or provision other than is allowed in the said Dietary Table, except on Christmas Day or by the direction in writing of the Medical Officer, as provided in Article 108 (*b*).

Art. 108.—Provided,

First.—That the Medical Officer may direct in writing such diet for any individual pauper as he may deem necessary, and the Master shall obey such direction until the next ordinary meeting of the Guardians, when he shall report the same in writing to the Guardians (*c*).

---

food in boxes or bags in the bedrooms, as such a practice is uncleanly, and likely to prove injurious to the health of the inmates.—*Instr. Letter*, February, 1842.

(*a*) In fixing the hours of rising and going to bed, and the employment of the infirm men and women, and the children, the Guardians, and the Master and Matron, ought to consult the Medical Officer for the Workhouse. This Article likewise permits the Guardians to fix the times at which the infirm men and women and the children shall have their meals, and also the manner in which their meals shall be furnished to them; for example, in their own rooms, if it be necessary.—*Instr. Letter*, February, 1842.

(*b*) With respect to the mode in which proposed alterations in the established dietary must be effected, see the General Dietary Order of the Poor Law Board, dated 16th February, 1848, *post*. And with regard to Workhouse Dietaries generally, see the report of Dr. Smith to Mr. Gathorne Hardy, dated 1st February, 1867, published by the Poor Law Board.

(*c*) This provision refers to the diet of individual paupers, and not to

Secondly.—That if the Medical Officer at any time certify that he deems a temporary change in the diet essential to the health of the paupers in the Workhouse, or of any class or classes thereof, the Guardians shall cause a copy of such certificate to be entered on the minutes of their proceedings, and may forthwith order, by a resolution, the said diet to be temporarily changed, according to the recommendation of the Medical Officer, and shall forthwith transmit a copy of such certificate and resolution to the Commissioners.

Thirdly.—That the Medical Officer shall be consulted by the Matron as to the nature of the food of the infants, and of their mothers when suckling, and the time at which such infants should be weaned.

Fourthly.—That the Guardians may, without any direction of the Medical Officer, make such allowance of food as may be necessary to paupers employed as nurses or in the household work; but they shall not allow to such paupers any fermented or spirituous liquors on account of the performance of such work, unless in pursuance of a written recommendation of the Medical Officer (*d*).

---

any class of paupers. The direction of the Medical Officer should be entered accordingly in the Workhouse Medical Relief Book, and he should specify therein the articles of diet to be supplied to the pauper.

(*d*) The orders of the Commissioners prescribe no dietary for the sick, but the quantity and nature of their food are left exclusively to the discretion of the Medical Officer; and in consequence of there being no fixed dietary for the sick, there is not only much confusion and error in the Master's accounts, but the Auditor has considerable difficulty in ascertaining the quantities of food actually consumed in the Workhouse. The Commissioners, by Art. 207, No. 9, have therefore required the Medical Officer for the Workhouse to frame the proper dietary for the sick paupers, in so many different scales as he shall deem expedient. They have recommended that the sick dietary should be similar to that used in hospitals, and containing four kinds of diet: viz, high, middle, low, and fever; and that the quantity of articles to be allowed for each should be minutely specified. The Commissioners further recommend that a copy of this dietary should be hung up in the infirmaries or sick-wards of the Workhouse; and they require that the Master's accounts should correspond with the entries made in the proper column of Form (Q.) by the Medical Officer. (See note to Art. 207, No. 9.)

Art. 109.—If any pauper require the Master or Matron to weigh the allowance of provisions served out at any meal, the Master or Matron shall forthwith weigh such allowance in the presence of the pauper complaining, and of two other persons (*a*).

Art. 110.—The clothing to be worn by the paupers in the Workhouse shall be made of such materials as the Board of Guardians may determine (*b*).

The second proviso to Art. 108 will enable the Guardians to adopt, without delay, such suggestion of the Medical Officer with respect to diet, as the prevalence of any epidemic or other disease may render advisable.—*Instr. Letter*, February, 1842.

The latter part of the 4th proviso may be acted upon, though the paupers are not at the time actually sick. If the Medical Officer consider that, owing to the nature of the work any pauper is employed upon, an allowance of fermented or spirituous liquors is necessary for the preservation of his health, and in writing recommends the allowance, the Guardians are at liberty to grant it.

(*a*) This article is intended to provide the means of satisfying every pauper that he receives the daily allowance of food assigned to him by the dietary, and it may be observed that the allowances to the paupers must be weighed and served out at each meal, and not one allowance for the whole of the meals during the day.

With reference to complaints of Workhouse inmates, the Poor Law Board in a circular dated 27th September, 1866, say that it appears to them very desirable that the inmates of Workhouses who may have complaints to make should have full information how and where to make them, so as to ensure attention. With this view the Board suggest that a printed notice should be hung up in each ward or room to the effect that any inmate who has a complaint to prefer should either address it in writing to the Clerk, or verbally to some member of the Visiting Committee when on his rounds through the Workhouse. The Board further suggest that a book should be kept, in which an entry of all such complaints should be made, together with a record of the steps taken by the Guardians in consequence.

(*b*) The clothing worn by the paupers need not be uniform either in colour or materials, and it should be stamped with the name of the Union, but so as not to be seen when worn. See 55 Geo. III. c. 137, s. 2, which enacts that the stamp or mark shall not be placed on any articles of wearing apparel, so as to be publicly visible on the exterior of the same.

With respect to the use of a penal dress in the Workhouse, see the Minute of the Poor Law Commissioners, in their 6th Annual Report, p. 98, which contains their reasons for disapproving of the practice of causing paupers to wear a distinguishing dress as a mark of disgrace. In the General Workhouse Rules issued by the Commissioners, in 1842, they permitted the Guardians to direct a dress different from that of the

Art. 111.—More than two paupers, any one of whom is above the age of seven years, shall not be allowed to occupy the same bed, unless in the case of a mother and infant children (c).

Art. 112.—The paupers of the several classes shall be kept employed according to their capacity and ability (d); and no pauper shall receive any compensation for his labour (e).

---

other inmates to be worn by disorderly or refractory paupers during a period of not more than forty-eight hours; but a similar provision is not contained in the present Order.—*Instr. Letter.*

(c) This Article does not admit of a mother and her infant sleeping in the same bed with another woman, nor does it admit of two adults and a child sleeping in the same bed. The practice of placing two adults to sleep in the same bed is very objectionable, and is on every account to be discouraged.

(d) It would be contrary to this Article, as well as to Art. 114 and Arts. 208, No. 6, and 210, No. 3, to send any of the inmates of the Workhouse, whether adults or children, out daily to work for farmers or in factories, whether for wages or otherwise. See also 56 Geo. III. c. 129, which however appears to apply only to adults. See 9 O. C. 64, as to the employment of Workhouse boys in a factory during the day.

As to the duty of the Master of the Workhouse in regard to the employment of the paupers, see Art. 208, No. 6.

See also note to Art. 112, and Arts. 208, No. 6, and 210, No. 3.

(e) Article 112 prohibits any pecuniary compensation for the labour of the inmates. Art. 108, No. 4, however, makes an exception as to extra allowances of food for paupers employed in the service of the house, as nurses, washerwomen, etc. The bodily exertions required of persons so employed, or the disagreeableness of the duty, may sometimes be such as to justify an extra allowance of this sort. In large Workhouses it is always advisable to employ a paid nurse; in many Workhouses paid household servants have been appointed.—*Instr. Letter*, February, 1842.

When it is considered expedient to employ a pauper inmate as a paid servant, the Guardians should appoint him or her as an assistant or otherwise. The person so appointed will then cease to be a pauper, and the cost of the wages (if any) and rations will then be charged to the common fund, in like manner as the other Workhouse Officers. If a task of work be prescribed under 5 & 6 Vict. c. 57, s. 5, for vagrants relieved in the Workhouse, the Guardians may, if they think fit, employ any able-bodied male pauper inmate of the Workhouse upon the work so prescribed, according to his capacity and ability, and require from him the performance of the same daily task of work. As regards a task of work for out-door poor, see note to Art. 99, *ante*, p. 75. Further upon this Article, see 56 O. C. (N. s.) 31.

Art. 113.—No pauper in the Workhouse shall be employed or set to work in pounding, grinding, or otherwise breaking bones, or in preparing bone-dust.

Art. 114.—The boys and girls who are inmates of the Workhouse shall, for three of the working hours at least, every day, be instructed in reading, writing, arithmetic, and the principles of the Christian Religion, and such other instruction shall be imparted to them as may fit them for service, and train them to habits of usefulness, industry, and virtue (*a*).

Art. 115.—Any pauper may quit the Workhouse upon giving to the Master, or (during his absence or inability to act) to the Matron, a reasonable notice of his wish to do so; and in the event of any able-bodied pauper, having a

---

As regards the religious instruction of children in the Workhouse, see the Order of 23rd August, 1859, *post*.

(*a*) The Poor Law Board leave the Guardians a discretion as to whether Workhouse children above a certain age shall be employed industrially during the whole of every alternate day, provided that the children be in the school at least eighteen hours in the course of the week, and not more than six hours in any one day, and that the manual occupations in which they are engaged are suitable for the purposes of industrial training.

Reference may here be made to the 14 & 15 Vict. c. 105, s. 6, and 29 & 30 Vict. c. 113, s. 16, which enable Guardians having adequate and greater provision for the reception of poor children in their Workhouse than they require, with the consent of the Poor Law Board, to contract with the Guardians of any other Union or Parish, for the reception, maintenance, and instruction therein of any poor children under the age of sixteen years, being orphans or deserted by their parents, or whose parents or surviving parent shall consent.

Reference may also be made to the 18 & 19 Vict. c. 34, as to the education of the young children of poor persons who are relieved out of the Workhouse, and the Circular dated 9th January, 1856, of the Poor Law Board, containing suggestions as to the proper mode of carrying it into execution. Also to the 25 & 26 Vict. c. 43, and 29 & 30 Vict. c. 113, s. 14, as to which, see *ante*, p. 29.

Where the Guardians of a Union or Parish represent to two Justices or a Magistrate that any child apparently under the age of fourteen years maintained in a Workhouse or Pauper School of a Union or Parish or in a District Pauper School is refractory, or is the child of parents either of whom has been convicted of a crime or offence punishable with penal servitude or imprisonment, and that it is desirable that he be sent to an industrial school under the Industrial Schools Act, 1866, the Justices or Magistrate may, if satisfied that it is expedient to deal with the child under that Act, order him to be sent to an industrial school. (29 & 30 Vict. c. 118, s. 17.)

family, so quitting the house, the whole of such family shall be sent with him, unless the Guardians shall, for any special reason, otherwise direct; and such directions shall be in conformity with the Regulations of the Commissioners with respect to relief in force at the time (*b*).

(*b*) By this Article, no pauper is allowed to quit the Workhouse without giving a *reasonable notice* of his or her wish to do so. The reasonableness of the notice must depend upon the circumstances under which it is given. In many of their former Orders the Commissioners fixed the length of the notice at *three hours*, but they now prefer the indeterminate expression used in this Article; inasmuch as the period of three hours might sometimes be too long and at other times too short. Some time after the giving of the notice is requisite, in order to enable the Master to restore to the pauper his own clothes (see Article 95), and to receive back those belonging to the Guardians. Some time likewise is required in order to enable the master to make the proper entries in the books. Moreover, a pauper cannot, in general, be discharged during the night, or at the time of meals, or during the performance of divine service. It may be added, that a longer time must be allowed to the Master, if several paupers give the notice simultaneously: but the Master will not be justified in throwing any unnecessary impediment in the way of a pauper's leaving the house in the shortest practicable time. Although paupers ought not to be discharged during the peformance of divine service, there is no power of detaining them during the whole of Sunday, if they should desire to leave the Workhouse on that day. The Commissioners believe that the Guardians, and the Master of the Workhouse as their Officer, have over orphan children, or children deserted by their parents, the same control which a guardian possesses over his ward; and that they may therefore detain in the Workhouse any such infant under the age of sixteen; provided that they have reasonable grounds for believing that leaving the Workhouse would be attended with injurious consequences to the child. *Reg* v. ——, 15 Q. B. 1061, shows that the Guardians are entitled to protect orphan children from personal injuries. The Guardians, however, are not authorized to detain in the Workhouse young persons above sixteen years of age, who have no friends, and are not going into service. Nor is there any power of detaining in the Workhouse mothers of bastard children who may be in the habit of quitting the Workhouse and returning to it after a few days' absence. But Lord Campbell, C.J., whilst Attorney-General, and Sir William Follet, advised the Poor Law Commissioners that the Guardians could not lawfully detain orphan children, or other children not having the benefit of parental care, in the Workhouse, without their consent so long as might be judged necessary for their protection, or until employment can be procured for them, unless they are apprenticed.

As regards the detention in a Workhouse of poor persons suffering from mental or other disease, it is enacted that when there shall be in any Workhouse a poor person suffering from mental disease, or from bodily disease of an infectious or contagious character, and the Medical Officer of the Workhouse upon examination reports in writing that such person is not in a proper state to leave the Workhouse without danger to himself or others, the Guardians may direct the Master to detain such person therein; or, if the Guardians be not sitting, the Master may, until the next meeting of the Guardians, detain him therein, and such person shall not be discharged from such Workhouse until the Medical Officer shall in writing certify that such discharge may take place; this does not prevent the removal of a lunatic to a Lunatic Asylum, etc., when such removal is otherwise required by law, nor the removal of any poor person after the parent or next of kin shall have given to the Guardians such an undertaking as they shall deem satisfactory to provide for the removal, charge, and maintenance of such person with due care and attention while the malady continues. (30 & 31 Vict. c. 106, s. 22.)

It may be added that unless the case be brought within the above enactment, the Guardians have no legal power to detain paupers in the Workhouse who give notice to leave it; as for instance a wife, the husband being in the House, and unable to leave owing to sickness or other cause.

It may be observed, that persons with infectious diseases going abroad, and exposing others to the infection, are punishable for a misdemeanour. (*Rex* v. *Vantandillo*, 4 M. & S. 73.) But now see the provisions on the subject in the Sanitary Act, 1866, 29 & 30 Vict. c. 90, s. 38, in Glen's 'Law of Public Health and Local Government.' Fourth edition, p. 594.

When a pauper has committed an offence, or been guilty of a misbehaviour in the Workhouse, punishable by confinement under Art. 130 or 131, his giving the proper notice to quit the Workhouse will not prevent the completion of such punishment, provided the confinement does not extend beyond the period mentioned in the seventh section of 54 Geo. III. c. 170. and the 93rd sect. of 4 & 5 Wm. IV. c. 76, viz. twenty-four hours, or such further space of time as may be necessary in order to bring such pauper before a justice of the peace. Art. 115 further provides that when any able-bodied pauper having a family quits the house, the whole of such family shall be sent with him or her, unless the Board of Guardians shall, for any special reason, otherwise direct. Upon this provision, it may be remarked, that the mother of a legitimate child, or of an illegitimate child, should, on leaving the Workhouse, take her child with her.

It seems doubtful whether the Guardians have the power to prevent the wife from leaving the Workhouse without her husband; but the husband can, if he thinks fit, detain her in the Workhouse by his marital authority; and the Guardians would be justified in refusing her permission to quit the Workhouse under such circumstances.—*Instr. Letter*, February, 1842. If the husband should refuse to exercise his marital control over the wife in this respect, the Guardians may discharge him from the Workhouse also. The course which the Guardians should adopt must, however, depend upon the circumstances of each case, and no general rule can be laid down; and it may be added that the Guardians cannot compel the wife of a pauper to enter the Workhouse, if she does not seek for relief for herself.

With regard to an infant under the age of sixteen, it is to be observed that the Court of Queen's Bench has decided that up to that age a female child has no right to withdraw herself from the custody of her

Art. 116.—Provided nevertheless, that the Guardians may, by any general or special direction, authorize the Master to allow a pauper, without giving any such notice as is required in Art. 115, to quit the Workhouse, and to return after a temporary absence only; and every such allowance shall be reported by the Master to the Guardians at their next ordinary meeting (*a*).

---

father against his will. (*Reg.* v. *Howes*, 30 L. J. M. C. 48.) It would seem, therefore, that a female child under the age of sixteen cannot discharge herself from the Workhouse against the will of her parent who is in the Workhouse. As regards the compulsory discharge of a pauper from the Workhouse by the Guardians, see 39 O. C. (N. S.) 112.

If an inmate of a Workhouse be subpœnaed as a witness in a court of law, he must be permitted to leave the Workhouse for the purpose of attending the Court; and in that case, if he should so desire, it will be proper he should be furnished with his own clothes, in which to appear in Court. If a pauper, for whose removal to the parish of his settlement an Order of Justices has been obtained, be in the Workhouse, and give notice of his intention to leave, he cannot be detained against his will on the ground that he is under an order of removal, but must be permitted to leave. The Master of the Workhouse has nothing whatever to do with the question of removal, which is one for the Guardians alone. Sometimes benevolent persons apply to Boards of Guardians to be permitted to adopt children from the Workhouse whose parentage is unknown; though there is no legal objection to the Guardians giving up the possession of the children under such circumstances, they should satisfy themselves that the proposal is for the child's advantage before consenting to it. Under this Article the Guardians are enabled to retain in the Workhouse the wife or other member of a family of an ablebodied man, on the head of the family discharging himself; but in that case they must give a special direction in the matter, and report the circumstances to the Poor Law Board for their sanction, under Art. 6 of the General Prohibitory Order, *post*. With respect to the power of the Master over persons with infectious diseases who may be in the Workhouse, see note on Art. 98.

(*a*) In general, any pauper who quits the Workhouse, having given the notice under Art. 115, is understood to have ceased to be an inmate of it; and if he should be subsequently re-admitted (see Art. 88), he will go through the process required by Arts. 91–97. But the proviso in Art. 116 prescribes a mode by which a pauper may be allowed to quit the Workhouse temporarily without ceasing to be an inmate of it, and without being subject upon his return to the regulations in Arts. 91–97. The following may serve as examples of the "urgent or special reasons" for which a pauper may be permitted to quit the Workhouse; viz. (1.) In order to search for work in the neighbourhood. (2.) To visit a relation. (3.) To attend a baptism at the parish church (see note on Art. 124). This permission ought to be given only from time to time, as the occasion may arise, and not at stated intervals, for example, once

Art. 117 (a).—Provided also, that nothing herein contained shall prevent the Master from allowing the paupers of each sex under the age of fifteen, subject to such restrictions as the Guardians may impose, to quit the Workhouse, under the care and guidance of himself, or the Matron, Schoolmaster, Schoolmistress, Porter, or some one of the assistants and servants of the Workhouse, for the purpose of exercise.

Art. 118.—Any person may visit any pauper in the Workhouse by permission of the Master, or (in his absence) of the Matron, subject to such conditions and restrictions as the Guardians may prescribe; such interview shall take place in a room separate from the other inmates of the Workhouse, and in the presence of the Master, Matron, or Porter, except where a sick pauper is visited (b).

---

a week or a fortnight. A permission to leave the house at stated intervals is found in practice to be abused. With respect to the penalty for abuses of the permission to quit the Workhouse temporarily see note on Art. 126. If an adult person should abscond from the Workhouse without giving any notice, for example, by climbing over a wall, or dropping from a window, he is not punishable unless he should carry away clothes or other effects of the Guardians, in which case he may be convicted under the 55 Geo. III. c. 137, or if he do any wilful damage to the property of the Guardians, he may be punished under 24 & 25 Vict. c. 97, ss. 5. 11, 12, 39. The Guardians and their Officers are not empowered to capture any person absconding from the Workhouse and bring him back against his will; and if he return voluntarily, they are not empowered to punish him after his return.—*Instr. Letter*, February, 1842.

If the Guardians have given the authority contemplated to the Master, he may grant leave of absence from the Workhouse to any boy or girl in the school who, upon sufficient grounds, may apply for leave. The Master must, however, report the allowance to the Guardians at their next ordinary meeting. The Schoolmaster or Schoolmistress have no authority to grant leave of absence to any of the children. It is desirable that, as far as the circumstances will admit, the Board of Guardians should reserve to themselves the exclusive power of giving leave of absence to children when not under the care of their parents. (57 O. C. (N. S.) p. 96.)

(a) The proviso in this Article allows the children to leave the Workhouse for the purpose of exercise under proper care. By Art. 212, No. 3, it is made the duty of the Schoolmaster and Schoolmistress to accompany the children on those occasions, unless the Guardians should otherwise direct.—*Instr. Letter*, February, 1842.

(b) This article allows any pauper in the Workhouse to receive the

Art. 119 (e).—No written or printed paper of an improper tendency, or which may be likely to produce insubordination, shall be allowed to circulate, or be read aloud, among the inmates of the Workhouse.

Art. 120.—No pauper shall play at cards, or at any game of chance, in the Workhouse; and the Master may take

---

visit of a stranger; but requires that, except in the case of a sick pauper, the interview shall take place in a separate room and in the presence of the Master or Matron. The necessity for this restriction arises from several causes, among which the following may be specified as the most prominent; namely, a fear of the introduction of spirits by visitors; the abuses which would ensue if the female inmates of a Workhouse were generally permitted to have private interviews with men; the probability that the minds of young persons in the Workhouse would be perverted by persons who might visit them. Accordingly, this restriction is not intended to offer any obstacle to the innocent and proper visits of relations and friends; and the Master or other officer present ought not to listen to the conversation between the visitor and the pauper, unless there should be a reasonable ground for suspecting the conversation to be of an improper character. It is desirable that there should be fixed days in the week on which paupers should be allowed to receive visits; and that they should not, in general, be visited on other days, except in cases of sickness or necessity.—*Instr. Letter*, February, 1842. Under this Article the Guardians may permit the visit of any person for any lawful purpose to any sick pauper, subject to such restrictions and conditions as they may think fit to impose.

(e) The words "printed paper" comprehend any newspaper, handbill, book, pamphlet, etc.—It will be observed, that the prohibition only extends to papers of an *improper tendency*, or which may be likely to produce insubordination. By Art. 214, No. 4, it is the duty of the Porter to prevent the admission into the Workhouse of any letter or printed paper falling within the prohibition in Art. 119. The Master is not empowered to examine letters written by the pauper inmates, and such letters should be sent to the post; nor is he empowered to detain or open letters addressed to a pauper, unless he have reason to suspect that the communication is of an "*improper tendency*." Paupers may be permitted to receive writing materials sent by their friends.—*Instr. Letter*, February, 1842.

The Poor Law Board have stated that if the Guardians should be of opinion that a collection of books for the use of the Workhouse inmates is desirable, they are at liberty to exercise their own judgment in regard to purchasing what shall appear to them to be requisite; and it will be for the Auditor to decide whether they have exceeded their legal powers in the particular case when the item comes before him at his audit. With regard, however, to future annual payments for the maintenance of the library, the Board consider it to be quite clear that the Guardians cannot bind their successors to expend any sum for such a purpose hereafter. (57 O. C. (N. s.) p. 85.)

from any pauper, and keep until his departure from the Workhouse, any cards, dice, or other articles applicable to games of chance, which may be in his possession (*a*).

Art. 121.—No pauper shall smoke in any room of the Workhouse except by the special direction of the Medical Officer, or shall have any matches or other articles of a highly combustible nature in his possession, and the Master may take from any person any articles of such a nature (*b*).

Art. 122 (*c*).—Any licensed Minister of the religious persuasion of an inmate of the Workhouse, who may at any

---

(*a*) The Commissioners state, that it is desirable that the prohibition in this Article should be applied to the inmates of the vagrant ward, as well as to the other paupers. See note to Art. 99, No. 9. The prohibition is as to "games of chance," and therefore it would not apply to chess, draughts, or dominoes, which are not games of that nature.

(*b*) The practice of smoking in the rooms of the Workhouse not only tends to uncleanliness, but is also offensive to many of the other inmates. The prohibition of matches, gunpowder, and the like, is necessary for protecting the house against fire.—*Instr. Letter*, February, 1842. The Article does not expressly apply to smoking in the yards of the Workhouse, but it is competent to the Guardians to make an order to prevent the practice of smoking in the yards, and they may also prohibit the officers of the Workhouse from smoking either in the Workhouse or the yards. If their order be disobeyed by any pauper, and he do not refrain from smoking when ordered to do so by the Workhouse Master or other officer of the Workhouse, he will be guilty of an offence within the meaning of Art. 127. As to the supply of tobacco and snuff to paupers in the Workhouse, see note to Art. 207, No. 8. The Medical Officer possesses no authority to order tobacco for any class of paupers generally. If he considers it to be absolutely necessary for any pauper on the ground of health, it should be inserted as an extra in the proper column of the Workhouse Medical Relief Book against the name of the pauper. When given, it should be entered in the Master's portion of the book, and transferred, like other extras, to the weekly provisions' consumption, and the other provision accounts of the Workhouse.

(*c*) With respect to this Article, see sect. 19 of the 4 & 5 Wm. IV. c. 76, which enacts that "No rules, orders, or regulations of the said Commissioners, nor any bye-laws at present in force or to be hereafter made, shall oblige any inmate of any Workhouse to attend any religious service which may be celebrated in a mode which may be contrary to the religious feelings of such inmate, nor shall authorize the education of any child in such Workhouse in any religious creed other than that professed by the parents or surviving parent of such child, and to which such parents or parent shall object, or, in the case of an orphan, to which the godfather or godmother of such orphan shall so object." And that " It shall and may be lawful for any licensed Minister of the religious persuasion of any inmate of such Workhouse, at all times in

time in the day, on the request of any inmate, enter the Workhouse for the purpose of affording religious assistance to him, or for the purpose of instructing his child or children in the principles of his religion, shall give such assistance or instruction so as not to interfere with the good order and discipline of the other inmates of the Workhouse, and such religious assistance or instruction shall be strictly confined to inmates who are of the religious persuasion of such Minister, and to the children of such inmates, except in the cases in which the Guardians may lawfully permit religious assistance and instruction to be given to any paupers who are Protestant Dissenters, by licensed Ministers who are Protestant Dissenters.

---

the day, on the request of such inmate, to visit such Workhouse for the purpose of affording religious assistance to such inmate, and also for the purpose of instructing his child or children in the principles of their religion." The words " Licensed Minister" in the 4 & 5 Wm. IV. c. 76, and "Minister" in sect. 43 of 7 & 8 Vict. c. 101, are by sect. 74 of the latter Act to be construed to mean and include every person in holy orders, and also every person teaching or preaching in any congregation for religious worship whose place of meeting is certified and recorded according to law. See also the opinion of the Crown lawyers upon the construction of 4 & 5 Wm. IV. c. 76, s. 19, in the 5th Annual Report of the Poor Law Commissioners, p. 75. They stated as follows:—" The remedial nature of the enactment in the 19th section obviously requires the most liberal construction; and we are therefore of opinion that the words 'Licensed Minister,' as there used, must be deemed to extend to and include Roman Catholic Clergymen and Clergymen of the Established Church." No decision has been pronounced upon the point; but the Court of Queen's Bench, in *Reg.* v. *Chelsea Guardians*, seemed inclined to think that the Act contemplated a request to be visited at all reasonable times, and that it was not necessary that there should be a particular request for each visit.

The following report of the case of *Reg.* v. *the Guardians of St. Luke's, Chelsea*, is contained in Knight and Co.'s 'Official Advertiser' of the 16th December, 1861:—

"THE QUEEN *v.* THE GUARDIANS OF ST. LUKE'S, CHELSEA.

" Nov. 11.—*Roman Catholic Inmates of Workhouse. Religious Assistance and Instruction. Mandamus.*—In this case a rule had been granted calling upon the Guardians of the Poor of the parish of St. Luke, Chelsea, to show cause why a *mandamus* should not issue, commanding them from time to time, and at all reasonable times of the day, to permit the Rev. Edward Bagshawe, a priest of the Oratory at Brompton, he being a licensed minister of the Roman Catholic Church, to visit the St. Luke's Workhouse for the purpose of affording due religious assistance to certain paupers, twenty in number, therein named, of the religious persuasion of the said Rev. E. Bagshawe. The application was founded upon the proviso to the 19th section of the Poor Law Amendment Act (the 4th & 5th of William IV. c. 76). In the course of the argument the Court suggested that an arrangement should, if possible, be come to between the parties, and the case was allowed to stand over for that purpose. The rule was subsequently discharged, without costs, upon the following terms of arrangement:—

"A Roman Catholic priest shall be permitted to visit the Roman Catholic inmates of St. Luke's, Chelsea, Workhouse, according to the following regulations:—

"1. *Able-bodied Inmates.*

"I. Each inmate may name a Roman Catholic priest and request his attendance, and the request once made need not be repeated.

"II. The request must be made known to or through the Master, or if to the priest himself, notice of it must be given to the Master by the priest before he acts upon it.

"III. The priest may visit the inmates at any time between 6 and 8 P.M. four days in the week, viz. Mondays, Tuesdays, Thursdays, and Fridays. They must be seen separately.

"IV. The inmates may go to church once or twice on every Sunday so long as this privilege is not abused.

"2. *Sick and Infirm Inmates.*

"V. The sick and infirm, after request once made according to the regulations laid down for the able-bodied inmates, may be visited at all practicable and convenient times.

"3. *Roman Catholic Inmates in general.*

"VI. The inmates may be supplied with the following books:—The Bible, the Poor Man's Catechism, the First Catechism, the Oratory Prayers and the Missal, the Imitation of Jesus Christ, and any others to be approved of by the Guardians."

By a "licensed Minister" of a Protestant Dissenting sect, the Commissioners understand a Minister who is recognized in his ministerial character by the members of such sect, and who has complied with all the requisitions of the law, and is therefore subject to no penalty in respect of the public exercise of his ministerial functions; but see 7 & 8 Vict. c. 101, s. 74, *ante*, p. 93.) It appears to the Commissioners that the section of the 4 & 5 Wm. IV. c. 76, above quoted, does not contemplate the attendance of Members of the Established Church at the divine service performed by a Dissenting Minister in a Workhouse. If any adult members of the Established Church should desire to attend the service of a Dissenting Minister, the Commissioners would not interfere to prevent their attendance, provided that no improper influence was used to induce them to attend, although they consider it objectionable; but the Commissioners think that children, being members of the Established Church, should never be permitted to attend on such occasions, and they would, in case of necessity, prohibit any such practice by an Order. See a full statement of the views of the Commissioners

Art. 123 (a).—No work, except the necessary household work and cooking, shall be performed by the paupers on Sunday, Good Friday, and Christmas Day.

Art. 124 (b).—Prayers shall be read before breakfast and after supper every day, and Divine Service shall be per-

on this subject to the Liskeard Guardians, 7th Annual Report, p. 230. —*Instr. Letter,* February, 1842. As regards the religious education or training of orphan children in the Workhouse, it is to be observed that, as a rule, where the father has not left nor expressed any direction or instruction as to the religion in which his infant children are to be educated, that the Court, in a case before it, said that it will assume that his wishes were that his children should be educated in his own religion. (In *re North,* 11 Jurist, 7.) The following case further illustrates this point :—A father being a beneficed clergyman of the Church of England, appointed his widow and a clergyman guardians of his infant children. The widow became a member of the sect of Plymouth Brethren. On the application of the other guardian of the children, the Court of Appeal, affirming the decision of Stuart, V.C. (1 L. R. Eq. 431), ordered the children, who were respectively in their fifteenth and twelfth years, to be brought up as members of the Church of England, and restrained their mother from taking them to a chapel of the Plymouth Brethren. In such a case the Court will pay no regard to the fact that the father was well affected towards Dissenters, and associated with them; nor will it be influenced by the wishes of the infants on the subject. (In *re Newberry,* 1 L. R. Ch. App, 263.) As to the age at which the children in the Workhouse may determine what place of worship they will attend, see O. C. vol. vii. p. 232. It is not intended that the visits of Ministers of religion should be subject to the restrictions imposed by Art. 118 on the visits of other persons. The Guardians are not restricted from permitting the attendance of duly licensed Dissenting Ministers at the Workhouse, at stated periods, for the purpose of performing religious services for such Dissenting inmates as may be desirous to attend their ministrations. But such attendances must be so given as not to interfere with the good order or discipline of the other inmates of the Workhouse. The Guardians also are not prohibited by law from permitting licensed Ministers of the religious persuasion of any inmate from visiting the Workhouse at stated times, or from performing religious services for such Dissenting inmates as may be desirous to attend their ministrations. Such religious instruction or assistance contemplated by the 4 & 5 Wm IV. c. 76, s. 19, must be strictly confined to persons who are Protestant Dissenters, and must be so given as not to interfere with the good order or discipline of the other inmates of the Workhouse.

(a) No work, except as is excepted in this Article, should be performed by the paupers on any general fast-day appointed by authority.

(b) The Master and the other Officers of the Workhouse ought, as far as possible, to attend the morning and evening prayers in the Workhouse. By Article 208, No. 4, it will be the duty of the Master to read the prayers both morning and evening and he ought only to cause

formed every Sunday, Good Friday, and Christmas Day in the Workhouse (unless the Guardians, with the consent of the Commissioners, otherwise direct), and at such prayers and Divine Service all the paupers shall attend, except the sick, persons of unsound mind, the young children, and such as are too infirm to do so : provided that those paupers who may object so to attend, on account of their professing religious principles differing from those of the Established Church, shall also be exempt from such attendance.

Art. 125 (*a*).—The Guardians may authorize any inmates of the Workhouse, being members of the Established Church, to attend Public Worship at a Parish church or chapel, on every Sunday, Good Friday, and Christmas Day, under the control and inspection of the Master or Porter, or other officer.

---

them to be read by others in case he should be prevented by conscientious scruples, or should be incapacitated through some defect of speech. By Art. 211, No. 1, it will be the duty of the Chaplain to perform Divine Service in the Workhouse every Sunday, Good Friday, and Christmas Day, unless the Guardians, with the consent of the Commissioners, otherwise direct. Where the Guardians have appointed a Chaplain, it is in general desirable that Divine Service should be performed in the Workhouse on Sunday by the Chaplain, and that the inmates who are members of the Established Church should not go out to attend Divine Service. Children ought, in general to be baptized at church ; and they ought to be baptized in the Workhouse only under circumstances which would justify the administration of baptism in a private house. Of this necessity the Chaplain must judge. The Sacrament of the Lord's Supper should not be administered in the Workhouse, except to the sick and disabled inmates, but to them it should be administered as often as the Chaplain may deem requisite : any of the other inmates whom he may judge fit to communicate with them should be permitted to do so. The churching of women should take place in the parish church. —*Instr. Letter*, February, 1842. Where, however, there is a Workhouse chapel, the Communion might be celebrated in it without impropriety, with the consent of the Bishop of the diocese ; but even in that case those inmates who desire it should be allowed to attend the parish church to receive the Sacrament at Easter and Christmas. At the same time, if the Bishop of the diocese sanction the administration of the Sacrament exclusively in the Workhouse, the Commissioners consider this approbation a sufficient authority for the Chaplain.

(*a*) It will be observed that the provision contained in this Article is permissive only, and that the Guardians are not compelled to permit the paupers to leave the house for the purpose of attending Divine Service at the parish church. See the observations of the Poor Law Comissioners in the note to Art. 124.

Art. 126.—The Guardians may also authorize any inmates of the Workhouse, being dissenters from the Established Church, to attend Public Worship at any dissenting chapel in the neighbourhood of the Workhouse, on every Sunday, Good Friday, and Christmas Day (*b*).

PUNISHMENTS FOR MISBEHAVIOUR OF THE PAUPERS (*c*).

Art. 127.—Any pauper, being an inmate of the Workhouse, who shall neglect to observe such of the regulations in this Order as are applicable to him as such inmate;—

(*b*) A similar remark to that contained in the note to Art. 124, as to leaving the Workhouse on Sundays, applies also to Protestant Dissenters, where they are visited in the Workhouse by Ministers of their own persuasion. There is, however, greater difficulty in the case of Roman Catholics; inasmuch as Mass cannot be solemnized in a Workhouse, unless it should contain an altar consecrated for the purpose. By Art. 125, it is required, that when the members of the Established Church attend Divine Service out of the Workhouse, they should be under the control and inspection of the Master or Porter, or other officer. This condition is necessarily omitted in Art. 126, because the Master or Porter could not accompany both the members of the Established Church and the Dissenters. The attendance of the Master or Porter is rendered imperative in the former case; inasmuch as in the Workhouses to which this Order applies, the inmates who are members of the Established Church greatly outnumber the members of other religious denominations. In the latter case, it will be the duty of the Guardians to make such regulations as will prevent any abuse of the permission by Dissenters who are inmates of the Workhouse; such as inducing the Ministers of the different congregations to certify the attendance of the inmates professing to frequent their chapels, and to state the times of the commencement and end of the service. Any pauper permitted to quit the Workhouse under Art. 116 or Arts. 125 and 126, and returning after the appointed time of absence, or misbehaving in going to, at, or returning from Public Worship, may be punished as disorderly by virtue of Art. 127. Moreover, in cases where permission to leave the Workhouse has been abused, the Guardians may properly exercise their discretion of refusing the pauper temporary leave of absence from the Workhouse for some time afterwards, as a month or six weeks, if he should continue an inmate of it.—*Instr. Letter*, February, 1842.

(*c*) Arts. 127-147 contain the regulations respecting the punishment of paupers, both adult and children, while inmates of the Workhouse, for misbehaviour. The general power of making "Regulations to be enforced in Workhouses, for the government thereof, and the preservation of good order therein," which has been conferred on the Commissioners by sections 15 and 42 of the 4 & 5 Wm. IV. c. 76, must be held to include the power of authorizing the proper Officers to inflict punish-

Or who shall make any noise when silence is ordered to be kept;

Or shall use obscene or profane language;

Or shall by word or deed insult or revile any person;

Or shall threaten to strike or to assault any person;

Or shall not duly cleanse his person;

Or shall refuse or neglect to work, after having been required to do so;

Or shall pretend sickness;

Or shall play at cards or other game of chance;

Or shall refuse to go into his proper ward or yard, or shall enter, or attempt to enter, without permission,

---

ment by which such Regulations may be "enforced." But, independently of these provisions, the necessity of inflicting certain punishments within the walls of a Workhouse is distinctly recognized by the law. The 54 Geo. III. c. 170, s. 7, by limiting the duration of the restraint which may be imposed on an inmate of a Workhouse, implies the legality of restraint within those limits, and by prohibiting the corporal punishment of adults, seems to recognize as lawful other reasonable punishments. In the 4 & 5 Wm. IV. c. 76 (section 93), these wholesome restrictions of the power of Workhouse Masters are repeated. From this clause the same inferences must undoubtedly be drawn as from 54 Geo. III. c. 170, s. 7; with this difference, however, that while the earlier statute may perhaps be held to apply specially to Workhouses regulated by local Acts of Parliament, section 93 certainly extends to all Workhouses. The powers possessed by Officers for restraining inmates of Workhouses guilty of misbehaviour appear to have been considered insufficient, and the 55 Geo. III. c. 137, s. 5, provides a more severe punishment by confinement, with hard labour, for any time not exceeding twenty-one days. It will be observed that this clause does not assert that no *punishment* can be inflicted on such an offender, but it asserts that no *sufficient* punishment was provided by the then existing law. Acting on the spirit of all these provisions, it appears desirable to impose slight punishments within the walls of the Workhouse itself for all trifling offences, and not to harass the Justices with complaints which must often relate to trifling matters, or to press for the rigorous measure of commitment to hard labour, at a great expense to the country, except when absolutely necessary. It will be observed that the word "*misbehaviour*," in the 55 Geo. III. c. 137, s. 5, whilst it includes the instances of misbehaviour enumerated by the Order of the Commissioners, also comprehends any kind of misbehaviour not specified in such Order. It will be desirable, therefore, that the Master, in all cases unprovided for in the Order of the Commissioners, or whenever he may entertain doubts as to his authority, should lay a complaint before the Magistrates under the provision just cited.—*Instr. Letter.*

the ward or yard appropriated to any class of paupers other than that to which he belongs ;

Or shall climb over any fence or boundary wall surrounding any portion of the Workhouse premises, or shall attempt to leave the Workhouse otherwise than through the ordinary entrance ;

Or shall misbehave in going to, at, or returning from Public Worship out of the Workhouse, or at Divine Service or Prayers in the Workhouse;

Or, having received temporary leave of absence, and wearing the Workhouse clothes, shall return to the Workhouse after the appointed time of absence, without reasonable cause for the delay ;

Or shall wilfully disobey any lawful order of any officer of the Workhouse;

Shall be deemed DISORDERLY.

Art. 128.—Any pauper, being an inmate of the Workhouse, who shall, within seven days, repeat any one, or commit more than one, of the offences specified in Art. 127 ;

Or who shall by word or deed insult or revile the Master or Matron, or any other officer of the Workhouse, or any of the Guardians ;

Or shall wilfully disobey any lawful order of the Master or Matron after such order shall have been repeated ;

Or shall unlawfully strike or otherwise unlawfully assault any person ;

Or shall wilfully or mischievously damage or soil any property whatsoever belonging to the Guardians ;

Or shall wilfully waste or spoil any provisions, stock, tools, or materials for work, belonging to the Guardians ;

Or shall be drunk ;

Or shall act or write indecently or obscenely ;

Or shall wilfully disturb other persons at Public Worship out of the Workhouse, or at Divine Service or Prayers in the Workhouse;

Shall be deemed REFRACTORY.

Art. 129.—The Master may, with or without the direction of the Guardians, punish any disorderly pauper by substituting, during a time not greater than forty-eight hours, for his dinner, as prescribed by the Dietary, a meal consisting of eight ounces of bread, or one pound of cooked potatoes or boiled rice, and also by withholding from him, during the same period, all butter, cheese, tea, sugar, or broth, which such pauper would otherwise receive, at any meal during the time aforesaid (a).

Art. 130.—The Guardians may, by a special direction to be entered on their minutes, order any refractory pauper to be punished by confinement in a separate room, with or without an alteration of diet, similar in kind and duration to that prescribed in Art. 129 for disorderly paupers; but no pauper shall be so confined for a longer period than twenty-four hours; or, if it be deemed right that such pauper should be carried before a Justice of the Peace, and if such period of twenty-four hours should be insufficient for that purpose, then for such further time as may be necessary for such purpose (b).

(a) By this Article the Master is authorized to make certain changes in the diet of disorderly paupers without any order of the Board of Guardians, either general or specific. With respect to the punishment of paupers who have been sick or are pregnant, or above sixty years of age, see Art. 134. Note that it is only *disorderly* paupers that are to be punished under this Article.

(b) In certain very rare cases it is possible that the Master may be unable to exercise his lawful power, or to carry into effect the regulations of the Commissioners, without using force towards some refractory pauper. In all such cases he should, if possible, avoid laying hands on the pauper, but he should call in the aid of the Porter or other officer. In such cases, too, it may often be desirable that the Master should cause such refractory paupers to be taken before a magistrate.—*Instr. Letter*, February, 1842. See also Art. 134, excepting certain cases from this rule, and Art. 129. Under this Article the period of confinement cannot be spread over a period of more than twenty-four consecutive hours; but the duration of the altered diet may extend to a period of forty-eight consecutive hours. In answer to an inquiry on this point, the Poor Law Board have stated that they are of opinion that the Guardians cannot order confinement for twelve hours each day during four consecutive days; and they also think that the Guardians cannot spread the confinement, referred to in Art. 130 of the General Consolidated Order, over more than a continued period of twenty-four hours. (O. C. 55 (N. S.) 64.)

Art. 131.—If any offence, whereby a pauper becomes refractory under Art. 128, be accompanied by any of the following circumstances of aggravation (that is to say), if such pauper
>Persist in using violence against any person;
>Or persist in creating a noise or disturbance, so as to annoy other inmates;
>Or endeavour to excite other paupers to acts of insubordination;
>Or persist in acting indecently or obscenely in the presence of any other inmate;
>Or persist in mischievously breaking or damaging any goods or property of the Guardians;

the Master may, without any direction of the Guardians, immediately place such refractory pauper in confinement for any time not exceeding twelve hours; which confinement shall, however, be reckoned as part of any punishment afterwards imposed by the Guardians for the same offence (c).

Art. 132.—Every refractory pauper shall be deemed to be also disorderly, and may be punished as such; but no pauper who may have been punished for any offence as disorderly shall afterwards be punished for the same offence as refractory, and no pauper who may have been punished for

---

(c) The Master is restrained by the Order from confining any pauper on his own authority, unless such pauper shall be refractory with any of the circumstances of aggravation specified in this Article. The Commissioners have thought it expedient to make these exceptions, since, without a precaution of this kind, a pauper might annoy the inmates by continued turbulence, or scandalize them by gross indecency. Subsequent punishment, though it might hinder the recurrence of such misconduct, could do nothing to protect those who would suffer from it at the moment. Cases sometimes occur, too, in which wanton mischief to property, or growing insubordination, must at once be stopped. It is therefore as a preventive of such evils that the Commissioners have permitted the Master to retain a limited power of confinement on his own authority and responsibility.—*Instr. Letter*, February, 1842.

Further, with regard to the power of the Master to confine a pauper inmate of the Workhouse, see the provision in the 4 & 5 Wm. IV. c. 76, s. 93.

any offence as refractory shall afterwards be punished for the same offence as disorderly (*a*).

Art. 133.—No pauper shall be punished by confinement or alteration in diet for any offence not committed in the Workhouse since his last admission, except in such cases as are expressly specified in Articles 127 and 128.

Art. 134.—No pauper who may have been under medical care, or who may have been entered in the medical weekly return as sick or infirm, at any time in the course of the seven days next preceding the punishment, or who may be reasonably supposed to be under twelve or above sixty years of age, or who may be pronounced by the Medical Officer to be pregnant, or who may be suckling a child, shall be punished by alteration of diet, or by confinement, unless the Medical Officer shall have previously certified in writing that no injury to the health of such pauper is reasonably to be apprehended from the proposed punishment; and any modification diminishing such punishment which the Medical Officer may suggest shall be adopted by the Master (*b*).

Art. 135.—No pauper shall be confined between eight o'clock in the evening and six o'clock in the morning, without being furnished with a bed and bedding suitable to the season, and with the other proper conveniences.

Art. 136.—No child under twelve years of age shall be punished by confinement in a dark room, or during the night (*c*).

(*a*) A refractory pauper may be punished merely as disorderly if the Master thinks it expedient to take this course, instead of first reporting the case for the decision of the Board of Guardians. This option will induce the Master to employ the minor punishment whenever it is likely to prove sufficient to prevent the repetition of the offence. The offence and punishment will nevertheless be duly brought under the notice of the Guardians by means of the book ordered to be kept by Art. 143.—*Instr. Letter*, February, 1842.

(*b*) Great caution should be used in inflicting any punishment by confinement or change of diet on paupers, whose health might in any manner be affected thereby.

(*c*) Arts. 136–142 contain regulations respecting the corporal correction of children. The Master must be deemed to be responsible for all punishments inflicted on adult inmates. With regard to the male

Art. 137.—No corporal punishment shall be inflicted on any male child, except by the Schoolmaster or Master.

Art. 138.—No corporal punishment shall be inflicted on any female child.

Art. 139.—No corporal punishment shall be inflicted on any male child, except with a rod or other instrument such as may have been approved of by the Guardians or the Visiting Committee (*d*).

Art. 140.—No corporal punishment shall be inflicted on any male child until two hours shall have elapsed from the commission of the offence for which such punishment is inflicted.

Art. 141.—Whenever any male child is punished by corporal correction, the Master and Schoolmaster shall, if possible, be both present.

Art. 142.—No male child shall be punished by flogging whose age may be reasonably supposed to exceed fourteen years (*e*).

Art. 143.—The Master shall keep a book, to be furnished him by the Guardians, in the Form (O) hereunto annexed, in which he shall duly enter,

Firstly, All cases of refractory or disorderly paupers, whether children or adults, reported to the Guardians for their decision thereon.

---

children, the Master and Schoolmaster have a concurrent power of control. The female children are to be considered as in the more immediate care of the Matron and Schoolmistress. The prohibition of the corporal punishment of adults, in the statutes before referred to, implies the legality of such punishment in the case of children. The expediency of such a mode of correction is a more difficult subject, and all classes of society are somewhat divided in opinion respecting it. The Commissioners are satisfied that good temper, joined to firmness and self-command, will enable a skilful teacher to manage children with little or no corporal punishment.—*Instr. Letter*, February, 1842.

(*d*) See note to Art. 142 as to the infliction of corporal punishment on a boy above fourteen years of age.

(*e*) The word "flogging" in this Article, would seem to contemplate an exposure of the person of the individual. Hence it is considered that a "caning" over the shoulders, which is a corporal punishment, would not be a "flogging," and that such a punishment might therefore be inflicted upon a boy above fourteen years of age.

Secondly, All cases of paupers, whether children or adults, who may have been punished without the direction of the Guardians, with the particulars of their respective offences and punishments (a).

Art. 144.—The person who punishes any child with corporal correction shall forthwith report to the Master the particulars of the offence and punishment; and the Master shall enter the same in the book specified in Art. 143.

Art. 145.—Such book shall be laid on the table at every ordinary meeting of the Guardians; and every entry made in such book since the last ordinary meeting shall be read to the Board by the Clerk.

The Guardians shall thereupon, in the first place, give direction as to the confinement or other punishment of any refractory or disorderly pauper reported for their decision, and such direction shall be entered on the minutes of the proceedings of the day, and a copy thereof shall be inserted by the Clerk in the book specified in Art. 143.

The Guardians, in the second place, shall take into their consideration the cases in which punishments are reported to have been already inflicted by the Master or other officer, and shall require the Master to bring before them any pauper so punished, who may have signified a wish to see the Guardians. If the Guardians in any case are of opinion that the officer has acted illegally or improperly, such opinion shall be entered on the minutes, and shall be communicated to the Master, and a copy of the minute of such opinion shall be forwarded to the Commissioners by the Clerk.

Art. 146.—If any pauper above the age of fourteen years unlawfully introduce or attempt to introduce any spirituous or fermented liquor into the Workhouse, or abscond from

---

(a) The record which is directed by this Article to be kept is of the utmost importance for the prevention of abuse. The details of offences and punishments must be accurately and punctually entered in the book; and if any case should not be properly reported, the Commissioners will always presume that such omission originated in a sense of the expediency of concealment.—*Instr. Letter*, February, 1842.

the Workhouse with clothes belonging to the Guardians, the Master may cause such pauper to be forthwith taken before a Justice of the Peace, to be dealt with according to law; and whether he do so or not, he shall report every such case to the Guardians at their next ordinary meeting (*b*).

Art. 147.—The Master shall cause a legible copy of Arts. 127, 128, 129, 130, and 131 to be kept suspended in the dining-hall of the Workhouse, or in the room in which the inmates usually eat their meals, and also in the Board-room of the Guardians (*c*).

VISITING COMMITTEE.

Art. 148.—The Guardians shall appoint one or more *Visiting Committees* from their own body; and each of such committees shall carefully examine the Workhouse or Workhouses of the Union once in every week at the least, inspect the last reports of the Chaplain and Medical Officer, examine the stores, afford, so far as is practicable, to the inmates an opportunity of making any complaints, and investigate any complaints that may be made to them (*d*).

(*b*) With respect to the introduction of spirits into a Workhouse, see 4 & 5 Wm. IV. c. 76, ss. 91, 92, 93, 94; and with respect to the punishment of any pauper who shall abscond from the Workhouse with any clothes belonging to the Guardians, see 55 George III. c. 137, s. 2, and note on Art. 116.

According to the provision in the 4 & 5 Wm. IV. c. 76, s. 93, the Master of a Workhouse is only empowered to confine a pauper inmate for twenty-four hours, or such further space of time as may be necessary to have him carried before a magistrate; and this authority cannot be extended so as to authorize the Master to continue the confinement of the pauper for any further time.

(*c*) It is also necessary for the Master to hang up in some one of the most public places in the Workhouse copies of the 92nd and 93rd sections of the 4 & 5 Wm. IV. c. 76, regarding the illegal introduction of spirituous liquors into the Workhouse.

(*d*) This Article directs the Guardians to appoint *one or more* Visiting Committees for the Workhouse, and defines the functions of the Committee. Any member or members of the Visiting Committee may visit the Workhouse at any time at which the Committee could visit it collectively; unless, indeed the Guardians should have given the Committee only a limited authority to visit it, so as to confine that authority

Art. 149 (a).—The Visiting Committee shall from time to time write such answers as the facts may warrant to the following queries, which are to be printed in a book, entitled the VISITORS' BOOK, to be provided by the Guardians, and kept in every Workhouse for that purpose, and to be submitted regularly to the Guardians at their ordinary meetings:—

Q. 1.—Is the Workhouse, with its wards, offices, yards, and appurtenances, clean and well ventilated in every part?—and is the bedding in proper order?—if not, state the defect or omission.

Q. 2.—Do the inmates of the Workhouse, of all classes, appear clean in their persons, and decent and orderly in their behaviour, and is their clothing regularly changed?

---

to a majority, or to any fixed number or portion of that Committee. The Guardians may order that each member of the Visiting Committee shall be admitted at all times to inspect the Workhouse. It will be observed that the powers of the Visiting Committee are confined to the purposes specified in this Article, and that they do not extend to other purposes, such as the ordering of stores, repairs of the house, etc.— *Instr. Letter*, February, 1842. Guardians who are not members of the Visiting Committee cannot claim as of right to visit the Workhouse. The Board of Guardians may, however, grant permission to do so in any case, if they think fit. The Visiting Committee must consist of a specified number of Guardians, individually named, selected from the General Board, and deputed by them to visit the Workhouse within the stated periods. There is no particular time named when the appointment of the Visiting Committee should be made; and indeed there appears to be nothing to prevent the appointment of a fresh committee at each meeting of the Guardians, their powers being limited till the next meeting. If the Guardians neglect to appoint a Visiting Committee, the Poor Law Board may appoint a paid Visitor. (See 10 & 11 Vict. c. 109, s. 24.) No one should make entries in the Visitors' Book but the appointed quorum of the Committee, if a quorum has been appointed. It is expedient to appoint a quorum, to be empowered to act as the Visiting Committee; but if none be appointed, all the members of the Committee must act together, and not singly. A single member may, however, visit the house on the appointed days, in the absence of the other members of the Committee.

The Master and Matron of the Workhouse need not necessarily accompany the Visiting Committee when they visit the several wards; but as a general rule it is desirable that they should accompany the Committee or individual members of it when they visit the wards.

(a) See Note to Art. 101.

Q. 3.—Are the inmates of each sex employed and kept at work as directed by the Guardians, and is such work unobjectionable in its nature?—if any improvement can be suggested in their employment, state the same.

Q. 4.—Are the infirm of each sex properly attended to, according to their several conditions?

Q. 5.—Are the boys and girls in the school properly instructed as required by the regulations of the Commissioners, and is their industrial training properly attended to?

Q. 6.—Are the young children properly nursed and taken care of, and do they appear in a clean and healthy state? Is there any child not vaccinated?

Q. 7.—Is regular attendance given by the Medical Officer?—Are the inmates of the Sick Wards properly tended?—Are the nurses efficient?—Is there any infectious disease in the Workhouse?

Q. 8.—Is there any dangerous lunatic or idiot in the Workhouse?

Q. 9.—Is Divine Service regularly performed?—Are prayers regularly read?

Q. 10.—Is the established Dietary duly observed;—and are the prescribed hours of meals regularly adhered to?

Q. 11.—Are the provisions and other supplies of the qualities contracted for?

Q. 12.—Is the classification properly observed according to Arts. 98 and 99?

Q. 13.—Is any complaint made by any pauper against any officer, or in respect of the provisions or accommodations?—if so, state the name of the complainant, and the subject of the complaint.

Q. 14.—Does the present number of inmates in the Workhouse exceed that fixed by the Poor Law Commissioners? (*b*)

(*b*) Reference may here be made to the 30 Geo. III. c. 49, s. 1, which empowers Justices to visit, inspect, and examine Workhouses; which power is saved to them by the 4 & 5 Wm. IV. c. 76, s. 43, in respect to

Repairs and Alterations of the Workhouse.

Art. 150 (a).—The Guardians shall, once at least in every year, and as often as may be necessary for cleanliness, cause all the rooms, wards, offices, and privies belonging to the Workhouse to be limewashed.

Art. 151.—The Guardians shall cause the Workhouse and all its furniture and appurtenances to be kept in good and substantial repair; and shall, from time to time, remedy without delay any such defect in the repair of the house, its drainage, warmth, or ventilation, or in the furniture or fixtures thereof, as may tend to injure the health of the inmates (b).

Government of the Workhouse by the Guardians.

Art. 152.—We do declare that, subject to the rules and regulations herein contained, the guidance, government, and control of every Workhouse, and of the officers, servants, assistants, and paupers within such Workhouse, shall be exercised by the Guardians of the Union (c).

Workhouses under the regulations of the Poor Law Commissioners, and the further power of enforcing the observance of these regulations conferred upon them.

(a) By Art. 208, No. 24, it is the duty of the Master to take care that the wards, rooms, larder, kitchen, and all the offices of the Workhouse, and all the utensils and furniture thereof, are kept clean, and in good order; and when any defect in the same occurs, to report it to the Guardians; and by Art. 210, No. 13, it is the especial duty of the Matron to assist the Master in cleansing and ventilating the sleeping-wards and dining-hall, and all parts of the premises.

(b) By Art. 207, No. 6, it is the duty of the Medical Officer to report in writing to the Guardians any defect in the drainage, ventilation, warmth, or other arrangement of the Workhouse which he may deem to be detrimental to the health of the inmates; and it is desirable that the Guardians should take the proper steps for remedying any defect to which their attention may be thus called. The 4 & 5 Wm. IV. c. 76, s. 23, and 30 & 31 Vict. c. 106, s. 13, subject the Guardians to the control, orders, and regulations of the Poor Law Board in their expenditure of the money of the ratepayers for the enlargement or alteration of the Workhouse.

(c) The 38th section of 4 & 5 Wm. IV. c. 76, enacts that no Guardian, except as is therein excepted, shall have power to act in virtue of

APPOINTMENT OF OFFICERS (d).

Art. 153.—The Guardians shall, whenever it may be requisite, or whenever a vacancy may occur, appoint fit persons to hold the under-mentioned offices, and to perform the duties respectively assigned to them; namely,

1. Clerk to the Guardians.
2. Treasurer of the Union.
3. Chaplain.
4. Medical Officer for the Workhouse.
5. District Medical Officer.
6. Master of the Workhouse.
7. Matron of the Workhouse.
8. Schoolmaster.
9. Schoolmistress.
10. Porter.
11. Nurse.
12. Relieving Officer.
13. Superintendent of Out-door Labour.

And also such assistants as the Guardians, with the consent of the Commissioners, may deem necessary for the efficient performance of the duties of any of the said offices (e).

---

his office, except as a member, and at a meeting of the Board: therefore the powers given by this Article must be exercised by the Guardians as a Board.

(d) As regards the appointment of the Collector of the Guardians, see the general orders of the Poor Law Board, dated 7th Oct. 1865, and 27th Nov. 1866, *post*.

As regards the appointment by the Guardians of certain other classes of Workhouse officers, see the General Order of the 19th August, 1867, *post*.

(e) In the Consolidated Orders issued to Unions declared since 1847, this Article proceeds as follows:—" And the said Guardians shall from time to time afterwards, whenever a vacancy may occur, appoint a fit person to supply such vacancy, except in the case of the Superintendent of Out-door Labour, whose office shall be filled as and when the Guardians may find it requisite to employ such an officer."

The power of the Commissioners to authorize and direct the Guardians to appoint officers, is partly founded upon their power of making regulations for the government of Workhouses, and the preservation of good order therein, derived from ss. 15 and 42 of the 4 & 5 Wm. IV. c. 76; and partly upon s. 46, which enables the Commissioners, by order under their hands and seal, to direct the Guardians of any Parish or Union to appoint paid Officers, with such qualifications as the Commissioners shall think necessary, for superintending or assisting in the administration of the relief or employment of the poor, and otherwise carrying the provisions of the Act into execution. The same section further empowers the Commissioners to direct the mode of appointment, and determine the continuance in office, or dismissal of such Officers; and when the Commissioners shall see occasion to regulate the amount of salaries payable to such Officers respectively, and the time and mode of payment thereof.

No legal doubt seems to have been entertained as to the power of the Commissioners to authorize or direct the appointment of any officer named in Art. 153, except the Chaplain. An Order of the Commissioners, directing a Board of Guardians to appoint a Chaplain, was moved by a writ of certiorari into the Court of Queen's Bench; but the Court decided that the Commissioners possessed the power, and consequently that the Order was valid. See the Seventh Annual Report of the Commissioners, pp. 23, 24. (*Reg.* v. *The Guardians of the Poor of the Braintree Union*, 10 L. J. R. (N. s.) M. C. 76.)—*Instr. Letter*, February, 1842.

As regards the appointment of a Chaplain to the Workhouse, the following case sets at rest the claim of the Incumbent of the parish in which the Workhouse is situated to give his consent before the Chaplain can perform the duties required of him:—

This was a suit instituted by the Rev. J. W. Molyneux, perpetual curate of St. Gregory's, with St. Peter's annexed, in Sudbury, against the Rev. W. S. Bagshaw, for reading prayers and preaching in the chapel annexed to the Workhouse of the Sudbury Union, which was situate within the parish of Mr. Molyneux, without his consent as the Incumbent thereof. Articles of accusation had been brought in, and their admission was opposed, on the 27th of April last, by the defendant.

The case was then argued by the Queen's Advocate and Dr. Tristram for the promoter; and by Dr. Deane, Q.C., and Dr. Twiss, Q.C., for the defendant.

His Lordship, in delivering judgment to-day, said he had no difficulty in arriving at what he considered to be the right conclusion in this case. The real question for him to decide was whether it was an ecclesiastical offence for a duly appointed Chaplain of a Union Workhouse to read prayers and preach when required by the Union authorities, without the consent of the Incumbent of the parish, to the inmates of the Workhouse who could not attend service at the parish church; for, although it did not clearly appear in the articles that Mr. Bagshaw was the Chaplain of the Workhouse, yet he was admitted to be so in argument by the counsel for the promoter. In *Reg.* v. *The Braintree Guardians*, it was decided by the Queen's Bench that it was the intention of the Legislature that there should be Chaplains appointed to Union Workhouses, and an ecclesiastical court was bound by that decision. If the appointment of Chaplain was authorized by law, he was of opinion that a clergyman, properly appointed Chaplain, might lawfully perform the full duties of a Chaplain by reading prayers and preaching to the inmates of the Union without the consent of the Incumbent of the parish. He was bound to do so if required by the proper authorities. His Lordship rejected the articles and condemned the promoter in costs.

Dr. Tristram, for the promoter, said the case was one of great importance to the Church, and he therefore asked the Court to give leave to the promoter to appeal to the Judicial Committee.

The Court granted leave to appeal on a further article being brought in alleging that Mr. Bagshaw had been appointed Chaplain of the Workhouse, and that he was required by the authorities of the Union to perform the services complained of. (*Molyneux* v. *Bagshaw*, 9 Jur. (N. S.) 553; 11 Weekly Reporter, 687; 8 L. J. (N. S.) 331.) The intention to appeal was abandoned, so that this judgment must be taken as final.

With respect to the Workhouse Officers named in this Article, the Commissioners remark, that the ordinary and convenient practice, and that which they prefer, is, that the Master and Matron should be husband and wife. The Commissioners have, in some cases, consented, on special grounds, to a different arrangement; but they are always reluctant to allow any departure from the practice of appointing a man and his wife as Master and Matron. See, however, Art. 189, determining the appointment of a Master or Matron, when either of them shall be removed from office by death or otherwise. It is desirable that the Master and Matron should be man and wife. In reference to their children, if they have any, the Poor Law Board, in a Circular dated the 8th December, 1856, have stated that where necessity may seem to require, they will assent to their being allowed to have their children residing in the Workhouse, under proper restrictions. But they add, in such case they will think it right to require some equivalent for the cost of maintaining each child, to be paid by the Master to the Guardians. With respect to other Workhouse Officers, in order to avoid the disappointment and inconvenience to them and to the Guardians, which may be occasioned by the refusal of the Board to sanction so much of an engagement as would permit the residence of the officer's child in the Workhouse, the Board, in the same Circular, requested the Guardians, when they elected such officers, to intimate clearly to any successful candidate who may have a child dependent upon him or her, that such child will not be permitted to reside in the Workhouse.

The Commissioners do not in general object to the Medical Officer for the Workhouse being also the Medical Officer for a district of the Union. —*Instr. Letter.*

With respect to the Clerk, it seems desirable in general that a Solicitor or Attorney should be appointed to the office, as a considerable amount of legal business falls to be transacted by the Clerk.

The offices of Schoolmaster and Schoolmistress should in no case be conjoined with any other office. With regard to these officers, see Art. 212, *post*, and notes thereon.

As the Treasurer is a Union officer, a Firm should not be appointed to the office, and this because the law casts upon him duties to perform, and also liabilities, which can only attach to some individual person, and which a Firm or Company cannot undertake. If the Guardians desire to keep their account with a Banking Company or Firm, they should appoint the Manager of the Bank or one of the Firm as their Treasurer;

Art. 154.—The officers so appointed to or holding any of the said offices, as well as all persons temporarily discharging the duties of such offices, shall respectively perform such duties as may he required of them by the Rules and Regulations of the Commissioners in force at the time, to-

the person so appointed can then give the required security to the Guardians in his individual capacity.

A Superintendent of out-door labour will only be appointed in those Unions to which the out-door labour test order has been issued. (See Art. 217 and note.) With respect to the suspension of this Officer when his services are not required, see the Supplemental Out-door Labour Test Order, *post*.

As regards the genuineness of written testimony to character and competency presented to Boards of Guardians by candidates for office, the Poor Law Board, on the 12th May, 1858, issued the following Circular to Boards of Guardians:—"I am directed by the Poor Law Board to bring under the notice of the Board of Guardians the case of the *Queen* v. *Collings*, which was tried at the last Lincoln Assizes. The indictment charged the accused with having unlawfully uttered false and counterfeit letters and writings, with the intent to procure for himself the appointment of Schoolmaster of the Workhouse of the Spalding Union. He pleaded guilty, and was sentenced by the Court to 18 months' imprisonment with hard labour.

"The Board think it right to draw the attention of all Boards of Guardians to this case, as a warning to show how necessary it is to take every precaution in their power to ascertain the authenticity of testimonials presented to them."

With reference to the above Circular it may be added, that a person forged testimonials as to his character, whereby he obtained a situation as Police Constable, and having been convicted of forgery, upon a case reserved, it was held by the Court of Criminal Appeal that he was properly convicted of forgery at common law. (*Reg.* v. *Moah*, 4 Jur. (N. s.) 464.) So uttering a forged testimonial to character, knowing it to be forged, with intent to deceive and thereby obtain a situation of emolument is a misdemeanour at common law. (*Reg.* v. *Sharman*, 23 L. J. (N. s.) M. C. 51.

This, though a grave offence, is not by any means so serious an offence as forgery by the statute; and in proceedings against the offender, it is not necessary to show that there was an intention to obtain money or to defraud any person in the ordinary acceptation of the term "fraud;" it is sufficient to show that there was an intention to deceive on the part of the offender, to obtain a conviction for the offence.

By 4 & 5 Wm. IV. c. 76, s. 48, no person shall be eligible to hold any parish office, or have the management of the poor in any way whatever, who shall have been convicted of felony, fraud, or perjury. With regard to the word "fraud," see note to Article 24, *ante*, page 14.

Pauper inmates and others who are appointed permanently as servants in the Workhouse come within the term "assistants," and to them the provisions of the Order of the 19th April, 1867, *post*, would apply.

gether with all such other duties, conformable with the nature of their respective offices, as the Guardians may lawfully require them to perform.

Provided always, that every regulation applying to any officer holding his office under this Order, shall apply to any officer of the like denomination appointed by the Guardians, although such officer may have been appointed before this Order shall have come into force (*a*).

Mode of Appointment.

Art. 155 (*b*).—Every officer and assistant, to be appointed under this Order, shall be appointed by a majority of the

---

(*a*) The proviso to this Article is omitted in the Consolidated Orders issued subsequent to this Order.

(*b*) So far as the appointment of officers is concerned, this Article overrides Art. 38, *ante*, p. 24.

It is necessary that a majority of the Guardians present should concur in the choice of the Officer; unless there be only three, in which case they must be unanimous. See 4 & 5 Wm. IV. c. 76, s. 38, by which no act of any meeting of Guardians shall be valid unless three members shall be present and concur therein. If one candidate (there being more than two candidates) have a larger number of votes than any other candidate, and if a *majority* of the Guardians present vote for other candidates, he is not duly appointed. According to the decision of the Court of Queen's Bench in *Ex parte Eynsham*, 12 A. & E. (N. s.) 398; 3 N. S. C. 507; 18 L. J. Q. B. 210; and *Reg.* v. *Christchurch, Spitalfields*, 26 L. J. M. C. 68; 7 E. & B. 409; and *Reg.* v. *Griffiths*. 17 Q. B. 164, it must be held that this Article requires that a majority of the votes of all the Guardians actually present at the meeting should be given in favour of a candidate before he can be regarded as duly elected. It is therefore necessary that those Guardians who, though present, do not vote, should be counted, in order to ascertain the majority of the whole body present at the meeting. See Official Circular of Poor Law Board, 55 (N. s.), p. 61. If there should be only two candidates, the one who has the largest number of actual votes will not be duly elected, if that number does not constitute an actual majority of the Guardians present. See also 12 & 13 Vict. c. 103, s. 19, as to the Presiding Chairman giving a second or casting vote in the case of an equality of votes on any question. When more than two candidates are proposed for an office, and neither of them have a majority of votes at the first voting, the Guardians should agree to strike off, in succession, the candidate who shall have the smallest number of votes, until some one candidate has more than the half of the votes given. The 12 & 13 Vict. c. 103, s. 19, which gives a second or casting vote to the presiding Chairman at a meeting of a Board of Guardians, applies to "*any* question at a meeting of the

Guardians present at a meeting of the Board, consisting of more than three Guardians, or by three Guardians if no more be present. Every such appointment shall, as soon as the same has been made, be reported to the Commissioners by the Clerk (*a*).

Art. 156.—No appointment to any of the Offices specified in Art. 153 shall be made under this Order, unless a notice, that the question of making such appointment will be brought before the Board, has been given and entered on the minutes, at one of the two ordinary meetings of the Board next preceding the meeting at which the appointment is made, or unless an advertisement giving notice of the consideration of such appointment shall have appeared in some public paper by the direction of the Guardians at least seven days before the day on which such appointment is made: Provided that no such notice or advertisement shall be necessary for the appointment of an assistant or temporary substitute (*b*).

Guardians," and therefore includes an election of Officers under this Article. See also note to Art. 38. According to *Saunders* v. *Owen*, 2 Salk. 467, which is supported by the subsequent case of *Reg.* v. *Grimshaw*, 10 Q. B. 747, an appointment to an office need not be in writing. But of course a record of the appointment having been made, should be entered in the minutes of the Guardians.

This Article has been slightly varied in some of the Consolidated Orders issued subsequent to the Order of the 24th July, 1847.

(*a*) By Art. 5 of the General Order of 9th August, 1867, *post*, the Guardians may require candidates to attend personally before the Board for examination, and may pay their reasonable expenses.

(*b*) This Article is somewhat varied in the Consolidated Order, issued to Unions declared since 1847.

The object of it is intended to prevent surprises in the appointment of the Officers, and to secure to the Union the advantages of allowing time for candidates to come forward and obtain a consideration of their claims. In addition to the regulations in this Article, the Commissioners suggest to the Guardians the expediency of making a bye-law requiring that special notice of every intended election should be sent by the Clerk to all the Guardians some days before the day of election. But all regulations made by the Guardians must, in order to be legally valid and binding, be submitted to and confirmed by the Commissioners. See s. 22 of the 4 & 5 Wm. IV. c. 76.—*Instr. Letter*. It will not be necessary to advertise the appointment in a newspaper, if notice of the appointment be given at one of the two preceding meetings. The

Art. 157.—The Guardians shall not, by advertisement, or other public notice, printed or written, invite tenders for the supply of medicines, or for the medical attendance on the paupers of the Union, unless such advertisement or notice shall specify the district or place for which such supply of medicines and such attendance is required, together with the amount of salary or other remuneration (c).

Art. 158.—The Guardians may from time to time divide the Union into districts for general and medical relief, with the consent of the Commissioners; and on any change in the division of the Union into districts for general and medical relief, or in the assignment of Relieving Officers and Medical Officers to such districts, the Clerk shall report every such change to the Commissioners for their approbation (d).

Art. 159.—The Guardians shall not assign to any Medical Officer a district which exceeds in extent the area of fifteen thousand statute acres, or which contains a population exceeding the number of fifteen thousand persons, according to the then last enumeration of the population published by authority of Parliament (e).

---

most orderly and formal mode is for the Chairman of the meeting at which the notice is to be given to announce precisely the proposal to elect at the next meeting or at the next but one, as the case may be. The fact of the announcement having been so made should be entered on the minutes. It will suffice if the notice is given at either one of the two ordinary meetings next before the appointment to be made.

(c) This Article does not prohibit advertisements for the services of Medical Officers, provided such advertisements specify the remuneration fixed or approved by the Poor Law Board. The competition of the candidates should turn upon their respective characters and skill, and not on the sum at which they may be severally willing to undertake the office.

(d) The Relief and Medical Districts cannot be made co-extensive unless the Relief Districts in respect to area and population are within the limits prescribed by Art. 159; and even in that case it would not seem desirable that they should be co-extensive, unless indeed the area and population is so small as not to require a further subdivision of the District; but see note to Art. 159.

The Guardians may transfer a Medical or Relieving Officer from one district to another district without the officer vacating his appointment; but the transfer could only be made with the officer's consent.

(e) In many Districts containing almost exclusively a poor popula-

Art. 160.—Provided that if it be impracticable, consistently with the proper attendance on the sick poor, for the Guardians to divide the Union into districts containing respectively an area and population less than is specified in Art. 159, then and in such case the Guardians shall cause a special minute to be made and entered on the usual record of their proceedings, stating the reasons which in their opinion make it necessary to form a district exceeding the said limits, and shall transmit a copy of such minute to the Commissioners for their consideration, and if the Commissioners signify their approval thereof to such Guardians, then and in such case, but not otherwise, such Guardians may proceed to assign the said district to a Medical Officer.

Art. 161 (*a*).—Provided also, that the limit of fifteen thousand statute acres, prescribed in Art. 159, shall not apply to any medical district situate wholly or in part within the principality of Wales; but no medical district situate wholly or in part within that principality shall be assigned to any Medical Officer residing more than seven miles from any part of any parish included within such district, unless such district shall have been specially sanctioned by the Commissioners in the same manner as is directed in Art. 160.

---

tion, even the limit of 15,000 persons may admit of a number of patients too large for the care of one Medical Officer; especially if the District consist partly of town and partly of rural Parishes. Under such circumstances, it would generally be for the Guardians to divide the District between two or more duly qualified medical practitioners. In like manner it may happen that a District consisting of an area less than 15,000 acres may contain a large population, and that the Guardians may be able to divide it with advantage. The Commissioners therefore do not by the limits fixed in this Article imply that no District is objectionable, or that every District will be sanctioned by them, which is within these limits.—*Instr. Letter.* The General Order of the Poor Law Board, dated 25th May, 1857, Art. 5, *post*, contains a provision enabling the Guardians to make a change in the extent of any Medical District when it is not assented to by the Medical Officer, by determining his appointment on six months' notice. The appointment must, however, have been made after the date of that Order.

(*a*) This Article is omitted in the Consolidated Orders subsequently

Qualifications of Officers (*b*).

Art. 162.—No person shall hold the office of Clerk, Treasurer, Master, or Relieving Officer, under this Order, who has not reached the age of twenty-one years (*c*).

Art. 163.—No person shall hold the office of Master of a Workhouse, or Matron of a Workhouse having no Master, unless he or she be able to keep accounts.

Art. 164.—No person shall hold the office of Relieving Officer unless he be able to keep accounts, and unless he reside in the district for which he may be appointed to act, devote his whole time to the performance of the duties of

---

issued to Unions which are not in Wales. The measure of acreage adopted in Art. 159 cannot be applied to Wales, as there are no available means of obtaining the requisite information in that part of the country; the Commissioners accordingly prescribed for Wales a limit, not of area, but of distance, which, though less convenient, is the best which the case permitted. Moreover, the physical circumstances of Wales, and the small number of resident medical practitioners, render it necessary to permit the formation of Medical Districts larger than those in most parts of England.

(*b*) The 5 & 6 Vict. c. 57, s. 14, enacts "that no person during the time for which he may serve or hold the office of Assistant-Overseer of any Parish, nor any paid Officer engaged in the administration of the laws for the Relief of the Poor, nor any person who, having been a paid Officer, shall have been dismissed within five years previously from such Office, under the provisions of the 4 & 5 Wm. IV. c. 76, shall be capable of serving as a Guardian; and no person receiving any fixed salary or emolument from the poor-rates in any Parish or Union, shall be capable of serving as a Guardian in such Parish or Union." This however does not prevent a Justice of the Peace for the county, who is *ex officio* a Guardian (see 4 & 5 Wm. IV. c. 76, s. 38), from being appointed to a Union office. He would, however, whilst holding such office, be disqualified from acting as an *ex officio* Guardian.

By 4 & 5 Wm. IV. c. 76, s. 77, no person employed in the administration of the Poor Laws shall furnish for his own profit goods or provisions given in parochial relief. It is possible that a Churchwarden, who in that capacity is an overseer (43 Eliz. c. 2, s. 1), might be deemed to come within this provision; but on public grounds, it is inexpedient that a person should hold the office of Churchwarden, and at the same time be an Officer of the Union, as, for instance, a Medical Officer.

(*c*) An infant cannot be appointed to an office of pecuniary trust. (See *Claridge* v. *Evelyn*, 5 B. & Ald. 81.) Though the regulation prevents the appointment of a person under 21 years of age to any of the offices mentioned, it does not prevent the Guardians from laying down a rule that candidates for office shall be of any specified greater age.

his office, and abstain from following any trade or profession, and from entering into any other service (*a*).

Art. 165.—No person shall hold the office of Nurse who is not able to read written directions upon medicines.

Art. 166.—Provided always, that the Guardians may, with the consent of the Commissioners previously obtained, but not otherwise, dispense with any of the conditions specified in Articles 162, 163, 164, and 165.

Art. 167.—No person shall be appointed to the office of Master, Matron, Schoolmaster, Schoolmistress, Porter, or Relieving Officer, under this Order, who does not agree to give one month's notice previous to resigning the office, or to forfeit one month's amount of salary, to be deducted as liquidated damages from the amount of salary due at the time of such resignation (*b*).

Art. 168 (*c*).—No person shall hold the office of Medical

(*a*) It will be held a breach of this regulation if a Relieving Officer carries on any business under the name of his wife; or if he shall have any interest in any business carried on in the name of any other person. But this does not extend to his wife carrying on the business of a dressmaker or milliner, etc. As to the duty of a Relieving Officer to attend as a witness in the case of an order of removal being applied for, see 54 O. C. (N. S.) p. 48. It would also be an infraction of the regulations, the employment of Relieving Officers in searching for and apprehending persons who may have deserted their families, leaving them chargeable to the poor-rate.

(*b*) It has been found inconvenient that Union Officers should quit their situations suddenly, and without giving any notice to the Guardians. The present Article is intended to guard against this inconvenience; but it does not apply to Officers elected under an Order bearing date previous to the date of the last General Orders of the Commissioners. With respect to the mode in which an Officer may resign his office, it is to be observed that the resignation need not necessarily be in writing, and that it will suffice if the Officer verbally tenders his resignation to the Guardians at a meeting of the Board. Moreover, the mere resignation is of itself sufficient to vacate the office, and acceptance by the Guardians is not indispensably necessary to render the resignation complete. But observe that the stipulation contemplated should be made in writing *at the time of the appointment* of the Officer, otherwise the provision in the Order will be of no avail. A notice of intended resignation should be given to the Guardians at a meeting of the Board, and not to their Clerk as their agent, during the interval of their meeting.

(*c*) The Commissioners think it desirable that every Medical Officer should possess both a medical and surgical qualification, and therefore they have required the three sorts of double qualification which are specified in Nos. 1, 2, and 3, of this Article. With respect to the second qualification in No. 3, see 55 Geo. III. c. 194 (the Apothecaries Act). The Commissioners thought themselves bound to consider the qualification stated in No. 4 as virtually a double qualification, according to the decision of the Court of Exchequer in *Stearenson* v. *Oliver*, 8 Mee. & Wels. 234. The qualification is limited to warrants or commissions, dated previously to the 1st August, 1826; inasmuch as the Act of 6 Geo. IV. c. 133 (which brought persons possessing this qualification within the benefit of the Apothecaries Act) expired on that day. Partners cannot be appointed *joint* Medical Officers of a District, but the fact that they are partners will be no objection to their being appointed individually as Medical Officers of distinct Districts in the same or in any other Union. There is nothing to prevent a Medical Officer of a District being also appointed to the Union Workhouse, if his residence is conveniently situate.—*Instr. Letter.* Further, with regard to this subject, see the Order of 10th December, 1859 (*post*), as to the medical qualifications of Medical Officers.

As regards the continuance in office of Medical Officers who at the time of their appointment were not duly qualified according to the regulations of the Poor Law Board, see Arts. 3 and 4 of the General Order of 25th May, 1857 (*post*).

The Medical Act (21 & 22 Vict. c. 90, s. 36) enacts, that after the 1st January, 1859, extended by 22 Vict. c. 21, s. 1, to 1st July, 1859, and again extended by 23 Vict. c. 7, s. 3, to 1st January, 1861, no person shall hold any appointment as a Physician, Surgeon, or other Medical Officer, in any Lunatic Asylum, House of Industry, Parochial or Union Workhouse or Poorhouse, Parish Union, or other Public Establishment, Body, or Institution, or as a Medical Officer of Health, unless he be registered under the Act. By section 33 of 21 & 22 Vict. c. 90, it is provided that no person who, on the 1st October, 1858, was acting as Medical Officer under an Order of the Poor Law Commissioners or Poor Law Board, should be disqualified to hold his office by reason of his not being registered before the 1st January, 1859, unless he shall have failed to be registered within six months from the passing of the Act, that is, the 2nd February, 1859; but see 22 Vict. c. 21, s. 2, and 23 Vict. c. 7, s. 4, which contain a further provision on the subject.

It is therefore incumbent upon the Guardians to ascertain that their Medical Officers are registered under the Act. This they will readily ascertain by reference to the Register published annually by the General Council under sect. 27 of the Act; or they should require the Medical Officer to produce to them evidence of his being so registered. The Poor Law Board have since (10th December, 1859) issued a General Order (*see post*) on the subject of the qualifications required for the appointment of Medical Officers, which however applies only to appointments made subsequently to the 1st March, 1860.

The Consolidated Orders subsequently issued contain, in lieu of Article 168 in the text of the General Consolidated Order, the following Article on the subject of the qualifications of Medical Officers:—

" Art. 167.—No person shall hold the office of Medical Officer under

Officer under this Order unless he possess one of the four following qualifications; that is to say,—

Art. 168.—1. A diploma or degree as surgeon from a Royal College or University in England, Scotland, or Ireland, together with a degree in medicine from an University in England, legally authorized to grant such degree, or together with a diploma or licence of the Royal College of Physicians of London.

2. A diploma or degree of surgeon from a Royal College or University in England, Scotland, or Ireland, together with a certificate to practise as an apothecary from the Society of Apothecaries of London.

3. A diploma or degree as surgeon from a Royal College or University in England, Scotland, or Ireland, such person having been in actual practice as an apothecary on the first day of August, one thousand eight hundred and fifteen.

4. A warrant or commission as surgeon or assistant-surgeon in her Majesty's Navy, or as surgeon or assistant-surgeon or apothecary in her Majesty's Army, or as surgeon or assistant-surgeon in the service of the

---

this Order, unless he be duly registered under "The Medical Act of 1858," and be qualified by law to practise both medicine and surgery in England and Wales, such qualification being established by the production to the Board of Guardians of a diploma, certificate of a degree, licence, or other instrument granted or issued by competent legal authority, in Great Britain or Ireland, testifying to the medical or surgical, or medical and surgical, qualification or qualifications of the Candidate for such office:

"Provided that evidence that any Candidate was in practice as an apothecary on the first day of August, one thousand eight hundred and fifteen, shall be taken to be equivalent to a certificate to practise from the Society of Apothecaries of London:

"Provided also that any person being registered as aforesaid, who shall possess a warrant or commission as surgeon or assistant-surgeon in Her Majesty's Navy, or as surgeon or assistant-surgeon or apothecary in Her Majesty's Army, or as a surgeon or assistant-surgeon in the service of the Honourable East India Company, dated previous to the first day of August, one thousand eight hundred and twenty-six, shall be qualified to be appointed to the office of Medical Officer as aforesaid."

Honourable East India Company, dated previous to the first day of August, one thousand eight hundred and twenty-six.

Art. 169.—Provided always, that if it be impracticable, consistently with the proper attendance on the sick poor, for the Guardians to procure a person residing within the district in which he is to act, and duly qualified in one of the four modes recited in Art. 168, to attend on the poor in such district, or that the only person resident within such district, and so qualified, shall have been dismissed from office by the Commissioners, or shall be unfit or incompetent to hold the office of Medical Officer, then and in such case the Guardians shall cause a special minute to be made and entered on the usual record of their proceedings, stating the reasons which, in their opinion, make it necessary to employ a person not qualified as required by Art. 168, and shall forthwith transmit a copy of such minute to the Commissioners for their consideration; and the Commissioners may permit the employment by such Guardians of any person duly licensed to practise as a medical man, although such person be not qualified in one of the four modes required by Art 168 (*a*).

Art. 170 (*b*).—Provided also, that the Guardians may, with the consent of the Commissioners, continue in office any Medical Officer duly licensed to practise as a medical man already employed by any such Guardians, although such Medical Officer may not be qualified in one of the four modes required by Art. 168 (*c*).

(*a*) It will be seen that if there be not a person resident *within* the District who possesses a double qualification, the Guardians can now appoint a medical man who is duly qualified to practise as such, and who is resident within the District, though there may be others residing *near to* the District possessing double qualifications. Further with respect to this Article, see Articles 3 and 4 of the General Order of the 25th May, 1857, *post.*

(*b*) If a person possessing only a single qualification altogether ceases to be a Medical Officer of the Union, he cannot be re-appointed to the same or any other District, unless under the provisions of Art. 169.

(*c*) This article is omitted in the Consolidated Orders issued subsequently to this Order.

Art. 171.—No person shall hold the office of Chaplain under this Order without the consent of the Bishop of the diocese to his appointment, signified in writing (*a*).

REMUNERATION OF THE OFFICERS.

Art. 172 (*b*).—The Guardians shall pay to the several officers and assistants appointed to or holding any office or employment under this Order, such salaries or remuneration as the Commissioners may from time to time direct or approve.

(*a*) The consent of the Bishop will be obtained by the Guardians, and forwarded by their Clerk to the Poor Law Board.—*Instr. Letter*, February, 1842. If the Bishop simply signifies his consent in writing, it will be sufficient. No formal licence is requisite. The appointment of a Chaplain to a Union Workhouse is not an appointment to a Benefice, for which a special licence is required. With reference to the payment of a fee to the secretary of the Bishop for the consent, the Poor Law Commissioners, in 9 Off. Cir. 178, stated that "the consent of the Bishop to the appointment of the Chaplain to a Union Workhouse is a requisite as much for the benefit of the Clergyman seeking to obtain that office, as of the Guardians requiring his services therein. When, therefore the proposed Chaplain applies for such consent and obtains it, and a fee is thereupon demanded of him by the Bishop's secretary, the Board think, that whether the latter could have lawfully insisted upon payment of the fee or not, the Chaplain has no legal claim upon the Guardians to be reimbursed the amount."

Where the Workhouse is in a peculiar, the Bishop to whose diocese the peculiar belongs, and not the Ordinary of the peculiar, will give the consent.—*Instr. Letter*, February, 1842.

A Clergyman of the Church of England duly appointed Chaplain of a Workhouse, may perform the service of the Church of England in a Workhouse, without the consent of the Incumbent of the parish in which the Workhouse is locally situated. (*Molyneux* v. *Bagshaw*, *ante*, p. 110.)

(*b*) The power of the Commissioners to determine the salaries of the Officers is derived from sect. 46 of the 4 & 5 Wm. IV. c. 76. See the Minute of the Commissioners, dated 31st October, 1840, in their Seventh Annual Report, p. 123. In all cases in which the Commissioners fix the salary or remuneration of an officer, or sanction the salary or remuneration proposed by the Guardians, they understand that no perquisites or extra charges or emoluments are to be allowed over and above such salary or remuneration. Thus the Workhouse Master should be required to account for the produce of bones, hog-wash, kitchen-stuff, and other refuse sold from, or consumed in, the house. Unless an agreement to that effect be made at the time of the appointment of any Workhouse Officer, no part of his family is to be maintained within the Workhouse. The maintenance of any children or other relations who may stay with him should be paid for by him, and the costs deducted from the charge of establishment maintenance at the end of the quarter. Upon this point, see note to Article 153. Moreover the quantity of each article of consumption allowed to each Officer daily should be specified by the Guardians, and entered on their minutes. Unless this is done, the Auditor will be unable to check the provision accounts of the Workhouse Master.

The Workhouse or other Officers of the Union are not entitled to call upon the Medical Officer to attend them when they are sick, as a part of the duty of the latter. If they do so, the Medical Officer will be entitled to require them to remunerate him for his attendance as private patients. Where, however, the illness is contracted in the discharge of their duties, the Guardians might, under the proviso to this Article and with the consent of the Poor Law Board, pay the bill of the Medical Attendant.

It must be remembered that the Workhouse Officers are not entitled to sell their rations or give them away when they do not consume the whole of what is allowed them by the terms of their appointment, nor are they at liberty to make a private arrangement with the tradesmen who supply the Workhouse with provisions, for the supply of a better quality of provisions for the use of the Officers than that which is allowed, without the special sanction of the Board of Guardians. The Commissioners are of opinion that a private arrangement with a tradesman, or the receipt of any compensation from such tradesman for a smaller quantity of any article than an officer thinks himself entitled to, is most objectionable; and they will be prepared to deal with any such transaction as an offence approaching to fraud. The rations allowed to the Master and Matron are for their own consumption only, and they are not entitled to supply their friends and other persons calling upon them with refreshments from the Workhouse stores. It may be remarked here, that the half of the salaries of the Medical Officers, and half the cost of medicines and surgical appliances when provided by the Guardians, and the whole of the salaries of the Schoolmasters and Schoolmistresses, will be repaid to the Guardians by Government. The Guardians, however, must, in the first instance, pay these salaries, and the salaries of the two last-mentioned officers should be *exclusive* of board and lodging in the Workhouse; otherwise the whole amount will not be repaid to the Guardians by Government. See the Circulars of the Poor Law Board on this subject. Gratuities for extraordinary services can only be paid under this Article to Officers "appointed to or holding any office or employment under this order," and such gratuities when paid must be charged in the accounts in the same manner as the salaries of the Officers. The regulation in Art. 172 does not apply to persons appointed temporarily to an office by the Guardians during a vacancy in the particular office. As to temporary substitutes, see Article 193 (*post*).

Here attention may be directed to the 27 & 28 Vict. c. 42; 29 & 30 Vict. c. 113, ss. 1, 2; 30 Vict. c. 6, s. 76; and 30 & 31 Vict. c. 106, ss. 18, 19, 20; which empower Guardians, with the consent of the Poor Law Board, to grant superannuation allowances to officers in their service. The allowance shall not exceed in any case two-thirds of the Officer's salary on his retirement; and the retiring Officer must be at least sixty

Provided that the Guardians, with the approval of the Commissioners, may pay to any officer or person employed by such Guardians a reasonable compensation on account of extraordinary services, or other unforeseen circumstances connected with the duties of such officer or person or the necessities of the Union (*a*).

Art. 173.—The salary of every officer or assistant appointed to, or holding, any office or employment under this Order, shall be payable up to the day on which he ceases to hold such office or employment, and no longer (*b*).

---

years of age, and have served as an Officer of some Union or Parish for twenty years at the least. Mr. Austin's edition of the Superannuation Acts may be usefully consulted.

(*a*) Under the statute law, there is no power to give gratuities out of the rates. (*Ex parte Mellish*, 8 L. J. (N. S.) 47.)

(*b*) But see Art. 175 respecting the payment of the salary of an Officer who has been suspended from his office, and is afterwards dismissed by the Poor Law Board. This Article does not apply to Officers appointed to or holding office under any other Order, as, for instance, a collector of poor-rates who is appointed under a separate Order (*post*).

It may be useful here to state, that with regard to Government salaries, the Lords Commissioners of Her Majesty's Treasury, by a Treasury minute, dated 1st July, 1837, have directed that in all cases where payment of salary is to be made for a broken period upon annual rates of pay or allowance, the amount due shall be calculated with reference to the number of days in the quarter in which such broken period occurs. The quarter ending

31st March	contains	90 days.
(in leap years).	,,	91 ,,
30th June	,,	91 ,,
30th September	,,	92 ,,
31st December	,,	92 ,,

It seems to be desirable that a like rule should be observed with regard to Poor Law Officers' salaries; but of course, if the quarters are made to terminate at different periods from the above, the number of days in each quarter will vary according to the circumstances.

In the Consolidated Orders issued to Unions, declared since 1847, in lieu of Article 173, the following is substituted :—

" The salary of every officer or assistant, appointed to or holding any office or employment under this Order, shall be payable up to the day on which he ceases to hold such office or employment, and no longer, and shall be paid at the several quarters ending at the usual Feast-days in the year; namely, Midsummer Day, Michaelmas Day, Christmas Day, and Lady Day: provided, nevertheless, that in the case of any officer whose duty it is to render accounts to the Board of Guardians, it shall be competent for the Guardians to defer in whole or in part the payment of

Art. 174.—If no remuneration or salary be expressly assigned to the treasurer, the profit arising from the use of money from time to time left in his hands shall be deemed to be the payment of his services (*c*).

Art. 175 (*d*).—An officer who may be suspended, and who may without the previous removal of such suspension be dismissed by the Commissioners, shall not be entitled to any salary from the date of such suspension.

Art. 176.—The Guardians shall not pay to any Officer bound to account, to be hereafter appointed, who may have been removed, or who may be under suspension from his office, any salary claimed by such officer until his accounts shall have been audited by the Auditor (*e*).

---

the salary of any such officer until his accounts shall have been audited and allowed by the Auditor, after which audit and allowance, the sum due up to the date of his accounts so audited shall be forthwith paid."

As to the quarterly or other periodical payment of Officers, see Articles 2 & 3 of the General Order of the 19th August, 1867, *post*.

(*c*) The Guardians cannot pay interest to their Treasurer on sums which they may overdraw, and charge such interest on the poor-rates. On this subject see note to Art. 81.

(*d*) But it would seem that, if the officer resign his office after his suspension, he will be entitled to payment of his salary up to the date of his resignation.

The Consolidated Orders subsequently issued contain, in lieu of Art. 175, the following :—

"An officer who may be suspended, and who may upon such suspension be dismissed by the Poor Law Board, shall not be entitled to any salary from the date of such suspension; and no officer who shall be temporarily suspended from his office by reason of his services not being required, shall be entitled to any salary pending such temporary suspension."

(*e*) After Art. 176, the following Articles relating to the expenses attending the election of Guardians are introduced in the Consolidated Orders subsequently issued :—

"Art. 173.—The Guardians shall pay, as compensation to the Clerk, or to the person appointed under the authority of this Order to act as such, in the performance of the duties hereby prescribed for the conduct of every election of Guardians, such a sum, not exceeding —— pounds, as the Guardians shall determine, which sum shall include the remuneration of the persons who may have been appointed to assist him in conducting and completing the election, and shall be defrayed out of the common fund of the Union.

"Art. 174.—The Guardians shall in the case of every contested election pay one farthing per head on the population of the parish in

Art. 177.—No salary of any District Medical Officer shall include the remuneration for operations and services of the following classes performed by such Medical Officer in that capacity for any out-door pauper, but such operations and services shall be paid for by the Guardians, according to the rates specified in this Article.

	£.	s.	d.
1. Treatment of Compound Fractures of the Thigh			
2. Treatment of Compound Fractures or Compound Dislocation of the Leg	5	0	0
3. Amputation of Leg, Arm, Foot, or Hand.			
4. The Operation for Strangulated Hernia			
5. Treatment of Simple Fractures or Simple Dislocations of the Thigh or Leg	3	0	0
6. Amputation of a Finger or Toe	2	0	0
7. Treatment of Dislocations or Fractures of the Arm	1	0	0

The above rates shall include the payment for the supply of all kinds of apparatus and splints (*a*).

---

which the contest shall have taken place, if the population shall be more than five hundred, and one halfpenny per head on the population of the parish in which the contest shall have taken place, if the population be not more than five hundred, to the said Clerk, or other person as aforesaid, in addition to the compensation mentioned in Art. 173, which sum shall be charged by the said Guardians to the account of such parish; and for the purpose of ascertaining the last-mentioned sums, the population of the parish shall be taken to be as stated in the census which, at the time of such election, shall have been last made under the authority of any Act of Parliament.

"Art. 175.—The cost of providing the several Forms marked (A.), (D.) and (E.) hereunto annexed, shall be defrayed out of the common fund of the Union.

"Art. 176.—The cost of providing the Form marked (C.) hereunto annexed, shall be charged by the said Guardians to the respective parishes in whose behalf the same may be required."

(*a*) The operations enumerated in Art. 177 are intended to provide for cases of urgency (principally those arising from accidents), which cannot be sent to a public hospital with safety and propriety. The payments for operations are limited to operations on out-door poor, and do not include those performed in the Workhouse. It appeared to the Commissioners that the continued attendance at the house of the patient in severe surgical cases usually forms the most burdensome part of the extra service of the medical man; whereas the constant visits of the

Medical Officer to the Workhouse enable him to attend a patient in the Workhouse without always making a visit for that express purpose. Moreover, when a patient can be removed to a Workhouse, or when he has long been the subject of medical treatment in the Workhouse, he may in general be removed with safety or propriety to an infirmary or hospital; and the Commissioners think it desirable that, where the distance or other circumstances do not present serious obstacles, paupers should enjoy the practised skill and combined judgment of the medical men usually connected with such establishments. While, therefore, the Commissioners would discourage the performance of important surgical operations in Workhouses, they are ready to sanction any reasonable subscription to an hospital or similar establishment by a Board of Guardians on behalf of the Union. The payments are intended to cover not only the operation, but also the attendance after the operation, which in severe cases of this sort ought usually to be numerous. Cases in which the patient does not survive the operation thirty-six hours, or in which he does not receive several subsequent attendances, are only to be paid for at the rate of one-half of the amount prescribed by Art. 177 (see Art. 179).—*Instr. Letter.*

Hernia reduced without a surgical operation does not entitle the Medical Officer to the fee of £5; and with respect to fractures, it may be here stated, for the information of non-medical readers, that a fracture is called compound when the end or ends of the bone or bones have penetrated the soft parts, so as to come in contact with the air, which alters the whole process set up by nature for the cure of a simple fracture,—giving rise at the same time to such a degree of constitutional irritation as usually leads to the death of old people. A comminuted fracture is a term applied to a fracture when the bone is broken into several pieces; also to any substance which has been ground into minute particles.

The following are within the regulation in No. 5:—Fracture of the neck of the thigh-bone, or of the malleolus externus. And the following are not within it:—Fractures of the knee-cap or patella, or of the tarsus, metatarsus, or toes.

The following are within the regulation No. 7:—Dislocation of the shoulder, elbow, and wrist; fracture of the humerus, ulna (or elbow-joint, which is formed by the bones of the arm), and radius. And the following are not within it:—Fracture of the ribs, clavicle, scapula, and acromion; carpus, metacarpus, and fingers or thumbs. Compound fractures of the *arm* are to be paid for at the same rate as simple fractures. Compound or simple fractures of the bones of the face do not come within the scope of the regulation, nor does the operation for fistula, lithotomy, lithotrity,—removing a cancer in the breast, tapping for dropsy, or the removal of tumours on any part of the body.

Medical men who are not Medical Officers of the Union are not entitled to any fees under this Order for operations performed upon, and services rendered to, paupers; but the Guardians, if they think fit, can nevertheless pay such medical men for their services such a sum as may be fair and reasonable. The fees are payable in respect to operations performed upon non-settled as well as upon settled paupers; and they must be charged to the same account as that to which the relief of the

Art. 178.—Provided that, except in cases of sudden accident immediately threatening life, no Medical Officer shall be entitled to receive such remuneration for any amputation, unless he shall have obtained, at his own cost, the advice of some member of the Royal College of Surgeons of London, or some fellow or licentiate of the Royal College of Physicians of London, before performing such amputation, and unless he shall also produce to the Guardians a certificate from such member of the Royal College of Surgeons, or such fellow or licentiate, stating that, in his opinion, it was right and proper that such amputation should be then performed (a).

---

particular pauper is charged. The same observation applies to extra allowances under Article 181, *post*.

Reference may here be made to the 11 and 12 Vict. c. 110, s. 2, which enables Guardians, if they think proper, to pay for any medical or other assistance which shall be rendered to any poor person on the happening of any accident, bodily casualty, or sudden illness, although no order may have been given for the same by them or any of their officers.

As regards the performance of surgical operations and services not specified in Art. 177, see Art. 181, which allows of an extra payment being made, with the approval of the Poor Law Board, for cases which may have presented peculiar difficulty, or required and received long attendance from the Medical Officer.

In some Unions, Articles 177, 178, 179, 180, 181, 182, and 183, have been suspended by subsequent Orders of the Poor Law Board.

(a) It is not necessary that the certificate be obtained and produced to the Guardians previous to the operation, but the Medical Officer must have obtained the advice upon which the certificate is founded before he performs the operation. As regards the Medical Officer obtaining assistance in performing operations, the following is an extract from a letter of the Poor Law Board, which was published in the 'Lancet' of 21st November, 1857 :—" As regards the application which you have made for an order for three medical men to assist you in the amputation, I am directed to state that the more regular course under circumstances such as you describe, is, that the Medical Officer himself (when he deems it needful to do so) should obtain any additional professional aid which may in his judgment be necessary, and after the operation has been performed, submit the facts to the Guardians. It then rests with them to determine whether the case was of such unusual and exceptional character as to warrant them in making a special allowance for the assistance so rendered." The Guardians should pay for the assistance so rendered themselves, and the case would not come within Article 181, if the payments be not made to the Medical Officer but to the persons by whom the assistance was rendered.

Art. 179.—Provided also, that if, in any case, the patient has not survived the operation more than thirty-six hours, and has not required and received several attendances after the operation by the Medical Officer who has performed the same, such Medical Officer shall be entitled only to one-half of the payments respectively prescribed above.

Art. 180.—Provided also, that if several of the fees specified in Art. 177 become payable with respect to the same person at the same time, and in consequence of the same cause or injury, the Medical Officer shall be entitled only to one of such fees, and if they be unequal, to the highest.

Art. 181.—In any surgical case not provided for in Art. 177, which has presented peculiar difficulty, or required and received long attendance from the District Medical Officer, the Guardians may make to the said Medical Officer such reasonable extra allowance as they may think fit, and the Commissioners may approve (b).

Art. 182.—In cases in which any Medical Officer, either for the Workhouse or a district, shall be called on by order of a person legally qualified to make such order to attend any woman in or immediately after childbirth, or shall,

---

After the 1st January, 1861, "no certificate required by any Act now in force, or that may hereafter be passed, from any Physician, Surgeon, Licentiate in Medicine and Surgery, or other Medical Practitioner, shall be valid, unless the person signing the same be registered under this Act." (21 & 22 Vict. c. 90, s. 37; 22 Vict. c. 21, s. 1; 23 Vict. c. 7, s. 3.) By s. 34 of the 21 and 22 Vict. c. 90, the words "legally qualified Medical Practitioner," or "duly qualified Medical Practitioner," or any words imputing a person recognized by law as a Medical Practitioner, or member of the medical profession, when used in any Act of Parliament, are to be construed to mean a person registered under that Act. As a general rule, it is thought not desirable that a medical man who is a Guardian of the Union should give certificates under this Article in his own Union.

It is only in cases of "amputation" that a certificate is required under this Article, therefore it is not requisite that a certificate should be obtained with regard to other surgical operations; as, for instance, the operation for strangulated hernia.

(b) Note that it is only surgical cases which fall under this rule. Other cases may be dealt with under Art. 172. See also 11 & 12 Vict. c. 110, s. 2, which enables the Guardians to give discretionary compensation in certain cases.

under circumstances of difficulty or danger, without any order, visit any such woman actually receiving relief, or whom the Guardians may subsequently decide to have been in a destitute condition, such Medical Officer shall be paid for his attendance and medicines by a sum of not less than ten shillings, nor more than twenty shillings, according as the Guardians may agree with such officer (a).

Art. 183.—Provided that in any special case in which great difficulty may have occurred in the delivery, or long

---

(a) Observe that the Medical Officer must have an order for his attendance, signed by a person legally qualified to make such an order; further upon this point, see Official Circulars, 4, p. 102, and 6, pp. 40, 90. When the accouchement takes place without the attendance of the Medical Officer, and the woman goes on satisfactorily till some time afterwards, and then falls ill, and is attended by the Medical Officer, it is considered that the case falls within his general contract, and that he is not entitled to a special fee for his attendance; for the words "immediately after childbirth" do not apply to such a case. Those words contemplate attendance within a reasonable time afterwards, and not after the lapse of three or four days. They must be taken to mean so immediately after childbirth that the Medical Officer may render the patient that medical assistance which is requisite in cases of childbirth as soon as the child is born, or within a short time afterwards. A lengthened attendance *previous* to childbirth, for illness consequent upon the woman's pregnancy, does not entitle the Medical Officer to a special fee. The attendance must be *at* and *subsequent* to the birth. The term "childbirth" applies only to cases in which the child was or might have been born alive; hence the delivery of a seven months' child comes within the term "childbirth." Attendances in a case of a miscarriage, or in consequence of symptoms of premature labour, or if the woman was only four or five months gone with child, do not entitle the Medical Officer to an extra fee. This regulation contains no provision for a case in which the woman is delivered by one Medical Officer and receives subsequent medical attendance from another. It contemplates the delivery and subsequent attendance being paid for to the *same* officer by a single fee; but it is considered that the Medical Officer will be entitled to the fee even though, upon his arrival at the house, he find that the woman has been delivered and has subsequently died. The delivery of a woman of twins does not entitle the Medical Officer to a double fee for his attendance, unless the circumstances attending the delivery be of such a special character as to bring the case within Article 183.

As regards the duty of the Master of the Workhouse to give an order, or rather to send for the Medical Officer of the Workhouse, see Art. 208, No. 14. By Art. 210, No. 12, the Matron is "to take proper care of the sick paupers."

subsequent attendance in respect of some puerperal malady or affection may have been requisite, any District Medical Officer shall receive the sum of two pounds (*b*).

SECURITY OF THE OFFICERS.

Art. 184.—Every Treasurer, Master, Matron of a Workhouse in which there is no Master, Collector, or Relieving Officer, every person hereafter appointed as Clerk, and every other officer whom the Guardians shall require so to do, shall respectively give a bond conditioned for the due and faithful performance of the duties of the office, with two sufficient sureties, not, in the case of any security to be hereafter entered into, being Officers of the same Union; and every Officer who shall have entered into any such security shall give immediate notice to the Guardians of the death, insolvency, or bankruptcy of either of such sureties, and shall, when required by the Guardians, produce a certificate, signed by two householders, that his sureties are alive, and believed by them to be solvent, and such officer shall supply a fresh surety in the place of any such surety who may die or become bankrupt or insolvent (*c*).

(*b*) Note that it is only a *District* Medical Officer that is entitled to an increased fee under this Article, and it must be read as a proviso to the preceding Article 182; so that there must be all the incidents required by that Article, accompanied by the circumstances referred to in it, to entitle the Medical Officer to the increased fee. A case of arm presentation is to be considered as a special case of great difficulty, entitling the medical officer to a fee of two pounds under this Article: so also the delivery by the use of forceps. Long subsequent attendance in respect of a puerperal malady or affection, such as diseased breasts, would entitle the Medical Officer to the extra fee; but not so if the attendance is merely on account of the general debility of the woman.

This Article does not contemplate the repayment to the Medical Officer of any fee paid to another medical man whom he may have called to his assistance in a special case.

(*c*) This Article requires the Guardians to take proper security from the Treasurer, the Master of the Workhouse, the Matron where there is no Master, Collector, or Relieving Officer, and every person appointed as Clerk, and also every other officer whom the Guardians shall require to give security, and to renew the security from time to time; and Art. 87 renders it necessary that the bonds so taken by the Guardians should be produced once a year for the inspection of the Auditor. The latter provision is highly desirable, in order to ensure the preservation of the bonds in the proper hands. As the security is given in pursuance of the regulations of the Commissioners, the instrument by which it is given is exempt from stamp duty (section 86 of 4 & 5 Wm. IV. c. 76). The Article requires that the sureties shall not be officers of the same Union, but the prohibition does not extend to an Officer of a parish in the Union, as a Collector or Assistant-Overseer, as such officers are not Officers of the Union. Though it does not prevent the officers naming members of the Boards of Guardians as sureties to their bonds, still it is not desirable, if it can be avoided, that individual Guardians should become sureties for their officers ; inasmuch as, in the event of proceedings being taken on the bond, the Guardian would be placed in the anomalous position of a member of a body causing proceedings to be taken against himself for the recovery of the penalty named in the bond. There is nothing in the Order which would prevent a person who is security for a paid officer being appointed himself a paid officer of the same Union ; but in such a case it would be proper that the bond should be cancelled, and a fresh security taken. As to the preparation of officers' bonds, see Art. 202, No. 4, and note. As to the liability of the sureties of a Union Treasurer for cheques cashed by an officer of the Union, see *Lichfield Union* v. *Greene*, 1 H. & N. 884; 26 L. J. R. (N.S.) Exch. 140; and 21 J. P. 198 That case shows that if payment of an order of the Guardians upon their Treasurer be taken in notes of a Country Bank, and the Bank afterwards stops payment, the Treasurer and his sureties are discharged.

The sureties to a bond given to the Guardians cannot be released from their obligation without the Guardians' consent ; but if, after satisfying themselves as to the state of the accounts of the Officer, the Guardians should deem themselves justified in cancelling the bond and taking fresh sureties, it is open to them to do so ; they ought not, however, to give up the bond unless they are so satisfied, and unless a fresh security of at least equal responsibility be provided. (56 O. C. (N.S.) 69.)

Where an officer has resigned, the Guardians are entitled to retain possession of his bond as long as they think proper. They may, however, give it up when a reasonable time has elapsed after the determination of his office, and he has duly accounted for all the money he has received.

The following decision of the Judicial Committee of the Privy Council with regard to the liability of sureties is very important in its bearing on the securities of Union Officers :—

1. That a plea that the respondents were guilty of negligence and want of due care in checking and properly examining the accounts of the person employed, and that the surety was thereby released and discharged from the penalty of the bond, was no defence to the action on the bond.

2. That the mere passive inactivity of the person to whom a guarantee is given, his neglect to call the principal debtor to account in reasonable time, and to enforce payment against him, does not discharge the surety ; that there must be some positive act done by him to the prejudice of

Art. 185.—Provided that the Guardians may, if they think fit, take the security of any society or company expressly authorized by statute to guarantee or secure the faithful discharge of the duties of such officers (*a*).

Art. 186.—Provided also, that the Guardians may, with the consent of the Commissioners, dispense with such security in the case of any banking firm acting as Treasurer, or in the case of a Treasurer, being a banker, or partner of such firm (*b*).

CONTINUANCE IN OFFICE AND SUSPENSION OF OFFICERS.—SUPPLY OF VACANCIES.

Art. 187.—Every officer appointed to or holding any office under this Order, other than a Medical Officer (*c*), shall continue to hold the same until he die, or resign, or be removed by the Commissioners, or be proved to be insane, to the satisfaction of the Commissioners (*d*).

---

the surety, or such degree of negligence as to imply connivance amounting to fraud.

3. That the surety guarantees the honesty of the person employed, and is not entitled to be relieved from his obligation because the employer fails to use all the means in his power to guard against the consequences of dishonesty. (*Black v. Ottoman Bank*, 8 Jur. (N.S.) 801).

(*a*) The British Guarantee Association was dissolved on the 1st December, 1862, and the European Assurance Society is now the only Society or Company authorized by statute to guarantee the fidelity of Poor Law Officers. The Poor Law Board, on the 4th June, 1860, approved of the form of guarantee to be given by the European Assurance Society. The Poor Law Board recommend, in all cases in which a security of a Guarantee Society is given on behalf of any officer to a Board of Guardians, that the Guardians should take care to have the receipt for the annual premium placed by such officer in their hands as soon as it is paid, and deposited for safe custody with the policy.

(*b*) Circumstances have occurred with respect to local banks in some parts of England, which have since caused the Poor Law Board to decline to consent to security being dispensed with in any case, except when the Bank of England may be appointed Treasurer. In the Consolidated Orders subsequently issued this Article is omitted.

(*c*) As to the Medical Officer, see the General Order of the 25th May, 1857.

(*d*) The Guardians cannot agree with an officer on his appointment that the appointment shall be determined on notice being given by either party; though it is competent for the Guardians to agree with an officer that he shall give a month's notice of his intention to resign his office

Art. 188.—Provided always, that every Porter, Nurse, Assistant, or Servant may be dismissed by the Guardians without the consent of the Commissioners; but every such dismissal, and the grounds thereof, shall be reported to the Commissioners (*a*).

Art. 189.—If any Master or Matron hereafter appointed be husband and wife, and one of them should be dismissed

---

(see Art. 167). They cannot remove him by giving notice that his services will be discontinued, inasmuch as such a course would be inconsistent with the 46th section of the 4 & 5 Wm. IV. c. 76, which empowers the Poor Law Board to determine the continuance in office or dismissal of paid officers. By sect. 48, the Board are empowered, as and when they shall think proper, by order under their hands and seal (either upon or without any suggestion or complaint in that behalf from the Overseers or Guardians of any Parish or Union), to remove any Master of any Workhouse, or Assistant-Overseer, or other paid officer of any Parish or Union, whom they shall deem unfit for or incompetent to discharge the duties of any such office, or who shall at any time refuse or wilfully neglect to obey and carry into effect any of the Rules, Orders, or Regulations of the said Board, and to require, from time to time, the persons competent in that behalf to appoint a fit and proper person in his room, and any person so removed is not competent to be appointed to or to fill any paid office connected with the relief of the poor in any such Parish or Union, except with the consent of the Board under their hands and seal.—*Instr. Letter.*

The Bankruptcy of an officer does not vacate the office; nor would Bankruptcy be a legal disqualification for office, though there may be circumstances which would render a Bankrupt an unfit person to be appointed to a paid office under the Guardians.

The exception to this Article, as to the tenure of office by Medical Officers, has been overruled by the General Order of the Poor Law Board, dated 25th May, 1857 (*post*).

In the Orders subsequently issued, this Article, after the words "or resign," is as follows:—"Or be proved to be insane by evidence which the Board shall deem sufficient, or shall become legally disqualified to hold such office, or be removed by the Poor Law Board."

The Poor Law Board, and not the Bishop of the diocese, have the power to remove the Chaplain of a Union Workhouse, he being an officer under the 46th and 48th ss. of 4 & 5 Wm. IV. c. 76, as interpreted by s. 109 of that Act. (*Ex parte Molyneux*, 27 J. P. 56; 7 L. T. (N. S.) 599.)

(*a*) The regulations requiring that the dismissals of the Porter, Nurse, and Assistants, and the grounds of them, should be reported to the Poor Law Board, is inserted in order to enable the Board to judge if a person so dismissed from one Union should be allowed to be appointed in another Union. As regards assistants or servants in the Workhouse, see however the Order of 19th April, 1867, *post*.

by Order of the Commissioners, or should otherwise vacate his or her office, or should die, the other or survivor shall, at the expiration of the then current quarter, cease to hold his or her office of Master or Matron, as the case may be (*b*).

Art. 190.—No officer of a Workhouse who may have been dismissed by any Order of the Commissioners, shall, after such dismissal, remain upon the Workhouse premises, or enter therein for the purpose of interfering in the management of such Workhouse, unless the Commissioners have consented to his subsequent appointment to an office in such Workhouse, under the provisions of the said first-recited Act, or to his temporary employment therein.

Art. 191.—Every Medical Officer duly appointed shall, unless the period for which he is appointed be entered on the Minutes of the Guardians at the time of making such appointment, or be acknowledged in writing by such Medical Officer, continue in office until he may die or resign, or become legally disqualified to hold such office, or be removed therefrom by the Commissioners (*c*).

Art. 192 (*d*).—The Guardians may at their discretion suspend from the discharge of his or her duties any Master,

---

(*b*) It is obviously desirable that, in every case where practicable, the Master and Matron should be man and wife, and that they should be without incumbrance. See note to Art. 153, *ante*, p. 111.

(*c*) This Article was rescinded by a General Order of the Poor Law Board, dated 15th February, 1855, which made new provisions with respect to the Medical Officer's tenure of office; and that Order has been again rescinded, except as to appointments made prior to the 24th June, 1857, by a General Order, dated 25th May, 1857 (*post*). The Consolidated Orders subsequently issued contain the following provision with reference to the tenure of the office of Medical Officer :—

" Every Medical Officer duly appointed shall hold his office according to the provisions contained in the General Order of this Board, bearing date the twenty-fifth day of May, one thousand eight hundred and fifty-seven."

(*d*) Respecting the salaries of officers suspended or dismissed, see Art. 175, *ante*, p. 125.

The Guardians cannot under this Article suspend either their Clerk or their Treasurer from office. The proper course for them to adopt in a case of any misconduct on the part of these officers is to report the

Matron, Schoolmaster, Schoolmistress, Medical Officer, Relieving Officer, or Superintendent of Out-door Labour; and the Guardians shall, in case of every such suspension, forthwith report the same, together with the cause thereof, to the Commissioners; and if the Commissioners remove the suspension of such officer by the Guardians, he or she shall forthwith resume the performance of his or her duties.

Art. 193.—If any officer, or assistant, appointed to or holding any office or employment under this Order, be at any time prevented by sickness or accident, or other sufficient reason, from the performance of his duties, the Guardians may appoint a fit person to act as his temporary substitute, and may pay him a reasonable compensation for his services; and every such appointment shall be reported to the Commissioners as soon as the same shall have been made (*a*).

---

fact of their misconduct to the Poor Law Board, who, if they think fit, can suspend them from the performance of their duties, previous to causing the matter of complaint to be investigated by a Poor Law Inspector. The bankruptcy of the Treasurer does not vacate the office. In such case he must tender his resignation to the Guardians before they can proceed to another election. The Guardians, if they suspend an officer, may at any time remove the suspension without the intervention of the Poor Law Board.

(*a*) If any of the officers who reside in the Workhouse should be temporarily incapable of performing their duties, the Guardians may under this Article employ a temporary substitute, and pay him for his services. It is not necessary that they should obtain the sanction of the Poor Law Board before they make the payment. It will be understood that if the Chaplain keep a curate, he will not be entitled to perform his duties in the Workhouse by his curate without the consent of the Guardians.—*Instr. Letter*, 5th February, 1842. The Guardians can grant temporary leave of absence to any officer; and, in general, no Workhouse Officer should absent himself from his duties without the permission of the Guardians. The officers ought not to be absent singly, and still less simultaneously, from the Workhouse, without sufficient cause. The Master ought always to sleep in the Workhouse.—*Ib.* This Article is not applicable to the case in which the Clerk may be occasionally prevented from attending personally to his duties at the Board for a single day. Such a case may be properly met by the appointment of the Vice-Chairman, or some other Guardian, to perform the duties of the Clerk for the particular occasion under Art. 194. Such occasional absence on the part of the Clerk ought not, however, to take place except for sufficient cause. But it applies to a Relieving Officer who

Art. 194.—The Vice-Chairman, or some Guardian to be appointed by the Guardians, may perform any of the duties assigned to the Clerk until any vacancy in the office shall have been filled, or until a substitute be appointed in the case of the sickness, accident, or absence of the Clerk (*b*).

Art. 195.—When any officer may die, resign, or become legally disqualified to perform the duties of his office, the Guardians shall, as soon as conveniently may be after such death, resignation, or disqualification, give notice thereof to the Commissioners, and proceed to make a new appointment to the office so vacant in the manner prescribed by the above regulations (*c*).

Art. 196.—If any officer give notice of an intended resignation to take effect on a future day, the Guardians may elect a successor to such officer, in conformity with the above regulations, at any time subsequent to such notice.

Art. 197.—In the case of any Medical Officer who holds his office for a specified term, the Guardians may provide for the continuance of such officer, or appoint his successor, within the three calendar months next before the expiration of such term (*d*).

Personal Discharge of Duties.

Art. 198.—In every case not otherwise provided for by this Order, every officer shall perform his duties in person, and shall not intrust the same to a deputy, except with the

---

may obtain leave of absence from his duties; unless a substitute be appointed to act for him, there will be no one legally responsible for the discharge of his duties during his absence.

As regards the substitute of a Medical Officer, see Art. 200, *post*.

(*b*) See the preceding note as to the absence of the Clerk from the meetings of the Board. If a Guardian be appointed a paid substitute for an officer under this Article, he will be a paid officer engaged in the administration of the Poor Laws within the meaning of 5 & 6 Vict. c. 57, s. 14, and as such, will be incapable of acting as a Guardian.

(*c*) Respecting the mode of appointment, see Articles 155, 156.

(*d*) Further provision as to the tenure of a Medical Officer's office is made by the General Order of the Poor Law Board, dated 25th May, 1857 (*post*).

special permission of the Commissioners on the application of the Guardians (a).

Art. 199.—Every Medical Officer shall be bound to visit and attend personally, as far as may be practicable, the poor persons intrusted to his care, and shall be responsible for the attendance on them (b).

Art. 200.—Every Medical Officer shall, as soon as may be after his appointment, name to the Guardians some legally qualified medical practitioner to whom application for medicines or attendance may be made, in the case of his absence from home, or other hindrance to his personal attendance, and who will supply the same at the cost of such Medical Officer, and the name and residence of every medical practitioner so named shall be forwarded by the Clerk to each Relieving Officer, and to the Overseers of every parish in the district of such Medical Officer (c).

(a) As regards the Clerk, see note to Art. 193; and as regards the Medical Officer, see Art. 200, and note.

(b) The Medical Officer cannot expressly delegate to his assistant in his general practice the duties of his office, however well qualified, legally or otherwise, such assistant may be. Though an assistant may visit a patient or aid his principal in the performance of his duties, no diminution or subdivision of the duty of personal attendance and personal responsibility on the part of the Medical Officer will be recognized on that account.

(c) It is not necessary that the substitute should possess one of the double qualifications named in Art. 168; and if any Medical Officer has a partner or assistant who is a duly qualified medical man, he may name such partner or assistant as his substitute under this Article, or indeed any Medical Officer of the Union may be appointed the substitute for another Medical Officer under this Article. The substitute of a Medical Officer must, however, be duly registered under "The Medical Act" (21 & 22 Vict. c. 90). The Medical Officer will be considered by the Poor Law Board as responsible for the skill and diligence of the person named by him as his substitute. Though the appointment is not by this Article made subject to the approval of the Guardians, they have the power to object to the appointment of any person of whom they may not approve; and it is certainly expedient that the provision which the Medical Officer may make for the discharge of his duties in his unavoidable absence from home or other hindrance, should be such as to secure the confidence of the Guardians. The Medical Officer can at any time rescind his nomination of a substitute, and name some other medical practitioner in his stead. A Guardian of the Union may be the appointed substitute of a Medical Officer. (56 O. C. (N. s.) 80.) As

DUTIES OF THE OFFICERS.

Art. 201 (*d*).—And we do hereby define and specify the duties of the several Officers appointed to or holding their offices under this Order, and direct the execution thereof to be as follows :—

DUTIES OF THE CLERK (*e*).

Art. 202.—The following shall be the duties of the Clerk :—

No. 1.—To attend all meetings of the Board of Guardians, and to keep punctually minutes of the proceedings at every meeting, to enter the said minutes in a book, and to submit the same so entered to the presiding Chairman at the succeeding meeting for his signature (*f*).

---

to a Guardian who is a medical man giving certificates under Article 178, see the note to that Art., page 128.

(*d*) The duties of the officers are defined with so much minuteness in the Articles, that the latter do not appear to require a detailed explanation. The Commissioners, however, remark, that every officer is presumed to know his own duties, and that his ignorance of them cannot be allowed as any excuse for neglect or error. The officers will be bound to learn their duties from the regulations of the Commissioners, a copy of which they can obtain by application to the Guardians; and if they should desire to obtain further information, they can apply to the Guardians or the Poor Law Board, who will always be ready to afford it. The Commissioners also caution the officers against supposing that they will be held responsible only for *intentional* breaches of duty, and that mere negligence will be considered as a venial offence. The officers are bound to perform the duties prescribed by the regulations, and a culpable omission to perform those duties is equally mischievous with intentional breaches of the regulations, and will be visited with equally severe punishment.—*Instr. Letter.*

(*e*) Other duties than are here described will have to be discharged by the Clerk, under the Assessment Committee Acts (25 & 26 Vict. c. 103; 27 & 28 Vict. c. 39), for which reference must be made to the several provisions of those Acts.

By the 5 & 6 Vict. c. 109, s. 6, the Clerk to a Board of Guardians is exempt from serving the office of Parish Constable.

(*f*) The Clerk cannot delegate his duty of attending the meetings of the Board of Guardians to another person; but if his absence should be sanctioned by the Guardians on any occasion, they can, if they think fit, accept the services of a substitute, or the Chairman or some other Guardian may act as Clerk during the absence of that officer.

With respect to the minutes of the Guardians, it may be remarked, that they are intended to be a true record of the proceedings of the Board, and the confirmation or affirmation of them by the succeeding Board will merely authenticate the accuracy of the record, without affecting the acts of the previous meeting, which in general require no subsequent confirmation or affirmation. Every discussion of any subject at a meeting of the Board, followed by a resolution, whether such resolution be for adopting, rejecting, or postponing the consideration of the matter submitted to the Board, should be placed on record in the minutes of the day, and also every complaint made by a pauper against any officer of the Union, together with the decision of the Guardians upon it, and notes of the evidence of the witnesses who may have been examined. And generally every occurrence, whether an *ex parte* statement or otherwise, and whether finally disposed of or not, should be placed on the minutes of the meeting at which it came under the notice of the Guardians. Mere discussions, opinions expressed, and remarks made by individual Guardians on any matter, ought to be excluded from the minutes; so also unseconded motions, which are not to be entered as a matter of right (2 Off. Cir. 178), but nevertheless may, if the Guardians so direct. A motion duly made and seconded ought to be entered in the minutes if the Guardians divide upon it, whatever the result of the division may be. If, however, the motion, after being seconded, be withdrawn without a division upon it, it ought not to appear on the minutes. The minutes are the official record of the proceedings of the Board of Guardians; and as the protest of an individual Guardian against any resolution of the Board does not form a part of such proceedings, the Guardian protesting cannot require his protest or the reasons of his dissent to be entered on the minutes. But even if his protest were so entered, it would have no legal effect, so as to control any resolution which a majority of the Guardians may have passed. The reading of a letter by an individual Guardian is not such a proceeding of the Board of Guardians as to warrant its insertion on the minutes, unless by a special vote the Board of Guardians should direct it to be so entered.

Rough minutes of the proceedings of the Guardians should not be made on loose sheets of paper; but where it is the practice to make rough minutes, a book should be used for the purpose, and a fair copy be made in the fair minute-book before the next meeting, in order that the minutes may be read over from such book and be signed by the Chairman at the commencement of the proceedings of the next meeting, agreeably to Article 41. See page 28.

As regards the minute-book of the Assessment Committee, required to be kept under 25 & 26 Vict. c. 103, s. 11, it should be borne in mind that the object of the Legislature was to secure a full and complete account of the proceedings of the Committee, so that any ratepayer might ascertain by an inspection and perusal of the minute-book, what steps had been taken by the Committee in matters which might come before them in which the ratepayer is interested. Every case of objection to a valuation list, and the decision upon it, should therefore be entered in the minutes of the Committee, as well as the receipt of every letter addressed to the Committee, and the answer to it. The letters addressed

Art. 102.—No. 2. To keep, check, and examine all accounts, books of accounts, minutes, books, and other documents as required of him by the Regulations of the Commissioners, or relating to the business of the Guardians, and from time to time to produce all such books and documents, together with the necessary vouchers, and the bonds of any officers, with any certificates relating thereto, which may be in his custody, to the Auditor of the Union, at the place of audit, and at the time and in such manner as may be required, by the Regulations of the Commissioners (a).

to the Committee need not be copied on the minutes verbatim, and the letters of the Committee may be copied into a special letter-book.

With regard to the presence of the Clerk at the meetings of the Guardians, see 9 O. C. 23. If there should be any special reason for requiring the Clerk to retire whilst the Guardians are deliberating upon any business before them, there is nothing to prevent the Guardians from requiring him to retire. In such a case, however, the Guardians cannot require the Clerk to record on their minutes anything that has been done by the Guardians during his absence, and not within his own knowledge. As a rule, however, the Clerk, as a responsible officer, should always be present at the meetings of the Guardians, in order that he may enter upon the minutes a faithful record of the proceedings of the Guardians. No individual Guardian possesses by virtue of his office any right to take copies or make extracts from the minutes; but the Board can authorize any individual Guardian to make a copy or extract from any document in their custody; neither can a Guardian claim as of right to search or inspect the minute-book of the Guardians. The usual practice is to allow copies or extracts to be taken by individual Guardians without express authority. If an individual Guardian cannot, as of right, demand a copy or extract from the minutes, still less can any ratepayer in the Union who is not a Guardian.

(a) With respect to the books of account alluded to in this section, see the General Order of Accounts of 14th January, 1867, *post*, and with respect to the production of officers' bonds, see Arts. 86 & 87 of this Order. See also Art. 203, No. 5, in respect to the duty of the Treasurer to produce any bonds which may be in his possession to the Auditor for his inspection. The inspection contemplated by Art. 25 of the Order of Accounts may be general in its character, but it should be such an inspection as will enable the Clerk not only to ascertain that the books are all kept and in the proper form, but also to detect any errors which may appear on the face of the book or account inspected. The arithmetical examination of the Master's books is not a duty, the performance of which is required from the Clerk; it is incumbent upon the Auditor to make such examination. (7 O. C. 220.)

With respect to the Clerk's attendance at the audit of the accounts,

Art. 202.—No 3. To peruse and conduct the correspondence of the Guardians according to their directions, and to preserve the same, as well as all Orders of the Commissioners, and letters received, together with copies of all letters sent, and all letters, books, papers, and documents belonging to the Union, or intrusted to him by the Guardians, and to make all necessary copies thereof (*a*).

it may be observed here that he is not bound to attend the audit of the Parish Officer's accounts, unless he be specially summoned by the Auditor. It may also be observed in this place, that the Guardians cannot retain possession of any parish books or documents contrary to the wish of the Parish, as the 58 Geo. III. c. 69, s. 6, directs that all such books, accounts, and documents shall be kept by such person and persons, and deposited in such place and manner as the inhabitants in vestry assembled shall direct. But where there is a Vestry Clerk appointed under the 13 & 14 Vict. c. 57, it is the duty of that officer to keep the parish books, deeds, and documents. See that Act, which is included in Glen's 'Small Tenements Rating Act,' 4th edition. With respect to the supply of the books of account for the Officers of the Union, it may be stated that the Guardians are only to provide the books required by the Officers of the Union. The Parish Officers must provide the books required for the parish accounts. See Art. 56 of the General Order for Accounts, of 14th January, 1867, *post*.

The Commissioners of Inland Revenue consider that the Clerk to the Guardians is the " proper officer " to make a return of the salaries of the paid Officers of the Union for the purpose of the Income Tax assessment, under 5 & 6 Vict. c. 35, s. 154.

(*a*) The Clerk is not required to wait for the special direction of the Board of Guardians to answer official letters involving the transactions of mere routine business, but if the reply he may have to give depend upon any decision to which the Guardians may come on the matter to which the letter relates being submitted to them, in that case he should take the special directions of the Board of Guardians before answering the letter. In any case he should be prepared to submit to the Guardians at each ordinary meeting all letters he may have received since their last meeting, and copies of the answers he may have given to them. Every letter written by the Clerk on any matter connected with his office, however unimportant the subject of it may be, should be copied into the letter-book of the Guardians in a legible hand. The following directions should be implicitly attended to in conducting official correspondence with the Poor Law Board, not only on the part of the Clerk, but on the part of all other persons. A departure from any of them not only causes great inconvenience in the transaction of the business of the Board, but prevents a prompt reply being given to the particular communication in respect of the transmission of which the directions have not been observed :—1. No document, except returns signed by the Clerk, should be transmitted to the Board, unaccompanied by a letter authenticating it. 2. Every distinct subject of communication, whether relating to the Union or to any separate parish in it, should form a distinct letter on a separate sheet of foolscap paper. 3. Where previous communications have taken place on the same subject, the official number and date of the last communication should be quoted. 4. The name of the Union and day of meeting of the Guardians, and, where the meetings are held otherwise than weekly, the date of the meeting next following the communication, should be placed at the head of all communications from the Guardians to the Poor Law Board. 5. All communications and packages from the country which are directed to the office of the Poor Law Board, as far as the arrangements of the Post Office will permit, should be transmitted through the post, and be directed under cover, "To the Poor Law Board, Whitehall, London."

When a Board of Guardians or Clerk of one Union wishes to communicate with a Relieving Officer of another Union, or where a Relieving Officer of one Union wishes to communicate with a Board of Guardians or with the Clerk of another Union, the letter should pass through the Clerks of both Unions.

The Clerk, having the legal custody of the accounts and books of the Union, if he be served with a subpœna *duces tecum* as a witness on any matter relating to the settlement of a pauper, or other business affecting the Union, must attend and produce all books, documents, and papers in his possession which may be required of him. (See *Reg.* v. *Greenaway* and *Reg.* v. *Carey*, 14 Law J. Rep. (N. S.), M. C. 190). These cases, however, referred to the Overseer of a parish; the Court held that an attachment would lie against an Overseer, and also against the Solicitor of the Parish, for refusing to produce the rate-books of such parish at Petty Sessions, in obedience to a Crown Office subpœna, in an inquiry touching the settlement of a pauper. But the Clerk will not be justified in allowing any strangers to inspect the books of the Union, or to make extracts from them, without the authority of the Board of Guardians. It is no part of the duty of the Clerk, or of any other Officer of the Union, to attend, when called upon by the Officers of any parish in the Union, before the magistrates in Petty Sessions as witnesses in any matter which has reference solely to the business of the particular parish, and not to their duties as Officers of the Union. If they receive a subpœna they will, of course, be bound to attend, as in the case of any other person who is not an Officer of the Union; but ordinarily the Relieving Officers should attend without putting the Parish Officers to the expense and trouble of a subpœna, if they can do so without materially interfering with the discharge of their duties. But it seems that, as a Relieving Officer is required to devote his whole time to the duties of his office (see Art. 164), he cannot claim to be paid for his attendance before the Justices on any parish matter. He can, however, claim his reasonable expenses; further on this point, see 39 O. C. (N. S.) 112.

All Union books which are closed should be in such custody as the Guardians direct under Art. 58 of the Accounts Order, of 14th January, 1867, *post.* It may also be here stated that no person, whether he

Art. 202.—No. 4. To prepare all written contracts and agreements to be entered into by any parties with the Guardians, and to see that the same are duly executed, and to prepare all bonds or other securities to be given by any of the officers of the Union, and to see that the same are duly executed by such officers and their sureties (*a*).

No. 5. To receive all requisitions of Guardians for extraordinary meetings, and to summon such meetings accordingly; and to make, sign, and send all notices required to be given to the Guardians, by this or any other order of the Commissioners (*b*).

No. 6. To countersign all orders legally made by the Guardians on Overseers for the payment of money, and all orders legally drawn by the Guardians upon the Treasurer (*c*).

---

be a Guardian or an Officer of the Union has an absolute right to inspect any document belonging to the Union in the custody of the Clerk; and that the proper course is to apply to the Guardians to grant permission, which should be expressed by a resolution entered on the minutes.

(*a*) In most cases the Clerk will merely have to fill up the blanks, in the printed forms of contracts and bonds, which may be procured from the publishers of such documents. The Clerk is not bound to leave his residence to witness the execution of bonds and contracts. When the parties to them, whether principals or sureties, do not attend the Board of Guardians for the purpose, some special directions should be given by the Clerk or by the Guardians respecting the execution, and information should be supplied as to the addresses of the attesting witnesses. If, owing to the sureties residing at a distance, it be necessary to incur any expense in obtaining their signatures, it would seem that the officer, and not the Guardians, must be at the expense; but it is different if the expense be incurred merely in satisfying the Guardians of the sufficiency of the surety. If it be necessary to incur any such expenses, they must be borne by the Guardians, and not by the officer, unless there be a previous stipulation to the contrary. The Clerk is to prepare only such bonds and securities as are given by the Officers of the Union; therefore it is not his duty to prepare bonds of Assistant-Overseers appointed under 59 Geo. III. c. 12, s. 7, given under 7 & 8 Vict. c. 101, s. 61, unless indeed such bonds can be considered as "written contracts," within the meaning of the first part of this regulation, and the Clerk is required by the Guardians to prepare them; but see note to Art. 87, *ante*, p. 58.

(*b*) See Arts. 34 and 35.

(*c*) See Arts. 82–84. If a cheque or order be drawn for an illegal

Art. 202.—No. 7. To ascertain, before every ordinary meeting of the Board, the balance due to or from the Union, in account with the Treasurer, and to enter the same in the minute-book (*d*).

No. 8. At the first meeting of the Guardians in each quarter, to lay before the Guardians, or some committee appointed by them, the non-settled poor account, and the non-resident poor account, posted in his ledger to the end of the preceding quarter; and to take the directions of the Guardians respecting the remittance of cheques or post-office orders to the Guardians of any other Union or Parish, or the transmission of accounts due from other Unions or Parishes, and requests for payment.

No. 9. Within fourteen days from the close of each quarter, to transmit by post all accounts of relief administered in the course of the preceding quarter to non-settled poor to the Guardians of the Unions and Parishes on account of which such relief was given; and to state in every account so transmitted the names and classes of the several paupers to whom the relief in question has been administered (*e*).

---

purpose (*i.e.* for a purpose for which the poor-rates are not legally applicable), the Clerk, although the cheque or order may be signed by the Chairman and two other Guardians, and he may be directed by the Board of Guardians to affix his signature, is not bound to do so. It should be remembered that Guardians who sign an order, drawn to defray expenditure which is illegal, will be personally liable for the amount of the order upon the Auditor's surcharge. The counter-signature of the Clerk should be written on the order after the signature by the Guardians. By countersigning the order, the Clerk attests the correctness of the document. (54 O. C. (N. S.) 43) The orders of the Guardians upon the Treasurer for payment of money, ought not to be countersigned by any other than the Clerk; if they be not properly countersigned by him, the Treasurer will not be bound to pay them.

(*d*) This information will be ascertained from the Treasurer's book. See Art. 18 of the Order for Accounts, *post*.

(*e*) See Arts. 77-80, which relate to the relief of non-settled and non-resident poor. It is of great importance that the above regulations (8 and 9) should be attended to; for (*The Guardians of the Wycombe Union v. The Guardians of the Eton Union*, 1 Hurl. & Norm. 687,

L

Art. 202.—No. 10. To communicate to the several officers and persons engaged in the administration of relief within the Union all orders and directions of the Commissioners, or of the Guardians, and, so far as may be, to give the instructions requisite for the prompt and correct execution of all such orders and directions, and to report to the Guardians any neglect or failure therein which may come to his knowledge (*a*).

No. 11. (*This Article is rescinded by order of the Poor Law Board of* 20*th February*, 1866, *post.*)

No. 12. To prepare and transmit all reports, answers, or returns as to any question, or matter connected with or relating to the administration of the laws for the relief of the poor in the Union, or to any other business of the Union, which are required by the regulations of the Commissioners, or which the Commissioners or any Assistant-Commissioner may lawfully require from him (*b*).

No. 13. To conduct duly and impartially, and in strict

---

26 L. J., (N. S.) M. C. 97) it must be taken that where Boards of Guardians do not send quarterly the account of relief granted to non-settled paupers, the account cannot be recovered in a court of law from the Union wherein the paupers are settled. On this point see *ante*, p. 54.

(*a*) This rule renders it the duty of the Clerk to convey to the Overseers the contribution orders of the Guardians, and any unavoidable expenses which he may incur in personally serving the orders should be defrayed out of the common fund; but there is no objection to the Relieving Officers delivering such orders if they are willing to do so, and if the delivery of them does not interfere with their ordinary duties. But now see Art. 4. No. 2, of the General Order of the Poor Law Board, dated 7th October, 1865, *post*.

(*b*) The Clerk by this rule is bound to answer all inquiries made of him by the Poor Law Board relating to the business of the Union. With respect to the weekly returns of the pauperism of the Union with which he is required to furnish the Poor Law Board and the Poor Law Inspector of the district, see the Circular Letters of the Poor Law Board, dated respectively 10th November, 1855, and 15th March, 1856. See also the 16 & 17 Vict. c. 97, s. 64, as to the duty of the Clerk to make the annual return of lunatics chargeable on 1st January. Those insane persons only who are actually chargeable on the 1st January should be included in the return. The time limited by the statute (1st February) for sending in the return should not be exceeded.

conformity with the regulations in force at the time, the annual or any other Election of Guardians (*c*).

No. 14. To observe and execute all lawful orders and directions of the Guardians applicable to his office (*d*).

Duties of the Treasurer of the Union.

Art. 203.—The following shall be the duties of the Treasurer of the Union:—

No. 1. To receive all moneys tendered to be paid to the Guardians, and to place the same to their credit (*e*).

(*c*) As to the election of Guardians, see Articles 1–27, and the Orders of the 14th January, 1867, and 21st February, 1868, *post*.

(*d*) The regulations do not make it the duty of the Clerk to attend committees of the Guardians, and to take minutes of their proceedings; but Art. 202, No. 14, prescribes that the Clerk shall observe and execute all lawful orders and directions of the Guardians applicable to his office. The Guardians may, if they think fit, direct the Clerk to attend a committee of their number legally appointed, and take minutes of their proceedings. The Clerk, under this rule, will be bound to prepare statistical returns and calculations on any matter relating to the relief of the poor of his Union, when ordered so to do by the Board of Guardians; but he is not bound to obey any order or directions which the Guardians cannot legally give. The office of the Clerk does not of itself confer upon him any power to interfere with the management or discipline of the Workhouse, or to admit paupers to see persons maintained in the house; but as the officer or agent of the Guardians, he may interfere to see that their orders as regards the management of the house are carried out, if authorized by the Guardians to do so. The Clerk cannot order, of his own authority, relief to be given to a destitute person; it has, however, been held that the Clerk is an officer having authority (*i. e.* when acting under the directions of the Guardians in the particular matter) to order the giving of relief, so as to establish a settlement by admission in a Township within the Union. (*Reg.* v. *Wigan*, 19 L. J. R. (N.S.) M. C. 18.)

The Clerk is the confidential officer of the Guardians, representing them in regard to the general business of the Union in the intervals of their meetings, and as such it is his duty to bring under their notice any neglect of duty on the part of any officer which may come within his knowledge.

(*e*) If the full amount of a contribution order, or the full amount of an instalment thereof, be not tendered to him, the Treasurer, under ordinary circumstances, should not refuse to receive the money. As a general rule, however, he should require the calls to be paid in full, according to the exigency of the contribution orders of the Guardians. In such a case he should give a receipt for a payment on account, and place the amount of it to the credit of the Union. If cheques on bankers

Art. 203.—No. 2 (*a*). To pay out of any moneys for the time being in his hands belonging to the Guardians, all orders for money which shall be drawn upon him, in conformity with Art. 84, when the same shall be presented at the house or usual place of business of the Treasurer, and within the usual hours of business.

No. 3. To keep an account, under the proper dates, of all moneys received and paid by him as such Treasurer, to balance the same at Lady Day and Michaelmas in every year, and to render an account of such moneys to the Guardians when required by them to do so (*b*).

No. 4. Whenever there are not funds belonging to the Guardians in his hands as Treasurer of the Union, to report in writing the fact of such deficiency to the Commissioners (*c*).

No. 5.—To submit a proper account, together with the

---

be tendered by Overseers to the Treasurer instead of "money" (cash), he will not be bound to accept such cheques in payment of a contribution order; but if he do so, it will be at his own risk; and he may properly refuse to sign a receipt for the payment until the cheques are cashed.

As regards moneys tendered to him by the Collector of the Guardians, see Art. 4 No. 6 of the General Order of the Poor Law Board, dated 7th October, 1865, *post*.

The Treasurer is also to receive any money certified by the District Auditor to be due under 7 & 8 Vict. c. 101, s. 32, which enacts that "the person from whom any money is so certified to be due shall, within seven days, pay or cause to be paid such money to the Treasurer of the Guardians of the Union or Parish, if there be any such Treasurer."

(*a*) As to the form in which these orders are to be drawn, see the General Order of 7th April, 1857 (*post*). That order restrains the Treasurer from paying any order of the Guardians not drawn in conformity therewith.

(*b*) With regard to this regulation see Art. 18 of the General Order for Accounts of 14th January, 1867, *post*.

(*c*) The Poor Law Board find that this regulation has been frequently overlooked by Treasurers, and in some instances they have been informed that it had not been brought to the notice of those officers. The Board attach much importance to the regulation, and trust that it may be carefully attended to in future.—*Letter of Poor Law Board to Union Treasurers*, 7th April, 1857.

bonds of any officers which may be in his custody, to the Auditor at the place of audit, and at the time and in such manner as may be required by the regulations of the Commissioners (*d*).

No. 6. To receive the moneys payable to him as Treasurer of the Union, under any Act of Parliament or other authority of law (*e*).

Art. 204.—Provided that the regulations in Art. 203 shall

(*d*) See Art. 87, as to the production of Officers' bonds to the Auditor. The 4 & 5 Wm. IV. c. 76, s. 47, requires the Treasurer to submit to the Auditor a full and distinct account of all moneys received, held, or expended by him on account of the Union. This account may be the Treasurer's Book, if the entries are made in such a manner as to show with preciseness for whom and to whom the Treasurer received and paid the money of the Guardians. Further, with regard to the audit of the Treasurer's account, see Art. 18 of the Order for accounts of 14th January, 1867, *post*.

(*e*) The Treasurer ought not to allow his account with the Guardians to be overdrawn; and if he advances money to them, he does so at his own risk, as the Guardians cannot legally borrow money for their current expenses upon the security of the rates, or pay interest upon money so borrowed. (See note to Articles 1 & 2 of Order of 26th February, 1866, *post*.) The regulation in No. 4 is introduced for the purpose of enabling the Commissioners to warn the Guardians of their duty, in case they should have failed to obtain the requisite supplies of money from the Overseers. It is also desirable when the funds in the Treasurer's hands are low, that he should communicate the fact to the Guardians.—*Instr. Letter*. When any Parish of a Union has an account with the Treasurer, independent of the Union account, the Treasurer ought not to transfer money from the former to the latter without an order of the Overseers.—*Ib*. Money in the Treasurer's hands, arising from the sale of Parish property, ought not to be appropriated without an order under the seal of the Poor Law Board. See 5 & 6 Wm. IV. c. 69, s. 3.—*Ib*. The orders issued by the Board for the sale of Parish property expressly require the proceeds of the sale to be paid to the Treasurer to abide the further order of the Board. The Poor Law Board having had occasion to communicate with the Commissioners of Inland Revenue, on the subject of the Liability to Stamp Duty of Receipts given by the Treasurers of Boards of Guardians, on the payment to them by Overseers of contributions ordered by the Guardians, the Board have been informed, that it is the opinion of the Commissioners that such Receipts are exempt from Stamp Duty by virtue of the provisions of the 4 & 5 Wm. IV. c. 76, s. 86, the Treasurer being an Officer appointed in pursuance of that Act, and the contributions paid to him by the Overseers being likewise made in pursuance of the same statute. —*Instr. Letter*, 24th March, 1854. On this point, see also the notes to Art. 84, *ante*, p. 56.

not be applicable to cases in which the Governor and Company of the Bank of England may act as Treasurer of the Union or Bankers to the Guardians (*a*).

DUTIES OF A MEDICAL OFFICER.

Art. 205.—The following shall be the duties of every Medical Officer appointed by the Guardians, whether he be the Medical Officer for a Workhouse or for a District:—

No. 1. To give to the Guardians, when required, any reasonable information respecting the case of any pauper who is or has been under his care; to make any such written report relative to any sickness prevalent among the paupers under his care, as the Guardians or the Commissioners may require of him; and to attend any meeting of the Board of Guardians when requested by them to do so.(*b*).

No. 2. To give a certificate respecting children whom it is proposed to apprentice, in conformity with Articles 59 and 61.

No. 3. To give a certificate under his hand in every case to the Guardians, or the Relieving Officer, or the pau-

---

(*a*) This article is omitted in the Orders issued subsequent to the present Order, when it is inapplicable to the particular Union.

(*b*) Concerning information to be given by the Medical Officer to the Relieving Officer, see Art. 215, No. 4. The Guardians, when they require the attendance of a Medical Officer at any meeting, must make a special request for his attendance, as a general notice to attend all the meetings of the Guardians will not come within this regulation.

The following may here be noted:—A., the Clerk to a Board of Guardians of a Union of which B. was Medical Officer, and C. Relieving Officer. A pauper was to be removed to another district, and had previously to be examined by B. A., in pursuance of directions from the Board of Guardians, called twice on B. for the purpose of getting him to see the pauper, but could not get him to do so. A. then went to C., and asked him to try and get B. to examine the pauper, telling C. at the same time that when he, A., saw B. on the preceding evening, B. " was not sober," whereupon C. served B. with a final order to examine the pauper, and B. did so. In an action by B. against A. for slander, it was held that the communication between A. and C. was privileged, and that B. must be non-suited. (*Sutton* v. *Plumridge*, 16 L. T. (N. S.) 741.)

per on whom he is attending, of the sickness of such pauper or other cause of his attendance, when required to do so (c).

Art. 205.—No. 4. In keeping the books prescribed by this Order, to employ, so far as is practicable, the terms used or recommended in the regulations and statistical nosology issued by the Registrar-General; and also to show when the visit or attendance made or given to

---

(c) That is, when required to give such certificate by the Guardians of the Union of which he is an officer. It is optional with him to give the certificate to Boards of Guardians or Relieving Officers of other Unions. The certificate need not be in any particular form. It will suffice if it be in the form in which ordinary medical certificates are usually given. This Article will include a certificate as to a lunatic pauper discharged from a lunatic asylum upon trial, under 16 & 17 Vict. c. 97, s. 79, if the Guardians or Relieving Officer require the Medical Officer to give a certificate in such a case; but the case would be different if he be summoned to attend a Justice when he makes an Order for the removal of a lunatic to an asylum under that Act. Apparently, the regulation will include a certificate of illness in the case of a member of a benefit club, where the Medical Officer may attend in sickness on a pauper, if such a certificate be required of him by the Guardians, or the Relieving Officer, or the pauper. It forms no part of the official duty of a Medical Officer to attend the Justices to prove that the sickness or disability of a pauper is likely to produce permanent disability, so as to render such pauper removable to the parish of his settlement under the 9 & 10 Vict. c. 66, s. 4. He must be summoned or subpœnaed to attend before the Justices the same as any other witness whose evidence is necessary, and he will be entitled to be recompensed accordingly for his attendance.

It is enacted by the Friendly Societies Amendment Act, 21 & 22 Vict. c. 101, s. 2, that in any society in which a sum of money may be insured, payable on the death of a child under the age of ten years, for the funeral expenses of such child, the sum so insured cannot lawfully be paid, unless the person who shall apply for payment produces a certificate, signed by a qualified Medical Practitioner, stating the probable cause of death of such child. If the child shall have been attended immediately before its death by the Medical Officer of any Union on account of such Union, he shall deliver to the parents or friends of the deceased child, upon their application, a certificate stating the probable cause of death of the child, and shall not be entitled to receive any fee for the same; and if such child shall not have been attended by such Medical Officer, nor by any qualified Medical Practitioner, the Medical Officer of the Union or Parish in which such child shall have been resident shall deliver to the parents or friends of the deceased child, upon their application, a certificate stating the probable cause of death of the child, and shall be entitled to receive from the parties applying for the same a fee of one shilling.

any pauper was made or given by any person employed by himself (*a*).

Duties of a District Medical Officer.

Art. 206.—The following shall be the duties of a District Medical Officer:—

No. 1. To attend duly and punctually upon all poor persons requiring medical attendance within the District of the Union assigned to him, and, according to his agreement, to supply the requisite medicines (*b*) to such persons, whenever he may be lawfully required to furnish such attendance or medicines by a written or printed Order of the Guardians, or of a Relieving Officer of the Union, or of an Overseer (*c*).

(*a*) See the statistical nosology of the Registrar-General of Births, Deaths and Marriages.

(*b*) Questions have arisen as to the propriety of using methylated spirit in the preparation of medical tinctures and extracts supplied by Medical Officers to their pauper patients, instead of pure spirit; it may therefore be useful to state that the Royal College of Physicians by a minute dated the 25th November, 1857, have publicly expressed their disapproval of the practice. The permission of the Inland Revenue Commissioners to use methylated spirit, it is stated by those Commissioners, in a circular letter dated February, 1858, does not countenance the use of such spirits in any manner not countenanced by the Colleges of Physicians of London, Edinburgh, or Dublin. As to the definition of the word "medicines" see Art. 227, *post*.

(*c*) The Medical Officer is bound, if a domiciliary visit be necessary, to visit his patients at their own homes; and if serious inconvenience is likely to be caused to any pauper by coming to the Medical Officer, the visits should be so made. It does not follow, however, that the Medical Officer is to visit every sick pauper, when the pauper can himself, without injury or danger to his health, attend at the Medical Officer's surgery; but if the Medical Officer refuses or neglects to visit, he must be prepared to show that he was justified in the particular case.

In cases of midwifery the Medical Officer is not permitted to employ a midwife as his substitute. If a midwife be employed, she must be employed by and paid by the Guardians, and not by the Medical Officer. In cases of childbirth, the practice of employing only female midwives in place of the Medical Officer, is one which, if adopted by the Guardians, should be exercised with due caution; and the Guardians should direct their officers in all cases of difficulty or danger at once to authorize the attendance of the Medical Officer. (57 O. C. (N.S.) 88). Further with regard to Midwifery Orders, the Board say (54 O. C. (N. S.(44), that " Medical assistance only forms a part of relief to the destitute poor, and that the same rules and principles apply to it as those which are applicable to any other kind of relief. Neither the Guardians of the Union nor the Relieving Officer are bound to relieve; nor, indeed, are they justified in relieving any person whose circumstances they have ascertained to be such as not to require relief. In cases in which there is good reason to believe that the applicant is able to pay for medical assistance himself, the Board usually recommend the Guardians, as the midwifery fee allowed to Medical Officers is an extra one, to cause it to be understood that relief of the nature in question will be granted by way of loan; and that the repayment of the whole, or of such part of the fee as the Guardians might determine, would be rigidly enforced by them; and to direct the Relieving Officer to notify the fact to every one who may apply to him for an order. The Board of Guardians may certainly notify that they require to have a fortnight or three weeks' previous notice of the intended application for the medical order; but if it have been omitted, and any case of sudden or urgent necessity arise, and aid is required by a person in a state of destitution, the Relieving Officer will not be justified in refusing to supply the requisite relief."

It is immaterial whether the poor person is in the receipt of other relief when a medical order is given; the fact of the person applying for such order and its being granted constitutes him *de facto* a pauper, and the Medical Officer is bound to attend. If he thinks that he is able to procure medical aid in his illness from his own resources, he should, nevertheless, continue his attendance till the next meeting of the Guardians, to whom he should report the circumstance, and take their further directions upon the case. The obligation upon those who have the administration of relief to supply necessary medical assistance to a person labouring under dangerous illness, though such person may not have received or have stood in need of relief previous to his illness, is established by the decision in *R.* v. *Warren*, Russ. & R. Crown Cases, 48. It may also be observed, that a Medical Officer is bound to attend members of sick clubs, if he receives a regular order from a Relieving Officer or Overseer, or from the Board of Guardians, and that the Guardians, and not the Medical Officer, are the persons who have to decide whether a person is in such destitute circumstances as to entitle him to medical aid at the cost of the poor-rates.

It not unfrequently happens that servants hired for a term fall sick whilst in service and apply for medical aid or other necessaries at the cost of poor-rates. In reference to such cases it may be observed, that as in the absence of any special agreement the master is not legally bound to provide his servant with medical or surgical aid in sickness, the case must be treated as one of ordinary destitution, and such relief, medical or otherwise, as may be necessary, supplied by the Guardians or their officers, as the case may require. (See O. C. No. 20, pp. 297, 298.) The Guardians can advance no claim on the master in respect of the giving of such relief to his servant; but they might give the relief by way of loan, and then, under the 4 & 5 Wm. IV. c. 76, s. 59, attach in the hands of the master any wages which may be due or which may be subsequently earned, and so repay the cost of the relief. *Sellen*

v. *Norman*, 4 Car. & P. 80; *Rex* v. *Saunders*, 7 Car. & P. 277; *Reg.* v. *Smith*, 8 Car. & P. 153, show that a master is not by the general law bound to provide medical advice for his servant; but that the case is different with respect to an apprentice, and a master is bound, during the illness of his apprentice, to provide him with proper medicines.

If by the terms of the Medical Officer's appointment he is required to supply medicines to the sick poor, it is his duty to supply the medicines which he prescribes, in such a state that they admit of being conveyed to his pauper patients. If the medicine is fluid, he must supply a bottle or some other vessel; if solid, a box, etc. He may, however, require the paupers to preserve them, and return them when done with. Medical Officers are not bound by any regulation in this Order to forward, or cause to be forwarded, to the residences of the sick paupers the medicines which they may prescribe. If the paupers are able to go themselves for the medicines, or if they can send any member of their family or any other person, they may reasonably be expected to do so. In general, the Medical Officers co-operate in forwarding the medicines, so far as the means of sending medicine in their general practice may be available, without incurring additional expense. But if the paupers themselves are unable to go or send for the medicines, and if the Medical Officers cannot forward them without employing special messengers for the purpose, it becomes the duty of the Relieving Officers to provide for the conveyance of the medicine to the paupers, who must in no case be left without the medicine prescribed for them by the Medical Officer.

As regards the supply of expensive medicines to the sick poor see note to Art. 227, *post.*

A Medical Officer is not bound to attend any case without a regular order, but if he be sent for and attends the case without an order, or treats the patients as being under his care, he will be held responsible for any neglect which may occur, and will not be permitted to plead in justification the want of an order.

An Overseer of the Poor is bound to administer relief in cases of "sudden and urgent necessity;" his order to the Medical Officer to attend a case of sickness which is of "sudden and urgent necessity," is therefore of equal force with the order of the Relieving Officer. If the Medical Officer should refuse to attend, upon the order of an Overseer, on the plea that the case is not one of "sudden and urgent necessity," he must be prepared to justify his refusal on that ground; but in general it would be advisable for him to attend the case, and afterwards represent the facts to the Board of Guardians, and take their directions as to his further attendance.

As regards the liability of an Overseer when he gives an order for medical attendance in a case in which he was not justified in doing so, it has been held, upon an action brought in the County Court at Crewkerne (*Wills* v. *Smith*), that the Overseer incurred no personal liability. The following is a copy of the judgment in that case:—
"Mr. Smith was Overseer of North Perrott, and Mr. G. F. Wills was one of the surgeons of the Yeovil Union, acting in the Parish of North Perrott, and the action had been brought to recover six shillings and sixpence for medical charges and attendance on a boy, for whom the defendant, in his official capacity, had ordered relief. The questions

were, whether it was a case of emergency, and whether the boy was a pauper, in which cases the Overseer would be justified in ordering relief. These questions had been gone into at the hearing of the case at the former Court, and the result was, that defendant had ordered the relief believing it to be a case of necessity, and also believing the boy to be a pauper. But although these positions had not been made out, yet it was clear that no fraud was intended, and that the defendant had acted in what he considered to be the strict discharge of his duty. The relief too would have been gratuitous if rendered under the proper orders of the Overseer, and therefore the plaintiff had sustained no loss. No claim therefore, after all that had transpired, should be founded upon the personal liability of the defendant; and taking all the circumstances into consideration, the verdict must be in his favour."

A Medical Officer is not empowered by the Orders of the Poor Law Board to order food or articles of diet, as meat, milk, wine, or porter, for his pauper patients. Any direction that he may give to that effect will only amount to an expression of opinion on his part, that relief in food or other necessaries is required. The power of granting relief rests with the Guardians, and in cases of sudden and urgent necessity with the Relieving Officer, and any certificate given by the Medical Officer for the allowance of extra nourishment to any of his patients can only be regarded as a recommendation or statement of his opinion as to what is required. If the certificate were to be taken in any other sense, it would have the effect of constituting the Medical Officer the absolute judge, not only of the kind of relief to be afforded, but also of the ability of the patient to provide it out of his own resources, which is entirely for the Guardians' consideration, in whom the discretion of giving or withholding relief of every kind is vested by law. The Guardians ought of course to be very guarded in the exercise of their discretion in this respect, and they should caution their officers also to be on their guard if any case should occur in which, acting on a sense of duty, they may deem it right to disregard either wholly or in part the Medical Officer's certificate, for by so doing they would incur responsibility which could only be justified by a knowledge that the circumstances of the individual were really such as to make the particular relief, certified as being necessary by the Medical Officer, improper to be given at the cost of the Union. If in any instance the Relieving Officer should, from his knowledge of the circumstances of the particular case, deem it to be his duty not to carry the directions of the Medical Officer into full effect, he ought with the least possible delay to report the facts to the Board of Guardians, and state to them his reasons for so acting, in order that they may decide whether he has exercised a sound discretion in the matter, and give directions accordingly.

The following are the observations of an eminent medical authority on the due supply of extra nourishment to the sick poor:—

"The well-doing of the sick poor and the interests of all who are concerned in their recovery, depend far more upon an adequate and well-regulated provision for *diet in sickness*, than upon the best and most liberal supply of drugs.

"A dietetic provision for the sick need not be inconsistent with the circumstances and habits of the class and place to which they belong;

Art. 206.—No. 2. On the exhibition to him of a ticket, according to Art. 76, and on application made on behalf of the party to whom such ticket was given, to afford such medical attendance and medicines as he would be bound to supply if he had received in each case an Order from the Guardians to afford such attendance and medicines.

---

but it should be sufficient to restore them to health, to lift them out of the weakness and helplessness which attend a protracted convalescence, and to fit them as speedily as possible for work.

"The miserable want of proper sick-diet in some cases, and the injudicious supply of improper articles by private charity in other cases, while interfering seriously with the object and the success of medical treatment, lead to an immense amount of chronic disease, infirmity, and mendicancy among that numerous class which is always hovering on the confines of pauperism."

If any pauper refuses to adopt the remedies prescribed for his disease, the Medical Officer should report such fact to the Board of Guardians, and continue his attendance on the pauper, or at all events watch the case till he obtains the directions of the Guardians for his future guidance in regard to it.

By the 16 & 17 Vict. c. 97, s. 66, every pauper lunatic not in an asylum, registered hospital, or licensed house, is required to be visited by the Medical Officer of or for the Parish or Union, or District of a Parish or Union, in which such lunatic is resident, who is entitled to a fee of two shillings and sixpence for each visit to a pauper not in a Workhouse. Within seven days after the end of every quarter, the Medical Officer is to prepare and sign a list, in the form prescribed by the Act, of the lunatics he shall have visited, and deliver such list to the Clerk to the Guardians. If at any time during the quarter the lunatic is chargeable to the poor-rates, the Medical Officer is bound to visit and report the case, and is entitled to his fee for so doing. If the lunatic be not so chargeable, no duty is cast upon the Medical Officer, and of course he cannot claim a fee if he visit in such case.

With regard to the calling in of another medical man to attend upon a pauper under the care of the Medical Officer, see the observations of Erle, C. J., in *Haigh* v. *North Bierley*, 5 Jur. (N. S.) 511 ; 28 L. J. (N. S.) Q. B. 65. "Suppose," he said, "the Guardians were dissatisfied with the opinion pronounced by their Medical Officer, might they not call in another medical man ?"

If the relief be given to parents for themselves and for their children, the latter are paupers, whom, according to 16 & 17 Vict. c. 97, s. 66, the Medical Officer is to visit ; but if the relief be given for the parents alone, the children are not paupers, and if lunatics, need not be visited and returned in the list of lunatics.

The Poor Law Board, in a Circular dated 2nd April, 1868, with reference to Arts. 199, 200, *ante*, request the co-operation of the Guardians in discouraging altogether the employment by Medical Officers of unqualified assistants.

Art. 206.—No. 3. To inform the Relieving Officer of any poor person whom he may attend without an order (*a*).

No. 4. To make a return to the Guardians at each ordinary meeting, in a book prepared according to the Form marked (P.) hereunto annexed (*b*), and to insert therein the date of every attendance, and the other particulars required by such Form, in conformity with Art. 205, No. 4.

Provided, however, that the Medical Officer may, with the consent of the Guardians, but not otherwise, make the entries which he is directed to make in such book on detached sheets of paper, according to the same Form, and cause the same to be laid before the Guardians at every ordinary meeting, instead of such book; and the Guardians shall, in that case, cause such sheets to be bound up at the end of the year.

DUTIES OF THE MEDICAL OFFICER FOR THE WORKHOUSE.

Art. 207.—The following shall be the duties of the Medical Officer for the Workhouse:— (*c*)

No. 1. To attend at the Workhouse at the periods fixed by the Guardians, and also when sent for by the Master or Matron.

No. 2 (*d*). To attend duly and punctually upon all poor persons in the Workhouse requiring medical attendance, and according to his agreement to supply the requisite medicines to such persons.

(*a*) See Art. 215, No. 4.

(*b*) See the substituted form in the Order of the Poor Law Board, dated 26th February, 1866, *post*.

(*c*) The Poor Law Board have, by a General Order, dated 4th April, 1868, *post*, prescribed certain additional duties as regards Workhouse Medical Officers.

(*d*) See the Notes on Art. 206, No. 1. See last note on preceding page.

In answer to a question whether the Medical Officer would be justified in using force in order to perform an operation which he considered necessary for the recovery of a diseased pauper inmate of the Workhouse, such pauper refusing to submit to the operation, the Commis-

Art. 207.—No. 3. To examine the state of the paupers on their admission into the Workhouse, and to give the requisite directions to the Master according to Articles 91 and 92.

No. 4. To give directions and make suggestions as to the diet, classification, and treatment of the sick paupers, and paupers of unsound mind, and to report to the Guardians any pauper of unsound mind in the Workhouse whom he may deem to be dangerous, or fit to be sent to a Lunatic Asylum (*a*).

---

sioners have stated that the question appeared to them to turn upon the point whether the pauper was competent to exercise a discretion of his own; and that if any medical practitioner could certify that the pauper was not of sound mind, they thought that the Guardians would be justified in authorizing those means to be used which they were informed could alone save his life. On the other hand, they stated that if the patient was of sound mind, he must be allowed to judge for himself in the matter.

(*a*) As regards the diet of the paupers, see Art. 108, which empowers the Medical Officers of the Workhouse to direct in writing such diet for any individual pauper as he may deem necessary. And as regards the duty of the Medical Officer in the cases of paupers suffering from mental disease or bodily disease of an infectious or contagious character, see 30 & 31 Vict. c. 106, s. 22, *ante*, p. 87.

In regard to a lunatic pauper in a Workhouse, the Commissioners in Lunacy have stated that it appeared to them, that so far as the Medical Officer of the Workhouse is concerned, he must give notice in writing of the lunacy of the pauper, under the 48th sect. of the 8 & 9 Vict. c. 126 (now 16 & 17 Vict. c. 97, s. 67), to the Relieving Officer of the Union in which the Parish to which the pauper may be chargeable is comprised, and that such Relieving Officer must take the requisite proceedings. They consider that no entry by the Medical Officer in his books, nor any notice by him to the Master, would suffice as a substitution for the notice to the Relieving Officer. The notice should be given to the Relieving Officer of the District in which the Workhouse is situate. (See note to Art. 101, p. 77.) With respect to dangerous lunatics in the Workhouse, see note to Art. 101, and 25 & 26 Vict. c. 111, s. 20. Sect. 38 of the 25 & 26 Vict. c. 111, contains the following provisions in reference to the pauper lunatics under confinement:—Two of the Commissioners in Lunacy, as regards any hospital or licensed house, and two of the Committee of Governors of any hospital, and two of the visitors of any licensed house, as regards any licensed house within their jurisdiction, may permit any pauper patient therein to be absent therefrom upon trial, for such period as they may think fit, and may make, or order to be made, an allowance to him not exceeding his charge in such hospital or house which shall be charged for him, and be payable as if he were actually therein, but shall be paid to him or for his benefit, as they may direct. If he do not return at the expiration of the time, and a medical certificate that his detention as a lunatic is no longer necessary, be not sent to the Proprietor or Superintendent, he may at any time within fourteen days after the expiration of the period be retaken. This corresponds with the provision contained in the 16 & 17 Vict. c. 97, s. 79, in regard to pauper lunatics in asylums.

The 16 & 17 Vict. c. 97, s. 67, imposes upon the Relieving Officers the duty of causing lunatics to be removed to asylums; and that is therefore part of their ordinary duties coming within the terms of their appointment. With reference to Unions and Parishes in the Metropolis, the Poor Law Board in a circular letter dated the 26th Nov. 1867, urge upon the consideration of the Guardians the propriety of endeavouring to provide that some Justice, having proper jurisdiction, should attend at the place where the lunatic may be living, whether at his own place of abode or at the Workhouse, to hear and investigate the case, and make the proper order of removal. Should this be found impracticable, the Board say that they do not doubt that the magistrates sitting at police courts will, so far as may be possible, arrange that the examination may be taken in a private room; they add that where a justice cannot be found conveniently to attend, the Clergyman of the parish and the Relieving Officer may be applied to for this purpose, though they consider it undesirable that the latter course should be resorted to, except there be a very strong necessity; and that due care must be taken that the proper medical assistance is rendered in these cases, and that the investigation, while free from the excitement of an open Court, is so conducted as that no doubts may arise as to the order having been issued after full deliberation, and with all necessary regularity. Under sect. 30 of the same statute, the Relieving Officer, on receiving notice from the visitors of any asylum of the discharge of a pauper lunatic therefrom, is to cause such lunatic to be removed to the Workhouse of the Union. If he should incur any expense in conveying to or removing pauper lunatics from an asylum, his proper course is to enter the amount in his Receipt and Payment Book, and submit the charge to the Auditor at the audit, who must determine as to its lawfulness and reasonableness; and this because the duty is cast upon the Relieving Officer by statute, and not by any order or direction of the Guardians.

It is not expedient that the Relieving Officer should himself accompany the lunatic to the asylum when it is at a distance, as by so doing he must leave his relief district, which he ought not to do without special leave from the Guardians.

Sect. 19 of the 25 & 26 Vict. c. 111, directs so much of the statute 16 & 17 Vict. c. 97, s. 67, as requires the Relieving Officer, and Overseer when there is no Relieving Officer, who shall have knowledge that any pauper, resident in a Parish, is or is deemed to be a lunatic, *and a proper person to be sent to an Asylum*, to give notice thereof to a Justice of the Peace, to be construed as if the words in italics had been omitted. Henceforth, therefore, it will suffice for the Relieving Officer, or Overseer (as the case may be), to have knowledge that there is a pauper resident in the Parish who is a lunatic; and it will not be necessary that he should have knowledge that the lunatic is a proper person to be sent to

Art. 207.—No. 5. To give all necessary instructions as to the diet or treatment of children and women suckling children, and to vaccinate such of the children as may require vaccination (a).

No. 6. To report in writing to the Guardians any defect in the diet, drainage, ventilation, warmth, or other arrangements of the Workhouse, or any excess in the number of any class of inmates, which he may deem to be detrimental to the health of the inmates (b).

No. 7. To report in writing to the Guardians any defect which he may observe in the arrangements of the infirmary, and in the performance of their duties by the nurses of the sick (b).

No. 8. To make a return to the Guardians, at each ordinary meeting, in a book prepared according to the Form (Q.) hereunto annexed, and to insert therein the date of every attendance, in conformity with Art. 205,

---

an asylum. The same clause in the statute 16 & 17 Vict. c. 97, requires the Justices to be satisfied that the lunatic is a proper person to be sent to an asylum; and this provision remains unaltered.

It will be the duty of the Medical Officer of the Workhouse, under 25 & 26 Vict. c. 111, s. 21, to make the quarterly returns required by 16 & 17 Vict. c. 97, s. 66, in regard to lunatic paupers in the Workhouse; but no provision is made for payment of a fee in such case. Sect. 21 of 25 & 26 Vict. c. 111, makes an addition to the form for the Quarterly List of lunatic paupers made out by the Medical Officers, by providing for a return of those who may be in the Workhouse, as to whom the Medical Officer is to certify whether the Workhouse is or is not sufficient for the accommodation of the lunatics detained therein, and whether or not the lunatics detained therein are proper persons to be kept in a Workhouse.

(a) Sect. 6 of 30 & 31 Vict. c. 84, now provides for the payment of a fee for vaccination performed in the Workhouse. It not unfrequently arises that the parents of children in a Workhouse will not allow the Medical Officer to vaccinate their children, and in answer to an inquiry as to whether the Guardians had power to cause such children to be vaccinated without the consent of the parents in such a case, the Commissioners have stated that they are of opinion that the Guardians have, without the permission of the parent, the right to vaccinate any child in their custody, during any danger of contagion from the small-pox.

(b) See Art. 1 of the Order of 4th April, 1868, post.

and the other particulars required by such Form to be inserted by the Medical Officer, and to enter in such return the death of every pauper who shall die in the Workhouse, together with the apparent cause thereof (a).

Art. 207.—No. 9 (b). To enter in the commencement of such Book, according to the Form (R.) hereunto annexed, the proper dietary for the sick paupers in the house in so many different scales as he shall deem expedient.

Duties of the Master (c).

Art. 208.—The following shall be the duties of the Master:—

(a) Compliance with the latter part of this rule will not supersede the necessity for giving a certificate of the apparent cause of the death of a pauper to the Registrar of Births and Deaths. It is only required that a statement of the apparent cause of the death should be inserted in the return. In no case do the Commissioners desire a post-mortem examination to take place solely for the purpose of satisfying this Rule. Excepting by the direction of a Coroner when holding an inquest, or of the Board of Guardians for any special urgent and peculiar reason which they may deem of sufficient importance to render such an examination necessary, or at the request of the nearest relatives of the deceased, the Commissioners deem that the Medical Officer would not be justified in making a post-mortem examination. They add, that they think that the Guardians would hardly be justified in directing in any particular case that a post-mortem examination should take place if the nearest relatives of the deceased objected clearly and decisively to that course.

Allowances of tobacco or snuff recommended for paupers should be entered in the proper columns of the Workhouse Medical Relief Book, and the period over which the allowance is to extend, should be specified. When the entry has been once made, it need not be repeated every week.

It has been held that a register of attendances, etc., kept by the Medical Officer of a Poor Law Union, and laid before the Board of Guardians weekly for inspection, in obedience to rules made by the Poor Law Commissioners under 4 & 5 Wm. IV. c. 76, s. 15, is not receivable in evidence for the party making it, as a public official book. (*Merrick* v. *Watley*, 8 A. & E. 170.)

(b) A copy of the Dietary so framed should be hung up in the Infirmaries or Sick Wards of the Workhouse.

(c) The Master of a Workhouse is answerable for the general order of the whole establishment; and minute personal attention on his part can alone detect and remedy defects in the discipline and cleanliness of

Art. 208.—No. 1. To admit paupers into the Workhouse,

the house. At the same time, decency requires that much of the detailed management of the female inmates, and of the children, should devolve on the Matron and her assistants. The close and accurate inspection of sleeping apartments actually occupied by women, and the treatment of the infants and younger children, ought to be performed by a female. If the authority of the Master be required to enforce obedience, he should at once be appealed to; but the Commissioners are desirous that all his duties should be discharged with the strictest regard to propriety. The habits of many of the inmates of a Workhouse will often be coarse and depraved, but the conduct of every officer of such an establishment should correspond with what those habits ought to be, rather than with what they actually are.—*Instr. Letter.*

The temper and discretion required for the judicious discharge of the duties of a Workhouse Master, and the confidence necessarily placed in his integrity, make it essential that the greatest care should be exercised in the choice of that officer. The Master, too, is in some degree dependent on the aid afforded him by the other officers of the establishment, and the appointment of an honest and efficient Porter is of the utmost importance. With this view the Commissioners advise the Guardians, whenever the Workhouse is not of very small dimensions, to appoint a paid Porter, and not to be satisfied with directing one of the paupers of the house to perform the functions allotted to that officer. The Commissioners believe it to be of rare occurrence that a pauper can be safely trusted to exercise the powers, and perform the duties, of the Porter, under the regulations of the Commissioners. For large Workhouses, and particularly Workhouses in towns (where applications for relief are frequently made by persons in urgent necessity, at all hours of the day and night), the Commissioners always require the Guardians to appoint a paid officer to perform the duties of Porter.—*Ib.*

The Commissioners likewise strongly disapprove of the practice of having recourse to a pauper as the instructor of either the male or female children. In no department of the Workhouse is a careful selection of the person employed of greater importance than in the offices of Schoolmaster and Schoolmistress. Their incompetence, and those habits which are generally the cause or consequence of pauperism, affect not only the present comfort and conduct of the children entrusted to their care, but exercise a most pernicious influence on the subsequent welfare of those children, and on the likelihood of their permanent chargeability.—*Ib.*

With respect to the Schoolmaster or Schoolmistress, the Commissioners remark, that in many instances differences have arisen between these officers and the Master or Matron; and as a want of harmony between the principal officers of the establishment cannot fail to impair their efficiency, and disturb the general discipline of the house, the Commissioners are desirous of inculcating upon all these officers the necessity of the utmost forbearance and command of temper in their mutual relations.—*Ib.*

By 5 & 6 Vict. c. 109, s. 6, the Master of a Workhouse is exempt from serving the office of parish constable, and by 13 & 14 Vict. c. 101, s. 6, from serving the office of overseer or any other parochial office.

in obedience to the orders specified in Art. 88, and also every person applying for admission who may appear to him to require relief through any sudden or urgent necessity, and to cause every pauper, upon admission, to be examined by the Medical Officer, as is directed in Art. 91 (*a*).

Art. 208.—No. 2. To cause every male pauper above the age of seven years, upon admission, to be searched, cleansed, and clothed, and to be placed in the proper ward (*b*).

No. 3.—To enforce industry, order, punctuality, and cleanliness, and the observance of all regulations for the government of the Workhouse by the paupers, and by the several officers, assistants, and servants therein (*c*).

(*a*) See notes to Art. 88. In discharging the duty imposed upon him by this Article, the Master is bound to exercise a sound and careful judgment, to the best of his ability, with reference to the condition of the applicant, as disclosed to him at the time. It would, however, be right that he should give due weight to any communication which he shall be satisfied has been sent to him by an Inspector of Police with reference to the case of any applicant for relief. Further, the fact of a person having been refused relief by the Relieving Officer would not of itself justify the Master of the Workhouse in declining to admit the applicant. Before refusing admission, in any case, it will be the duty of the Master to satisfy himself that the person applying does not, at the time of application, require relief through any sudden or urgent necessity. (55 O. C. (N.S.) 64.)

Having once admitted a pauper into the Workhouse, the Master cannot afterwards refer the case to the Relieving Officer, but should report it to the Guardians at their next meeting, and take their directions for his future guidance.

(*b*) The Master has no authority to detain or open letters addressed to pauper inmates of the Workhouse, unless indeed he should have reason to believe that the communication is of an improper tendency; nor can he prevent paupers from receiving presents of money; he should, however, report the fact of a pauper being in possession of money to the Board of Guardians. The Master is to decide, in the first instance, to which class a pauper on his admission to the Workhouse shall be assigned; but in the event of a doubt arising as to a pauper's proper class, he should be guided by the opinion of the Medical Officer, until the case is laid before the Guardians for their decision.

(*c*) With reference to this Article, it may be observed that the Master can, without any special authority from the Board of Guardians, in re-

Art. 208.—No. 4. To read prayers to the paupers before breakfast, and after supper, every day, or cause prayers to be read, according to Art. 124 (*a*).

No. 5. To cause the paupers to be inspected, and their names called over, in conformity with Art. 103, in order that it may be seen that each individual is clean and in a proper state.

No. 6. To provide for and enforce the employment of the able-bodied adult paupers, during the hours of labour; to assist in training the youths in such employment as will best fit them for gaining their own living; to keep the partially disabled paupers occupied to the extent of their ability; and to allow none who are capable of employment to be idle at any time (*b*).

No. 7. To visit the sleeping wards of the male paupers at eleven o'clock in the forenoon of every day, and see that such wards have been all duly cleansed and are properly ventilated (*c*).

No. 8. To see that the meals of the paupers are duly provided, dressed, and served, according to the directions

---

gard to each case, take proceedings before the Justices for the punishment of disorderly paupers in the Workhouse; but when the circumstances allow of delay, it will be proper for him to take the directions of the Guardians before instituting the proceedings. If the offender will not go voluntarily before the Justices, a summons or warrant, as the case may require, must be obtained; and until it can be executed, the offender may be detained in the Workhouse. (See 54 Geo. III. c. 170, s. 7, and 4 & 5 Wm. IV. c. 76, s. 93.)

(*a*) When the Master is unable to read prayers himself, it will be proper for the Schoolmaster to read them; and where there is no Schoolmaster, for the Porter or one of the best-conducted paupers.

(*b*) Particular attention should be paid to enforcing a task of work, under the 5 & 6 Vict. c. 57, s. 5, from vagrants and tramps relieved in the Workhouse with a night's lodging and supper or breakfast. See Note to Art. 99, No. 9, and 29 & 30 Vict. c. 113, s. 15, *ante*, p. 75, and the Minute of the Poor Law Board on vagrancy, First Annual Report, p. 29. As to the employment of the inmates of the Workhouse generally, see Articles 102 and 112, and notes; see also note to Art. 112, and Arts. 114 and 210, No. 3.

(*c*) He must also see that the beds are all made up and in proper order.

in Articles 104 and 107, and to superintend the distribution of the food (*d*).

Art. 208.—No. 9. To say, or cause to be said, grace before and after meals (*e*).

No. 10. To visit all the wards of the male paupers before nine o'clock every night in winter, and ten o'clock in summer, and see that all the male paupers are in bed, and that all fires and lights therein are extinguished, except so far as may be necessary for the sick.

No. 11. To receive from the Porter the keys of the Workhouse at nine o'clock every night, and to deliver them to him again at six o'clock every morning, or at such hours as shall from time to time be fixed by the Guardians.

No. 12. To see that the male paupers are properly clothed, and that their clothes are kept in proper repair (*f*).

No. 13. To cause the birth of every child born in the Workhouse to be registered by the Registrar of Births and Deaths within the space of one week after such child shall have been born; and also to enter such birth in a register kept according to Form (S.) hereunto annexed (*g*).

No. 14. To send for the Medical Officer in case any pauper is taken ill or becomes insane, and to take care that all sick and insane paupers are duly visited by the

---

(*d*) See Note to Art. 41, No. 4, *ante*, p. 31, as to supplying food to paupers waiting to see the Board of Guardians at the Workhouse.

(*e*) See Note to Art. 208, No. 4, which is also applicable to this regulation.

(*f*) As regards clothing the paupers, see Art. 95 and note, p. 67.

(*g*) See the substituted form in the Order of the Poor Law Board dated 26th Feb. 1866, *post*. The births of still-born children must be entered in this Register, as well as the births of children born alive. The Registration Act is silent as to still-born children. In the "Regulations for Registrars of Births and Deaths," as approved by the Secretary of State, the following direction is given (p. 11):—"Still-born children must not be registered; but if a child is born alive, and dies how soon soever after birth, both the birth and the death must be registered separately in the proper form."

Medical Officer, and are provided with such medicines and attendance, diet, and other necessaries, as the Medical Officer or the Guardians direct, and to apprise the nearest relation in the Workhouse of the sickness of any pauper, and, in the case of dangerous sickness, to send for the Chaplain, and any relative or friend of the pauper, resident within a reasonable distance, whom the pauper may desire to see (*a*).

Art. 208.—No. 15 (*b*). To take care that no pauper at the approach of death shall be left unattended either during the day or the night.

No. 16. To give immediate information of the death of any pauper in the Workhouse to the Medical Officer, and to the nearest relations of the deceased who may be known to him, and who may reside within a reasonable distance; and if the body be not removed within a reasonable time, to provide for the interment thereof (*c*).

(*a*) If the illness be of a dangerous nature, care should be taken to send a *written* communication to the Medical Officer, and not a verbal message merely. But generally the Master will act advisedly when he sends written communications in every case, as verbal messages are liable to be misunderstood. As to orders in midwifery cases, see Art. 182. As to the removal of dangerous lunatics to an asylum, see the 16 & 17 Vict. c. 97, s. 67, which makes it the duty of the Relieving Officer to whom the Justices' order for the removal of any pauper lunatic to a lunatic asylum is addressed, to convey, or cause the lunatic to be conveyed, to the asylum. See also 25 & 26 Vict. c. 111, s. 20, on the same point.

(*b*) If a pauper be seriously and dangerously ill, the Master will of course take care that some one sits up in attendance during the night, notwithstanding that the death of the pauper may not be immediately expected.

(*c*) It does not appear in what manner this notice is to be given, and whether he is expected to send the notice by post. If the pauper's friends all reside at a distance, it would seem but proper that the Master should send them notice of the death by post, if their address be known to him.

The following remarks respecting the burial of paupers dying in the Workhouse may be here inserted:—With respect to the place of burial of a pauper, it is to be observed that for the purposes of burial the question of settlement is wholly immaterial, the obligation to bury having existed long before the statute which created the present form of pauper

settlement. The 7 & 8 Vict. c. 101, s. 31, gives a full and complete right to the Guardians to bury the body of a pauper dying in the Workhouse in the churchyard of the Parish in which the Workhouse is situate, unless the deceased person, or the husband or wife, or next of kin shall have otherwise desired; and it is incumbent upon the Guardians under that statute, when the burial of a poor person takes place under their direction, to pay to the persons entitled the fee or fees which by the custom of the Parish in which the burial takes place can be legally claimed. But the Commissioners advise that, with a view of consulting the prevalent wishes of the poor on this subject, the body of every pauper of the Union dying in the Workhouse should in general be interred in the churchyard of his own Parish, unless the Incumbent of that Parish should object. The Commissioners think that the most convenient course is to remove the body in a hearse; but it seems that any male inmates of the Workhouse, of suitable age and strength, may be required by the Guardians to assist in carrying a coffin from the Workhouse to a neighbouring burial-ground.—*Instr. Letter*.

Under the above-mentioned Act the Guardians are the persons empowered to take the requisite proceedings in regard to the burial of a poor person, and neither the friends of the deceased nor the Guardians of the individual Parish, or the Overseers, have any authority to give directions for a burial under the provisions of the Act. As, during the intervals of the meetings of the Guardians, their officers have no authority to interfere in the burial of paupers without the express instructions of the Guardians, it is recommended that precise and definite regulations, prescribing the course to be taken by their officers as regards the burial of poor persons, should be drawn up by the Guardians and entered on their minutes. If in any case the Master of the Workhouse being duly authorized should pay the cost of the burial of a pauper dying therein, he should charge the cost in his accounts.

If the Guardians keep a hearse for carrying the bodies of paupers to the place of burial, upon a declaration being made by the Master of the Workhouse that it is used for the sole purpose of burying paupers who die in the Union, the Commissioners of Inland Revenue will abstain from assessing duty upon the hearse, though, in strict point of law, it is not exempt from duty. As regards the liability to such duty, see note to Art. 215, No. 6, *post*, p. 186.

As to the place of burial, see also 18 & 19 Vict. c. 79, s. 2, which enables Boards of Guardians to enter into agreements with Cemetery Companies or Burial Boards for the burial of paupers, and the 20 & 21 Vict. c. 81, s. 6, as to the consecration of land to be set apart especially for the burial of paupers.

By the 7 & 8 Vict. c. 101, s. 56, the Workhouse is constructively situated in the parishes to which the paupers are respectively chargeable, but now by the Union Chargeability Act, 1865, 28 & 29 Vict. c. 79, s. 10, for the purposes of the burial of any poor person dying in the Workhouse of any Union, such Workhouse shall be considered as situated in the Parish in the Union where such poor person resided last, previously to his removal to the Workhouse; therefore only the fees payable by custom on the burial of a parishioner can be claimed when the dead body of a pauper is removed from the Workhouse to the parish of chargeability for burial. With regard to the payment of burial fees under 7 & 8 Vict. c. 101, s. 31, the rule is that where the burial takes place under the direction of the Guardians or any of their officers duly authorized, the fee or fees payable by the custom of the Parish "shall be paid out of the Poor-rates" for the burial, to the person or persons entitled by the custom to receive any fee.

The Poor Law Commissioners said in their Official Circular, generally, the effect of the whole provision in 7 & 8 Vict. c. 101, s. 31, appears to them to be as follows:—1. As a general rule, all bodies buried by Guardians are to be buried in the churchyard or in a consecrated burial-ground, and this in the parish, or township, of the death. 2. But the burial in such churchyard or consecrated burial-ground may be dispensed with by the desire of the deceased, or husband, wife, or next of kin. 3. If the burial in the churchyard or consecrated burial-ground be dispensed with in compliance with such desire, the Guardians may apparently authorize the burial anywhere, i. e. in unconsecrated ground, or in ground out of the parish of the death. 4. Also the Guardians may authoritatively direct the burial to take place in the parish where the deceased was chargeable. But this is a departure from the general law, and is in this clause made the exception. It is only authorized when the deceased or his relatives have desired it, or the Guardians see particular cause for it. This case may arise when there is an objection of the deceased or his friends to burial in the churchyard or consecrated burial-ground of the parish. And if there be any burial-ground of the parish or township (i. e. belonging to the township) which is not consecrated, the Guardians may bury the body in such burial-ground. (10 O. C. (N. S.) 149.)

There is no provision of the law which makes it the duty of a Master of a Workhouse to admit the corpse of a person, who has not died therein, into the Workhouse. Such corpse must remain in the custody of the persons who have possession of it until some proper place of deposit can be found for its reception. The Workhouse is not necessarily a place for its deposit, and in some cases it might be improper that it should be received therein. But in many cases there may be no objection to its reception, especially in cases where the Guardians take upon themselves the charge of the burial, and where they have provided a proper dead-house.

If the unclaimed bodies of paupers who die in a Workhouse be given up for the purposes of anatomical examination, the regulations contained in the Schools of Anatomy Act (2 & 3 Wm. IV. c. 75) must be strictly adhered to by the Master, otherwise he will subject himself to the penalties provided by that Act,—namely, imprisonment for a term not exceeding three months, or a fine not exceeding £50; but see *Reg.* v. *Feest*, 27 L. J. R. (N. S.) M. C 164, on this point.

With respect to the holding of Coroners' inquests in Workhouses, the Commissioners have stated that there may be particular cases in which the Guardians would be justified in allowing an inquest to be held in the Workhouse on the body of a person found dead not within its walls, —as where the inconvenience of a refusal would be great. In such cases the Guardians would no doubt think it their duty to allow the inquest being so held; but whenever they do so, it will be proper that they

Art. 208.—No. 17. When requisite, to cause the death of every pauper dying in the Workhouse to be duly registered by the Registrar of Births and Deaths within five days after the day of such death; and also to enter such death in a register kept according to Form (T.) hereunto annexed (*a*).

No. 18. To deliver an inventory of the clothes and other property of any pauper who may have died in the Workhouse, to the Guardians at their next ordinary meeting (*b*).

---

should give the permission as a voluntary act, and not as the admission of a right. If the Medical Officer is required by the Coroner to perform the post-mortem examination, he will be entitled to claim the usual remuneration for his services, irrespective of his office of Medical Officer. The Coroner by the law of England has an absolute right to enter with the inquest any house in which a dead body may be on which he proposes to hold an inquest (see the third edition of Jervis 'On the Office and Duties of Coroner,' by Lovesy), and he should therefore not be denied admission to the Workhouse for such a purpose. If he supplies the names of the inquest, they should be entered by the Porter in his book. If he do not give their names, the Porter should enter in the book the name of the Coroner, and specify that he was accompanied by the inquest. With respect to money found in the possession of any pauper dying in the Workhouse, it is enacted by the 12 & 13 Vict. c. 103, s. 16, that the Guardians of the Union or Parish wherein such pauper shall die may reimburse themselves the expenses incurred by them in and about the burial of such pauper, and in and about the maintenance of such pauper at any time during the twelve months previous to the decease. If there be any overplus, and the relief has not been advanced by way of loan, the Guardians are bound to return the amount of such overplus to any executor or administrator legally appointed. Money found on the body of a pauper who has died in the Workhouse, and on whose body a coroner's inquest has been holden, cannot be applied to defraying the expenses of the inquest, which are payable out of the county rates.

It may be further added, that the Guardians of a Union are not under any legal obligation to bury the dead bodies of persons dying in Public Hospitals. (*Reg.* v. *Stewart*, 12 A. & E. 773.) The exercise of the power given by the 7 & 8 Vict. c. 101, s. 31, is discretionary on the part of the Guardians, who may decline to undertake the burial of any dead body, not being in the Workhouse, if they think fit so to do.

(*a*) See the substituted form in the Order of the Poor Law Board, dated 26th February, 1866, *post*.

(*b*) As to the appropriation of the effects of a deceased pauper, see note to No. 16; and as to the disposal of the clothing of deceased paupers, see 7 O. C. p. 167.

Art. 208.—No. 19. To keep such portion of the Workhouse Medical Relief Book prescribed in this Order as is assigned to him in the Form marked (Q.), and to keep all books or accounts which he is, or hereafter may be, by any Order of the Commissioners, directed and required to keep; to allow the same to be constantly open to the inspection of any of the Guardians of the Union, and to submit the same to the Guardians at their ordinary meetings (a).

No. 20. To submit to the Guardians, at every ordinary meeting, an estimate of such provisions and other articles as are required for the use of the Workhouse, and to receive and execute the directions of the Guardians thereupon.

No. 21. To receive all provisions and other articles purchased or procured for the use of the Workhouse, and before placing them in store to examine and compare them with the bills of parcels or invoices severally relating thereto; and after having proved the accuracy of such bills or invoices, to authenticate the same with his signature, and submit them to the Guardians at their next ordinary meeting.

No. 22. To receive and take charge of all provisions, clothing, linen, and other articles belonging to the Workhouse, or confided to his care by the Guardians, and issue the same to the Matron or other persons as may be required (b).

No. 23. To report to the Guardians from time to time the names of such children as the Schoolmaster may recommend as fit to be put out to service, or other employment, and to take the necessary steps for

---

(a) See Article 19 of the General Order for Accounts for the books required to be kept by the Master of a Workhouse.

(b) The refuse of the Workhouse must be sold and brought to account for the benefit of the establishment. In no case will the Master be justified in appropriating the produce of the sale of such refuse, or of old unserviceable stores, to his own use. (See note to Art. 172, *ante*, p. 122.)

carrying into effect the directions of the Guardians thereon (c).

Art. 208.—No. 24. To take care that the wards, rooms, larder, kitchen, and all other offices of the Workhouse, and all the utensils and furniture thereof, be kept clean and in good order; and as often as any defect in the same, or in the state of the Workhouse, shall occur, to report the same in writing to the Guardians at their next ordinary meeting (d).

No. 25. To submit to the Guardians, at every ordinary meeting, a report of the number of the inmates in the Workhouse, according to the Form (U.) hereunto annexed.

No 26. To bring before the Visiting committee or the Guardians any pauper inmate desirous of making a complaint or application to the Guardians.

No. 27 (e). To report forthwith to the Medical Officer and to the Guardians, in writing, all cases in which any restraint or compulsion may have been used towards any pauper inmate of unsound mind in the Workhouse.

No. 28. To keep a book, in which he shall enter all his written reports to the Guardians or to the Medical Officer, and to lay the same before the Guardians at every ordinary meeting.

No. 29. To inform the Visiting Committee and the Guardians of the state of the Workhouse in every department, and to report in writing to the Guardians any negligence or other misconduct on the part of any of the subordinate officers or servants of the establishment; and generally to observe and fulfil all lawful orders and directions to the Guardians suitable to his office.

(c) The Master must make this report, whether or not the parents of the children be in the Workhouse.

(d) See note to Article 41 (fifthly), *ante*, p. 32.

(e) No pauper who requires habitual or frequent restraint, and is consequently dangerous to himself or others, is to be retained in the Workhouse for a longer period than fourteen days. (See Article 101.)

Art 209.—The Master shall not, except in case of necessity, purchase or procure any articles for the use of the Workhouse, nor order any alterations or repairs of any part of the premises, or of the furniture or other articles belonging thereto, nor pay any moneys on account of the Workhouse, or of the Union, without the authority of the Guardians, nor apply any articles belonging to the Guardians to purposes other than those authorized or approved of by such Guardians (*a*).

Duties of the Matron.

Art. 210.—The following shall be the duties of the Matron :—

No. 1. In the absence of the Master, or during his inability to act, to act as his substitute in the admission of paupers into the Workhouse, according to Articles 88 and 208, Nos. 1 and 2, and to cause every pauper upon such admission to be examined by the Medical Officer, as is directed in Art. 91.

No. 2. To cause the pauper children under the age of seven years, and the female paupers, to be searched, cleansed, and clothed upon their admission, and to be placed in their proper wards.

No. 3. To provide for and enforce the employment of the able-bodied female paupers during the hours of labour, and to keep the partially disabled female paupers occupied to the extent of their ability, and to assist the Schoolmistress in training up the children so as best to fit them for service (*b*).

No. 4. To call over the names of the paupers, as is directed in Art. 103, to inspect their persons, and see that each individual is clean.

No. 5. To visit the sleeping wards of the female paupers at eleven o'clock in the forenoon of every day, and to

---

(*a*) See note to Article 41 (fifthly), *ante*, p. 32.
(*b*) See note to Article 112, and Articles 114 and 208, No. 6.

see that such wards have been all duly cleansed, and are properly ventilated.

Art. 210.—No. 6. To visit all the wards of the females and children (c) every night before nine o'clock, and to ascertain that all the paupers in such wards are in bed, and all fires and lights not necessary for the sick or for women suckling their children, therein extinguished.

No. 7. To pay particular attention to the moral conduct and orderly behaviour of the females and children, and to see that they are clean and decent in their dress and persons.

No. 8. To superintend and give the necessary directions for making and mending the linen and clothing supplied to the male paupers, and all the clothing supplied to the female paupers and children, and to take care that all such clothing be properly numbered and marked on the inside with the name of the Union.

No. 9. To see that every pauper in the Workhouse has clean linen and stockings once a week, and that all the beds and bedding be kept in a clean and wholesome state.

No. 10. To take charge of the linen and stockings for the use of the paupers, and the other linen in use in the Workhouse, and to apply the same to such purposes as shall be authorized or approved of by the Guardians, and to no other.

No. 11. To superintend and give the necessary directions concerning the washing, drying, and getting up of the linen, stockings, and blankets, and to see that the same be not dried in the sleeping wards or in the sick wards.

No. 12. To take proper care of the children and sick paupers, and to provide the proper diet for the same, and for women suckling infants, and to furnish them with such changes of clothes and linen as may be necessary.

(c) The word "children" includes only those in Class 7, specified in Article 98.

Art. 210.—No. 13. To assist the Master in the general management and superintendence of the Workhouse, and especially in—

    Enforcing the observance of good order, cleanliness, punctuality, industry, and decency of demeanour among the paupers;

    Cleansing and ventilating the sleeping wards and the dining-hall, and all other parts of the premises;

    Placing in store and taking charge of the provisions, clothing, linen, and other articles belonging to the Union.

No. 14. When requested by the Porter, in pursuance of Art. 214, No. 5, to search any female entering or leaving the Workhouse under the circumstances described in that Article.

No 15. To report to the Master any negligence or other misconduct on the part of any of the female officers or servants of the establishment, or any case in which restraint or compulsion may have been used towards any female inmate of unsound mind.

No. 16. And generally to observe and fulfil all lawful orders and directions of the Guardians suitable to her office.

Duties of the Chaplain (*a*).

Art. 211.—The following shall be the duties of the Chaplain:—

No. 1. To read prayers and preach a sermon to the pau-

(*a*) With respect to religious ministrations in Workhouses by Dissenting ministers, see Art. 122 and note thereon. In former editions of this Work, it was said that to "read prayers" meant to read without change or mutilation, the whole morning service or the afternoon service, as commonly read in churches, with the litany and commandments, etc., as usual on Sunday mornings, and that every clergyman's engagements at his ordination bind him to a strict observance of this rule. The Queen's Advocate, Sir J. D. Harding, has however, it is understood, advised that the words "to read prayers" do not compel the Chaplain to read verbatim on every Sunday the whole order for

pers and other inmates of the Workhouse on every Sunday, and on Good Friday and Christmas Day, unless the Guardians, with the consent of the Commissioners, may otherwise direct (*b*).

Art. 211.—No. 2. To examine the children (*c*), and to catechize such as belong to the Church of England, at least once in every month, and to make a record of the same, and state the dates of his attendance, the general progress and condition of the children, and the moral

---

morning prayer, as commonly read in churches. The Chaplain is not required to baptize children in the Workhouse, except under circumstances which would justify the administration of baptism in a private house; nor is he required to church women who may be confined in the Workhouse. The children should be baptized in the parish church, and the mothers should be churched there also. It is necessary that the particulars of baptisms in the Workhouse should be entered in the registry in the custody of the Rector or Vicar of the Parish in which the Workhouse is situated. See 52 Geo. III. c. 146, s. 11; but apparently no fee can be demanded for making such entry.

The pauper inmates should be allowed to receive the Holy Communion at the parish church; and where there is no Workhouse chapel used exclusively for the purpose of divine worship, this rite should not be administered in the Workhouse, except to the sick and disabled. Where there is a chapel, the Communion may be celebrated in it, with the consent of the Bishop of the diocese; but even in that case those inmates who desire it should be allowed to attend the parish church at Easter and Christmas. (See also note to Article 124, p. 96.)

In many Unions the Workhouse chapel is licensed by the Bishop of the diocese, but in others not. Such a chapel cannot be consecrated by the Bishop unless the freehold be conveyed to the Ecclesiastical Commissioners, and this the Guardians have no power to do. Further upon these points see the case and opinion of Dr. Adams in the Report of the Poor Law Commissioners on the further amendment of the Poor Law, page 112.

The Chaplain of the Workhouse has no duty to perform under the 52 Geo. III. c. 146, s. 7, in transmitting an account of the baptisms performed in the Workhouse to the Registrar of the diocese. (4 O. C. 84.)

(*b*) The following opinion of Dr. Adams may here be quoted from the 'Report of the Poor Law Commissioners on the Amendment of the Law,' p. 112:—"I think that, with the Bishop's licence, it is not requisite that any part of the Workhouse should be consecrated to sanction a clergyman of the establishment in the performance of any of the duties required of the Chaplain of the Workhouse by the Poor Law Commissioners."

(*c*) This applies to the general as well as to the religious examination of the Workhouse children. (See 53 Off. Cir. (N.S.) 21.)

and religious state of the inmates generally, in a book to be kept for that purpose, to be laid before the Guardians at their next ordinary meeting, and to be termed "THE CHAPLAIN'S REPORT" (a).

Art. 211.—No. 3. To visit the sick paupers, and to administer religious consolation to them in the Workhouse, at such periods as the Guardians may appoint, and when applied to for that purpose by the Master or Matron.

DUTIES OF THE SCHOOLMASTER AND SCHOOLMISTRESS (b).

Art. 212.—The following shall be the duties of the School-

(a) The Chaplain's Report-Book should be kept in the custody of the Workhouse Master, unless the Guardians should give directions to the contrary.

(b) With the view to encouraging the appointment of competent persons to these offices, the repayment of their salaries to the Union is made conditional upon their obtaining certificates of efficiency, competency, probation, or permission, as the case may be.

The following are the regulations on this subject:—

Poor Law Schools are periodically visited by Inspectors, who report thereon to the Board, who thereupon issue to the Schoolmaster or Schoolmistress a certificate in the various grades and divisions, according to the proficiency exhibited by the Teacher.

The amount to be repaid to the Union from the Parliamentary Grant is regulated by the grade of the certificate which the Teacher obtains, and by the number of children in the school, according to the following scale:—

Grades and Divisions of Certificates for Service in Poor Law Schools.	MASTERS.		MISTRESSES.		Sum to be allowed in respect of each Scholar in addition to the Minimum Allowance.
	Minimum Allowance from the Grant.	Maximum Allowance from the Grant.	Minimum Allowance from the Grant.	Maximum Allowance from the Grant.	
	£.	£.	£.	£.	s.
First Grade { 1	30	60	24	48	12
2	30	55	24	44	11
3	30	50	24	40	10
Second Grade { 1	25	45	20	36	7
2	25	40	20	32	6
3	25	35	20	28	5
Third Grade { 1	20	30	16	24	4
2	20	25	16	20	3
3	20	20	16	16	—
Fourth Grade .	15	15	12	12	—

master and Schoolmistress for the Workhouse, or either of them:—

Art. 212.—No. 1. To instruct the boys and girls according to the directions in Art. 114.

The Poor Law Board have laid down the following conditions of payment:—

The whole amount issued to each Union from the Treasury must be paid by the Guardians to the Teacher.

If the salary at which the Guardians have engaged the Teacher exceeds the amount issued from the Treasury, the difference must continue to be paid to the Teacher out of the poor-rate, until the Poor Law Board has agreed to the engagement of the same or another teacher at a reduced salary.

If the Teacher does not reside in the Workhouse, and is not provided with rations, the Guardians must allow the Teacher the sum of £15 a year in lieu thereof out of the poor-rate.

The Teacher must have convenient and respectably furnished apartments; rations, the same in kind and quality as are supplied to the Master of a Workhouse; must be subjected to no menial offices; must have proper assistance in the management of the children when not in school.

If the Inspectors report that any Poor Law School is not furnished with the necessary books and school apparatus, the Guardians must provide them.

Industrial Instructors', as well as Schoolmasters' and Schoolmistress' salaries, are, under certain conditions, repaid to the Guardians upon the special report of the School Inspectors.

The Poor Law Board, in a Circular dated the 12th March, 1867, state that they are of opinion that the following scale would be a simple, and at the same time a fair and proper one :—

That when the Guardians provide board and lodging two-thirds of the Officer's salary should be allowed from the Grant. When they do not provide board and lodging, one-half of the salary should be so allowed.

Thus in either case about one-half of the salary, inclusive of board and lodging, would be borne by the Guardians, and one-half be repaid to them out of the fund provided by Parliament. If, however, the services of the Officer are given solely for the instruction of the children, as in the case of a Band Master or Drill Master, the whole salary may properly be allowed from the Parliamentary Grant. As regards the number of officers for whom the payments should be made, the Board are of opinion that an Industrial Teacher should not be allowed for less than about thirty children, unless in schools in which such a Teacher is employed instead of a Schoolmaster or Schoolmistress. There should also be not less than six children under instruction to entitle the Guardians to a payment on account of the Teacher's salary. The inspectors in reporting on the Industrial Teachers will ascertain that they do not merely employ the boys and girls in assisting them in their work, but that they give them *bonâ fide* instruction, and that the children exhibit a satisfactory proficiency or skill in the trade taught.

Art. 212.—No. 2. To regulate the discipline and arrangements of the school, and the industrial and moral training of the children, subject to the direction of the Guardians (*a*).

No 3. To accompany the children when they quit the Workhouse for exercise, or for attendance at public worship, unless the Guardians shall otherwise direct.

No. 4. To keep the children clean in their persons, and orderly and decorous in their conduct (*b*).

No. 5. To assist the Master and Matron respectively in maintaining due subordination in the Workhouse.

(*a*) Under this regulation it is the duty of the Schoolmaster and Schoolmistress to superintend the children out of school-hours, as well as during the periods when they are actually under instruction. As to granting leave of absence to children attending Workhouse schools, see note to Art. 116.

The Schoolmistress is not required by the regulations either to give notice to the Master of her intention to be absent temporarily from the Workhouse, or to ask his permission when quitting it. It is, however, competent to the Guardians, under Art. 152, to frame a regulation upon the subject if they consider it expedient to do so. (57 O. C. (N. S.), p. 94.)

(*b*) The Master and Matron respectively must see that the boys and girls are properly clothed (Art. 208, No. 12 ; Art. 210, No. 10); but if the Schoolmaster or Schoolmistress should observe that the children's clothing requires repairing or washing, they should direct the attention of the Master or Matron to the matter.

It is the duty of the Schoolmaster and Schoolmistress to superintend and take charge of the boys and girls respectively who are attending school out of school-hours, as well as when they are under instruction.

By Art. 210, No. 7, it is the duty of the Matron to see that the children are clean and decent in their persons; and under Art. 212, No. 4, the duty of the Schoolmistress in this respect is limited to the children in her school; that of the Matron extends to all the children in the Workhouse. The Matron should make the requisite arrangements for the actual washing, etc., of the children, in which duty some respectable inmate of the Workhouse might be employed. The Schoolmistress should not be required personally to assist, beyond giving a general superintendence as regards the children under her care; but blame would attach to her as well as to the Matron, if any just ground of complaint as to cleanliness should exist. Generally, it may be added that in any details in which the regulations do not contain specific directions, the Guardians may themselves lay down such rules as may appear to them advisable, provided they are not inconsistent with the regulations.

Duties of a Nurse (c).

Art. 213.—The following shall be the duties of a Nurse for the Workhouse:—

No. 1. To attend upon the sick in the sick and lying-in wards, and to administer to them all medicines and medical applications, according to the directions of the Medical Officer.

No. 2. To inform the Medical Officer of any defects which may be observed in the arrangements of the sick or lying-in ward.

No. 3. To take care that a light is kept at night in the sick ward.

(c) The Poor Law Board referring to these duties say that it is obvious that they require, in any Workhouse where there are many sick patients, great care and attention on the part of the nurse. The office is one of very serious responsibility and labour, and requires to be filled by a person of experience in the treatment of the sick, of great respectability of character, and of diligent and decorous habits. Such person cannot discharge the duties of the office singly, but must have the assistance of others of both sexes; and there is scarcely less need of the same qualities in the persons who are to be the Assistants than of those required for the chief officer. Hence the Board say it is necessary that the Nurses should be adequately remunerated, and that they should be appointed after a strict investigation of their qualifications for the office. But the Board consider it of the highest importance that the Assistants to the Nurse should also be paid officers. By appointing paid Assistants the Guardians will have an opportunity of selecting persons whose qualifications for the office can be properly ascertained, and they will also be able to hold such officers responsible for negligence or misconduct, as in the case of the superior officers of the Workhouse. The Board recommend the Guardians, as far as possible, to discontinue the practice of appointing pauper inmates of the Workhouse to act as Assistant Nurses in the infirmary or sick ward. Where the arrangements of the Workhouse will permit, it is very desirable that special accommodation should be provided for the Nurse and the paid Assistants, so that they may be always ready to attend upon the patients, and be removed as much as possible from the distraction which the proceedings in a large Workhouse are calculated to produce.—*Instr. Letter*, 5th May, 1865. See also note to Art. 98, *ante*, p. 70.

General reference may also be made in this place to the report of the Medical Officer of the Poor Law Board on the sufficiency of the arrangements for the care and treatment of the sick in various Workhouses in different parts of England, dated 15th April, 1867, and to the Order of 4th April, 1868, *post*.

DUTIES OF THE PORTER.

Art. 214.—The following shall be the duties of the Porter of the Workhouse:—

No. 1. To keep the gate and to prevent any person, not being an officer of the Workhouse, or of the Union, an Assistant Poor Law Commissioner, or any person authorized by law, or by the Commissioners or Guardians, from entering into or going out of the house without the leave of the Master or Matron.

No. 2. To keep a book in which he shall enter the name and business of every officer or other person who shall go into the Workhouse, and the name of every officer or other person who shall go out thereof, together with the time of such officer's or person's going in or out (*a*).

No. 3. To receive all paupers who apply or present themselves for admission in conformity with Art. 88, and, if the Master and Matron be both absent, to place such paupers in the receiving ward until the Master or Matron return (*b*).

(*a*) The names of the Workhouse and all other Union officers must be entered in the Porter's book every time they leave the Workhouse and return, however frequently that may be in the course of the day. The Porter is to enter the ingress and egress of the following persons:— The Guardians on board or other days; the Clerk and those having business at his office; the Relieving Officer; the Master, Matron, and other officers, with their friends visiting them; persons coming in with goods, fuel, etc.; paupers admitted into the house; paupers discharged therefrom; mendicants admitted and discharged; persons attending funerals; applicants on board-days; the Chaplain; the Medical Officer; all persons going to church or chapel, and returning therefrom; and also the visits of the Poor Law Inspectors; School Inspectors; Commissioners in Lunacy; and all other persons having a statutory right to visit the Workhouse.

So also if the Register Office be within the walls of the Workhouse, the Porter must enter in his book the names of all persons resorting to the office for registration or other purposes.

With regard to the entry of the name of the Coroner when he enters the Workhouse with the inquest, see note to Article 208, No. 16, p. 169.

(*b*) It is considered that the latter part of this Article applies to all paupers who present themselves for admission, whether with or without

Art. 214.—No. 4. To examine all parcels and goods before they are received into the Workhouse, and prevent the admission of any spirituous or fermented liquors, or other articles contrary to any of the regulations contained in this order, or otherwise contrary to law (c).

No. 5. To search any male pauper entering or leaving the Workhouse whom he may suspect of having possession of any spirits or other prohibited articles, and to require any other person entering the Workhouse whom he may suspect of having possession of any such spirits or prohibited articles to satisfy him to the contrary before he permit such person to be admitted; and, in the case of any female, to cause the Matron to be called, for the purpose of searching her, if necessary (d).

No. 6. To examine all parcels taken by any pauper out of the Workhouse, and to prevent the undue removal of any article from the premises.

No. 7. To lock all the outer doors, and take the keys to the Master, at nine o'clock every night, and to receive them back from him every morning at six o'clock, or

---

an order, and whether their cases be of "sudden or urgent necessity," or not. When the Master returns, it will be for him to decide whether they shall be allowed to remain in the house.

(c) If the Register Office be within the walls of the Workhouse, the Porter is not required to examine parcels relating to registration business which may be sent there addressed to or intended for the Superintendent Registrar.

(d) The following are examples of prohibited articles:—Spirituous or fermented liquors; letters or printed papers, as books, pamphlets, etc., being of an improper tendency; cards or dice; matches or other highly combustible articles. The Porter cannot take from paupers money or trinkets which he may find in their possession; but he ought to report the finding of any such upon a pauper to the Master, who should then make his report to the Guardians, as the circumstances of the case may require. This rule does not authorize the detaining or opening letters addressed to pauper inmates of the house; neither does it require the Porter to search the Workhouse officers for prohibited articles, these officers being entitled to introduce spirituous liquors into the Workhouse for their own use; nor does it authorize the Porter to search persons who present themselves as visitors to the inmates of the Workhouse. (See also Art. 210, No. 14.)

at such hours as shall from time to time be fixed by the Guardians; and if any application for admission to the Workhouse be made after the keys shall have been so taken to the Master, to apprise the Master forthwith of such application.

No. 8. To assist the Master and Matron in preserving order, and in enforcing obedience and due subordination in the Workhouse.

No. 9. To inform the Master of all things affecting the security and order of the Workhouse, and to obey all lawful directions of the Master or Matron, and of the Guardians, suitable to his office.

Duties of a Relieving Officer (a).

Art. 215.—The following shall be the duties of a Relieving Officer:—

No. 1. To attend all ordinary meetings of the Guardians, and to attend all other meetings when summoned by the Clerk.

No. 2. To receive all applications for relief made to him within his district, or relating to any Parish situated within his district, and forthwith to examine into the circumstances of every case by visiting the house of the applicant (if situated within his district), and by

---

(a) A Relieving Officer must never be absent from his district without the express permission of the Guardians, and without leaving some one in charge. It is considered undesirable that Relieving Officers should be employed by the Guardians in the transaction of any business which requires them to be absent from their district. They have no duty to discharge in respect to obtaining orders of removal of poor persons to the places of their settlement, and they therefore should abstain from all interference in such cases: as regards the removal of Irish and Scotch paupers to Ireland and Scotland. (See, however, the statutes 8 & 9 Vict. c. 117; 24 & 25 Vict. c. 76; 25 & 26 Vict. c. 113, and 27 & 28 Vict. c. 89.) With regard to the duty of a Relieving Officer in respect of the removal of lunatic paupers to and from Lunatic Asylums, see note to Article 207, No. 4, *ante*, p. 159.

By 5 & 6 Vict. c. 109, s. 6, a Relieving Officer is exempt from serving as Parish Constable, and by 13 & 14 Vict. c. 101, s. 6, from serving as Overseer or any other parochial office.

making all necessary inquiries into the state of health, the ability to work, the condition and family, and the means of such applicant, and to report the result of such inquiries in the prescribed form to the Guardians at their next ordinary meeting; and also to visit from time to time, as requisite, all paupers receiving relief, and to report concerning the same as the Guardians may direct (*b*).

(*b*) It is important for the Relieving Officer to observe that it is his duty to visit at their dwellings all persons who have applied for relief as soon as possible after he has received the application. The Relieving Officer should moreover observe that he is responsible for all persons who apply for or receive relief in his district, and that he cannot discharge himself of this responsibility by any agreement or understanding between himself or the Guardians, and the Guardians or Relieving Officer of another Union. (See the Minute of the Commissioners on the relief of non-resident paupers, in their Seventh Annual Report, and also the provisions of this order relating to the relief of non-settled and non-resident poor, Arts. 77–80.)

The Relieving Officer is not bound to attend the case of an applicant for relief unless the person be actually destitute in some Parish or place in his district. He is not required to relieve a pauper settled in a Parish in his district when such pauper resides in a Parish in another Relieving Officer's district, even though such Parish be in the same Union; but it is considered that if they live within so short a distance, so as to enable the Relieving Officer, without interference with the duties which he has to discharge within his district, to visit them, it is his duty to do so and relieve them himself. As regards the relief of poor persons residing in places which were extra-parochial, see the 20 Vict. c. 19, under which such places are now constituted Parishes, and the greater part of them added to Unions.

If an application be made to the Relieving Officer on behalf of a poor person at the time the Board is sitting, he should forthwith report the case to the Guardians, and take their directions upon it, and this notwithstanding that he may not have had time to inquire into the case; and he must report to the Guardians every fresh application he receives, though in any particular case they may have already refused to allow relief to the applicant. The Relieving Officer is not required to make any written suggestion as to the amount of relief which, in his opinion, each case requires; but he should be prepared to state his opinion orally upon the subject to the Board of Guardians when called upon to do so. He is bound to give the Guardians all necessary information in his possession which may contribute to the efficient discharge of their duties as regards the relief of the poor; and it will be proper that he should make them acquainted with all cases of destitution which come under his observation, even though the destitute persons may not have applied to him for relief. Sometimes persons who are in the custody of the law

Art. 215.—No. 3. In any case of sickness or accident requiring relief by medical attendance, to procure such attendance by giving an order on the District Medical Officer, in the Form (V.) hereunto annexed, or by such other means as the urgency of the case may require (*a*).

No. 4. To ascertain from time to time, from the District Medical Officer, the names of any poor persons whom such Medical Officer may have attended or supplied with medicines without having received an order from himself to that effect (*b*).

---

are in a state of destitution, and in such cases, if the prisoner be within the district of the Relieving Officer, it would be incumbent upon him to receive the application for relief in the usual manner, and report it to the Guardians. But see 4 O. C. 46, as to supplying relief to a child born in a prison.

(*a*) If the ailment be such as to afford reasonable ground for the attendance of a medical man, and the applicant be unable to procure medical aid for himself and family, the Relieving Officer should give the order, but not otherwise. In cases requiring *immediate* medical or surgical attendance, when the services of the Medical Officer of the district cannot be promptly obtained, the Relieving Officer may upon the emergency employ any other medical man to attend the case; but the Medical Officer of the district should be directed to take charge of it as soon as practicable. With regard to the grant of midwifery orders for the wives of labourers, it may be here stated that medical aid is a part of general relief, and must be administered according to the same rules. Neither the Guardians nor the Relieving Officer are bound to relieve, nor are they justified in relieving, any person whose circumstances they have ascertained to be such as not to require relief at the cost of the poor-rates. They will not properly discharge their duties if, by a fear of incurring responsibility, they are deterred from withholding relief where the position, station, and circumstances of the applicants have satisfied them that it ought not to be allowed; but the safest course, in such cases, is for the Guardians to give notice that, whenever the circumstances of the applicant render him a fit object, the medical aid would be granted by way of loan, and the repayment of the whole of medical fee would be enforced.

(*b*) In case the Medical Officers should have attended any paupers without an order from the Relieving Officer (as, for example, under an order from the Board of Guardians, or from an Overseer, it will be the duty of the Relieving Officer to ascertain the names of such paupers, and to visit them.

The Vaccination Act, 30 & 31 Vict. c. 84, s. 11, contemplates that a Relieving Officer may in writing "refer any child" to the Public Vaccinator for vaccination.

Art. 215.—No. 5. In every case of a poor person receiving medical relief, as soon as may be, and from time to time afterwards, to visit the house of such person, and, until the next ordinary meeting of the Guardians, to supply such relief (not being in money) as the case on his own view, or on the certificate of the District Medical Officer, may seem to require (*c*).

No. 6. In every case of sudden or urgent necessity, to afford such relief to the destitute person as may be requisite, either by giving such person an order of admission into the Workhouse, and conveying him thereto if necessary, or by affording him relief out of the Workhouse, provided that the same be not given in money, whether such destitute person be settled in any Parish comprised in the Union or not (*d*).

(*c*) This regulation is in accordance with the provisions of the 4 & 5 Wm. IV. c. 76, s. 54, which directs that in such cases, any relief given by an Overseer shall be given " in articles of absolute necessity, but not in money." The Relieving Officer will not be excused from a personal visit to the house of the sick person, even though the disease under which such person labours is of an infectious or contagious nature, as fever, small-pox, etc. He is as much bound as the Medical Officer to visit fever and other infectious or contagious cases. With respect to the duty of the Relieving Officer in the administration of relief to sick paupers upon the certificate of the Medical Officer, it is to be observed that the visit which the Relieving Officer is required to make under this regulation should, as a general rule, take place before he orders the relief stated in the certificate to be required by the pauper. When his other duties do not allow of his at once visiting the case, he is authorized to afford relief on the certificate of the Medical Officer as relief urgently needed, and he should then visit the case as soon afterwards as may be possible. A Relieving Officer must in all such cases be responsible for the exercise of the discretion granted to him by the provisions of the Consolidated Order.

(*d*) In cases of sudden or urgent necessity, the Commissioners remark that it is the duty of the Relieving Officer to administer the appropriate relief needed (such as food, lodging, or medical assistance), and not to save his own trouble by giving money to a pauper at a moment when he may be unable to use it. If the Relieving Officer gives an order for the Workhouse, and affords the means of conveyance to it, he is considered to have furnished adequate relief, provided the person be in a fit state for removal, and be not in actual want of food. In the latter case, immediate out-relief in kind should be given, according to

Art. 215.—No. 7. To report to the Guardians at their next ordinary meeting all cases reported to him by an Overseer in conformity with Art. 218, and to obey the

the necessities of the pauper. If the sickness be of a serious nature, the removal of the pauper should not be effected without a medical certificate, if it can be obtained without delay, and without apprehension of danger to the pauper by having to wait for it.—*Instr. Letter.*

The exercise of a Relieving Officer's discretion under this Article is controlled by the provisions of the Order of 21st December, 1844, *post;* and in dealing with cases of able-bodied paupers under circumstances of "urgent necessity," those provisions must be observed. If the case be "sudden *and* urgent," out-door relief in kind may be given. If it be only "sudden" *or* "urgent," an order for the Workhouse should be given, and the pauper conveyed thither if necessary.

If in any case, owing to the sickness, tender age of the children, the distance of the residence of the family from the Workhouse, or any other cause, any members of the family are unable to walk to the Workhouse, and have not the means of conveyance to it, it will be the Relieving Officer's duty to provide for their conveyance, and the expense he incurs in so doing he will charge as out-relief given under circumstances of "sudden or urgent necessity," under the circumstances above assumed. It will be the duty of the Relieving Officer to take this course, though the order of admission to the Workhouse may have been given by the Guardians, and though they may not have given any directions in regard to the conveyance of the family to the Workhouse.

Some Boards of Guardians provide a carriage for the conveyance of paupers to or from the Workhouse, and it may be here stated that 16 & 17 Vict. c. 90 operates as a repeal of 6 & 7 Wm. IV. c. 65, s. 3, and that a carriage so used does not come within the 5th Exception to Schedule D. of 16 & 17 Vict. c. 90. The Commissioners of Inland Revenue have so advised the Poor Law Board. (See also Note to Art. 208, No. 16, *ante*, p. 167.

If an Overseer in a case of sudden and urgent necessity gives an order for the Workhouse, and incurs an expense in sending the pauper to the Workhouse, he should charge the expense in his own accounts, and submit it to the auditor; but in what way the Parish is to obtain reimbursement from the common fund of the Union is certainly not clear.

If a pauper refuses an offer of relief in the Workhouse, and if, in consequence of such refusal, the case should become one of "sudden or urgent necessity," so as to render relief of some kind absolutely necessary, the Relieving Officer in that case would be bound to afford relief out of the house in articles of absolute necessity until the next meeting of the Guardians. It will, however, be necessary that the Relieving Officer should act with great care and discretion in all such cases, and it will be his duty to report the circumstances to the Guardians, and take their further directions for his future guidance. It should also be observed that it is the duty of the Relieving Officer, under this regulation, to administer relief without reference to the place where the applicant had last slept.

directions of the Guardians with reference to the relief administered in such cases (*a*).

Art. 215.—No. 8. To perform the duties with respect to pauper apprentices prescribed by Arts. 60, 61, and 62.

As regards the burial of paupers, it should be observed that a Relieving Officer is not legally bound to interfere in any way unless "duly authorized" (7 & 8 Vict. c. 101, s. 31) to direct the burial at the expense of the poor-rates; *i.e.* he must either have a general authority from the Guardians, or a special authority in regard to the particular burial ; and the authority should be expressed by a resolution of the Guardians, duly recorded in their minutes. Such a resolution may be passed by the Guardians in the following terms:—"Resolved, that in pursuance of the 7 & 8 Vict. c. 101, s. 31, this Board hereby authorize the Relieving Officers of this Union, between the intervals of the meetings of the Guardians, to bury, at the expense of the poor-rates, any dead bodies within their respective districts, and also any deceased paupers who at the time of death were in receipt of relief from this Board. It is also ordered that the Relieving Officers report such cases, and produce vouchers for the amount expended, at the next meeting of the Guardians for their sanction."

In Parishes in which the military are stationed, it will sometimes happen that soldiers becoming lunatics, on their discharge from the service, are taken to the Poor Law authorities to be relieved. In such cases, if the lunatic be destitute, it is the duty of the Relieving Officer to undertake the case in the same way as the case of any ordinary applicant for relief.

It is sometimes found that aged poor persons will not accept relief in a Workhouse, even though they are in such a state of mind and body as to be incapable of taking care of themselves out of it. Such cases are extremely difficult to deal with, as the Guardians cannot compel destitute persons to enter the Workhouse against their will. The only available course of proceeding appears to be for the Guardians to order the Relieving Officer to stop the allowance of out-door relief, and, if the pauper refuses to enter the Workhouse, to direct the officer to watch the case, and afford such temporary relief in kind as the urgency of it may render necessary during the intervals of the Guardians' meetings.

Guardians sometimes determine, from prudential and philanthropic motives, to take children who are not being properly brought up by their parents or other relations, into the Workhouse, though no application may have been made to them to do so. In reference to such cases, it should be stated that, if the children are not really destitute, the Guardians would not be legally justified in interfering with them, notwithstanding that they may have reason to apprehend that they will be brought up to a life of immorality. If they be really destitute, the case will, of course be different, and the Guardians, in dealing with it, will be guided by a due consideration of the facts of each case as they may arise.

(*a*) The intention of this rule is, that the Relieving Officer shall report to the Guardians all cases reported to him by an Overseer, in con-

Art. 215.—No. 9 (a). To give all reasonable aid and assistance at the request of any other Relieving Officer of the Union, by examining into the case of any applicant for relief, or administering relief to any pauper whose name has been entered on the books of such other Relieving Officer, and who may be within his own district.

No. 10. Duly and punctually to supply the weekly allowances of all paupers belonging to his district, or being within the same, and to pay or administer the relief of all paupers within his district to the amount and in the manner in which he may have been lawfully ordered by the Guardians to pay or administer the same (b).

---

formity with Art. 1 of the General Order, on duties of Overseers, dated 22nd April, 1842 (*post*). In the regulations issued to new Unions this rule stands thus :—" To report to the Guardians, at their next ordinary meeting, all cases of relief given by an Overseer which may be reported to him by an Overseer, and to obey the directions of the Guardians with reference to the relief administered in such cases."

(a) The Relieving Officer is not bound to give such aid and assistance to the Relieving Officers of other Unions. It may be here observed that a Relieving Officer is not required to write to the Officers of other Unions advising relief to be given to paupers belonging to such other Unions, and removable thereto, but who are resident within his district. Any urgent case of want should be relieved at once, without any reference to the question of the pauper's settlement. As regards the mode of conducting the official correspondence with Officers of other Unions regarding relief cases, as well as other matters, see note to Art. 202, No. 3. The Clerk to the Board of Guardians is the proper officer to correspond in all matters relating to the relief of the poor, and the Relieving Officers should therefore abstain from doing so. See the remarks on the subject, *ante*, p. 143.

(b) The Relieving Officer must in all cases pay the paupers at the times and places he is directed to do so by the Board of Guardians ; and he has no authority, between the intervals of the Guardians' meetings, to vary the amount of relief which has been ordered by the Guardians ; but if he should do so, he must be prepared to show either obvious or manifest fraud on the part of the pauper, or a cessation of the circumstances under which the relief was given, as, in the case of illness, that the pauper has recovered or obtained employment at adequate wages. When the ground of withholding the relief is the cessation of the illness of the pauper, a medical certificate will be indispensable. On the other hand, the Relieving Officer has the power to allow additional relief in kind in cases of sudden and urgent necessity. On this point see

7 O. C. 232. The Relieving Officer cannot order the discharge of a pauper from the Workhouse who has been once received therein. The Relieving Officer should confine himself to the relief of paupers who are actually residing within his district. He is not required to relieve any destitute person who may be residing in the district of another Relieving Officer. The officer who receives the application from the pauper and is ordered by the Guardians to administer the relief, should do so, and charge the costs in his accounts accordingly. It will then be for the Guardians to charge the relief to the common fund. Moreover, a Relieving Officer has nothing to do with determining how relief to a pauper should be charged in the accounts of the Guardians. Questions of chargeability must be decided by the Guardians in the first instance. He must deal with the cases of the several paupers with respect to their relief according as their necessities may require, without reference to any question as their chargeability. (See also note (b) to Art. 215, No. 2.)

Relief to non-resident paupers belonging to a parish in his district may be administered by the Relieving Officer, if their names are entered in his Application and Report Book, and if they live within so short a distance as to enable him to visit and relieve them himself without interfering with the duties which he has to discharge within his district. In that case he would account for the relief given in the same manner as that allowed to paupers living within his district. If the non-resident paupers live at a distance, the Relieving Officers should not make the payments to them, but they should be relieved in the manner provided for by Articles 77, 78, 79, and 80, and the repayments of such relief should be made by the Guardians. On no account should the Relieving Officer enter in his accounts relief which he does not pay himself.

As the Guardians cannot lawfully give out-door relief to able-bodied paupers without the sanction of the Poor Law Board, the Relieving Officer will be liable to be called upon by the Auditor to repay out of his own pocket any relief which he may have given under the orders of the Guardians, contrary to the provisions of the General Prohibitory Order. When he is ordered by the Guardians to give out-door relief to able-bodied paupers whose cases do not come within any of the exceptions to Art. 1 of the Prohibitory Order, he ought to satisfy himself that the Clerk reports the cases to the Board for their sanction before the expiration of fifteen days from the day on which the relief is ordered to be given. Relieving Officers cannot lawfully give money to casual poor persons and wayfarers, to enable them to remove to another Union or Parish. If any Union or Parish Officer endeavours illegally to remove the burden of maintenance to another Parish or Union, or without any such intention defrays or gives money to defray the travelling expenses of the wayfarer, he will not only meet with the severest displeasure of the Commissioners, but also be liable to be indicted and proceeded against under the 9 & 10 Vict. c. 66, s. 6, which imposes a penalty, not exceeding five pounds and not less than forty shillings, upon any Officer of any Parish or Union who shall, contrary to law, with intent to cause any poor person to become chargeable to any Parish to which such person was not then chargeable, convey any poor person out of the Parish for which such officer acts, or cause or procure any poor person to

Art. 215.—No. 11. To visit, relieve, and otherwise attend to non-settled poor, being within his district, according to the directions of the Guardians, whose officer he is, and in no other way, subject always to the obligation imposed on him in cases of sudden or urgent necessity.

be so conveyed, provided in consequence thereof such poor person becomes chargeable to some other Parish. But it is legal for a Relieving Officer, after having received the proper written directions from the Guardians so to do, to defray the cost of the conveyance of a sick pauper to a hospital or infirmary at a distance, and the cost of his relief therein, and probably also the cost of the return journey.

By the 28 & 29 Vict. c. 79, s. 6, where the Guardians of any Union or Parish shall be satisfied that any pauper is settled within and removable to their Union or Parish, and shall consent, under their common seal, to receive such pauper without an order of removal, the Guardians seeking to remove such pauper may do so without any such order.

With reference to the above provision the Poor Law Board say :—

" Henceforth the respective Boards of Guardians will communicate mutually as to the removal of any pauper who may become chargeable, and if the facts be agreed upon and the settlement and removal be admitted, the pauper may be removed without the necessity of any depositions or order of justices, and consequently without the expense which attends those proceedings.

" The Guardians will under these provisions have to ascertain for themselves both the settlement and the removability of the paupers, and where they are removable, the Board of Guardians where the paupers are living will have to remove them.

" It will necessarily become a question for the consideration of the Guardians, to determine what course they shall adopt in carrying this measure into execution. The Board recommend them to make no lasting arrangement at present. They think it will be most advisable that the Boards of Guardians should await the experience of some few months, at least, before they undertake to provide for anything beyond the cases which may arise. But the Board must at once state that they would most strongly object to any proposal for making the Master of the Workhouse or the Relieving Officer act as Removing Officer.

" It is highly injurious to the management and relief of the poor, that either of those Officers should be absent from the Workhouse or his district for any purpose which is not in the discharge of his regular duties. Neglect of the poor, under such circumstances, is too probable an event to enable the Board to sanction any such arrangement." (*Instr. Letter*, 28th February, 1866.

In this place it may be mentioned, that by sect. 3, c. 24, of the Coast-Guard Regulations issued by the Admiralty, provision is made for granting travelling allowances to widows and children of Coast-Guardsmen to enable them to return to the parishes to which they belong.

Reference may here be made to the minutes of the Poor Law Commissioners on the subject of relief in clothing, and relief to members of Friendly Societies (Sixth Annual Report, 1840, pp. 93, 97.)

Art. 215.—No. 12. To set apart one or more pages in his out-door relief list, in which he shall duly and punctually enter up the payments made by authority of his own Board of Guardians to non-settled poor, and to take credit for such payments in his receipt and expenditure book (*a*).

No. 13. To present his weekly accounts to the Clerk for his inspection and authentication before every ordinary meeting of the Guardians, and to the Guardians, at such meeting, for their approval.

No. 14. To submit to the Auditor of the Union all his books, accounts, and vouchers, at the place of audit, and at such time and in such manner as may be required by the Regulations of the Commissioners (*b*).

No. 15. To assist the Clerk in conducting and completing the annual or other election of Guardians, according to the Regulations of the Commissioners (*c*).

No. 16. To observe and execute all lawful orders and directions of the Guardians applicable to his office (*d*).

(*a*) That is, poor persons chargeable to, or in the receipt of relief from the Guardians of other Unions.

(*b*) This duty is not contingent upon the Relieving Officer receiving notice of the day appointed for the audit. He is bound to inform himself of the time of the audit, of which notice will be given by the Clerk. (4 O. C. 79.)

(*c*) The Relieving Officer is not entitled to any extra remuneration for this service, unless it be specially awarded to him by the Guardians, with the sanction of the Poor Law Board, under Article 172.

(*d*) The order or direction of the Guardians should be expressed in the form of a resolution duly recorded in the minutes of the day.

As regards the attendance of the Relieving Officers before the Magistrates in Petty Sessions upon any matter relating solely to the business of any particular Parish when so required by the Parish Officers, see note to Art. 202, No. 2. As regards the attendance of Relieving Officers as witnesses, the Poor Law Board have stated that, as the whole time of the Relieving Officer is engaged by the Guardians, he is not legally entitled to claim compensation for his personal attendance as a witness in any case in which either the Guardians of the Union or the Parish Officers may require his evidence. But that he may properly claim to be reimbursed any reasonable extra expenses which he may be put to in attending the Court to give evidence. As a general rule, the Board consider that a Relieving Officer should attend in any such case without

Art. 216.—The Relieving Officer shall in no case take credit in his accounts, or enter as paid or given by way of relief, any money or other articles which have not been paid or given previously to the taking of such credit, or the making of such entry; and he shall not take credit in such accounts for any money paid to any tradesman or other person without producing, at the next ordinary meeting of the Guardians, a bill from such tradesman or person, with voucher of payment (*a*).

Duties of a Superintendent of Out-door Labour.

Art. 217.—The duties of a Superintendent of Out-door Labour shall be to superintend any able-bodied paupers, not inmates of the Workhouse, who may be set to work by the Guardians, to take care that they perform the work respectively assigned to them, and to report truly to the Guardians respecting the performance of such work (*b*).

---

putting the Parish Officers to the expense and trouble of procuring and serving either a summons or a subpœna, if he can do so without materially interfering with the discharge of the duties of his office. (See also the case, *Re Eastern Counties Railway Company and Overseers of Moulton*, 25 L. J. R. (N. S.) M. C. 49; 54 O. C. (N. S.) 48.) In 39 O. C. (N. S.) 112, on the same point, the Poor Law Board say that by the 7 & 8 Vict. c. 101, s. 70, Justices have the power of determining what is a fair and reasonable remuneration to be paid to witnesses who attend before them in poor removal cases. With regard to the Relieving Officer they say, as he is bound to give up his whole time to the service of the Union, this remuneration should not be more than sufficient to cover the expenses which he may incur in the attendance, as for instance, the refreshment which he may require, and the actual cost of his travelling. But with regard to the Clerk to the Guardians, as he is not bound to give up his whole time to the service of the Union, the Board consider that he should be paid a reasonable remuneration for his attendance in the same way that other witnesses are paid. What is a reasonable remuneration will be a question for the Justices to determine in reference to the circumstances of each case.

(*a*) Any departure from the strict injunction contained in this rule, on being discovered, will meet with the severest displeasure of the Poor Law Board, and may lead to the loss of the officer's situation.

(*b*) See the provisions of the Supplemental Out-door Labour Test Order (*post*), which however has only been issued to the Unions, the names of which follow the Order.

RECEIPT AND PAYMENT OF MONEY BY OFFICERS.

Art. 218.—No Clerk, Relieving Officer, Master, or other officer appointed to or holding any office under this Order, shall, directly or indirectly, receive or bargain to receive any gratuity, per-centage, or allowance of any kind with reference to any contract with the Guardians, or in respect of any payment made or to be made for goods supplied or work executed according to the order of such Guardians or on their behalf.

Art. 219.—No Clerk shall, directly or indirectly, cause to be paid to himself, or shall pay away on his own account or for his own benefit, any cheque drawn by the Guardians, and made payable to any person other than himself.

Art. 220.—Every Clerk, receiving any cheque or money from the Guardians on account of any other party, shall transmit the same within fourteen days to the proper persons, and shall produce the receipt or acknowledgment for the same at the next ordinary meeting after the same has come to his hands (c).

Art. 221.—Every officer of the Union who may receive money on behalf of the Guardians thereof, shall forthwith pay the same into the hands of the Treasurer of the Union, to the credit of the Guardians, notwithstanding that any salary or balance may be due from the Union to such officer (d).

(c) See Art. 51, and note, p. 39, as to the attendance of contractors and tradesmen to receive payment of their accounts.

(d) This Article is imperative even though the officer, if a Relieving Officer, may not at the time have sufficient money in his hands belonging to the Guardians to pay the poor with. The word "forthwith" must be taken to signify "with all convenient speed;" and the Article must be most strictly observed by the whole of the officers. The words "immediately on demand," in a covenant to pay money, must bear a reasonable construction; and in the particular case it was held that the obligee was entitled to a reasonable time to pay the money and make inquiries as to whom he might safely pay it. (*Toms* v. *Wilson*, 9 Jur. (N. S.) 492.)

Art. 222.—No Relieving Officer or other officer of any Guardians, nor any Assistant Overseer or Collector, shall receive money for the relief of any non-settled pauper on behalf of any officer, or of the Guardians of any other Parish or Union, or shall constitute himself in any way the agent of any officer or Guardians of such other Parish or Union, except as is provided in this Order (*a*).

Art. 223.—If any money be transmitted to any officer, contrary to the provisions of this Order, such officer shall forthwith pay such money into the hands of the Treasurer of the Union whose officer he is, and shall report to the Guardians at their next meeting the fact that such money has been so received and paid, and shall make a true entry accordingly in his accounts.

EXPLANATION OF TERMS.

Art. 224.—Whenever the word "Parish" is used in this Order, it shall be taken to include any place maintaining its own poor, whether parochial or extra-parochial (*b*).

Art. 225.—Whenever the word "Overseer" is used in this Order, it shall be taken to include any person acting or legally bound to act in the discharge of any of the duties

---

(*a*) This Article only prohibits the receipt of money by any officer to be applied by such officer in relieving any non-settled pauper. It does not prevent an officer from receiving money in repayment of relief already afforded by order of his Board of Guardians to a non-settled pauper. But in the event of money so coming into an officer's hands, it will be his duty to pay it over to the Treasurer, as directed by Arts. 221 and 223. As regards the administration of relief to non-settled poor, see Art. 77–80.

(*b*) By the 29 & 30 Vict. c. 113, s. 18, in all statutes, except there shall be something in the context inconsistent herewith, the word "Parish" shall, among other meanings applicable to it, signify a place for which a separate Poor Rate is or can be made, or for which a separate Overseer is or can be appointed.

As to extra-parochial places, see the 20 Vict. c. 19, by which such places are constituted Parishes for all the purposes of the Assessment to the Poor Rate, the Relief of the Poor, the County, Police, or Borough Rate, the Burial of the Dead, the Removal of Nuisances, the Registration of Parliamentary and Municipal Voters, and the Registration of Births and Deaths.

usually performed by Overseers of the Poor, so far as such duties are referred to in this Order (c).

Art. 226.—Whenever the word "Commissioners" is used in this Order, it shall be taken to mean the Poor Law Commissioners (d).

Art. 227.—Whenever the word "medicines" is used in this Order, it shall be taken to include all medical and surgical appliances; whenever the words "medical attendance" are used in this Order, they shall be taken to include surgical attendance; and whenever the words "medical relief" are used in this Order, they shall be taken to include relief by surgical as well as medical attendance (e).

(c) The word "Overseer," therefore, will include a Churchwarden, who by virtue of his office is an Overseer of the poor, and it will also include an Assistant Overseer, having the duties of an Overseer delegated to him in his warrant of appointment, under the 59 Geo. III. c. 12, s. 7.

(d) This Article is omitted in the Consolidated Orders subsequently issued.

The powers of the Poor Law Commissioners having ceased, the word "Commissioners" is now to be taken to mean "the Poor Law Board." (12 & 13 Vict. c. 103, s. 21.)

(e) The supply of an expensive medicine, such as Cod Liver Oil, may be made the subject of a special agreement with the Guardians on the appointment of the Medical Officer.

The Poor Law Board, in a circular dated 12th April, 1865, referring to the Report of the House of Commons on Poor Relief (Session 1864), and to the recommendation of the Committee that in future Cod Liver Oil, Quinine, and other expensive medicines shall be provided at the expense of the Guardians, subject to the orders and regulations of the Poor Law Board, request the Guardians to consider whether an alteration in the medical arrangements as regards the supply of the medicines referred to cannot be made whenever a new appointment of a Medical Officer may become necessary; or, with the consent of the present Medical Officers, during the continuance of their existing contracts.

With regard to the mode in which the proposed object can most conveniently be effected the Board are of opinion,—1. That it may be advisable to provide a store of Cod Liver Oil at the Workhouse, or at some other convenient places of deposit in the Union, and to supply it to the sick poor on the prescription of the Medical Officers, through the Relieving Officers, in the same way as Wine, or other extras recommended by the Medical Officers in the way of nourishment, are now supplied. 2. That Quinine and other expensive medicines may be supplied—either by an order of the Medical Officer on a Chemist, the cost of the medicines so ordered being paid for by the Guardians to such

Art. 228.—Whenever the words "Medical Officer" are used in this Order, they shall be taken to include any person duly licensed as a medical man, who may have contracted or agreed with any Guardians for the supply of medicines, or for medical attendance (*a*).

Art. 229.—Whenever the words Clerk (*b*), Master, or Matron are used in this Order, they shall be taken to mean the Clerk to the Guardians, and the Master or Matron of the Workhouse respectively.

Art. 230.—The term "non-resident poor" in this Order shall be taken to mean all paupers in receipt of relief allowed on account of any Union in relation to which the term is used, but not residing therein.

Art. 231.—The term "non-settled poor" in this Order shall be taken to mean all paupers residing in the Union

---

Chemist as goods or provisions supplied in relief, or, by the Medical Officers themselves, who may send in an account quarterly to the Guardians of the cost of the medicines in question which they may have supplied to their pauper patients.

The former plan the Board say may probably be convenient in the town Unions; the latter in the country Unions. And they add that Cod-Liver Oil, and any other medicines intended to be so supplied, should be specified and excepted from the provisions of the medical contract, which require generally that Medical Officers should themselves provide the requisite medicines and medical appliances for their pauper patients.

An "Elastic Bandage" would come within the term "surgical appliance" (58 O. C. (N. S.) 103), though the proper interpretation of the words, when applied to articles of use or wear, would seem to include only such things as a medical practitioner would supply to his private patients, and not such as he would recommend the patient to obtain from tradesmen or dealers themselves. Leeches would also come within the meaning of the same term. (4 O. C. 88.)

A "Truss" is a surgical appliance within the meaning of this Article; so also is a Pessary, which is in the nature of a Truss; but a specific payment for them to the Medical Officer may be provided for under his agreement.

(*a*) But see the Medical Act, 21 & 22 Vict. c. 96, and note to Article 168, page 118.

(*b*) The definition in this Article of the word "Clerk" is omitted in the Consolidated Order issued to new Unions, and is defined in the following substantive Article:—"The word 'Clerk' shall mean the Clerk to the Guardians, and shall extend in this order to the person who may be appointed, under Article 2, to act as such in the performance of the duties hereby prescribed relating to the election of Guardians."

in relation to which the term is used, but to whom relief is allowed on account of some Parish or Union other than that in which they reside (c).

Art. 232.—Whenever, in describing any person or party, matter or thing, the word importing the singular number or the masculine gender only is used in this Order, the same shall be taken to include, and shall be applied to, several persons or parties, as well as one person or party, and females as well as males, and several matters or things as well as one matter or thing, respectively, unless there be something in the subject or context repugnant to such construction.

Art. 233.—Whenever in this Order any Article is referred to by its number, the Article of this Order bearing that number shall be taken to be signified thereby.

SCHEDULES.

FORM A.—*Election of Guardians of the Poor.* (See Art. 6.)—(*This Form of Notice has been rescinded by the General Order of the 14th January,* 1867, *and again by the Order of 21st February,* 1868, *which latter Order prescribes another Form of Notice.*)

(c) This definition of "non-settled poor" does not include "irremovable poor," under the 9 & 10 Vict. c. 66, who are "non-settled," in relation to the Union from which they are "irremovable."

In the Consolidated Orders subsequently issued, the following additional Article is inserted:—"The word 'child' shall signify a person under the age of twenty-one years."

All classes of poor (with the exception of lunatics made chargeable to the county, and certain classes of poor in Unions and Parishes within the Metropolitan district) are now chargeable to the common fund. The Union Chargeability Act, 1865, 28 & 29 Vict. c. 79, s. 1, repeals so much of 4 & 5 Wm. IV. c. 76, s. 26, as requires Parishes in Unions to defray expenses of their own poor. Henceforth "all the cost of the relief to the poor, and the expenses of the burial of the dead body of any poor person under the direction of the Guardians, or of any of their officers duly authorized (see 7 & 8 Vict. c. 101, s. 31) in such Union thenceforth incurred, and all charges thenceforth incurred by the Guardians of such Union in respect of vaccination (see 30 & 31 Vict. c. 84), and registration fees and expenses (see 6 & 7 Wm. IV. c. 86, s. 29), shall be charged upon the common fund thereof."

FORM B.—*Nomination Paper.* (See Art. 8.)

Parish of ——— }
——— UNION. } This ——— day of ———, 18—.

Names of Persons nominated to be Guardians.	Residence of the Persons nominated.	Quality or Calling of Persons nominated.

I, being* ——— duly qualified to vote in the Parish aforesaid, nominate the above to be Guardian (*or* Guardians) for the said Parish.

——— Signature } of Nominator.
——— Address }

FORM C.—*Voting Paper.* (See Art. 10.) *This Form of Voting Paper has been rescinded by the General Order of the 14th January,* 1867, *which prescribes another Form of Notice. See Art.* 2 *of that Order, post,* p. 232.

FORM D.—*Notice to Guardians Elected.* (See Art. 23.)

(In consequence of the provision in the 14 & 15 Vict. c. 105, s. 2, with respect to the continuance in office of Guardians until the 15th April, inclusive, in each year, notwithstanding the election of their successors, the Poor Law Board, by a General Order, dated the 22nd March, 1852, *post*, have substituted an amended Form of Notice to Guardians elected, for the Form originally contained in this Order.)

FORM E. (See Art. 24.)

——— UNION.

I do hereby certify that the Election of Guardians of the

---

* *Note.*—Only one person is empowered to sign this paper, and after the word *being* he must insert (*a ratepayer*) or (*owner of property*), according to his qualification.

Poor for the several Parishes in the ——— Union was conducted in conformity with the Order of the Poor Law Commissioners, and that the Entries contained in the Schedule hereunto written are true.

Parishes (arranged alphabetically.)	Names of Persons nominated as Guardians.	Residence.	Quality or Calling.	No. of Votes given for each Candidate.	Names of the Guardians elected.	Names of the Guardians qualified to act in the Parishes where no Guardian has been elected.

Given under my hand this ——— day of ———
——— Clerk to the Guardians of the Poor of the ——— Union.

FORM F. (See Art. 34.)

To the Clerk of the Guardians of the ——— Union.

Requisition for an Extraordinary Meeting of Guardians.

We, the undersigned, being two of the Guardians of the Poor of the ——— Union, do hereby require an Extraordinary Meeting of the Guardians of the said ——— Union to be summoned, to be holden at ——— on ——— the ——— day of ——— 18—, at ——— o'clock in the forenoon, to take into consideration [*set out the business.*]

———
——— } Guardians.

FORM G.—*Notice of Change of Period, Time or Place of Meeting.* (See Art. 35.)

——— day of ——— 18—.

To *A. B.*, Guardian of the Poor of the ——— Union.

Sir,—You are hereby informed that the next Ordinary Meeting of the Guardians of the Poor of the ——— Union will take place at ——— on ——— day the ——— day of ——— 18—, at ——— o'clock in the ———noon, for the transaction of business; and that the Ordinary Meetings of the said Guardians will henceforth be held [*weekly or fortnightly, as the case may be,*] at the same place, on the same day of the week, and at the same hour.

———— Signature of Clerk to the Guardians.

FORM II.—*Notice of an Adjourned Meeting of Guardians.*
(See Art. 35.)

———— day of ———— 18——.

To *A. B.*, Guardian of the Poor of the ———— Union.

Sir,—This is to give you notice, that an adjourned meeting of the Guardians of the Poor of the ———— Union will be held at ———— on ———— the ———— day of ———— 18——, which meeting you are hereby requested to attend.

———— Signature of Clerk to the Guardians.

FORM I.—*Notice of an Extraordinary Meeting of Guardians.*
(See Art. 35.)

———— day of ———— 18——.

To *A. B.*, Guardian of the Poor of the ———— Union.

Sir,—I am directed by *C. D.* and *E. F.*, two of the Guardians of the Poor of the ———— Union, to summon an Extraordinary Meeting of the Guardians of the Poor of the said Union, at ———— on ———— the day of ———— 18——. at ———— o'clock in the forenoon, to take into consideration [*set out the business*], which meeting you are hereby requested to attend.

———— Signature of Clerk to the Guardians.

FORM K.—*Out-Relief Ticket.* (See Art. 43.)

———— UNION.
Weekly Relief ordered the ———— day of ———— 18——.

Name.	Money.	Loaves. lb. each.	For what Period.
	Other Articles.		

———— Signature of Relieving Officer.

FORM L.—*Ticket for Permanent Medical List.*
(See Art. 76.)

```
                                           _____ UNION.
Date _____
Good until the _____ day of _____ 18____
Name of Pauper _____
Residence of Pauper _____
Name of Medical Officer _____
Residence _____
Usual hour at which he is at home _____
```

FORM M.—*Order for Contributions.* (See Art. 83.) *And the substituted Form in the Order of the Poor Law Board, dated 26th February, 1866, post.*

Form N. (See Art. 102.)

	Time of Rising.	Interval for Breakfast.	Time for Work.	Interval for Dinner.	Time for Work.	Interval for Supper.	Time for going to bed.
From 25th March to 29th Sept....	½ before 6	From ½ past 6 to 7	From 7 to 12	From 12 to 1	From 1 to 6	From 6 to 7	8 o'clock
From 29th Sept. to 25th March	½ before 7	From ½ past 7 to 8	From 8 to 12	From 12 to 1	From 1 to 6	From 6 to 7	8 o'clock

Form O.—*Workhouse Punishment Book.* (See Art. 143.)

No. of the Case.	Name.	Offence.	Date of Offence.	Punishment inflicted by Master or other Officer.	Opinion of the Guardians thereon.	Punishment ordered by Board of Guardians.	Date of Punishment.	Initials of Clerk.	Observations.

Form P (a).—*District Medical Relief Book.* (See Art. 206, No. 4.)—(*See the substituted Form in the Order of the Poor Law Board of 26th Feb., 1866, post.*)

Form Q.—*Workhouse Medical*

(A.) To be filled up by the Medical Officer.

Initials of Medical Officer in attendance on every Case.	Name of the Sick Pauper	When admitted to Sick Ward.	When discharged.	Nature of Disease.	Days. when attended.							Males. The No.* of the Dietary on which placed.							Females. The No.* of the Dietary on which placed.							Extras.			
					S	M	T	W	Th	F	Sat	S	M	T	W	Th	F	Sat	S	M	T	W	Th	F	Sat	What ordered.	When ordered.	When discontinued.	State or Termination of the Case, and in the event of Death the apparent cause of.
					Total No. each Day																					Total Quantity consumed.			

* Dietaries for the sick are to be numbered thus:—No. 1. House

As regards the Sick Paupers on Diet No. 1 (House Diet), the will appear in the "Daily Provisions' Consumption Account," for ing date the 17th day of March, 1847.

The Number of the Paupers on each description of the Dietaries the close of each week to a Summary at the end of the

WEEKLY

No. of the Dietary.	Description of Classes in the Diet Table.	Sunday.
1	House Diet.—Males	
1	House Diet.—Females	
2	Full Diet.—Males	
2	Full Diet.—Females	
3	Low Diet.—Males	
3	Low Diet.—Females	
4	Fever Diet.—Males	
4	Fever Diet.—Females	
	Total Number of Sick Paupers...	

Schedule.—Form Q.

...lief Book (See Art. 207, No. 8.)

(B. To be filled up by the Master of the Workhouse, with the Articles actually given.

Quantity of Provisions consumed.								Extras provided.					
Bread.	Meat.	Bacon.	Cheese.	Rice.	Oatmeal.	Milk.		Ale.	Porter.	Wine.	Brandy.	Gin.	Remarks.
lbs.	lbs.	lbs.	lbs.	lbs.	lbs.	pints.		pints	pints	pints	pints.	pints.	

...et. No. 2. Full Diet, No. 3. Low Diet. No. 4. Fever Diet.

...tras only should be entered in this book, since their ordinary Diet ...hich see Form 26 of the General order of the Commissioners, bear-

...d according to the several Sexes is to be carried by the Master at ...ook, to be prepared in the following Form :—

...MMARY.

	Number of Patients each Day.						Collective Number of days.
Monday.	Tuesday.	Wednesday.	Thursday.	Friday.	Saturday.		

Form R. (See Art. 207, No. 9.)

*DIETARY FOR SICK PAUPERS.

No. 1	House Diet being the ordinary diet for the paupers in the house.								
No. 2		Breakfast.		Dinner.				Supper.	
2	Full Diet...	ounces.	pints.	ounces.	pints.	ounces.	ounces.	pints.	ounces.	pints.
2	Males									
2	Females ...									
		Breakfast.		Dinner.				Supper.	
3	Low Diet...	ounces.	pints.	ounces.	pints.	ounces.	ounces.	pints.	ounces.	pints.
3	Males.									
3	Females ...									
		Breakfast.		Dinner.				Supper.	
4	Fever Diet	ounces.	pints.	ounces.	pints.	ounces.	ounces.	pints.	ounces.	pints.
4	Males									
4	Females. ...									

N.B. Sugar, Arrow-Root, Sago, Butter, Milk, Wine, Spirits, Porter, and Beer, are in all cases to be treated as extras, to be expressly ordered when required, and the quantity is to be then specified in the proper column of this book.

* If thought proper by the Medical Officer, any additional number of Dietaries may be introduced, and numbered consecutively.

Form S. (See Art. 208, No. 13.)—(*See the substituted Form in the Order of the Poor Law Board of 26th Feb., 1866, post.*)

Form T. (See Art. 208, No. 17.)—(*See the substituted Form in the Order of the Poor Law Board of 26th Feb., 1866, post.*)

FORM U. (See Art. 208, No. 25.)

—— UNION WORKHOUSE. *Week ending* —— 18—.

WARDS.	Beds therein.	Number of Occupants each Night.							Total.	Observations.
		S.	M.	T.	W.	Th.	F.	Sat.		
Able-bodied Men ...										
Old Men										
Boys										
Male Infirmary										
—— Infectious										
—— Receiving										
Total										
Able-bodied Women										
Old Women										
Girls										
Female Infirmary ...										
Lying-in Ward										
Female Infectious ...										
—— Receiving......										
Total										

The foregoing is a true statement.

—— Master.
—— Matron.

FORM V.—*The Medical Relief Order Check Book.*
(See Art. 215, No. 3.)

No.——	No.——
To ——, Medical Officer.	To ——, Medical Officer, —— Union.
Name, _____	Sir,
Age, _____	You are hereby requested to visit and undertake the treatment of the undermentioned cases.
Residence, _____	Name, _____
Nature of Case, _____	Age, _____
Forwarded by —— at —— o'clock in the —— of the —— day of —— 18—.	Residence, _____
	Nature of Case,* _____
—— Relieving Officer.	Forwarded by —— at —— o'clock in the —— of the —— day of —— 18—.
	—— Relieving Officer.

* This is to be filled up so as to distinguish—
  1. Midwifery Cases.
  2. Fractures and Accidents.
  3. Cases of urgency, which require immediate attention.

SCHEDULE,

Containing the Names of the Unions to which the annexed Order applies.

Aberaeron.
Abergavenny.
Aberystwith.
*Abingdon.
Alban's, St.
Alcester.
Alderbury.
*Alnwick.
Alresford.
Alton.
*Altrincham.
Amersham.
Amesbury.
Ampthill.
*Andover.
*Anglesey.
Asaph, St.
*Ashbourne.
Ashby-de-la-Zouch.
Ashford, East.
Ashford, West.
Ashton-under-Lyne.
Aston.
*Atcham.
Atherstone.
*Auckland.
Austell, St.
*Axbridge.
Axminster.
*Aylesbury.
*Aylsham.

*Bakewell.
Bala.
*Banbury.
Bangor & Beaumaris.

Barnet.
*Barnstaple.
Barrow-upon-Soar.
*Basford.
*Basingstoke.
Bath.
Battle.
Beaminster.
Bedale.
*Bedford.
Bedminster.
*Belford.
*Bellingham.
*Belper.
Berkhampstead.
Berwick-upon-Tweed.
*Beverley.
*Bicester.
Bideford.
Biggleswade.
Billericay.
*Billesdon.
*Bingham.
Bishop Stortford.
Blaby.
Blackburn.
*Blandford.
Blean.
*Blofield.
*Blything.
Bodmin.
Bolton.
Bootle.
*Bosmere and Claydon.
Boston.
*Boughton, Great.

*Bourn.
Brackley.
Bradfield.
Bradford (Wilts).
Bradford (York).
Braintree.
Brampton.
*Brecknock.
Brentford.
Bridge. [bridge.
*Bridgend and Cow-
*Bridgewater.
Bridgnorth.
*Bridlington.
Bridport.
*Brixworth.
Bromley.
Bromsgrove.
*Bromyard.
Buckingham.
*Builth.
Buntingford.
Burnley.
*Burton-upon-Trent.
Bury.

*Caistor.
Calne.
Cambridge.
Camelford.
*Cardiff.
Cardigan.
Carlisle.
Carmarthen.
Carnarvon.
*Castle Ward.

---

* The asterisks refer to the order relating to the payment of the expenses attending the election of Guardians, as to which see *post*, p. 219.

Catherington.
Caxton & Arrington,
Cerne.
Chailey.
Chapel-en-le-Frith.
*Chard.
Cheadle.
*Chelmsford.
Cheltenham.
*Chepstow.
Chertsey.
*Chesterfield.
Chester-le-Street.
*Chesterton.
Chippenham.
*Chipping Norton.
Chipping Sodbury.
Chorley.
Chorlton.
Christchurch.
Church Stretton.
*Cirencester.
Cleobury Mortimer.
Clifton.
*Clitheroe.
Clun.
Clutton.
*Cockermouth.
Colchester.
Columb, St., Major.
*Congleton.
Conway.
Cookham.
Corwen.
Cosford.
Cranbrook.
Crediton.
Crickhowel.
Cricklade and Wootton Bassett.
Croydon.

Cuckfield.
*Darlington.
Dartford.
Daventry.
*Depwade.
Derby.
Devizes.
Dewsbury.
*Docking.†
Dolgelly.
*Doncaster.
*Dorchester.
Dore.
Dorking.
Dover.
*Downham.
Drayton.
*Driffield.
Droitwich.
Droxford.
Dudley.
Dulverton.
Dunmow.
Durham.
Dursley.

Easington.
Easingwold.
Eastbourne.
East Grinstead.
Easthampstead.
*East Retford.
Eastry.
East Ward.
Ecclesall Bierlow.
Edmonton.
Elham.
Ellesmere.
Ely.
Epping.

Epsom.
*Erpingham.
Eton.
Evesham.
Faith, St.
Falmouth.
Fareham.
*Faringdon.
Farnham.
Faversham.
Festiniog.
Foleshill.
Fordingbridge.
*Freebridge Lynn.
Frome.
Fulham.
Fylde.

*Gainsborough.
Garstang.
Gateshead.
Germans, St.
*Glanford Brigg.
*Glendale.
Glossop.†
*Gloucester.
Godstone.
Goole.
*Grantham.
Gravesend and Milton.
Greenwich.
Guildford.
Guiltcross.
Guisborough.

Hackney.
Hailsham.
·Halifax.
Halstead.
Haltwhistle.

---

† Docking is a Union for settlement, and Glossop a Union for rating and settlement.

Hambledon.
Hardingstone.
*Hartismere.
Hartley Wintney.
Haslingden.
Hastings.
Hatfield.
Havant.
*Haverfordwest.
Hay.
Hayfield.
Headington.
*Helmsley Blackmoor.
Helston.
Hemel Hempstead.
Hendon.
Henley.
*Henstead.
*Hereford.
Hertford.
*Hexham.   [don-
Highworth and Swin-
Hinckley.
Hitchin.
Holbeach.
Holborn.
Hollingbourn.
Holsworthy.
Holywell.
Honiton.
Hoo.
*Horncastle.
Horsham.
Houghton-le-Spring.
*Howden.
Hoxne.
*Huddersfield.
Hungerford.
*Huntingdon.
Hursley.

Ipswich.
Ives, St.

Keighley.
*Kendal.
Kettering.
Keynsham.
Kidderminster.
Kingsbridge.
Kingsclere.
King's Lynn.
King's Norton.
Kingston-upon-
 Thames.
Kington.
Knighton.

Lampeter.
Lancaster.
Lanchester.
Langport.
Launceston.
Ledbury.
Leek.
Leicester.
Leigh.
Leighton Buzzard.
Leominster.
Lewes.
Lewisham.
*Lexden & Winstree.
*Leyburn.
Lichfield.
*Lincoln.
Linton.
Liskeard.
Llandilo Fawr.
Llandovery.
Llanelly.
Llanfyllin.
Llanrwst.
*Loddon & Clavering.
*London, City of.
London, East.
London, West.
Longtown.

Loughborough.
*Louth.
*Ludlow.
Luton.
*Lutterworth.
Lymington.

*Macclesfield.
Machynlleth.
Madeley.
Maidstone.
*Maldon.
Malling.
Malmsbury.
*Malton.
Mansfield.
Market Bosworth.
*Market Harborough.
Marlborough.
Martley.
Medway.
Melksham.
*Melton Mowbray.
Mere.
Meriden.
Merthyr Tydvil.
Midhurst.
Mildenhall.
Milton.
*Mitford and Laun-
 ditch.
*Monmouth.
*Morpeth.

*Nantwich.
*Narbeth.
Neath.
Neot's, St.
*Newark.
Newbury.
Newcastle-in-Emlyn.
Newcastle-under-Lyne.
Newcastle-upon-Tyne.

Newent.
New Forest.
Newhaven.
Newmarket.
*Newport (Monmouth).
Newport (Salop).
*Newport Pagnell.
*Newton Abbott.
Newtown and Llanidloes.
*Northallerton.
Northampton.
North Aylesford.
Northleach.
*Northwich.
North Witchford.
Nottingham.†
Nuneaton.

Oakham.
Okehampton.
Olave's, St.
Ongar.
Ormskirk.
Orsett.
*Oundle.

Pateley Bridge.
Patrington.
Pembroke.
Penkridge.
*Penrith.
Penzance.
*Pershore.
*Peterborough.
Petersfield.
Petworth.
Pewsey.
Pickering.
*Plomesgate.
Plympton, St. Mary.
*Pocklington.
Pont-y-Pool.

Poole.
Poplar.
Portsea Island.
Potterspury.
Prescot.
Presteigne.
Preston.
*Pwllheli.

Radford.
Reading.
Redruth.
Reeth.
Reigate.
Rhayader.
Richmond (Surrey).
*Richmond (Yorkshire).
Ringwood.
Risbridge.
Rochdale.
Rochford.
Romford.
Romney Marsh.
Romsey.
Ross.
*Rothbury.
Rotherham.
Royston.
*Rugby.
*Runcorn.
Ruthin.
Rye.

*Saffron Walden.
Salford.
Saviour's, St.
*Scarborough.
Sculcoates.
Sedbergh.
Sedgefield.
Seisdon.
Selby.

*Settle.
Sevenoaks.
Shaftesbury.
*Shardlow.
Sheffield.
Sheppey.
Shepton Mallett.
Sherborne.
Shiffnall.
*Shipston-upon-Stour.
*Skipton.
*Skirlaugh.
*Sleaford.
Solihull.
Southam.
South Molton.
South Shields.
South Stoneham.
*Southwell.
Spalding.
*Spilsby.
Stafford.
Staines.
*Stamford.
Stepney.
Steyning.
Stockbridge.
Stockport.
*Stockton.
Stokesley.
Stone.
Stourbridge.
*Stow.
Stow-on-the-Wold.
Strand.
*Stratford-upon-Avon.
Stratton.
Stroud.
Sturminster.
*Sudbury.
Sunderland.
*Swaffham.
Swansea.

† The Election Expenses Order of 24th July, 1847, does not apply to Nottingham.

P

Tamworth.	Uxbridge.	Weymouth.
*Taunton.		Wheatenhurst.
Tavistock.	Wakefield.	Whitby.
*Teesdale.	Wallingford.	Whitchurch.†
Tenbury.	Walsal.	Whitechapel.
*Tendring.	*Walsingham.	Whitehaven.
Tenterden.	Wandsworth and	Wigan.
Tetbury.	Clapham.	*Wigton.
Tewkesbury.	Wangford.	*Williton.
Thakeham.	*Wantage.	Wilton.
*Thame.	Ware.	Wimborne and Cranborne.
Thanet, Isle of.	Wareham & Purbeck.	
*Thetford.	Warminster.	*Wincanton.
*Thingoe.	Warrington.	Winchcombe.
*Thirsk.	*Warwick.	*Winchester, New.
*Thomas, St.	Watford.	Windsor.
Thornbury.	Wayland.	Winslow.
Thorne.	Weardale.	*Wirrall.
Thrapston.	Wellingborough.	Wisbeach.
Ticehurst.	Wellington (Salop).	Witham.
Tisbury.	Wellington (Som.)	*Witney.
Tiverton.	Wells.	Woburn.
Todmorden.	Welwyn.	Wokingham.
Tonbridge.	Wem.	Wolstanton and Burslem.
Torrington.	Weobly.	
Totnes.	Westbourne.	Wolverhampton.
Towcester.	West Bromwich.	*Woodbridge.
Tregaron.	Westbury-upon-Severn.	*Woodstock.
Truro.		Worcester.
Tynemouth.	Westbury and Whorwelsdown.	Worksop.
		Wortley.
Uckfield.	West Derby.	*Wrexham.
Ulverstone.	West Firle.	*Wycombe.
*Uppingham.	West Ham.	
Upton-upon-Severn.	*West Hampnett.	*Yeovil.
Uttoxeter.	West Ward.	*York.

Given under our Hands and Seal of Office, this Twenty-fourth day of July, in the year One thousand eight hundred and forty-seven.

(L. S.)

(Signed) GEO. NICHOLLS.
     GEORGE CORNEWALL LEWIS.
     EDMUND W. HEAD.

† This refers to the Whitchurch Union in the County of Southampton.

Similar CONSOLIDATED ORDERS were subsequently issued to the following Unions on the dates undermentioned; and the remuneration to the Clerk for conducting the annual election of Guardians is in each case fixed at £10, with the exception of the Isle of Wight and Norwich Unions, in which the remuneration is fixed at £15, and in the Westminster and Woolwich Unions at £20 respectively; and in the case of contested elections at the same rate as is specified in Article 4 of the Election Expenses Order of 24th July, 1847, *post*, p. 219.

Barnsley	12th June, 1850.
Barton-upon-Irwell	24th January, 1850.
Bedwellty	19th March, 1849.
Bierley, North	14th February, 1849.
Birkenhead	8th April, 1861.
Bramley	7th January, 1863.
Gower	19th October, 1857.
Hartlepool	4th April, 1859.
Hawarden	25th February, 1853.
Hemsworth	29th October, 1850.
Holyhead	15th February, 1853.
Kirkby Moorside	9th February, 1850.
Knaresborough	28th June, 1854.
Norwich*	27th October, 1863.
Oldham	22nd November, 1847.
Ouseburn, Great	4th August, 1854.
Penistone	2nd February, 1850.
Pontefract	1st March, 1862.
Pontypridd	29th December, 1862.
Prestwich	2nd August, 1850.
Ripon	8th February, 1853.
Samford	16th March, 1849.
Tadcaster	7th March, 1862.
Westminster	13th April, 1868.

---

* See the Norwich Poor Act, 1863, 26 & 27 Vict. c. xciii.

Wetherby	4th March, 1861.
Wharfedale	7th March, 1861.
Whitchurch (Salop)	19th February, 1853.
Wight, Isle of	18th September, 1865.
Woolwich	8th April, 1868.

ORDERS ISSUED TO INCORPORATIONS.

Consolidated Orders modified to meet the provisions of the local Acts in each place, and omitting the provisions relating to the Election of Guardians, have been issued to the following:—

Bristol	24th April, 1856.
Amended	16th July, 1857.
Canterbury	13th June, 1856.
Exeter	20th September, 1856.
Amended	16th June, 1860.
Coventry	22nd August, 1859.

Similar Orders, but omitting the provisions relating to the apprenticeship of pauper children as well as those relating to the election of Guardians, have been issued to

Alverstoke	28th February, 1852.
Birmingham	16th January, 1850.
Chichester	27th March, 1852.
Amended	19th January, 1854.
Farnborough	18th June, 1852.
Headley	6th July, 1852.
Kingston-upon-Hull	2nd March, 1850.
Oswestry	16th November, 1850.
Plymouth	6th August, 1853.
Amended	24th April, 1855.
Southampton	26th February, 1850.
Stoke Damerel	31st January, 1855.

A similar order, but omitting the provisions relating to the Custody of Bonds as well as those relating to the Apprenticeship of Pauper Children and the Election of Guardians, has been issued to

Salisbury	27th February, 1858.

Orders containing Rules and Regulations for the Government of the Workhouse and the Appointment and Duties of Workhouse Officers have been issued to

Ash	20th March, 1837.
Barwick-in-Elmet (Wrkh^{se} rules)	19th May, 1848.
Caton (Workhouse rules) . .	12th February, 1850.
Montgomery and Pool . . .	22nd June, 1846.
Oxford	16th August, 1843.
Shrewsbury	27th April, 1850.

Orders have been issued to the Chester Incorporation for

Government of the Workhouse .	13th August, 1844.
Appointm^t, etc., of Relievg Offic^{rs}	14th December, 1850.
Medical Relief Regulations . .	9th August, 1851.

In the Bury St. Edmund's, East and West Flegg, Forehoe, Mutford and Lothingland, and Tunstead and Happing Incorporations, the following General Orders of the Poor Law Commissioners are in force:—

Workhouse Rules and Regulations	5th February, 1842.
Medical Regulations	12th March, 1842.
Proceed^{gs} of Boards of Guardians	20th April, 1842.
Duties of Officers	21st April, 1842.

THE CONSOLIDATED ORDER—PARISHES.

(8*th December*, 1847.)

To the Guardians of the Poor *of the several* **Parishes** *and* **Township** *named in the Schedule hereunto annexed.*

To the Churchwardens and Overseers of the said several Parishes and Township;—

To the Clerk or Clerks to the Justices of the Petty Sessions held for the Division or Divisions in which the said Parishes and Township are situate;—

And to all others whom it may concern.

WE, the Poor Law Commissioners, in pursuance of the authorities vested in Us by an Act passed in the fifth year of the reign of his late Majesty King William the Fourth, intituled "*An Act for the Amendment and better Administration of the Laws relating to the Poor in England and Wales,*" and by all other Acts amending the same, do hereby rescind every Order, whether General or Special, heretofore issued by the Poor Law Commissioners to the Parishes and Township named in the Schedule hereunto annexed, which relates to the several subjects herein provided for, except so far as the same may have related to the apprenticeship of any poor person not yet completed, or may have required or authorized the appointment of any officer, or the giving of any security, or the making of any contract not yet executed, or the making of any orders by the Guardians for contributions and payments not yet obeyed, or may have defined the salaries of any officers, or have prescribed the districts within which the duties of any officer shall be performed, or may have provided for the class of paupers or their number to be received into any particular Workhouse, or may have made special provisions in respect of the administration of medical relief, and the payment of the salaries or fees of medical officers, or may have provided for the election of Guardians in any case where such election shall not have been completed when this Order shall come into force, and except the Orders regulating the mode of election of Guardians in the Parishes of St. Mary Lambeth and Stoke-upon-Trent, and the Township of Leeds.

(*This Order is, with the exception of the substitution of the word "Parish" for "Union," similar to the General Consolidated Order to Unions, ante, p. 1. In this Order, however, Art. 161 of the Order of the 24th July, 1847, is omitted, it being inapplicable.*)

SCHEDULE,

Containing the Names of the Parishes and Township to which the annexed Order applies.

- Alston-with-Garrigill.
- East Stonehouse.
- Leeds.
- St. George-in-the-East (*a*).
- St. Martin-in-the-Fields (*b*).
- St. Mary Abbots, Kensington.
- St. Mary, Lambeth.
- St. Mary Magdalen, Bermondsey.
- St. Mary, Rotherhithe.
- St. George the Martyr, Southwark (*c*).
- St. Giles, Camberwell.
- St. Luke, Chelsea.
- St. Matthew, Bethnal Green.
- Paddington.
- Stoke-upon-Trent.
- Whittlesea, St. Mary and St. Andrew.
- Great Yarmouth.

Given under our Hands and Seal of Office, this Eighth day of December, in the year One thousand eight hundred and forty-seven.

L. S.

(Signed) GEORGE NICHOLLS.
EDMUND W. HEAD.

(*a*) Art. 159, suspended 10th May, 1855.
(*b*) Since added to the Strand Union.
(*c*) An Order containing Regulations for the Treatment of Lunatics at Mitcham, was issued on the 30th April, 1862.

CONSOLIDATED ORDERS have subsequently been issued, on the dates undermentioned, to the following Parishes, in each of which relief to the poor is administered under a separate Board of Guardians; the remuneration to the Clerk for conducting the Annual Election of Guardians is in each case fixed at £10 to those places marked *, at £20 to those places marked †; and in the case of contested elections, at the same rate as is specified in Art. 3 of the Election Expenses Order of the 8th December, 1847 (p. 219, *post*), to be paid to the Clerks of all Parishes mentioned in the Schedule of that Order, with the exception of St. Mary and St. Andrew, Whittlesea.

*Hampstead, St. John:—
  Election of Guardians . . . . 20th January, 1849.
  Meetings and Proceedings of Guardians; Appointment and Duties of Officers other than the Workhouse Officers . . . . 24th May, 1848.
  Workhouse Regulations; Appointment and Duties of Workhouse Officers . . . . . 19th August, 1850.
*Holbeck . . . . 24th Sept., 1862.
*Hunslet . . . . 24th Sept., 1862.
  „ Election Expenses suspended . . . . 17th October, 1866.
Manchester . . . . 31st May, 1850.
  „ Election Expenses suspended . . . 29th July, 1856.
  Arts. 172, 173, 174, 175, 176, 177, 178, regarding the payment of fees to the Medical Officers, have been suspended.
*Mile End Old Town . . . . 4th April, 1857.
*Saddleworth . . . . 18th July, 1853.
†St. George, Hanover Square . . . . 7th August, 1867.
†St. Giles and St. George, Bloomsbury . . . . 20th April, 1868.
†St. James, Clerkenwell . . . . 31st January, 1868.
†St. Leonard, Shoreditch . . . . 15th January, 1868.
†St. Luke, Middlesex . . . . 4th March, 1868.
†St. Margaret and St. John the Evangelist, Westminster . . . . 23rd Sept., 1867.
†St. Mary, Islington . . . . 4th July, 1867.
†St. Marylebone . . . . 31st July, 1867.

†St. Mary, Newington . . . . {4th Sept., 1867.
28th October, 1867.
†St. Pancras . . . . 8th June, 1867.
Toxteth Park . . . . 16th June, 1857.
„ Election Expenses suspended . . 13th January, 1858.

An Order containing Rules and Regulations for the government of the Workhouse, and the appointment and duties of Workhouse officers, was issued to

Liverpool . . . . 27th April, 1843.

Regulations have been issued for the Government of the Schools of the Workhouses of the following places;—

Brighton	Warren Farm		5 January, 1863.
Cardiff	Ely		19 November, 1867.
Lambeth	Norwood Schools		23 June, 1852.
Leeds	Beckett St.	„	8 March, 1854.
Liverpool	Kirkdale	„	7 August, 1856.
Manchester	Swinton	„	6 July, 1852.
Marylebone, St.	Southall	„	{1 June, 1860. 31 July, 1867.
Mile End Old Town (*including accounts by Matron*)			11 December, 1861.
Newport (Mon.)	Caerleon Schools		24 August, 1859.
Oxford	Cowley	„	24 November, 1854.
Shoreditch	Brentwood	„	{28 July, 1854, and 10 March, 1859. 15 January, 1868.
St. George-in-the-East	Plashet	„	14 June, 1852.
St. George the Martyr	Mitcham	„	18 August, 1855.
St. Giles & St. George, Bloomsbury	Isleworth	„	{8 March, 1866. 12 November, 1866.
St. James, Clerkenwell	Highgate Hill	„	11 December, 1860.
St. James, Westm^r	Battersea	„	6 July, 1852.
St. Mary, Islington		„	{29 March, 1867. 19 November, 1867.
Strand	Edmonton	„	3 January, 1856.
Whitechapel	Forest Lane	„	17 March, 1854.

Regulations for the Government of District Schools have been issued to the Managers of the following Districts:—

Central London	23rd February, 1852.
Farnham and Hartley Wintney	17th January, 1852.
Finsbury	
Forest Gate	
Kensington	
Lincolnshire and Nottinghamshire	
North Surrey	22nd May, 1851.
Reading and Wokingham	10th February, 1852.
South East Shropshire	16th August, 1851.
South Metropolitan	18th July, 1854.
West London	

Districts in the Metropolis formed under 30 Vict. c. 6:—

METROPOLITAN ASYLUM DISTRICT	15th May, 1867.	Declaration.
	18th June, 1867.	Rules and Regulations.
	17th July, 1867.	Amending ditto.

SICK ASYLUM DISTRICTS:—

Central London	2nd May, 1868.	Declaration.
	10th June, 1868.	Rules and Regulations.
Kensington	28th Jan., 1868.	Declaration.
	29th Feb., 1868.	Rules and Regulations.
Newington	18th Jan., 1868.	Declaration.
	7th Feb., 1868.	Rules and Regulations.
Poplar and Stepney	23rd April, 1868.	Declaration.
	16th May, 1868.	Rules and Regulations.
Rotherhithe	18th Jan., 1868.	Declaration.
	18th Feb., 1868.	Rules and Regulations.

ELECTION EXPENSES ORDER—UNIONS.

(24th July, 1847.)

To the Guardians of the Poor *of the several* **Unions** *named in the Schedules hereunto annexed;—*

To the Churchwardens and Overseers of the Poor of the several Parishes comprised in the said several Unions;—

To the Clerk or Clerks to the Justices of the Petty Sessions held for the Division or Divisions in which the said several Unions are situate;—
And to all others whom it may concern.

WE, the Poor Law Commissioners, do hereby, under the authority of an Act passed in the fifth year of the reign of his late Majesty King William the Fourth, intituled " *An Act for the Amendment and better Administration of the Laws relating to the Poor in England and Wales,*" rescind all such of the provisions contained in any Order or Orders under the hands and seal of the Poor Law Commissioners as direct the payment of expenses to be incurred in the election of Guardians of the Poor for the several Parishes comprised in the several Unions named in the Schedules hereunto annexed.

And whereas by a General Order under the hands and seal of the Poor Law Commissioners, bearing even date herewith, addressed to the Guardians of the Poor of the said several Unions, the said Commissioners have (amongst other things) prescribed the manner of conducting the future election of Guardians of the Poor for the several Parishes comprised in the said Unions; and it is expedient that provision should be made for the payment of the expenses to be incurred in such elections.

Now, therefore, We, the said Poor Law Commissioners, do hereby order and direct in regard thereto, with reference to each of the said Unions named in the said Schedules as follows:—That the expenses of every future election of Guardians of the Poor of the several Parishes comprised in the said Unions shall be defrayed by the Guardians of the said Unions in the manner hereinafter set forth; that is to say,—

Art. 1.—The cost of providing the several Forms marked (A.), (D.), and (E.), contained in the said Order, being the Notice of Election (*a*), the Notice to the Guardians elected, and the Certificate of the Election, shall be defrayed out of the common fund of the Union.

Art. 2.—The cost of providing the Form marked (C), contained in the said Order, being the Voting Paper, shall be defrayed out of the funds in the possession of the said Guardians belonging to the respective Parishes to which the Voting Papers shall relate.

Art. 3 (*b*).—The compensation which shall be paid to the Clerk, or to the person appointed under the authority of the said recited Order to act as such in the performance of the duties thereby prescribed, shall include the remuneration of the persons who may have been appointed or employed to assist him in conducting and completing the election, and shall, in respect of the

---

(*a*) See now the notice of Election in the Order of 21st Feb., 1868.

(*b*) This Article applies to special as well as to general elections, and under it the Guardians may award such compensation as they may think fit, within the limit prescribed, to the Clerk for conducting special elections of Guardians; and the amount is to be charged in the same manner and to the same fund as the expenses incurred in the annual election, as directed by the above Order. As regards the discretionary power of the Guardians under this Article, see *Ex parte Metcalfe*, 6 E. & B. 287. In that case the Court refused to order a Local Board of Health to pay a reasonable compensation to the person conducting the first election of the Local Board, upon a suggestion that an inadequate sum had been allowed; as the Local Board had a discretion as to what sum it was reasonable to allow, and the exercise of their discretion in this respect is not a subject to review.

several unions named in the following Schedule marked (A.), be such sum, not exceeding *Ten Pounds*, as the Guardians shall determine, and shall, in respect of the several Unions named in the following Schedule marked (B.), be such sum, not exceeding *Fifteen Pounds*, as the Guardians shall determine, and such sums respectively shall be defrayed out of the common fund of the Unions.

Art. 4 (*c*).—And in the case of every contested election, one farthing per head on the population of the Parish in which the contest shall have taken place, if the population shall be more than five hundred, and one halfpenny per head on the population of the Parish in which the contest shall have taken place, if the population be not more than five hundred, shall be paid to the said Clerk or other person as aforesaid in addition to such compensation, and shall be defrayed out of the funds in the possession of the said Guardians belonging to such Parish. And for the purpose of ascertaining the last-mentioned sums, the population of the Parish shall be taken to be as stated in the Census which at the time of such election shall have been last made under the authority of any Act of Parliament.

And We do hereby declare, that whenever the word

(*c*) Sometimes after the voting papers are prepared, candidates withdraw from the election, in consequence of which no contest arises. As to the allowance to the Clerk in such a case, see 24 O. C. 55, and 39 O. C. (N. S.) 104. It seems however that if the voting papers be actually issued, the Clerk would be entitled to payment according to this Article. The sum to which the Clerk will be entitled under this Article will be calculated according to the last published census, until the result of any new census, which in the meantime may have been taken, shall have been presented to Parliament and published.

In the case of a Parish divided into wards for the purposes of the election of Guardians, inasmuch as each ward is declared to be a separate Parish for all the purposes of the election of Guardians, in computing the amount of compensation to be allowed under this Article, the calculation should be made upon the population of the ward only. It will, however, not always be easy to ascertain the population in such cases with accuracy. The number of inhabited houses would apparently be some guide.

"Parish" is used in this Order, it shall be taken to signify any Place in the Union separately maintaining its own Poor.

SCHEDULE A.

Containing the Names of the Unions in which the sum is not to exceed Ten Pounds.

(The Unions in this Schedule are those contained in the Schedule to the General Consolidated Order of 24th July, 1847, which are not distinguished by an asterisk. *See page* 206.)

SCHEDULE B.

Containing the Names of Unions in which the sum is not to exceed Fifteen Pounds.

(The Unions in this Schedule are those contained in the Schedule to the General Consolidated Order of 24th July. 1847, which are distinguished by an asterisk. *See page* 206.)

Given under our Hands and Seal of Office, this Twenty-fourth day of July, in the year One thousand eight hundred and forty-seven.

(L. S.)

(Signed) GEO. NICHOLLS.
G. C. LEWIS.
EDMUND W. HEAD.

The Consolidated Orders, subsequently issued to the following Unions, contain clauses providing for the expenses attending the elections of Guardians. See note to Article 173 of the Consolidated Order. The payments for conducting the Elections in such Unions are stated, *ante,* p. 211.

The following are the Unions referred to:—

Barnsley.	Oldham.
Barton-upon-Irwell.	Penistone.
Bedwellty.	Pontefract.
Birkenhead.	Pontypridd.
Bramley.	Prestwich.
Gower.	Ripon.
Great Ouseburn.	Samford.
Hartlepool.	Tadcaster.
Hawarden.	Westminster.
Hemsworth.	Wetherby.
Holyhead.	Wharfedale.
Kirkby Moorside.	Whitchurch (Salop).
Knaresborough.	Wight, Isle of
North Bierley.	Woolwich.
Norwich.	

So much of the Order of 24th July, 1847, as relates to the compensation to be paid to the Clerk for conducting and completing the election of Guardians has been suspended in the following Unions:—Salford, 25 October, 1856; Leicester, 13 March, 1857; Chorlton, 20 December, 1858; Bradford (York), 1 January, 1867; Nottingham, 7 August, 1856; Newent, 27 September, 1859; West Derby, 4 February, 1868.

ELECTION EXPENSES ORDER—PARISHES.

(8th December, 1847.)

To the Guardians of the Poor *of the several* **Parishes** *named in the Schedule hereunto annexed;*—

To the Clerk or Clerks to the Justices of the Petty Sessions held for the Division or Divisions in which the said several Parishes are situate;—

And to all others whom it may concern.

WHEREAS, by a General Order, under the hands and seal of the Poor Law Commissioners, bearing even date herewith, addressed, amongst others, to the Guardians of the Poor of the several Parishes named in the Schedule hereto, the said Commissioners have (amongst other things) prescribed the manner of conducting the Election of Guardians of the Poor for the said several Parishes; and it is expedient that provision should be made for the payment of the expenses to be incurred in such Elections.

Now, therefore, We, the said Poor Law Commissioners, do hereby order and direct henceforth in regard thereto, with reference to each of the said Parishes, as follows:—That the expenses of every Election of Guardians of the Poor of the said several Parishes shall be defrayed by the Guardians of the said Parishes in the manner hereinafter set forth; that is to say,—

Art. 1.—The cost of providing the several forms contained in the said Orders shall be defrayed by the said Guardians out of the funds in their possession belonging to the said Parish.

Art. 2.—The compensation which shall be paid to the Clerk, or to the person appointed under the authority of the said recited Orders to act as such in the performance of the duties thereby prescribed, shall include the remuneration of the persons who may have been appointed or employed to assist him in conducting and completing the Election, and shall, in respect of the said several Parishes, be such sum, not exceeding *Ten Pounds*, as the Guardians shall determine, and shall be defrayed by the said Guardians out of the said funds.

Art. 3.—And in the case of every contested Election in the Parish of Saint Mary and Saint Andrew Whittlesea *Threepence*, and in every other of the said Parishes *Twopence*, in respect of each person separately assessed to the Poor-rate of the Parish shall be paid to the said Clerk or other person as aforesaid in addition to such compensation, and shall be defrayed by the said Guardians out of the said funds.

SCHEDULE,

Containing the Names of the Parishes to which the present Order applies.

Alston-with-Garrigill.
Bermondsey, St. Mary Magdalen.
East Stonehouse.
Paddington.
St. Matthew, Bethnal Green.
St. George-in-the-East.
St. Martin-in-the-Fields (a).
St. Mary Abbotts, Kensington.
St. Mary, Rotherhithe.
Whittlesea, St. Mary and St. Andrew.
Great Yarmouth.

Given under our Hands and Seal of Office, this Eighth day of December, in the year One thousand eight hundred and forty-seven.

(Signed)   GEO. NICHOLLS.
                 EDMUND W. HEAD.

L. S.

(a) Since added to the Strand Union.

Election Expenses Orders have subsequently been issued to the following Parishes:—

Parishes.	Dates of Orders.	Payments allowed.
Camberwell, St. Giles	4th May, 1859	10*l.* and 2*d.* for each person assessed.
Chelsea, St. Luke	13th Mar. 1851	do. do.
Lambeth, St. Mary	14th Dec. 1849	do. do.
Leeds	8th Dec. 1847 Suspended 9th Feb. 1860	20*l.* and 2*d.* for each person separately or jointly assessed.
Stoke-upon-Trent	16th Sep. 1847	10*l.* and 2*d.* for each person separately assessed.

The rates of payment for conducting the elections in Hampstead, Holbeck, Hunslet, Mile End Old Town; Saddleworth; St. George, Hanover Square; St. James, Clerkenwell; St. Leonard, Shoreditch; St. Luke, Middlesex; St. Margaret and St. John, Westminster; St. Mary, Islington; St. Mary, Newington; St. Marylebone; St. Pancras,—are mentioned *ante,* p. 216.

NOTICE TO GUARDIANS ELECTED ORDER.
(22nd March, 1852.)

To the Guardians of the Poor *of the several Unions* (a) *set forth in the First and Second Schedules hereunto annexed;—*

To the Churchwardens and Overseers of the Poor of the several Parishes and Places comprised within the said several Unions;—

To the Clerk or Clerks to the Justices of the Petty Sessions held for the Division or Divisions in which the said several Unions are respectively situate;—

And to all others whom it may concern.

WHEREAS the Poor Law Commissioners, by an Order bearing date the 24th day of July, 1847, being a general rule addressed (amongst others) to the Guardians of the Poor of the several Unions mentioned in the First Schedule hereunto annexed, and the Poor Law Board, by divers Orders, the dates whereof are respectively set forth in the Second Schedule hereunto annexed, addressed to the several Unions therein also set forth, did among other matters, order and direct that the Clerk to the Guardians, when he shall have ascertained that any Candidate is duly elected as Guardian, shall notify the fact of his having been so elected by delivering or sending, or causing to be delivered or sent, to him a notice in the Form (D.) thereunto annexed, which said Form is the following:—

(a) This Order was not issued to single Parishes under separate Boards of Guardians, but only to Unions.

Notice to Guardians elected.

——— Union.
 Parish of ———.

 Sir,—I do hereby give you notice, and declare, that you have been duly elected a Guardian of the Poor for the Parish of ——— in the ——— Union, and that the next meeting of the Board of Guardians of the said Union will be held at ——— on ——— next, at the hour of ———.
 Signed this ——— day of ———
     ——— Clerk to the Guardians of the Poor of
        the ——— Union.
 To Mr. ——— of ———.

And whereas in the Act passed in the last Session of Parliament, intituled "*An Act to continue an Act of the Fourteenth Year of Her Majesty for charging the Maintenance of certain poor Persons in Unions in England and Wales upon the Common Fund: and to make certain Amendments in the Laws for the Relief of the Poor,*" it was enacted, that the Guardians elected for the several Parishes in any Union formed or to be formed under the Act of the fifth year of King William the Fourth, Chapter Seventy-six, or for the several Wards in any Parish divided into Wards, should continue to act as such until the Fifteenth day of April inclusive in each year, notwithstanding their successors might have been elected previously to that day; and from and after the said Fifteenth day of April every Guardian newly elected for any such Parish or Ward should act as such Guardian for the ensuing year.

And whereas it is expedient that the said Form of Notice should be altered so as to render it conformable to the said enactment,

Now, therefore, We, the Poor Law Board, in pursuance of the powers given in and by the Statutes in that behalf made and provided, do hereby alter so much of the said recited General Order, and so much of the several Orders which are referred to in the Second Schedule hereunto annexed, as prescribes the Form of Notice to Guardians elected as above set forth; and We do hereby Order and Direct, that such Form shall be as follows; that is to say,—

FORM (D.)

Notice to Guardians elected.

—— Union.

Parish [*or* Township] of ——.

Sir,—I do hereby give you notice, and declare that you have been duly elected a Guardian of the Poor for the Parish [*or* Township] of —— in the —— Union, and that the first meeting of the Board of Guardians of the said Union at which you will be lawfully entitled to attend and act as Guardian will be held at —— on —— day, the —— [*add* instant, *or* April next], at the hour of ——.

Signed this —— day of ——.

—— Clerk to the Guardians of the Poor of the —— Union.

To Mr. —— of ——.

FIRST SCHEDULE to which the above Order refers.

(The Unions in this Schedule are, with the exception of those mentioned in the Second Schedule hereunder, those specified in the Schedule to the General Consolidated Order of 24th July, 1847, *ante*, p. 206.)

SECOND SCHEDULE to which the above Order refers.

Barnsley	12th June, 1850.
Barton-upon-Irwell	24th January, 1850.
Bedwellty	19 March, 1849.
Hemsworth	29 October, 1850.
Kirkby Moorside	9th February, 1850.
North Bierley	14 February, 1849.
Oldham	22nd November, 1847.
Penistone	2nd February, 1850.
Prestwich	2nd August, 1850.
Samford	16th March, 1849.

Given under our Hands and Seal of Office, this Twenty-second day of March, in the year One thousand eight hundred and fifty-two.

JOHN TROLLOPE, *President.*
S. H. WALPOLE.
B. DISRAELI.

COURTENAY, *Secretary.*

*** Consolidated Orders issued subsequently to the date of this Order are in accordance therewith.

ELECTION OF GUARDIANS AMENDMENT ORDER.

(14*th January*, 1867.)

To the Guardians of the Poor *of the several* **Unions** *named in the Schedules hereunto annexed :—*

To the Churchwardens and Overseers of the Poor of the several Parishes, Townships, and Places comprised in the said Unions ;—

To the Clerk or Clerks to the Justices of the Petty Sessions held for the Division or Divisions in which the said Unions are respectively situate ;—

And to all others whom it may concern.

WHEREAS, by a General Order bearing date the 24th day of July, 1847, addressed to the several Unions mentioned in the Second Schedule hereunto annexed, and by divers subsequent Orders addressed to the several Unions mentioned in the Third Schedule hereunto annexed, the dates whereof are therein set forth, the Poor Law Commissioners and the Poor Law Board respectively have made sundry rules and regulations as to the mode of conducting the Election of Guardians in such Unions; and it is expedient that certain alterations should be made in such rules and regulations.

Now therefore, We, the Poor Law Board, acting under the authority of the Statutes in that behalf made and provided, hereby Order, as regards the general election of Guardians of such Unions in future, as follows :—

Art. 1.—So much of the several Orders as provides for the Notice of Election (*a*) and the form of the Voting

---

(*a*) See Art. 6 of the General Consolidated Order, *ante*, p. 5.

Paper (*a*) shall be rescinded, and the Notice shall be according to the form set forth in the First Schedule hereunto annexed, or to the like effect.

Art. 2.—The form of Voting Paper to be used hereafter shall be according to the form in the said Schedule set forth.

Art. 3.—No Nomination Paper delivered, except through the post (*b*), to the Clerk or to any person appointed to receive the same, or at the office, address, or residence of such Clerk or other person, before the hour of Nine o'clock in the morning, or after the hour of Eight o'clock in the evening, shall be valid (*c*).

Art. 4.—As soon as practicable after the receipt of the Nomination Papers the Clerk shall make out two lists, containing the names and residence of the persons nominated for the several Parishes in the Union, and shall cause one list to be suspended in the Board Room of the Guardians, and the other to be affixed to the principal external door of the Workhouse of the Union, if any, and where there are several Workhouses in the Union, of that which contains the Board Room or is situated nearest to it.

Art. 5.—If a greater number of Candidates be nominated for any Parish than the number of Guardians required to be elected for it (*d*), the Clerk shall, as soon as practicable, make out a list in writing of the Candi-

---

(*a*) See Art. 10 of the Consolidated Order, *ante*, p. 10.

(*b*) The delivery through the post will remain as before.—*Instr. Letter*, 22nd Jan. and 1st Feb., 1867. (See Note to Art. 8, *ante*, p. 8.)

(*c*) As to the days on which Nomination Papers are to be delivered, see Art. 8 of the above Order, *ante*, p. 8.

(*d*) The number of Guardians to be elected for each Parish is prescribed by the Declaration Order forming the Union; or if the number in any case has been increased since the Union was formed, by a special Order of the Poor Law Commissioners or Poor Law Board. The Declaration Order also prescribes the qualification for the office of Guardian in the Union in accordance with 4 & 5 Wm. IV. c. 76, s. 38, *i. e.* the being rated to the Poor Rate at an annual rental not exceeding £40 in any case.

dates, and the names and addresses of the several Nominators of them, and keep such list open in the Board Room of the Guardians until the close of the Election; and every person entitled to vote at the Election for such Parish may apply at such room during any day after the list shall have been made out, except when the Board of Guardians are holding their meeting therein, between the hours stated in Art. 3, for an inspection of such list, and may copy the same or any part thereof.

Art. 6.—If any person nominated, or any person on his behalf, give at least one clear day's notice in writing, to the Clerk before the delivery or collection of the Voting Papers, of an intention to send some Agent to accompany each or any Deliverer (*e*) or Collector (*f*) of the Voting Papers, the Clerk shall make suitable arrangements to enable such Agent to accompany each person appointed to deliver or collect the Papers accordingly (*g*).

Art. 7.—The Guardians shall provide, for the use of every person appointed to collect the Voting Papers, a box or bag (*h*) having a small opening for the reception of the papers, which shall be delivered by the Clerk to such person locked, and such person shall deposit every Voting Paper received by him, or allow the Voter to deposit his own Paper, in the box or bag through the opening, and shall deliver the box or bag to the Clerk on the day of collecting the Papers, and the Clerk shall open the same at the casting up of the Votes, and not before.

(*e*) See Art. 11 of the General Consolidated Order, *ante*, p. 10.
(*f*) See Art. 17 of the same Order, *ante*, p. 12.
(*g*) This Article follows the provision in the Local Government Act, 21 & 22 Vict. c. 89, s. 21. (See 'Glen's Law of Public Health and Local Government,' p. 58, 4th Edition.)
(*h*) The boxes or bags will be provided by the Guardians at the cost of the common fund.

Art. 8.—The Clerk shall allow each Candidate, or some person on his behalf, to be present at the casting up of the votes, and shall declare at the close of such casting up the number of votes allowed by him to every Candidate, and shall, if he reject any Voting Paper, mark thereon the act of its rejection, and declare the ground of such rejection, if required to do so by any person whose Voting Paper shall be rejected (*a*).

Art. 9.—The Nomination and Voting Papers when delivered by the Clerk to the Board of Guardians (*b*) shall be open to the inspection of any person who may have nominated a Candidate or of any Candidate at the election for which there was a contest, or to any person appointed in writing on behalf of such Nominator or Candidate, during the hours of Ten o'clock in the forenoon and Six o'clock in the afternoon on any day except Sunday during the six calendar months next ensuing the First Meeting of the Board of Guardians after the annual election (*c*).

(*a*) The Board trust that the improvements in the form of the Voting Paper will prevent many of the accidents which have rendered Voting Papers delivered to the Clerk invalid. At the same time the knowledge of the ground for the rejection will render the person whose Paper is rejected less likely to be dissatisfied than has been the case under the present course of proceeding, where the Clerk may have rejected the Papers upon very sufficient grounds, but without expressing them. These provisions are not intended to give either to the Candidates or the Voters any right to interrupt or disturb the Clerk in the discharge of his duty. He will not be compelled to allow any discussion before him upon the Voting Papers, nor his course to be delayed by the interposition of any person or documents not called for by himself.—*Instr. Letter*, 22nd January, 1867.

As to the casting up of the votes, see Art. 21 of the General Consolidated Order, *ante*, p. 13.

(*b*) See Art. 24 of the General Consolidated Order, *ante*, p. 14, as to the delivery of the Voting Papers to the Guardians after the election.

(*c*) This article does not empower the Candidates to take copies of the Voting Papers; but the Guardians may allow them to be copied if they think fit. There can, however, be no reason why the Candidate may not make notes in writing of the result of his inspection of the Voting Papers.

EXPLANATION OF TERMS.

Art. 10.—Whenever in describing any person or party, matter or thing, the word importing the singular number or the masculine gender only is used in this Order, the same shall be taken to include, and shall be applied to, several persons or parties as well as one person or party, and females as well as males, and several matters or things as well as one matter or thing, respectively, unless there be something in the subject or context repugnant to such construction.

Art. 11.—The term "Clerk" shall signify the Clerk or person acting as such in the conduct of the Election; and the term "Parish" shall include Wards (*d*) in those Unions where Parishes have been divided into Wards for the Election of Guardians.

FIRST SCHEDULE.

FORM A.

NOTICE OF ELECTION.

(*This Form has been substituted by the Form prescribed in the Schedule to the General Order of* 21*st February*, 1868, *see post,* p. 244.)

(*d*) See *post,* p. 248.

FORM B.

Voting Paper for the Election of Guardians for the year 186 .

———— UNION.

Voting Paper for the Parish of

No. of Voting Paper.	Name and Address of Voter.	Number of Votes.	
		As Owner.	As Ratepayer.

Directions to the Voters.

The Voter is entitled to vote for   Guardian [*or* Guardians], and no more.

The Voter, if able to write, must himself write his initials against the name of every person for whom he votes, and must himself sign this paper.

The name of a Firm or Partnership will be of no avail. The signature by a wife for her husband, whether in his name or her own, will be useless.

If the Voter cannot write, he must affix his mark, but such mark must be attested, and the name of the Voter filled in by a witness, and such witness must write the initials of the Voter against the name of every person for whom the Voter intends to vote.

If a Proxy vote, he must in like manner write his own initials, sign his own name, and state in writing the name of the person for whom he is Proxy; thus—*John Smith* for *Richard Williams.*

This paper must be carefully preserved by the Voter, as no second paper will be given. When it is filled up, it must be kept ready for delivery to Mr.   , who will call for the voting paper on the   day of   , between the hours of   before noon, and of   afternoon. No other person is authorized to receive the voting paper. The Voter may deliver the paper open or sealed up in an envelope, and may himself deposit it in the box or bag used for the collection.

If the voting paper be not ready for the person appointed to collect it when called for, the vote will be lost. It will also be lost if more than   name   be returned in the list, with the initials of the Voter placed against such name , or if the voting paper be not signed by the Voter, or if the mark of the Voter be not attested when attestation is required.

Initials of the Voter against the Name of the Person for whom the vote is intended to be given.	Names of the Persons nominated as Guardians.	Residence of the Persons nominated.	Quality or Calling of the Persons nominated.	Opinion of the Clerk as to the disqualification.

I vote for the persons in the above list against whose names the initials are placed as above.

(Place for Signature of the Voter)
(Place for the mark if the Voter cannot write)
Name of the Voter who cannot write
Witness to the mark
Address of the Witness
(Place for Signature where the Voter votes by Proxy)
for

WARNING.—It is enacted by the statute 14 & 15 Vict. c. 105, s. 3, that " If any person, pending or after the Election of any Guardian or Guardians, shall wilfully, fraudulently, and with intent to affect the result of such Election, commit any of the Acts following ; that is to say, fabricate in whole or in part, alter, deface, destroy, abstract, or purloin any Nomination or Voting Paper used therein; or personate any person entitled to vote at such Election; or falsely assume to act in the name or on the behalf of any person so entitled to vote; or interrupt the distribution or collection of the Voting Papers; or distribute or collect the same under a false pretence of being lawfully authorized to do so," he will be liable to be sent to prison for three months with hard labour.

SECOND SCHEDULE.

[The Unions in this Schedule are those contained in the Schedule to the General Consolidated Order of 24th July, 1847, *ante*, p. 206, with the exception of the Nottingham Union, as to which, see *ante*, p. 2 note.]

THIRD SCHEDULE.

[The Unions in this Schedule are those mentioned in the Table, *ante*, p. 211, with the exception of Norwich, Westminster, and Woolwich Unions.]

Given under our Hands and Seal of Office, this Fourteenth day of January, in the year One thousand eight hundred and sixty-seven.

GATHORNE HARDY, *President*.
S. H. WALPOLE.
B. DISRAELI.

RALPH A. EARLE, *Secretary*.

A similar General Order to the foregoing was issued on the 1st February, 1867, to the following places:—

Alston-with-Garrigill.
East Stonehouse.
Great Yarmouth.
Holbeck.
Hunslet.
Leeds.

Manchester.
Mile End Old Town.
Paddington.
Saddleworth.
St. George-in-the-East.
St. George the Martyr, Southwark.

Election of Guardians Amendment Order, 1867.

St. Giles, Camberwell.
St. John, Hampstead.
St. Leonard, Shoreditch.
St. Luke, Chelsea.
St Martin-in-the-Fields (*a*).
St. Mary Abbotts, Kensington.
St. Mary, Lambeth.
St. Mary Magdalen, Bermondsey.
St. Mary, Rotherhithe.
St. Matthew, Bethnal Green.
Stoke-upon-Trent.
Toxteth Park.
Whittlesea, St. Mary and St. Andrew.

(*a*) Since added to the Strand Union.

ELECTION AMENDMENT ORDER.
(21*st February*, 1868.)

To the Guardians of the Poor *of the several* **Unions, Parishes,** *and* **Townships** *respectively named in the Third Schedule hereunto annexed :—*

To the Churchwardens and Overseers of the Poor of the said several Parishes and Townships, and the several Parishes and Places comprised in the said Unions;—

To the Clerk or Clerks to the Justices of the Petty Sessions held for the Division or Divisions in which the said Unions, Parishes, and Townships are respectively situate ;—

And to all others whom it may concern.

WHEREAS by divers Orders directed to the several Unions, Parishes, and Townships respectively named in the Third Schedule hereunto annexed, the Qualification of Guardians for such Unions, Parishes, and Townships respectively has been declared,

And whereas by two General Orders bearing date the 14th day of January, 1867, and the 1st day of February in the same year, and by sundry other Orders issued subsequently, addressed respectively to the said several Unions, Parishes, and Townships, the Poor Law Board directed that the Notice of Election might be prepared and issued in the form therein set forth,

And whereas by Section 4 of "The Poor Law Amendment Act, 1867," it is enacted that the Qualification of a Guardian described by the Poor Law Amendment Act, 1834, shall be determined with reference to the annual rateable Value (*a*) of the Property in respect of which his Qualification is claimed,

And whereas it is expedient that the several Orders pre-

(*a*) It is the rateable value, and not the gross estimated rental, that is here referred to.

scribing the Qualification of Guardians as aforesaid and the Notice of Election should be altered.

Now therefore, We, the Poor Law Board, acting under the authority of the Statutes in that behalf made and provided, do hereby alter all the said Orders which prescribe the Qualification of a Guardian of the Poor in the said Unions and Parishes, and do Order that the same shall be determined with reference to the annual rateable Value of the Property in respect of which his Qualification is claimed, instead of with reference to the annual rental or annual value.

And we further Order and Direct that the Notices of Election in the Schedules hereunto annexed shall be substituted for those set forth in the several Orders above referred to (*a*).

Whenever the word "*Parish*" is used in this Order, it shall be taken to signify any place for which a separate Poor Rate is or can be made, or for which a separate Overseer is or can be appointed (*b*).

FIRST SCHEDULE.
FORM (A).
NOTICE OF ELECTION.
FOR UNIONS.

Election of Guardians of the Poor for the year 186 .

—— UNION.

I, the undersigned, Clerk to the Guardians of the Poor of the above-named Union, with reference to the ensuing Election of Guardians of the Poor for the several Parishes in the said Union, do hereby give notice as follows:—

1.—The number of Guardians of the Poor to be elected for the Parishes in the said Union is as follows:—

(*a*) See *ante*, pp. 5 and 231.
(*b*) See 29 & 30 Vict. c. 113, s. 18.

B

For the Parish of	Guardians.
For the Parish of	Guardians.
For the Parish of	Guardians.

2.—Any person, not otherwise disqualified by law, who shall be rated to the Poor Rate in any Parish in the Union in respect of hereditaments of the annual rateable value of not less than   Pounds, is qualified to be nominated for the office of Guardian at the said Election by any person then qualified to vote.

3.—Nominations of Guardians must be made according to the form below, which is the form prescribed by the Poor Law Board. Such nominations must be sent after the Fourteenth, but on or before the   day of March instant, to me,   , or to Mr.   at   for the Parish of   , or to Mr.   at   for the Parish of   , who alone are authorized to receive the same. Nominations sent before the said Fourteenth (a), or after the said   day of March instant, or sent to any other person, will be invalid; and so also if they be delivered at the address, office, or residence of the Clerk or other persons above named, before the hour of nine o'clock in the morning or after the hour of eight o'clock in the evening, unless sent through the post.

4.—On the   day of   I shall cause a list of the names of the persons nominated as Candidates for the several Parishes to be suspended in the Board Room of the Guardians, and to be affixed to the principal door of the Workhouse at   .

5.—If more than the above-mentioned number of Guardians be nominated for any Parish, I shall cause a list of the Candidates and of the names and addresses of their several Nominators to be made out, and to be kept in the Board Room of the Union, which list will be open to the inspection of every person qualified to vote on any day when the Board of Guardians are not holding their Meet-

---

(a) This should be the 15th, and the notice when issued should be altered accordingly.

ing between the hours mentioned above. I shall also cause Voting Papers to be delivered on the   day of April at the address in such Parish of each Ratepayer, Owner, and Proxy qualified to vote; and on the   day of April I shall cause such Voting Papers to be collected.

6.—On the   day of April I shall attend at the Board Room of this Union at the hour of   , and I shall on that day, and, if necessary, the following days, proceed to ascertain the number of votes given for each Candidate.

7.—If any Voter do not receive a Voting Paper on the said   day of April, he may apply to me before the   day of April for one; and if any Voting Paper be not collected on the said   day of April through the default of the Collector, the Voter in person may deliver it to me before noon on the   day of April.

8.—Any person put in nomination for the Office of Guardian may, at any time during the proceedings in the Election, tender to me in writing his refusal to serve the office, and the Election, so far as regards that person, will be no further proceeded with.

Form of Nomination Paper.

Parish of ⎱
——————— ⎰ This   day of   , 186 .
Union.

Names of Persons nominated to be Guardians.	Residence of the Persons nominated.	Quality or Calling of Persons nominated.

I, being*   duly qualified to vote in the Parish aforesaid, nominate the above to be Guardian [or Guardians] for the said Parish.

——————— Signature ⎱ of Nominator.
——————— Address ⎰

* *Note.*—Only one person is empowered to sign this paper, and after the word *being* he must insert (*a ratepayer*) or (*owner of property*) according to his qualification.

One of these words only must be used.

Given under my hand, this   day of March, 186 .

———————— Clerk to the said Guardians.

WARNING.—It is enacted by the Statute 14 & 15 Vict. c. 105, s. 3, that—" If any person, pending or after the Election of any Guardian or Guardians, shall wilfully, fraudulently, and with intent to affect the result of such Election, commit any of the acts following; that is to say, fabricate in whole or in part, alter, deface, destroy, abstract, or purloin any Nomination or Voting Paper used therein; or personate any person entitled to vote at such Election; or falsely assume to act in the name or on the behalf of any person so entitled to vote; or interrupt the distribution or collection of the Voting Papers; or distribute or collect the same under a false pretence of being lawfully authorized to do so," he will be liable to be sent to prison for three months with hard labour.

SECOND SCHEDULE.

FORM (A).

NOTICE OF ELECTION.

FOR PARISHES AND TOWNSHIPS.

Election of Guardians of the Poor for the year 186 .

—— Parish [*or* Township].

I, the undersigned, Clerk to the Guardians of the Poor of the above-named Parish [*or* Township], with reference to the ensuing Election of Guardians of the Poor for the said Parish [*or* Township], do hereby give notice as follows,—

1.—The number of Guardians of the Poor to be elected for the said Parish [*or* Township] is

[*Where the Parish is divided into Wards the number of Guardians for each Ward is to be stated.*]

2.—Any person not otherwise disqualified by law, who shall be rated to the Poor Rate in the Parish [*or* Township] in respect of hereditaments of the annual rateable value of not less than   Pounds, is qualified to be nominated for the office of Guardians at the said Election by any person then qualified to vote.

3.—Nominations of Guardians must be made according to the Form below, which is the Form prescribed by the Poor Law Board. Such nominations must be sent after the Fourteenth, but on or before the   day of March instant, to me,   , or to Mr.   , at   , or to Mr.   at   , who alone are authorized to receive the same. Nominations sent before the said Fourteenth (*a*), or after the said   day of March instant, or sent to any other person, will be invalid; and so also if they be delivered at the address, office, or residence of the Clerk or other persons above named, before the hour of nine o'clock in the morning or after the hour of eight o'clock in the evening, unless sent by the post.

4.—On the   day of   I shall cause a list of the names of the persons nominated as Candidates for the Parish [*or* Township] to be suspended in the Board Room of the Guardians, and to be affixed to the principal door of the Workhouse at   .

5.—If more than the above-mentioned number of Guardians be nominated for the Parish [Township *or* Ward] I shall cause a list of the Candidates and of the names and addresses of their several Nominators to be made out, and to be kept in the Board Room of the Parish [*or* Township], which list will be open to the inspection of every person qualified to vote on any day when the Board of Guardians are not holding their Meeting, between the hours mentioned above. I shall also cause Voting Papers to be delivered on the   day of April, at the address in the Parish [Township *or* Ward] of each ratepayer, owner, and proxy qualified to vote; and on the   day of April I shall cause such Voting Papers to be collected.

6.—On the   day of April I shall attend at the Board Room of this Parish [*or* Township] at the hour of   , and I shall on that day, and, if necessary, the

---

(*a*) This should be the 15th, and the notice when issued should be altered accordingly.

following days, proceed to ascertain the number of votes given for each Candidate.

7.—If any Voter do not receive a Voting Paper on the said   day of April, he may apply to me before the   day of April for one; and if any Voting Paper be not collected on the said   day of April through the default of the Collector, the Voter in person may deliver it to me before noon on the   day of April.

8.—Any person put in nomination for the office of Guardian may, at any time during the proceedings in the Election, tender to me in writing his refusal to serve the office, and the Election, so far as regards that person, will be no further proceeded with.

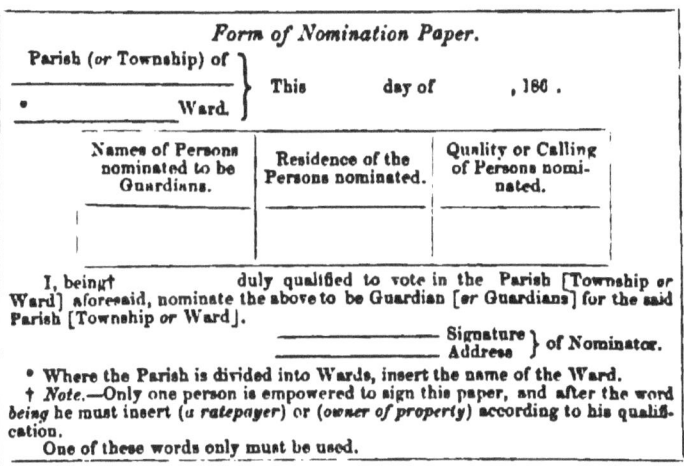

Given under my hand, this   day of March, 186 .
————, Clerk to the said Guardians.

WARNING.—It is enacted by the Statute 14 & 15 Vict. c. 105, s. 3, that—" If any person, pending or after the Election of any Guardian or Guardians, shall wilfully, fraudulently, and with intent to affect the result of such Election, commit any of the acts following; that is to say, fabricate in whole or in part, alter, deface, destroy, abstract, or purloin any Nomination or Voting Paper used therein ; or personate any person entitled to vote at such Election; or falsely assume to act in the name or on the behalf of any person so entitled to vote; or interrupt the distribution or collection of the Voting Papers; or distribute or collect the same under a false pretence of being lawfully authorized to do so," he will be liable to be sent to prison for three months with hard labour.

THIRD SCHEDULE.
Names of the Unions.

[The Unions contained in this Schedule are those mentioned in the Consolidated Order, *ante*, p. 206, excepting Nottingham; and in the Table set forth on p. 211, *ante*, excepting Norwich, Westminster, and Woolwich.]

Names of the Parishes or Townships.

Alston-with-Garrigill.
East Stonehouse.
Holbeck.
Hunslet.
Manchester.
Mile End Old Town.
Paddington.
Saddleworth.
St. George-in-the-East.
St. George, Hanover Square.
St. George-the-Martyr, Southwark.
St. Giles, Camberwell.
St. James, Clerkenwell.
St. John, Hampstead.
St. Leonard, Shoreditch.
St. Luke, Chelsea.
St. Margaret and St. John the Evangelist, Westminster.
St. Martin-in-the-Fields.*
St. Mary Abbots, Kensington.
St. Mary, Islington.
St. Mary, Lambeth.
St. Marylebone.
St. Mary Magdalen, Bermondsey.
St. Mary, Newington.
St. Mary, Rotherhithe.
St. Matthew, Bethnal Green.
St. Pancras.
Stoke-upon-Trent.
Toxteth Park.
Whittlesea, St. Mary and St. Andrew.
Yarmouth, Great.

Given under our Hands and Seal of Office, this Twenty-first day of February, in the year One thousand eight hundred and sixty-eight.

(L. S.)

DEVON, *President.*
GATHORNE HARDY.
MARLBOROUGH.

G. SCLATER-BOOTH, *Secretary.*

---

* Since added to the Strand Union.

FORM OF ORDER FOR DIVISION OF PARISHES INTO WARDS FOR ELECTION OF GUARDIANS (a).

𝕿𝖔 𝖙𝖍𝖊 𝕲𝖚𝖆𝖗𝖉𝖎𝖆𝖓𝖘 𝖔𝖋 𝖙𝖍𝖊 𝕻𝖔𝖔𝖗 *of the* —— 𝖀𝖓𝖎𝖔𝖓, *in the County of* —— ; —

To the Churchwardens and Overseers of the Poor of the Parish of ——, *comprised in the said Union;—*

To the Churchwardens and Overseers of the Poor of the several other Parishes comprised in the said Union;—

To the Clerk or Clerks to the Justices of the Petty Sessions held for the Division or Divisions in which the said Union is situate;—

And to all others whom it may concern.

WHEREAS, by an Order bearing date the —— day of —— One thousand eight hundred and ——, the Poor Law Commissioners ordered and declared that the Parishes and Places described in the margin thereof, should be united, for the administration of the laws for the relief of the Poor, by the name of the —— Union.

And whereas the Parish of —— was included amongst the Parishes and Places so named in the said Order as aforesaid.

And whereas by the said recited Order the Poor Law Commissioners determined the number of Guardians of the Poor to be elected for each of the said Parishes, and determined that —— Guardians of the Poor should be elected for the said Parish of ——.

(a) This Order can be issued only in those cases in which the population of the parish exceeds 20,000. See the 7 & 8 Vict. c. 101, s. 19.

And whereas the said Parish of —— contains more than twenty thousand persons, according to the enumeration of the population last published by authority of Parliament, and it appears to Us, the Poor Law Board, to be expedient that the said Parish should be divided into Wards for the purpose of the conduct of the Election of Guardians of the Poor for the same.

Now, therefore, We, the said Poor Law Board, in pursuance of the powers given in and by the Statutes in that case made and provided, do hereby Order and Direct, that for the purpose of the conduct of the Election of Guardians of the Poor the said Parish of —— shall be divided into the —— Wards hereinafter described, each of which Wards now contains a number of rated houses not less than four hundred, and the said Wards shall be named respectively—
—— Ward;

The —— Ward shall be bounded by, etc.

And for all the purposes of such Election of Guardians, We do hereby Direct, that each of the said Wards shall be considered as a separate Parish (*b*).

And having due regard to the value of the rateable property therein, We do determine the number of Guardians to be elected for each of the said Wards to be as follows, (that is to say,)

That —— Guardians shall be elected for the —— Ward;

And We do hereby further Order and Direct, that the Guardians to be elected for the said several Wards shall be elected in such manner and form, and at such time, as the Poor Law Commissioners have, by their Order, bearing date the (Twenty-fourth day of July), One thousand eight hundred and (forty-seven), determined in respect to the annual Election of Guardians for the Parishes comprised within the said —— Union.

And We hereby also further Order, that the several

(*b*) See 29 & 30 Vict. c. 113, s. 18, as to the definition of the word "Parish."

forms of notices and documents, and all the proceedings by the said last-mentioned Order prescribed in respect of such Election of Guardians, shall be altered by the addition or substitution of the term *Ward*, with the name thereof, to or for the term *Parish*, wherever the same shall be rendered requisite by the nature of the proceedings.

Given under our Hand and Seal of Office, this —— day of ——, in the year One thousand eight hundred and ——.

———, *President.*

———, *Secretary.*

Orders dividing Parishes into Wards have been issued to the following Unions and Parishes:—

Unions, etc.	Parishes; Wards*; and No. of Guardians.	Date of Orders.
Ashton-under-Lyne.	*Asht.-u.-Lyne.* Audenshaw . . . . . 1; Hartshead . . . . . 3; Knott Lanes . . . . 1; East Ward of the Town's Division . . . . . 3; West Ward of the Town's Division 2	6 Mar. 1849.
Blackburn . .	*Blackburn.* St. Mary's . . . . . 1; St. John's . . . . . 1; Trinity . . . . . . 1; Park . . . . 2; St. Peter's . . . . . 2; St. Paul's 2	2 Oct. 1851.
Cheltenham .	*Cheltenham.* East . . . . 3; North . . . . 3; West . . . . 3; Middle . . . . . . 3; South 3	15 Feb. 1850.
Hackney . .	*St. John's.* Hackney . . . . . . 3; Homerton . . . . . 2; South Hackney . . . 4; Dalston . . . . . . 3; Stamford Hill . . . 2; West Hackney . . . 3; De Beauvoir Town . . 3	2 Mar. 1850. 6 Sept. 1856. 3 Jan. 1852. 10 Aug. 1861.

* See Art. 11 of the General Order of 14th January, 1867, *ante*, p. 235.

Division of Parishes into Wards. 251

Unions, etc.	Parishes; Wards; and No. of Guardians.	Date of Orders.
Hunslet ...	St.Mary. Hunslet. { The East Ward ... 3 The North Ward ... 3 The West Ward ... 3	17 Dec. 1862.
Lambeth ...	{ Bishop's ... 3 Marsh and Wall ... 6 Out Liberty ... 8 Prince's Liberty ... 3	21 May, 1846.
Leeds ...	Leeds. { East ... 2 Kirkgate ... 2 Mill Hill ... 3 North ... 2 North-east ... 2 North-west ... 2 South ... 2 West ... 3	21 Nov. 1844.
Leicester ...	St.Margt. { No. I. ... 4 No. II. ... 5 No. III. ... 4 No. IV. ... 4	25 Feb. 1851.
Nottingham .	St. Mary. { First ... 6 Second ... 6 Third ... 3 Fourth ... 3 Fifth ... 6	13 Feb. 1865.
Oldham ...	Oldham. { Clarksfield ... 1 Mumps ... 1 St. James's ... 1 St. Mary's ... 1 St. Peter's ... 1 Waterhead Mill ... 1 Werneth ... 1 Westwood ... 1	30 Nov. 1864.
Preston ...	Preston. { Christ Church ... 2 Fishwick ... 2 St. John's ... 2 St. Peter's ... 2 St. George's ... 2 Trinity ... 2	29 Feb. 1848.
Rochdale ..	Spotland. { Spotland, nearer side ... 2 Spotland, further side ... 2 Whitworth ... 2 Brandwood ... 1	4 Feb. 1865.
St. George's, Hanover Square	St. Geo. Han. Sq. { Dover ... 1 Conduit ... 1 Grosvenor ... 3 Brook ... 3 Curzon ... 2 Knightsbridge ... 4 Out ... 4	11 July, 1867.

Election of Guardians.

Unions, etc.	Parishes; Wards; and No. of Guardians.		Date of Orders.
St. James's, Clerkenwell.	St. Jas.Clwl.	Pentonville . . . . . 3 St. Philip's . . . . . 4 St. Mark's . . . . . 3 St. James's . . . . . 4 St. John's 4	8 Jan. 1868.
St. Leonard, Shoreditch.	St. Leon. Sh.	Holywell . . . . . . 2 St. Leonard's . . . 2 Hoxton New Town . . 4 Hoxton Old Town . . 4 Haggerstone, East . . 3 Haggerstone, West . . 3	18 Dec. 1867.
St. Luke, Middlesex.	St. Lu. Mid.	City Road East . . . 3 City Road West . . . 4 Old Street . . . . 3 East Finsbury . . . . 4 West Finsbury 4	4 Feb. 1868.
St. Margaret and St. John, Westminster.	S.M.&S.J.W.	Knightsbridge . . . . 4 St. Margaret . . . . 5 St. John 7	26 Aug. 1867.
St. Mary, Islington.	St. Mary, Isl.	Canonbury and St. Peter's 4 Highbury . . . . . 4 Holloway, Lower . . . 2 Holloway, Upper . . . 3 St. Mary's . . . . . 2 Thornhill and Barnsbury 3	4 June, 1867.
St. Marylebone.	St. Mybe.	Grove and Regent's Park 4 Portland and Cavendish . 5 Portman . . . . . . 5 St. John's Wood . . . 4	28 June, 1867.
St. Matthew, Bethnal Green.	St. Mat.B.gn.	East . . . . 6 North . . . . 6 South . . . . 6 West 6	9 Feb. 1864.
St. Pancras . .	St. Pancras.	No. 1 . . . . 2 No. 2 . . . . 2 No. 3 . . . . 3 No. 4 . . . . 3 No. 5 . . . . 2 No. 6 . . . . 2 No. 7 . . . . 2 No. 8 8	7 May, 1867.

Unions, etc.	Parishes; Wards; and No. of Guardians.		Date of Orders.
Stoke-upon-Trent.	Parish of Stoke-u.-Trent.	Shelton . . . . . . 5 North . . . . 6 South-west . . . . . 5 Fenton . . . . . . 3 South-east 5	16 Dec. 1845.
Stourbridge .	Foreign of W. Kingswinford.	Brierley Hill . . . . 3 Brockmoor . . . . . 1 Pensnett . . . . . . 2 Quarry Bank . . . . 1 St. Mary's . . . . . 2 Wordsley 2	10 Feb. 1853.
Walsall . . .	Foreign of W.	Bloxwich . . . . . 2 Walsall Wood . . . . 1 The Foreign 4	15 Dec. 1866.
Great Yarmouth.	Gt. Yarmth.	North . . . . 3 Market . . . . . . 3 Regent . . . . . . 3 St. George's . . . . 3 Nelson 4	3 Jan. 1852.

The City of Norwich is divided by the Local Act into 16 Wards, or Districts, for the election of Guardians, numbered respectively 1 to 16. Wards 1 to 5 and 10 to 12 each returns 2 Guardians; Wards 6, 7, 9, 13 to 16 each returns 3 Guardians; Ward 8 returns 5 Guardians.

FORM OF ORDER FOR A FRESH ELECTION OF A GUARDIAN (a).

To the Guardians of the Poor *of the* —— **Union,** *in the County of* —— ;—

To the Churchwardens and Overseers of the Poor of the Parish of ——, *in the said Union ;—*

To the Clerk or Clerks to the Justices of the Petty Sessions held for the Division or Divisions in which the said Union is situate ;—

And to all others whom it may concern.

WHEREAS by an Order, being a General Rule, bearing date the 24th day of July, 1847, addressed (among others) to the Guardians of the Poor of the —— Union, the Poor Law Commissioners prescribed the manner of conducting the Election of Guardians of the Poor for the several Parishes and places comprised in the said Union, and directed that the proceedings thereat should take place at the times therein mentioned.

And whereas, by a certain Order of the said Commissioners in that behalf, one Guardian is directed to be elected for the Parish of ——, comprised in the said Union.

(a) This Order is only issued when a vacancy in the office of Guardians occurs previous to the expiration of the parochial year (25th March), when the General Elections take place. It is of course varied according to the circumstances occasioning the vacancy. Orders for fresh elections of Guardians are issued under the authority of the 5 & 6 Vict. c. 57, s. 11 ; which enacts that in every case of omission to elect, or of vacancy in any Board of Guardians, by death, resignation, or disqualification, the Poor Law Board shall be deemed to be empowered to order a new election for the completion of the Board of Guardians.

When there is a Special Election, it is not necessary to send a copy of the return Form (E.), *ante,* p. 198, to every parish in the Union. It will suffice if it be sent to the Parish for which the Special Election is held.

And whereas ——, the Guardian elected for the said Parish, hath tendered his resignation of the said office for the acceptance of the Poor Law Board, for certain causes which they have deemed reasonable, and they have accepted such resignation, and it is necessary, for the due and proper administration of the relief of the Poor in the said Union, that one Guardian should be elected for the said Parish.

(Or, *if the vacancy occur by the death of the elected Guardian :*)—And whereas ——, the Guardian elected for the said Parish, is deceased, and there is at present no Guardian for the said Parish, and it is necessary, for the due and proper administration of the relief of the Poor in the said Union, that one Guardian should be elected for the said Parish.

(Or, *if there was default in the election of a Guardian :*)—And whereas, by reason of default of election, there is at present no Guardian for the said Parish of —— for the present year, and it is necessary, for the due and proper administration of the relief of the Poor in the said Union, that one Guardian should be elected for the said Parish.

(Or, *if the vacancy occurred by the elected Guardian having ceased to be rated :*)—And whereas ——, the Guardian elected for the said Parish has ceased to be rated to the Poor Rate in any Parish or Place within the said Union, and is disqualified to act as such Guardian, and there being now no Guardian for the said Parish, it is necessary for the due and proper administration of the relief of the Poor in the said Union, that one Guardian should be elected for the said Parish.

(Or, *if the Guardian has become incapacitated for holding the office :*)—And whereas —— has been elected a Guardian for the said Parish, but, by reason of his holding the office of —— in the said —— Union, he is incapable of serving as a Guardian, and there being now no Guardian for the said Parish, it is necessary, for the due and proper administration of the relief of the Poor in the said Union, that one Guardian should be elected for the said Parish.

Now We, the Poor Law Board, do hereby Order and Direct, that an Election of one Guardian for the said Parish of —— shall take place, in the manner and according to the form prescribed in the above recited Order.

And We do hereby further Order and Direct, that the days on which the proceedings above mentioned, in the matter of the said Election, are to take place, shall be the following, that is to say,

The day for publishing the notice of the Election shall be the —— day of —— next.

The last day for receiving nominations of a Guardian shall be the —— day of —— next.

The day on which the voting papers shall be delivered in the event of any contest, shall be the —— day of —— next.

The day on which the voting papers shall be collected shall be the —— day of —— next.

The day on which voting papers may be received if there should be a default of delivery, and the day on which voting papers may be delivered to the Clerk if there should be a default in the collection, shall be the —— day of —— next.

The day on which the votes shall be cast up shall be the —— day of —— next.

And We hereby Order and Direct, that the Clerk to the Guardians of the said Union do perform such of the duties imposed upon him by the said recited Order, and all other duties suitable to his office, which it may be requisite for him to perform in conducting and completing the Election hereby ordered and directed to take place; provided however, that the notice of Election to be given by the said Clerk shall be affixed on the outward gate of the Workhouse now occupied by the said Guardians on behalf of the said Union, and on such places in the said Parish as are ordinarily made use of for affixing thereon notices of parochial business.

Given under our Hand and Seal of Office, this —— day of ——, in the year 186 .

——, *President.*

——, *Secretary.*

FORM OF RELIEF COMMITTEES ORDER.

To the Guardians of the Poor *of the —— Union, in the County of ——;—*

To the Churchwardens and Overseers of the Poor of the several Parishes, Townships, and Places comprised in the said Union;—

To the Clerk or Clerks to the Justices of the Petty Sessions held for the Division or Divisions in which the said Union is situate;—

And to all others whom it may concern.

WHEREAS by a General Order, addressed (amongst others) to the Guardians of the Poor of the —— Union, in the County of ——, bearing date the 24th day of July, in the year 1847, the Poor Law Commissioners made certain provisions to regulate the Meetings of the Guardians of the Poor of the said Union, and the proceedings of the Board of such Guardians, by reason whereof the relief to all the paupers belonging to the said Union is exclusively controlled and managed by the whole of the said Guardians sitting as one Board.

And whereas in the said Union the number of paupers requiring relief is at this time very large, and it is expedient that other provisions should be made in such behalf.

Now, therefore, in pursuance of the powers given in and by an Act passed in the fifth year of the reign of his late Majesty King William the Fourth, intituled "*An Act for the Amendment and better Administration of the Laws relating to the Poor in England and Wales,*" We, the Poor Law Board, do hereby Order and direct as follows; viz.—(a)

(a) The Order contemplates that the determination of the relief Committee in the cases adjudicated upon shall be reported to the Board of Guardians at the earliest convenient period. When a Committee is

First.—That the Guardians of the Poor of the said Union may, at any ordinary meeting, form committees of themselves, and may from time to time assign to any one of such Committees the whole or part of the District of any of the Relieving Officers of the said Union, in order that such Committee may hear and determine all applications for relief on account of poor persons residing or being in the District which may have been so assigned to such Committee, and may give all directions respecting the continuance of relief to poor persons belonging to such District, in such manner as the Guardians acting as a Board may now, or shall hereafter, be authorized to do.

Secondly.—That all the proceedings of such Committee shall be entered into the Application and Report Book of the Relieving Officer of the District, and into some other book to be kept for this purpose, by the presiding Chairman thereof, and such book shall be laid before the Board of Guardians at the same or at their next ordinary meeting, after each sitting of the said Committee, as may be the more convenient; and thereupon the Clerk to the said Guardians shall enter on the minutes of the said Board of Guardians the fact of the same having been so laid before them.

Provided that nothing in this Order contained shall at any time prevent the Guardians acting as a Board, from rescinding or altering any Order of such Committee in regard to relief not previously administered, or from considering and deciding on any application from any poor person, or determining on the continuance or cessation of any weekly or other allowance which shall not have been actually given.

---

sitting at the same time as the General Board, the report should be made then and there. On receiving the report, it would be competent to the Guardians to reverse or modify the decision of the Committee in any case in which the relief ordered had not already been given; but the revision of the decisions of the Committee should not take place until the Committee have gone through and reported upon the whole of the cases.

Given under our hand and Seal of Office, this —— day of ——, in the year 186 .

——, *President*.

——, *Secretary*.

Orders similar to the foregoing have been issued to the following Unions and Parishes:—

Altrincham	8th February, 1856.
Asaph, St.	14th June, 1856.
Ashton-under-Lyne	24th November, 1847.
Barnsley	23rd October, 1850.
Barton-upon-Irwell	26th May, 1864.
Basford	12th November, 1852.
Belper	26th October, 1863.
Bethnal Green	29th February, 1868.
Birmingham	10th December, 1861.
Blackburn	{ 30th January, 1862. { 18th February, 1862.
Blything	24th October, 1856.
Bolton	6th January, 1848.
Bradford (Yorkshire)	27th November, 1847.
Bury	{ 17th November, 1859. { 16th June, 1862.
Cambridge	7th March, 1856.
Cardiff	7th May, 1859.
Carlisle	19th March, 1853.
Chelmsford	22nd February, 1858.
Chesterton	22nd March, 1856.
Chorlton	29th December, 1858.
Clitheroe	3rd October, 1857.
Cockermouth	18th August, 1855.
Cosford	11th March, 1856.
Coventry	14th December, 1860.
Depwade	17th June, 1856.
Ely	23rd July, 1856.
Fulham	7th February, 1855.
Fylde	25th August, 1859.
Glanford Brigg	31st October, 1860.
Glossop	7th October, 1862.
Greenwich	22nd October, 1856.
Halifax	2nd March, 1847.

Haslingden	19th March, 1862.
Hexham	8th November, 1862.
Hitchin	13th November, 1856.
Huddersfield	10th May, 1853.
Keighley	2nd December, 1857.
Lambeth, St. Mary's	2nd March, 1855.
Lancaster	9th January, 1847.
Leigh	26th January, 1848.
Lexden and Winstree	18th March, 1856.
Linton	6th September, 1856.
Maidstone	11th July, 1861.
Manchester	19th June, 1850.
Mansfield	21st May, 1862.
Monmouth	21st June, 1867.
Newmarket	19th April, 1856.
Nottingham	29th November, 1856.
Oldham	22nd November, 1847.
Poplar	29th October, 1866.
Preston	6th May, 1848.
Prestwich	27th June, 1862.
Pwllheli	1st August, 1848.
Rochdale	29th January, 1859.
Saffron Walden	18th February, 1856.
Salford	4th May, 1848.
Sheffield	23rd February, 1854.
South Shields	22nd January, 1857.
Stockport	17th February, 1862.
Sudbury	22nd March, 1856.
Thingoe	14th July, 1856.
Todmorden	10th July, 1848.
Toxteth Park	20th August, 1857.
Tynemouth	11th March, 1857.
Wandsworth and Clapham	16th March, 1855.
Wangford	16th April, 1856.
Warrington	4th May, 1861.
Warwick	30th August, 1858.
West Derby	13th November, 1856.
West Ham	14th April, 1859.
Wigan	15th May, 1848.
Wigton	16th January, 1856.
Wisbeach	4th November, 1852.
Wycombe	28th May, 1866.

FORM OF DISTRICT RELIEF COMMITTEES ORDER (a).

To the **Guardians of the Poor** *of the* —— **Union**, *in the County of* —— ;—

To the Churchwardens and Overseers of the Poor of the Parishes of ——, *in the said Union ;—*

To the Clerk or Clerks to the Justices of the Petty Sessions held for the Division or Divisions in which the said Union is situate ;—

And to all others whom it may concern.

WHEREAS the Parishes of —— are comprised in the —— Union, in the County of ——, and are situated at a greater distance than four miles from the place of meeting of the Board of Guardians of the said Union:

Now We, the Poor Law Board, by virtue of the powers given in and by the statutes in that behalf made and provided, and on the application of the said Board of Guardians, do hereby form the said Parishes into a District for the purposes hereinafter mentioned, with reference to relief to the poor persons therein requiring the same.

And We do hereby Direct the said Guardians, from time to time, to appoint a Committee of their Members for such

---

(a) With respect to this Order, see the 5 & 6 Vict. c. 57, s. 7, which enacts that whenever the whole of any Parish or Parishes is situated at a greater distance than four miles from the place of meeting of the Board of Guardians of the Union of which such Parish or Parishes may form part, it shall be lawful for the Commissioners, on the application of the Board of Guardians, to form such Parish or Parishes into a district, and to direct the said Guardians from time to time to appoint a committee of their members to receive applications of poor persons requiring relief in such districts, to examine into the cases of such poor persons, and to report to the said Guardians thereon.

District, to receive applications of poor persons therein requiring relief, and to examine into the cases of such poor persons, and to report to the said Guardians thereon.

And We do hereby further Order and Direct that the said Committee shall, when formed, appoint some convenient time and place within the said District, whereat all applications to such District Committee shall be made and heard, and shall communicate the same to the Clerk of the Guardians of the said Union, who shall cause notice thereof to be published in the said Parishes.

And We do further Direct that the said Committee shall, at every meeting, appoint some one of themselves to preside thereat, as Chairman, during that meeting, and shall take means to have minutes of their proceedings kept, so that the same may be duly reported to the Board of Guardians of the said Union.

And We do hereby further Order and Direct:—

First.—That the Relieving Officers of the said Union within whose District the said Parishes or either of them shall be situated, shall attend upon the said Committee, as and when the said Committee shall hold their meetings, and shall examine into the cases for relief which shall be brought before the said Committee, and shall report thereon to such Committee in like manner, as prescribed by the Poor Law Commissioners, in their General Order,* dated the Seventeenth day of March, One thousand eight hundred and forty-seven, and in their General Order, dated the Twenty-fourth day of July, One thousand eight hundred and forty-seven, in regard to all applications for relief made to the Board of Guardians.

Secondly.—That each Relieving Officer shall enter into his Application and Report Book the recommendations of the said District Committee, and report the same, with the cases, to the next meeting of the Board of Guardians.

Provided, nevertheless, that the examination or recom-

---

* But see now Accounts Order of 14th January, 1867, *post*.

mendation of any case by the said Committee, shall not exonerate or discharge any such Relieving Officer from the duty imposed upon him, to relieve, or otherwise deal with every case occurring within his District, requiring relief, according to the manner prescribed by the said last-mentioned General Order.

And We hereby further Order and Direct, that the Clerk to the said Guardians shall enter upon the minutes of the Board the reports of the said Committee, and shall also enter the recommendations of such Committee, contained in the Application and Report Book of the said Relieving Officer, in the Relief Order Book.

> Given under our Hand and Seal of Office, this —— day of ——, in the year One thousand eight hundred and ——.
>
> ————, *President.*
>
> ————, *Secretary.*

Orders similar to the foregoing have been issued to the following Unions:—

Altrincham	30th November, 1849.
Ashton-under-Lyne	13th February, 1862.
Cardiff	12th April, 1862.
Cockermouth	18th August, 1855.
Congleton	1st August, 1846.
Holywell	14th February, 1856.
Runcorn	14th July, 1860.
Stockton	30th June, 1849.
Teesdale	12th July, 1848.
Williton	13th January, 1843.

CONSOLIDATED ORDER AMENDMENT ORDER,

(26th February, 1866.)

To the Guardians of the Poor of the several Unions named in the Schedules hereunto annexed ;—

To the Churchwardens and Overseers of the several Parishes and Places comprised within the said Unions ;

To the Clerk or Clerks to the Justices of the Petty Sessions held for the Division or Divisions in which the Parishes and Places comprised within the said Unions are situate ;—

And to all others whom it may concern.

WHEREAS, by reason of the passing of the "Union Chargeability Act, 1865," it is expedient that certain alterations should be made in the General Order of the Poor Law Commissioners, bearing date the 24th day of July, 1847, issued to the several Unions named in the Schedule (A.) hereunto annexed, and in the similar Orders made and issued by the said Poor Law Commissioners and the Poor Law Board respectively to the several Unions named in the Schedule (B.) hereunto annexed.

Now therefore, We, the Poor Law Board, in pursuance of the powers given in and by the Statutes in that behalf made and provided, hereby, from and after the Seventh day of March next, rescind the following Articles in the said Orders; that is to say :—

> "Art. 81.—The Clerk shall, four weeks at least before the Twenty-fifth day of March and the Twenty-ninth day of September respectively in each year, refer to and ascertain the cost to each Parish in the Union for the

maintenance of the Poor, and other separate charges, as well as for the common charges incurred in the half of the last year corresponding to the half year next coming, and shall estimate and, as near as may be, divide amongst the Parishes any extraordinary charges to which the Union may be liable in the coming half year, and he shall also estimate the probable balance due to or from the Parish at the end of the current half year, and shall then prepare the orders on the several Parishes for the sums which, upon such computation, it shall appear necessary for them to contribute to the expenses of the Union for the coming half year; and the orders so prepared shall be laid before the Guardians, for their consideration, three weeks at least before the expiration of the current half year.

"Art. 82.—The Guardians shall make orders on the Overseers or other proper authorities of every Parish of the Union, from time to time, for the payment to the Guardians of all such sums as may be required by them for the relief of the Poor of the Parish, and for the contribution of the Parish to the common fund of the Union, and for any other expenses chargeable by the Guardians on the Parish; and in such orders the contributions shall be directed to be paid in one sum or by instalments, on days specified, as to the Guardians may seem fit."

So much of the Articles in the said Orders as requires the Clerk of the Guardians—

"To conduct all applications by or on behalf of the Guardians to any Justice or Justices at their Special, Petty, or General Sessions, and if he be an attorney or solicitor, to perform and execute all legal business connected with the Union, or in which the Guardians shall be engaged, except prosecutions at the assizes, actions at law, suits in equity, or parliamentary business, without charge for anything beyond disbursements."

And so much of the said Orders as prescribes the Forms in the Schedules to the said Orders, termed "Order for Contributions," "District Medical Relief Book," "Register of Births in the Workhouse," and "Register of Deaths in the Workhouse."

We hereby Order, from and after the said Seventh day of March next, as follows (*a*):—

Art. 1.—The Clerk shall, as soon as convenient before the 25th day of March next, and thenceforth four weeks at least before the 29th day of September and the 25th day of March respectively in each year, estimate the probable amount of the expenditure in the relief of the poor, and other charges by the Guardians on behalf of the Union, as well as any separate expenditure (*b*) chargeable against any Parish therein during the then next ensuing half year, and estimate the probable balance due to or from each Parish at the end of the current half year, and shall apportion the sums to be contributed by the several Parishes comprised in the Union,

---

(*a*) The 28 & 29 Vict. c. 79, s. 11, requires the Poor Law Board to make such orders as may be requisite to render its provisions applicable to the proceedings and accounts of the Guardians and Overseers; and the Board accordingly have issued this General Order, making such alterations in the General Consolidated Order as they think necessary.

The alterations the Board say are not numerous, and will not require any particular explanation, but the Board have given their attention to the general provision relating to the duties of the Clerk. It is most probable that the alteration of the law will simplify the keeping of the accounts in the Union, and thus to some extent diminish the labours of that officer. But as questions of fact and law, which arise out of the removal and settlement of the paupers of the Union, will now fall within the scope of his duties, and if he be an attorney he must undertake the conduct of the litigation which may arise out of them, the Board have deemed it right to reconsider the terms of the Article in the Consolidated Order which refers to this subject, and have enlarged the exception so as to enable the Clerk to make full charges for much of the business which may arise out of this change in the law. They have also had in their recollection the business which has been cast upon the Board of Guardians and their Clerk, as their professional adviser, in litigations arising out of the Union Assessment Committee Acts.—*Instr. Letter*, 28th February, 1866.

(*b*) The County rate is a separate charge in respect of each Parish, and therefore comes under the words "separate expenditure."

according to the law for the time being in force therein, and shall prepare the orders on the Overseers or other proper authorities of the several Parishes for the payment of such respective contributions, and of any such separate expenditure as aforesaid, and the orders so prepared shall be laid before the Guardians for their consideration a reasonable time before the expiration of the current half year (c).

(c) It is important that the Guardians should be careful to keep constantly a sufficient balance in the Treasurer's hands to defray the current expenses of the Union; and for this purpose that they should make, from time to time, sufficient orders for contributions upon the Overseers of the several Parishes, and enforce the orders in case the payment should be delayed. The Guardians must call for contributions from each Parish fully sufficient to meet the expenditure incurred in respect of it; and no such arrears should be allowed to accrue, in any case, as would cast the burdens of one Parish on the other Parishes of the Union.—*Instr. Letter.*

As to this and the following Article, see the correspondence in the Official Circular, Nos. 14 & 15 (N. s.), p. 217.

It has been the long-established doctrine (see *Tawney's* case, 2 Salk. 531; *R.* v. *Goodcheap*, 6 T. R. 159; *R.* v. *Wacell*, 1 Doug. 151; *R.* v. *Dursley*, 5 Ad. & E. 15) that Overseers cannot levy retrospective rates, that is, that they cannot levy rates to defray debts incurred by Parish Officers of former years, unless in cases where they are expressly authorized to do so by Act of Parliament, as in 41 Geo. III. c. 23, s. 9, and also in 11 & 12 Vict. c. 91, ss. 1 and 2. The same rule has been held to apply to a Board of Guardians, who cannot, under the powers conferred upon them by Articles 1 and 2 of the Order of 26th February, 1866, make an order upon the Overseers for the payment of money to defray debts or liabilities incurred in a former year. (See the case of *Waddington* v. *The Guardians of the City of London Union*, in the second volume of Glen's 'Poor Law Statutes.') In delivering the judgment of the Court of Error in that case, Baron Watson made special reference to this work in quoting the Orders of the Poor Law Commissioners and Poor Law Board upon which the judgment was founded.

A judgment was afterwards obtained by one of the creditors against the Guardians, and a bill was thereupon filed by the Attorney-General and the Guardians against the Judgment Creditor and the Sheriff of London, praying that it might be declared that the lands and hereditaments and the goods and chattels in and about the Union Workhouse and premises were held by the Guardians in trust for and on behalf of the Union, and that the same were not liable to satisfy the claims of the Creditor and his judgment, and that the Defendants might be restrained from levying writs of *fieri facias* and *elegit*, and levying execution against the goods, chattels, lands, hereditaments, moneys, or property of the Guardians. Upon demurrer, it was held by Wood, V.C., that

Art. 2.—The Guardians shall make orders on the Overseers or other proper authorities of every Parish in the Union at the commencement of each half year ending on the days above mentioned, and from time to time as occasion may arise, for the payment to the Guardians of all such sums as may be required by them as the contribution of the Parish to the common fund of the Union, and for any other expenses separately chargeable by the Guardians on the Parish; and in such orders the contributions shall be directed to be paid in one sum or by instalments, on days to be specified in such orders, as to the Guardians may seem fit (*a*).

---

money raised by rates for the relief of the poor is not applicable to the discharge of the claims of Judgment Creditors of the Board of Guardians in respect of debts incurred prior to the year for which the rate was raised; and *semble*, that such money is applicable to the discharge of debts incurred within the year for which the rate was raised. *Attorney-General* v. *Wilkinson*, 5 Jur. (N.S.) 538.

As to the validity of a contribution order, see *Hale* v. *The Guardians of the City of London Union*, 6 Jur. (N.S.) 74; 29 L. J. (N.S.) M. C. 5; 6 C. B. 863. In that case a contribution order was made without taking into account a balance due *to* the particular Parish, and the Court held that the order was illegally made, and could not be enforced; but when an estimate made under Article 1 of the sum which will be required for the ensuing half-year includes a balance existing at the beginning of the half-year, which balance is made up of balances from preceding half-years, the order for contribution is valid under s. 6 of 22 & 23 Vict. c. 49. (*City of London Union* v. *Acocks*, 8 C. B. (N.S.) 760; 24 J. P. 502.)

Further, with reference to Article 1 of the Order of 26th February, 1866, see 22 & 23 Vict. c. 49, s. 6, in the second volume of Glen's 'Poor Law Statutes.'

(*a*) As to the mode of computing contributions of Parishes to the common fund, see the new provisions on the subject in 24 & 25 Vict. c. 55, ss. 9, 10, and 25 & 26 Vict. c. 103, s. 30, and 28 & 29 Vict. c. 79, by s. 12 of which the Guardians shall distribute the charges upon the common fund during and at the close of every half year in the proportions according to which the Orders for the contributions to the common fund were made upon the several Parishes comprised in such Unions at the commencement of such half year, notwithstanding the change which may be made in the valuation list of any Parish during such period.

With reference to the above, the Poor Law Board say:—" The statute 24 & 25 Vict. c. 55, s. 9, required the contributions to the common fund to be calculated according to the rateable value of the several Parishes comprised in the Union, and s. 10 referred the Guardians to the County or Borough Rate for a basis; but by the Union Assessment Committee Act of 1862 the Valuation Lists, when approved for all the Parishes in the Union, were substituted as the proper basis for that calculation. Between the time when the contributions are calculated and the end of the half year for which they are required, differences may arise in the valuations, as shown by the County Rate or the Valuation Lists, and doubts have been entertained as to the proper basis for adjusting the charges upon the several Parishes of the Union. These doubts are removed, and it is now directed that the Guardians shall distribute the charges at the close of every half year, in the proportions according to which the orders for the contributions were made at its commencement."—*Instr. Letter*, 28th February, 1866.

It will be noticed that in the Form of Contribution Order the Guardians are not required to specify how much is called for on account of common fund, and how much on account of separate charges. This was not necessary, for in distributing the common charges under 28 & 29 Vict. c. 79, s. 12, the Guardians will do so upon the basis given by the statute, and that basis will be in their own possession. If its correctness should be questioned when the audit of their accounts takes place, that will be the time to settle the question before the auditor.

If there are Churchwardens, they should be named in the order where they are Overseers *ex officio*, *i.e.* in Parishes, but not in Townships, etc.

The Clerk will first form an estimate of the expenditure for the whole Union during the ensuing half-year. Having done so, he will then calculate what amount thereof each Parish must contribute according to its annual rateable value. The next step will be to estimate the probable balance in favour of or against each Parish, and deduct or add, as the case may be, the amount thereof from or to the amount of the common charges apportioned to each Parish to contribute; then the separate charges likely to be incurred on account of each Parish during the half-year must be ascertained, and the aggregate of the sums so found will be the sums for which the contribution orders are to be made.

The contribution orders may be made payable in one, two, or more instalments, as the Guardians think fit; but it is not desirable that the instalments should be more than two, as if they are, unnecessary trouble and expense is occasioned to the Overseers.

It will be seen that this Order requires that the contribution orders shall be made at the commencement of each half-year ending on Michaelmas and Lady Day respectively. This obviates the difficulty experienced under the former order, when the orders were made prior to the termination of the half-year ended at Lady Day, and the old Overseers went out of office before the money was paid to the Treasurer of the Guardians, as it was thought by the Poor Law Board to be very doubtful whether, as regards an order of contribution made upon existing Overseers, succeeding Overseers could be proceeded against for any neglect to pay to the Union Treasurer the money required by the order. (7 O. C. 217.) The order must be addressed to all the Churchwardens and Overseers by name, though it need not necessarily be served on more than one of them. (See 12 & 13 Vict. c. 103, s. 7.)

If the order include any sum to be provided under the Cattle Diseases

Act, 29 & 30 Vict. c. 110, by s. 5 of that Act it is required to state in the order the amount in the pound of contribution required for Cattle Act expenses.

If the Parish Officers should fail to pay the money required, the Guardians may proceed against them before the justices for a disobedience to the orders of the Commissioners, under section 98 of the 4 & 5 Wm. IV. c. 76, or they may have recourse to the remedy afforded to the Guardians by the 2 & 3 Vict. c. 84, s. 1. In case of its being necessary for the Guardians to proceed adversely against the Parish Officers the Commissioners recommend a recourse to the remedial proceeding afforded by the latter statute, rather than to the penal proceeding authorized by the former.—*Instr. Letter.* With respect to this enactment, see *Newbold* v. *Coltman*, 6 Exch. Rep. 189, in which it was held that the justices act ministerially and not judicially in proceedings at special sessions under the Act. If by reason of the neglect of the Overseers to pay the moneys called for by the Guardians, any relief directed by the Guardians to be given be delayed or withheld during a period of seven days, proceedings can be taken against the Overseers under the statute 7 & 8 Vict. c. 101, s. 63, which enacts that if the Overseers of any Parish wilfully neglect to make or collect sufficient rates for the relief of the poor, or to pay such moneys to the Guardians of any Parish or Union as such Guardians may require, and if by reason of such neglect any relief directed by the Board of Guardians to be given to any poor person be delayed or withheld during a period of seven days, every such Overseer shall, upon conviction thereof, forfeit and pay for every such offence any sum not exceeding £20. The powers conferred on the Guardians by the 2 & 3 Vict. c. 84, render them responsible for securing a sufficient supply of funds from the Parish Officers; and if the Guardians should fail to obtain from the Parish Officers funds sufficient to defray the current expenditure of the Parish, they have no other legal power to procure funds to supply the deficiency. The Guardians are not in general empowered to borrow money on the security of the rates (except in the cases and for the purposes specially provided for by the statutes, such as the building of or procuring Workhouses under 4 & 5 Wm. IV. c. 76, and enabling poor persons to emigrate, under the same Act, and the making a survey or valuation of a Parish, under 6 & 7 Wm. IV. c. 96), or to pay interest for the money borrowed.—*Instr. Letter,* April, 1842. But see *Reg.* v. *Bangor,* 16 L. J. R. (N. s.) 58, and 11 Jur. 587, as to charging the poor-rates under the 6 & 7 Wm. IV. c. 96; and also *Reg.* v. *Hurstbourne-Tarrant,* 27 L. J. R. (N. s.) M. C. 214. If proceedings be instituted under the 2 & 3 Vict. c. 84, s. 1, the Clerk, acting upon his own responsibility, has no authority to stay those proceedings, but should apply to the Board of Guardians for further directions.

With reference to these proceedings, s. 9 of 14 & 15 Vict. c. 105, is one of much importance to those Unions which extend into several separate jurisdictions. The Treasurer of a Union may reside or have his place of business in one jurisdiction, while the Overseer or officer who ought to pay money to the Treasurer may live in another jurisdiction; and doubts have been entertained, when it has been necessary to take legal proceedings for default of payment, as to what justices were empowered to hear the complaint and enforce the payment. Under this section the justices of the county, district, or place in which the Overseer or officer shall reside at the time of the default, or in which the Treasurer shall reside or have his place of business, shall have jurisdiction to hear and determine the complaint. Those justices should therefore be applied to whose jurisdiction will be most convenient for the several parties in the particular case.

The 4 & 5 Wm. IV. c. 76, renders the Overseers liable to certain penalties if they wilfully neglect or disobey a contribution order of the Guardians; and the 2 & 3 Vict. c. 84, s. 1, applies to the recovery of the money called for by such an order, and of the costs incurred in enforcing payment. The two provisions being entirely distinct (that is to say, the one being penal and the other remedial), a conviction under the 4 & 5 Wm. IV. c. 76, for a disobedience of the order, will not interfere with any subsequent proceedings which may be taken by the Guardians to enforce or recover payment of the money under the 2 & 3 Vict. c. 84, s. 1. (56 O. C. (N. S.) 74.) In a case where a person had refused to exercise the office of Parish Officer and make a rate, though he had been appointed Churchwarden of a chapelry within the Union, the Clerk to the Guardians, by the direction of the Board of Guardians, obtained a warrant of justices to levy the amount claimed off the plaintiff's goods, under 2 & 3 Vict. c. 84, s. 1. Upon trespass brought by the plaintiff for this distress, it was held that the alleged trespass was an act done in pursuance of the provisions of the 4 & 5 Wm. IV. c. 76, and that therefore the defendant was entitled to notice of action and to the other provisions afforded by the 104th section of that Act. (*Carter* v. *Filliter*, 1 Car. & M. 498.)

By Art. 203, No. 4, the Treasurer is required, whenever there shall not be funds belonging to the Guardians in his hands, to report in writing the fact of such deficiency to the Poor Law Board.

It is considered that certified balances paid to the Treasurer of the Guardians under the 7 & 8 Vict. c. 101, s. 32, may be applied towards payment of the contribution order made upon the Overseers of the particular Parish; for the statute enacts that " such money shall be applied by the Guardians to the use of all or any of the Parishes included in such Union, according as all or any of such Parishes may be interested in the sum so paid."

It is provided by the 12 & 13 Vict. c. 103, s. 7, that where the Guardians of any Union or Parish shall make any order for the payment of money upon Overseers or other officers of any Parish upon whom they are empowered by law to make it, and a copy of such order shall be served upon any one of such Overseers or other officers, it shall be lawful for the said Guardians to enforce such order against the person so served, as fully and as effectually as if a copy thereof had also been served upon every one of such Overseers or other officers. A further provision is made by the 14 & 15 Vict. c. 105, s. 9, which enacts that where the Overseer or any other officer of any Parish, or any officer of a Union, shall neglect to pay in due course of law money lawfully payable by him as such Overseer or officer to the Treasurer of such Union or Parish, residing or having his place of business in a county, district, or place different from that in which such Overseer or officer shall reside at the

And as regards the duties of the Clerk, We hereby further Order that from and after the 25th day of March next it shall be his duty—

Art. 3.—To conduct all applications by or on behalf of the Guardians to any Justice or Justices at Petty or Special Sessions, or out of Sessions; and, if he be an attorney or solicitor, to perform and execute, without charge for anything beyond disbursements, all legal business connected with the Union, or in which the Guardians shall be engaged, except prosecutions at the Assizes or Quarter or General Sessions, or Central Criminal Court, all other proceedings at the said Quarter or General Sessions, actions and other proceedings in the Superior Courts of Law, suits and other proceedings in the Superior Courts of Equity, and Parliamentary business (*a*).

---

time of any such default, and by reason of such neglect such Overseer or officer shall be liable to be summoned before a justice or justices, any justice or justices of either county, district, or place, shall have jurisdiction to hear and determine the complaint.

(*a*) It is to be observed that business relating to the survey and valuation of Parishes, the sale of Parish property, and the application of the sale proceeds, is the business of the Guardians under the statutes relating thereto, and therefore the Clerk is not entitled to make an extra charge for conducting the correspondence which arises out of, or for advising or assisting the Guardians in the performance of any of the acts or duties which become necessary in the furtherance of this business. Further on this point, see 53 Off. Cir. (N. s.) p. 23.

It is the duty of the Clerk under this Article to obtain the necessary evidence of settlement, and to make the application to the Justices on behalf of the Guardians for orders of removal. If he should incur any expense in so doing, he should make out an account thereof to the Guardians, who can repay the amount so far as they may be proper. His duty, however, does not extend to the actual removal of the paupers, for which the Guardians should make proper arrangements.

As regards orders of maintenance under 43 Eliz. c. 2, s. 7, it will be his duty to make the application to the Justices, and the Application and Report Book of the Relieving Officer will supply the information as to the relatives.

In order to bring the business within the exception to this Article, there must be an actual entry of the cause in the particular Court. If the proceeding be abandoned before the cause is entered in the Court, the business will not come within the exception.

In appeals to the Quarter Sessions against orders of removal, the proceedings are to be deemed proceedings at the Quarter Sessions from the time when the Guardians give their Clerk instructions to commence the appeal, or to support an order of removal obtained by the Guardians when it is appealed against.

The Poor Law Board consider that if a Clerk to a Board of Guardians be a solicitor or attorney, they would not be justified in employing any other solicitor or attorney instead of their Clerk to transact any business which by this Article it is made the duty of the Clerk to transact on behalf of the Guardians.

The prosecution of persons under the Vagrant Act for deserting their families and leaving them chargeable to the poor-rates should be conducted by the Guardians or by their Clerk under their directions, as they can pay the cost of such prosecutions according to the 7 & 8 Vict. c. 101, s. 59, and 28 & 29 Vict. c. 79, s. 9. It is, however, open to any person to prosecute offenders against the Vagrant Act, as the Act does not cast that duty upon any one in particular. It would seem that the limitation in the 11 & 12 Vict. c. 43, s. 11, would not apply to an offence under s. 3 of the Vagrant Act if there is a continuing chargeability of the family, and it can be proved that the head of it is able, wholly or in part, to maintain his or her family by work or other means, and wilfully refuses or neglects to do so. As to the application of Jervis's Act to a prosecution under s. 4 of the Vagrant Act, see *Reere* v. *Yeates*, 31 L. J. M. C. 241; 1 H. & C. 435, in Glen's 'Jervis's Acts,' 3rd ed. Neither the Guardians nor the Overseers should interfere with prosecutions for other offences against the Vagrant Act.

Proceedings to effect the removal of Scotch or Irish paupers, under the 8 & 9 Vict. c. 117, s. 2; the 24 & 25 Vict. c. 76; the 25 & 26 Vict. c. 113; and the 26 & 27 Vict. c. 89, also fall within the scope of the Clerk's duties, as prescribed by this Article; so also proceedings in Lunacy, when the pauper lunatics are confined in Lunatic Asylums (except, of course, appeals to Quarter Sessions). (See 24 & 25 Vict. c. 55, s. 6.) Under the 24 & 25 Vict. c. 55, s. 7, it is not necessary that a complaint should be made by three Guardians personally before the Justices. It should be made by the Clerk in accordance with this Article, under the authority of a resolution duly passed at a meeting of the Guardians. The statement of grounds required by 16 & 17 Vict. c. 97, s. 107, should be signed by three Guardians at a meeting of the Board of Guardians.

This rule includes applications for orders of maintenance under the 43 Elizabeth; for compelling payment of contributions to the Union by Overseers; and generally all those cases in which summary remedies through the intervention of Justices are given generally, and of which the Guardians may have occasion to avail themselves; it also includes applications for orders of removal to Petty Sessions, such being now the business of the Guardians under the 28 & 29 Vict. c. 79. Criminal proceedings in Petty Sessions taken on behalf of the Guardians in their official character are within the scope of the Clerk's duties under this rule. So where the proceedings are for the protection of the Guardians in the exercise of their official functions,—as for absconding from the Workhouse with the Union clothing, misbehaviour in the Workhouse, or proceedings against officers for purloining, embezzling, or misapplying the property of the Union, or disobeying the orders of the Guar-

Art. 4.—He shall take care in every case that his bill for legal business against the Guardians shall be duly taxed before the same shall be paid (*a*).

---

dians, or against persons for illegally introducing spirituous liquors into the Workhouse,—so would conveyancing business connected with the sale of property belonging to the Guardians, or the purchase of property as for the enlargement of the Workhouse premises. So also would be appeals to Special Sessions under 27 & 28 Vict. c. 39, ss. 1, 2. In making applications to the Justices, the Clerk must attend such Justices whenever the attendance may be required, according to the circumstances affecting the jurisdiction of the Justices, whether within or out of the Union. Of course there is nothing to prevent the Overseers from employing the Clerk, if he be an attorney or solicitor, to transact any legal business in which they may be engaged on behalf of their particular Parish; but he cannot act, or rather ought not to act, professionally as the advocate or agent on behalf of a particular Parish, in any matter in which the interests of that Parish and the interests of the whole of the Parishes in the Union are conflicting. If the Clerk be one of a firm, the firm cannot be employed to do work for the Guardians, and be paid their professional charges, when such work falls within this Article as one of the duties of the Clerk which he is to discharge without charge beyond disbursements out of pocket. See as to this, in regard to Justices, *Broughton* v. *Broughton*, 25 L. J. R. 250, Chanc. An action in the County Court is not within the exception to the rule, those courts not being superior courts of law or of equity.

Any Clerk or other officer to any Board of Guardians, if duly empowered by such Board, may make or resist any application, claim, or complaint, or take and conduct any proceedings on behalf of such Board before any Justice or Justices of the Peace at petty or special sessions, or out of sessions, although such Clerk or officer be not an attorney or solicitor, or have not obtained a stamped certificate. (7 & 8 Vict. c. 101, s. 68.) The privilege is not, however, extended by that Act to proceedings at general or quarter-sessions. Upon this point, see *Reg.* v. *Buchanan*, 8 Q. B. 883.

If the Board of Guardians are the local authority for the removal of nuisances for any Parish within the Union, it is incumbent upon the Clerk to conduct the proceedings which the Guardians as such local authority may direct in any case.

Lastly, with reference to this regulation, it is to be observed that agency-charges are disbursements within the meaning of it.

With reference to proceedings between two Unions in a court of law conducted by the respective Clerks who are attorneys, and the right to costs in such case as against the unsuccessful party, the following cases may be consulted: *Attorney-General* v. *Shillibeer*, 19 L. J. Exch. 115; 4 Exch. 606; 14 L. T. 273. See also *Galloway* v. *Corporation of London*, 4 L. R. Eq. 90.

(*a*) With reference to the taxation of bills of law costs, see 7 & 8 Vict. c. 101, s. 39, and the General Order, *post*.

Art. 5.—The following Forms shall be substituted for those above mentioned; that is to say:—

Order for Contributions (*b*).

To *A. B.* and *C. D.*, Overseers (*or**   ) of the Parish of

You are hereby ordered and directed to pay to *F. G.*, of   , Treasurer of the Guardians of the Poor of the   Union, at   , on the   day of   , the sum of   Pounds   Shillings and   Pence, [*or* on the following days, that is to say, on the   day of   the sum of   Pounds   Shillings and   Pence; and on the   day of   , the sum of   Pounds   Shillings and   Pence], from the Poor Rates of the Parish of   , as the contribution of the Parish to the common fund of the Union, and for such other expenses as are chargeable by the said Guardians on the said Parish separately, and to take the receipt of the said *F. G.*, indorsed upon this paper, for the said sum [*or* sums].

Given under our hands, at a meeting of the Guardians of the Poor of the said   Union, held on the   day of   18 .

(Signed)   *X. Y.*   Presiding Chairman.
W. X.
U. V. } Guardians.

────── Countersignature of the Clerk to the Guardians.

* Here insert the names of any parties in the Parish authorized to make the Poor Rate in place of the Overseers.

───────────────────────────────

(*b*) Substituted for Form M., *ante*, p. 201.

District Medical Officer's
_____ Union.

Name of Pauper.	Age.	Residence.	Nature of Disease.	___ Medical Officer of the ___ District.	Week ending ___ day of ___ 186 .			Week ending ___ day of ___ 186 .	
					Days when attended, or when Medicines were furnished.*	Necessaries ordered to be given to the Patient.	Present State or Termination of the Case.	Days when attended, or when Medicines were furnished.*	Necessaries ordered to be given to the Patient.
					S M T W Th F Sat			S M T W Th F Sat	

* Attendances at the Patient's own house are to be denoted by the Letter (H.). Attendance without seeing the Patient, by the Letter (M.). Any Attendance given by a Substitute or

Register of Births in the Workhouse (b).
_____ Union.   _____ Master.

Date of Birth.	Whether Male or Female.	Name of Parents, or Mother.	From what Parish Parent admitted.†	When and where baptized.	In what Name baptized.	Remarks.

† *Note.*—In the case of a Vagrant admitted into the Workhouse who becomes a Mother therein, the word Vagrant must be inserted.

(a) Substituted for Form P., *ante*, p. 201.
(b) Substituted for Form S., *ante*, p. 204.

Relief Book (a).

Week ending —— day of —— 186 .				Week ending —— day of —— 186 .				Observations.
Days when attended, or when Medicines were furnished.*			Necessaries ordered to be given to the Patient.	Present State or Termination of the Case.	Days when attended, or when Medicines were furnished.*			Necessaries ordered to be given to the Patient.	Present State or Termination of the Case.	
S	M T W Th F	Sat			S	M T W Th F	Sat			

...ances at the Surgery or Medical Officer's residence by the Letter (S.). Medicine supplied ... other Person instead of the Medical Officer, is to be entered in *red* ink.

Register of Deaths in the Workhouse (c).

—————— Union. —————— Master.

Date of Death.	Name.	Age.	From what Parish admitted.*	Where buried.

* *Note.*—In the case of a Vagrant admitted into the Workhouse who dies therein, the words admitted as a Vagrant should be inserted.

(c) Substituted for Form T., *ante*, p. 204.

Art. 6.—The word "Parish" in this Order shall mean every place for which a separate poor rate is made (*a*).

Art. 7.—The word "Overseers" shall be taken to include any person acting or legally bound to act in the discharge of any of the duties usually performed by Overseers, so far as they are referred to herein (*a*).

SCHEDULE (A.).

[The Unions in this Schedule are those mentioned in the General Consolidated Order, *ante*, p. 206.]

SCHEDULE (B.).

[The Unions in this Schedule are those mentioned (excepting Norwich, Westminster, and Woolwich) in the Table, *ante*, p. 211.]

Given under our Hands and Seal of Office, this Twenty-sixth day of February, in the year One thousand eight hundred and sixty-six.

                                C. P. VILLIERS, *President*.
                                G. GREY.
                                W. E. GLADSTONE.

ENFIELD, *Secretary*.

(*a*) These definitions are necessary, because since 28 & 29 Vict. c. 79, Parishes in Unions no longer separately maintain their own poor, which is the interpretation of the word "Parish" in 4 & 5 Wm. IV. c. 76, s. 109.

ORDER RELATING TO GUARDIANS' ORDER UPON TREASURER (b).

(7th April, 1857.)

To the Guardians of the Poor of the several **Unions, Parishes,** and **Townships** named in the Schedules hereunto annexed;—

> To the Treasurers of the said several Unions, Parishes, and Townships;—
>
> To the Clerk or Clerks to the Justices of the Petty Sessions held for the Division or Divisions in which the said several Unions, Parishes, and Townships are respectively situate;—
>
> And to all others whom it may concern.

WHEREAS, by a General Order of the Poor Law Commissioners, bearing date the Twenty-fourth day of July, One thousand eight hundred and forty-seven, addressed to the Guardians of the Poor of the several Unions named in

---

(b) The Poor Law Board having observed with much regret the frauds which have been committed by the Officers of some Unions upon Boards of Guardians, and considering that the Form of Order for payment of money commonly used by the Guardians offers undue facility for the commission of such frauds, deemed it right to issue this General Order. The Board have now required that in all cases the Order shall be made payable to the person in whose favour it is drawn, or *to his order*. Thus, the creditor of the Guardians must obtain the Order, and the payment can only be made to him, or to some person through his indorsement, unless his name be forged upon it. The Board believe that if Art. 51 of the General Consolidated Order were in all cases duly and punctually observed, the affairs of the Guardians would be conducted in many Unions with greater regularity than is now the case, and there would be greater security for their creditors, and less risk of improper dealing with their Cheques and Orders for payment.—*Instr. Letter*, 7th April, 1857.

the First Schedule hereunto annexed, and by divers other Orders, the dates whereof are respectively set forth in the Second Schedule hereunto annexed, addressed to the Guardians of the Poor of the several Unions, Parishes, and Townships therein named; and by a General Order bearing date the Eighth day of December, One thousand eight hundred and forty-seven, addressed to the Guardians of the Poor of the several Parishes and Townships named in the Third Schedule hereunto annexed, certain Regulations were made with reference to the proceedings and duties of such Guardians;

And whereas, among other matters, it is provided therein that the Guardians shall pay every sum greater than Five Pounds by an Order, which shall be drawn upon their Treasurer, and shall be signed by the presiding Chairman and two other Guardians at a meeting, and shall be countersigned by the Clerk;

And whereas it is expedient to prescribe a form in which all Orders shall in future be drawn by the said Guardians upon their Treasurers as hereinafter mentioned;

Art. 1.—Now, therefore, We, the Poor Law Board, in pursuance of the powers given in and by the Statutes in that behalf made and provided, do hereby, with respect to the several Unions, Parishes, and Townships in the said Schedules mentioned, Order and Direct that every Order which shall be drawn by the said Guardians of the several Unions, Parishes, and Townships for a sum greater than Five Pounds, upon their respective Treasurers, shall, from and after the Twenty-fourth day of June next, be in the following form, that is to say: (*a*)—

(*a*) If the order be presented to the Treasurer for payment indorsed by procuration, he will not be bound to pay it until he is satisfied that the person who has indorsed it had authority to do so. There appears, however, to be no reason why the general law of agency should not apply to the indorsement of orders drawn by a Board of Guardians upon their Treasurer. In *Attwood* v. *Mannings*, 7 B. & C. 283, Bayley, J.,

———— (Date.)
———— (Place of Meeting.)

To *A. B.*, Treasurer of the Guardians of the Poor of the ———— Union [Parish or Township], in the Count — of ————, at ————.

Pay to *C. D.*, or Order, the sum of ———— Pounds ———— Shillings and ———— Pence, and charge the same to the Account of the said Guardians.

(Signed)

————, *Presiding Chairman.*

——— ⎱ *Guardians of the Poor*
——— ⎰ *of the said Union [Pa-*
        rish or Township].

Countersigned by ————,
Clerk to the said Guardians.

N.B.—The Guardians request that this Order may be presented for payment within fourteen days from the date hereof, to the Treasurer at his house or usual place of business, and within the usual hours of business (*b*).

with reference to a bill of exchange accepted by procuration, said that a person taking such a bill ought to exercise due caution, for he must take it upon the credit of the party who assumes the authority to accept, and it would be only reasonable prudence to require the production of that authority.

If the prescribed form of order be departed from in drawing the order, the exemption from stamp duty will be lost. The Order does not apply to orders for the payment of sums amounting to or under five pounds; and therefore, if such an order be drawn, it will not be exempt from stamp duty.

(*b*) This will merely operate as a request, and will have no legal effect as regards the Order itself. In a Circular of the Poor Law Board, dated 24th March, 1854, they state, that having had occasion to communicate with the Commissioners of Inland Revenue on the subject of the liability to stamp duty of receipts given by the Treasurers of Boards of Guardians, on the payment to them by Overseers of the Poor of contributions ordered by the Guardians, the Board have been informed that it is the opinion of the Commissioners that such receipts are exempt from stamp duty by virtue of the provisions of the 4 & 5 Wm. IV. c. 76, s. 86, the Treasurer being an officer appointed in pursuance of that Act, and the contributions paid to him by the Overseers being likewise made in pursuance of the same statute, and they requested the Guardians to communicate such opinion to their Treasurer. It may be added, that in the case of orders drawn by Guardians in favour of their Relieving Officers for the payment of relief, that as such orders will contain the

Art. 2.—And We do hereby Order the Treasurer of the said Guardians to pay out of the moneys for the time being in his hands belonging to them, all orders for money which shall be drawn upon him in the above form, when the same shall be presented at his house or usual place of business, and within the usual hours of business.

FIRST SCHEDULE.

[The Unions are those which are contained in the Schedule to the General Consolidated Order, dated the 24th July, 1847, *ante*, p. 206.]

SECOND SCHEDULE.

Names of Unions, Parishes, and Townships not included in the General Orders.	Dates of Orders issued subsequently to the General Orders.
Barnsley	12th June, 1850.
Barton-upon-Irwell	24th January, 1850.
Bedwellty	19th March, 1849.
Great Ouseburn	4th August, 1854.
Hampstead, St. John	24th May, 1848.
Hawarden	25th February, 1853.
Hemsworth	29th October, 1850.
Holyhead	15th February, 1853.
Kirkby Moorside	9th February, 1850.
Knaresborough	28th June, 1854.
Manchester	31st May, 1850.
North Bierley	14th February, 1849.
Oldham	22nd November, 1847.
Penistone	2nd February, 1850.
Prestwich	2nd August, 1850.
Ripon	8th February, 1853.
Saddleworth	18th July, 1853.
Samford	16th March, 1849.
Whitchurch (Salop)	19th February, 1853.

indorsement of the Relieving Officer, they will suffice to prove the receipt of the money by him on account of the Guardians. If, however, the Guardians should require that the Relieving Officers should give a receipt for the cheques when they are handed to them, such receipts would not appear to be exempt from stamp duty.

THIRD SCHEDULE.

Names of Parishes and Townships referred to in the annexed Order included in the General Order dated the 8th December, 1847:—

Alston-with-Garrigill.	St. Mary, Lambeth.
East Stonehouse.	St. Mary, Magdalen, Bermondsey.
Leeds.	
St. George-in-the-East.	St. Mary, Rotherhithe.
St. George-the-Martyr, Southwark.	St. Matthew, Bethnal Green.
	Paddington.
St. Giles, Camberwell.	Stoke-upon-Trent.
St. Luke, Chelsea.	Whittlesea, St. Mary and St. Andrew.
St. Martin-in-the-Fields (a).	
St. Mary Abbots, Kensington.	Great Yarmouth.

Given under our Hands and Seal of Office, this Seventh day of April, in the year One thousand eight hundred and fifty-seven.

       E. P. BOUVERIE, *President*.
       G. GREY.
       G. C. LEWIS.

R. W. GREY, *Secretary*.

*** A separate General Order was issued on the same date to the incorporated Hundreds of East and West Flegg, Forehoe, and Tunstead and Happing in the county of Norfolk, and the Mutford and Lothingland Incorporation in the county of Suffolk, and to Plymouth, on 13th June, 1857; and a similar Order was issued to the Oswestry Incorporation on the 23rd July, 1862.

All Consolidated Orders issued subsequently to 7th April, 1857, are in accordance with the above Order.

(a) Since added to the Strand Union.

WORKHOUSE DIETARIES—GENERAL ORDER.
(16th February, 1848.)

---

*To the **Guardians of the Poor** of the several **Unions** named in the Schedule hereunto annexed.*

To the Clerk or Clerks to the Justices of the Petty Sessions held for the Division or Divisions in which the said Unions are situate;—

And to all others whom it may concern.

WHEREAS the Poor Law Commissioners have, by various Orders under their Hands and Seals, issued to the several Unions named in the Schedule hereunto annexed, the dates whereof are set forth in the said Schedule, ordered and directed that the Paupers of the respective Classes and Sexes who might then or thereafter be received and maintained in every Workhouse of the said respective Unions should, during the period of their residence therein, be fed, dieted, and maintained with the food and in the manner described in the Table or Tables set forth in each Order respectively.

Now we, the Commissioners for administering the Laws for Relief of the Poor in England, do hereby confirm all the said Orders now in force in the said several Unions; and do Order and Direct, that the same shall continue to be acted upon and obeyed in the Unions to which the same have been respectively directed, until the said Commissioners shall, with reference to any one or more of such Unions, by their Order, otherwise Direct.

Provided, however, that if the Guardians of any Union shall at any time or times deem it expedient that a change should be made, either temporarily or permanently, in the nature or quantity of the food specified in the Order last issued to such Union, or in the manner therein described, and shall send a complete and accurate statement of the proposed alteration, in writing, signed by the presiding Chairman of the meeting of the Board whereat the resolution for making such alteration was adopted, to the said Commissioners, and the said Commissioners shall sanction and approve of such alteration, the Guardians may, when the same shall have been so sanctioned and approved of, but not before, cause the same to be adopted and used in the Workhouse or Workhouses of the said Union, as the case may be, without any further Order of the said Commissioners in that behalf.

Provided also, that nothing herein contained shall be taken to rescind or alter any Provision or Regulation of the Poor Law Commissioners contained in their General Order bearing date the Twenty-fourth day of July, One thousand eight hundred and forty-seven, and addressed to the said several Unions herein referred to, which applies to the subject of the diet of the Paupers in the Workhouse or Workhouses of such Unions.

SCHEDULE above referred to.

(The Unions in this Schedule are those which are contained in the Schedule to the General Consolidated Order of the 24th July, 1847, *ante*, p. 206, excepting the following Unions:—

Anglesey.	Bury.	Dolgelly.
Auckland.		Dulverton.
	Camelford.	Durham.
Bala.	Cardigan.	
Bolton.	Carlisle.	Easington.
Broughton, Great.	Chorley.	East Ward.
Bradford (York).	Congleton.	
Builth.	Conway.	Fylde.
Burnley.		

Garstang.
Glossop.

Haslingden.
Hemel Hempstead.
Holsworthy.
Houghton-le-Spring.
Huddersfield.

Keighley.
Kingston-upon-Thames.
Knighton.

Lampeter.
Lancaster.
Leigh.
Llandilo-Fawr.
Llanwrst.
Loddon and Clavering.

London, City of.
London, West.

Machynlleth.
Merthyr Tydvil.

Newcastle-in-Emlyn.
Nottingham.

Olave's, St.
Ormskirk.

Pateley Bridge.
Penrith.
Pocklington.
Presteigne.
Preston.
Pwllheli.

Reading.

Rhayader.
Rochdale.
Romsey.
Runcorn.
Ruthin.

Salford.
Settle.
Stratton.

Todmorden.
Tregaron.

Wakefield.
Welwyn.
West Derby.
Wigan.
Wisbeach.
Wortley.)

Given under our Hands and Seal of Office, this Sixteenth day of February, in the year One thousand eight hundred and forty-eight.

(L. S.)

CHAS. BULLER, JR., *President.*
G. GREY.
C. WOOD.

FORM OF SPECIAL DIETARY ORDER.

To the Guardians of the Poor *of the* —— **Union** *in the Count— of* ——;—

To the Clerk or Clerks to the Justices of the Petty Sessions held for the Division or Divisions in which the said Union is situate;

And to all others whom it may concern.

We, the Poor Law Board, do hereby Order and Direct, that the Paupers maintained in the Workhouse of the —— Union, in the Count— of ——, shall be dieted with the food and in the manner described and set forth herein, viz.—(*here follows the Table*).

And we do hereby empower the Guardians of the Poor of the said Union to allow to each infirm person resident in the said Workhouse a sufficient quantity of tea for breakfast [*and for supper*], not exceeding one pint per meal, sweetened with an allowance of sugar, not exceeding half an ounce to each pint of tea, together with an allowance of butter not exceeding —— ounces per week, in lieu of the —— for breakfast [*and* —— *for supper*] prescribed by the above Table.

And We do hereby further Order and Direct, that children, under the age of nine years, resident in the said Workhouse, shall be fed, dieted, and maintained with such food and in such manner as the said Guardians shall direct; and that children of the age of nine years, and under the age of —— years, shall be allowed the same quantities as are prescribed in the above table for women.

And We do also Order and direct, that the sick paupers, resident in the said Workhouse, shall be dieted in such manner as the Medical Officer for the said Workhouse shall direct.

And We do hereby further Order and Direct, that the Master of the Workhouse shall cause two or more copies of this our Order, legibly written, or printed in large type, to be hung up in the most public places of such Workhouse, and renewed from time to time, so that such copies may be always kept fair and legible (a).

Provided, however, that if the said Guardians of the Poor shall, at any time or times, deem it expedient that a change should be made, either temporarily or permanently, in the nature or quantity of the food specified in this Order, or in the manner herein described, and shall send a complete and accurate statement of the proposed alteration, in writing, signed by the presiding Chairman of the meeting of the Board of the said Guardians whereat the resolutions for making the alteration was adopted, to the said Poor Law Board, and the said Poor Law Board shall sanction and approve of such alteration, the said Guardians may, when the same shall have been so sanctioned and approved of, but not before, cause the same to be adopted and used in the said Workhouse without any further Order of the said Poor Law Board in that behalf.

Provided also, that nothing herein contained shall be taken to rescind or alter any provision or regulation of the Poor Law Commissioners contained in their General Order, bearing date the Twenty-fourth day of July, One thousand eight hundred and forty-seven, addressed to the Guardians of the Poor of the said Union.

Given under our Hand and Seal of Office, this —— day of ——, in the year One thousand eight hundred and sixty—.

——, *President*.

——, *Secretary*.

(*a*) There is no Order which requires that the Dietary Tables for Children should be printed and exhibited in the Workhouse. The Guardians therefore may do as they think best in the matter; but it would seem expedient that the same publicity should be given to the Dietaries of the Children as is given to the Dietaries for the Adults.

The following are the forms in which amended dietary tables are sanctioned by the Poor Law Board:—

―――― Union.

At a **Meeting of the Board of Guardians** of the ―――― Union held on the ―――― day of ――――, 186―, it was resolved that the following amended Dietary Table for the Paupers, of the respective classes and sexes hereunder described, in the Workhouse of this Union, be submitted for the sanction and approval of the Poor Law Board, pursuant to the General Dietary Order of that Board, dated the 16th of February, 1848:

Dietary for the Able-bodied Paupers.

		Breakfast.			Dinner.					Supper.		
Sunday	Men	…	…	…	…	…	…	…	…	…	…	…
	Women	…	…	…	…	…	…	…	…	…	…	…
Monday	Men	…	…	…	…	…	…	…	…	…	…	…
	Women	…	…	…	…	…	…	…	…	…	…	…
Tuesday	Men	…	…	…	…	…	…	…	…	…	…	…
	Women	…	…	…	…	…	…	…	…	…	…	…
Wednesday	Men	…	…	…	…	…	…	…	…	…	…	…
	Women	…	…	…	…	…	…	…	…	…	…	…
Thursday	Men	…	…	…	…	…	…	…	…	…	…	…
	Women	…	…	…	…	…	…	…	…	…	…	…
Friday	Men	…	…	…	…	…	…	…	…	…	…	…
	Women	…	…	…	…	…	…	…	…	…	…	…
Saturday	Men	…	…	…	…	…	…	…	…	…	…	…
	Women	…	…	…	…	…	…	…	…	…	…	…

Children between 9 and 16 years of age to be allowed the same diet as Women.

The Sick to be dieted as directed by the Medical Officer.

――――, *Presiding Chairman.*

I consider the allowances in the above amended dietary to be sufficient.

――――, *Medical Officer.*

Poor Law Board, ――――, 186―.

The Poor Law Board sanction the above amended dietary table.

――――, *Secretary.*

If the proposed Dietary should contain Soup, Broth, Porridge, Gruel, or any other Liquid Food, or puddings, the names and quantities of the several ingredients to be used to every gallon of such Liquid Food, or to every pound of such Puddings, should be entered in the Form below. It will not be necessary that the quantities of Salt, Sugar, Pepper, Spices, or any other Ingredients used for the purpose of giving flavour rather than nourishment should be specified.

Soup.*		Broth.*		Porridge.†	
Name and Description of Ingredient.	Quantity of each Ingredient to a Gallon.	Name and Description of Ingredient.	Quantity of each Ingredient to a Gallon.	Name and Description of Ingredient.	Quantity of each Ingredient to a Gallon.
	oz. | pts.		oz. | pts		oz. | pts

* State whether the Meat is allowed to remain in the Soup or Broth, or if the Soup or Broth be made with the Liquor in which the Meat was boiled on the previous day.
† The Form also contains columns for the insertion of the requisite particulars as to Gruel, Puddings, etc.

_____ *Clerk to the Guardians.*

186

In like manner separate Dietary Tables for the aged and infirm are to be submitted for the sanction of the Poor Law Board.

With reference to the Dietary for the aged and infirm, the Board say that they think it desirable that they should be allowed tea at breakfast and supper, and that the quantity should be one pint to each person, with half-an-ounce of sugar, and one or two ounces of milk to each pint; also that they should have an allowance of half-an-ounce of butter at each of their meals.

As regards the Dietary Tables for Children in the Workhouse, they are to be framed as follows:—

———— UNION.

At a meeting of the Board of Guardians of the ———— Union, held on the ———— day of ———— 18 , it was resolved that the following Dietary Tables for the Pauper Children from 2 to 9 years of age, hereunder described in the Workhouse of the said Union, be submitted for the approval of the Poor Law Board.

TABLE A.
Children from 2 to 5.

	BREAKFAST.		DINNER.				SUPPER.	
Sunday								
Monday								
Tuesday								
Wednesday								
Thursday								
Friday								
Saturday								

TABLE B.
Children from 5 to 9.

	BREAKFAST.		DINNER.				SUPPER.	
Sunday								
Monday								
Tuesday								
Wednesday								
Thursday								
Friday								
Saturday								

Children under 2 years of age to be dieted at discretion.
The Sick to be dieted as directed by the Medical Officer.

———————— *Presiding Chairman.*

I consider the allowances in the above Dietaries to be sufficient.

———————— *Medical Officer.*

The Poor Law Board approve of the above Dietary Tables.

Poor Law Board, 186 .

______________ *Secretary.*

A table of ingredients in soup, etc., similar to that on page 290, *ante*, is also to be prepared with reference to Children's Dietaries.

The Poor Law Board have, by a Circular dated 22nd April, 1856, recommended that distinct dietary tables should be formed for children under 9 years of age,—one for those from 2 to 5 years old, and another for those from 5 to 9. They direct that the dietaries should be prepared by the Guardians, with the assistance of the Medical Officer; and when prepared, submitted for their approval. With a view of affording the Guardians some assistance in carrying out the suggestion, the Board recommended for the consideration of the Guardians and the Medical Officer, the following Dietary Tables :—

	TABLE A. Children from 2 to 5.									TABLE B. Children from 5 to 9.								
	Breakfast.		Dinner.				Supper.			Breakfast.		Dinner.				Supper.		
	Bread.	Milk.	Meat.	Potatoes.	Suet Pudding.	Rice Pudding.	Bread.	Butter.	Milk and Water.	Bread.	Milk.	Meat.	Potatoes.	Suet Pudding.	Rice Pudding.	Bread.	Butter.	Milk and Water.
	oz.	Pts.	oz.	oz.	oz.	oz.	oz.	oz.	Pts.	oz.	Pts.	oz.	oz.	oz.	oz.	oz.	oz.	Pts.
Sunday	4	½	3	8	–	–	4	¼	½	5	½	3½	8	–	–	5	¼	½
Monday	4	½	–	–	8	–	4	¼	½	5	½	–	–	–	–	5	¼	½
Tuesday......	4	½	3	8	–	–	4	¼	½	5	½	3½	8	10	–	5	¼	½
Wednesday .	4	½	–	–	–	8	4	¼	½	5	½	–	–	–	10	5	¼	½
Thursday ...	4	½	3	8	–	–	4	¼	½	5	½	3½	8	–	–	5	¼	½
Friday	4	½	–	–	8	–	4	¼	½	5	½	–	–	10	–	5	¼	½
Saturday ...	4	½	3	8	–	–	4	¼	½	5	½	3½	8	–	–	5	¼	½

Suet Pudding—9½ oz. Flour and 1½ oz. Suet to a pound.
Rice Pudding—5½ oz. Rice to a pound.
Milk and Water—Half Milk.

METROPOLITAN CASUAL POOR DIETARY ORDER.

(3rd March, 1866.)

To the Guardians of the Poor *of the several* **Unions** *and* **Parishes** *named in the Schedule hereunto annexed;—*

To the Masters of the respective Workhouses of the said Unions and Parishes;—

To the Clerk or Clerks to the Justices of the Petty Sessions held for the Division or Divisions in which the said Unions and Parishes are situate:—

And to all others whom it may concern.

We, the Poor Law Board, in pursuance of the powers given in and by the Statutes in that behalf, hereby Order and Direct, that, notwithstanding any provision contained in any General or other Order heretofore issued by the Poor Law Commissioners or the Poor Law Board to the Guardians of the Poor of the respective Unions and Parishes named in the Schedule hereunto annexed, the destitute wayfarers, wanderers, and foundlings admitted into the vagrant wards of the Workhouses belonging to the said several Unions and Parishes shall henceforth be dieted with the food and in the manner described and set forth herein, namely,—

SUPPER. { For all persons above 9 years of age . . . . { 6 oz. of bread and a pint of gruel.
For children under 9 years of age . . . . { 4 oz. of bread and half a pint of gruel.

BREAKFAST { For all persons above 9 years of age . . . . { 6 oz. of bread and a pint of gruel.
For children under 9 years of age . . . . { 4 oz. of bread and half a pint of gruel.

The pint of gruel for supper for all persons above 9 years of age to be withdrawn from the 25th of March to the 29th of September in each year.

And We hereby Order and Direct that, as regards each of the said Unions and Parishes, the Master of the Workhouse, or, where the vagrant wards are detached from the Workhouse, the Superintendent of the vagrant wards, shall cause two or more copies of this our Order, legibly written or printed in large type, to be hung up in the vagrant wards of the Workhouse, and renewed from time to time, so that such copies may be always kept fair and legible.

The term "Guardians" in this Order shall be taken to apply to any "Governors," "Directors of the Poor," "Trustees," "Managers," or "Acting Guardians," entitled to act in the ordering of relief from the Poor Rates under any Local Act of Parliament.

SCHEDULE,

Containing the Names of the Unions and Parishes to which this Order applies.

Names of Unions.	Names of Unions.
Fulham.	Olave's, St.
Greenwich.	Poplar.
Hackney.	Saviour's, St.
Holborn.	Stepney.
Lewisham.	Strand.
London, City of.	Wandsworth and Clapham.
London, East.	Whitechapel.
London, West.	

Names of Parishes.	Names of Parishes.
Bethnal Green, St. Matthew.	Martin, St., in the Fields (a).
Chelsea, St. Luke.	Mile End Old Town.
Clerkenwell, St. James.	Marylebone, St.
George, St., Hanover Square.	Paddington.
George, St., in the East.	Pancras, St.
Giles, St., in the Fields, and St. George, Bloomsbury.	Shoreditch, St. Leonard.
	Bermondsey, St. Mary Magdalen.
Hampstead, St. John.	Camberwell, St. Giles.
Islington, St. Mary.	George, St., the Martyr, Southwark.
James, St., Westminster (b).	
Kensington, St. Mary Abbots.	Lambeth, St. Mary.
Luke, St., Middlesex.	Newington, St. Mary.
Margaret, St., and St. John the Evangelist, Westminster.	Rotherhithe, St. Mary.

Given under our Hands and Seal of Office, this Third day of March, in the year One thousand eight hundred and sixty-six.

       C. P. VILLIERS, *President.*
       G. GREY.
       W. E. GLADSTONE.

H. FLEMING, *Secretary.*

(*a*) This Parish has since been added to the Strand Union.
(*b*) Now with the Parish of St. Anne, Soho, forming the Westminster Union.

INSANE PERSONS AND STRAYED CHILDREN ORDER.

(3rd December, 1841.)

To the Guardians of the Poor *of the several* **Unions** *and* **Parishes** *under a Board of Guardians named in the Schedule hereunto annexed ;—*

To the Churchwardens and Overseers of the several Parishes and Places comprised within the said Unions, and of the several other Parishes named in the said Schedule ;—

To the Clerk or Clerks to the Justices of the Petty Sessions held for the Division or Divisions in which the Parishes and Places comprised within the said Unions and the other Parishes named in the said Schedule are situate ;—

And to all others whom it may concern.

IN pursuance of the authorities vested in Us by an Act of Parliament, passed in the fifth year of the reign of King William the Fourth, intituled "*An Act for the Amendment and better Administration of the Laws relating to the Poor in England and Wales,*" We, the Poor Law Commissioners, do hereby Order and Direct, as follows :—

Art. 1.—Whenever any child supposed to have strayed, or any insane person wandering abroad whose friends or relations are unknown, shall have been received into any Workhouse belonging to any of the Unions or Parishes mentioned in the Schedule hereunto annexed, the Master or other person having charge of such Workhouse shall properly fill up four Notices in the Forms marked A or B respectively, hereto annexed, and shall forthwith cause one of such Notices to be affixed on the outer gate of the said Workhouse, and shall forward one other of the same so filled up to each of the three Police Stations, whether of the Metropolitan or City Police, nearest to the place where such child or insane person shall be understood to have been found.

Art. 2.—If at the expiration of twenty-four hours from the reception of such child or insane person into such Workhouse, no claim or inquiry respecting the same shall have been made at the Workhouse in which such child or insane person shall have been received, the Master or other person having charge of such Workhouse shall send a copy of the notice, already filled up as hereinbefore directed, to the Clerk to the Guardians of the Parish or Union to which such Workhouse may belong, and such Clerk shall immediately cause to be prepared forty-eight copies of the notice so filled up and forwarded to him, and shall forthwith transmit thirty-six copies of such notice to the Commissioners of the Metropolitan Police, at their Chief Office, and twelve copies of such notice to the Commissioner of Police for the City of London, at his office.

Art. 3.—In the construction of this present Order—
1.—The word "*Child*" shall be taken to signify every person being or appearing to be under twelve years of age.
2.—The words "*Insane Person*" shall be taken to signify any idiot or other person of unsound mind.

FORM A.

CHILD FOUND.
Where
When
Sex
Name (if known)
Apparent Age
Complexion
Hair (Colour of)
Particular Marks on the person
Dress and Marks thereon
Any Statement made by the Child as to its abode
Now in _____ Workhouse.
_____ Day of _____ 18 .

FORM B.

INSANE PERSON FOUND.
Where _____
When _____
Sex _____
Name (if known) _____
Apparent Age _____
Complexion _____
Hair (Colour of) _____
Particular marks on the person _____
Dress and Marks thereon _____
Any Statement made by the Insane person as to his or her abode—
_____
Now in _____ Workhouse.
_____ Day of _____ 18 .

Schedule containing the Names of the Unions and Parishes to which the present Order applies.

LIST OF UNIONS AND PARISHES.	
UNIONS.	PARISHES.
Hackney. Holborn. Kensington. London, City of. London, East. London, West. Olave's, St.	George, St., in the East. Martin, St., in the Fields (a). Matthew, St., Bethnal Green. } In the County of Middlesex.
Poplar. Saviour's, St. Stepney. Strand. Wandsworth and Clapham. Whitechapel.	George, St., the Martyr, Southwark. Giles, St., Camberwell. Mary, St., Lambeth. Mary Magdalen, St., Bermondsey. Mary, St., Rotherhithe. } In the County of Surrey.

Given under our Hands and Seal of Office, this Third day of December, in the year One thousand eight hundred and forty-one.

    (Signed) G. C. LEWIS.
         EDMUND W. HEAD.

(a) Since added to the Strand Union.

RELIGIOUS INSTRUCTION ORDER (b).

(23rd *August*, 1859.)

To the Guardians of the Poor *of the several* **Unions** *named in the Schedules hereunto annexed ;—*

To the Churchwardens and Overseers of the Poor of the several Parishes comprised in the said Unions ;—

To the Clerk or Clerks to the Justices of the Petty Sessions held for the Division or Divisions in which the said Unions are respectively situate ;—

And to all others whom it may concern.

WHEREAS, by the Act passed in the fifth year of the reign of King William the Fourth, Chapter Seventy-six, it was, among other things, enacted, that no Rules, Orders, or Regulations of the Poor Law Commissioners, nor any byelaws then in force, or to be thereafter made, should oblige any inmate of any Workhouse to attend any religious service celebrated in a mode contrary to the religious principles of such inmate, nor should authorize the education of

---

(b) With reference to the above Order, the Poor Law Board, in their Circular Letter accompanying it, state that they have recently had under their consideration the regulations at present in force on the subject of the classification of the pauper inmates of Workhouses according to their religious persuasion and the provisions now made for securing religious instruction for such of the inmates as are orphans. The Board have come to the conclusion that it is necessary to give more precise and definite instructions upon the above-mentioned points than those which at present exist, and they have accordingly decided upon issuing an Order, of which a copy accompanies this letter. The Board do not doubt that Boards of Guardians will give such directions to the Master and Matron as will secure a prompt and systematic compliance with the provisions of the present Order.

Further, with reference to this Order, see 4 & 5 Wm. IV. c. 76, s. 19, and 29 & 30 Vict. c. 113, s. 14.

any child in a Workhouse in any religious creed other than that professed by the parents or surviving parent of such child, and to which such parents or parent should object, or in the case of an orphan, to which the godfather or godmother of such orphan should object; and it was also provided that it should and might be lawful for any licensed minister of the religious persuasion of any inmate of such Workhouse, at all times in the day, on the request of such inmate, to visit such Workhouse for the purpose of affording religious assistance to such inmate, and also for the purpose of instructing his child or children in the principles of their religion;

And whereas, by an Order bearing date the Seventeenth day of March, One thousand eight hundred and forty-seven, being a General Order, issued to the several Unions mentioned in the First Schedule hereunto annexed, and by various special Orders subsequently issued to the several Unions mentioned in the Second Schedule hereunto annexed, the Poor Law Commissioners and Poor Law Board respectively have ordered and directed that the Master of every Workhouse of the respective Unions shall punctually enter up and accurately keep a certain Book, termed the In-door Relief List, in which shall be entered for each Parish of the Union, in the form therein numbered 22 (except as regards the Order relating to the Hartlepool Union, wherein such form is numbered 21), the several particulars set forth in the said form;

And whereas the religious persuasion of each pauper inmate of the Workhouse is one of the particulars set forth in that form;

And whereas it is desirable that provision should be made for the entry in such column of the religious persuasion of every orphan child whose godfather or godmother does not give information with regard to the religion of such orphan, and that other means should be taken for securing religious instruction to orphans in Workhouses than exist at present:

Now therefore, We, the Poor Law Board, under the authority of the Statutes in that behalf made and provided, hereby Order and Direct as follows:—

Article 1.—That whenever there shall be in the Workhouse any orphan child under the age of fourteen years, the Master of the said Workhouse shall enter in such Indoor Relief List, as the religious persuasion of such orphan, the religious creed which was professed by the father of such orphan at the time of his death, if the Master know or can ascertain the same by reasonable inquiry; or, if the same cannot be so ascertained, the creed professed by the mother of such orphan at the time of her death, if the same be known to the said Master, or can be by him in like manner ascertained:

Provided always, that if the godfather or godmother of such orphan shall make any objection, this article shall not have any force or application.

Article 2.—Such orphan, while an inmate of the Workhouse, shall not be instructed in any other religious creed than that so entered, unless he or she, being above the age of twelve years, shall desire to receive instruction in some other creed, and unless he or she be considered by the Poor Law Board to be competent to exercise a reasonable judgment upon the subject.

Article 3.—The Master of the Workhouse shall, subject to the directions of the Guardians of the Union, take all practicable steps in order to procure the attendance at the Workhouse from time to time, for the purpose of affording religious instruction to such orphan, of some Minister of the religious persuasion of the said orphan, as ascertained according to the provisions of this Order, or according to the information of the godfather or godmother;

Provided always, that such attendance shall take place at such times as shall not be inconsistent with the discipline and good order of the Workhouse.

Article 4.—The provisions herein contained applicable to the Master of the Workhouse shall extend to the Matron in cases in which there shall be no Master, or in which he shall be absent, or his office shall be vacant.

SCHEDULES referred to in the foregoing Order.

FIRST SCHEDULE.

(The Unions in this Schedule are those which are included in the General Consolidated Order, *ante*, p. 206.)

SECOND SCHEDULE.

Names of Unions.	Dates of Orders.
Barnsley	23rd April, 1850.
Barton-upon Irwell . .	26th January, 1850.
Bedwelty	28th November, 1849.
Gower	9th November, 1857.
Great Ouseburn . . .	6th July, 1854.
Hartlepool	26th May, 1859.
Hawarden	5th March, 1853.
Hemsworth	22nd November, 1850.
Holyhead	19th February, 1853.
Kirkby Moorside . . .	23rd December, 1848.
Knaresborough . . .	16th June, 1854.
North Bierley	14th February, 1849.
Oldham	20th November, 1848.
Penistone	22nd November, 1849.
Prestwich	3rd August, 1850.
Ripon	8th February, 1853.
Samford	27th March, 1849.
Whitchurch (Salop) . .	25th February, 1853.

Given under our Hands and Seal of Office, this Twenty-third day of August, in the year One thousand eight hundred and fifty-nine.

C. P. VILLIERS, *President*.
G. C. LEWIS.
W. E. GLADSTONE.

H. FLEMING, *Secretary*.

COLLECTOR OF THE GUARDIANS ORDER.

(7th October, 1865) (a).

To the Guardians of the Poor *of the several* **Unions, Parishes,** *and* **Places** *named in the Schedules hereunto annexed;—*

To the Clerk or Clerks to the Justices of the Petty Sessions held for the Division or Divisions in which the said Unions, Parishes, and Places are situate;—

And to all others whom it may concern.

WHEREAS it is oftentimes expedient that Guardians of the Poor should appoint an Officer to collect and receive moneys from time to time due and payable to them or on their account.

Now, therefore, We, the Poor Law Board, acting under the authority of the Statutes in that behalf made and provided, hereby Order and Direct the Guardians of the Poor of the several Unions, Parishes, and Places named in the Schedules (B.) and (C.) hereunto annexed, as and when they shall see occasion to do so, to appoint a fit and proper

---

(a) In their Circular-Letter, accompanying the above Order of the 7th October, 1865, the Poor Law Board state as their reason for issuing it that they have been frequently applied to on the subject of the inconveniences experienced by Boards of Guardians in many Unions in regard to the collection of moneys payable to them, by reason of the want of a proper officer for such purpose. The Board, moreover, anticipate that after the complete establishment of Union Chargeability, the demands for such an officer will increase.

This Order it will be seen has no reference to Overseers. It is confined to debts or demands due to the Guardians, and does not apply to the Poor-rate.

person to collect the moneys due and payable to such Guardians, to be termed Collector of the Guardians (a).

And We further Order, with respect to such appointment, as follows; that is to say:—

MODE OF APPOINTMENT.

Art. 1.—Every Officer to be appointed under this Order shall be appointed by a majority of the Guardians present at a meeting of the Board, and voting on the question of such appointment.

Every such appointment shall, as soon as the same has been made, be reported to the Poor Law Board by the Clerk to the Guardians.

Art. 2.—Previous to an appointment to the aforesaid office being made under this Order, a notice that the question of making such appointment will be brought before the Board of Guardians shall be given and entered on their minutes at one of the two ordinary meetings of the said Board next preceding the meeting at which the appointment is made, or an advertisement, giving notice of the consideration of such appointment, shall be inserted in some public newspaper, by the direction of the Guardians, at least seven days before the day on which such appointment is made. Provided that no such notice or advertisement shall be necessary for the appointment of a temporary substitute.

QUALIFICATION.

Art. 3.—Every person who shall be appointed to the office of Collector under this Order shall agree to give one month's notice previous to resigning the office, or to forfeit one month's amount of salary, to be deducted as liquidated damages from the amount of salary due at the time of such resignation (b).

(a) By the General Order of 7th November, 1866, *post*, p. 312, the Guardians may appoint more than one Collector for the above purposes.

(b) A Relieving Officer may be appointed Collector with the consent of the Poor Law Board, under Art. 166 of the Consolidated Order, *ante*, p. 118, but not the Clerk to the Guardians, as the two offices would be incompatible in the same person.

Duties of the Officer.

Art. 4.—The duties of the Collector shall be:—

No. 1. To collect, under the directions of the Guardians, all sums of money from time to time due and payable to them other than such as under their orders or otherwise shall be payable to their Treasurer.

No. 2. To serve the orders of contributions upon the Overseers when required by the Guardians to do so.

No. 3. To assist the Clerk to the Guardians in filling up receipts, keeping books, and making returns which relate to any matter concerning the moneys payable to the Guardians which he may have collected or may have been required to collect.

No. 4. To produce to the Guardians or their Clerk respectively, whenever required by them or him, the account books in his custody by virtue of his office as such Collector, and to balance the same, and to furnish them with a true list of all defaulters in the payment of moneys due to them, and under their directions to attend the proceedings against such defaulters.

No. 5. To keep punctually a book according to the Form set forth in the Schedule (A.) No. 1, hereunto annexed, and to duly enter therein all sums received and all sums paid by him, and to give in respect of all moneys received by him a receipt in the Form in the said Schedule (A.) No. 2 (*c*).

No. 6. To pay all sums received by him to the Treasurer of the said Guardians monthly, or at any shorter period if required by them to do so; and whenever the same shall amount to £50 or upwards, to pay the same to the said Treasurer as soon as practicable after the receipt thereof.

No. 7. To submit to the Guardians at their ordinary meeting an account of the payments and disbursements

---

(*c*) See, however, Art. 17 of the General Order for Accounts, *post*.

made by him on their behalf, with proper vouchers where the same can be obtained, once a month, or at a shorter interval if he find it necessary to do so.

No. 8. To attend every meeting of the Guardians when required by them to do so, and every meeting of the Finance Committee, if there be one, and to obey all lawful orders and directions of such Guardians and Committee relating to his office.

No. 9. To attend the Auditor at the Audit of the accounts of the Guardians, and to obey all the Regulations contained in the Orders of Accounts issued to the Unions and Parishes named in the said Schedules (B.) and (C.) hereunto annexed, which relate to the attendance and accounting of officers at the Audit (a).

REMUNERATION OF THE OFFICER.

Art. 5.—The Board of Guardians shall pay to the officer appointed to the office of Collector under this Order such salary, either by a fixed sum or by a poundage, as the Poor Law Board shall from time to time direct or approve; and shall also repay the amount expended or disbursed by him on their behalf according to the account rendered by him, so far as it shall be found to have been duly and properly incurred.

Art. 6.—The salary of such officer shall be payable from the day on which he commences the performances of his duties up to the day on which he shall cease to hold such office, and no longer, and shall be paid by quarterly payments at the several quarters ending at the usual Feast Days in the year, namely, Lady Day, Midsummer Day, Michaelmas Day, and Christmas Day, with a proportionate sum to be paid to his executors or administrators in case he shall die while holding such office; and in the case of a pay-

---

(a) It will be seen that the Order does not relate to the collection of the Poor-rate, and that it does not interfere with the duties of Collectors of Poor-rates appointed by the Guardians, or with the duties of Assistant Overseers appointed under 59 Geo. III. c. 12, s. 7.

ment by poundage, the same shall be calculated by the said Guardians at such several quarters upon the amount which the said Guardians shall ascertain to have been collected by such Collector in the quarter then last ended, and the same shall be paid by the said Guardians at such times accordingly.

Art. 7.—It shall be competent for the Guardians to defer, in whole or in part, the payment of the salary of such Collector, until his accounts shall have been audited and allowed by the Auditor, after which audit and allowance the sum due up to the date of his accounts so audited shall forthwith be paid.

Art. 8.—No such Collector who may be suspended, and who shall upon such suspension resign, or be removed by the Poor Law Board, shall be entitled to any salary from the date of such suspension; and no such officer who shall be temporarily suspended from his office, by reason of his services not being required, shall be entitled to any salary pending such temporary suspension.

SECURITY.

Art. 9.—The person appointed to such office shall give a bond in such penal sum as the said Guardians shall think fit, in the names of himself and two sufficient sureties, not being officers of the same Union or Parish as that for which he shall be appointed, conditioned for the due and faithful performance of the duties of the office; and every such Collector shall give immediate notice to the said Guardians of the death, insolvency, or bankruptcy of either of such sureties, and shall, when required by the said Guardians, produce a certificate signed by two householders, that his sureties are alive, and believed by them to be solvent, and shall supply a fresh surety in the place of any such surety who may die, or become bankrupt or insolvent: Provided that the Guardians may, if they think fit, take the security of any society or company expressly authorized by statute to guarantee or secure the faithful discharge of the duties of any Poor Law officer.

Art. 10.—The Auditor shall, in the statement required by the General Orders of the Poor Law Commissioners and the Poor Law Board in that behalf, to be transmitted to them of the securities of the officers of the said Unions or Parishes, include the name of the Collector for the time being appointed under this Order, together with the particulars in the said General Orders required, and shall report thereon to the Board of Guardians, in like manner as therein set forth with reference to the securities of other officers.

CONTINUANCE IN OFFICE AND SUSPENSION OF OFFICER.—SUPPLY OF VACANCY.

Art. 11.—Every Collector shall hold the said office until he shall die, or resign, or be removed by the Poor Law Board, or be proved to be insane by evidence which such Board shall deem sufficient, unless the Guardians shall deem it advisable to discontinue the office, and shall inform the said Board accordingly; and upon such death, resignation, removal, or insanity of any such officer, the said Guardians shall give notice thereof to the Poor Law Board, and proceed to appoint some person in his place, according to the provisions of this Order; and in every case of a resignation, the Clerk of the said Guardians shall transmit to the Poor Law Board a statement of the cause of such resignation, so far as it may be known to them.

Art. 12.—The said Guardians may, at their discretion, suspend from the discharge of his duties any such Collector, and shall, in case of every such suspension, forthwith report the same, together with the cause thereof, to the Poor Law Board, for their decision thereon, and if the Poor Law Board remove such suspension, he shall forthwith resume the performance of his duties.

Art. 13.—If any such Collector be at any time prevented by sickness or accident, or other sufficient reason, from the performance of his duties, the Guardians may appoint a fit person to act as his temporary substitute, and may pay such person a reasonable compensation for his services; and every such appointment, with a statement of the circumstances which have led to it, shall be reported to the Poor Law Board, as soon as the same shall have been made, by the Clerk to the Guardians.

Art. 14. The word "Parish" in this Order shall mean every place which maintains its own poor separately, or for which a separate poor rate is made.

Art. 15.—The word "Overseer" shall be taken to include any person acting or legally bound to act in the discharge of any of the duties usually performed by Overseers, so far as they are referred to herein.

SCHEDULE (A.)

No. 1.—*Form of Collector's Book.*

UNION [or PARISH].

RECEIPTS.					PAYMENTS TO THE TREASURER.		
Date.	No. of Receipt.	From whom received.	On what account.	Amount.	Date.	On what account.	Amount.
				£. s. d.			£. s. d.

310   Collector of the Guardians Order.

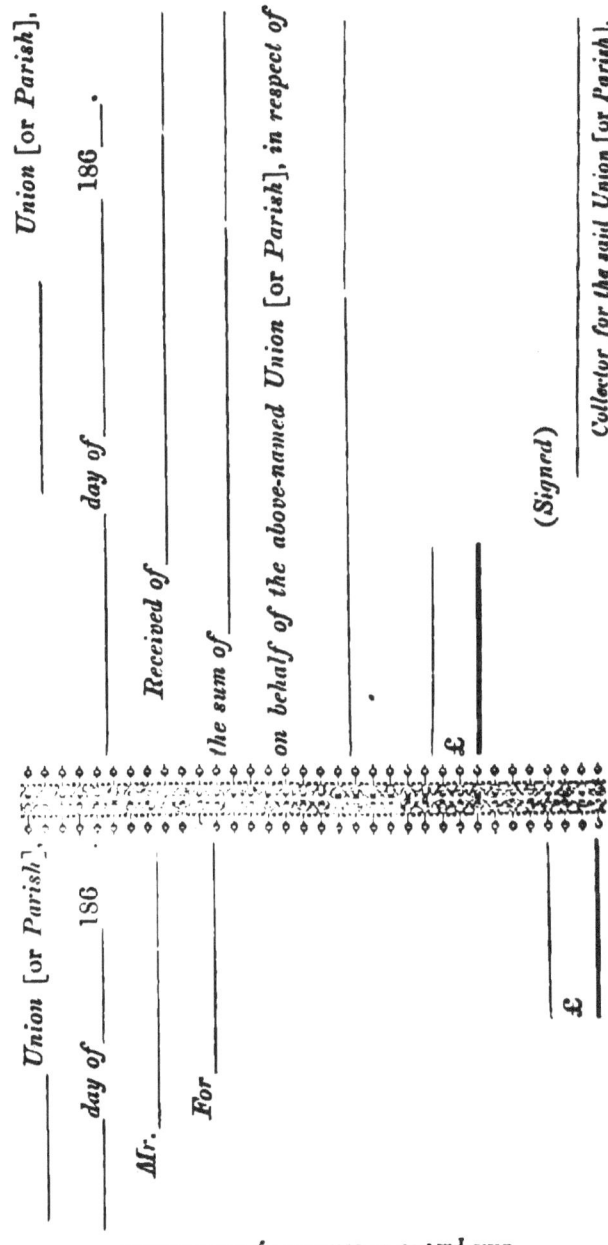

SCHEDULE (B.)

Containing the Names of the Unions to which the foregoing Order refers.

[The Unions in this Schedule are those contained in the Schedule to the General Consolidated Order, *ante*, p. 206, and those mentioned in the Table of Consolidated Orders separately issued, *post*, p. 211, except Norwich, Westminster, and Woolwich Unions.]

SCHEDULE (C.)

Containing the Names of the Parishes, Townships, and Places referred to in the foregoing Order.

Alston-with-Garrigill.
East Stonehouse.
Holbeck.
Hunslet.
Leeds.
Manchester.
Mile End Old Town.
Paddington.
Saddleworth.
St. George-in-the-East.
St. George-the-Martyr, Southwark.
St. Giles, Camberwell.
St. John, Hampstead.
St. Leonard, Shoreditch.
St. Luke, Chelsea.
St. Martin-in-the-Fields (a).
St. Mary Abbots, Kensington.
St. Mary, Lambeth.
St. Mary Magdalen, Bermondsey.
St. Mary, Rotherhithe.
St. Matthew, Bethnal Green.
Stoke-upon-Trent.
Toxteth Park.
Whittlesea, St. Mary and St. Andrew.
Yarmouth, Great.

Given under our Hands and Seal of Office, this Seventh day of October, in the year One thousand eight hundred and sixty-five.

(L. S.)

C. P. VILLIERS, *President.*
G. GREY.
W. E. GLADSTONE.

ENFIELD, *Secretary.*

(a) This Parish has since been added to the Strand Union

COLLECTORS OF GUARDIANS ORDER.

(27*th November*, 1866.)

To the Guardians of the Poor *of the several* **Unions, Parishes,** *and* **Places** *named in the Schedules hereunto annexed;—*

To the Clerk or Clerks to the Justices of the Petty Sessions held for the Division or Divisions in which the said Unions, Parishes, and Places are situate;—

And to all others whom it may concern.

WHEREAS, by a General Order under the Hands and Seal of the Poor Law Board, dated the Seventh day of October One thousand eight hundred and sixty-five, addressed to the Guardians of the Poor of the several Unions, Parishes, and Places named in the Schedules (B.) and (C.) thereunto annexed, being the same as those named in the Schedules (A.) and (B.) hereunto annexed, the said Poor Law Board ordered and directed the said Guardians, as and when they should see occasion to do so, to appoint a fit and proper person to collect the moneys due and payable to such Guardians, to be termed Collector of the Guardians.

And whereas it is expedient that the Guardians of some of the Unions and Parishes should be empowered to appoint more than one such Collector.

Now, therefore, We, the said Poor Law Board, acting under the authority of the Statutes in that behalf made and provided, hereby Order and Direct that as and when any Board of Guardians shall see occasion to do so, they may appoint more than one Collector for the above purpose.

And We hereby further Direct that all the Regulations and Provisions contained in the said recited Order shall apply to the Collectors to be appointed under the authority of this Order.

SCHEDULE (A.)

Containing the Names of the Unions to which the foregoing Order refers.

[The Unions are the same as those mentioned in the Schedule (A.) to the Order of the 7th October, 1865, *ante*, p. 311.]

SCHEDULE (B.)

Containing the Names of the Parishes, Townships, and Places referred to in the foregoing Order.

[The Parishes are the same as those mentioned in the Schedule (B.) to the Order of the 7th October, 1865, *ante*, p. 311.]

Given under our Hands and Seal of Office, this Twenty-seventh day of November, in the year One thousand eight hundred and sixty-six.

GATHORNE HARDY, *President.*
S. H. WALPOLE.
B. DISRAELI.

H. FLEMING, *Secretary.*

APPOINTMENT OF ASSISTANT OFFICERS ORDER.

(19th *August*, 1867.)

To the **Guardians** of the **Poor** *of the several* **Unions** *and* **Parishes** *named in the Schedules hereunto annexed;—*

To the Clerk or Clerks to the Justices of the Petty Sessions held for the Division or Divisions in which the said Unions and Parishes are respectively situate;—

And to all others whom it may concern.

WHEREAS, by divers General and other Orders, addressed to the several Unions and Parishes named in the Schedules hereunto annexed, the Poor Law Commissioners and the Poor Law Board respectively made certain regulations with reference to the appointments of Officers and Assistants, and their Salaries and continuance in office; and it is expedient that certain alterations should be made in such regulations.

Now therefore, We, the Poor Law Board, acting under the authority of the Poor Law Amendment Act, 1834 (*a*), and the other Statutes in that behalf made and provided, hereby Order as follows:—

Art. 1.—The Guardians may employ such persons as they shall deem requisite in or about the Workhouse or Workhouse Premises, or on the Land occupied for the employment of the pauper inmates of the Workhouse, or otherwise in or about the relief of the In-door Poor, upon such

---

(*a*) See 30 & 31 Vict. c. 106, s. 30.

terms and conditions as shall appear to them to be suitable (*b*).

Art. 2.—So much of any Order (*c*) as would require the Guardians to report to this Board the appointment, salary, removal, or discharge of any such person employed by them as aforesaid, or as would provide for the quarterly or other periodical payment of any such person engaged at daily, weekly, or monthly wages, or by the piece or job, is hereby rescinded (*d*).

Art. 3.—The foregoing Articles of this Order (except so much thereof as relates to their quarterly or other periodical payments (*e*)) shall not apply to the following Officers or Persons; that is to say,—

    Clerk to the Guardians.

(*b*) As to the appointment of other Workhouse Officers, see *ante*, p. 109.

(*c*) See Art. 155 of the General Consolidated Order, *ante*, p. 113.

(*d*) The Poor Law Board say that it will be seen that the effect of this Order is, with certain exceptions, to dispense with the necessity of reporting the appointment, removal, discharge, or salaries for the approval of the Board in future. It will still, however, be necessary that such Report should be made in respect of the appointments of the superior Officers required for the relief of this class of Poor, and of those subordinate appointments the charge of which wholly or in part is now borne by the Consolidated Fund. The Guardians must, nevertheless, carefully record the appointments which they make, the salaries which they agree to pay, and the stipulations which they enter into with the persons engaged by them, so that the Auditor may have no difficulty in respect of the payments made to such persons when the accounts of the Guardians are laid before him.

As the Metropolitan Poor Act of 1867 casts upon the Common Poor Fund of the Metropolis the salaries of the Officers employed by the Guardians of the Metropolitan Unions and Parishes in and about the relief of the Poor, provided the appointments of the Officers have been sanctioned by the Poor Law Board, it will be competent for those Guardians to act under the previous Orders applicable to them, and continue to report the appointments of all their Officers to this Board. In such cases the Guardians will waive the advantages granted by the first and second Articles of this Order.

The Board observe that this Order does not dispense with the annual return of the List of Officers and of the rest of the staff of the Guardians with which the Board require to be supplied, in order that they may be informed from time to time of the actual number of persons in the employment of the Guardians, and the nature of their duties and services.—*Instr. Letter, 20th August,* 1867.

(*e*) See *ante*, p. 124, note.

Chaplain.

Medical Officer for the Workhouse and his Assistants.

Dispensers and Persons engaged in preparing and dispensing Medicines.

Master of the Workhouse.

Matron of the Workhouse.

Porter.

Nurse and Assistant Nurses.

Schoolmaster and Schoolmistress, and other persons engaged in teaching or instructing pauper children.

Art. 4.—The provisions of the said Orders relating to the security to be given by Officers shall apply to every person employed under this Order (*a*).

Art. 5.—When the Guardians propose to make an appointment of any officer, assistant, or servant under any of the Orders aforesaid or any other Order of the Poor Law Board, they may by special resolution require any Candidate to attend personally before their Board for examination, and may pay such reasonable expenses incurred by such Candidate as they shall deem proper (*b*).

Art. 6.—The word "Unions" in this Order shall be taken to include not only Unions of Parishes formed under the provisions of the hereinbefore mentioned Act, but also Unions of Parishes incorporated or united for the relief or

---

(*a*) See Articles 184–186 of the General Consolidated Order, *ante*, p. 131.

(*b*) With reference to this Article the Poor Law Board say that they have taken this opportunity of providing for a subject which is constantly causing much annoyance to Boards of Guardians. In making appointments to offices the Guardians sometimes require the personal attendance of all or some of the candidates. Difficulties have occasionally occurred in providing for the expenses of candidates who attend from a distance. Boards of Guardians often pay their expenses, but many Auditors disallow the amount as not being legally chargeable upon the rates, and this Board, when appealed to, have considered themselves bound to uphold the legality of the Auditor's decision. The Board have therefore introduced a provision which they believe will remove the objection, and enable the Guardians to deal with this subject in the manner which, in the exercise of their judgment, they deem most advisable in the particular cases which may occur.—*Instr. Letter, 20th August*, 1867.

maintenance of the Poor under any Local Act of Parliament.

The word "Guardians" in this Order shall be taken to include not only Guardians appointed or entitled to act under the provisions of the said hereinbefore mentioned Act, but also any Governors, Deputy Governors, Assistants, Directors, Managers, Acting Guardians, Vestrymen, or other officers appointed or entitled to act as Managers of the Poor and in the distribution or ordering of relief to the Poor from the Poor Rate under any Local Act of Parliament.

Whenever the word "Parish" is used in this Order, it shall be taken to signify any place for which a separate Poor Rate is or can be made, or for which a separate Overseer is or can be appointed (c).

The word "Workhouse" shall include every School, Infirmary, or Hospital provided by the Guardians for the reception of paupers.

SCHEDULES to which the foregoing Order refers.

Names of the Unions.

[The Unions contained in the Schedule to this Order are those mentioned in the Schedule to the General Consolidated Order, *ante*, p. 206, and the Unions mentioned in the Table of Consolidated Orders separately issued, *ante*, p. 211; except Norwich, Westminster, and Woolwich Unions]; and also the following places which are under Local Acts, namely:—

Bristol.	Exeter.	Oswestry.
Bury St. Edmund's.	Flegg, East and West.	Oxford.
Canterbury.	Kingston-upon-Hull.	Salisbury.
Chester.	Montgomery and Pool.	Shrewsbury.
Chichester.	Mutford and Lothingland.	Southampton.
Coventry.		Tunstead and Happing.

(c) See 29 & 30 Vict. c. 113, s. 18.

Names of the Parishes.

- Alston-with-Garrigill.
- Birmingham.
- Brighton.
- East Stonehouse.
- Holbeck.
- Hunslet.
- Leeds.
- Liverpool.
- Manchester.
- Mile End Old Town.
- Paddington.
- Plymouth.
- Saddleworth.
- St. George-in-the-East.
- St. George, Hanover Square.
- St. George-the-Martyr, Southwark.
- St. Giles and St. George, Bloomsbury.
- St. Giles, Camberwell.
- St. James, Clerkenwell.
- St. James, Westminster (*b*).
- St. John, Hampstead.
- St. Leonard, Shoreditch.
- St. Luke, Chelsea.
- St. Luke, Middlesex.
- St. Martin-in-the-Fields (*a*).
- St. Mary Abbots, Kensington.
- St. Mary, Islington.
- St. Mary, Lambeth.
- St. Marylebone.
- St. Mary Magdalen, Bermondsey.
- St. Mary, Newington.
- St. Mary, Rotherhithe.
- St. Matthew, Bethnal Green.
- St. Pancras.
- Stoke Damerel.
- Stoke-upon-Trent.
- Toxteth Park.
- Whittlesea, St. Mary and St. Andrew.
- Yarmouth, Great.

Given under our Hands and Seal of Office, this Nineteenth day of August, in the year One thousand eight hundred and sixty-seven.

DEVON, *President*.
B. DISRAELI.
GATHORNE HARDY.

G. SCLATER-BOOTH, *Secretary*.

(*a*) Since added to the Strand Union.
(*b*) Now with the Parish of St. Anne, Soho, forming the Westminster Union.

FORM OF PAY-CLERK OF THE POOR ORDER (c).

To the Guardians of the Poor *of the* **Parish** *of* ———, *in the County of* ——— ;—

> *To the Churchwardens and Overseers of the Poor of the said Parish ;—*
>
> *To the Clerk or Clerks to the Justices of the Petty Sessions held for the Division or Divisions in which the said Parish is situate ;—*
>
> *And to all others whom it may concern.*

WE, the Poor Law Board, acting under the authority of the several Statutes in this behalf made and provided, do hereby Order and Direct the Guardians of the Poor of the ——————— in the County of ———, *within one calendar month from the date hereof,* to appoint a fit and proper person for the distribution of relief to the Poor of the said ———, to be termed the Pay-Clerk of the Poor of the said ———.

And We do further Order, with respect to such appointment, as follows ; that is to say,—

QUALIFICATION.

Art. 1.—Every person who shall be appointed to the office of Pay-Clerk under this Order shall agree to give one month's notice previous to resigning the office, or to forfeit one month's amount of salary, to be deducted, as liquidated damages, from the amount of salary due at the time of such resignation.

(c) This form of Order is in accordance with the Order issued to the Township of Toxteth Park ; but the form of Order differs in some of the Unions.

MODE OF APPOINTMENT.

Art. 2.—Every person who shall be appointed to the office of Pay-Clerk under this Order, shall be appointed in like manner and subject to the same Rules and Regulations as are required for the appointment of Officers under an Order of the Poor Law Board, bearing date the —— day of ——, One thousand eight hundred and ——, and addressed to the Guardians of the Poor of the said —— (*a*).

DUTIES OF THE OFFICER (*b*).

Art. 3.—The duties of the Pay-Clerk shall be as follows; namely,—

> No. 1. To attend at the office provided by the said Guardians for the distribution of relief to paupers, at such times as the said Guardians shall require, and to distribute from the funds and stores under his care the relief ordered by them to be given to the paupers of the said ——, on receiving from the several Relieving Officers of the said —— tickets according to the Form (A.) hereunto annexed, in which the relief ordered by the said Guardians to be given to the poor persons presenting the same at such office shall have been properly entered.
>
> No. 2. To keep punctually and accurately a book, to be called "The Pay Book," in the Form (B.) hereunto annexed, and enter therein the sums of money given in relief, and the value of relief in kind given by him to every person presenting a ticket for relief as aforesaid, such entry to be made after, and not before, the relief shall have been actually given; and to keep a

---

(*a*) See Art. 155, etc., of the General Consolidated Order, *ante*, p. 113.
(*b*) The duties of the Pay-Clerk must be strictly confined to those prescribed by the Order; and he must not be employed in any of the duties which appertain to the other officers. He is not empowered to give orders for relief, and must therefore abstain from doing so; and the books which he is to keep do not supersede in any way the books to be kept by any other officer.

separate account in such book of the relief paid to the non-settled poor.

Art. 3.—No. 3. To keep punctually and accurately a book, to be called "The Pay-Clerk's Receipt and Expenditure Book," in the Form (C.) hereunto annexed, and to enter therein all moneys received and disbursed by him, and all tickets for relief discharged by him; and to balance such account weekly.

No. 4. To present his accounts weekly to the Clerk to the Guardians of the said —— for his inspection and authentication, before every ordinary meeting of the Guardians, and to the Guardians, at such meeting, for their approval.

No. 5. To submit to the Auditor all his books, accounts, and vouchers, at the time and place of audit.

No. 6. To attend the meetings of the Guardians of the said ——, when required by them.

No. 7. To observe and execute all lawful orders and directions of the Guardians applicable to his office.

No. 8. To perform all the duties prescribed by any Rules, Orders, and Regulations which may be issued by the Poor Law Board applicable to his office.

Remuneration of the Officer.

Art. 4.—The Board of Guardians shall pay to the Officer appointed under this Order to the office of Pay-Clerk, an annual salary of —— pounds, and charge the same to the said ——.

Art. 5.—The salary of such Officer shall be payable up to the day on which he ceases to hold such office, and no longer, and shall be paid by quarterly payments at the several quarters ending at the usual Feast Days in the year, namely, Christmas-day, Lady-day, Midsummer-day, and Michaelmas-day, with a proportionate sum to be paid to his executors or administrators in case he shall die while holding such office; but it shall be competent for the Guardians to defer in whole or in part the payment of the salary of such Pay-Clerk until his accounts shall have been audited and allowed by the Auditor, after which audit and allowance the sum due up to the date of his accounts so audited shall forthwith be paid.

No Pay-Clerk who may be suspended, and who shall, upon such suspension, resign or be removed by the Poor Law Board, shall be entitled to any salary from the date of such suspension; and no such Officer who shall be temporarily suspended from his office by reason of his services not being required, shall be entitled to any salary pending any such temporary suspension.

Art. 6.—The said Officer shall not, directly or indirectly, receive or bargain to receive any gratuity, percentage, or allowance of any kind with reference to any contract with the Guardians, or in respect of any payment made or to be made for goods supplied or work executed according to the order of such Guardians, or on their behalf.

SECURITY.

Art. 7.—The person appointed to such office shall give a bond in such penal sum as the said Guardians shall think fit, in the names of himself and two sufficient sureties, not being Officers of the aforesaid ———, conditioned for the due and faithful performance of the duties of the office; and he shall give immediate notice to the said Guardians of the death, insolvency, or bankruptcy of either of such sureties, and shall, when required by the said Guardians, produce a certificate, signed by two householders, that his sureties are alive and believed by them to be solvent, and shall supply a fresh surety in the place of any such surety who may die, or become bankrupt or insolvent: Provided that the Guardians may, if they think fit, take the security of any society or company expressly authorized by statute to guarantee or secure the faithful discharge of the duties of any Poor Law Officer (a).

(a) See Art. 185, *ante*, p. 133.

CONTINUANCE IN OFFICE AND SUSPENSION OF OFFICER.
—SUPPLY OF VACANCY.

Art. 8.—Every Officer appointed under this Order shall hold the said office until he shall die, or resign, or be removed by the Poor Law Board, or be proved to be insane, by evidence which such Board shall deem sufficient; and upon such death, resignation, removal, or insanity of any such Officer, the said Guardians shall give notice thereof to the Poor Law Board, and proceed to appoint some person in his place, according to the provisions of this Order, and in every case of a resignation the said Guardians shall transmit to the Poor Law Board a statement of the cause of such resignation, so far as it may be known to them.

Art. 9.—The said Guardians may, at their discretion, suspend from the discharge of his duties any such Pay-Clerk, and shall, in case of every such suspension, forthwith report the same, together with the cause thereof, to the Poor Law Board, for their decision thereon; and if the Poor Law Board remove the suspension of such Pay-Clerk by the Guardians, he shall forthwith resume the performance of his duties.

Art. 10.—If any Officer appointed under this Order be at any time prevented by sickness or accident, or other sufficient reason, from the performance of his duties, the Guardians may appoint a fit person to act as his temporary substitute, and may pay such person a reasonable compensation for his services; and every such appointment, with a statement of the circumstances which have led to it, shall be reported to the Poor Law Board, as soon as the same shall have been made, by the Clerk to the Guardians.

Art. 11 (b).—The Auditor of the District comprising the said ——— shall, in the statement required by the General Order of the Poor Law Board, dated the 14th day of January, 1867, to be transmitted to the Poor Law Board

---

(b) This Article, however, is not in all the Orders issued authorizing the appointment of a Pay-Clerk.

of the securities of the Officers of the said ———, include the name of the Pay-Clerk for the time being appointed under the authority hereof, together with the particulars in the said General Order required, and shall report thereon to the Board of Guardians of the said ——— in like manner as therein set forth with reference to the securities of other Officers.

Art. 12.—Provided, that if at any time hereafter the Guardians should deem it advisable to discontinue the employment of a Pay-Clerk for the Parish, and shall give three months notice of such their intention to the person for the time being holding such office, and the Poor Law Board shall consent to rescind this Order, the office shall terminate at the expiration of such notice.

FORM (A).

Out-Relief Ticket.

Parish of _____.

Mr. _____ pay to _____

the following Relief, viz.

186 .

Week.	Money.	Loaves	Week.	Money.	Loaves	Week.	Money.	Loaves
1 (Date.)			1 (Date.)			1 (Date.)		
2 (Date.)			2 (Date.)			2 (Date.)		
3 (Date.)			3 (Date.)			3 (Date.)		

_____ Signature of Relieving Officer.

FORM (B.)

Pay Book.

———— of ————————.

Half-year ending ————————

————————, Pay-Clerk.

Name of the Pauper.	Where resident.	1st Week, ending	2nd Week, etc. to 13th Week.	Totals for the First Quarter.		1st Week, ending	2nd Week, etc. to 13th Week.	Totals for the Second Quarter.		Totals for the Half-year.	
		In Money. | In Kind.	In Money. | In Kind.	In Money.	In Kind.	In Money. | In Kind.	In Money. | In Kind.	In Money.	In Kind.	In Money.	In Kind.
Weekly Totals.											
				£. s. d.				£. s. d		£. s. d.	
								Correct		Correct.	
				Initials of Clerk }							

Instructions as to filling up this Form.

1. The same Person is on no account to be entered twice in the half-year.
2. In the Column headed "Name of the Pauper," the name of the head of the family alone is to be inserted.
3. For relief in kind enter its equivalent value in money.

FORM (C.)

The Pay-Clerk's Receipt and Expenditure Book.

—— of ———— ——

——————— Week of the Quarter ending ——————— 18 .

Pay-Clerk in account with the Board of Guardians of the
—— of ——————

Dr.		Cr.
Date.	Money received, and Tickets discharged.	Charge to the ———.

Given under our Hand and Seal of Office, this   day of   , in the year One thousand eight hundred and   .

Secretary.   *President.*

———

Orders authorizing the appointment of Pay-Clerks have been issued to the following places, on the dates undermentioned:—

    Birmingham . . . .   16th January, 1850.
    Bradford (Yorkshire) . . . . . . 23rd June, 1853.

Bethnal Green	12th December, 1867.
Chorlton (a)	18th July, 1862.
Manchester (b)	31st May, 1850.
Leeds	16th May, 1848.
Poplar	14th November, 1867.
Preston (for the Township of Preston only) (c)	9th March, 1860.
St. Leonard, Shoreditch	14th August, 1860.
Toxteth Park	19th November, 1857.
West Derby (two Townships and the municipal part of the Township of West Derby) (d) . . .	26th June, 1861.

*** In acting upon these Orders, the originals, in the possession of the respective Boards of Guardians, should be consulted.

(a) Salary increased by Orders dated 15th December, 1864, and 25th January, 1866.

(b) The Order here referred to is the Consolidated Order issued to Manchester, which contains the articles and forms relating to the Pay-Clerk.

(c) Salary increased, 23rd October, 1863.

(d) Altering salary, 6th November, 1867.

MEDICAL APPOINTMENTS ORDER.

(*25th May*, 1857.)

To the Guardians of the Poor *of the several* **Unions** *and* **Incorporations** *named in the Schedules hereunto annexed ;—*

To the Clerk or Clerks to the Justices of the Petty Sessions held for the Division or Divisions in which the said several Unions and Incorporations are respectively situate ;—

And to all others whom it may concern.

WHEREAS, by two Orders bearing date the Fifteenth and the Twenty-third days of February, One thousand eight hundred and fifty-five, respectively (*a*) addressed to the Guardians of the Poor of the several Unions set forth in the First Schedule hereunto annexed, and to the Guardians of the Poor of the several incorporated Hundreds set forth in the Second Schedule hereunto annexed, the Poor Law Board did rescind parts of certain General Orders previously issued, and did make certain Provisions regarding the period for which the Medical Officers of such Unions and

---

(*a*) As it was found in practice that the Orders of 15th and 23rd February, 1855, did not give full effect to the recommendation of the Select Committee of the House of Commons on the subject of medical relief, the Poor Law Board felt it incumbent upon them to issue the present Order in their place, for the purpose as well of carrying out the views of the Committee, as regards permanency of tenure, more completely and satisfactorily, as of making provision in certain other respects for cases with regard to which experience showed that difficulties might arise. The present Order came into operation on the 24th June, 1857, but the former Order continues in force in regard to all Officers who were appointed prior to that day. It will be seen that this Order applies to the Medical Officer of the Workhouse, and to the District Medical Officer separately.—*Instr. Letter.* 6th June, 1857.

Incorporations should hold their office; and it is expedient that such provisions should be altered:

Now therefore, We, the Poor Law Board, in pursuance of the powers given in and by the statutes in that behalf made and provided, do hereby, from the Twenty-fourth day of June next, rescind the said General Orders of the Fifteenth and Twenty-third days of February, One thousand eight hundred and fifty-five, except so far as they rescinded any part of former Orders, and except so far as they apply to Officers appointed prior to the said Twenty-fourth day of June next.

And We do hereby Order, with respect to every appointment of a Medical Officer in the said several Unions and Incorporations after the said Twenty-fourth day of June next, as follows:—

Art. 1.—Every Medical Officer of a Workhouse duly qualified at the time of his appointment according to the regulations of the Poor Law Board then in force, shall hold his office until he shall die, or resign, or be proved to be insane by evidence which the Poor Law Board shall deem sufficient, or become legally disqualified to hold such office, or be removed by the Poor Law Board (*b*).

Art. 2.—Every District Medical Officer duly qualified as aforesaid at the time of his appointment, and then being, or within two months after his appointment becoming, resident within the District for which he shall be appointed to act, shall hold his office until he shall die or resign, or be proved to be insane in the same manner as in the previous Article, or become legally disqualified to hold such office, or be removed by the said Board, or cease to reside within such District (*c*).

(*b*) Every Medical Officer of the Workhouse, duly qualified when appointed, is to hold his office during his life, or until he resign, or become insane, or legally disqualified to hold it, or be removed by the Poor Law Board.—*Instr. Letter*, 6th June, 1857.

(*c*) This Article applies to the District Medical Officer, who, being

Art. 3.—If a Medical Officer not fully qualified or not resident within his District at the time of his appointment, or within two months thereof, shall afterwards complete his qualification or become resident within such District, as the case may be, the Guardians may, upon such completion of his qualification or becoming resident respectively, after giving such notice as would be necessary in respect of an appointment in case the office were vacant, pass a resolution empowering such Medical Officer to hold his office for the time specified in Article 2, and if they transmit a copy of such resolution to the Poor Law Board, and if that Board consent, such Officer, being so duly qualified and resident, shall be entitled thenceforth to hold such office accordingly.

Art. 4.—If the Guardians shall elect a District Medical Officer, whether duly qualified as aforesaid or otherwise, not residing within his District at the time of his appointment, and not becoming resident therein within two months after it, or shall elect as such Medical Officer a person not duly qualified as aforesaid, but

---

duly qualified at the time of his appointment, is either then resident within his district, or becomes so within two months afterwards. Such Officer will continue to hold his office for the same period as the Workhouse Medical Officer, unless he ceases to reside within his district, when his office will determine. It would be very satisfactory to the Board if Boards of Guardians were always able to secure the services of duly qualified Medical Officers resident within their districts. This, however, is not uniformly the case, and Guardians are occasionally under the necessity of appointing as Medical Officers professional persons not duly qualified or non-resident. In assenting under such circumstances to such appointments, the Board have deemed it unadvisable to confer upon such officers a permanent tenure of office. They are of opinion that the most convenient course is to treat such instances as exceptional, and they have accordingly by Art. 4 required every Board of Guardians which may be under the necessity of making any such appointment, to report to them all the circumstances which render it necessary; and they have reserved to themselves the power of determining the period for which the Officer in this exceptional case shall hold his office. The Board of Guardians are further required to cause a special entry to be placed upon their minutes to show the grounds of their appointment in such case.—*Instr. Letter*, 6th June, 1857.

licensed to practise medicine, and residing within his District at such time, the Guardians shall employ as a District Medical Officer such person not residing within his District, or such person not duly qualified as aforesaid (as the case may be), for such time only as the Poor Law Board shall approve of or direct (*a*); and when the Guardians shall make any such election as in this Article specified, they shall cause a special Minute to be made and entered on the usual record of their proceedings, stating the reasons which in their opinion make it necessary to employ such person not residing within the District in which he is to act, or not duly qualified as aforesaid, and forthwith transmit a copy of such Minute to the said Board for their consideration.

Art. 5.—Where a change in the extent of the District of a Medical Officer shall be deemed necessary for the more convenient supply of Medical Relief to the Poor, or otherwise for the general benefit of the Union or Incorporation, and he shall decline to acquiesce therein, the Guardians may, with the consent of the Poor Law Board, but not otherwise, and after six months' notice in writing, signed by their Clerk, given to such Medical Officer, determine his office (*b*).

(*a*) In these cases, the usual practice of the Board is to sanction the employment for one year only.

(*b*) Article 5 provides for cases in which the medical arrangements of the Union are not satisfactory, from the fact that some districts are too extensive for the proper attention to the poor, or too small to secure adequate remuneration to the Medical Officer. In such cases changes in these districts, however necessary, cannot be effected if the Medical Officers being permanently appointed to their districts decline, as they would have a legal right to do, to assent to any change; therefore it has appeared to the Board advisable to guard against inconvenient results which might sometimes arise from the permanency of tenure as conferred by this Order upon Medical Officers. It is accordingly provided, that when the Guardians consider that a change in the extent of any district is necessary for the more convenient supply of medical relief to the poor, or otherwise for the general benefit of the Union, and the Medical Officer declines to acquiesce therein, the Guardians may, with the consent of this Board, determine the office of the Medical Officer. In order,

Art. 6.—Provided, that nothing herein contained shall prevent the Guardians in any case of emergency, or under any special circumstances, from appointing one or more Medical Officers to act temporarily for such time and upon such terms as the Poor Law Board shall approve (*a*).

Art. 7 (*b*).—When any Medical Officer shall cease to hold his office under any of the provisions herein contained, the Guardians shall proceed to make a new appointment to the office rendered vacant, in the manner prescribed by the Regulations of the Poor Law Commissioners or Poor Law Board in force at the time, unless by reason of any change in the extent of the District such office as previously constituted shall become unnecessary.

Art. 8.—If the Guardians shall have given notice to determine the continuance in office of any Medical Officer under this Order, and the Poor Law Board shall have consented thereto, the Guardians may appoint a successor to such Officer at any time subsequent to their receiving such consent; provided that nothing herein contained shall prevent such Officer from being re-appointed if otherwise eligible.

FIRST SCHEDULE.

Contains the names of the Unions mentioned in the Schedule to the General Consolidated Order of the 24th July, 1847 (*ante*, p. 206), and also the following Unions:—

---

however, that this change may not take place abruptly, or without due warning, a six months' notice in writing is to be given by the Guardians to the Officer.—*Instr. Letter*, 6th June, 1857.

(*a*) Art. 6 is intended to meet the cases of temporary appointments of Medical Officers in cases of emergency.—*Ib.*

(*b*) Art. 7, requiring the Guardians to fill up vacancies, corresponds with Art. 195 of the General Consolidated Order, and Art. 8, enabling the Guardians to appoint the successor to the Officer whose office is determined by them under the above provision before the determination of his office, corresponds with Art. 197 of the same Order.—*Ib.*

Barnsley.
Barton-upon-Irwell.
Bedwellty.
Great Ouseburn.
Hawarden.
Hemsworth.
Holyhead.
Kirkby Moorside.

Knaresborough.
North Bierley.
Oldham.
Penistone.
Prestwich.
Ripon.
Samford.

SECOND SCHEDULE.

Names of Incorporations referred to in the annexed Order.

The Incorporated Hundreds of
East and West Flegg . . .
Forehoe . . . . } in the county of Norfolk.
 and
Tunstead and Happing . .
And the Incorporated Hundred of
Mutford and Lothingland, in the county of Suffolk.

Given under our Hands and Seal of Office, this Twenty-fifth day of May, in the year One thousand eight hundred and fifty-seven.

    (Signed)   E. P. BOUVERIE, *President.*
                    G. GREY.
                    G. C. LEWIS.
COURTENAY, *Secretary.*

All Consolidated Orders issued subsequently to the 25th May, 1857, are in accordance with the above Order.

MEDICAL OFFICERS' QUALIFICATION ORDER.
(10*th December*, 1859.)

To the **Guardians of the Poor** *of the several* **Unions** *named in the Schedules hereunto annexed ;—*

To the Clerk or Clerks to the Justices of the Petty Sessions held for the Division or Divisions in which the said several Unions are respectively situate ;—

And to all others whom it may concern.

WHEREAS by a General Order, bearing date the Twenty-fourth day of July, One thousand eight hundred and forty-seven, addressed to the several Unions named in the First Schedule hereunto annexed, and by divers other Orders addressed to the several Unions named in the Second Schedule hereunto annexed, the Poor Law Commissioners and Poor Law Board respectively did prescribe the qualification for the office of Medical Officer in such Unions;

And whereas by "the Medical Act of 1858," it has been provided, that every person registered under that Act shall be entitled, according to his qualification or qualifications, to practise Medicine or Surgery, or Medicine and Surgery, as the case may be, in any part of Her Majesty's Dominions;

And whereas by the said Act it was also provided, that after the First day of January, One thousand eight hundred and fifty-nine, which time was extended by an Act of the 22nd Vict. c. 21, to the first day of July last, no person should hold any appointment as a Physician, Surgeon, or other Medical Officer, in any House of Industry, Parochial or Union Workhouse or Poorhouse, Parish, Union, or other public establishment, body, or institution, unless he be registered under the said Medical Act;

And whereas it is expedient that the regulations relating to the qualification for the office of Medical Officer in the Unions aforesaid should be altered for the future:

Now therefore we, the Poor Law Board, acting in pursuance of the powers given in and by the Statutes in that behalf made and provided, hereby rescind, as regards every appointment to be made after the first day of March next, so much of any orders and regulations issued to the Unions specified in the Schedules aforesaid as prescribes the qualification for the office of the Medical Officers thereof.

And we hereby order as follows:—

Art. 1.—After the said first day of March next, no person shall be qualified to be appointed to the office of Medical Officer under any of the Orders above referred to, unless he shall be registered as aforesaid, and shall be qualified by law to practise both Medicine and Surgery in England and Wales, such qualification being established by the production to the Board of Guardians of a Diploma, Certificate of a Degree, Licence, or other Instrument, granted or issued by competent legal authority in Great Britain or Ireland, testifying to the medical or surgical, or medical and surgical, qualification or qualifications of the candidate for such office (a).

(a) In the Circular dated 3rd January, 1860, accompanying this General Order, as to the Qualifications of Medical Officers, the Poor Law Board say that "the full qualification which has hitherto been required by the Board for such officers, has consisted of a competent knowledge of medicine and surgery, and the legal capacity to exercise both those branches of medical science in England. The then existing law did not enable any person to practise medicine in England, who did not possess a diploma or licence conferred upon him by some public constituted authority of that country, and consequently the qualification for Medical Officers was specially limited in the General Consolidated Order, in regard to medicine, in the manner prescribed in that Order. But the alteration in the law effected by 'the Medical Act of 1858,' has removed the previous restrictions upon persons possessed of qualifications emanating from authorities out of England, and has enabled the persons registered under that Act to practise, according to their respective qualifications, medicine or surgery, or medicine and surgery, in any part of Her Majesty's dominions. The Board have therefore deemed it advisable to modify the provisions of the General Consolidated Order, and to enable any person who can establish his qualification to practise both medicine and surgery by the production of proper testimonials, issued by competent legal authority in any part of the United Kingdom, to be a candidate for the office of Medical Officer in the Unions to which the Order is directed. The terms of the new Order appear to the Board to be sufficiently explicit in themselves to render any detailed explanation unnecessary. The Board think, however, that it will be convenient if they point out to the Guardians the nature of the testimonials which may be submitted to them, and what qualifications will be established by such testimonials. The following list will give the best information which the Board at present possesses on the subject:—

Authority granting the Qualification.	Name of Qualification.
The Royal College of Physicians of London	Licence in Medicine.
The Royal College of Physicians of Edinburgh	Licence in Medicine.
The Royal College of Surgeons of England	Licence in Surgery.
The Royal College of Surgeons of Edinburgh	Licence in Surgery.
The Faculty of Physicians and Surgeons of Glasgow	Licence in Surgery.
The Royal College of Surgeons of Ireland	Licence in Surgery.
The Society of Apothecaries, London	Licence in Medicine.
The University of London . . .	Degree in Medicine.
The University of Edinburgh . .	Degree in Medicine and Surgery.
The University of Oxford . . .	Degree in Medicine.
The University of Cambridge . .	Degree in Medicine.
The University of Glasgow . . .	Degree in Medicine. Degree or Licence in Surgery.
The University and King's College, Aberdeen	Degree in Medicine.
The Marischal College and University, Aberdeen	Degree in Medicine and Surgery.

The following have been since admitted:—
Apothecaries' Hall of Dublin, Medicine.
The University of St. Andrew, Medicine and Surgery.
The University of Dublin, Medicine and Surgery.
The King's and Queen's College, Ireland, Medicine.
The University of Durham, Medicine and Surgery.

The Guardians should bear in mind that the provisions of the Order are general, and include all diplomas, degrees, or licences " granted or issued by competent legal authority in Great Britain and Ireland," and

Art. 2.—Evidence that any candidate was in practice as an Apothecary on the First day of August, One thousand eight hundred and fifteen, shall be taken to be equivalent to a Certificate to practise from the Society of Apothecaries of London.

Art. 3.—Any person being registered as aforesaid, who shall possess a Warrant or Commission as Surgeon or Assistant Surgeon in Her Majesty's Navy (b), or as Surgeon or Assistant Surgeon in the service of the Honourable East India Company, dated previous to the first day of August, One thousand eight hundred and twenty-six, shall be qualified to be appointed to the office of Medical Officer as aforesaid.

Art. 4.—Nothing herein contained shall apply to the regulations contained in the General Order of this Board, bearing date the Twenty-fifth day of May, One thousand eight hundred and fifty-seven, which relate to the appointment or employment in special cases of persons not fully qualified.

---

the Poor Law Board will readily afford the best advice in their power to the Guardians, in any case in which a candidate for the Office of Medical Officer may submit to them testimonials of his qualification to practise medicine or surgery, emanating from any body not enumerated in this circular. In this Order the Board have only provided for the complete qualification of the Medical Officer; and any special cases which may occasionally occur where a fully qualified Candidate cannot be obtained, must be provided for by the Guardians under the provisions of the General Order bearing date the 25th of May, 1857. It will be observed that the Order will only operate in respect of appointments to be made after the first of March, 1860, and that it does not interfere with the registration of the Officer, which is an additional requisite imposed by the Medical Act of 1858.

Degrees in Medicine granted by Foreign Universities, although the persons upon whom they have been conferred may be registered in respect of them, cannot be recognized as conferring a qualification for the office of Medical Officer, inasmuch as they are not "granted by some competent authority in Great Britain or Ireland," as required by the Order.

(b) The words "or as Surgeon or Assistant Surgeon or Apothecary in Her Majesty's Army," were by a clerical error omitted in the original Order, but they are included in the subsequent Orders on this subject.

FIRST SCHEDULE.

Name of Unions referred to in the annexed Order are those which are included in the General Consolidated Order, *ante*, page 206.

SECOND SCHEDULE.

Names of Unions not included in the General Consolidated Order, dated the 24th July, 1847.	Dates of Orders issued subsequently to the General Consolidated Order.
Barnsley	12th June, 1850.
Barton-upon-Irwell	24th January, 1850.
Bedwellty	19th March, 1849.
Gower	19th October, 1857.
Great Ouseburn	4th August, 1854.
Hartlepool	4th April, 1859.
Hawarden	25th February, 1853.
Hemsworth	29th October, 1850.
Holyhead	15th February, 1853.
Kirkby Moorside	9th February, 1850.
Knaresborough	28th June, 1854.
North Bierley	14th February, 1849.
Oldham	22nd November, 1847.
Penistone	2nd February, 1850.
Prestwich	2nd August, 1850.
Ripon	8th February, 1853.
Samford	16 March, 1849.
Whitchurch (Salop)	19th February, 1853.

Given under our hands and Seal of office, this Tenth day of December, in the year One thousand eight hundred and fifty-nine.

      C. P. VILLIERS, *President*.
      G. C. LEWIS.
      W. E. GLADSTONE.

H. FLEMING, *Secretary*.

On the 27th January, 1860, a General Order similar to the preceding was issued to—

  The Incorporated Hundreds of East and West Flegg.
  Forehoe, and Tunstead and Happing.

On the 27th January, 1860, a similar General Order was also issued to the Parishes and Township mentioned in the Schedules to such Order, viz.—

First Schedule.

The Parishes and Townships mentioned in the Schedule to the General Consolidated Order of the 8th December, 1847, *ante*, page 215.

Second Schedule.

Manchester.
Mile End Old Town.
Saddleworth.
St. John, Hampstead.
St. Leonard, Shoreditch.
Toxteth Park.

And on the 9th February, 1860, a similar General Order was issued to the following Incorporations and Places under Local Acts:—

Alverstoke.
Barwick-in-Elmet.
Birmingham.
Bristol.
Canterbury.
Caton.
Chester.
Chichester.
Coventry.
Exeter.
Farnborough.
Headley.
Kingston-upon-Hull.
Liverpool.
Montgomery and Pool.
Norwich.
Oswestry.
Oxford.
Plymouth.
Salisbury.
Shrewsbury.
Southampton.
Stoke Damerel.
St. Giles-in-the-Fields and St. George, Bloomsbury.
St. James, Clerkenwell.
St. James, Westminster.
St. Luke, Middlesex.
St. Margaret and St. John the Evangelist, Westminster.
St. Marylebone.
St. Mary, Newington.
St. Pancras.

DUTIES OF WORKHOUSE MEDICAL OFFICERS ORDER.

(4th April, 1868.)

To the **Guardians of the Poor** of the several **Unions, Incorporations,** and **Parishes** named in the Schedule hereunto annexed;—

To the Medical Officers for the Workhouses of such Unions, Incorporations, and Parishes respectively;—

To the Clerk or Clerks to the Justices of the Petty Sessions held for the Division or Divisions in which the said Unions, Incorporations, and Parishes are respectively situate;—

And to all others whom it may concern.

WHEREAS, by two General Orders dated respectively the Twenty-fourth day of July, One thousand eight hundred and forty-seven, and the Eighth day of December in the same year, and by divers other Orders of the Poor Law Commissioners and the Poor Law Board, addressed to the several Unions, Incorporations, Parishes, and other Places named in the Schedule hereunto annexed, provisions are made for the appointment of an Officer for every Workhouse, termed "The Medical Officer for the Workhouse," and the duties to be performed by such Officer are therein set forth.

And whereas it is expedient that certain other duties should be prescribed to be performed by such Medical Officers,

Now therefore, We, the Poor Law Board, under the authority of the Statutes in that behalf made and provided, hereby Order and Direct, from and after the Twenty-fourth day of June next, as regards the Medical Officer for every Workhouse in the Unions, Incorporations, and Parishes named in the said Schedule, as follows; that is to say:—

Art. 1.—He shall keep a book, to be termed "The Workhouse Medical Officer's Report Book" (to be supplied by the Guardians), in which he shall enter in writing, duly and punctually and under the correct dates, every Report required by the said Orders to be made by him to the Board of Guardians as to the defects in the diet, drainage, ventilation, warmth, and other arrangements of the Workhouse; as to any excess in the number of any class of inmates which he may deem to be detrimental to health (a); as to every defect which he may observe in the arrangements of the Infirmary or Sick Wards, and in the performance of their duties by the Nurses of the Sick (b); and, further, a Report of any other matter which, in the discharge of the duties of his office, he shall consider to require the attention of the Guardians; and also such recommendations relating to any of the matters aforesaid as he may think it right to submit to the said Guardians.

Art. 2.—He shall cause this book to be delivered to the Clerk to the Guardians in sufficient time to allow it to be laid before the Board of Guardians at the ordinary meeting held at or next following the date of the Report, and to be produced to the Visiting Committee, and to the Inspectors of the Poor Law Board, when they shall require to see it.

Art. 3.—He shall enter on a card, to be affixed at or near the head of the bed of every patient upon whom he shall be in attendance, all medical or other extras which he shall deem necessary to be supplied.

Art. 4.—He shall report in writing to the Poor Law Board the case of every sudden and every accidental

---

(a) See Art. 207, No. 6, *ante*, p. 160.
(b) See Art. 207, No. 7, *ante*, p. 160.

death which may occur in the Workhouse within twenty-four hours after he shall receive information of the same, and the cause of the death so far as he is able to explain it (*a*).

Art. 5.—He shall report in writing to the Poor Law Board half-yearly, that is to say, on or about the First day of July and on or about the First day of January, upon the several matters set forth in the following Statement.

Art. 6.—The word "Guardians" in this Order shall be taken to include any Governor, Director, Manager, Acting Guardian, Vestryman, or other Officer in a Parish or Union appointed or entitled to act as a Manager of the Poor, and in the distribution of the relief to the Poor from the Poor Rate, under any General or Local Act of Parliament.

Statement of the Medical Officer for the Workhouse.

To the Poor Law Board.

_____ *Union* [*Incorporation* or *Parish*].
_____ *Workhouse*.

STATEMENT of the MEDICAL OFFICER for the above-named Workhouse, for the half-year ended on the   day of   186 , in answer to the following inquiries in reference to the said Workhouse.

1. Is there sufficient ventilation and warmth?
2. Has the accommodation during the preceding six months for the several classes of sick been sufficient?
3. Are the arrangements for cooking and distribution of food, as regards the sick, satisfactory?
4. Is the nursing satisfactorily performed?
5. Is there a sufficient supply of towels, vessels, bedding, clothing, and other conveniences for the use of the sick inmates?
6. Are the medical appliances sufficient and in good order?
Are there any water-beds or rack bedsteads? and,

(*a*). See Art. 208, No. 16, *ante*, p. 166.

if so, are they sufficient in number and in good order?
7. Are the lavatories and baths sufficient and in good order?
8. Are the supply and distribution of hot and cold water sufficiently provided for?

(Signed) _____ *Medical Officer.*

at _____

this _____ day of _____ 186

SCHEDULE to which the foregoing Order refers.

Names of the Unions and Incorporations.

(The Unions are those mentioned in the Schedule to the General Consolidated Order, *ante*, p. 206, and to which Consolidated Orders have been issued separately, *ante*, p. 211.) The Incorporations are the following:—

Bristol.	Flegg, East and West.	Oswestry.
Bury St. Edmund's.	Forehoe.	Oxford.
Canterbury.	Headley.	Salisbury.
Chester.	Kingston-upon-Hull.	Shrewsbury.
Chichester.	Montgomery and Pool.	Southampton.
Coventry.	Mutford and Lothing-	Tunstead and Happing.
Exeter.	land.	

Names of the Parishes and other Places.

Alston-with-Garrigill.	Paddington.
Birmingham.	Plymouth.
East Stonehouse.	Saddleworth.
Holbeck.	St. George-in-the-East.
Hunslet.	St. George, Hanover Square.
Leeds.	St. George-the-Martyr, Southwark.
Liverpool.	St. Giles-in-the-Fields and St.
Manchester.	George, Bloomsbury.
Mile End Old Town.	St. Giles, Camberwell.

St. James, Clerkenwell.
St. John, Hampstead.
St. Leonard, Shoreditch.
St. Luke, Chelsea.
St. Luke, Middlesex.
St. Margaret and St. John the Evangelist, Westminster.
St. Mary Abbots, Kensington.
St. Mary, Islington.
St. Mary, Lambeth.
St. Marylebone.
St. Mary Magdalen, Bermondsey.
St. Mary, Newington.
St. Mary, Rotherhithe.
St. Matthew, Bethnal Green.
St. Pancras.
Stoke Damerel.
Stoke-upon-Trent.
Toxteth Park.
Whittlesea, St. Mary and St. Andrew.
Yarmouth, Great.

Given under our Hands and Seal of Office, this Fourth day of April, in the year One thousand eight hundred and sixty-eight.

DEVON, *President.*
GATHORNE HARDY.
MARLBOROUGH.

M. E. HICKS BEACH, *Secretary.*

With reference to the foregoing Order, see the Circular Letter of the Poor Law Board, dated 20th April, 1868, explaining their reasons for its issue.

VACCINATION CONTRACT ORDER.

(15th February, 1868.)

To the Guardians of the Poor *of the several Unions named in the Schedule* (C.) *hereunto annexed;—*

To the Clerk or Clerks to the Justices of the Petty Sessions held for the Division or Divisions in which the said Unions are respectively situate;—

And to all others whom it may concern.

WHEREAS the Poor Law Board, by a General Order bearing date the Thirtieth day of November One thousand eight and fifty-three, and divers other Orders in that behalf, addressed to the Guardians of the Poor of the several Unions named in the Schedule (C.) hereunto annexed, did prescribe certain Forms of Contract which the said Guardians should adopt in making Contracts with the Medical Officers of the said Unions, or other legally qualified Medical Practitioners, under the provisions of the Act of the sixteenth and seventeenth years of the reign of Her Majesty, intituled "*An Act further to extend and make compulsory the Practice of Vaccination.*"

And whereas by reason of the passing of "The Vaccination Act, 1867," it is expedient that such Forms of Contract should be altered and modified, and that, with respect to all future Contracts, the said several Orders should be rescinded,

Now therefore, We, the Poor Law Board, in pursuance of "The Poor Law Amendment Act, 1834," and the several other Statutes in that behalf, hereby Order and Direct, that in respect of all Contracts to be entered into by the Guardians of the said several Unions, after the date hereof, the said Orders shall be rescinded.

And We hereby further Order and Direct, with reference to all the said Unions, that the following Form of Contract, with such modifications as the Guardians, with the approval of the Poor Law Board, may determine upon, shall be adopted by the said Guardians in making future Contracts with the Medical Officers of the said Unions, or other legally-qualified Medical Practitioners therein, under the provisions of the above-recited Acts;

ARTICLES OF AGREEMENT entered into this —— day of —— One thousand eight hundred and —— between —— of the one part, and the Guardians of the Poor of the —— Union, in the County of —— of the other part.

Whereas the said Guardians have, in pursuance of the several statutes in that behalf, with the approval of the Poor Law Board, divided the Union aforesaid into —— districts, for the purpose of vaccination, one of which districts comprises the parishes and places following; that is to say ——, and have appointed the places mentioned in the Schedule (A.) hereto annexed as convenient for the performance of such Vaccination; and the said Guardians have agreed with the said —— to enter into a proper contract for the performance of the vaccination;

Now, therefore, the said —— doth hereby covenant and agree with the said Guardians and their successors, that from and after the —— day of —— he will attend by himself or some medical practitioner legally qualified for that purpose as his substitute, at the times and places mentioned in the said Schedule (A.), or at such other times and places as the said Guardians shall, with the consent of the Poor Law Board, determine and cause to be indorsed thereon, and will then and there duly, and according to the requirements of the law, vaccinate every person resident in the district aforesaid who shall apply to or be brought to him for the purpose of being vaccinated, and will do and perform all such acts and things as to the best of his judgment, and in accordance with such requirements, shall seem necessary for the purpose of causing such vaccination to be successfully terminated;

And will in like manner vaccinate any child resident out of his district whom any Relieving Officer of the said Union shall in writing refer to him for vaccination;

And will attend at the times and places mentioned in the said Schedule (A.) to inspect the results of such vaccination in the persons so vaccinated, and will duly inspect such persons accordingly, and do such acts and give such directions, and otherwise treat the cases as upon such inspection shall appear to him to be necessary;

And will keep a book to be termed "The Vaccinator's Register," to be provided for him by the said Guardians, and will, as soon as practicable after he shall have vaccinated any person to whom this contract shall apply, and as soon as practicable after he shall have inspected the results of the vaccination of such person, make the entries respectively applicable to the vaccination and the Inspection of the results described in the Form set forth in the Schedule (B.) hereto annexed, and will, on the day next before the first ordinary meeting of the said Guardians in every calendar month [*or* quarter of the year, *as may be agreed upon between the parties*], deliver or cause to be delivered to their Clerk the book in which he shall have made such entries during the interval preceding such meeting.

And the said Guardians do, for themselves and their successors, covenant and agree with the said —— as follows; that is to say,—To pay to him, his executors or administrators, within one calendar month after Lady Day, Midsummer Day, Michaelmas Day, and Christmas Day respectively, during the subsistence of this Contract, and within one month after its termination, for every person to whom this Contract shall apply upon whom, in accordance with the regulations of the Lords of the Council in force at the time, and all other requirements of the law, the operation of primary vaccination shall be successfully performed by the said —— at the within-mentioned station at ——, the same being situated at [*or* within one mile from] his residence by the nearest public carriage road, the sum of [*here insert the sum agreed upon, not less than* 1s. 6d.]; and for every such person so vaccinated at the within-mentioned station at ——, the same being situated over one mile and under two miles distant from such residence, the sum of [*here insert the sum agreed upon, not less than* 2s.]; and for every such person so vaccinated at the within mentioned station at ——, the same being situated over two miles from such residence, the sum of [*here insert the sum agreed upon, not less than* 3s. 0d.]; and further, to pay to him, his executors or administrators, at the times herein-before mentioned, the sum of —— in respect of every person to whom this Contract shall apply upon whom the operation of primary Vaccination shall be successfully performed in accordance with such regulations and requirements as aforesaid by the said —— elsewhere than at a station herein mentioned.

And it is hereby mutually agreed by and between the parties hereto, that no sum of money shall be paid to the said —— in respect of any person whose name, together with the other particulars relating to the case, shall not be duly entered in the said Register, except in the case of any omission which shall be explained to the satisfaction of the said Guardians.

And it is hereby mutually agreed that this Contract may be put an end to by either of the parties hereto on giving twenty-eight days' notice in writing to the other party respectively of the intention to put an end to the same.

[*Here must be inserted some other stipulation or condition to which the Poor Law Board shall consent to secure the due vaccination of persons, the observance of the Provisions of the Vaccination Act with regard to the transmission of the Certificate of successful Vaccination, and the fulfilment of all other Provisions of the said Act on the part of the Public Vaccinator.*] (a).

SCHEDULES referred to in the above Articles of Agreement.

SCHEDULE (A.)

Times and Places appointed for Vaccination and Inspection respectively.			
Times.			Places.
Day of Attendance.		Hours of the Day.	
for Vaccination.	for Inspection.		At the Residence of the said
	This must be the same day in the following week.		at_____ At_____ At_____

(*a*) This has been added in consequence of the language of 30 & 31 Vict. c. 84, s. 7; and the Guardians will have to consider what conditions are necessary to effect the object of the section.

The following clause has been suggested for insertion in the Contract in this place, and appears to be free from objection, "Provided always that the said —— shall not be entitled to be paid his account from time to time to be rendered of fees for cases of Vaccination, unless he shall have punctually attended at the times and places for the purposes of Vaccination, as stated in the Schedule hereto, and also shall have duly and punctually registered and certified in relation to Vaccination (as he is required to do by the Vaccination Act, 1867) in respect of every person who shall have applied to him for such purpose during the whole period, or quarter of a year, to which his account or claim for fees from time to time rendered to the said Guardians shall relate."

Vaccination Contract Order.

SCHEDULE (B.)

Vaccinator's Register of the _____ District of the _____ Union.

Public Vaccinator _____ day of _____ 186 .

1	2	3	4	5		6	7	8	9	10	11	12		13	14	15
No. of case consecutive to 800, and then to be repeated.	Date of Vaccination.	Name.	In case of Re-vaccination of Adults, and Adolescents successfully vaccinated in early Life, Mark R.	Age.		Place of Residence.	Where Vaccinated.*	Name or No in Register of the subject with whose Lymph the Vaccination is performed,—or insert N.V.E. if the Lymph be sent by the National Vaccine Establishment,—or state other source, if any.	Initials of Person performing the Vaccination.	When and where inspected.*	Initials of the person inspecting.	Result.		Date of sending Certificate to the Registrar.	Fee due in respect of each case of successful primary Vaccination.	Fee due in respect of each case of successful Re-vaccination.
				Years.	Months.							Successful.	Unsuccessful.		£. s. d.	£. s. d.
														Total.		

* Whether at the Vaccinator's Residence, or at an appointed Station (and if so, which) or where else. [Until new Contracts are entered into pursuant to this Order, the Vaccination Registers will be kept according to existing Contracts.—W. C. O.]

In witness whereof the said —— hath hereunto set his hand and seal, and the said Guardians their Common Seal, the day and year first above written.

Signed, Sealed, and delivered by
the above-named ——
in the presence of ——
} (L. S.)

The Common Seal of the Guardians of the above-named Union was hereto affixed at a meeting of the Board of Guardians, held on the day of the date hereof by ——, Chairman of the Board at the said Meeting, in the presence of

Clerk to the Guardians of the said Union.

SCHEDULE (C.)

Names of Unions referred to in the foregoing Order.

The Unions are those mentioned in the Schedule to the General Consolidated Order, *ante*, p. 206, and to which Consolidated Orders have been issued separately, *ante*, p. 211, except the Westminster and Woolwich Unions, and the following Incorporations, namely:—

Flegg, East and West.   Mutford and Lothingland.
Forehoe.   Tunstead and Happing.

Given under our Hands and Seal of Office, this Fifteenth day of February, in the year One thousand eight hundred and sixty-eight.

(L. S.)

Devon, *President.*
Gathorne Hardy.
Marlborough.

G. Sclater-Booth, *Secretary.*

The Poor Law Board on the 7th March, 1868, issued a General Order similar to the foregoing, but adapted to the case of single Parishes, to the following Parishes, Townships, and other Places referred to in such Order.

SCHEDULE (C.)

Alston-with-Garrigill.
East Stonehouse.
Leeds.
Manchester.
Paddington.
Saddleworth.
St. George in the East.
St. George-the-Martyr, Southwark.
St. Giles, Camberwell.
St. John, Hampstead.
St. Luke, Chelsea.
St. Mary Abbots, Kensington.
St. Mary, Lambeth.
St. Mary Magdalen, Bermondsey.
St. Mary, Rotherhithe.
St. Matthew, Bethnal Green.
Stoke-upon-Trent.
Whittlesea, St. Mary and St. Andrew.
Yarmouth, Great.

SCHEDULE (D.)

Holbeck.
Hunslet.
Mile End Old Town.
St. George, Hanover Square.
St. James, Clerkenwell.
St. Leonard, Shoreditch.
St. Luke, Middlesex.
St. Margaret and St. John the Evangelist, Westminster.
St. Mary, Islington.
St. Marylebone.
St. Mary, Newington.
St. Pancras.
Stoke Damerel.
Toxteth Park.

An Order similar to the foregoing was issued on the 11th April, 1868, to the Bristol Incorporation.

REGULATIONS OF THE PRIVY COUNCIL AS TO VACCINATION.

The following Regulations in reference to Vaccination were issued by the Lords of Her Majesty's Most Honourable Privy Council, at the Council Chamber, Whitehall, on the 1st December, 1859, and 18th February, 1868.

1st December, 1859.

To the Guardians of the Poor of all Unions and Parishes, to the Churchwardens and Overseers of all Parishes, Townships, and places in which the Relief to the Poor is not administered by Guardians, in England and Wales, and to all Medical Practitioners.

Whereas by the Public Health Act, 1858, and by an Act since passed to perpetuate the same, it is enacted that the Privy Council may from time to time issue such regulations as they think fit, for securing the due qualification of persons to be thereafter contracted with by Guardians and Overseers of Unions and Parishes in England for the Vaccination of persons resident in such Unions and Parishes, and for securing the efficient performance of Vaccination by the persons already or thereafter to be contracted with as aforesaid:

Now, therefore, it is hereby ordered, by the Lords and others of Her Majesty's Most Honourable Privy Council (of whom the Vice-President of the Committee of the said Privy Council on Education is one) that on and after the first day of January, 1860, the following Regulations shall be in force; viz.—

1. Except where the Privy Council, for reasons brought to their notice, see fit in particular cases otherwise to allow, no person shall in future be admitted as a Contractor for Vaccination unless he possess the same qualifications as are required by the Orders of the Poor Law Commissioners as qualifications for a District Medical Officer, and produce a special Certificate, given under such conditions as the Privy Council from time to time fix, by some Public Vaccinator whom the Privy Council authorize to act for the purpose (a), and by whom he has been duly instructed or examined in the practice of Vaccination, and all that relates thereto;—

But the production of this special Certificate on occasion of the Contract being made may be dispensed with, if the Certificate, or some other which the Privy Council judge to be of like effect, have been among the certificates or testimonials necessary for obtaining any diploma, licence or degree, which the candidate possesses;—

And also, in respect of persons legally admitted to practise before this regulation comes into effect, the special Certificate may be dispensed with, on condition that the Contract, during one year from its making, continue subject to the approval of the Poor Law Board;—

And all persons now contracted with shall be deemed to be qualified to be again contracted with.

2. Under the same conditions as are appointed for the admission of a Contractor any person qualified to be a Contractor may, on the Contractor's application, be admitted by the Guardians or Overseers to act as his occasional deputy;—

But, if this admission be not part of the original Contract, it must be notified by indorsement upon the Contract; and at least fifteen days before it is intended to take effect, a copy of the proposed indorsement, together with all requisite evidence of the qualification of the person whom it is proposed to admit, must be transmitted to the Poor Law Board.

3. All Vaccinations and Inspections under Contract shall be performed by the Contractor in person, or by some other Contractor of the same Union or Parish acting for him, or by a deputy duly admitted as above;—

But at any Station where the Contractor is authorized (as above) to grant certificates, pupils and other candidates, aged not less than eighteen years, may, in his presence and under his direction, take part in vaccinating.

All Vaccinations and Inspections under Contract shall be performed in accordance with the annexed "Instructions for Vaccinators under Contract."

4. Until some new form of Vaccination Register be duly prescribed, the person who performs any Vaccination under Contract shall, on the

---

(a) See list of Vaccinators so authorized, *post*, p. 355.

day when he performs it, legibly write in his Register (as now provided) the letter R (for Revaccination) against the name of every person, adult or adolescent, who, having in early life been successfully vaccinated, is revaccinated; and shall also enter in some column, or in the margin of the Register, the source whence the lymph used in the vaccination was obtained,—

Thus: the name, or number (if any) in the Register, of the subject from whom the lymph was taken; or "N.V.E.," if the lymph was sent by the National Vaccine Establishment; or the name or description of any other source;—

And where the Vaccination or the Inspection is done by a person acting as Deputy for the Contractor, the Deputy shall write the initials of his name in the Register side by side with the entry of the case; viz. in the left margin of the page, if it be a Vaccination which he performs, or in the right margin of the page, if it be an inspection which he performs.

5. Guardians and Overseers, in their respective Unions and Parishes, shall forthwith take measures to bring the performance of public Vaccination into conformity with these regulations.

18*th February*, 1868.

To the Guardians of the Poor of all Unions and Parishes, to all Public Vaccinators, and to all others whom it may concern.

The Lords and others of Her Majesty's Most Honourable Privy Council (of whom the Vice-President of the Committee of the said Privy Council on Education is one) acting under the authority of the Vaccination Act of 1867, and all other authorities in this behalf, do hereby make and issue the following Regulations, in addition to those already in force, for securing the efficient performance of Public Vaccination, and in respect of the Revaccination of persons who apply to be revaccinated, that is to say—:

I.—PLACES AND TIMES FOR VACCINATION UNDER CONTRACT.

1. Except where the Privy Council, for reasons brought to its notice, sees fit in regard of any particular District to sanction a system of domiciliary Vaccination, every Vaccination-District shall have in it at least one public Station appointed for the performance of the Vaccinations under Contract; and where any such Station has been provided for a District, no person resident within two miles thereof, and not being an inmate of the Workhouse, shall be vaccinated under Contract elsewhere than at such Station (*b*), unless the Vaccinator in the particular case be of opinion (which, if so, he is hereby required to note in his Register) that, for some special reason, the person whom he purposes to vaccinate cannot properly be vaccinated at the Station.

2. Except under special authorization from the Privy Council as aforesaid, or in so far as may be expedient at times when there is im-

---

(*b*) This Regulation does not place any restriction in the Vaccination of persons resident within the District, but beyond two miles from the Station.

2 A

mediate danger of Small-pox, Vaccination under Contract shall not be appointed to be performed at any Station oftener than once a week (*a*).

3. And in any future Contract concerning a Vaccination-District which is partly or wholly within a town, there shall not, except under special authorization as aforesaid, be appointed within the town more than a single Station for the performance of the Vaccinations of the District.

II.—VACCINATION DISTRICTS IN TOWNS (*b*).

No part of the Metropolis, or of any City, or Municipal Borough, or Town Corporate, or other Town, shall, in respect of any future Contract, form by itself, or with any rural place, a separate District for Vaccination, except with the approval of the Privy Council, unless it contain an estimated population of at least 25,000 persons, or else be as much of the Metropolis, City, Borough, or Town, as is for purposes of Vaccination under the control of one Board of Guardians.

III.—OFFICE OF PUBLIC VACCINATOR.

After the expiration of the month of June next, no two or more persons shall be allowed to act severally as Vaccinators under Contract in any one and the same part or district of any Union or Parish (*c*).

IV.—REVACCINATION.

The performance of Revaccination by the Public Vaccinator on persons applying to him for that purpose shall be limited in each case by the following conditions:—(1) that, so far as the Public Vaccinator can ascertain, the applicant has attained the age of 15 years, or, if during any immediate danger of Small-pox, the age of 12 years, and has not before been successfully revaccinated; and (2) that, in the Public Vaccinator's judgment, the proposed Revaccination is not for any sufficient medical reason undesirable; and (3) that the Public Vaccinator can afford vaccine lymph for the purpose without in any degree postponing the claims which are made on him for the performance of Primary Vaccination in his District.

Educational Vaccinating Stations.

In order to provide for the granting of those Special Certificates of Proficiency in Vaccination, which, under the Regulations of the Privy Council, are required to be part of the Medical Qualification for enter-

---

(*a*) This Regulation will apply to future Contracts only.

(*b*) With reference to the words "other Town," this Article is to be read "no part .... of any .... town shall .... form by itself, or with any other rural place, a separate District for Vaccination ...." Therefore if a "town" in a Union be not divided, the rest of the Union may be formed into any number of Districts.

(*c*) This Article will not apply to the Deputy of the Contractor.

ing into contracts for the performance of Public Vaccination, or for acting as Deputy to a Contractor, the following arrangements are made:—

1. The Vaccinating Stations, enumerated in the subjoined list, are open, under conditions appointed by the Privy Council, for the purposes of Teaching and Examination;

2. The Public Vaccinators officiating at these Stations are authorized by the Privy Council to give the required Certificates of Proficiency in Vaccination to persons whom they have sufficiently instructed therein; and

3. The Public Vaccinators, whose names in the subjoined list are printed in *Italic Letters*, are also authorized to give such Certificates, after satisfactory Examination, to persons whom they have not themselves instructed.

Cities & Towns having Educational Vaccinating Stations.	Places used as Educational Vaccinating Stations.	Public Vaccinators authorized to give Certificates of Proficiency in Vaccination.	Days and Hours of attendance of the Public Vaccinators.
London	(Principal Station) Surrey Chapel, Blackfriars Road	Mr. *James Furness Marson*	Tuesday, Thursday; 1-3.
	(North-West Station) 13, Lisson Grove.	Mr. James George Gerrans	Monday, Thursday; 10-12.
	(West Station) 9, St. George's Road, Pimlico, S.W.	Dr. Edward Lowe Webb	Monday; 10-12.
	(East Station) 1, Well Strt., Wellclose Sq.	Mr. William Jones Lewis	Tuesday; 9-11.
	(North Station) Tottenham Court Chapel, Tottenham Court Road.	Mr. William E. G. Pearse	Monday, Wednesday; 1-2.
	(South-West Station) 46, Marsham Strt., Westminster.	Mr. William Edwin Grindley Pearse.	Monday, Thursday; 9-11.
Birmingham	The Genl. Dispensary	Mr. *John Garner*	Monday; 10-12.
Bristol	7, St. Augustine's Pl.	Mr. *William Yeoman Sheppard.*	Tuesday; 10-12.
Leeds	23, Boynton Street, Quarry Hill	Mr. *Frederick Holmes*	Tuesday; 2.
Liverpool	The Ladies' Charity, Parr Street	Mr. *Arthur Browne Steele.* Mr. *John Henry Wilson,* and Mr. *John Fenton,* acting conjointly, or at least two of them together.	Friday; 2.
Manchester	159, Rochdale Road	Mr. *Ellis Southern Guest.*	Monday; 2-4.
Newcastle-on-Tyne	11, Pilgrim Street	Mr. *G. C. Gilchrist.*	Tuesday; 2-3.
Sheffield			
Edinburgh	The Royal Dispensary	Dr. *William Husband*	Wednesday, Saturday; 12.
Glasgow	The Hall of the Faculty of Physicians and Surgeons	Dr. *James Dunlop*	Monday; 12.

By direction of the Lords of the Council.

OUT-DOOR RELIEF PROHIBITORY ORDER (a).

(21st December, 1844.)

To the Guardians of the Poor *of the several Unions named in the Schedule hereunto annexed;—*

To the Churchwardens and Overseers of the Poor of the several Parishes and Places comprised within the said respective Unions;

To the Clerk or Clerks to the Justices of the Petty Sessions held for the Division or Divisions in which the Parishes and Places comprised within the said respective Unions are situate;—

And to all others whom it may concern.

WE, the Poor Law Commissioners, in pursuance of the authorities vested in Us by an Act passed in the fifth year of the reign of his late Majesty King William the Fourth, intituled "*An Act for the Amendment and better Administration of the Laws relating to the Poor in England and Wales,*" do hereby rescind an Order, being a General Rule of the Poor Law Commissioners, bearing date the Second day of August, in the year of our Lord One thousand eight hundred and forty-one, except so far as the same rescinds any Order or Orders theretofore issued by the Poor Law Commissioners.

And We do hereby also rescind the Orders relative to the relief of able-bodied poor persons, issued by the Poor

---

(a) It is most desirable that the persons to whom relief is either granted or refused should be satisfied that the grant or refusal is determined by fixed rules, and not by partial or temporary considerations, and for this reason it is expedient that copies of the Prohibitory Order should be hung up in a conspicuous part of the Workhouse, and of the room in which the Guardians usually assemble.—*Instr. Letter*, Dec., 1839.

Law Commissioners to the several Unions hereunder mentioned, except so far as the same rescind any Order or Orders theretofore issued by the said Commissioners, or relate to the Out-door Labour Test for able-bodied Male Paupers: that is to say,—

> The Order bearing date the Ninth day of December, One thousand eight hundred and forty-one, and issued to the Guardians of the Poor of the Burgh of Bury Saint Edmund's;
>
> The Order bearing date the Tenth day of January, One thousand eight hundred and forty-two, and issued to the Guardians of the Poor of the Aberystwith Union;
>
> The Order bearing date the Fifteenth day of April One thousand eight hundred and forty-two, and issued to the Guardians of the Poor of the Ruthin Union;
>
> The Order bearing date the Thirtieth day of April, One thousand eight hundred and forty-two, and issued to the Guardians of the Poor of the Llanfyllin Union;
>
> The General Order bearing date the Thirtieth day of July, One thousand eight hundred and forty-two, and issued to the Guardians of the Poor of the Longtown Union, the Guardians of the Poor of the Whitehaven Union, and the Guardians of the Poor of the Wigton Union;
>
> The Order bearing date the Fifth day of August, One thousand eight hundred and forty-two, and issued to the Guardians of the Poor of the Cockermouth Union;
>
> The Order bearing date the Ninth day of September, One thousand eight hundred and forty-two, and issued to the Guardians of the Poor of the Richmond Union, in the County of York;
>
> The Order bearing date the Thirtieth day of November, One thousand eight hundred and forty-two, and issued to the Guardians of the Poor of the Ormskirk Union;
>
> The Order bearing date the Seventeenth day of December, One thousand eight hundred and forty-two, and issued to the Guardians of the Poor of the Hailsham Union;

The Order bearing date the Twenty-first day of January, One thousand eight hundred and forty-three, and issued to the Guardians of the Poor of the Chard Union;

And the General Order bearing date the Twenty-seventh day of June, One thousand eight hundred and forty-three, and issued to the Guardians of the Poor of the Saint Asaph Union; the Guardians of the Poor of the Bala Union; the Guardians of the Poor of the Bridgend and Cowbridge Union; the Guardians of the Poor of the Corwen Union; the Guardians of the Poor of the Festiniog Union; and the Guardians of the Poor of the Pwllheli Union:

Provided that nothing herein contained shall apply to any relief given under or prohibited by any of the said Orders hereby rescinded.

And We do hereby Order, Direct, and Declare, with respect to each and every of the Unions named in the Schedule hereunto annexed, as follows:—

Art. 1.—Every able-bodied person, male or female, requiring relief from any Parish within any of the said Unions, shall be relieved wholly in the Workhouse of the Union, together with such of the family of every such able-bodied person as may be resident with him or her, and may not be in employment, and together with the wife of every such able-bodied male person, if he be a married man, and if she be resident with him; save and except in the following cases (*a*):—

(*a*) The provisions of this Order, so far as they refer to poor persons requiring relief from "any parish," must now be read with reference to the provisions of the Union Chargeability Act, 1865, by which all such relief is now chargeable upon the common fund of the Union.

The only remark on the Prohibitory Clause which the Commissioners make is, that the Guardians under it are not bound to require any child of an able-bodied person who can support itself to accompany its parent into the Workhouse, if it appear expedient that such child should continue in employment.—*Instr. Letter*, 21st December, 1844.

All persons under sixteen years of age are not to be regarded as not able-bodied, thus—

Art. 1.—1st (exception).—Where such person shall require relief on account of sudden and urgent necessity (*b*).

2nd.—Where such person shall require relief on account of any sickness, accident, or bodily or men-

---

Girls of fourteen and fifteen years of age who are able to maintain themselves by their own labour are able-bodied.

So also a lad of fifteen, or even fourteen, years of age able to maintain himself by his own labour. But an orphan girl of twelve years of age cannot be considered as an able-bodied person. If the father be alive and the child be under sixteen years of age no question arises, as the relief is given to him and not to the child. If a child be out at service, it is not necessarily an able-bodied person within the meaning of Article 1. In deciding the question whether a child can or cannot be relieved out of the Workhouse without the sanction of the Poor Law Board, regard must be had to the age of the child, and not merely to the fact that it is able to take a place of service suited to its years and its strength; but no age has been fixed when a child is to be considered able-bodied, nor when an adult shall cease to be such. Under no circumstances should the practice be resorted to of allowing weekly relief to boys and girls whilst they are in employment and in the receipt of wages. The effect of such relief is to enable the employers to obtain the services of the children partly at the expense of the ratepayers, and also to prevent the children of independent labourers obtaining employment.

Neither are persons above sixty years of age necessarily to be regarded as "not able-bodied." It is a question of fact in each case, depending upon the physical strength and condition of the applicant for relief.

The Guardians must decide the question of able-bodied or not for themselves, according to the circumstances of each case; bearing in mind that an appeal ultimately lies to the auditor against their decision if they give exceptional relief to a destitute person who, at the time, is really able bodied.

(*b*) By "sudden and urgent necessity" (which words are used in section 54 of the 4 & 5 Wm. IV. c. 76), the Commissioners understand any case of destitution requiring instant relief. It is to be remarked further, that this exception does not authorize *permanent* out-door relief in any case. A case originally of sudden and urgent necessity, which subsequently requires continued relief, loses its character of suddenness and urgency. The relief subsequently required will be either ordinary relief, and therefore to be given in the Workhouse, or it may be extraordinary, and given, for example, under the second exception to Art. 1.—*Instr. Letter*. However, no general rule can be laid down for the interpretation of those words, further than that the circumstances contemplated must be of an exceptional character. See, however, note to Art. 215, No. 6, *ante*, p. 185.

tal infirmity affecting such person, or any of his or her family (*a*).

Art. 1.—3rd (exception).—Where such person shall require relief for the purpose of defraying the expenses, either wholly or in part, of the burial of any of his or her family (*b*).

Art. 1.—4th (exception).—Where such person, being a

(*a*) The second exception provides for the case of any able-bodied man who is himself insane or temporarily sick, or who has met with an accident, or any of whose family require to be relieved on the ground of insanity, infirmity, accident, or sickness.—*Instr. Letter.* The Guardians should bear in mind that when they resolve to give relief in consequence of the sickness of any member of the family of an able-bodied man, the amount of loss sustained, or additional expense incurred in consequence of such sickness, is, under ordinary circumstances, the proper standard by which to regulate the amount of the exceptional relief to be given. The case of a woman who is actually confined in childbirth will be a case of sickness coming within this exception, until she is recovered from her confinement, and is able to resume her usual occupation; but mere pregnancy is not within the exception, if it be not accompanied by sickness. The word "family" in this exception includes illegitimate children.

(*b*) Under this exception relief may be given to able-bodied persons for the funerals of any members of their families, without requiring them to come into the Workhouse.—*Instr. Letter.*

It is entirely optional with the Guardians whether they will undertake the burial of the dead body of any poor person or not under the 7 & 8 Vict. c. 101, s. 31, and they may prescribe the conditions under which alone they will consent to bury the body at the expense of the poor-rates. A Relieving Officer has of himself no authority to supply the means of burial in the intervals between the meetings of the Guardians; the Guardians may however give him a general authority to do so; but in that event he must act strictly in accordance with the terms of the authority given to him in regard to pauper funerals, as to such general authority see note to Art. 215, No. 6, of the General Consolidated Order, *ante*, p. 185. The words of the statute, "poor person," are not confined to a person actually chargeable to the poor-rates. If the Guardians have entered into a contract for pauper funerals, they, and not the Relieving Officers, should pay the contractor. *Reg. v. Vann*, 21 L. J. M. C. 39, shows that a parent is bound to provide Christian burial for the body of a deceased child if he has the means; but if he has not the means, though the body remains unburied and becomes a nuisance to the neighbourhood, he is not indictable for the nuisance, notwithstanding he could have obtained money for the burial expenses by way of loan from the Poor Law authorities, for he is not bound to incur a debt.

widow. shall be in the first six months of her widowhood (c).

5th.—Where such person shall be a widow, and have a legitimate child or legitimate children dependent upon her, and incapable of earning his, her, or their livelihood, and have no illegitimate child born after the commencement of her widowhood (d).

(c) The exception of widows during the first six months of their widowhood is adopted with a view of enabling persons thus situated to have an adequate interval for the purpose of making such arrangements for their support as their altered condition may require.—*Instr. Letter.* If an able-bodied widow have no child or children dependent upon her for support, out-door relief cannot be granted to her beyond the six months named in this Article, without the previous consent of the Poor Law Board, obtained under Art. 6. (Page 370, *post.*)

(d) The exception of widows with children, so far as it relates to able-bodied women in employment, is one respecting which the Guardians ought to exercise great circumspection in applying it in practice. The Guardians, when administering relief under it, ought to take into account, that when small weekly allowances in aid of wages are made, they too commonly serve to excuse relations from the payment of contributions to a larger amount; and that the out-door allowances, when given indiscriminately in widowhood, tend to put an end to provident habits, in respect of insurances in sick clubs or otherwise. It should, moreover, be borne in mind, that allowances made by the parish to able-bodied widows in employment do not always confer the advantages intended, inasmuch as their wages, as in the case of able-bodied men, are commonly reduced in consideration of the allowance from the parish; and that such reduction of the wages, combined with the excuse furnished to relations or friends for withholding their contributions, together with the pauper habits thus engendered, often renders such allowances to widows in aid of wages an injury rather than a benefit to them; whilst in some districts this class of able-bodied widows may be so numerous that their labour, thus depreciated at the expense of the ratepayers, may be substituted for the more highly paid labour of independent labourers. The Commissioners trust that the Guardians will seldom find that the ordinary rate of earnings of able-bodied women is so low as not to enable them to support one child at the least: and that the Guardians will not adopt any such general rule as that of relieving all widows with one, or with any fixed number of children, but will make a careful inquiry into every case thus to be relieved.—*Instr. Letter.* It only seems necessary to observe further in reference to this exception, that if a woman after her widowhood have an illegitimate child, her case will no longer be within the exception; but if the illegitimate child should afterwards die, her case will again fall within the exception, and the Guardians will be at liberty to give her out-door relief if they think fit so to do. And further, that if a woman have illegitimate children before her marriage, and afterwards becomes

Art. 1.—6th (exception).—Where such person shall be confined in any gaol or place of safe custody, subject always to the regulation contained in Article 4 (*a*).

7th.—Where such person shall be the wife, or child, of any able bodied man who shall be in the service of her Majesty as a soldier, sailor, or marine (*b*).

Art. 1.—8th (exception).—Where any able-bodied person, not being a soldier, sailor, or marine, shall not reside within the Union, but the wife, child, or children of such person shall reside within the same, the Board of Guardians of the Union, according to their discretion, may, subject to the

---

a widow and have no legitimate children dependent upon her, her case will not be within exception 5 to Article 1; but if she have legitimate children dependent upon her, her case, notwithstanding her having an illegitimate child born before marriage, will fall within the exception. But note the omission of the words "dependent upon her" in the last part of the exception. If a widow have an illegitimate child not dependent upon her, and legitimate children who are dependent upon her, her case will not come within the exception so long as the illegitimate child lives.

The fifth exception is to be construed as having reference to the actual widowhood of the woman, and not to the first widowhood, in a case in which the woman marries again, and becomes a second time a widow.

(*a*) It sometimes becomes necessary that the Guardians should be empowered to give relief to the wife and children in cases where the husband cannot be required to enter the Workhouse on account of his being in a place of legal confinement.—*Instr. Letter.* It may be added here, that it sometimes happens that a person in the custody of the law prior to committal for trial is in destitute circumstances and in need of relief. If in such a case application be made on his behalf to the Guardians or to the Relieving Officer, it is considered that the Guardians or that Officer should provide the prisoner with such relief in kind as may be absolutely necessary.

(*b*) The state of the law in reference to married women, explained in the note to the eighth exception, and the peculiar rights and obligations of soldiers, sailors, and marines, render it desirable to give great latitude to the proceedings of the Board of Guardians in respect of the families of persons in these departments of the Queen's service. The seventh exception, therefore, allows of relief of any kind being given to the wife or children of a soldier, sailor, or marine, whether in or out of the Workhouse, without requiring the husband to come into the Workhouse.—*Instr. Letter.* Reference may here be made to the 19 Vict. c. 15, ss. 8, 9, regulating the repayment to Boards of Guardians of the cost of relief given to Chelsea or Greenwich pensioners, and also of the cost of the maintenance of such as shall become insane.

regulation contained in Article 4, afford relief in the Workhouse to such wife, child, or children, or may allow out-door relief for any such child or children being within the age of nurture, and resident with the mother within the Union (c).

(c) The eighth exception provides for the case of a wife whose husband is absent from her, either by desertion or otherwise, and is necessary in consequence of the state of the law applicable to women thus situated. It has been held that in such cases relief to the children was not relief to the wife; consequently, the wife could not be compelled to come with her children into the Workhouse, although a new provision has been made by the statute 7 & 8 Vict. c. 101, s. 25, to be noticed at full hereafter, in respect of certain women separated from their husbands. If, however, under any circumstances she require relief for herself, the Guardians may require her to receive it in the Workhouse; and if she require relief for her children, the Guardians may require such of them as are above the age of nurture to receive it in the Workhouse, whether she do or do not come into the Workhouse. As regards, however, children under the age of nurture (to be within the age of nurture a child must be within seven years of age) who may be living with the mother, the Guardians cannot remove them from her; so that if she require relief for them and them only, the Guardians must, except in the cases hereafter provided for, give out-relief, if relief be necessary.— *Instr. Letter.* It is a well-recognized rule with regard to the maintenance of the poor, that while a child is under seven years of age, it shall not be separated from the mother for the purpose of being maintained by the parish in which it is settled; see the observations of Lord Campbell, C.J., on this point, in *Re Alice Race*, 3 Jur. (N. S.) Q. B. 336; and *Reg.* v. *Clarke*, 7 E. & B. 186; under seven, he said, is called the age of nurture; which is the peculiar nurture required by a child from its mother, which is entirely different from guardianship for nurture which belongs to the father in his lifetime, even from the birth of the child. With regard to relieving a child under the age of nurture, apart from its mother, and the liability of such child to be removed to the place of its settlement, reference may be made to *Reg.* v. *Combs*, 5 E. & B. 892; 25 L. J. R. (N. S.) M. C. 59; 2 Jur. (N. S.) 255. *Reg.* v. *Birmingham*, 5 Q. B. 210, shows that the mother cannot consent to the separation from her of her children who are within the age of nurture; it is the right of the children within that age to be with their mother. With reference to the relief of deserted wives and children, see the Circular of the Poor Law Commissioners, App. (A.), No. 6, p. 83, Fifth Annual Report of Poor Law Commissioners. If the wife or children of a soldier become destitute, she or they must be relieved, and neither the Guardians nor the Overseers can establish any legal claim against the husband for maintenance whilst he is in the service, nor can they attach his pay by way of reimbursement, as he is exempted from such liability by the provisions of the Annual Mutiny Act. It would be prudent in such cases, however, to declare the relief to be given by

Art. 2.—In every case in which out-door relief shall be given on account of sickness, accident, or infirmity to any able-bodied male person resident within any of the said Unions, or to any member of the family of any able-bodied male person, an extract from the Medical Officer's Weekly Report (if any such Officer shall have attended the case), stating the nature of such sickness, accident, or infirmity, shall be specially entered in the Minutes of the Proceedings of the Board of Guardians of the day on which the relief is ordered or subsequently allowed.

But if the Board of Guardians shall think fit, a certificate under the hand of a Medical Officer of the Union, or of the Medical Practitioner in attendance on the party, shall be laid before the Board, stating the nature of such sickness, accident, or infirmity, and a copy of the same shall be in like manner entered in the Minutes (*a*).

---

way of loan, and after he leaves the service perhaps some portion of it might be recovered. With regard to the relief of the families of men who are serving in the militia, see 52 O. C. (N. s.) pp. 9, 10.

Art. 1 requires that able-bodied women, deserted by their husbands, should only receive relief in the Workhouse. If such a woman requires relief for her children, any child under the age of nurture and residing with the mother may receive out-door relief; but the children above that age must be taken into the Workhouse. This is expressly provided for by the 8th exception to the Article in cases in which the husband has left the Union in which the wife resides. If, however, he has gone beyond the seas, under Art. 4 she is entitled to be relieved in the same manner and subject to the same conditions as if she were a widow.

(*a*) The regulation which requires the entry on the Minutes of the Medical Officer's Report, or a Medical Certificate in case of relief being given to an able-bodied pauper on account of sickness, accident, etc., has been introduced in consequence of a tendency which has displayed itself in various parts of the country, to make exceptions to the Prohibitory Order on too slight grounds, and the Commissioners think that this provision will have the useful effect of calling the special attention of the Guardians to every such case. If the pauper should not have been attended by a Medical Officer of the Union, a certificate may be given either by the Medical Practitioner who may have attended him, or by a Medical Officer of the Union who may visit him for the purpose. *Instr. Letter.* The entry in the Minutes here referred to, it will be perceived, refers to the Medical Reports or Certificates on which the orders of the Guardians for relief are founded, and is in no way interfered with by the Order for Accounts, *post*.

Art. 3.—No relief shall be given from the poor-rates of any parish comprised in any of the said Unions to any person who does not reside in some place within the Union, save and except in the following cases (*b*):—

> Art. 3.—1st (exception).—Where such person, being casually within such parish, shall become destitute (*c*).
>
> Art. 3.—2nd (exception).—Where such person shall require relief on account of any sickness, accident, or bodily or mental infirmity, affecting such person, or any of his or her family (*d*).

(*b*) Under the provisions of this Article, the Guardians may relieve a pauper residing within the Union, though not residing in the Parish to which he belongs; the Commissioners, however, are far from wishing to encourage even this species of non-resident relief. It is true that the frauds and evils which are incidental to non-resident relief, in consequence of the want of inspection and the difficulty of transmitting the relief, do not occur with reference to paupers resident within the Union, who are within the reach of the Relieving Officers, but, nevertheless, the ratepayers of the Parish charged with the relief, who by means of the quarterly list of paupers can, by personal observation of those who reside in their Parish, ascertain whether they are fit objects for relief, are deprived of this protection where the pauper for whom they pay is resident at a distant part of the Union. The relief of paupers out of their Parish, and out of the relieving District in which the Parish is comprised, is not unattended with difficulties, both of a legal and practical nature, which are sufficient to make it desirable that the Guardians should not, without sufficient ground, permit new cases of this nature even within the Union. The Commissioners have stated fully their views on the subject of non-resident relief, as respects both its legality and expediency, in a Minute dated the 26th of January, 1841. See their Seventh Annual Report, p. 106.—*Instr. Letter.* The foregoing observations of the Poor Law Commissioners on this Article must, however, now be read with reference to the Union Chargeability Act, 1865.

(*c*) The Commissioners have introduced this exception in order to meet the cases of vagrants, who may become casually destitute within the Union. It is the duty of the Guardians to relieve persons so situated, without reference to the place of their settlement or residence. The Commissioners have not introduced into this Article an exception on account of sudden and urgent necessity. (See note to Art. 1, exception 1.) Cases of sudden and urgent necessity manifestly require the prompt attention and vigilant inspection which can only be exercised by the Guardians and their Officers in the district where the necessity arises.—*Instr. Letter.*

(*d*) This exception corresponds to the second exception to Art. 1. The Commissioners introduced this exception on account of the difficulty which a want of the power of giving temporary relief to non-resi-

3rd.—Where such person shall be entitled to receive relief from any parish in which he or she may not be resident, under any order which Justices may by law be authorized to make (*a*).

Art. 3.—4th (exception).—Where such person, being a widow, shall be in the first six months of her widowhood (*b*).

---

dents in case of sickness has been found to create in some parts of the country. The Commissioners, however, caution the Guardians against giving temporary relief in cases of sickness to persons not resident within the Union, unless they are able to obtain accurate information concerning the case, and can ensure adequate and prompt relief, both medical and otherwise. It may be observed that this exception permits poor persons to be sent to establishments out of the Union intended for the treatment of their respective infirmities, as hospitals for the sick, asylums for the insane, and schools for the blind or deaf and dumb.—*Instr. Letter.* But since this Order was issued, the 9 & 10 Vict. c. 66, s. 4, has prevented the removal of a poor person who has become chargeable to a Parish, in which he is not settled, in consequence of temporary sickness. In such a case the Guardians cannot grant non-resident relief, as such relief as may be necessary is properly chargeable to the common fund of the Union in which the pauper is resident. The Guardians may, however, under this exception, grant non-resident relief to any poor person whose sickness, etc., is of a permanent character. Moreover, if the case of a pauper falls within the exception, and it be desirable to send the pauper to a hospital out of the Union for medical treatment, or to a sea-bathing infirmary for the benefit of sea-bathing, as is desirable in cases of scrofula, it would be legally competent for the Guardians to make the customary payment to the hospital in respect of the pauper, as the temporary sojourn of the pauper at the seaside under such circumstances would not constitute an interruption of residence in the Union.

(*a*) The third exception is intended expressly to except from the operation of the Order the cases of relief given to non-resident lunatics in asylums under orders of Justices, and to persons under orders of removal.—*Instr. Letter.*

(*b*) This exception is similar to the fourth exception to Art. 1, the reasons for which are stated in the note to that exception.—*Instr. Letter.* But see the 9 & 10 Vict. c. 66, s. 2, which makes a widow irremovable, and consequently chargeable to the Union in which she is residing for one year after her husband's death, provided she was living with him at the time of his death, and has not afterwards changed her residence. In such a case the Guardians cannot lawfully grant non-resident relief, and the statute consequently over-rides this exception. The case of a person who is a widow in a constructive sense, under the 7 & 8 Vict. c. 101, s. 25, does not come within this exception. The exception refers to the husband's death, and therefore it applies only to those who are widows in fact.

5th.—Where such person is a widow, who has a legitimate child dependent on her for support, and no illegitimate child born after the commencement of her widowhood, and who at the time of her husband's death was resident with him in some place other than the parish of her legal settlement, and not situated in the Union in which such parish may be comprised (*c*).

Art. 3.—6th (exception).—Where such person shall be a child under the age of sixteen, maintained in a Workhouse or Establishment for the education of pauper children not situate within the Union (*d*).

(*c*) This exception is that which the Legislature has introduced in the 7 & 8 Vict. c. 101, s. 26, and upon which the Commissioners made their remarks in their Circular Letter to Boards of Guardians, dated the 17th October, 1844. Upon that enactment the Commissioners in the Circular referred to observe, "That the widow must have been resident with her husband at the time of his death, not only out of the Parish of her settlement, but also out of the Union in which that Parish may be comprised. The object of the clause appears to be to avoid the disturbance of those connections and mode of life at a distance from the Union to which the family may have become accustomed, and which existed at the time of the husband's death. Where all the conditions exist which would enable the Guardians to grant non-resident relief, they are still to use their discretion as to whether non-resident relief to the widow is in each particular case desirable. The general objection to such relief, such as the difficulty of ascertaining the circumstances of paupers beyond the power of inspection of the Guardians or their Officers, and the further difficulties attendant on the transmission of relief to places where the Guardians have no authority and no official agency, will be weighed by the Guardians. This power is one entrusted to Boards of Guardians only. Overseers acquire no authority under this provision to administer non-resident relief to the class of widows described. It must be borne in mind by Guardians and their Officers that they are in nowise exempted from their previous obligation to relieve any widow who may be in their Parish or Union requiring relief, by the power thus given to the Guardians of the place of her settlement to afford her non-resident relief. And even when that power is exerted, if notwithstanding the relief sent to her by her Parish, she or her children require additional or further relief, the Officers of the place where she is are still bound, as heretofore, to afford her the relief which the circumstances require." The exception does not provide for relief in the particular Parish only in which the widow was residing at the time of her husband's death, but enables the Guardians to give non-resident relief to the widow anywhere in England.

(*d*) This exception removes the restriction upon Guardians from sending children to a Workhouse or Establishment for the training of

7th.—Where such person shall be the wife or child, residing within the Union, of some person not able-bodied, and not residing within the Union (a).

---

pauper children, which may be situated out of their Union, where, but for the prohibition of relief to non-residents contained in the Order, they might lawfully do so.—*Instr. Letter.* The 7 & 8 Vict. c. 101, s. 31, and 29 & 30 Vict. c. 113, s. 16, empower the Guardians of any Parish or Union to send infant poor, not above the age of sixteen years, being chargeable to such Parish or Union, who are orphans or are deserted by their parents, or whose parents or surviving parents or guardians are consenting thereto, to any district school formed under that Act. See also the 14 & 15 Vict. c. 105, s. 6, as to sending, with the consent of the Poor Law Board, certain children to a Workhouse belonging to another Union or Parish, where there is adequate accommodation. Reference may also be made to the 12 & 13 Vict. c. 103, s. 14, enabling Guardians to contract to receive into their Workhouses certain poor persons belonging to other Unions or Parishes within certain limits. It is further enacted by the 18 & 19 Vict. c. 34, s. 1, that the Guardians may lawfully grant relief out of the Workhouse to provide education for any child of any poor person lawfully relieved out of the Workhouse, between the ages of four and sixteen, in any school to be approved of by them, for such time and under such conditions as they shall see fit. In such cases, however, the Guardians cannot lay down any rule as to the school the children are to go to. They must leave the selection of the school to the parent of the child. See the Circular of the Poor Law Board on this subject, dated 9th January, 1856.

The sixth exception in Article 3 also applies to children sent to certified establishments for the instruction of the blind, deaf, dumb, lame, deformed, or idiotic persons. Under the 25 & 26 Vict. c. 43, s. 1, the Guardians may send any poor child who is an orphan, or deserted by his or her parents or surviving parent, or whose parents or surviving parent shall consent, to any school for the instruction of the blind, etc., certified by the Poor Law Board in the manner directed by the Act, and supported wholly or partially by voluntary subscriptions, the Managers of which shall be willing to receive such child, and may pay the expenses incurred in the maintenance, lodging, and education of such child, not exceeding the total sum which would have been charged for the maintenance of such child if relieved in the Workhouse during the period of maintenance in the institution, and cost of the conveyance of the child thereto, and, in case of death, the cost of burial. See also 29 & 30 Vict. c. 113, s. 14, as to educating pauper children in the religion to which they belong.

A list of the schools which have been certified by the Poor Law Board under 25 & 26 Vict. c. 43, will be found in the 'Union and Parish Officers' Almanack,' published by Messrs. Knight and Co.

As to adult blind or deaf and dumb paupers being sent to institutions established for the reception of such persons, see 30 & 31 Vict. c. 106, s. 21.

(*a*) This exception enables the Guardians to relieve the resident

Art. 3.—8th (exception).—Where such person shall have been in the receipt of relief from some parish in the Union from which such person seeks relief, at some time within the twelve calendar months next preceding the date of that one of the several Orders hereinbefore recited which was applicable to that Union, being settled in such parish, and not being resident within the Union at the time of the allowance of the relief.

Art. 4 (*b*).—Where the husband of any woman is beyond the seas, or in custody of the law, or in confinement in a licensed house or asylum as a lunatic or idiot, all relief which the Guardians shall give to his wife, or her child or children, shall be given to such woman in the same manner, and subject to the same conditions, as if she were a widow.

Art. 5.—It shall not be lawful for the Guardians, or any of their Officers, or for the Overseer or Overseers of any parish in the Union, to pay, wholly or in part, the rent of the house or lodging of any pauper, or to apply any portion

---

family of a non-resident man, provided he be not able-bodied, without requiring them to come into the Workhouse.—*Instr. Letter.*

(*b*) This Article is introduced in conformity with the provision contained in the 7 & 8 Vict. c. 101, s. 25, in regard to the relief of women separated from their husbands, in certain cases particularly specified, who are by that provision to be treated as widows in respect to relief to be afforded to them by Guardians. In the Circular Letter of the 17th October, 1844, on this subject, the Commissioners remark, "Married women whose children required and received relief were not before the passing of this Act liable to any conditions in respect of such relief, and could cast off their children upon the Parish, however well such women might be able to maintain their children, or to contribute to their maintenance. Widows, on the other hand, were liable to the like conditions and consequences of relief afforded to themselves and their children as the fathers of legitimate children are. The present Act declares that while the husband of any woman is beyond the seas (that is, *out of Great Britain*), or in custody of the law, or in confinement in any licensed house or asylum as a lunatic or idiot, all relief given to the wife, or to her child or children, shall, notwithstanding her coverture, be given to her in the same manner and subject to the same conditions as if she were a widow." (Sect. 25.) And again, "Where widows are obliged to receive relief for their children within the Union, or within the Workhouse, these married women will be subject to the like condition."—*Instr. Letter.*

of the relief ordered to be given to any pauper in payment of any such rent, or to retain any portion of such relief for the purpose of directly or indirectly discharging such rent, in full or in part, for any such pauper.

Provided always, that nothing in this Article contained shall apply to any shelter or temporary lodging, procured in any case of sudden and urgent necessity, or mental imbecility, or shall be taken to prevent the said Guardians, in regulating the amount of relief to be afforded to any particular person, from considering the expense to be incurred by such person in providing lodging (*a*).

Art. 6.—Provided always, that in case the Guardians of any of the said Unions depart in any particular instance from any of the regulations hereinbefore contained, and within fifteen days after such departure report the same, and the grounds thereof, to the Poor Law Commissioners, and the Poor Law Commissioners approve of such departure, then the relief granted in such particular instance shall, if otherwise lawful, not be deemed to be unlawful, or be subject to be disallowed (*b*).

(*a*) This Article is intended to prevent a practice which has prevailed in some parts of the country, whereby the poor-rates have been made a fund for the payment of rents directly to the landlords. In all cases where the pauper is so far destitute as to require a lodging, or the means of paying for one, if the Guardians do not deem it expedient in the particular case to require the party to come into the Workhouse, they should supply to the pauper the means of paying for such lodging.—*Instr. Letter*.

(*b*) The Commissioners state that it is possible, although not probable, that cases may occasionally arise which present very peculiar circumstances, and which do not fall within any of the exceptions contained in the present Order. The Commissioners think it desirable in cases of that kind, in which the immediate withdrawal or denial of out-door relief might appear likely to produce serious evil to the applicant, that the Guardians should give out-door relief or take a portion of the applicant's family into the Workhouse, and report the case within fifteen days to the Commissioners as a case of peculiar urgency, in order that they may give their opinion thereupon. The Commissioners have accordingly introduced this proviso, enabling the Guardians to pursue this course with respect to exceptional cases of this description.—*Instr. Letter*.

With respect to the allowance of relief given by the Relieving Officer

Art. 7.—No relief which may be contrary to any regulation in this Order shall be given by way of loan; and any relief which may be given to, or on account of, any person above the age of twenty-one, or to his wife, or any part of his or her family under the age of sixteen, under Art. 1, or any of the exceptions thereto, or under any of the exceptions to Art. 3, or under Art. 4, or under the proviso in Art. 6, may, if the Guardians think fit, be given by way of loan (*c*).

on the order of the Guardians under this Article, see note on Art. 215, No. 10 of the General Consolidated Order, *ante*, p, 188.

Observe that when out-door relief is given to able-bodied poor persons whose cases do not come within any of the exceptions to Art. 1, with the intention of setting such poor persons to work under the Supplemental Out-door Labour Test Order (*post*) in return for such relief, that unless the cases be reported to the Poor Law Board for their sanction under this Article, that the cost of the relief will be liable to be disallowed by the Auditor. The Labour Test Order, though it requires something more, does not dispense with the requirement of Art. 6 of this Order. The approval of the Poor Law Board to a departure from any of the regulations contained in this Order is signified by a letter signed by one of their secretaries or assistant-secretaries. On this point see 29 & 30 Vict. c. 113, s. 4.

(*c*) The first part of Art. 7 is introduced in order to put an end to a misapprehension of the law which existed in some Boards of Guardians, viz. that although the Prohibitory Order prevented them from *giving* out-door relief, they might nevertheless *lend* it. The second part of the Article enables the Guardians to make all the relief which may be given to persons above twenty-one years of age, or their families, a loan under the 58th section of the 4 & 5 Wm. IV. c. 76.—*Instr. Letter*. Servants falling sick whilst in the employment of their masters frequently apply for relief during their sickness, and unless there is a special agreement between the master and servant, the former is not liable to provide the latter with medical or surgical aid in case of sickness. If such an agreement existed in any case, it would give the servant a remedy against the master; but in no case have the Guardians any claim against the master for relief which they may give to his servant. In such a case the Guardians may give the relief on loan, and they may, under the 4 & 5 Wm. IV. c. 76, s. 59, attach in the hands of the master any future wages which the servant may earn. On this point see *ante*, p. 153. Medical relief, as the exact cost of it in any individual case cannot in general be severed from the total cost of medical relief in the Union, does not seem to be such relief as can be given by way of loan. But in some Unions it is nevertheless so given; and in the case of orders upon the Medical Officer to attend the wives of labourers in their confinement, for which a specific fee is paid, it is open to the Guardians to declare the relief to be given by way of loan. The Guardians should

Art. 8.—Whenever the word "Parish" is used in this Order, it shall be taken to include any place separately

notify to any such applicants that the relief would be granted by way of loan, and that the repayment of the whole, or such part as the Guardians might determine, would be strictly enforced by them. It must be borne in mind that unless the relief at the time that it is given be expressly declared to be given by way of loan, it cannot be recovered from the applicant afterwards. As to the application of property coming into the possession of paupers, in repayment of relief, see the 11 & 12 Vict. c. 110, s. 10, and 12 & 13 Vict. c. 103, s. 16. The distinction between relief by way of loan and a loan should also be borne in mind. The Guardians are not empowered to lend money to any one, whether destitute or not; all that they can legally do is to relieve destitution where it exits, and declare that the relief is given by way of loan, and not absolutely. The relief when so given should be administered by the Relieving Officer in the same manner as ordinary relief, and entered by him in his accounts. Afterwards it will rest with the Guardians to take the proper steps for its recovery; they may employ the Relieving Officer to collect the money; but if legal proceedings are necessary to enforce repayment, they should be conducted by the Clerk, pursuant to Art. 3, of the Order, *ante*, p. 272. As to the mode of obtaining repayment of relief given to out-pensioners of Greenwich and Chelsea Hospitals and lunatic pensioners, see 19 Vict. c. 15, ss. 8, 9. Under s. 8 of that Act the Secretary at War may agree with the Guardians for the repayment to them out of the pension of the amount of relief advanced to or expended on the pensioner's account, not exceeding in any case where relief has been administered to the pensioner's wife or one child only, whom he is bound to maintain, the amount of one-half; or where such relief has been administered to two or more such children, or to the pensioner's wife, and one or more such child or children, the amount of two-thirds of his pension. If the pensioner and his family be relieved in the Workhouse, the Guardians have no legal right to, and cannot claim, any larger amount of the pension than is equivalent to the actual cost of the paupers in the Workhouse. They cannot claim more than the charge made in respect of each of the other inmates. Sect. 9 of the Act relates to lunatic pensioners who are chargeable to the Poor Rates.

A poor person cannot be compelled to accept relief by way of loan to enable him to bury the dead body of one of his family, for he is not bound to accept a loan and render himself liable to be proceeded against, and lose his liberty, and be deprived of the means of maintaining his family by incurring a debt. There is no doubt, Lord Campbell, C. J., said, that if a parent has the means of providing Christian burial for his child, he is bound to do so; but he is not liable to be indicted for a nuisance if he has not the means of burying it. He cannot sell the child's body or cast it into a river; but unless he has the means of giving it Christian burial he does not commit a crime by leaving it unburied, although it may be a nuisance to the neighbourhood, for which, he added, the parish officers would probably be liable. (*Reg.* v. *Vass*, 21 L. J. (N.S.) M. C. 41.)

maintaining its own poor, whether parochial or extra-parochial.

Art. 9.—Whenever the word "Union" is used in this Order, it shall be taken to include not only an Union of Parishes formed under the provisions of the hereinbefore recited Act, but also any Union of Parishes incorporated or united for the relief or maintenance of the poor under any Local Act of Parliament (*a*).

Art. 10.—Whenever the word "Guardians" is used in this Order, it shall be taken to include not only Guardians appointed or entitled to act, under the provisions of the said hereinbefore recited Act, but also any Governors, Directors, Managers, or Acting Guardians entitled to act in the ordering of relief to the poor from the poor-rates under any Local Act of Parliament (*a*).

Art. 11.—Whenever in this Order any Article is referred to by its number, the Article of this Order bearing that number shall be taken to be signified thereby.

(*a*) Arts. 9 & 10.—These Articles are introduced because the Order is addressed to four Unions of Parishes formed, not under the 4 & 5 Wm. IV. c. 76, but under Local Acts of Parliament, viz. Bury St. Edmund's, East and West Flegg, Forehoe, and Tunstead and Happing. —*Instr. Letter*. The third, the Stamford Incorporation, was subsequently dissolved, and the Parishes reunited under the name of the Stamford Union, on the 24th February, 1849.

In concluding the remarks on this Order, it is desirable to call attention to a provision which has been made by the Legislature, with reference to the relief of Lascars and other natives of the territories under the government of the Council for India who may be found destitute in this country, and also with reference to the repayment of such relief out of the revenues of India. The provision referred to is contained in the "Merchant Shipping Act Amendment Act, 1855," 18 and 19 Vict. c. 91. The 16th clause of the 17 and 18 Vict. c. 120, contains a provision applicable to a somewhat similar class of persons to those specified in the 18 & 19 Vict. c. 91, namely, to natives of any country in Asia, Africa, or any of the Islands in the South Sea or Pacific Ocean, or of any other country not having any consul in the United Kingdom. This provision will be found in the first volume of Glen's Poor Law Statutes, pages 861–867.

SCHEDULE,

Containing the Names of the Unions to which the present Order applies.

Aberacron.	Battle.	Bromley.
Abergavenny.	Beaminster.	Bromsgrove.
Aberystwith.	Bedale.	Bromyard.
Abingdon.	Bedford.	Buckingham.
Alban's, St.	Bedminster.	Buntingford.
Alcester.	Belford.	Burton-upon-Trent.
Alderbury.	Belper.	Bury St. Edmund's.
Alnwick.	Bellingham.	
Alresford.	Berkhampstead.	Caistor.
Alton.	Berwick-upon-Tweed.	Calne.
Altrincham.	Beverley.	Cambridge.
Amersham.	Bicester.	Cardiff.
Amesbury.	Bideford.	Cardigan.
Ampthill.	Biggleswade.	Carmarthen.
Andover.	Billericay.	Castle Ward.
Asaph, St.	Billesdon.	Catherington.
Ashby-de-la-Zouch.	Bingham.	Caxton and Arrington.
Ashford, East.	Bishop Stortford.	Cerne.
Ashford, West.	Blaby.	Chailey.
Aston.	Blandford.	Chapel-en-le-Frith.
Atcham.	Blean.	Chard.
Atherstone.	Blofield.	Cheadle.
Auckland.	Blything.	Chelmsford.
Austell, St.	Bosmere and Claydon.	Cheltenham.
Axbridge.	Boston.	Chepstow.
Axminster.	Bourn.	Chesterfield.
Aylesbury.	Brackley.	Chesterton.
Aylesford, North.	Bradfield.	Chester-le-Street.
Aylsham.	Bradford (Wilts).	Chippenham.
	Braintree.	Chipping Norton.
Bakewell.	Brampton.	Chipping Sodbury.
Bala.	Brecknock.	Christchurch.
Bunbury.	Bridge.	Church Stretton.
Barnet.	Bridgend and Cow-	Cirencester.
Barnstaple.	bridge.	Cleobury Mortimer.
Barrow-upon-Soar.	Bridgnorth.	Clifton.
Basford.	Bridgwater.	Clun.
Basingstoke.	Bridport.	Clutton.
Bath.	Brixworth.	Cockermouth.

Colchester.
Columb, Major, St.
Cookham.
Corwen.
Cosford.
Cranbrook.
Crediton.
Crickhowel.
Cricklade and Wootton Bassett.
Croydon.
Cuckfield.

Darlington.
Dartford.
Daventry.
Depwade.
Derby.
Devizes.
Docking.
Doncaster.
Dorchester.
Dore.
Dorking.
Dover.
Downham.
Drayton.
Driffield.
Droitwich.
Droxford.
Dudley.
Dunmow.
Durham.
Dursley.

Easingwold.
Eastbourne.
East Grinstead.
Easthampstead.
East Retford.
East Ward.
Eastry.
Elham.

Ellesmere.
Ely.
Epping.
Epsom.
Erpingham.
Eton.
Evesham.

Faith, St.
Fareham.
Faringdon.
Faversham.
Festiniog.
Flegg, East and West.
Foleshill.
Fordingbridge.
Forehoe.
Freebridge Lynn.
Frome.

Gainsborough.
Germans, St.
Glanford Brigg.
Glendale.
Glossop.
Gloucester.
Godstone
Goole.
Grantham.
Gravesend & Milton.
Guildford.
Guiltcross.
Guisborough.

Hailsham.
Halstead.
Haltwhistle.
Hambledon.
Hardingstone.
Hartismere.
Hartley Wintney.
Hastings.
Havant.

Haverfordwest.
Hay.
Hayfield.
Headington.
Hemel Hempstead.
Henley.
Henstead.
Hereford.
Hertford.
Hexham.
Highworth and Swindon.
Hinckley.
Hitchin.
Holbeach.
Hollingbourn.
Holywell.
Honiton.
Hoo.
Horncastle.
Horsham.
Houghton-le-Spring.
Howden.
Hoxne.
Hungerford.
Huntingdon.
Hursley.

Ipswich.
Ives, St.

Kettering.
Keynsham.
Kidderminster.
Kingsbridge.
Kingsclere.
King's Norton.
Kington.
Knighton.

Lauchester.
Langport.
Launceston.
Ledbury.

Leek.
Leighton Buzzard.
Leominster.
Lewes.
Lexden & Winstree.
Leyburn.
Lichfield.
Lincoln.
Linton
Liskeard.
Llandilo Fawr.
Llandovery.
Llanelly.
Llanfyllin.
Loddon and Clavering.
Longtown.
Loughborough.
Louth.
Ludlow.
Luton.
Lutterworth.
Lymington.

Madeley.
Maidstone.
Maldon.
Malling.
Malmesbury.
Malton.
Mansfield.
Market Bosworth.
Market Harborough.
Marlborough.
Martley.
Medway.
Melksham.
Melton Mowbray.
Mere.
Meriden.
Midhurst.
Mildenhall.
Milton.
Mitford & Launditch.

Monmouth.
Morpeth.

Nantwich.
Narbeth.
Neath.
Neots, St.
Newark.
Newbury.
Newcastle-in-Emlyn.
Newcastle-under-Lyne.
Newent.
New Forest.
Newhaven.
Newmarket.
Newport (Monmouth).
Newport (Salop).
Newport Pagnell.
Newton Abbott.
Northampton.
Northleach.
Northwich.
North Witchford.
Nuneaton.

Oakham.
Okehampton.
Ongar.
Ormskirk.
Orsett.
Oundle.

Patrington.
Pembroke.
Penkridge.
Penrith.
Penzance.
Pershore.
Peterborough.
Petersfield.
Petworth.
Pewsey.
Pickering.

Plomesgate.
Plympton, St. Mary.
Pont-y-Pool.
Poole.
Portsea Island.
Potterspury.
Pwllheli.

Reading.
Redruth.
Reeth.
Reigate.
Richmond (Yorkshire).
Ringwood.
Risbridge.
Rochford.
Romford.
Romney Marsh.
Romsey.
Ross.
Rothbury.
Royston.
Rugby.
Ruthin.
Rye.

Saffron Walden.
Scarborough.
Sculcoates.
Sedgefield.
Seisdon.
Selby.
Sevenoaks.
Shaftesbury.
Shardlow.
Sheppey.
Shepton Mallett.
Sherborne.
Shiffnal.
Shipston-upon-Stour.
Skirlaugh.
Sleaford.

Solihull.
Southam.
South Molton.
South Shields.
South Stoneham.
Southwell.
Spalding.
Spilsby.
Stafford.
Staines.
Stamford.
Steyning.
Stockbridge.
Stone.
Stourbridge.
Stow.
Stow-on-the-Wold.
Stratford-upon-Avon.
Stroud.
Sturminster.
Sudbury.
Swaffham.
Swansea.

Tamworth.
Taunton.
Tavistock.
Teesdale.
Tenbury.
Tendring.
Tenterden.
Tetbury.
Tewkesbury.
Thakeham.
Thame.
Thanet, Isle of.
Thetford.
Thingoe.
Thirsk.
Thomas, St.

Thornbury.
Thorne.
Thrapston.
Ticehurst.
Tisbury.
Tiverton.
Tonbridge.
Torrington.
Totnes.
Towcester.
Tunstead and Happing.
Tynemouth.

Uckfield.
Uppingham.
Upton-upon-Severn.
Uttoxeter.
Uxbridge.

Wallingford.
Walsal.
Walsingham.
Wangford.
Wantage.
Ware.
Wareham & Purbeck.
Warminster.
Warwick.
Watford.
Wayland.
Weardale.
Wellingborough.
Wellington (Som.)
Wellington (Salop).
Wells.
Welwyn.
Wem.
Weobly.
Westbourne.
West Bromwich.

Westbury-upon-Severn.
Westbury and Whorwelsdown.
West Firle.
West Ham.
West Hampnett.
West Ward.
Weymouth.
Wheatenhurst.
Whitby.
Whitchurch.
Whitehaven.
Wigton.
Williton.
Wilton.
Wimborne and Cranborne.
Wincanton.
Winchcombe.
Winchester, New.
Windsor.
Winslow.
Wirrall.
Wisbeach.
Witham.
Witney.
Woburn.
Wokingham.
Wolverhampton.
Woodbridge.
Woodstock.
Wolstanton and Burslem.
Worcester.
Worksop.
Wrexham.
Wycombe.

Yeovil.

Given under our Hands and Seal of Office, this Twenty-first day of December, in the year of our Lord One thousand eight hundred and forty-four.

     (Signed) GEO. NICHOLLS.
           G. C. LEWIS.
           EDMUND W. HEAD.

On the 21st December, 1844, an Order similar to the foregoing, but omitting the words "and not situated in the Union in which such Parish may be comprised" (at the end of the 5th exception to Article 3), was issued to the following single Parishes in which relief to the poor is administered under Boards of Guardians:—

Alston-with-Garrigill,	Whittlesea, St. Mary and St.
East Stonehouse,	Andrew,
Stoke-upon-Trent,	Yarmouth, Great.

On the 17th August, 1852, a further General Order on the same subject was issued to the following Unions:—

Chertsey,	Kingston-upon-Thames,
Easington,	Stockton.

A General Prohibitory Order similar to the above, bearing date the 6th January, 1857, was issued to the

Camelford,	Helston, and
Dulverton,	Holsworthy Unions.

Orders prohibiting out-door relief to the able-bodied poor have also, since the issue of the General Order of the 21st December, 1844, been issued to the following Unions and Places on the dates under-mentioned:—

Ashbourne	5th December, 1849.
Bangor and Beaumaris	30th March, 1849.
Bedwellty	24th February, 1864.
Bodmin	15th May, 1851.
Bootle	13th June, 1856.
Bridlington	16th October, 1849.
Canterbury	5th April, 1851.
Carnarvon	30th March, 1849.
Chester	1st November, 1850.

Congleton	9th February, 1846.
Exeter	20th October, 1856.
Falmouth	13th January, 1853.
Farnham	6th March, 1848.
Gower	24th March, 1866.
Great Boughton	10th March, 1858.
Great Ouseburn	14th January, 1859.
Hartlepool	13th December, 1861.
Hatfield	5th May, 1845.
Hawarden	12th July, 1855.
Helmsley Blackmoor	21st July, 1852.
Kirkby Moorside	7th February, 1852.
Knaresborough	7th May, 1858.
Llanrwst	30th March, 1849.
Macclesfield	2nd October, 1852.
Newtown and Llanidloes	24th April, 1845.
Oswestry	16th November, 1850.
Pocklington	2nd July, 1856.
Pontypridd	26th February, 1866.
Ripon	28th February, 1856.
Samford	27th March, 1849.
Sedbergh	31st July, 1855.
Shrewsbury (a)	23rd May, 1851.
Stokesley	14th February, 1852.
Stratton	15th May, 1851.
Truro	13th January, 1853.
York	18th May, 1852.

To the City of Oxford an Order regulating the administration of out-door relief was issued on the 19th December, 1848.

Orders have also been issued to the following places, containing provisions of the Prohibitory, Out-door Relief Regulation, and Non-resident Relief Orders:—

Dolgelley	26th November, 1858.
Conway	28th November, 1859.

(a) This Order regulates the administration of out-door relief by the Select Vestry of each of the Parishes of St. Alkmond, St. Chad, Holy Cross and St. Giles, St. Julian, St. Mary, and Meole Brace within the Town of Shrewsbury and Liberties thereof, forming the Shrewsbury Poor United District.

Runcorn . . . . 5th May, 1860.
Machynlleth . . . . 13th December, 1861.
Northallerton . . . . 30th June, 1862.

In each of those cases the particular Order should be referred to, as it is not always in the precise terms of the Order given in the text, *ante*, page 356.

OUT-DOOR RELIEF REGULATION ORDER.

(14th December, 1852.)

To the Guardians of the Poor *of the several* Unions *and* Parishes *named in the Schedules hereunto annexed;—*

To the Churchwardens and Overseers of the Parishes comprised in the said Unions, and the said several other Parishes named in the said Schedules;—

To the Clerk or Clerks to the Justices of the Petty Sessions held for the Division or Divisions in which the said Unions and Parishes are situate;—

And to all others whom it may concern.

WHEREAS the Poor Law Board, by their Order bearing date the 25th day of August last, and addressed to the several Unions and Parishes named in the Schedules thereunto annexed, being the same as those mentioned in the Schedules hereunto annexed, did make certain rules and regulations for the administration of the relief to the outdoor poor, and it is expedient that the same should be modified:

Now, therefore, We, the Poor Law Board, in pursuance of the authorities vested in Us by an Act passed in the fifth year of the reign of his late Majesty King William the Fourth, intituled "*An Act for the Amendment and better Administration of the Laws relating to the Poor in England and Wales*," and by all other Acts amending the same, do hereby rescind the said Order, except so far as it rescinded any Order theretofore issued by the Poor Law Commissioners or Poor Law Board to the said Unions and Parishes named in the Schedules hereunto annexed (a), and except as to every matter done or commenced in obedience thereto; and We do hereby Order, Direct, and Declare, with respect to each and every of the said Unions and Parishes from and after the First day of January next, as follows:—

(a) The following is the rescinding clause of the Order of the 25th August, 1852, that is here referred to:—"We, the Poor Law Board, in pursuance, etc. etc., do hereby rescind so much of every Order, whether General or Special, heretofore issued by the Poor Law Commissioners or Poor Law Board to the several Unions and Parishes named in the Schedules hereunto annexed, as relates to the several subjects herein provided for."

The Poor Law Board, with reference to the Order of 25th August, 1852, stated that they thought it expedient to issue to certain Unions and Parishes, in many of which no regulations concerning out-door relief are now in force, a General Order regulating the administration of relief, and prescribing, among other things, an out-door labour test for able-bodied males.

The principle kept in view in all the provisions of this Order is that which was established by the 43rd Eliz. c. 2, namely, that the disabled poor should be relieved and the able-bodied be employed; which ruling principle of the Poor Law is laid down in these words by that statute, —the Churchwardens and Overseers shall "take order from time to time for setting to work the children of all such whose parents shall not, by the said Churchwardens and Overseers, or the greater part of them, be thought able to keep and maintain their children; and also for setting to work all such persons, married or unmarried, having no means to maintain them, and use (using) no ordinary and daily trade of life to get their living by; and also, to raise, weekly or otherwise, a convenient stock of flax, hemp, wool, thread, iron, and other ware and stuff, to set the poor on work; and also, competent sums of money for and towards the necessary relief of the lame, impotent, old, blind, and such other among them being poor and not able to work."

The Guardians at the present day stand in the place of the Churchwardens and Overseers, and the Poor Law Board therefore address to them the following remarks explanatory of the several Articles of the Order:—

The Board are of opinion that where there is a commodious and efficient Workhouse, it is best that the able-bodied paupers should be received and set to work therein; but, looking to the circumstances of most of the Unions and Parishes in London and in some other populous places, they have not thought it expedient in this Order to prohibit out-door relief to any class of paupers; at the same time they leave the Guardians at liberty to offer relief in the Workhouse only in every case in which they may consider it right to apply that test of destitution, or in which they consider that form of relief the most suitable to the necessity of the applicant and the circumstances of the case.—*Instr. Letter*, 25th August, 1852.

Art. 1.—Whenever the Guardians allow relief to any able-bodied male person, out of the Workhouse, one-half at least of the relief so allowed shall be given in articles of food or fuel, or in other articles of absolute necessity (*b*).

Art. 2.—In any case in which the Guardians allow relief for a longer period than one week to an indigent poor person, resident within their Union or Parish respectively, without requiring that such person shall be received into the Workhouse, such relief shall be given or administered weekly, or at such more frequent periods as they may deem expedient (*c*).

(*b*) The object of this provision is to prevent the misapplication of the relief furnished, and the general rule is to be observed whether work is exacted in return for the relief or not.—*Instr. Letter*, 25th August, 1852.

In this Article all words which relate to any other class of destitute poor than able-bodied males have been omitted, and, as it is now framed, the Guardians have therefore full discretion as to the description of relief to be given to indigent poor of every other class. The Board cannot, however, but observe, that whilst they have introduced this modification in deference to the numerous representations of the Boards of Guardians who have addressed them on the subject, they entertain a strong conviction, which is justified by the practice of several well-managed Unions and Parishes, that a certain portion of relief may properly be given in kind, with benefit to the ratepayers and advantage to the poor. The Board are induced, therefore, to express a confident hope that this mode of relief, the beneficial results of which are attested by experience, will be generally adopted by Boards of Guardians in the due exercise of that discretionary power with which they are invested. *Instr. Letter*, 14th December, 1852.

The Poor Law Board consider that Art. 1 of the General Order of the 14th December, 1852, does not apply to the case of a man who, though ordinarily able-bodied, is suffering from sickness at the time of his obtaining relief; nor to the case of a man who, being able-bodied, requires relief on account of the sickness of his wife or of any of his children under sixteen years of age.—57 O. C. (N.S.), 82.

(*c*) Art. 2 prevents the practice of delivering a large amount of relief to a pauper at once in cases in which it is intended that the relief shall be for a considerable period, and the amount is consequently more than the immediate destitution of the pauper requires. The object of the Board in this Article is mainly to save poor persons in the receipt of relief from being exposed to the temptation of expending at once money given to them beyond their present necessities.—*Instr. Letter*, 25th August, 1852.

Words have been introduced in Art. 2 limiting the obligation to administer the relief weekly to cases of poor persons resident within the

Art. 3.—It shall not be lawful for the Guardians or their officers (a)—

To establish any applicant for relief in trade or business;

Nor to redeem from pawn for any such applicant any tools, implements, or other articles;

Nor to purchase and give to such applicant any tools, implements, or other articles, except articles of clothing or bedding where urgently needed, and such articles as are hereinbefore referred to in Art. 1;

Nor to pay, directly or indirectly, the expense of the conveyance of any poor person, unless conveyed under the provisions of some Statute (b), or under an Order of Justices or other lawful authority, or in conformity with some Order or Regulation of the Poor Law Commissioners or the Poor Law Board, except in the following cases; viz.—

Art. 3.—1st. The case of a person conveyed to or from a district school, or an hospital or infirmary, or a lunatic asylum, or a house licensed or hospital registered for the reception of lunatics;

2nd. The case of a person conveyed to the Workhouse of the Union or Parish in which such person is at the time chargeable;

Union or Parish, so as to avoid any inconvenience or difficulty which might be experienced in extending the application of the Regulation to non-resident poor. The Board have also inserted words for the purpose of more clearly showing that there is nothing in this Article to prevent Guardians from directing that the relief ordered be given more frequently than once a week, if they think fit to direct that a portion only be given at a time. All that is necessary is, that each week's relief should be given within the week.—*Instr. Letter*, 14th December, 1852.

(a) This article is general in its terms, and it applies to in-door paupers as well as to those who are relieved out of the Workhouse. Moreover, it will be observed that it contains an absolute prohibition of the application of the poor-rates to any of the purposes mentioned; and that the Article cannot in any case be dispensed with under the provisions contained in Article 10 of this Order.

(b) The apprenticeship of pauper boys to the sea-service being authorized by statute, the expenses of their conveyance to the place where they are to be bound, or to sail from, would come within this exception. As to such apprenticeships see *ante*, p. 49.

Art. 3.—3rd. The case of a person conveyed to or from any other Workhouse or other house or establishment for the reception of poor persons, in which for the time being it shall be lawful for the Guardians to place such person;

Nor to give money to or on account of any such applicant for the purpose of effecting any of the objects in this Article mentioned;

Nor to pay, wholly or in part, the rent of the house or lodging of any pauper, nor to apply any portion of the relief ordered to be given to any pauper in payment of any such rent, nor to retain any portion of such relief for the purpose of directly or indirectly discharging such rent, in full or in part, for any such pauper;

Provided always, that nothing in this Article contained shall apply to any shelter or temporary lodging procured for a poor person in any case of sudden or urgent necessity or mental imbecility.

Art. 4.—No relief shall be given from the poor-rates of any of the said Parishes, or of any Parish comprised in any of the said Unions, to any person who does not reside in some place within such Parish or Union respectively, save and except in the following cases;—

1st. The case of a person casually within such Parish, and destitute.

2nd. The case of a person requiring relief on account of any sickness, accident, or bodily or mental infirmity, affecting him or her, or any of his or her family.

3rd. The case of a widow, having a legitimate child dependent on her for support, and no illegitimate child born after the commencement of her widowhood, and who at the time of her husband's death was resident with him in some place other than the Parish of her legal settlement, and not situated in the Union in which such Parish is comprised.

4th. The case of a child under the age of sixteen maintained in a Workhouse or Establishment for the education of poor children not situated within the Union or Parish.

Art. 4.—5th (exception).—The case of the wife or child residing within such Parish or Union of some person not residing therein.

6th. The case of a person who has been in the receipt of relief from such Parish, or from some Parish in the Union from which he or she seeks relief, at some time within the twelve calendar months next preceding the date of this Order (a).

Art. 5.—No relief shall be given to any able-bodied male person while he is employed for wages or other hire or remuneration by any person (b).

(a) Art. 4 imposes a restriction upon the allowance of relief to non-resident paupers, with certain exceptions, wherein a discretionary power, subject, however, to the restrictions imposed by the other Articles of this Order, is left to the Guardians. It is obvious that relief to non-resident paupers is a form of relief peculiarly open to abuse, and the Poor Law Commissioners have, in their Minute of the 26th January, 1841, Seventh Annual Report, p. 106, fully detailed the general objections and evils arising out of it. The present Order, however, in consideration of such relief having, in recent times, prevailed extensively, only provides for its gradual extinction, and still permits it in certain cases, where the denial might be most felt as a hardship. The relief of this kind which is authorized by the 7 & 8 Vict. c. 101, s. 26, to widows, is necessarily exempted from the rule. The Guardians will remember that, in cases where the non-resident pauper is irremovable by reason of the late Removal Act, there is no legal ground for their granting relief, which, if required, should be given by and charged upon the Union or Parish of the residence.—*Instr. Letter*, 25th August, 1852.

(b) Art. 5 prohibits the giving relief to able-bodied male paupers while employed for wages. The evils of such a system of relief have been found so great in practice as to be almost universally admitted, and are prominently indicated by the Legislature in the 4 & 5 Wm. IV. c. 76, s. 52, as forming the principal ground on which the Poor Law Commissioners were by that Act invested with the power and charged with the duty of making Regulations for the due administration of relief to able-bodied persons. The Board desire, however, to point out, that what is intended actually to prohibit, is the giving relief at the same identical time as that at which the person receiving it is in actual employment and in the receipt of wages (unless he falls within any of the exceptions afterwards set forth), and that relief given in any other case, as, for instance, in that of a man working for wages on one day and being without work the next, or working half the week and being

Art. 6.—Every able-bodied male person, if relieved out of the Workhouse, shall be set to work by the Guardians, and be kept employed under their direction and superintendence so long as he continues to receive relief (c).

Art. 7.—Provided that the regulations in Articles 5 and 6 shall not be imperative in the following cases:—

1st. The case of a person receiving relief on account of sudden and urgent necessity.

2nd. The case of a person receiving relief on account of any sickness, accident, or bodily or mental infirmity, affecting such person or any of his family.

3rd. The case of a person receiving relief for the purpose of defraying the expenses of the burial of any of his family.

4th. The case of the wife, child, or children of a person confined in any gaol or place of safe custody.

5th. The case of the wife, child, or children, resident

---

unemployed during the remainder, and being then in need of relief, is not prohibited by this Article.—*Instr. Letter*, 14th December, 1852.

(c) Article 6 prohibits the allowing relief to an able-bodied male pauper out of the Workhouse unless he be set to work, and kept at work by the Guardians as long as he continues to receive relief. Several cases, however, which are described in Art. 7, are exempted from the compulsory operation of this rule, though in all or any of them the Guardians may, if they think proper, upon a consideration of the circumstances, require work to be performed in return for the relief given. The Board must observe that every payment made by Guardians to paupers ought to assume the form of relief, not of wages, and consequently should be measured by the wants of the applicant, and not by the quantity of work done. It is, therefore, of primary importance that the paupers should labour under vigilant superintendence, and should be required to execute a task fixed according to their physical ability. The General Consolidated Orders provide, in the Unions and Parishes to which they have been issued, for the appointment, and prescribe the duties of a Superintendent of Labour (Arts. 153 and 217); and where superintendence is mentioned in this Order, it is assumed that a Superintendent of Labour is, or is to be, appointed under one of those Orders, or, where they have not been issued, by the general authority of the body administering relief in the Union or Parish, and the Board also assume that he shall be competent, under the direction of the Guardians, to enforce the performance of the required task.—*Instr. Letter*, 25th August, 1852. See also the Instructional Letter of 14th December, 1852.

within the Parish or Union, of a person not residing therein.

Art. 8.—The Guardians shall, within thirty days after they shall have proceeded to act in execution of Art. 6, report to the Poor Law Board the place or places at which able-bodied male paupers shall be set to work, the sort or sorts of work in which they or any of them shall be employed, the times and mode of work, and the provision made for superintending them while working, and shall forthwith discontinue or alter the same, if the Poor Law Board shall so require (*a*).

Art. 9.—No relief which shall be contrary to any regulation in this Order shall be given by way of loan, but any relief which may be given in conformity with the provisions of this Order to or on account of any person to whom relief may be lawfully given above the age of twenty-one, or to his wife, or any part of his or her family under the age of sixteen, may, if the Guardians shall think fit, be given by way of loan (*b*).

Art. 10.—If the Guardians shall, upon consideration of the special circumstances of any particular case, deem it expedient to depart from any of the Regulations hereinbefore contained (except those contained in Art. 3), and within Twenty-one days after such departure shall report the same, and the grounds thereof, to the Poor Law Board, the

---

(*a*) Article 8 directs that the Guardians shall, within thirty days after the time when they begin to put this test in operation, supply the Poor Law Board with full information as to the measures they have taken for giving effect to the provisions of the Order.—*Instr. Letter*, 25th August, 1852.

(*b*) Article 9. The strict observance of this Article is important for the correction of a prevalent error regarding relief by way of loan. It is not unfrequently supposed that there are cases in which, though the Guardians may not *give* relief, they may *lend* it. But this Article points out that what cannot legally be given must not be lent ; and that the power of lending is only to be exercised where the Guardians think fit to do something less than absolutely give the relief applied for in cases where the application is lawful. In such cases, and in such only, they may lend it ; and such loans should never be made without being in due time strictly recovered.—*Instr. Letter*, 25th August, 1852.

relief which may have been so given in such case by such Guardians before an answer to such report shall have been returned by the said Board, shall not be deemed to be contrary to the provisions of this Order; and if the Poor Law Board shall approve of such departure, and shall notify such approval to the Guardians, all relief given in such case after such notification, so far as the same shall be in accordance with the terms and conditions of such approval, shall be lawful, anything in this Order to the contrary notwithstanding (c).

Art. 11.—Whenever the word "Guardians" is used in this Order, it shall be taken to include not only Guardians appointed or entitled to act under the provisions of the said hereinbefore recited Act, but also any Governors, Directors, Managers, Acting Guardians, Vestrymen, or other officers in a Parish or Union, appointed or entitled to act as Managers of the Poor, and in the distribution or ordering

---

(c) The Board have introduced important modifications in Article 10, which is now in substance to the following effect, viz. that in any case in which the Guardians deem it expedient to depart from any of the provisions of the Order (with one exception), and to report the fact of such departure, with the reasons for it, within twenty-one days, to the Poor Law Board, the relief given by them in the interval between the date of such departure, and the receipt of an answer from this Board, shall not be deemed to involve any violation of this Order. The modification thus effected in the Article leaves to the Guardians full and unfettered discretion to deal, in the first instance, with any special case in which they may deem it expedient to give relief in a manner at variance with the provisions of this Order, and only requires them to report to the Board the fact of their having given such relief, and the grounds on which they have done so. As the exceptions provided in Articles 4 and 7 are so numerous as to meet almost all cases, it appears to the Board that the instances in which the Guardians will consider it necessary to avail themselves of the provisions of Article 10 for the purpose of giving relief, will, in all probability, be very few. While, therefore, the Board, on consideration of the special circumstances of many of the Unions and Parishes affected by the Order, and of the character of their population, have thought it expedient to introduce the modified provision now referred to, they trust that the judgment and experience of Boards of Guardians will lead them to abstain, as far as practicable, from any material departure from the sound principles of Poor Law administration upon which the Articles of this Order regulating relief are founded.—*Instr. Letter*, 14th December, 1852.

of the relief of the Poor from the Poor-rate, under any general or local Act.

Art. 12.—Whenever the word "Parish" is used in this Order, it shall be taken to include any place separately maintaining its own Poor, whether parochial or extra-parochial (*a*).

Art. 13.—Whenever in describing any person or party, matter or thing, the word importing the singular number only is used in this Order, the same shall be taken to include, and shall be applied to several persons or parties as well as one person or party, and several matters or things as well as one matter or thing respectively, unless there be something in the subject or context repugnant to such construction.

Art. 14.—Whenever in this Order any Article is referred to by its number, the Article of this Order bearing that number shall be taken to be signified thereby.

SCHEDULE (A).

Containing the Names of the Unions to which the above Order applies.

Anglesey.	Bradford, in the West Riding, Yorkshire.	City of London.
Ashton-under-Lyne.		Chorley.
	Brentford.	Chorlton.
Barnsley.	Builth.	Clitheroe.
Barton-under-Irwell.	Burnley.	*Conway.
Bierley, North.	Bury.	Coventry.
Blackburn.		
Bolton.	Carlisle.	Dewsbury.
Boughton, Great.†	Chichester.	*Dolgelly.

(*a*) But see 29 & 30 Vict. c. 113, s. 18, as to the meaning of the word "Parish."

* So much of this Order as relates to the mode of administering relief to poor persons in these Unions has been rescinded. (See the special Orders issued in these cases, page 379.)

† This Order is rescinded as regards the Great Boughton Union: see Order of 10th March, 1858, *ante*, p. 379.

Dulverton.
East London.
Ecclesall Bierlow.
Edmonton.
Fulham.
Fylde, The.
Garstang.
Gateshead.
Greenwich.
Hackney.
Halifax.
Haslingden.
Hemsworth.
Hendon.
Holborn.
Huddersfield.
Keighley.
Kendal.
King's Lynn.
Kingston-upon-Hull.
Lampeter.
Lancaster.
Leicester.

Leigh.
Lewisham.
*Machynlleth.
Merthyr Tydvil.
Mutford and Lothingland.
Newcastle-upon-Tyne.
*Northallerton.
Nottingham.
Norwich.
Oldham.
Pateley Bridge.
Penistone.
Poplar.
Prescot.
Presteigne.
Preston.
Prestwich.
Radford.
Rhayader.
Richmond in the county of Surrey.
Rochdale.
Rotherham.

*Runcorn.
St. Olave's.
St. Saviour's.
Salford.
Salisbury.
Settle.
Sheffield.
Skipton.
Southampton.
Stepney.
Stockport.
Strand.
Sunderland.
Todmorden.
Tregaron.
Ulverstone.
Wakefield.
Wandsworth and Clapham.
Warrington.
West Derby.
West London.
Whitechapel.
Wigan.
Wight, Isle of.
Wortley.

SCHEDULE (B.)

Containing the Names of the Parishes to which the above Order applies.

Leeds.
Liverpool.
Manchester.
Paddington.
St. George-in-the-East.
St. George-the-Martyr, Southwark.
St. Giles, Camberwell.
St. John, Hampstead.
St. Luke, Chelsea.
St. Martin-in-the-Fields (*a*).
St. Mary Abbots, Kensington.
St. Mary, Lambeth.
St. Mary Magdalen, Bermondsey.
St. Mary, Rotherhithe.
St. Matthew, Bethnal Green.

(*a*) Since added to the Strand Union.

Given under our Hands and Seal of Office, this Fourteenth day of December, in the year One thousand eight hundred and fifty-two.

       JOHN TROLLOPE, *President.*
       S. H. WALPOLE.
       B. DISRAELI.

COURTENAY, *Secretary.*

Orders similar to the above have also been issued to the following Unions and places:—

Abingdon	24th January, 1866.
Birkenhead	9th December, 1861.
Bristol	24th April, 1856.
Exeter	20th September, 1856.
Holyhead	18th May, 1858.
St. Luke, Middlesex	23rd January, 1856.
Mile End Old Town	4th March, 1861.
Newington, St. Mary	4th July, 1855.
Plymouth	3rd January, 1856.
Saddleworth	5th May, 1858.
Toxteth Park	{ 27th November, 1857. { 31st March, 1858.
Wharfedale	20th April, 1861.
Wetherby	13th April, 1861.

An Order regulating the administration of out-door relief in the Parish of St. Pancras was issued on the 21st August, 1856.

FORM OF SUPPLEMENTAL OUT-DOOR LABOUR TEST ORDER (a).

To the Guardians of the Poor *of the —— Union, in the Count— of ——;—*

To the Churchwardens and Overseers of the Poor of the several Parishes and Places comprised in the said Union;—

To the Clerk or Clerks to the Justices of the Petty Sessions held for the Division or Divisions in which the said Union is situate;—

And to all others whom it may concern.

In pursuance of the powers and authorities given in and by the Statutes in that case made and provided, We, the Poor Law Board, do hereby Order, Direct, and Declare, with respect to the Relief of the Poor in the —— Union, in the Count— of ——, as follows:—

Art. 1.—Every able-bodied male pauper who may receive relief from any Parish within the Union, and may be relieved out of the Workhouse, with the approbation of the Poor Law Board, according to the 6th Article of an Order of the Poor Law Commissioners, dated the 21st day of December, 1844, shall be relieved in the following manner: that is to say,—

Half at least of the relief given to such pauper shall be given in food, clothing, and other articles of necessity.

No such pauper shall receive relief from the Guardians of the Union, or any of their Officers, or any Overseer of

---

(a) With respect to this Order, see the Minute of the Poor Law Commissioners respecting the means of enforcing an out-door labour test, dated 31st October, 1842, 9th Annual Report, p. 381.

any Parish in the Union, while he is employed for wages or other hire or remuneration by any person; but every such pauper so relieved shall be set to work by the Guardians.

Art. 2.—The Guardians shall, within fourteen days after the day when this Order comes into force, and from time to time afterwards, as the Poor Law Board may require, report to the Poor Law Board the place or places at which able-bodied male paupers shall be so set to work in the Union, the sort or sorts of work in which they or any of them shall be employed, the times and mode of work, and all such other matters relating to the employment of such able-bodied paupers as the said Guardians shall deem material to be communicated to the Poor Law Board, or as the Poor Law Board shall require (a).

Art. 3.—If the Guardians of the Union shall depart, in any particular instance, from any of the regulations hereinbefore contained, and shall, within fifteen days after such departure, report the same and the grounds thereof to the Poor Law Board, and if the Poor Law Board shall approve of such departure, then the relief granted in such particular instance shall, if otherwise lawful, not be deemed to be unlawful, or be subject to be disallowed.

Art. 4.—Whenever the word "Parish" is used in this Order, it shall be taken to signify any place separately maintaining its own poor;

And whereas provision is made in the General Order of the said Poor Law Commissioners, bearing date the Twenty-fourth day of July, One thousand eight hundred and forty-seven, addressed, among others, to the Guardians of the Poor of the said Union, for the appointment of an Officer, to be termed a Superintendent of Out-door Labour, and for the continuance in office of such Officer, and it is expe-

---

(a) The 4 & 5 Wm. IV. c. 76, s. 28, enables the Guardians to provide "utensils, materials for setting the poor on work" in the Union, and also authorizes the charging the cost and expenses so incurred to the common fund of the Union.

As regards the enforcement of a task of work for poor persons relieved out of the Workhouse, see 29 & 30 Vict. c. 113, s. 15, *ante*, p. 75.

dient to provide for the suspension of such Officer on other occasions than those provided for by the said last-mentioned Order:

We do therefore further Order and Direct, that if at any time the number of able-bodied male paupers requiring relief shall be so small as to render the services of such an Officer unnecessary, the Guardians may suspend him from the performance of his duties until a further occasion shall arise.

Given under our Hand and Seal of Office, this —— day of ——, in the year One thousand eight hundred and sixty—.

———, *President.*

———, *Secretary.*

Supplemental Out-door Labour Test Orders have been issued to the following Unions and Places:—

Abergavenny	2nd June, 1842.
Alderbury	14th February, 1849.
Alresford	2nd June, 1847.
Altrincham	13th March, 1857.
Andover	18th December, 1846.
Ashby-de-la-Zouch	15th January, 1858.
Auckland	9th February, 1858.
Austell, St.	30th January, 1867.
Axbridge	2nd March, 1847.
Axminster	20th June, 1844.
Aylesbury	24th January, 1848.
Aylsham	13th January, 1844.
Bakewell	10th December, 1864.
Banbury	21st January, 1868.
Barnet	12th January, 1849.
Barnstaple	22nd May, 1847.
Barrow-on-Soar	2nd June, 1847.
Basford	28th May, 1847.
Battle	2nd June, 1847.
Beaminster	2nd March, 1849.
Bedminster	17th March, 1847.
Berwick-upon-Tweed	5th April, 1850.

Beverley	24th January, 1854.
Bideford	5th June, 1847.
Billericay	30th November, 1849.
Birmingham	16th January, 1850.
Bosmere and Claydon	2nd February, 1850.
Boston	3rd February, 1847.
Bradford (Wilts)	15th August, 1852, and 8th February, 1845.
Braintree	20th January, 1849.
Brampton	7th March, 1855.
Bridgnorth	23rd March, 1858.
Bridgewater	21st December, 1846.
Bridport	6th March, 1848.
Bromsgrove	21st May, 1842, and 21st April, 1845.
Buntingford	24th January, 1843.
Calne	4th February, 1845.
Cambridge	3rd February, 1848.
Camelford	27th July, 1849.
Cardiff	31st December, 1857.
Catherington	2nd June, 1847.
Caxton and Arrington	12th January, 1847.
Chapel-en-le-Frith	21st May, 1842.
Chard	19th March, 1845.
Cheltenham	24th December, 1846.
Chepstow	27th March, 1858.
Chertsey	17th December, 1847.
Chesterfield	17th June, 1848.
Chesterton	14th February, 1849.
Chichester	27th March, 1852.
Chippenham	15th March, 1847.
Chipping Norton	22nd December, 1846.
Chipping Sodbury	23rd February, 1847.
Clifton	11th March, 1847.
Clutton	7th December, 1849.
Cockermouth	5th August, 1842.
Colchester	16th February, 1861.
Columb, St., Major	31st May, 1847.
Congleton	8th February, 1862.
Crediton	21st May, 1847.
Cuckfield	16th July, 1842, and 19th March, 1845.
Darlington	18th September, 1866.

Depwade	7th February, 1854.
Derby	12th December, 1867.
Downham	24th January, 1854.
Dudley	8th July, 1842, and 21st April, 1845.
Dunmow	31st May, 1847.
Dursley	1st April, 1847.
Easington	30th April, 1842.
Easingwold	13th February, 1850.
East Grinstead	2nd February, 1850.
East Stonehouse	16th December, 1848.
Ely	19th January, 1854.
Evesham	16th January, 1850.
Faith, St.	6th January, 1848.
Falmouth	1st May, 1849.
Faversham	25th January, 1868.
Foleshill	13th December, 1847.
Freebridge Lynn	31st January, 1854.
Glossop	19th January, 1848.
Gloucester	1st April, 1847.
Goole	24th November, 1849.
Gravesend and Milton	12th February, 1855.
Guildford	2nd June, 1847.
Guiltcross	17th March, 1853.
Hailsham	17th December, 1842, and 19th March, 1845.
Halstead	20th January, 1849.
Hambledon	5th June, 1847.
Hayfield	4th February, 1862.
Hartismere	24th January, 1850.
Helston	29th January, 1846.
Highworth and Swindon	28th January, 1845.
Hinckley	15th April, 1863.
Holbeach	25th January, 1854.
Holsworthy	31st July, 1849.
Horsham	25th January, 1845.
Hoxne	10th February, 1846.
Huntingdon	25th January, 1854.
Ipswich	22nd February, 1855.
Ives, St.	13th January, 1854.
Kettering	25th January, 1847.
Kidderminster	12th January, 1849.
Kingsbridge	31st May, 1847.

King's Norton	7th February, 1849.
Leek	17th December, 1857.
Leighton Buzzard	3rd March, 1855.
Linton	7th January, 1854.
Longtown	30th July, 1842.
Loughborough	9th December, 1857.
Luton	28th November, 1854.
Lymington	12th January, 1849.
Macclesfield	3rd June, 1856.
Maidstone	27th February, 1857.
Maldon	7th December, 1847.
Malmesbury	24th January, 1850.
Mansfield	28th May, 1847.
Melksham	30th March, 1847.
Mere	25th February, 1847.
Mildenhall	16th January, 1854.
Nantwich	23rd January, 1843.
Newark	24th January, 1854.
Newbury	14th January, 1848.
New Forest	19th January, 1848.
Newmarket	30th December, 1846.
Newport (Monmouth)	12th January, 1849.
Newport Pagnell	15th December, 1843.
Newport (Salop)	15th July, 1843.
Newtown and Llanidloes	25th June, 1857.
Northampton	28th January, 1848.
North Aylesford	25th January, 1868.
North Witchford	24th January, 1854.
Nuneaton	30th December, 1847.
Ongar	22nd June, 1847.
Ormskirk	20th June, 1862.
Oxford	19th December, 1848.
Peterborough	18th March, 1851.
Petersfield	2nd June, 1847.
Pontypool	5th June, 1852.
Poole	21st January, 1850.
Portsea Island	18th February, 1858.
Richmond (Yorks)	9th September, 1842.
Risbridge	21st January, 1850.
Romford	24th January, 1854.
Romsey	24th December, 1866.
Royston	10th January, 1854.
Rye	9th July, 1842.

Saffron Walden	25th January, 1854.
Sculcoates	30th January, 1862.
Shepton Mallet	7th February, 1844.
Skipton	18th June, 1842.
South Molton	29th October, 1846.
South Shields	2nd September, 1843.
Spalding	10th December, 1849.
Stockton	12th January, 1858.
Stoke-upon-Trent	28th February, 1860.
Stourbridge	21st April, 1845.
Stratton	28th July, 1849.
Sudbury	25th February, 1848.
Taunton	20th January, 1849.
Tavistock	21st May, 1847.
Teesdale	15th April, 1848.
Tendring	8th February, 1856.
Tewkesbury	31st July, 1861.
Thame	11th January, 1847.
Thetford	7th April, 1852.
Thornbury	16th February, 1848.
Ticehurst	4th June, 1847.
Tiverton	22nd May, 1847.
Tonbridge	13th February, 1857.
Torrington	28th November, 1846.
Tynemouth	19th February, 1850.
Uppingham	24th January, 1850.
Uxbridge	6th January, 1848.
Walsall	21st April, 1845.
Walsingham	30th January, 1861.
Wangford	23rd December, 1848.
Ware	2nd March, 1855.
Wareham and Purbeck	10th January, 1848.
Warwick	21st December, 1867.
Watford	8th March, 1849.
Wellington (Salop)	20th March, 1843.
Wellington (Somerset)	22nd March, 1847.
Wells	13th March, 1847.
Wem	24th January, 1850.
West Bromwich	21st April, 1845.
Westbury and Whorwelsdown	5th August, 1842.
West Ham	16th January, 1854.
Weymouth	31st December, 1867.
Whitby	28th November, 1848.

Whitehaven	30th July, 1842.
Wigton	2nd March, 1855.
Wilton	16th December, 1848.
Wincanton	2nd March, 1847.
Windsor	12th January, 1849.
Wirral	3rd May, 1849.
Wisbeach	13th January, 1854.
Witney	1st February, 1848.
Woburn	6th February, 1868.
Wokingham	30th December, 1846.
Wolstanton and Burslem	7th March, 1862.
Woodbridge	11th June, 1847.
Woodstock	26th January, 1858.
Worcester	20th January, 1849.
Wycombe	9th November, 1849.
Yarmouth, Great	28th February, 1855.

DUTIES OF OVERSEERS ORDER.

(22nd *April*, 1842.)

To the Guardians of the Poor *of the several* **Unions** *named in the Schedules hereunto annexed ;—*

To the Churchwardens and Overseers of the several Parishes and Places comprised within the said Unions ;

To the Clerk or Clerks to the Justices of the Petty Sessions held for the Division or Divisions in which the Parishes and Places comprised within the said Unions are situate ;—

And to all others whom it may concern.

WE, the Poor Law Commissioners, in pursuance of the authorities vested in Us by an Act passed in the fifth year of the Reign of his late Majesty King William the Fourth, intituled "*An Act for the Amendment and better Administration of the Laws relating to the Poor in England and Wales,*" do hereby Order, Direct, and Declare, with respect to each and every of the Unions named in the Schedule hereunto annexed, as follows :—

DUTIES OF THE OVERSEERS.

Art. 1.—If any Overseer of the Poor of any Parish shall, in any case of sudden and urgent necessity (*a*), have given temporary relief to any poor person in articles of necessity, or, in any case of sudden and dangerous illness, shall have given an order for medical relief, the said Overseer shall forthwith report such case in writing to the Relieving

---

(*a*) See 4 & 5 Wm. IV. c. 76, s. 54.

Officer of the district or to the Board of Guardians of the Union, and the amount of such relief, or the fact of having made such order.

Art. 2.—If any Overseer of the Poor of any Parish receive an Order under the hands and seal of two Justices, according to the provisions of the said Act (*a*), directing relief to be given to any aged or infirm person, without such person being required to reside in any Workhouse, he shall forthwith transmit the same to the Relieving Officer of the district to be laid before the Guardians at their next meeting, that they may be enabled without delay to give to the Relieving Officer the necessary directions as to the amount and nature of the relief to be given.

Art. 3.—If any Overseer receive an order for medical relief from any Justice in case of sudden and dangerous illness (*b*), he shall, as soon as may be after complying with such order, report the fact of his having received the same, and the manner in which he has complied with it, in writing to the Relieving Officer of the District, or to the Board of Guardians of the Union.

Art. 4.—To perform such duties in connection with the Election of Guardians for the Union as may be imposed upon the Overseers by any Regulations of the Poor Law Commissioners in force at the time (*c*).

Art. 5.—And We do further Order and Direct the Overseers of the Poor of every Parish in the Union—

> Firstly.—From time to time to provide *Rate Books* according to the Form (A.) hereunto annexed; and duly and punctually to make the entries therein of the several matters mentioned in the headings of the several columns of the said Form; and to cause every rate for

---

(*a*) See 4 & 5 Wm. IV. c. 76, s. 27; *Reg.* v. *Totnes*, 14 L. J. R. (N.S.) M. C. 148; 7 A. and E. (N.S.) 690; and *Reg.* v. *Durham*, 4 N. S. C. 437.
(*b*) See 4 & 5 Wm. IV. c. 76, s. 54, and Art. 215, No. 7, p. 186, *ante*.
(*c*) See Arts. 1, 5, and 26 of Consolidated Order, *ante*.

the relief of the poor in the Parish, and the allowance of such rate by the Justices, to be recorded in the said Rate Book (*d*).

Secondly.—To pay over from time to time, out of the poor-rates collected, all such sums as by any Order of the Guardians expressed to them in writing, according to the Form set forth in the Order of the Poor Law Commissioners, bearing date the twentieth day of April instant, shall be directed to be provided from the poor-rates of the Parish; and to pay over such sums to such person or persons, at such times and places as by the same Order shall be directed, and to take the receipt of such person or persons; and to produce such order and such receipt as their vouchers for such payments before the Auditor of the said Union in passing their quarterly accounts (*e*).

Art. 5.—Thirdly.—(*This had reference to the accounts of the Overseers, and it is not now in force.*)

Art. 5.—Fourthly.—To enter in some book, to be from time to time provided for that purpose, the names and addresses of the owners and proxies who shall send statements of their claims to vote, and the assessment of the poor-rate on the property in respect whereof

---

(*d*) The form of Rate Book prescribed by this Order was altered by the Poor Law Accounts Order of the 17th March, 1847; and again by an Order of the 18th November, 1850, to meet the requirements of the Small Tenements Rating Act, 13 & 14 Vict. c. 99. The new Order of Accounts of 14th January, 1867, *post*, prescribes the form of Rate Book now to be used.

(*e*) The Order here referred to has been rescinded by the Consolidated General Order of the 24th July, 1847, Arts. 81, 82, and 83 of which contained provisions regarding making of Contribution Orders on the Overseers. The form in which the Contribution Order is required to be made is now prescribed by the order of the Poor Law Board, dated 26th February, 1866. The Overseers should be careful to pay money to the Treasurer of the Union, in obedience to an Order of the Guardians of the Union, only upon the receipt of the Treasurer himself; as otherwise, if the money be misapplied before it comes into the hands of the Treasurer, the Overseers may be held personally responsible for the amount; besides which, any other receipt but that of the Treasurer himself will not suffice at the audit.

they respectively claim to vote, which book may be kept in the Form marked (B.) hereto annexed (*a*).

EXPLANATION OF TERMS.

Art. 6.—Whenever the word "Union" is used in this Order, it shall be taken to include not only an Union of Parishes formed under the provisions of the hereinbefore recited Act, but also any union of Parishes incorporated or united for the relief or maintenance of the Poor under any Local Act of Parliament.

Art. 7.—Whenever the word "Guardian" is used in this Order, it shall be taken to include not only Guardians appointed or entitled to act under the provisions of the said hereinbefore recited Act, but also any Governors, Directors, Managers, or Acting Guardians entitled to act in the ordering of relief to the poor from the poor-rates under any Local Act of Parliament (*b*).

Art. 8.—Whenever the word "Parish" is used in this Order, it shall be taken to include any place maintaining its own poor, whether parochial or extra-parochial (*c*).

(*a*) With respect to the duties of the Overseers in relation to the annual elections of Guardians, see Arts. 1, 5, and 26 of the Consolidated General Order of 24th July, 1847, *ante*.

The Overseers may object to the names of any persons entered on the Register of Owners whom they shall believe to be dead, or to be disqualified from voting as such Owners, and shall give public notice (on or near the doors of all churches or chapels within the Parish, and at all the usual places of affixing notices of Parochial business, 7 & 8 Vict. c. 101, s. 15) of the names to which they have made objections on some day between the 5th and 15th days of February, and shall send a copy of such notice to the Clerk of the Guardians, who shall hear and decide such objections at the time of his revision of the Register, in like manner as in the case of other objections (30 & 31 Vict. c. 106, s. 7).

The Overseers may from time to time make a fresh Register of Owners who have claimed to vote for Guardians and of Proxies as they shall find necessary, causing the names to be copied from the former Register, and the two to be carefully collated and verified. (*Ibid*, s. 8.)

(*b*) This latter definition of the word Guardian has reference to the Incorporations mentioned on the next page.

(*c*) See 20 Vict. c. 19, as to places which were formerly extra-parochial, but which are now parishes for the purposes mentioned in that Act; also 29 & 30 Vict. c. 113, s. 18.

Art. 9.—Whenever the word "Overseer" is used in this Order, it shall be taken to include any person acting or legally bound to act in the discharge of any of the duties usually performed by Overseers of the Poor, so far as such duties are referred to in this Order.

FORM (A).

[This Form is now superseded, see the General Order for Accounts, *post.*]

FORM (B.) (*See Art. 5, Fourthly.*)

Book for Registry of Owners of Property and Proxies.

—— Union. Parish of ——.

No.	Name of Order.	Address.	Property in respect whereof right to vote is claimed.	No. of reference to Rate Book.	Aggregate Amount of Assessment.	Name of Proxy.	Address of Proxy.	No.	Date on which Claim received.

We do certify that the above is a full and correct register and entry of the claims to vote of owners of property and proxies in the said Parish.

(Signed) } Overseers.

Schedule containing the Names of the Unions to which the present Order applies.

(The Unions in this Schedule are those specified in the Schedule to the General Consolidated Order of 24th July, 1847, *ante*, p. 206, [excepting Ashbourne, Ashton-under-Lyne, Farnham, Fulham, and Rochdale], and also Bury St. Edmunds, East and West Flegg, Forehoe, Mutford and Lothingland, and Tunstead and Happing Incorporations.)

Given under our Hands and Seal of Office, this Twenty-second day of April, in the year One thousand eight hundred and forty-two.

(Signed) G. C. LEWIS.
EDMUND W. HEAD.

A General Order similar to the foregoing was issued on the 11th May, 1842, to the following single Parishes:—

Alston-with-Garrigill.	St. Mary, Lambeth.
East Stonehouse.	St. Mary Magdalen, Bermondsey.
St. George-the-Martyr, Southwark.	St. Mary, Rotherhithe.
	St. Matthew, Bethnal Green.
St. George-in-the-East.	Stoke-upon-Trent.
St. Giles, Camberwell.	Whittlesea, St. Mary and St. Andrew.
Liverpool.	
St. Luke, Chelsea.	Great Yarmouth.
St. Martin-in-the-Fields (a).	

On the 22nd February, 1858, a General Order, nearly similar to the foregoing, was issued by the Poor Law Board to the following Parishes, Townships, and Hamlet, namely:—

Parish of Paddington.	Township of Leeds.
Parish of Saint John, Hampstead.	Township of Manchester.
	Township of Saddleworth.
Parish of Saint Mary Abbott's, Kensington.	Township of Toxteth Park.
	Hamlet of Mile End Old Town.

And on the 28th April, 1858, a General Order similar to that of the 22nd February, 1858, was issued to the Unions which were declared subsequently to the issue of the General Order of 22nd April, 1842; namely,—

Ashbourne.	Kirkby Moorside.
Barnsley.	Knaresborough.
Barton-upon-Irwell.	North Bierley.
Bedwellty.	Oldham.
Farnham.	Penistone.
Fulham.	Prestwich.
Gower.	Ripon.
Great Ouseburn.	Rochdale.
Hawarden.	Samford.
Hemsworth.	Whitchurch (Salop.)
Holyhead.	

(a) Since added to the Strand Union.

FORM OF COLLECTOR OF POOR-RATES ORDER.

To the Guardians of the Poor *of the* —— **Union** (*a*), *in the County of* —— ;—

To the Churchwardens and Overseers of the Poor of the Parish of ——, *in the said Union;*—

To the Clerk or Clerks to the Justices of the Petty Sessions held for the Division or Divisions in which the said Union is situate;

And to all others whom it may concern.

WE, the Poor Law Board, acting under the authority of the several Statutes in that behalf made and provided, having received an application from the Guardians of the Poor of the —— Union, in the County of ——, to direct the appointment of a paid Collector of the Poor-rates in the Parish of —— within the said Union, hereby Order and Direct the said Guardians, *within one calendar month from the date hereof,* to appoint a fit and proper person to collect the rates assessed for the relief of the Poor in the said Parish, to be termed Collector of the Poor-rates.

And We further Order, with respect to such appointment, as follows; that is to say (*b*),—

(*a*) The instances in which Orders for the appointment of Collectors of Poor-rates for individual parishes have been issued are so numerous that it is considered unnecessary to insert a list of them in this work.

(*b*) In many instances the Order for the appointment of a Collector of Poor-rates, and prescribing his duties, etc., varies from the present form of Order. In each case it is therefore necessary that the Order actually issued should be consulted.

Mode of Appointment.

Art. 1.—Every Officer to be appointed under this Order shall be appointed by a majority of the Guardians present at a meeting of the Board, and voting on the question of such appointment.

Every such appointment shall, as soon as the same has been made, be reported to the Poor Law Board by the Clerk.

Art. 2.—Previous to an appointment to the aforesaid Office being made under this Order, a notice that the question of making such appointment will be brought before the Board of Guardians, shall be given and entered on their minutes, at one of the two ordinary meetings of the said Board next preceding the meeting at which the appointment is made, or an advertisement, giving notice of the consideration of such appointment, shall be inserted in some public newspaper, by the direction of the Guardians, at least seven days before the day on which such appointment is made. Provided that no such notice or advertisement shall be necessary for the appointment of a temporary substitute.

Qualification.

Art. 3.—Every person who shall be appointed to the office of Collector under this Order shall agree to give one month's notice previous to resigning the office, or to forfeit one month's amount of salary, to be deducted, as liquidated damages, from the amount of salary due at the time of such resignation.

Duties of the Officer.

Art. 4.—The duties of the Collector shall be:—

No. 1. To assist the Churchwardens and Overseers in making, assessing, and levying the Poor-rates of the said Parish.

No. 2. To collect the Poor-rates from the parties assessed thereto in the said Parish (*a*).

(*a*) The Collector is not bound to take the Rate Book with him when

Art. 4.—No. 3. To assist the said Churchwardens and Overseers in filling up receipts, keeping all books, and making all returns which relate to any matter concerning the Poor-rates of the said Parish.

No. 4. At all times, when required by such Churchwardens and Overseers, to produce to them respectively the Rate Books and other Account Books in his custody relating to the said Parish, and to balance the said rates, and to furnish the said Churchwardens and Overseers of the Poor and the Board of Guardians with a true list of all defaulters in the payment of Poor-rates due to such Parish, and under their direction to institute and attend to proceedings against such defaulters (*b*).

No. 5. To attend the meetings of the Guardians of the said Union, when required by them, and to obey all lawful orders and directions of such Guardians, and of the majority of the said Churchwardens and Overseers of the Poor (*c*).

No. 6. To perform all the duties prescribed by the Poor Law Commissioners in their General Order dated the

---

he collects the rate; but any ratepayer can obtain an inspection of the books in the manner provided for by 17 Geo. II. c. 3, s. 2; 17 Geo. II. c. 38, s. 1; 6 & 7 Wm. IV. c. 96, s. 5; and 6 & 7 Vict. c. 18, s. 16. The duties of the Collector under this Order are confined to the collection of the Poor-rate; and therefore it forms no part of his duty to make and collect a gas-rate under the 3 & 4 Wm. IV. c. 90. As regards the collection of the county-rate in a parish situate partly within and partly without a borough, see the provision in the 15 & 16 Vict. c. 81, s. 32.

(*b*) The Collector, it will be perceived, is to institute and attend to proceedings against defaulters under the direction of the Churchwardens and Overseers. He should therefore do so under the direction of the majority of the Overseers. (See 7 & 8 Vict. c. 101, s. 61.) According to the form in 12 Vict. c. 14, the summons should, however, be in the name of the Overseers.

(*c*) With reference to this regulation, the Poor Law Board say that a direction of the Guardians to the Collectors to produce their Rate and other books when they attend before the Guardians, appears to be a "lawful Order" within the meaning of the regulation. (56 O. C. (N. s.) 67.)

Seventeenth day of March, One thousand eight hundred and forty-seven, and in the General Order of the Poor Law Law Board bearing date the Sixteenth day of March, One thousand eight hundred and fifty-four (*a*), so far as the same relate to the office of Collector, and all Rules, Orders, and Regulations to be hereafter issued by the Poor Law Board applicable to his office.

REMUNERATION OF THE OFFICER.

Art. 5. The Board of Guardians shall pay to the officer appointed to the office of Collector under this Order a salary of ―― pounds per annum, and charge the same to the said Parish (*b*).

Art. 6.—The salary of such Officer shall be payable up to the day on which he ceases to hold such office, and no longer, and shall be paid by quarterly payments at the several quarters ending at the usual Feast Days in the year, namely, Christmas Day, Lady Day, Midsummer Day, and Michaelmas Day, with a proportionate sum to be paid to his executors or administrators in case he shall die while holding such office; but it shall be competent for the Guardians to defer, in whole or in part, the payment of the salary of such Collector until his accounts shall have been audited and allowed by the Auditor, after which audit and allowance the sum due up to the date of his accounts so audited shall forthwith be paid.

Art. 7.—No Collector who may be suspended, and who shall, upon such suspension, resign, or be removed by the Poor Law Board, shall be entitled to any salary from the date of such suspension; and no such Officer who shall be

---

(*a*) This must now be read with reference to the Accounts Order of 14th January, 1868, *post*.

(*b*) Sometimes the Order provides that the Collector shall be paid by a poundage on the Poor-rates collected. It may be stated here that the salary or other remuneration of the Collector appointed under this Order must be paid by the Guardians, and charged by them to the particular parish, and not by the Overseers of the Parish.

temporarily suspended from his office, by reason of his services not being required, shall be entitled to any salary pending such temporary suspension.

SECURITY.

Art. 8.—The person appointed to such office shall give a bond in such penal sum as the said Guardians shall think fit, in the names of himself and two sufficient sureties, not being officers of the aforesaid Union, conditioned for the due and faithful performance of the duties of the office; and every such Collector shall give immediate notice to the said Guardians of the death, insolvency, or bankruptcy of either of such sureties, and shall, when required by the said Guardians, produce a certificate, signed by two householders, that his sureties are alive and believed by them to be solvent, and shall supply a fresh surety in the place of any such surety who may die, or become bankrupt or insolvent. Provided that the Guardians may, if they think fit, take the security of any society or company expressly authorized by Statute to guarantee or secure the faithful discharge of the duties of any Poor Law Officer.

CONTINUANCE IN OFFICE AND SUSPENSION OF OFFICER. —SUPPLY OF VACANCY.

Art. 9.—Every Collector shall hold the said office until he shall die or resign or be removed by the Poor Law Board, or be proved to be insane by evidence which such Board shall deem sufficient; and upon such death, resignation, removal, or insanity of any such Officer, the said Guardians shall give notice thereof to the Poor Law Board, and proceed to appoint some person in his place, according to the provisions of this Order; and in every case of a resignation, the said Guardians shall transmit to the Poor Law Board a statement of the cause of such resignation, so far as it may be known to them.

Art. 10.—The said Guardians may, at their discretion,

suspend from the discharge of his duties any such Collector, and shall, in case of every such suspension, forthwith report the same, together with the cause thereof, to the Poor Law Board, for their decision thereon; and if the Poor Law Board remove the suspension of such Collector by the Guardians, he shall forthwith resume the performance of his duties.

Art. 11.—If any such Collector be at any time prevented, by sickness or accident, or other sufficient reason, from the performance of his duties, the Guardians may appoint a fit person to act as his temporary substitute, and may pay such person a reasonable compensation for his services; and every such appointment, with a statement of the circumstances which have led to it, shall be reported to the Poor Law Board, as soon as the same shall have been made, by the Clerk to the Guardians.

Given under our Hand and Seal of Office, etc.

ORDER RELATING TO COLLECTORS OF POOR-RATES.

(15th *November*, 1867.)

𝕿o t𝖍e 𝕲uar𝖉ians of t𝖍e 𝕻oor *of the several* 𝖀nions *named in the Schedule hereunto annexed;—*

    To the Churchwardens and Overseers of the Poor of the several Parishes comprised in the said Unions;—

    To the Clerk or Clerks to the Justices of the Petty Sessions held for the Division or Divisions in which the said Unions are situate;—

And to all others whom it may concern.

WHEREAS the Poor Law Commissioners and the Poor Law Board respectively have, by divers Orders in that behalf heretofore issued, ordered the Guardians of the Poor of the several Unions named in the Schedule hereunto annexed to appoint Collectors of the Poor-rates, or Assistant Overseers with the duty of collecting the Poor-rates, in all or some of the Parishes comprised in such Unions, and have specified the duties to be executed by such officers, and have regulated the amount of salaries payable to them, and the time and mode of payment thereof, and the proportions in which the respective Parishes for which they are appointed shall contribute to the payment,

AND WHEREAS the said Board have, by a General Order bearing date the 14th day of January, 1867, and by sundry other Orders, prescribed the mode in which such Collectors and Assistant Overseers shall make out and keep their accounts in relation to the collection of the Poor-rates,

AND WHEREAS by reason of the provisions of "The Representation of the People Act, 1867," the labour incurred in the making out and collecting of the Poor-rate in certain Parishes may be increased, and a greater demand may be made upon such Collectors and Assistant Overseers as aforesaid, in respect of their services in such Parishes; and in such cases it is desirable that an increase should be made in the salaries or other compensation paid to the Collectors, and Assistant Overseers appointed and acting under such Orders in any Parish affected by the provisions of the said Act in respect of such additional services,

Now THEREFORE, We, the Poor Law Board, acting under the powers given in and by the Statutes in that behalf, do hereby Order as follows; that is to say,— (a)

Art. 1.—The Guardians of the Poor of the said several Unions may, if they think proper, make a reasonable increase in the salaries or other compensation now legally paid by them to such Officers as aforesaid of such amount and for such a period as to the said Guardians shall appear suitable, and may from time to time renew, alter, or increase such compensation.

Art. 2.—Every Resolution of the Guardians under this Order shall be reported to the Poor Law Board for their approval, and shall be of no force until approved of by them.

Art. 3.—If the Poor Law Board think proper at any time to direct the increase authorized to be made by this Order in any case to be discontinued, the payment of such increase shall cease from such time as the Board shall specify.

Art. 4.—Provided, that if the Board of Guardians shall deem it expedient to make any change in the Districts for which any such Collector or Assistant Overseer shall be now acting, and such Officer, and, when necessary, his Sureties, shall consent thereto, their proposal shall be submitted to the Poor Law Board, and if they approve of the same

---

(a) With reference to this Order, see the Circular Letter of the Poor Law Board, dated 16th November, 1867, in their 20th Annual Report.

such change may be effected either with an Order of the Board or without it, as the case may require.

Art. 5.—Every such Collector or Assistant Overseer shall give his aid and assistance to the Overseers of the Parish for which he acts in making out and serving the notices of Poor-rates in arrear required to be made out and served by the 28th section of the said Act, and in making out the list of persons in arrear of their Poor-rates required by the 29th section of the said Act to be made out and served by such Overseers respectively.

Art. 6.—Notwithstanding anything herein contained, the provisions of the said General and other Orders as to the keeping of the accounts of the said Officers, and of every other Order relating to the duties of such Officers, and the powers, authorities, and duties of the said Guardians, and of the Overseers of the Parishes for which they are acting, shall continue in full force.

Art. 7.—The word "*Unions*" in this Order shall be taken to include not only Unions of Parishes formed under the provisions of "The Poor Law Amendment Act, 1834," but also Unions of Parishes incorporated or united for the relief or maintenance of the Poor under any Local Act of Parliament.

The word "*Guardians*" in this Order shall be taken to include not only Guardians appointed or entitled to act under the provisions of the said "Poor Law Amendment Act, 1834," but also any Guardians appointed or entitled to act as Managers of the Poor under any Local Act of Parliament.

Whenever the word "*Parish*" is used in this Order it shall be taken to signify any place for which a separate Poor-rate is or can be made, or for which a separate Overseer is or can be appointed.

SCHEDULE.

Names of Unions to which this Order applies (a).

Aberystwith.
Abingdon.
Amersham.
Andover.
Anglesey.
Asaph, St.
Ashford, East.
Aston.
Atcham.

Bangor & Beaumaris.
Bath.
Battle.
Bedford.
Bedminster.
Berwick-upon-Tweed.
Beverley.
Birkenhead.
Blackburn.
Blean.
Bodmin.
Bolton.
Bosmere and Claydon.
Boston.
Boughton, Great.
Bradford (York).
Bramley.
Brecknock.
Bridge.
Bridgend and Cowbridge.
Buckingham.
Bury.

Caistor.
Cambridge.
Cardiff.

Cardigan.
Carlisle.
Carmarthen.
Carnarvon.
Cheltenham.
Chichester.
Chippenham.
Chorlton.
Christchurch.
Cirencester.
Clifton.
Clitheroe.
Cockermouth.
Colchester.
Conway.
Cookham.
Cuckfield.

Darlington.
Derby.
Devizes.
Dewsbury.
Doncaster.
Dover.
Dudley.
Durham.

Eastry.
Ecclesall Bierlow.
Elham.
Ellesmere.
Evesham.

Falmouth.
Frome.
Fulham.

Gainsborough.
Gateshead.
Gloucester.
Gravesend and Milton.
Guildford.
Guisborough.

Hackney.
Halifax.
Hartismere.
Hartlepool.
Haverfordwest.
Headington.
Hereford.
Hertford.
Highworth & Swindon.
Holborn.
Holyhead.
Holywell.
Honiton.
Horsham.
Huddersfield.
Huntingdon.

Ipswich.

Kendal.
Kidderminster.
Kingsbridge.
King's Norton.

Launceston.
Leicester.
Leominster.
Lewisham.
Liskeard.
Llanelly.

(a) The Unions in this Schedule comprise one or more Parishes within a Parliamentary Borough.

London, City.
London, East.
London, West.
Lymington.

Macclesfield.
Machynlleth.
Madeley.
Maidstone.
Malton.
Mansfield.
Medway.
Merthyr Tydvil.
Monmouth.
Morpeth.

Neath.
Newcastle-under-Lyme.
Newhaven.
Newport (Monmouth).
Newton Abbot.
Newtown and Llanidloes.
Northallerton.
Northampton.
North Aylesford.
Nottingham.

Olave's, St.
Oldham.
Oxford.

Pembroke.
Penzance.
Peterborough.
Petersfield.
Pontefract.

Pontypridd.
Poole.
Portsea Island.
Preston.
Prestwich.
Pwllheli.

Reading.
Rhayader.
Richmond (York).
Ripon.
Romney Marsh.
Ruthin.
Rye.

Salford.
Saviour's, St.
Scarborough.
Sculcoates.
Sheffield.
Shiffnal.
Southampton.
South Shields.
South Stoneham.
Southwell.
Stafford.
Stamford.
Stepney.
Steyning.
Stockport.
Stockton.
Strand.
Stroud.
Sunderland.
Swansea.

Tamworth.

Taunton.
Tavistock.
Tewkesbury.
Thakeham.
Thetford.
Thirsk.
Thomas, St.
Tiverton.
Truro.
Tynemouth.

Wakefield.
Walsall.
Wareham and Purbeck.
Warrington.
Warwick.
Wells.
West Bromwich.
Westbury and Whorwelsdown.
West Derby.
West Hampnett.
Weymouth.
Whitby.
Whitechapel.
Whitehaven.
Wigan.
Wilton.
Winchester, New.
Windsor.
Wolstanton and Burslem.
Wolverhampton.
Woodbridge.
Worcester.
Worksop.
Wycombe.

Given under our Hands and Seal of Office, this Fifteenth day of November, in the year One thousand eight hundred and sixty-seven.

DEVON, *President*.
B. DISRAELI.
GATHORNE HARDY.

G. SCLATER BOOTH, *Secretary*.

APPRENTICESHIP ORDER.

(29*th January*, 1845.)

To the Guardians of the Poor *of the several* **Unions** *and of the several* **Parishes** *named in the Schedule hereunto annexed, and the Officers of such Unions and Parishes ;—*

> *To the Churchwardens and Overseers of the several Parishes and Places comprised within the said Unions, and of the several other Parishes named in the said Schedule ;—*

> *To the Clerk or Clerks to the Justices of the Petty Sessions held for the Division or Divisions in which the Parishes and Places comprised within the said Unions, and the said other Parishes named in the said Schedule, are situate ;—*

And to all others whom it may concern.

IN pursuance of the powers vested in us by an Act passed in the fifth year of the reign of his late Majesty King William the Fourth, intituled "*An Act for the Amendment and better Administration of the Laws relating to the Poor in England and Wales,*" and an Act passed in the seventh and eighth year of the reign of her present Majesty Queen Victoria, intituled "*An Act for the further Amendment of the Laws relating to the Poor in England,*" We, the Poor Law Commissioners, do make the following Rules and Regulations in regard to the Apprenticing of Poor Children of the several Unions named in the Schedule A. hereunto annexed, and of the Parishes named in the Schedule B. hereunto annexed.

THE PARTIES.

Art. 1.—No child under the age of *nine* years shall be bound apprentice;

And no child that cannot read and write his own name.

No child shall be so bound to a person who is not a Housekeeper, or assessed to the Poor Rate in his own name;

- Or who is a journeyman, or a person not carrying on trade or business on his own account;
- Or who is under the age of twenty-one;
- Or a married woman.

THE PREMIUM.

Art. 2.—No premium other than clothing for the apprentice shall be given upon the binding of any person above the age of *fourteen*, unless such person be maimed, deformed, or suffering from some permanent bodily infirmity, so that the nature of the work or trade which such person is fit to perform or exercise is restricted.

Art. 3.—Where any premium is given, it shall consist in part of clothes supplied to the apprentice at the commencement of the binding, and in part of money, one moiety whereof shall be paid to the master at the binding, and the residue at the termination of the first year of the binding.

TERM.

Art. 4.—No apprentice shall be bound for more than *eight* years.

CONSENT.

Art. 5.—No person above *fourteen* years of age shall be so bound without his *consent*;

And no child under the age of *sixteen* years shall be so bound without the consent of the father of such child, or if the father be dead, or be disqualified to give such consent, as hereinafter provided, or if such child be a bastard, without the consent of the mother, if living, of such child.

Provided, that where the parent of such child, whose consent would be otherwise requisite, is transported beyond the seas, or is in the custody of the law, having been convicted of some *felony*, or for the space of six calendar months before the time of executing the indenture has deserted such child, or for such space of time has been in the service of Her Majesty, or of the East India Company, in foreign parts, such parent, if the father, shall be deemed to be disqualified as hereinbefore stated, and if it be the mother, no such consent shall be required.

PLACE OF SERVICE.

Art. 6.—No child shall be bound to a master whose place of business, whereat the child is to work and live, shall be distant more than *thirty* miles from the place in which the child is residing at the time of the binding;

Unless in any particular case the Poor Law Commissioners shall, on application to them, otherwise permit.

PRELIMINARIES TO THE BINDING.

Art. 7.—If the child, whom it is proposed to bind apprentice, be in the Workhouse, and under the age of *fourteen*, the Guardians shall require a certificate in writing from the Medical Officer of the Workhouse, or from some Medical Man duly licensed to practise, as to the fitness in regard to bodily health and strength of such child to be bound apprentice to the proposed trade, and shall also ascertain from the Master of the Workhouse the capacity of the child for such binding in other respects.

Art. 8.—If the child be not in the Workhouse, but in the Union or Parish, by the Guardians of which it is proposed that it shall be bound, a Relieving Officer or some other person authorized by the persons proposing to bind such child, shall examine into the circumstances of the case, the condition of the child, and of his parents, if any, and the residence of the proposed master, the nature of his trade, the number of other apprentices, if any, then bound to him, and generally as to the fitness of the particular binding, and shall report the result of his inquiry to the Board of Guardians.

Art. 9.—If the Board of Guardians think proper to proceed with the binding, they shall, when the child is under the age of *fourteen*, direct such child to be taken to a Medical Man duly licensed to practise, to be examined as to his fitness in respect of bodily health and strength for the proposed trade or business; in order that such Medical Man may certify in writing according to his judgment in the matter, which certificate shall be produced, previously to the binding, to the Guardians.

Art. 10.—If the child be residing in some other Parish or Union, the Guardians who propose to bind him shall not proceed to do so unless they receive such a report as is required in Art. 8 from the Relieving Officer or some other Officer administering the relief of the poor of the district in which such child is residing, and a certificate from some medical practitioner of the neighbourhood of the child's residence to the effect required in Art. 9.

Art. 11.—When a premium is proposed to be given, in a case within the provision of Art. 2, the Guardians shall require a certificate in writing of some medical practitioner, certifying that the person is maimed, deformed, or disabled, to the extent specified in such Article, and shall cause a copy of such certificate to be entered on their minutes before they proceed to execute the indenture.

Art. 12.—When such certificate, as is required by Articles 7, 9, and 10, is received, or in case from the age of the child no such certificate is required, the Guardians shall direct that the child, and the proposed master, or some person on his behalf, and in case the child be under the age of *sixteen*, the parent or person in whose custody such child shall be then living, shall attend some meeting of the Board to be then appointed.

Art. 13.—At such meeting, if such parties appear, the said Guardians shall examine into the circumstances of the case; and if, after making all due inquiries, and hearing the objections (if any be made) on the part of the relatives or friends of such child, they shall deem it proper that the binding shall be effected, they may forthwith cause the indentures to be prepared, and in such manner and with such sanction as the law shall require to be executed, provided that when the same shall have been executed by the master and the other parties lawfully authorized, the same shall be signed by the child, as hereinafter provided.

Art. 14.—If the proposed master reside out of the Union or Parish on account of which the binding is to be effected, but in some other Union or Parish under a Board of Guardians, whether formed under the provisions of the first-recited Act or of the Act of the twenty-second year of the reign of King George the Third, intituled "*An Act for the better Relief and Employment of the Poor,*" or of any local Act, the Guardians shall, before proceeding to effect the binding, communicate in writing the proposal to the Guardians of such other Union or Parish, and request to be informed whether such binding is open to any objection, and if no objection be reported by such Guardians within the space of one calendar month, or, if the objection does not appear to the Guardians proposing to bind the child to be sufficient to prevent the binding, the same may be proceeded with; and when the indentures shall have been executed the Guardians who executed the same shall cause notice thereof in writing to be sent to the Guardians of the Union or Parish wherein the said apprentice is to reside.

INDENTURE.

Art. 15.—The indenture shall be executed in duplicate by the master and the Guardians, or the persons lawfully authorized to do so, and shall not be valid unless signed by the proposed apprentice, without aid or assistance, in the presence of the said Guardians; and the consent of the parent, where requisite, shall be testified by such parent signing with his name or mark, to be properly attested, the foot of the said indenture, and where such consent is dispensed with under the provision contained in Article 5, the cause of such dispensation shall be stated at the foot of the indenture, by any Clerk or other Officer acting as Clerk to the said Guardians.

Art. 16.—The indenture shall contain mention of the place or places at which the apprentice is to work and live.

Art. 17.—One part of such indenture, when executed, shall be kept by the Guardians; the other shall be delivered to the master.

DUTIES OF THE MASTER.

Art. 18.—And we do hereby prescribe the duties of the master to whom such poor child may be apprenticed, and the terms and conditions to be inserted in the said indentures, as follows:—

No. 1.—The master shall teach the child the trade, business, or employment set forth in the indenture, unless the Board of Guardians authorize the substitution of another trade or business.

No. 2.—He shall maintain the said child with proper food and nourishment.

No. 3.—He shall provide a proper lodging for the said child.

No. 4.—He shall supply to the said child one suit of proper clothing every year during the term of the binding.

No. 5.—He shall, in case the said child be affected with any disease or sickness, or meet with any accident, procure, at his own cost, adequate medical or surgical assistance, to be supplied by some duly qualified medical man, for such child.

No. 6.—He shall, once at least on every Sunday, cause the child to attend some place of divine worship, if there be any such within a reasonable distance, according to the religious persuasion in which the child has been brought up, so, however, that no child shall be required by the master to attend any place of worship to which his parents or surviving parent may object, nor, when he shall be above the age of *sixteen*, any place to which he may himself object.

No. 7.—Where such parents or parent or next of kin shall desire it, he shall allow the said child, while under the age of *sixteen*, to attend any Sunday or other school which shall be situated within the same Parish, or within *two* miles distance from his residence, on every Sunday, and, if there be no such school which such child can attend, shall, at some reasonable hour on every Sunday allow any minister of the religious persuasion of the child to have access to such child for the purpose of imparting religious instruction.

No. 8.—Where the apprentice continues bound after the age of *seventeen* years, the master shall pay to such apprentice, for and in respect of every week that he duly and properly serves the said master, as a remuneration. a sum to be inserted in the indenture, or to be agreed upon by the Guardians and the said master when that time arrives, or, if they cannot agree, to be settled by some person to be then chosen by the said master and such Guardians, and, until such sum be agreed upon or settled, not less than one *fourth* of the amount then commonly paid as wages to journeymen in the said trade, business, or employment.

No. 9.—The master shall, by himself or by his agent, produce the apprentice to the Board of Guardians by whom such apprentice was bound, or to their successors in office, at their ordinary meeting next preceding the end of the first year of the binding, and before the receipt of the remainder of the premium, if any be due, and shall in like manner produce the said apprentice at some one of their ordinary meetings, to be held at or about the middle of the term, and whenever afterwards required to do so by the said Guardians or their successors,

Provided that, if the apprentice reside out of the Union or Parish by the Guardians whereof he was bound, the apprentice shall be produced, as herein before directed, to any Board of Guardians of the Union or Parish, as described in Art. 14, or if there be no such Board of Guardians then to the Overseers of the Parish in which the apprentice may be residing.

No. 10.—The master shall not cause the said apprentice to work or live more than *ten miles* from the place or places mentioned in the indenture, according to Art. 16, without the leave of the Guardians so binding him, or their successors.

Art. 19.—These duties of the master shall be enforced by covenants and conditions to be inserted in the said indenture so to be executed by him.

Art. 20.—The master shall also covenant not to assign nor to cancel the indenture, without the consent of the Guardians or their successors, previously obtained, under a penalty to be specified in the said covenant, and to pay to the said Guardians or their successors all costs and expenses that they may incur in consequence of the said apprentice not being supplied with medical or surgical assistance by the master, in case the same shall be at any time requisite.

Art. 21.—The indenture shall be made subject to the following provisoes :—

1.—That if the master take the benefit of any Act for the relief of insolvent debtors, or be discharged under any such Act, such indenture shall forthwith become of no further force or effect.

2.—That if, on a conviction for a breach of any one of the aforesaid covenants before a Justice of the Peace, in pursuance of the provisions of the Statute in such case made and provided, the Guardians who may be parties to the said indenture, or their successors, shall declare by a resolution that the indenture shall be determined, and shall transmit a copy of such resolution, under the hand of their clerk or the person for the time being acting as such, by the post or otherwise, to the said master, such indenture shall, except in respect of all rights and liabilities then accrued, forthwith become of no further force or effect.

EXPLANATION OF TERMS.

Art. 22.—The word *Union* in this Order shall be taken to include any Union of Parishes incorporated or united for the relief or maintenance of the poor under any Local Act of Parliament.

Art. 23.—The word *Guardians* in this Order shall be taken to include any Governors, Deputy Governors, Assistants, Directors, Managers, Acting Guardians, Trustees of the Poor, or Select Vestrymen, entitled to act in the ordering of relief to the poor from the poor-rate under any Local Act of Parliament.

Art. 24.—Whenever the word *Parish* is used in this Order, it shall be taken to include any place maintaining its own poor, whether parochial or extra-parochial.

Art. 25.—The word *Child* in this Order shall signify any person under the age of twenty-one years.

Art. 26.—Whenever, in describing any person or party, matter, or thing, the word importing the singular number or the masculine gender only is used in this Order, the same shall be taken to include, and shall be applied to several persons or parties as well as one person or party, and females as well as males, and several matters or things as well as one matter or thing, respectively, unless there be something in the subject or context repugnant to such construction.

Art. 27.—Whenever in this Order any article is referred to by its number, the article of this Order bearing that number shall be taken to be signified thereby.

Art. 28.—Provided that nothing herein contained shall apply to the apprenticing of poor children to the Sea Service.

Art. 29.—And, in pursuance of the provisions contained in the said first-recited Act, We do Direct, that wherever any Justice or Justices shall, under any authority of law, assent or consent, order or allow, of the binding of any poor child as apprentice, such Justice or Justices shall certify at the foot of the indenture and the counterpart thereof, in the form and manner following; that is to say,

"I or We, (*as the case may be*) Justice *or* Justices of
"the Peace of and in the County (*or other jurisdiction,*
"*as the case may be*) of   , who have assented to,
"ordered, *or* allowed the above binding, do hereby cer-
"tify that we have examined and ascertained that the
"Rules, Orders, and Regulations of the Poor Law
"Commissioners, for the binding of poor children ap-
"prentices, and applicable to the above-named Parish,
"(*or other place, as the case may be*) contained in their
"General Order bearing date the Twenty-ninth day of
"January One thousand eight hundred and forty-five,
"have been complied with.

"Signed this   day of

_____Signature."

SCHEDULE A.

Containing the names of the Unions to which the present Order applies.

Bury St. Edmund's.	Oswestry.
Chester.	Oxford.
Chichester.	Plymouth.
Flegg, East and West, Hundred.	Southampton.
Forehoe Hundred.	Tunstead and Happing Hundred.
Mutford and Lothingland Hundred.	

SCHEDULE B.

Containing the Names of the Parishes to which the present Order applies.

Birmingham.   Kingston-upon-Hull.   Stoke Damerell.

Given under our Hands and Seal of Office, this twenty-ninth day of January, in the year One thousand eight hundred and forty-five.

(Signed) Geo. Nicholls.
G. C. Lewis.

A General Order, similar in its terms to the foregoing, was issued by the Poor Law Commissioners on the 29th January, 1845, addressed to all those Parishes which were not then placed under the Poor Law Amendment Act of 1834.

It is still in force in the Parishes in the following Gilbert's Incorporations:—

Caton	Lancashire.
Brinton	Norfolk.
Alverstoke	} Southampton.
Farnborough	
Headley	
Alstonefield	Stafford.
Ash	Surrey.
Arundel	} Sussex.
East Preston	
Bainbridge	North York.
Barwick	} West York.
Carlton	
Great Preston	

And also in the following Parishes in which relief to the Poor continues to be administered under the 43 Eliz. c. 2.

Arkholm-with-Cawood	} Lancashire.
Burrow-with-Burrow	
Cantsfield	
Ireby	
Leck	
Melling-with-Drayton	
Roburndale	
Tunstal	
Whittington	

South Stoke and Offham	⎫
Kingston	⎬ Sussex.
North Stoke	⎪
Heene	⎭
Bishop Dale	⎫
Carperby	⎬ North York.
Newbiggin	⎪
Thornton Rust	⎭
Thorp Stapleton	West York.
Middletown	⎫
Rhos Goch	⎪
Uppington	⎬ Montgomery.
Trewen	⎪
Castle Caereinion	⎪
Cyfronydd	⎭

The Order is also in force in the Parish of Brighton, and in the Parishes in the Shrewsbury, and Montgomery and Pool Incorporations.

On the 31st December, 1844, a General Order similar to the foregoing was issued, which now only remains in force in the Parish of Liverpool.

TAXATION OF BILLS OF COSTS ORDER.
(21st November, 1844.)

To the Clerks of the Peace *of the several Counties, Ridings, Divisions, and Places in England and Wales;—*

To the Guardians of the Poor of the several Unions and Parishes in England and Wales;

To the Overseers of the Poor of the several Parishes and Places in England and Wales;

And to all others whom it may concern.

WHEREAS it was enacted by the Act passed in the last Session of Parliament, intituled "*An Act for the further Amendment of the Laws relating to the Poor in England,*" that, on application of any Overseer, or of any Board of Guardians, or of any Attorney-at-Law, it should be the duty of the Clerk of the Peace of the County or Place, or his deputy, if thereunto required, to tax any bill due to any Solicitor or Attorney in respect of business performed on behalf of any Parish or Union situate wholly or in part within such County or Place; and that the allowance of any sum on such taxation should be *primâ facie* evidence of the reasonableness of the amount, but not of the legality of the charge; and that the Clerk of the Peace should be allowed for such taxation after the rate to be fixed from time to time by the Master of the Crown Office, and declared by an Order of the said Commissioners;

And whereas the Master of the Crown Office has fixed the rate of allowance to the Clerk of the Peace in respect of such taxation as herein declared:

Now, therefore, WE, THE POOR LAW COMMISSIONERS,

in pursuance of the statute aforesaid, do hereby declare, that the Clerk of the Peace of every County or Place in England and Wales, shall be allowed for the taxation of every bill due to any Solicitor or Attorney, in respect of business performed on behalf of any Parish or Union after the rate of *Fourpence per sheet*, or folio, of *seventy-two words each*.

Given under our Hands and Seal of Office, this twenty-first day of November, in the year One thousand eight hundred and forty-four.

(Signed) GEO. NICHOLLS.
EDMUND W. HEAD.

The attention of the Poor Law Board having been directed to the charges made by some Clerks of the Peace, and their Deputies, for taxing bills of costs due to Solicitors and Attorneys in respect of business performed on behalf of Parishes or Unions, they, on the 8th April, 1857, addressed a Circular to those Clerks, in which they stated that as those charges have frequently been in excess of the sums allowed by the established Scale, they deemed it advisable to transmit again to the several Clerks of the Peace a copy of the General Order issued by the Poor Law Commissioners on the 21st November, 1844, in pursuance of the statute 7 & 8 Vict. c. 101, s. 39, and they requested their attention to the terms of the Order in the event of their being called upon thereafter to tax any such bills.

The statute above referred to enacts that on application of any Overseer, or of any Board of Guardians, or of any Attorney-at-law, it shall be the duty of the Clerk of the Peace of the County or Place, or his Deputy, if thereunto required, to tax any bill due to any Solicitor or Attorney in respect of business performed on behalf of any Parish or Union situated wholly or in part within such City or Place; and the allowance of any sum on such taxation shall be *primâ facie* evidence of the reasonableness of the amount, but not of the legality of the charge; and the Clerk of the Peace shall be allowed for such taxation after the rate to be fixed from time to time by the Master of the Crown Office, and declared by an Order of the Poor Law Commissioners; and if any such bill be not taxed before it is presented to the Auditor, the Auditor's decision on the reasonableness as well as the legality of the charges shall be final. With regard to the latter point, namely, the finality of the Auditor's decision, see *Reg.* v. *Napton*, 25 L. J. R. (N.S.) Q. B. 296; *Reg.* v. *Hunt*, 6 El. & Bl. 408; 2 Jur. (N.S.) 1138. See also *Attorney-General* v. *Shillibeer*, 4 Exch. Rep. 606, as to Solicitor's costs when he is paid by a salary; and *In re Barber*, 14 Mee. & W. 726.

Taxation by the Clerk of the Peace or other taxing officer is not, however, absolutely compulsory upon the Overseers in all cases; for instance, as to costs incurred in punishing persons keeping disorderly houses, under the 25 Geo. II. c. 36, s. 5, the "Constable or other Officer shall be allowed all the reasonable expenses of such prosecution, to be ascertained by any two Justices of the Peace of the county, riding, division, or liberty where the offence shall have been committed, and shall be paid the same by the Overseers of the Poor of such parish or place."

The Clerk of the Peace does not appear to be bound to tax bills of costs, unless some qualified person attend before him to produce papers and give such explanations of the items as may be required. This however would occasion great extra expense, and would not be generally necessary. Usually the bills are forwarded to him for taxation, and any communications required are given by letter. When this is done, it would seem that a reasonable sum may be charged for the extra trouble beyond the sum of 4d. per folio fixed by the Order, which was intended to have reference to the taxing merely.

The ratepayers not being persons liable "to pay" within the meaning of the 6 & 7 Vict. c. 73, s. 31 (Attorneys and Solicitors Act), cannot apply for a reference of an Attorney's bill to taxation under the 7 & 8 Vict. c. 101, s. 39, and this Order. (See *In re Barber*, 14 Mee. & W. 720.)

It has always been the practice of the Master of the Crown Office, on the taxation of bills of costs, to count figures as words; and, in reckoning the charge to be made under this Order, the Clerk of the Peace is entitled to do so likewise. It would seem that if a table of fees be fixed under the 57 Geo. III. c. 91, it would nevertheless be competent for the Clerk of the Peace to demand and receive the fees payable under the 7 & 8 Vict. c. 101, and the above Order, though they may exceed in amount the fee which would, but for the latter Act and Order, have been payable by the table of fees under the 57 Geo. III. c. 91.

It has been held that, under the 7 & 8 Vict. c. 73, s. 37, an Attorney's bill for agency business is taxable. (*Smith* v. *Dimes*, 4 Exch Rep. 32.)

According to the practice of the Crown Office no fee is payable to the Clerk of the Peace for "appointment to tax;" but for obtaining an "appointment to tax," which necessitates the attendance of a clerk, and occasionally occupies some time, a fee of 3s. 4d. is always allowed in the Court of Queen's Bench to an Attorney; so also the Clerk of the Peace is not entitled to charge for "allocation and fee therein" where he is paid for taxing, but for the latter payment only.

GENERAL ORDER FOR ACCOUNTS.

(14*th January*, 1867.)

To the Guardians of the Poor *of the several Unions named in the Schedule* (H.) *hereunto annexed ;—*

To the Churchwardens and Overseers of the Poor of the several Parishes and Places comprised within the said Unions ; —

To the Clerk or Clerks to the Justices of the Petty Sessions held for the Division or Divisions in which the Parishes comprised within the said Unions are situate ;—

And to all others whom it may concern (a).

WHEREAS it is enacted in "The Union Chargeability Act, 1865," that the Poor Law Board shall, as soon as convenient, make all such Orders as may be requisite to render the provisions of that Act applicable to the proceedings and accounts of the Guardians of Unions and of Overseers of Parishes comprised therein.

Now, therefore, We, the Poor Law Board, in pursuance of the authorities vested in us by an Act of Parliament

---

(a) The Poor Law Board issued this General Order in compliance with the direction contained in the 11th section of the Statute 28th & 29th Vict. c. 79, to render the Accounts of the Guardians conformable to the provisions of that Act. The Board have by this Order removed all the regulations in the former Orders of Accounts which referred to parochial chargeability, but they have not removed the parochial division of paupers, as they have considered that for many purposes it will prove convenient to retain the entry and classification of paupers with reference to the Parishes in which they reside or from which they are removed into the Workhouse.—*Instr. Letter*, 22nd January, 1867.

The Board have had portions of the Order applicable to the Overseers, Treasurer, Master of the Workhouse, and Relieving Officer printed for distribution among those Officers for their immediate guidance.

passed in the fifth year of the reign of King William the Fourth, intituled "*An Act for the Amendment and better Administration of the Laws relating to the Poor in England and Wales,*" hereby, from the Twenty-fifth day of March next, rescind all such Orders, and all such parts of any Orders, heretofore issued by the Poor Law Commissioners or the Poor Law Board to the several Unions named in the Schedule (H.) hereunto annexed, as relate to the keeping, examining, closing, auditing, allowing, and publishing of the Accounts of the said Unions, and of the Parishes therein, and of the Officers thereof, or to the keeping of any Books of Account relating to such Unions or Parishes by any Officer thereof (*a*), other than a Chaplain (*b*) or Medical Officer (*c*), or to the accounting of any such Officer to the Auditor, or to any other party, so far as this present Order applies to the keeping of the same or similar Books, and to the accounting of such Officers, except as hereinafter excepted.

And We hereby, nevertheless, Order, that until the Twenty-ninth day of September next the Guardians of any such Union, and the Officers thereof, and the Overseers of the Parishes therein, may keep their Accounts and Books of Account in the Forms now used by them respectively, or adapt them where necessary to the Forms herein prescribed, as nearly as may be.

And subject thereto, in every case in which the Poor Law Board shall not assent to a departure from any of the Regulations contained in this Order, and in reference to such of the Officers in the said Unions to whom this Order shall be applicable not yet appointed, as shall from time to time be appointed hereafter.

(*a*) The General Orders rescinded by this Order are the following: General Order for Accounts, 17th March, 1847; Form of Poor-rate Order, 18th November, 1850; Collection of Poor-rate Order, 16th March, 1854. This Order also rescinds the Special Orders on the same subjects.

(*b*) See Art. 211, No. 2, of the Consolidated Order, *ante*, p. 175.

(*c*) See Art. 206, No. 4, *ante*, p. 157, and Art. 207, Nos. 8 and 9; *ante*, pp. 160, 161, of the General Consolidated Order.

We hereby, from the said Twenty-fifth day of March next, Order and Direct as follows:—

KEEPING OF ACCOUNTS.

PAROCHIAL ACCOUNTS.

Overseers.

Art. 1.—The Overseers (*d*) of every Parish in the Union shall (except so far as such books are kept under their direction by any Collector) punctually enter and accurately keep according to the forms and direction in the Schedule A. hereunto annexed:—

> *A Rate Book* (*e*). In this book shall be inserted the particulars of the assessment and collection of the Poor-rate of the Parish, as set forth in the *Form* of Rate Book; and in addition to the declaration required by the Union Assessment Committee Act, 1862 (*f*), or any Act amending the same (*g*), where the Valuation List for the Parish shall have been finally approved of, and elsewhere in addition to the declaration required by the Statute 6 & 7 Will. IV. c. 96, such Overseers shall, before any rate is presented to the Justices for their

---

(*d*) If a Vestry Clerk be appointed for the Parish under 13 & 14 Vict. c. 57, it will be his duty under sect. 7 of that Act, to assist the Overseers in making out their accounts whenever required by them to do so; and also to examine the accounts of the Assistant-Overseer or Collector of Poor-rates, and their returns of arrears. By the same section the Vestry Clerk is required to attend the audit of the accounts of the Overseers, and to conduct all correspondence arising therefrom, and also to perform other duties as is therein specified in connection with those of the Overseers. He is also to keep the Parish deeds and documents, and the Rate Books and accounts which are closed.

(*e*) The arrears of rates in column 2, which are not excused, are to be carried to column 13, headed "recoverable arrears of former rates;" and the sums of that column and the amount of the new rate as stated in columns 11 or 12 being added together, will constitute the "total amount actually to be collected" to be entered in column 14.—*Instr. Letter*, 17th March, 1847.

(*f*) See 25 & 26 Vict. c. 103, s. 28.

(*g*) See 27 & 28 Vict. c. 39, s. 11.

allowance, sign a declaration, in words at length, of the total amount of the rate so presented for allowance, according to the form or to the effect set forth in the said *Form.*

(a.)—The several columns of the *Rate Book* which contain the gross estimated rental and rateable value, and the rate in the pound assessed upon the several persons liable to be assessed, the recoverable arrears and the total amount to be collected, shall be added up at the foot of every page, and the several totals shall be ascertained and set forth at the foot of the rate, before the same shall be submitted to the Justices for their allowance (*a*).

(b.)—If the Overseers shall deem it convenient, the rate may be divided into several portions corresponding with the several divisions of the Parish, if any, so as to bring all the rateable property of each division together, and there may be separate series of numbers for the assessments in every division, and they may in like manner bring together in the rate separate classes of rateable property (*b*).

(c).—The Overseers may, if they think proper, bring together and assess under one number all or any portion of the properties situated in the Parish or in any separate division thereof, if there be any, belonging to the same person, and for which he shall be liable to be assessed as Owner (*c*).

(*a*) The amounts ascertained at the foot of each page may be carried on to the next page, or the several totals may be brought together at the end of the rate, for a gross total.—*Instr. Letter.*

It is the duty of the Auditor to ascertain that the columns of the Rate Book are correctly cast; but the mode of doing so is a matter which is left to his own discretion, subject to his general responsibility for the correctness of the sums brought by the Overseers into account.

(*b*) A Poor-rate may be in more books than one, *Scadding* v. *Lorant,* 19 L. J. M. C. 5.

(*c*) This Article is permissive and not compulsory. If one number should be adopted for the whole of the properties, the several occupations should nevertheless appear in the assessment, as well as the names of the occupiers and the rateable value of the several tenements, should

Provided that nothing herein contained shall apply to any Poor-rate made under the authority of a Local Act by persons other than the Overseers.

A Book of Receipts and Payments. On one side of this book shall be entered, according to the *Form* so named, an account of all moneys received by the Overseers, by virtue of their office, on behalf of the Parish, and on the other side of such book the Overseers shall enter, in like manner, with the proper dates, an account of all moneys paid and expended by them, by virtue of their office, on behalf of the Parish, and shall sign the same in the place prescribed in the said Form (*d*).

And at the foot of every such account the Overseers shall insert, before each audit, a "*Memorandum*" in respect of each rate allowed by Justices during the half-year, containing the particulars set out in the Form (*e*).

---

be set out separately. It would, however, only be necessary to prepare one receipt in the Rate Receipt Check Book in respect of the rate upon all the properties brought together and assessed. If an owner occupy his own property, and is also rated for small tenements under the 13 & 14 Vict. c. 99, he should be assessed under a separate number in respect of the property in his own occupation.

(*d*) Every transaction, excepting receipts from Poor-rate, should be entered under its true date in this book. Moneys received from the Poor-rate cannot be entered in this manner, but the total amount received on account of each rate during the half-year, should be entered in one sum. In the *memorandum* at the foot of the account for the half-year should be entered in respect of each rate—1. the total amount of the rate; 2. the amount legally excused in such rate; 3. the amount not recoverable; and 4. the sum remaining to be accounted for.—*Instr. Letter.*

(*e*) The Auditor should not pass an account unless the particulars required by the *memorandum* are inserted.

The 7 & 8 Vict. c. 101, s. 33, renders it illegal for Parish Officers to alter their accounts after being duly made up for audit; when they are laid before the Auditor, it then rests with him to decide upon the legality of every item therein; but see *Reg.* v. *Denbighshire JJ.*, 33 L. T. 145, and the observations thereon, *post.*

The Overseers should be careful not to enter in the Receipt and Payment Book as receipts anything which they have not actually received, and to confine their entries to *actual* receipts and payments on account of the Parish. The account should show the balance of any money in their hands actually received at the time the account is closed; and the *memorandum* will show the balance due to the Parish in respect of uncollected rates.

Art. 2.—The Overseers shall make out, in the Form so named, *A Balance Sheet of the Receipts and Payments* for every half-year, according to the said Receipt and Payment Book (*a*), and shall sign the same in the place prescribed in the said Form, and deliver such Balance Sheet, and a duplicate thereof, to the Auditor at the audit of their accounts, to be by him examined and signed. One of these sheets shall be delivered to the Clerk of the Guardians as hereinafter directed (*b*), and the other shall, together with the Book of Receipts and Payments, be laid by the Overseers before the next meeting of the Vestry (*c*), and such Balance Sheet shall be preserved among the other parochial documents, and be open to the inspection of the ratepayers of the Parish (*d*).

Art. 3.—In every case in which there are more than thirty ratepayers on the Rate Book, and in which there is no Collector, the Overseer shall, and in cases where there is a less number of ratepayers the Overseers may, use:—

1. *A Rate Receipt Check Book*, the leaves of which shall contain the *Form* set forth in the Schedule. The receipts and notes thereof shall be numbered consecutively with numbers corresponding with those in the Rate Book (*e*).

(*a*) The balance sheet is to contain the total amount of each class of the Overseer's receipts and payments for the half-year, arranged in the order and under the heads indicated in the Form.—*Instr. Letter*. By Art. 26, *post*, the Overseer's accounts are to be made up and balanced to the 25th March and the 29th September in each year.

(*b*) See Art. 45, *post*.

(*c*) It will not be necessary for the Overseers to call a Vestry meeting for this special purpose. It will suffice if they lay the documents before the *next* Vestry that is held after the audit.

(*d*) As to the custody of Parish documents, etc., see 58 Geo. III. c. 69, s. 6, 13 & 14 Vict. c. 57, s. 7, and 24 & 25 Vict. c. 125, s. 2. The Workhouse of a Union is not an improper repository for documents of a Parish within the Union so as to make them inadmissible in evidence when produced thence: *Slater* v. *Hodgson*, 9 Q. B. 727; 2 N. S. C. 488; and in *Reg.* v. *Eaton*, 10 Jur. 222, it was said that the Parish chest is the proper place of custody of the rate books of a Parish.

(*e*) The Overseers are not bound to use a Rate Receipt Check Book

They may also, where they deem it expedient, use—

2. *A General Receipt Check Book,* for any sum received on account of such Parish other than in respect of rates (*f*).

If the Overseers think fit, they may cause a *Demand Note* to be printed in the *Rate Receipt Check Book,* according to the Form in the said Schedule, which may be detached and left with the ratepayer or at his address when the payment of the rate is demanded, which Demand Note shall be numbered so as to correspond with the number of the receipt, and may show the particulars of the claims or the purposes for which the rate is made, if the Overseers think proper to have the same inserted therein.

Art. 4.—When the whole or the balance of the amount due for Poor-rate shall be received from any person assessed, at that time and not before, the receipt applicable to such person's assessment shall be detached from the Rate Receipt Check Book, and the same shall be delivered, stamped with an adhesive stamp where the amount of the payment shall render such stamp necessary, to the person paying the same, and the note shall be retained in the book.

In the receipt and in the note thereof so retained the true date of the payment of the money shall be inserted.

When payment of any rate shall be received by instalments, the fact of every payment shall be noted on the back of the receipt and on the note thereof, and the receipt shall

---

when there are less than thirty ratepayers on the Rate Book. Collectors, however, being paid officers, are in all cases bound by Article 7 to keep the Rate Receipt Check Book.—*Instr. Letter.*

Articles 3, 4, & 7 of this Order contemplate that when the amount of the rate paid requires a stamped receipt, it should be given by the Overseers or Collectors receiving the money. Such a receipt should therefore be given in all such cases, and adhesive stamps used. A tender of a Poor-rate in copper money to any amount exceeding one shilling at the same time, is not a legal tender; and if country bank notes or checks upon bankers be taken in payment of rates, they are at the risk of the persons who take them, as they do not constitute a legal tender.

(*f*) No form for this book is prescribed by the Order.

not be given to the person paying the rate until the whole amount of the rate shall have been received, but an acknowledgment of the amount received shall be given in writing upon the Demand Note, or otherwise, as it shall be found convenient.

Art. 5.—The Overseers of every Parish shall, whenever they are required so to do by the Auditor for the time being, or by the Poor Law Board, accurately and truly make out a *Terrier* of the lands and tenements, and an *Inventory* of stock, moneys, goods, and effects belonging to such Parish, or given or applicable in aid of the Poor-rates thereof, according to the Forms so named (*a*).

Collector of the Parish (*b*).

Art. 6.—Every Collector appointed for a Parish shall enter up so much of any Books or Forms of the Overseers relating to the Valuation List (*c*), or to the collection of the Poor-rate, as he may be directed to enter up by the Overseers for the time being, and shall enter in the *Rate Book* all such particulars of every assessment as he shall be directed by such Overseers to enter therein; and every such Collector shall attend before the Auditor at the same time as the Overseers of the Parish for which he acts:

(*a*) The Terrier and Inventory are to be made out only when the Auditor or Poor Law Board require them.

(*b*) As to the term "Collector" see Art. 60, *post*. The Board have made several additions to the forms of account kept by the Collectors of the Poor-rate, with the hope of providing more effectual security to the ratepayers of parishes who are provided with such officers. They are sensible of the great difficulty that attends this subject in large Parishes where, owing to the vast number of ratepayers and the various contingencies which attend their circumstances, the collection of the rates is attended with delays and losses, and affords much opportunity for the exercise of fraud or embezzlement. Greater vigilance on the part of the Overseers, the Guardians, and the Auditor is required to protect the ratepayers from the results of such misconduct, and the Board have now introduced into the forms of account kept by these officers additional checks which they trust will prove some aid to the examination and investigation of their accounts.—*Instr. Letter*, 22nd January, 1867.

(*c*) See the Union Assessment Committee Acts, 25 & 26 Vict. c. 103, and 27 & 28 Vict. c. 39, in Glen's 'Poor Law Statutes,' vol. ii.

Provided that the signature of any such Collector to any book presented to the Auditor shall not be taken to stand for or to supply the place of the signature of any Overseer which may be otherwise required by this Order (*d*).

Art. 7.—Every such Collector shall in all cases fill up and use, as is herein-before directed in the case of Overseers of Parishes in which there are more than thirty ratepayers on the Rate Book (*e*), a *Rate Receipt Check Book*, in the form herein-before prescribed.

Provided that if the Guardians or the Overseers direct, he shall keep an additional book, to be termed *The Instalment Rate Receipt Check Book*, according to the Form in the said Schedule (A.) annexed, which shall be used by him as and when he receives any sum on account of the rate short of the full amount due. The receipt therefrom shall be given to the person paying, and the amount and date shall be entered in the note of this book, and upon the receipt in the other book.

Art. 8.—Every Collector, before he shall proceed to collect any rate, shall prepare receipts in one book, or in several, if so directed by the Overseers, in the aforesaid Form, numbered both on the receipt and the note thereof with the same number consecutively throughout the book, and properly fill in the same respectively with the names of the several ratepayers, and the sum to be collected from each, and submit every such Rate Receipt Check Book, so numbered and filled up, to the Overseers of the Parish for which such rate is to be collected, before he proceeds to collect the rate ; and such Overseers shall cause the correctness of the numbering, and the correspondence of the sums, and of the names filled in, with the Rate Book to which they relate, to be ascertained, and on the leaf next after the last

---

(*d*) If a Vestry Clerk has been appointed for the Parish under the 13 & 14 Vict. c. 57, certain duties with regard to the accounts of the Collector will devolve upon him under sect. 7 of that Act. See Glen's ' Small Tenement Rating and Vestries Act,' 5th ed.

(*e*) See Art. 3, *ante*, p. 438.

of the receipts so made out in respect of any one rate, the said Overseers shall certify the fact that such Receipt Check Book has been examined and ascertained to be correct, and shall state in words at length the number of the receipts filled up for the rate then to be collected; which certificate shall be in the Form set forth in the Schedule, and shall be signed by the said Overseers and correctly dated (a).

If upon the closing of any rate there shall remain in the Rate Receipt Check Book any receipts made out for such rate unused, the Collector to whom such book shall belong shall enter upon each of such receipts the reason of its not having been used, and date and sign such entry.

Art. 9.—The Collector shall every week pay over all moneys collected by him, or in his hands, belonging to the Parish, whenever the amount exceeds Five Pounds, to the Banker to whom the Overseers may direct, to be placed to the account of one or more of them; or, if directed by one of the Overseers, to the Treasurer of the Guardians of the Union, or to any other authority, in payment of any Order from such Guardians or other authority then due, and in the absence of any such direction, shall pay the same to one of the said Overseers in person; provided that as often as at any time in the course of any week the sum or sums of money in the hands of such Collector belonging to the Parish shall together exceed Fifty Pounds, he shall forthwith pay over such sum or sums in the manner herein-before directed.

Art. 10.—Every such Collector shall keep a book (b), to

(a) The Certificate should be signed by a majority of the Churchwardens and Overseers, or Overseers, as the case may be (see Art. 59, *post*), and it may be attached to each separate Rate Receipt Check Book, without waiting for the whole of them to be verified.

If there be a Vestry Clerk appointed under the 13 & 14 Vict. c. 57, he may assist the Overseers in the performance of their duties under this Article; but the Overseers will nevertheless remain responsible for their adoption of his acts, and their signatures to the Certificate.

(b) This book is prescribed for the purpose of showing the amount in the Collector's hands at any time.

be called the *Collecting and Deposit Book*, according to the Form so named, in which shall be entered accurately, and under their true dates, all sums received and deposited and paid by him as such Collector respectively, and also the number of every receipt given by such Collector out of the *Rate Receipt Check Book*, or the *Instalment Rate Receipt Check Book* (as the case may be), and he shall balance such book monthly, at the times specified in the following Article, and the Overseer shall enter his initials against every sum stated to be deposited with him, which he shall receive.

Art. 11.—Every such Collector shall keep a book containing blank Forms of *Monthly Statements*, according to the Form in the Schedule (A.), and shall every month fill up one of such statements with the several particulars set forth in the said Form, which statement shall be made up to the last day of every calendar month inclusive; except in the case of the month of March, when it shall be made up to the 25th, and in that of the month of September, when it shall be made up to the 29th; so that any receipts or payments on the remaining days of those months respectively shall be included in the next monthly statement; and he shall forthwith deliver a copy of such statement, signed by himself, to one of the Overseers, and another to the Board of Guardians at their ordinary meeting next after the day when the same shall be made up.

Provided that the Board of Guardians or the Overseers may, if they think fit, require a statement, containing the several particulars set forth in the said Form to be made out and delivered to them respectively every week or fortnight.

The Overseer who receives the statement shall enter his initials in the column against the amount stated to be paid to the Overseers, if he shall have received the sum there mentioned; and both he and the Clerk to the Guardians respectively shall mark on such statement the date of his receipt thereof, and preserve the copies delivered to him, and produce the same to the Auditor at the next audit (*a*).

Art. 12.—The Collector shall previous to each audit make out *An Unpaid Rates Statement*, containing a statement of the rates allowed during the last half-year, with the dates of their allowance, and showing the name of every person rated to the relief of the poor in respect of whom there shall be at the end of the half-year for which the audit is being held, any arrear of the rate or rates made before that in the course of collection on the last day of that half-year, with the other particulars set forth in the *Form* in the Schedule hereunto annexed. He shall submit it to one of the Overseers for his signature, and shall produce the same to the Auditor at the audit (*b*).

Art. 13.—In every case in which there shall be more than one Collector employed in the collection of any one rate,

---

(*a*) The Collector's Monthly Statement, which will be made up from the materials contained in the "Collecting and Deposit Book," is, in pursuance of Art. 11, to be delivered by every Collector to one or more of the Overseers, and by every Collector appointed under an Order of the Commissioners it is also to be delivered to the Board of Guardians. The object of this statement is to inform the Overseers and the Board of Guardians of the state of the Collector's account at the close of each month. The Commissioners request the particular attention of Overseers and Boards of Guardians to the necessity of superintending the proceedings of persons employed in collecting the Poor-rates. Full opportunity for doing so will be given by the *Statement* now prescribed, and proper vigilance on the part of the local authorities may prevent loss.—*Instr. Letter*, 17th March, 1847.

(*b*) Under sect. 32 of the 7 & 8 Vict. c. 101, the Overseers are liable for any money which may be lost through their neglect ; and the Auditor is empowered to surcharge them therewith. The object of this statement is to enable the Auditor to ascertain whether any, and what amount of Poor-rates may have been so lost ; and, also, whether any Poor-rates remain uncollected, which are recoverable, and which ought to have been collected. It is necessary for Overseers to bear this in mind, as by sect. 61 of 7 & 8 Vict. c. 101, every Collector or Assistant-Overseer is bound to obey the majority of the Overseers of the Parish for which he acts in all matters relating to the collection of the rates ; and it must, at the same time, be remembered that the responsibility of the Overseers for the payment of contributions and other matters, is not diminished by the appointment of a Collector or Assistant-Overseer, whom they themselves have the power of controlling. —*Instr. Letter*, 17th March, 1847.

the provisions in the several articles herein-before made shall apply to the portion of such rate assigned to each Collector as if such portion were one entire rate.

Art. 14.—Provided that nothing herein contained relating to the Collector shall apply to a Collector appointed under any Local Act by any other authority than the Overseers, and provided also that where the Poor Law Board have made any special provision in respect of the making or collecting of the Poor-rate in any parish, the Order containing such provision shall not be rescinded or affected by anything herein contained.

GENERAL ACCOUNTS OF THE UNION.

Clerk's Books.

Art. 15.—The Clerk to the Board of Guardians shall enter from time to time at proper dates in the Minute Book of the Guardians a statement of the books and accounts inspected and examined by him (c), and of all orders drawn on the Treasurer (d), and of moneys paid or received, and all minutes relating to the allocation or division of charges, or any other pecuniary transaction of the Board of Guardians on behalf of the Union, or of any Parish therein; and shall insert marginal notes of reference to the folios of the respective Ledgers in which the items relating to any of such orders, payments, receipts, or other transactions are entered.

Art. 16.—The Clerk shall punctually enter and accurately keep the following Books of Account, according to the Forms and directions in the Schedule B. hereunto annexed:—

A General Ledger (e), in which items of the various trans-

(c) See Art. 25, *post*.
(d) See Arts. 1 and 2 of the Order of the 26th Feb. 1866, *ante*, p. 266.
(e) No entry should be made in the Ledger unless it be authorized by an entry in the Minute Book; therefore the allocation of the common charges should be recorded in the Minutes of the Guardians as having been authorized by them, before it is entered in the Ledger. The allo-

actions relating to the receipt or payment of moneys by the Guardians, and the supply of goods, provisions, or necessaries, or the execution of works, or performance of services, on behalf of the Union or of any Parish therein, contained in the Minute Book, shall be entered and posted up, according to their proper dates, under the following heads of account, and such additional heads as may be or may from time to time become necessary :—

    In-Maintenance (*a*).
    Out-Relief (*b*).
    Non-resident Poor Account (*c*).
    Non-settled Poor Account (*d*).
    Relief declared on Loan (*e*).
    Lunatics Account (*f*).
    Extra Medical Fees (*g*).
    Emigration Expenses (*h*).
    Vaccination Expenses (*i*).

---

cation will of necessity be entered in the Minutes of the day after the half-year's accounts are closed, *i.e.* some day after the close of the half-year.

(*a*) See Articles 62 and 63, *post*, as to the words "Provisions," "Necessaries," and "In-Maintenance," and what should be included in the latter.

(*b*) See Art. 63, *post*, as to what should be included in "Out-Relief." Expenses connected with the removal of paupers to their places of settlement, and expenses connected with the removal of poor persons to or from the Workhouse, should be charged to out-relief.

(*c*) See Articles 77-80, *ante*, pp. 51, 54.

(*d*) "Non-settled Poor" are those who are residing in the Union, and are relieved by the Guardians on account of other Unions.

(*e*) See 4 & 5 Wm. IV. c. 76, s. 58; and Art. 7 of the General Prohibitory Order. *ante*, p. 371, and Art. 9 of the Out-door Relief Regulation Order, *ante*, p. 388.

(*f*) See 16 & 17 Vict. c. 97, and 24 & 25 Vict. c. 55, s. 6. Expenses incurred in removing lunatics to or from asylums, and expenses connected with the charging of lunatics to the county, should be charged to this account.

(*g*) See Art. 177, *ante*, p. 126.

(*h*) See 4 & 5 Wm. IV. c. 76, s. 62; 7 & 8 Vict. c. 101, s. 29, and 29 & 30 Vict. c. 113, s. 9.

(*i*) See 30 & 31 Vict. c. 84.

(*j*) See 6 & 7 Wm. IV. c. 86, s. 29; 7 Wm. IV. & 1 Vict. c. 22, ss. 25 and 27 in Glen's 'Registration of Births, Deaths, and Marriages Laws.'

Registration Expenses (*j*).
County rate (*k*).
Salaries and Superannuations Account (*l*).
Rations Account.
Building and Repairs Account (*m*).
Workhouse Loan Account (*n*).
Furniture and Property Account.
Provisions Account.
Clothing Account.
Necessaries and Miscellaneous Account.
Parish Property Account.
Invoice Account.
Invoice Account, and if the Board of Guardians so direct, Tradesmen's Accounts (*o*).
Collector's Account (*p*).
Treasurer's Account.
General or Common Fund Account.
General Balance.

With the respective dates of such transactions, and references to the folios of the Minute Book in which the entries relating to such transactions are contained,

---

(*k*) See 15 & 16 Vict. c. 81.
(*l*) See 27 & 28 Vict. c. 42; and 29 & 30 Vict. c. 113, ss. 1, 2; and 30 & 31 Vict. c. 106, s. 18.
(*m*) See 4 & 5 Wm. IV. c. 76, s. 24. The word "repairs" refers only to the building and fixtures.
(*n*) See 4 & 5 Wm. IV. c. 76, s. 24.
(*o*) With regard to the "Invoice Account," or "Tradesmen's Accounts," the Commissioners recommend that the invoices entered in the Master's *Day Book* (Book of Receipts and Payments, *post*), should be posted, either to the credit of an "Invoice Account," or, if the Board of Guardians so direct, to the credit of separate "Tradesmen's Account," and to the debit of the "Provisions Account," the "Common Charges Account," (General or Common Fund Account), or such other proper accounts as each case may require.—*Instr. Letter.*

Cod-Liver Oil, and other expensive medicines, Chloride of Lime, etc., obtained for in-door and out-door purposes, should appear in these accounts.

(*p*) See the Collectors of the Guardians Orders, *ante*, p. 303, and Art. 17, *post*.

and to the folios of the corresponding credits and debits respectively (*a*).

He shall keep an account in such Ledger, or in a separate Ledger, as the Guardians shall direct, to be called *The Parochial Ledger* (*b*), with every Parish in the Union.

He shall keep another account in such Ledger, or in a separate Ledger of the same form, to be called *The Non-settled Poor Ledger* (*c*), with every other Union and Parish chargeable with the relief granted to the non-settled Poor in the Union; and every such account shall be debited with the amounts to be charged against, and credited with the amounts discharged by, such Union and Parish.

He shall also keep the following books :—

1. *The Relief Order Book*, in which shall be entered the names of all persons applying for relief, whether through

---

(*a*) If the Union be in the Metropolis, it will also be necessary to keep in the Ledger an "Asylum Account with the managers of asylums, under the Metropolitan Poor Act, 1867."

(*b*) The Parochial Ledger is intended to contain the accounts of the several Parishes with the Union, to the debit of which accounts are to be posted the portions of the several classes of expenditure chargeable to such Parishes; and to the credit of which are to be posted the contributions paid by the Overseers to the Treasurer of the Union, and any other sums to the credit of which the Parishes may be entitled, such, for example, as balances struck by the Auditors, and paid over to the Treasurer, in pursuance of 7 & 8 Vict. c. 101, s. 32. The Parochial Ledger will be adopted in such Unions only as contain a sufficient number of Parishes to make it desirable to do so. In small Unions it will, probably, be found most convenient to open accounts with the several Parishes in the General Ledger, as has been the custom under the former Order.—*Instr. Letter*, March, 1847.

(*c*) See Articles 77–80, *ante*, pp. 51–54. The Commissioners think that it may be found convenient in Unions, in which there are accounts for relief to non-settled poor against many other Unions, to keep such accounts in a separate Ledger, so that the account against each of such Unions for several years may appear at one view, and also be separated from the General Accounts of the Union advancing the relief.

With regard to the necessity for keeping the Parochial Ledger, and the Ledger for Non-settled Poor in separate books, the Clerk will take the directions of the Board of Guardians. No extra trouble will be imposed upon him by the mere separation of the books.—*Instr. Letter*, March, 1847.

the Relieving Officer or directly to the Board, with a minute of the order made on such application in each case, and the particulars set forth in the Form in the said Schedule (*d*).

2. *The Order Check Book* (*e*). This book shall be kept according to the Form so named, and shall contain all orders given by the Guardians for provisions, stores, repairs, and for other articles or work, and notes of such orders, and forms of the invoices to accompany commodities supplied, or to be delivered when work is done; such orders, when signed by the Clerk, together with the form of invoice, shall be detached from the said book, and issued to the tradesmen or other persons dealt with or employed, to be returned and disposed of in the manner described thereon; and the notes, certified by the Clerk's initials, shall be retained in the said book.

3. *The Pauper Classification Book*, in which, at the end of every half-year shall be entered, in the columns appropriated for that purpose, the number of persons

---

(*d*) If Relief Committees shall have been appointed for districts in the Union (see the form of Order, *ante*, p. 261), the provision to Art. 24, *post*, will apply to the relief order books kept by such Committee.

The Relief Order Book is to contain entries of those cases in which the Board of Guardians order relief to be given, or allow relief provisionally given by the Relieving Officers. It will not be necessary that minutes of any orders for relief entered in this book should be entered also in the ordinary Minute Book, but minutes may be made therein referring to the particulars recorded in this book; care should be taken that the entries in this book correspond with those in the *Application and Report Book*, on which it is a check, the latter being ordinarily in the custody of the Relieving Officer.—*Instr. Letter*, March, 1847.

(*e*) This book is to be used in every case in which orders are given by the Board of Guardians for articles to be supplied, or for work or repairs to be done.—*Instr. Letter*. The order of the Guardians for the supply of goods must precede all expenditure; and no Officer has authority to order goods of any description, and afterwards to obtain the confirmation of the Guardians of his act. It will be observed that the language of this Article is general, and that it applies to all goods, etc., supplied to the Guardians. Further with regard to this Article, see note to Art. 41 (fifthly), *ante*, p. 32.

of each class relieved during the half-year, and the other particulars set forth therein (*a*).

4. *The Petty Cash Book* (*b*), in which shall be entered promptly, and in the order of date, an account of the sums received by the Clerk for Petty Disbursements, and of the sums, not exceeding £5 each, paid by him thereout, by direction of the Board of Guardians, or on his own authority in any case of urgency, which account shall be balanced quarterly, and laid before the Board of Guardians at their ordinary meetings, and the Clerk shall submit and account for the same to the Auditor at the time of the audit.

Collector of the Guardians (*c*).

Art. 17.—Every Collector of the Guardians shall keep punctually and accurately a book according to the Form set forth in the Schedule (C.) hereunto annexed, and shall duly enter therein all sums received and all sums paid by him. This account he shall balance quarterly. He shall give in

---

(*a*) This book is to be made up from the statistical portion of the In-door and Out-door Relief Lists, the Non-resident Poor Accounts, and the Medical Relief Books. The number of paupers belonging to each Parish of the several classes relieved in the half-year being brought together in this book, will constitute the materials for making up the *Statistical Statement* (*post*, p. 467) which the Clerk, by Art. 30, is required to transmit to the Poor Law Board. See Articles 28 and 29, and the Notes at the foot of the Form.—*Instr. Letter*, March, 1847. It should also include Lunatics in Asylums or Licensed Houses. The Auditor should direct his special attention to this Book, especially to the second and third groups of paupers, and the explanatory Notes printed at the foot of the Form. With regard to the classification of children, it is to be observed that those who are under sixteen years of age should be classed with their parents. Those who are above sixteen should be classed as paupers independent of their parents.

(*b*) A corresponding account with the Clerk should also be opened in the Union Ledger. In this account the Clerk will be liable to be dealt with by the Auditor in like manner as any other accounting officer. As to the Clerk's liability to account to the Auditor, see Note to Art. 40, *post*, p. 474. If a cheque be drawn and given to the Clerk to pay bills under £5, both the cheque and the payments which he may so make, should be entered in his Petty Cash Book. Of course, if the Clerk neither receives nor pays moneys, he need not keep a Petty Cash Book.

(*c*) See the Collectors of Guardians Order, *ante*, pp. 303–312.

respect of all moneys received by him a receipt according to the Form in the said Schedule.

Treasurer's Book.

Art. 18.—The Treasurer of the Guardians shall keep, punctually and accurately, a Book according to the *Form* set forth in the Schedule (D.) hereunto annexed, in which shall be entered an account of all moneys received and paid by him on account of the Guardians. He shall balance this account quarterly, and shall cause the book to be laid before the Board of Guardians once every month, or oftener if required by the said Guardians to do so, and before the Auditor at the time of the audit (*d*).

IN-DOOR RELIEF.

WORKHOUSE ACCOUNTS.

Master's Books.

Art. 19.—The Master of every Workhouse of the Union shall punctually enter up and accurately keep the following Books and Accounts, according to the Forms and directions in the Schedule (E.) hereunto annexed.

1. *An Inventory.* In this book shall be entered a list of all the fixtures, furniture, utensils, bedding, house linen, and other effects in the Workhouse, and the stock and other like property belonging to the Guardians in the Workhouse, and on the Workhouse premises (not included in the Provisions, Clothing, Farm, Necessaries and Miscellaneous Accounts), and every particular relating to the use, sale, or disposal thereof; and such book shall be completed from time to time by the entry of

---

(*d*) It would be contrary to this Article for the Treasurer to keep more than one account with the Guardians, as, for instance, a Building Loan account and a General account, all the moneys he receives on account of the Guardians must be placed to the same general account.

articles purchased or otherwise obtained, and of articles condemned as worn out, sold, or otherwise disposed of, by the direction of the Board of Guardians.

2. *The Admission and Discharge Book* (a). In this book shall be kept an account of every pauper admitted into and of every pauper discharged from the Workhouse, which account shall be balanced weekly, or, if the Board of Guardians so direct, daily.

Where the Guardians direct a separate book to be kept for an account of the admission and discharge of vagrants relieved in the principal or auxiliary Workhouse, the same shall be kept in the Form set forth in the said Schedule; and when any vagrant shall have been relieved in any such Workhouse for the space of twenty-four hours and is not then discharged, or where he shall be previously taken into some other ward of the Workhouse, his name shall be transferred to the Admission and Discharge Book as in the case of any other pauper.

3. *The In-door Relief List*, in which shall be entered, in respect of each Parish of the Union, the names of the paupers admitted therefrom, with the number of days in each week of the half-year during which each such pauper has been in the Workhouse, and the other particulars set forth in the Form (b).

4. *The Abstract of the In-door Relief List*, in which shall be entered the aggregate number of days in each week of the half-year passed in the Workhouse by the paupers admitted from each Parish, and of the vagrants, and the total number of such days in respect of all the

---

(a) This book is so arranged as to show the numbers in the Workhouse at each meal, of the several classes into which the paupers are distributed in the "Daily Provisions Consumption Account." It will show also the number attached to the pauper's own clothes when they are put aside upon his admission, and also marked on the clothes given out to such pauper. Under the same number his name will be found in the "Clothing Register Book."—*Instr. Letter*, 17th March, 1847.

(b) See the provisions of the Religious Instruction Order of 23rd August, 1859, *ante*, p. 299.

Parishes in the Union, for each week and for the half-year.

5. *A Day Book*, in which shall be entered the amount of the invoices of all goods delivered and bills for all work done at the Workhouse, together with the several particulars relating thereto, in the Form in the Schedule set forth. The entries shall be made on the dates of the deliveries and receipts respectively, and this book shall be made up weekly.

The invoices and bills shall be entered and numbered in the order in which they are received, and shall be filed and preserved in the same order (*c*).

6. He shall also keep an account, to be termed *The Master's Account of Receipts and Payments*, according to the Form in the said Schedule, in which shall be entered all moneys received and paid by him on account of the said Guardians, under their proper dates. He shall balance this account once every month, or oftener if required to do so by the Guardians; and for all moneys received by him he shall give a receipt from a *Receipt Check Book* in the Form in the said Schedule set forth (*d*).

7. *A Quarterly Summary of the Day Book* shall be made and completed quarterly according to the Form in the

---

(*c*) This book is provided in order that the Master may record all the invoices of goods supplied, and of work done at the Workhouse. By Art. 25 the Clerk is required to examine the entries in this book, and to see that all the goods supplied are carried by the Master to the proper accounts in his books. It will be the Clerk's own duty to carry them to the proper accounts in the Ledger.—*Instr. Letter*, 17th March, 1847. The cash transactions of the master will be entered in his Receipt and Payment Book. The Master should on no account obliterate or interfere with the number which the invoice bears on its delivery to him, but should add a second number for the purposes of the Day Book. All provisions, of whatever kind (see Art. 62), including wine, spirits, or beer, should be entered in the Day Book in the column headed " provisions ;" and when wine, etc., is given out to the sick, the quantities will be mentioned in the Workhouse Medical Relief Book, and be from thence carried into the Provisions Consumption Accounts.

(*d*) See Art. 20, *post*, as to the Farm Account.

said Schedule; provided that the Guardians may, if they see fit, dispense with the keeping of so much of this summary as contains the entries under the separate names and trades.

8. *The Daily Provisions Consumption Account.* In this account shall be entered the number of paupers of the several classes at each meal in the Workhouse, and the quantities of the principal articles of provisions daily consumed by them. In this account may be shown the allowance claimed by the Master in respect of waste or unavoidable loss in the preparation or distribution of the provisions, and the quantities of any provisions supplied for any extraordinary occasion (*a*).

9. *The Weekly Provisions Consumption Account.* In this account shall be entered the quantities of the principal articles of provisions consumed by the paupers in the Workhouse, and also the quantities taken from the stores for the officers and servants of the Workhouse, in each week, and those supplied on extraordinary occasions or in out-door relief, if any (*b*).

(*a*) This Account is to facilitate the ascertaining of the quantities of the several principal articles of cooked or prepared provisions required, according to the Diet Table, for each meal; and also to record these quantities, together with the quantities of the articles in the form in which they are received into the House, that is, in their raw or unprepared state. It is essential that the Master should record the actual consumption of the raw provisions taken out of store and not returned thereto, rather than enter as the quantities consumed a mere weekly estimate or calculation made with reference to the Diet Table.—*Instr. Letter*, 17th March, 1847.

As regards waste in the distribution of provisions, if it arises notwithstanding all due care and attention in the distribution, a reasonable allowance should be made for it.

(*b*) This account is prescribed for the purpose of collecting together, in weekly totals, the quantities in their raw or unprepared state, of the several articles which appear by the "Daily" Account to have been used during each week. The weekly entry for such of the sick as have not the ordinary house diet, will be checked by the diet and the amount of extras, every article of which for the week should be entered opposite each name in the Workhouse Medical Relief Book. The blank columns in that book may be used for the entry of the articles of an ordinary

10. *The Provisions Receipt and Consumption Account.* In this account shall be entered the quantities of the several articles of provisions received and consumed weekly, and the quantities on hand at the commencement and end of every week, and the other particulars in such Form set forth (*c*).

11. *A Quarterly Summary of Provisions received and consumed.* This summary shall be made up from the said Provisions Receipt and Consumption Account, and shall be completed quarterly.

12. *A Quarterly Balance of the Provisions Account.* In this account shall be entered the total quantities and values of the several articles of provisions received and consumed in the quarter, and also the quantities and values of the several articles in store at the beginning and end of the quarter, and the other particulars set

---

kind not mentioned in the printed headings.—*Instr. Letter*, 17th March, 1847.

Though the Forms as set forth in this Order are framed to meet the common ordinary supply of relief, and the Master's books apply to the supply of provisions to the in-door poor, there is nothing to prevent the introduction of other matters into the books, where provisions are supplied to other paupers. The Commissioners see no objection to the Master inserting the quantity of provisions given out of the Workhouse stores during every week for out-door relief in the weekly Provisions Consumption Account, after the entry for the sick, and in such case the total to be carried to the "Provisions Receipt and Consumption Account" will consist of the quantities consumed in the house, and that consumed in out-door relief; or, if it be considered more convenient, an intermediate total, showing the quantity of provisions consumed in the house, might be made. To that must then be added the amount expended in out-door relief, and the gross total will then go on, through the Provisions Receipt and Consumption Account, and Quarterly Summary of Provisions received and consumed, the value of the whole amount when carried to the Ledger will, as heretofore, be distributed between in-maintenance and out-door relief, according to the separate amounts.—9 O. C. (N. s.) 130.

The day of admission and day of discharge of a pauper from the Workhouse, as shown by the Admission and Discharge Book, should both be reckoned in charging the cost of the maintenance of paupers.

(*c*) A considerable saving of time and labour to the Master will be effected, by requiring the calculations of the money value of the quantities of the several articles entered in this Account to be made quarterly instead of weekly.—*Instr. Letter*, 17th March, 1847.

forth in the Form in the Schedule, and the same shall be submitted to the Visiting Committee or some member thereof when so made up and balanced, who shall enter a memorandum at the foot of the account certifying to the same having been submitted to them or one of them (a).

13. *The Clothing Materials Receipt and Conversion Account.* In this account shall be entered a statement of all the articles of clothing materials and of bed and house linen (not made up), from time to time received into the Workhouse, and the several particulars of their conversion, and otherwise set forth in the Form in the Schedule (b).

14. *The Clothing Receipt and Expenditure Account.* In this account shall be entered on the one side the several articles of clothing received from tradesmen or made up in the house, and on the other side the several articles given out, together with the numbers marked thereon.

The articles shall, before they are given out, except when they are given out to paupers quitting the Workhouse or relieved out of the Workhouse, be marked on the inside with the name of the Union, and, as far as practicable, be numbered in suits, so that all the articles of a suit shall bear the same number.

(a) This Form is similar to that of the "Provisions Receipt and Consumption Account," excepting that money columns are added for the purpose of introducing the calculations referred to in the notice of that account. Should this account not balance on the first trial, it will at once be seen, by comparing the columns of totals, in reference to which article the error has arisen; and by tracing backwards the entries relating to that article, the error will readily be detected.—*Instr. Letter*, 17th March, 1847.

The object of Art. 19, Nos. 12, 15, and 19, is to secure that the accounts should be submitted to a member of the Committee, and that such submission should be recorded in each account.

(b) This book will be in the nature of a *Dr.* and *Cr.* account of every article of materials for clothing and bed and house linen. The Account will be debited with the several articles of materials supplied to the Workhouse from time to time, and credited with the quantities of such materials from time to time converted into clothing or bed and house linen.—*Instr. Letter*, 17th March, 1847.

The numbers shall begin with No. 1, and follow each other consecutively; but whenever any article shall have been condemned, or cut up for use in mending other articles, or supplied to paupers quitting the Workhouse, its number may be marked on another article of the same description, the previous number thereon, if any, being obliterated (c).

15. *The Clothing Materials Receipt and Conversion Account*, and *The Clothing Receipt and Expenditure Account*, shall be made up, balanced, and compared with the stock in store at the end of every half-year by the Master, in the presence of the Visiting Committee or some member thereof, when the accounts of the Union are closed, as hereinafter mentioned, and at such other times as the Board of Guardians may require, and to these accounts the like memorandum shall be entered as in the Quarterly Balance of the Provisions Account.

16. *The Clothing Register Book.* In this book shall be entered, under the number marked on the suit of clothes given out to each pauper admitted into the Workhouse, the name of the pauper, together with the dates of his

---

(c) The number of articles of clothing of each description purchased, or made up in the House, is to be entered in the proper column of this Account, when purchased or made up, in the same manner as the number of articles is entered in the present "Clothing Receipt Book." In reference to the expenditure of clothing, a different system to that hitherto pursued is introduced. It will be seen, that clothing is to be numbered in suits before it is given out. A suit for a man will probably consist of one coat, one waistcoat, one pair of trousers, two shirts, a pair of shoes, two pairs of stockings, one hat, and two handkerchiefs, all of which will bear the same number. When a suit is given out, the number marked thereon is to be entered in the column appropriated for that purpose, and the number of articles of each description comprised in the suit, is also to be entered in the proper columns. This account being balanced at the end of the half-year, will show the numbers of the several new articles remaining in store.—*Instr. Letter*, 17th March, 1847.

It sometimes happens that a pauper in the Workhouse is destitute of clothing, and cannot be discharged without a fresh supply. In such a case if the Guardians order clothing to be given to the pauper, it should be supplied from the Workhouse stores, and the cost charged in the In-Maintenance Account.

or her admission and discharge; and a ticket bearing such number shall be attached to the pauper's own clothes.

In addition to the number marked on the clothes, the Master shall insert in the said book a number to indicate the size of the suit.

The Guardians may if they see fit dispense with the keeping of this book (*a*).

17. *The Necessaries and Miscellaneous Account.* In this book the Master shall enter punctually, according to the proper dates, all articles, goods, and materials received by him for use or consumption in the Workhouse, other than provisions, clothing, materials for repairs, and such articles as are entered in the Inventory Book or the Farm Account. He shall also enter therein the consumption of such articles, goods, and materials in respect of the Workhouse, the paupers, and the officers and servants of the Workhouse, as the case may be. This account shall be kept weekly, unless the Guardians shall, in cases where the Workhouse is licensed to hold less than one hundred inmates, authorize its being kept monthly. It shall be kept in the form in the said Schedule (E.) hereunto set forth.

18. *A Quarterly Summary of the Necessaries and Miscel-*

(*a*) At the head of the several columns of this book, numbers will be inserted beginning with Number 1, and following each other consecutively; and when a suit of clothes is given out, the name of the person to whom it is given, with the date of his admission, will be entered under the number marked on the suit. In addition to this number, another number indicating the size of the suit, is to be inserted in the space set apart for it. When the person to whom the suit was given out is discharged, the date of his discharge is to be entered, and such entry will show that the suit is available for any other person whom it may fit; and the name of the other person to whom the same suit is given out, will be entered under the previous name. When any article of a suit is worn out, another article of the same size and description is to take its number, and be substituted for it. This article will, of course, be entered in the Clothing Receipt and Expenditure Account, in the manner already explained. The number should on no account be stamped on a conspicuous part of the garment, but it should be so placed, as not to be visible when the garment is worn.—*Instr. Letter,* 17th March, 1847.

laneous Account, shall be made by the Master at the end of every quarter from the Necessaries and Miscellaneous Account, according to the Form in such Schedule.

19. *A Quarterly Balance of the Necessaries and Miscellaneous Account.* In this account shall be entered the total quantities and values of the several articles, goods, and materials received and consumed in the quarter, and also the quantities and values of the same in store at the beginning and end of the quarter, in the Form set forth in the said Schedule, and shall submit the same to the Visiting Committee or some member thereof when so made up and balanced, who shall enter a memorandum at the foot of the account certifying to the same having been submitted to them or one of them.

Art. 20.—When the Guardians think proper to require it, he shall keep an account to be termed *A Farm Account*, in which he shall enter, under the correct dates, items of all articles, stock, implements, seeds, and other matters received by him for the use of the land belonging to the Workhouse, or maintained thereon for consumption in the Workhouse; and all payments made and all sums received by him on account thereof, or of the produce of such land and stock.

This account shall be kept in such Form as the Guardians shall prescribe, and shall be balanced by the Master quarterly, or oftener, if the Guardians so direct. It shall be laid by him before the Auditor together with the other books of the Master (*b*).

Art. 21.—When there is a Dispensary in the Workhouse or an Assistant Officer appointed to take charge of the medicine and medical appliances, the Master shall enter in his Day Book such medicines and medical appliances when re-

---

(*b*) It is imperative that this account should be balanced quarterly; but the Master's Account of Receipts and Payment (Art. 19, No. 6, *ante*) must be balanced monthly.

ceived by him under the head of Dispensary, and the Dispenser shall keep an account of his receipt, and the consumption or disposal of such medicines and medical appliances in a book to be framed according to such form as the Medical Officer of the Workhouse shall recommend and the Guardians shall order to be adopted, and he shall submit the same to the Auditor at the time of the audit for examination, and shall be answerable for the correctness of such account and of the entries therein (*a*).

Art. 22.—So much of this Order as relates to the duties of the Master of the Workhouse shall be applicable to and be binding upon the Matron of any Workhouse not having a Master, and also to and upon the Matron or other person having the charge of any Workhouse during the temporary absence of the Master, or any vacancy in the office of Master.

OUT-DOOR RELIEF.

Relieving Officer's Books (*b*).

Art. 23.—The Relieving Officer shall punctually enter up and accurately keep the following books and accounts, according to the Forms and directions in the Schedule F. hereunto annexed:—

1. *The Application and Report Book.* In this book shall be entered every distinct application made from time to time through the Relieving Officer for relief, and such of the particulars therein set forth as, on making the requisite examination into the circumstances of the case, he shall collect, as well as the medical relief or relief in kind (if any) already given by the Relieving Officer at his discretion, or reported to him to have

---

(*a*) Article 22, Nos. 17 to 21 are for the first time introduced into the Order of Accounts. Forms of Farm Account and Dispenser's Book may be obtained from the publishers.

(*b*) In some few extensive Parishes an Officer, termed "Pay Clerk of the Poor," is appointed, under the authority of an Order of the Poor Law Board, as to which see *ante*, p. 319.

been given by an Overseer, or any medical aid given to a woman in labour by the Medical Officer without an order.

A note of the decision or direction of the Board of Guardians shall be inserted at the Meeting of the Board, and authenticated by the initials of the Chairman or Clerk, in the column contained in the Form for this purpose.

Where any application is made to the Board of Guardians directly, and the Board order any relief to be administered by the Relieving Officer, he shall enter in this book the particulars of the case as he shall obtain them, and the same shall be dealt with in all respects as when the application is made to himself in the first place (c).

2. *The Out-door Relief List.* In this book shall be entered, in one of the Forms in the said Schedule set forth, the sums of relief in money, and the value of the relief in kind, given by the Relieving Officer to or for each pauper relieved by him in each week. The entries shall include only relief given to the pauper himself, or to some person properly authorized to receive it, and shall be made after the relief has been actually so given, and not before or otherwise. In this book shall also be entered, in the proper columns, the number of

---

(c) The notes at the foot of the Form contain full instructions as to the manner in which this book should be kept. A fresh entry of each pauper's case should be made in this book on each fresh application for relief, though no essential variation in the particulars of the case may have occurred since the making of the previous entry. When an inmate of a Workhouse wishes to apply for out-door relief, the application should be made to the Relieving Officer direct, and by him brought before the Board of Guardians. This may be done by the Workhouse Master referring the inmate to the Relieving Officer in the first place; or the Guardians, on the Master reporting the case, may direct the Relieving Officer to receive the application, and bring it, with the necessary particulars, before the Guardians at their next meeting.

Expenses incurred in the removal of Pauper Lunatics to Asylums should not be entered in this book, but in the "Receipt and Expenditure Book."

individuals of any of the several classes relieved in each case, and the other particulars in the Form in the Schedule set forth. The Relieving Officer shall enter up this book every week, and shall complete the same at the end of every half-year, taking care that no pauper appear in such Relief List more than once in the half-year, unless there shall be some alteration in the circumstances of the case.

He shall also keep a book, to be termed *The Out-door Relief List for Vagrants*, in which shall be entered the relief in money and kind given by him to every person relieved by him as a vagrant or casual pauper. He shall keep this book weekly, with the particulars, and according to the Form and instructions in the same Schedule set forth, and shall enter the total of the expenditure for each week in the corresponding week in the Out-door Relief List. Any Assistant Relieving Officer who administers relief to vagrants must supply this information to the Relieving Officer, and be responsible for its correctness (*a*).

3. *The Abstract of the Out-door Relief List.* In this form shall be entered the names of the several Parishes, and against them the total amount of each week's relief, in respect of the paupers resident therein, according to the Out-door Relief List. It shall be made up against each ordinary meeting of the Guardians, and shall remain in the custody of the Clerk (*b*).

(*a*) The cases of vagrants should be entered either in the " Application and Report Book," or in the " Out-door Relief List " for vagrants; and if sent to the Workhouse, this should be noted in the column headed "Nature of Relief." Relief given to them in the Workhouse should be entered by the Master in the Workhouse books, and not by the Relieving Officer in his " Out-door Relief List." As the Relieving Officer is only required to enter the relief which he himself gives to vagrants, he is not required to take cognizance of relief to vagrants given by Overseers in cases of sudden and urgent necessity under 4 & 5 Wm. IV. c. 76, s. 54. The Overseers must enter such relief in their own accounts, and take the decision of the Auditor upon it.

(*b*) This abstract is to be made up at the meetings of the Board of Guardians, and left in the custody of the Clerk, in order that he may

4. *The Receipt and Expenditure Book* (c). In this book the Relieving Officer shall keep, in the *Form* so named in the said Schedule, an account of all moneys received and disbursed by him, and of all tickets or orders for relief in kind issued by him, and also of all articles received and given out by him for the relief of the out-door poor in each parish in his district; and shall balance such account weekly. In this book the Relieving Officer shall also enter, at the end of every quarter's account, *a Summary of Receipts and Expenditure* for the quarter.

---

possess a duplicate of the out-door relief account against each parish, in the event of the "Out-door Relief List" itself being lost or destroyed. *Instr. Letter,* 17th March, 1847.

(c) The weekly accounts in money and in kind will not be entered separately in the "Receipt and Expenditure Book," as will appear by the "Out-door Relief List" from which they are posted. The relief in money and in kind which are carried out separately in the Out-door Relief List, at the end of each quarter, will be entered separately in the quarterly *Summary* in which the Relieving Officer's money account, and account of relief in kind, will be balanced separately.

With regard to relief to *Non-Resident* and *Non-Settled* poor, it should be observed of *Non-Resident* relief that it is of two kinds—namely, that which is paid through the Relieving Officer of the Board allowing it, and that which is paid by an order on the Treasurer or other means, as prescribed by the Commissioners. In the first case the pauper's name will appear in the "Out-door Relief List" as a matter of course, and will be charged by the Relieving Officer to the Parish in the same manner as relief to a resident pauper. In the second case, the Relieving Officer will have nothing to do with the matter, and the relief will ultimately be a credit to the Treasurer, and a debit of the Parish against which it is charged in the "Parochial Ledger."

Non-Settled Relief, so far as it appears in the accounts of the Union, by the Officers of which it is advanced, will be entered in a separate account, in the "Out-door Relief List," by the Relieving Officer who pays it, and will not be carried into any account against a particular Parish. Accounts should be opened in the "Out-door Relief" List for the several Unions to which the non-settled poor in the Relieving Officer's District belong; and the relief of such poor should be entered in such accounts in the same manner as the relief to the settled poor is entered under their several Parishes.—*Instr. Letter,* 17th March, 1867.

Payments made by Relieving Officers in conveying lunatic paupers to and from Lunatic Asylums should be entered in this book (see 16 & 17 Vict. c. 97, s. 77, and 80); and, indeed, all money which the Officer may receive from or on behalf of the Guardians, and from whatever source the receipt may come.

Art. 24.—Nothing herein contained shall affect the forms of the books of accounts kept by the Pay Clerk where any such officer shall act under the order of the Poor Law Board, nor affect the provisions contained in any Order of the Poor Law Commissioners or the Poor Law Board, whereby the Guardians are empowered to appoint committees to receive applications for relief.

EXAMINATION AND CLOSING OF ACCOUNTS.

Art. 25.—On the day next before every ordinary meeting of the Board of Guardians, or on the day of such meeting, but previous to the meeting, the Clerk shall examine the Master's Day Book, and shall compare the entries of invoices and bills with the invoices and bills themselves, and shall see that all the goods supplied and works done are carried by the Master to the proper accounts, and shall certify the correctness of the same by his initials. He shall also compare the entries of payments in the Master's Receipt and Payment Account with the vouchers, and ascertain that the Master has debited this account with all sums received by him, and produces proper vouchers for all payments made by him, and shall insert his initials at the foot of such account. And he shall inspect the other books required to be kept by the Master by this Order, so as to ascertain that they are duly kept in proper form and with due regularity.

The Clerk shall also, at the same time, examine the weekly account in each Relieving Officer's Out-door Relief Lists and Receipt and Expenditure Book, so as to ascertain the accuracy of the entries therein, and that the relief has been given in accordance with the orders of the Guardians by comparison with the Relief Order Book, and shall certify the correctness of the same by his initials.

The Clerk shall report to the Guardians at tne said meeting the result of his examinations.

And the Master and Relieving Officer shall respectively, subject to any direction of the Board of Guardians, present their Books and Accounts to the Clerk for his examination on such day as aforesaid (*a*).

Art. 26.—The Overseers of every Parish, and every Collector acting for any Parish, shall make up and balance to the 25th day of March and the 29th day of September in each year, all such books as they are required, by the Act passed in the 8th year of the reign of her Majesty Queen Victoria, intituled "*An Act for the Amendment of the Laws relating to the Poor in England*," to deposit for the inspection of the ratepayers at some house within the Parish seven days at least before the audit (*b*).

Art. 27.—All the accounts of the Union and of the Officers of the Union shall be closed at the end of every half-year, that is to say, up to the 25th day of March and the 29th day of September in each year, inclusively, when such days occur at the end of the week established by the practice of the Union, and at other times at the end of such week first completed next after such days respectively. And the several Officers keeping such accounts shall forthwith lay, or cause to be laid, their respective accounts so closed before the Board of Guardians (*c*).

(*a*) All that the Clerk is now required to do in reference to the Master's accounts, is to see that he has made the proper entries in the "Day Book," and has given credit in the proper books and accounts for all the goods supplied at the Workhouse. The examination of the Relieving Officers' accounts the Commissioners have considered indispensable. The examination, however, both of the Master's and the Relieving Officers' accounts, may now be made on the day, or on the day before the day of the Guardians' meeting.—*Instr. Letter*, 17th March, 1847.

At the Clerk's examination of the accounts of a Relieving Officer he should require vouchers for all payments taken credit for, as in the absence of vouchers he cannot certify to the correctness of the accounts. The vouchers will, of course, be returned to the Officer to be produced to the Auditor, and also to the Guardians, in accordance with the Art. 216 of the Consolidated Order, *ante*, p. 192. Further, with regard to this Art. see note (*a*) to Art. 202, No. 2 of that Order, *ante*, p. 141.

(*b*) See 7 & 8 Vict. c. 101, s. 33. The accounts are to be deposited seven clear days, *at least*, before the audit; and this, according to legal construction, excludes the day of deposit and the day of audit.

(*c*) See Art. 67, *post*, as to the definition of "the period of the week." Whatever be the day of the week for the closing of the accounts "established by the practice of the Union," that will be the day for the closing of the accounts of the half-year.

Article 20 of the former Order of Accounts was to be understood as having reference to the meeting of the Guardians, in which cases the accounts are closed up to the day of such meeting. This course the Board consider to be the more correct, and at the same time the more convenient; and they recommend that it should in future be adopted in all cases. But it must be observed that where the meetings of the Guardians are held fortnightly, the week's accounts should be closed at the end of the half-year, although there be no meeting of the Guardians in the week.—*Instr. Letter*, 15th March, 1856.

The week should terminate on the day preceding the meeting of the Guardians, and the Poor Law Board think that it is in every respect most convenient that the week should so terminate (as indicated in Art. 67, *post*), and that it is competent to the Guardians to establish this practice. The day of meeting of the Guardians is always to be excluded; and the whole of the Union Officers should close their accounts on the same day. Items of receipt and expenditure occurring after the date at which the amounts are closed should not be inserted in those accounts, but should go into the accounts for the following half-year.

The following tables, extracted from Mr. Lloyd Roberts' exemplification of the mode of keeping accounts under this Order, set forth the dates upon which the accounts of Unions, and of the Officers of Unions, must, for future half-years, be commenced and closed, according to the provisions of Arts. 27 and 67 of the Order:—

FIRST TABLE.—MICHAELMAS HALF-YEARS.

Commencing with.	Will end with.	Number of weeks in each Half-year.
March 26	September 30	27
,, 27	October 1	27
,, 28	,, 2	27
,, 29	,, 3	27
,, 30	,, 4	27
,, 31	,, 5	27
April 1	September 29	26

SECOND TABLE.—LADY DAY HALF-YEARS.

Commencing with.	Will end with.	Number of weeks in each Half-year.	In Leap Years.	
			Will end with.	Number of Weeks in each Half-year.
September 30	March 30	26	March 29	26
October 1	,, 31	26	,, 30	26
,, 2	,, 25	25	,, 31	26
,, 3	,, 26	25	,, 25	25
,, 4	,, 27	25	,, 26	25
,, 5	,, 28	25	,, 27	25
,, 6	,, 29	25	,, 28	25

Art. 28.—The Master of the Workhouse shall, at the end of every half-year, allow each Relieving Officer to inspect the In-door Relief List for the half-year last expired.

And each of the Relieving Officers shall forthwith, after the end of the half-year, inspect the names entered in such In-door Relief List, and shall write his initials in red ink against the name of every pauper who shall have been entered in the Out-door Relief List in the course of the said half-year.

Art. 29.—The Clerk or Medical Officer in possession of the District Medical Relief Books shall, at the end of every half-year, allow each of the Relieving Officers to inspect such books; and each of the Relieving Officers shall forthwith inspect the names in such books, and shall write his initials in red ink against the name of every pauper who shall not have received any other than medical relief during the half-year then last closed.

Art. 30.—The Clerk shall, at the close of each half-year, prepare in duplicate, from the accounts of the Union,— 1. A Statistical Statement, showing the number of paupers of all classes actually relieved in the course of the last half-year, and the other particulars, according to the Form and directions in the Schedule (B.) set forth; and—2. A Financial Statement, showing the account of the Receipt and Expenditure of the Union for the last half-year, together with the then outstanding liabilities, in the *Form* in the said Schedule (B.) set forth; which statements the Clerk shall submit to the Auditor at the time of his auditing the Union accounts (*a*).

(*a*) The half-yearly Financial Statement heretofore has shown only the receipts and expenditure by the Guardians for the half-year. The Board have thought it right that henceforth this Statement shall also show the liabilities of the Guardians outstanding at the end of the half-year to which the Statement relates. They have often felt that the ratepayers have not received the full information of the financial state of their Union when, though they learnt the amount of money received by the Board of Guardians and that which had been expended, they had no information as to the amount of outstanding liabilities due from the Union. The Statute 22 & 23 Vict. c. 49, has tended greatly

The Auditor, if satisfied of the correctness of such Statements, shall sign the same; and the Clerk shall forthwith transmit one copy of each Statement to the Poor Law Board, and preserve the other copy for the Board of Guardians.

Art. 31.—The Clerk shall, as soon as he shall receive notice from the Auditor of the day or days appointed by him for the auditing of the half-yearly Accounts of the Union, and the several Parishes comprised therein, cause the following notice to be affixed on the external gate or door of every Workhouse in the Union, and at some other place or places where Union notices are usually affixed, and shall continue the same so affixed until the audit is completed:—

"＿＿＿＿＿ UNION.

"Notice is hereby given, that the Half-yearly Statement of the Accounts of this Union, together with the *Relief Order Book* and the *Ledger*, will, on the   day of   be deposited at   ; and such Statement and Books will be open to be inspected, examined, and copied by any Owner of Property or Ratepayer in the said Union, at any reasonable hour in the day time, when the Board of Guardians is not sitting, until the   day of   ; and that on the last-mentioned day, at the hour of   the Accounts of the Union will be audited by   the Auditor of the District comprising this Union, at   when and where every such Owner of Property or Ratepayer, who may have any objection to any matter contained in the above-mentioned Accounts, may attend, and prefer his objection, and the same will be heard and determined by the Auditor.

"Dated

"Clerk to the Board of Guardians."

---

to check the running on of debts and claims against the Guardians; and the Board trust that this new form of Financial Statement will still further aid in the desirable end of keeping the charges incurred by the Guardians within the year for which they are elected to act as such.—*Instr. Letter*, 22nd January, 1867.

Art. 32.—The Clerk shall, three clear days (*a*) before the day appointed for auditing the Union Accounts, deposit the said Half-yearly Statement of the Accounts of the Union, together with the Relief Order Book and Ledger, in the Board Room of the Guardians of the Union, or such other place as the Board of Guardians may appoint, and shall permit the said Statement, Book, and Ledger to be inspected, examined, and copied by any Ratepayer or Owner of property in the Union, in the presence of the Clerk or some other person approved of by the Board of Guardians, at any reasonable hour in the day-time, when the Board of Guardians shall not be sitting, after the said Statement, Book, and Ledger shall have been so deposited, and previous to the day appointed for the auditing of the accounts of the Union.

Art. 33.—In case the auditing of any of the Union or Parish Accounts shall be adjourned for any longer period than from day to day, the Clerk, on receiving from the Auditor notice thereof, shall affix, in manner aforesaid, notice of the time and place of such adjournment, and of the Accounts remaining to be audited, as often as such adjournment shall be made.

Art. 34.—Every Master of a Workhouse shall, within seven days after the end of each half-year, insert in the proper columns, according to the *Form* in Schedule (B.) named, *the Parochial List and Statement of Account*, for every Parish in the Union, or with the consent of the Board of Guardians in a separate list containing similar columns, to be called *the List of In-door Poor*, the name of every pauper admitted from every such Parish who shall have been relieved in the Workhouse during the whole or any part of the previous half-year, together with the number of days each pauper has been maintained in the Workhouse; and every Relieving Officer shall, within fourteen days after the end of each half-year, enter in the proper columns of

---

(*a*) *I. e.* exclusive of Sunday, if it intervenes.

the said *List* for every Parish in his District, or with the consent of the Board of Guardians, in a separate list containing similar columns, to be called the *List of Out-door Poor*, the name of every pauper contained in the Out-door Relief Lists and District Medical Officer's books for the previous half-year, together with the amounts of relief in money and in kind given to each pauper.

Such Parochial Lists, when filled up by the Master and Relieving Officers respectively, shall be delivered by them to the Clerk, who shall examine the entries made therein, and shall certify to the accuracy thereof by his signature. The Clerk shall also make out, in the form given at the foot of such Parochial List, a complete Statement of the Account of every Parish with the Union and shall date and sign the same.

Art. 35.—The Relieving Officers of the Union shall, within thirty days after the end of each half-year, under the direction of the Board of Guardians or of the Clerk, deliver a copy of each of such lists and statement for every Parish in his District to the Overseers thereof, who shall lay the same before the next Vestry Meeting, and preserve the same with the Parish papers.

Art. 36.—The salaries of the several Officers of the Guardians, whether for the full quarter or for any portion thereof, shall be paid at the several quarters ending at the usual feast-days in the year, namely, Lady Day, Midsummer Day, Michaelmas Day, and Christmas Day; and where an Officer is paid according to a poundage or similar rate, the amount shall be calculated by the Guardians at those several quarter-days upon the amount which the said Guardians shall ascertain to have been collected or earned by such Officer in the quarter then ended; provided nevertheless, that in the case of any Officer whose duty it is to render accounts to the Board of Guardians or Auditor, such Officer shall submit his accounts for the quarter in question to the Guardians before such payment, and further that it shall be competent for the Guardians to defer in whole or in part the payment of the salary or other compensation of any such Officer until his accounts shall have been audited and allowed by the Auditor, after which audit and allowance the sum due up to the date of his accounts so audited shall be forthwith paid.

Art. 37.—Where any Officer shall be entitled to be paid any extra fees or emoluments, he shall make out his account thereof quarterly according to the above-mentioned days, and lay the same before the Guardians on those days, and his claim shall be deemed to accrue at the expiration of one calendar month next following such quarter-day, provided that the Guardians may, if they think fit, pay the same before the expiration of such month.

Auditing of Accounts.

Art. 38.—The Auditor shall audit the accounts of the Union and of the Parishes comprised therein, once in every half-year; that is to say, as soon as may be after the 25th day of March and the 29th day of September, respectively. Provided always, that if the Auditor shall be required by the Poor Law Board, to hold an extraordinary audit, either of the whole or of any portion of the accounts of the Union or any Parish therein, in addition to the ordinary audit, at any time between such two days, all the provisions herein contained, with reference to the ordinary audit, shall, as far as they may be applicable, apply to such extraordinary audit (*a*).

(*a*) The Poor Law Commissioners, in their Instructional Letter, state that a mere knowledge of accounts is only a small part of the requisite accomplishments of an Auditor. It is necessary that he should have a complete knowledge of the statutes and authorities by which the expenditure of the Poor-rates is regulated, and of the Poor Law Commissioners' rules, orders, and regulations, and be able to make sound and legal inferences from these authorities, so as to determine their effect in special cases. Some acquaintance with the law of contracts is necessary, and, above all, a large experience of the nature of the pecuniary transactions of the Guardians, Overseers, and other accountable officers, without which it is impossible for him to exercise his important function of ascertaining, as he is bound to do in every case, the reasonableness of every item. To come to correct conclusions in such matters is obviously impossible without a knowledge of the terms upon which transactions on the like scale and conditions are usually effected. It may be added, with reference to the above, that, as a general rule, it is not desirable that an Auditor should express any opinion as to the payment out of the Poor-rates of any expenses which may afterwards come before him at an audit, and in regard to which he may then have to give his decision. It forms no part of his duty to give advice to Union or Parish Officers as to the legality of any particular expenses which they may contemplate charging in their accounts; and as his advice, if given, may embarrass him in his subsequent proceedings, it is advisable that he should in general abstain from expressing any opinion upon an item of expenditure except at the audit, when he must decide as to the legality or otherwise of the charge.

The notice of Audit to be given to the Overseers fourteen days before the Audit, under 7 & 8 Vict. c. 101, s. 33, is as follows:—

POOR LAW AMENDMENT ACT, 1844.
(7 & 8 Vict. c. 101.)

NOTICE OF AUDIT.

——— Union.

To the Overseers of the Poor or other Officers employed in carrying the Laws for the Relief of the Poor into execution in the Parish or Township of .

I, the undersigned, Auditor of the District within which the above named Union is situate, hereby give notice, that I have appointed the Audit of the Accounts of the said Union, and of the Parishes therein comprised, for the Half-year ended the ——— day of ———, 186 , to be held on ———, the ——— day of ———, 186 , at ——— o'clock in the forenoon, *at the Board-room of the Guardians of the said Union*, when and where you are required to attend, and produce your Books of Account, Rate Books, and Vouchers.

You are also required to have your Rate Books and other Accounts made up and balanced, *seven clear days* before the day fixed for the Audit, and to deposit them, for the inspection of all Persons liable to be rated to the relief of the Poor, at the house of a Churchwarden, Overseer, Collector, or Assistant-Overseer, or at some other house within the Parish. You are likewise required to affix, at the usual place or places of giving Parish notices, notice of the time and place of Audit as above notified by me, and of the place where the Rate Books and other Accounts are deposited.

Outgoing Overseers must pay the balance due from them to the succeeding Overseers, and produce their receipt for the same at the Audit.

Dated this ——— day of ———, 186 .

——— *District Auditor.*

Overseers are required to produce at the Audit:—
The Rate Books, with all the Columns properly filled up, cast up, and balanced.
The Valuation and Supplemental Valuation Lists.
The Rate Receipt Check Books.
The General Receipt Check Book.

Art. 39.—The Auditor in respect of every ordinary audit shall give to the Clerk to the Guardians fourteen days' notice in writing of the time and place on and at which he intends to commence the audit of the accounts of the Union, and of the Parishes therein (*a*).

Art. 40.—The Officers of the Union, and the Overseers and Officers of the Parishes therein, who by law are bound to account to such Auditor, shall attend at the time and place appointed by him for the audit of their accounts, and shall submit to the Auditor all books, documents, appointments in writing, contracts, bills, orders for payment, receipts, and other vouchers containing or relating to their accounts, together with the Banker's Pass Books where the Overseers keep their accounts with a Banker; and the same shall at the time of the audit be open to the inspection of any owner of property or ratepayer interested in such accounts, but to such extent and in such manner only as

---

The Overseers' Book of Receipts and Payments duly filled up, balanced, and signed by the Churchwardens and Overseers.
The Balance Sheet in Duplicate duly filled up.
Receipts and Vouchers for all payments made by them.
The Overseers' Banker's Pass Book.
The Collectors' or Assistant-Overseers' Monthly Statements.
Assistant-Overseers and Collectors are, in addition to the above, to produce,—
The Book of Monthly Statements.
The Collecting and Deposit Book.
The Instalment Rate Receipt Check Book, if any.
The Unpaid Rates' Statement, and
A Certificate of Proof that each of the Sureties named in the Bond is living, and is not bankrupt or insolvent.
It is requisite that one at least of the Overseers, whose Accounts are to be audited, shall *personally* attend the Audit (as well as the Assistant-Overseer or Collector, if any).
It is necessary that notices and advertisements of special audits to be held under this Article should be given in all respects as in the case of ordinary audits. (7 & 8 Vict. c. 101, s. 33.)

(*a*) There is nothing in the 7 & 8 Vict. c. 101, s. 33, or in the Order of Accounts, which prevents the Auditor from giving notice of audit before the 29th of September and 25th of March respectively. The 11 & 12 Vict. c. 91, s. 7, further provides that the notice of audit shall be published in a newspaper circulating in the Union. The expenses attending these advertisements are repaid to the Auditors by the Poor Law Board. The salaries of the Auditors are also paid by the Poor Law Board out of the Consolidated Fund.

will not in the judgment of the said Auditor interfere with the audit (*a*).

Art. 41.—In auditing the accounts, the Auditor shall see that they have been kept and are presented in proper form; that the particular items of receipt and expenditure are stated in sufficient detail, and that the payments are supported by adequate vouchers and authority; and he shall ascertain whether all sums received, or which ought to have been received, are brought into account; and he shall examine whether the expenditure is in all cases such as might lawfully be made; and he shall reduce such payments and charges as are exorbitant, shall surcharge moneys not duly accounted for, or lost by negligence, upon the person who ought to account for the same, or whose negligence or improper conduct has caused the loss, and shall disallow and strike out such payments as are contrary to the Orders, Rules, and Regulations of the Poor Law Board, or are not otherwise authorized by law (*b*).

(*a*) The Clerk to the Guardians is not ordinarily an "accounting officer;" but if he be entrusted with money to pay petty cash accounts, he is bound to render an account of his payments, and in so far would be an officer bound to account to the Auditor. As to the Clerk's Petty Cash Account, see Art. 16, No. 4, *ante*, p. 450.

Amongst other books, the Auditor may call for the production of the Overseers' Banker's Pass Book, for the purpose of verifying the entries in the Collecting and Deposit Book. The Pass Book is not, however, a book of account which the Overseers are required to deposit for the inspection of the ratepayers under 7 & 8 Vict. c. 101, s. 33.

With regard to the attendance of the Officers at the audit, it is to be observed, as regards the Overseers, that the Assistant-Overseer, if there be one, may attend the audit of the accounts of the Overseers on their behalf, but that it is competent for the Auditor to require the attendance of one or more of the Overseers when he deems their attendance necessary. He may also allow an Overseer to attend by deputy, but he should only do so in exceptional cases. Art. 202, No. 2, of the Consolidated Order, *ante*, p. 141, and this Article, prescribe the Clerk's duty in this respect.

(*b*) In strictness, the duty of the Auditor under this Article is to ascertain not merely whether the payments for which the Officers take credit were directed or sanctioned by proper authority, but also whether the facts of such payments having been made be established by adequate vouchers. (56 O. C. (N. S.) 68.) The 11 & 12 Vict. c. 91, s. 8, requires notice to be given by the Auditor to any person (not being an accounting Officer) before he shall surcharge such person in respect of

Art. 42.—When he disallows any payment or surcharges any sum upon any person, he shall declare the ground of his decision, and offer to state such ground in writing, if required by the person aggrieved to do so, in the proper book of account forthwith, or so soon as the arrangements for the business of his audit will permit.

Art. 43.—He shall examine and collate the several books and papers of account of the several accounting parties; and shall ascertain that the several entries correspond with and balance each other, where such balance may be required; but in the case of any error caused by inadvertence or accident in the account of any Officer, he may require such Officer to correct the same, and such Officer shall make the necessary correction, and the Auditor shall then deal with the account so corrected. But if such Officer shall refuse to do so, the Auditor shall himself make the correction, and report the circumstances of the case to the Poor Law Board.

Art. 44.—He shall compute the several accounts so as to verify the arithmetical accuracy thereof, and the balance due to or from the Overseers or the Officers rendering the same at the time to which the audit relates; and he shall state the balance in words at length, and certify the same by his signature or initials, and add the date of the audit, and when he certifies any sum or other matter to be due he shall, as far as practicable, enter his certificate and his reasons for the same (when they are required) in some part of the book of account, which shall be free from other writing (*c*).

---

any improper payment which he may have authorized, so that such person having received the notice may appear before the Auditor and defend his act. If the notice required by the statute be omitted to be given, any surcharge which the Auditor may make upon the person intended to be affected by it will be null and void.

"Disallow and strike out," per Mr. Justice Blackburn in *Reg.* v. *City of London Union, Easter Term*, 1862, "does not mean that you are to draw your pen through it (the item); but it means that you are to express in words that you do disallow it, and cause it to be struck out. It is not requisite to strike out the figures if he (the Auditor) writes by the side of them 'disallowed.'"

(*c*) With regard to the mode of certifying balances, see 11 & 12 Vict. c. 91, s. 5.

Art. 45.—He shall at each audit compare the Balance Sheets herein-before directed to be delivered to him by the Overseers of every Parish, with the entries in the Books of Receipts and Payments of the Overseers; and having certified by his signature or initials at the foot of such Balance Sheets that it is in conformity with the said book, shall deliver one duplicate of such Balance Sheets to the Clerk to the Board of Guardians, who shall preserve it, together with the other Balance Sheets of the same half-year, with the books and papers of the Guardians, and shall deliver the other to the Overseers (*a*).

Art. 46.—The Auditor shall receive any objection made by a ratepayer or any person aggrieved against the accounts undergoing audit, or any item or charge therein, or any vouchers or authority for the same, and shall examine into the merits of such objection, and make a decision respecting the same, stating the grounds thereof, and offering to enter the same in the book of account then being examined, if required to do so, as in the case of a disallowance or surcharge (*b*).

Art. 47.—If he shall doubt the correctness of any account, or any item or charge in any account, he shall require the Officer rendering the account, or any other person holding or accountable for any money, books, deeds or chattels, relating to the Poor-rates or the relief of the poor, to appear before him, and shall call upon such person to produce any accounts, books, or papers which he may lawfully require; and he shall examine such Officer or person as may then appear, and such accounts, books, and papers as may be produced before him, respecting such account, item, or charge (*c*).

(*a*) See Art. 2, *ante*, p. 438.
(*b*) The Auditor's decision, if it be adverse to the objection, may afterwards be appealed against. (See 7 & 8 Vict. c. 101, ss. 35, 36.)
(*c*) If it be necessary for the purpose contemplated by this Article that the Audit should be adjourned, or if on any other account it should be necessary to adjourn the Audit, the adjournment should be to a day certain, and never *sine die*.

The following Table of average waste in the consumption of Workhouse provisions in certain Unions in the same county may be useful as a guide to what ought to be allowed as waste :—

Unions.	Waste in the lb.		
	Bread.	Butter.	Cheese.
A	1 oz.	1 oz.	1 oz.
B	1 "	1 "	1 "
C	1 "	1¼ "	1 "
D	1 "	1 "	1 "
E	1 "	1 "	1 "
F	2 "	1¼ "	1¼ "
G	1 "	1 "	1 "
H	1 "	1 "	1¼ "
I	¼ "	1 "	
K	2 "	1¼ "	1¼ "
L	1 "	1 "	1 "
M	1 "	2 "	1 "
N	1 "	1 "	1 "
O	1¼ "		
P	2 "	1¼ "	1¼ "
Q	1 "	1 "	1 "
R	1 "	1 "	1 "

Ordinarily, each pound of flour in baking into bread will yield 1 lb. 5½ oz. of bread, and barley-meal will yield 1 lb. 8½ oz. of bread. A sack of flour weighs 280 lbs., and flour of the first quality will produce about 90 to 96 4 lb. loaves per sack. Inferior flour will not produce more than 80 to 86 4 lb. loaves per sack.

According to actual experiments carefully superintended, the following results have been obtained in bread-making in a Union Workhouse :—

56 lbs. of barley-meal, when baked, produced 81 lbs. of bread, being an increase of 44·64 per 100 lbs.

28 lbs. of wheat-flour, when baked, produced 35 lbs. of bread, being an increase of 25 lbs. per 100 lbs.

The yield of bread will, however, vary according to circumstances, such as the quality of the flour used, the nature of the oven, and the skill of the baker.

It has been found, taking the aggregate of bakings in Union Workhouses in a district, that 1629 lbs. of wheat-flour produced 2054 lbs. of bread, or an increase of 26·13 per 100 lbs., and that 716 lbs. of barley-meal produced 942½ lbs., or an increase of 31·63 per 100 lbs.

In making allowances for waste, the Master should be guided by the results of actually weighing the food before it is cooked or served out, and not by entering an assumed average allowance for waste. In no case should he compensate errors in his previous accounts by making other erroneous entries for the purpose of neutralizing the errors.

Art. 48.—If the Auditor find that any money, goods, or chattels belonging to the Union, or any Parish therein, have been purloined, embezzled, wasted, or misapplied (*a*), or that any deficiency or loss has been incurred by the negligence or misconduct of any Officer or other person accounting, and shall surcharge (*b*) such Officer or person with such amount or value in his account, he shall submit a statement of such surcharge to the Board of Guardians as soon as he conveniently can do so.

Art. 49.—The Auditor having audited the several accounts in the Ledger, shall sign a certificate at the foot of the balance-sheet therein, to the following effect:—

"I have examined the several accounts of which the foregoing is the balance-sheet, and I have compared the several payments credited to the Treasurer with the vouchers, and I hereby certify that the entries appear to be correct and legal. And that [when the balance in the Treasurer's book does not agree with the balance in the Ledger], subject to the explanation below [the difference to be explained at the foot of the certificate], the balance of the Treasurer's account, viz. £   , agrees with the balance which by his own book appears to have been in his hands at the time of closing such account; and I find from the information laid before me that the amount of the outstanding liabilities of the Union at that time was £   .

" Dated   (Signed)   "*Auditor.*"

And in the other books the Auditor shall enter a certificate of his having audited the same, and sign and date the same (*c*).

(*a*) See 4 & 5 Wm. IV. c. 76, s. 97.
(*b*) See 7 & 8 Vict. c. 101, s. 32.
(*c*) The certificate at the foot of the account in the Receipt and Payment Book will be a sufficient compliance with this provision as regards that account.

The signature of the Auditor may be impressed with a stamp. In the case of *Bennett* v. *Brumfitt*, 3 L. R. C. P. 29; 37 L. J. C. P. 25, where notice of objection to a voter's name being on the Register, the signature of the objector was engraved in *facsimile* on a stamp, and impressed on the notice of objection by the objector, per Bovill, C.J., "it

Art. 50.—The Auditor shall, at the close of each audit of the accounts of the Union, transmit to the Poor Law Board statements in the *Forms* in the Schedule (G.) hereunto annexed of the books directed by this Order to be kept by the Overseers, Collectors, and Union Officers, showing which is not kept, or is imperfectly kept, or kept in a Form different from that prescribed by the Poor Law Board, and shall deliver copies thereof to the Board of Guardians (*d*), and shall send to the Poor Law Board a Certificate in the Form therein contained in respect of each Union, and of the Parishes therein, where he finds that there has been no default.

Art. 51.—The Auditor shall, at the close of every audit of the accounts of the Union next after the 25th day of March in every year, transmit to the Poor Law Board a statement, in the *Form* in the said Schedule (G.), setting forth the name of each Union Officer, Collector of Poor-rates (*e*), Vestry Clerk, and other Officer in the Union required to give security, and whether such security, together with any certificate or proof that each of the sureties named therein is living, and is not bankrupt or insolvent, was produced to him at such audit, or the security is otherwise in force; and also in the column headed "Observations," stating any defects which he may discover in such securities.

And the Auditor shall, at the close of such audit, deliver a copy of such statement to the Board of Guardians.

---

was clear that such a signature would be a good signature under the Statute of Frauds and under the Wills Act, and he was of opinion that it was also a good signature under this statute (6 Vict. c. 18, s. 17). The signature in every case was made not by the hand alone, but by some instrument. It was written either with a pen or a pencil, or a brush, and he could see no distinction between using a stamp by the personal hand of the maker of the signature, and using a pen or a pencil, or a paint-brush. If written with a pencil, it could not be contended not to be his signature, and so if written with a paint-brush. It was the act of the party, and to his (the C.J.'s) mind was his signature." Willes, J., concurred.

(*d*) The provision which requires the Auditors to send to the Board of Guardians copies of these reports, is suspended for the present. (See the Suspensory Order, *post*, p. 544.)

(*e*) This will apply to the bond of an Assistant-Overseer. (See Art. 60, *post*, p. 482.)

52.—The personal representatives of an Officer accountable under this Order, dying before the half-yearly audit of his accounts, shall, so far as they may be by law required, account, in conformity with the provisions herein contained in the place of such deceased Officer; and all regulations affecting the accounts of such Officer shall, so far as may be otherwise lawful, affect the accounts of the personal representatives of such Officer (*a*).

Art. 53.—If any person, being Clerk to the Board of Guardians, Treasurer, Master of the Workhouse, Collector appointed by the Guardians, or Relieving or other Officer of the said Guardians, accountable under this Order, shall resign his office or be removed therefrom before the audit of his accounts shall have been held and closed, such person shall lay before the Board of Guardians, at a time to be fixed by them, a true and complete account of all moneys, matters, and things committed to the charge of, or collected, received, held, or distributed by such person on behalf of the Union or any Parish therein, in such form as he would have had to produce them before the Auditor at the end of the current half-year, if he had so long continued in office; and shall deliver over all balances, books, papers, matters, and things in his hands, to the Board of Guardians, or to the person whom they may appoint to receive the same; subject always to the liability of such person to account to the Auditor at the next audit, and without prejudice to the power of the Auditor to allow or disallow the account of such person or any charge therein, or to surcharge him in respect of any charge to which he might be liable.

54.—Every person voluntarily undertaking to fulfil either wholly or in part the duties of any Officer affected by this

---

(*a*) If an accounting Officer die after the audit, the Auditor's certificate cannot be enforced; but if there should be default on the part of the Officer, so as to operate as a forfeiture of his bond, the loss may be recovered from his sureties. No certificate made against the legal representative of a deceased Officer in respect of any disallowance or surcharge can be enforced by the Auditor. The Auditor should, however, audit such accounts as may be rendered by the personal representatives of the deceased, and certify the balance due upon the face of those accounts, which will be recoverable from the sureties if it be not paid.

Order, shall, so far as relates to the accounts prescribed by this Order to be kept or presented by any such Officer, keep and present such accounts in the same form and manner as any such Officer is by this Order directed to keep and present such accounts.

Art. 55.—The Clerk shall, at all reasonable times, at the request in writing of any owner of property or ratepayer in the Union, permit him to inspect the Statements of the Union or Parish accounts in the possession of the Guardians for the twelve months prior to the last audit.

And, in reference to the purchase and custody of Books and Papers for the Accounts, We hereby order and direct as follows:—

Art. 56.—The proper books and papers of account for the Clerk, the Master of the Workhouse, the Medical Officers, and the Relieving and other Officers of the Union, shall be purchased by the Board of Guardians, and paid for out of their common fund. Those required for the Overseers or Collector of the Parish shall be paid for out of the Poor-rate of the Parish.

Art. 57.—The books and papers of account belonging to the Guardians in current use shall, except where special provision is otherwise made, remain in the custody of the proper Officers accounting, and shall be produced and exhibited at the ordinary meetings of the Guardians and whenever else the Board of Guardians may require their production, as well as on other lawful occasions.

Art. 58.—The books and papers of the Guardians containing the accounts which are closed, shall be deposited for safe custody with such person, and at such a place as the Board of Guardians may from time to time direct (*b*).

(*b*) The Guardians have entire control over the books and papers of the Union, and when they have accumulated to such an extent as to cause inconvenience in finding proper depositories for them, the Guardians may, if they think fit, cause such of them as appear to be of no further use to be sold as waste paper; care should, however, be taken that no books (such as the Minute Books, Ledgers, Registers, the Relief Lists, the Workhouse Admission and Discharge Books) which may partake of books of record, which may be required by way of legal evidence

And in reference to the meaning of certain words used in this Order, We hereby order and direct as follows :—

Art. 59.—Whenever the word "Overseers" is used in this Order, it shall be taken to mean Overseers of the Poor and Churchwardens, so far as they are authorized or required by law to act in the management or relief of the Poor, or in the collection or distribution of the Poor-rate in any Parish, and to apply to the majority of the whole body of Churchwardens and Overseers or of the Overseers only, as the case may be.

Art. 60.—The term "Collector" in the construing of this Order shall be taken to apply to any person appointed under any Act of Parliament, or any Order of the Poor Law Board, to collect the rates for the relief of the poor in any Parish or Parishes, whether such person shall be designated Collector of Poor-rates or Assistant-Overseer, or be called by any other name whatever, or the Collector of the Guardians, as the context shall require.

Art. 61. Whenever the word "Parish" is used in this Order, or in any other Order issued by the Poor Law Board, it shall be taken to apply to any place for which a separate Poor-rate shall or can be made, or for which a separate Overseer is or can be appointed.

Art. 62.—The word "Provisions" shall include all articles of food specified in the Dietary Tables or supplied in rations to the officers and servants of the Workhouse, or expressly ordered for any inmate upon the recommendation of the Medical Officer. The word "Necessaries" shall include all articles supplied to any inmate specially, either by way of

---

at any time hereafter, should be parted with. The Clerk has no authority to destroy any of the Union papers without the direction of the Board of Guardians, and such direction should be duly recorded in the Minute Book, and the papers specifically mentioned in the Minute. The best course to pursue in such a case is for the Guardians to appoint a Committee of their number, to ascertain, with the assistance of the Clerk of the Union, what books and documents should not be longer preserved. All the official correspondence of the Guardians should however be carefully preserved; and the most convenient course will be to have such correspondence from time to time bound in volumes, with an index prefixed to each of names and subjects.

nourishment or as stimulant, or in bodily relief, which are not entered in the Provisions Accounts.

Art. 63.—The word "In-maintenance" shall apply to all the expense incurred in and about the maintenance, treatment, and relief of the paupers in the Workhouse exclusive of the repairs and furniture of the Workhouse, and the salaries, remuneration, and rations of the officers and servants, but inclusive of the charges for apprentice fees, outfits, burials(a), and the necessary expenses incurred in the warming, cleansing, and lighting the Workhouse, and otherwise keeping it fit for daily use. The word "Out-relief" shall apply to the cost of all relief, schooling, and other expenses incurred in and about the paupers relieved out of the Workhouse, exclusive of the salaries of officers and the charges for relief stations.

Art. 64.—Whenever the word "Chairman" is used in this Order, it shall be taken to mean any person acting as Chairman for the time being.

Art. 65.—Whenever in this Order any Article is referred to by its number, the Article of this Order bearing the number referred to shall be taken to be signified thereby.

Art. 66.—Whenever in this Order the word importing the singular number or the masculine gender only is used, it shall be taken to include and apply to several persons as well as one, and to females as well as males, unless there be something in the subject or context repugnant to such construction.

Art. 67.—For the purposes of this Order, except where otherwise provided, the year shall commence on the Twenty-sixth day of March in every year, and the period of the week shall be deemed to include the seven days which commence in the day of the week on which the meeting of the Board of Guardians is held, unless there be anything in the context inconsistent with such interpretation.

(a) The cost of In-door funerals should be defrayed by the Guardians, and not by the Master of the Workhouse or Relieving Officer.

When the Guardians claim repayment from another Union of the cost of relief given to a pauper in the Workhouse, such claim should be confined to the cost of "In-Maintenance," as defined by this Article.

SCHEDULE
Containing the Forms of the Parish Accounts

The Rate

Form of heading to the "Rate."

An Assessment for the Relief of the Poor of the Parish of   , in the Count of   , and for other purposes chargeable thereon, according to law, made this (*b*)   day of   , in the year of our Lord One thousand eight hundred and   , after the rate of   in the pound.

	ARREARS.						RATE.				
No.	Due, or if excused.	If excused, write the word "excused."	Name of Occupier.	Name of Owner.	Description of Property rated.	Name or Situation of Property.	Estimated Extent.	Gross estimated Rental.	Rateable Value.	Rate at — in the Pound.	Amount of Rate assessed upon and payable by the Owner, instead of the Occupier, by virtue of the Statute or Statutes in that behalf.
1	2	3	4	5	6	7	8	9	10	11	12
	£. s. d.						A. R. P.	£. s. d.	£. s. d.	£. s. d.	£. s. d.

Totals.

Form of Declaration at the foot of the "Rate."

We declare that adding the columns 11 and 12 together, the total of the above Rate amounts to the sum of   pounds shillings and   pence.

We,   do declare the several particulars specified in the respective columns of the above Rate to be true and correct so far as we have been able to ascertain them, to which end we have used our best endeavours.

or We, the undersigned, do hereby declare that one of us, or some person on our behalf, has examined and compared the several particulars in the respective columns of the above Rate with the Valuation List made under the authority of the Union Assessment Committee Act of 1862, in force *in this Parish*, and the several hereditaments are, to the best of our belief, rated according to the value appearing in such Valuation List.

   ————————, *Overseer.*
   ————————, *Overseer.*
   ————————, *Churchwarden.*
   ————————, *Churchwarden.*

(*a*) See Art. 1, *ante*, p. 435.
(*b*) The date of the Rate should be the day when it is signed by the Churchwardens and Overseers, and not the day when it is allowed by the Justices.

⁎⁎⁎ Under the 43 Eliz. c. 2, it is necessary that an actual majority of the Church-Resp., 34 L. J. M. C. 49; 11 Jur. (N. S.) 65; 18 C. B. 52, that an Assistant-Overseer if he is appointed by the Vestry to perform all the duties of the Overseers. It will, should sign the Rate. See 25 & 26 Vict. c. 103, s. 28, and 27 & 28 Vict. c. 39, s. 11, with

Column 12 of the Poor Rate will be inapplicable in the case of any Vict. c. 102, s. 7, in the 'Representation of the People Act,' 1867, by

(A.)
to be kept by *the Overseers and Collectors.*
Book (*a*).

Recoverable Arrears of former Rates.	COLLECTION.					
	Total amount to be Collected.	Amount actually Collected.	Uncollected at balancing this book.			
			Recoverable Arrears at balancing the book.	Irrecoverable at balancing the book.		
				Amount legally excused.	Otherwise not recoverable.	
					Amount.	Causes.
13	14	15	16	17	18 (*c*)	19
£. *s. d.*	£. *s. d.*	£. *s. d.*	£. *s. d.*	£. *s. d.*	£. *s. d.*	

(*c*) Rates reduced on appeal under 27 & 28 Vict. c. 39, s. 1, should be inserted in this column, with the necessary explanation in column 19.

wardens and Overseers should sign the Rate, and it seems from *Baker,* App., *Lock,* appointed under 59 Geo. III. c. 12, s. 12, may sign the Rate as one of the Overseers however, be best in all cases that a majority of the Churchwardens and Overseers regard to the Declaration to be added to the Rate by the Overseers.—*W. C. G.*

Parish wholly or partly in a Parliamentary Borough. See 30 & 31 Glen and Lovesy.

Overseers' Book of
_____ Union.

The Overseers' Account for the Half-year

Dates.	Items.				Totals.		
		£.	s.	d.	£.	s.	d.
	Memorandum.*						
	Rate allowed on day of on						
	£ at per £1						
	Arrears brought forward						
	Total						
	Amount of Rates legally excused . .						
	Ditto, ditto, not recoverable						
	Amount collected						
	Balance						

* Here insert the amounts of the Rates made during this half-year.

We declare the entries in the above Account and Memorandum to be
subscribed our names, this

I find the Balance of this Account to be _____ pounds,
as the case may be) the Churchwardens and Overseers *or* the Overseers,
successors before this day.

Dated _____

NOTE.—This Account, as well as the Rate Books and other Accounts of the Over-
at least before the day fixed for the Audit. (See 7 & 8 Vict. c. 101, s. 33.)

Schedule A.—Parochial Accounts.—Overseers.

Receipts and Payments (a).

Parish of _____

ending the _____ day of _____ 186 .

Dates.	Items.			Totals.		
		£.	s. d.	£.	s.	d.
	PAYMENTS.					

true, just, and complete; and in verification thereof, we have hereunto
day of   , 186 .

_____ } *Churchwardens.*

_____ } *Overseers.*

_____ shillings, and _____ pence, against (or in favour of,
of which sum I find that _____ has been paid by them to their

_____ *Auditor.*

seers, must be made up and balanced and deposited for inspection seven clear days

(a) See Art. 1, *ante*, p. 437.

Balance Sheet of the Overseers' Receipts and Pay-
_____ UNION.

RECEIVED.	£.	s.	d.
Balance (if any) against the Overseers at the end of the last Half-year, when the same has not been paid to the Treasurer of the Union			
From the Poor Rate			
Received in aid of the Poor Rate:— £. s. d.			
Total received			
Balance (if any) in favour of the Overseers at the end of this Half-year			

Signed this   day of

I hereby certify that this Balance Sheet is correct.

This_____ day of_____

(a) See Art. 2, *ante*, p. 438.
(b) The Overseers who are appointed at Lady Day cannot legally pay any sums due out of which such sums can be paid; but they may pay any debts contracted for months prior to the termination of the year of office of such immediate predecessors.

ments for the Half-year ended   186   (*a*).

Parish of_____

PAID.	£.	*s.*	*d.*
Balance (if any) in favour of the Overseers at the end of the last Half-year (*b*)			
Contributions paid to the Treasurer of the Union . .			
Separate Expenditure:—			
County, Borough, Hundred, or Police Rate paid by Overseers			
Constables' Expenses			
Other smaller payments:— £. *s.* *d.*			
Total expended			
Balance (if any) against the Overseers at the end of this Half-year (*b*)			

_____ } *Churchwardens.*

_____ } *Overseers.*

_____ *Auditor.*

which may seem to be due to their predecessors unless there be any arrears of Rate by their immediate predecessors, and not discharged, which fell due within three

490   General Order for Accounts.

The Rate Receipt Check Book (a).

____ UNION.
____ No. ____

RECEIPT.

Parish of ____ the ____ day of ____ 186 ___

Received of ____

the sum of ____

in respect of the Poor Rate of the above Parish, viz.: £   s.   d.

Rate made the ____ day of ____ 186 , on £ ____ Assessment, at ____ in the Pound . . .

Arrear of former Rate . .

Total . .

(Signed) ____

____ UNION. No. ____

NOTE.

Parish of ____

the ____

M ____

Rate made on the ____ day of ____

Arrear £ ____

£ ____

This part is to be retained by the Overseers.

____ UNION. No. ____

DEMAND NOTE.

Parish of ____

Mr. ____ Street.

The Overseers of the Poor demand payment of the Poor Rate, made the ____ day of ____ 186 , and of the arrears of former Rates as below now due from you.

£.   s.   d.

Amount of Rate at in the Pound }

Arrears . .

Total . .

(b) Particulars of the Rate, or Purposes for which the above Rate has been made at ____ in the Pound respectively.

(Signed) ____

(a) See Art. 3, *ante*, p. 138. If the Poor Rate be made to meet a contribution order of the Guardians and for general purposes, it will suffice to state that fact. It is not necessary to specify the amount in the £ to meet the contribution order. The rate in the £ required to meet a Highway precept should be stated separately.

(b) State how much for relief of the Poor, for County or Borough Rate, for Highways, and other matters.

Schedule A.—*Parochial Accounts.*—*Overseers.* 491

Form of Certificate to be signed by the Overseers.

We, the Overseers of the Poor of the (Parish or Township aforesaid), do hereby certify that we have examined this Receipt Check Book, and have ascertained the correctness of the numbering and the correspondence of the sums and names in such receipts with the Rate Book, and we certify that the Number of Receipts in this Book so filled up for this Rate amounts to (e).

Dated this ———— day of ————

Signed ————————

———————— Overseers.

(e) Here state the number in words at length.

The Instalment Rate Receipt Check Book (d).

UNION.		INSTALMENT RECEIPT.	UNION.
NO.			No. (e)

Parish of ———————— the ———— day of ———— 186 .

Parish of ————————

Mr. ————————

Received of ————————

on account of Poor Rate.

the sum of ————————

£ ————

on behalf of the above Parish, on account of Poor Rate now due.

£ ————

(Signed) ———————— Collector.

See Memorandum on the Note in the Rate Receipt Check Book. They are not to be necessarily the same as in the Rate Receipt Check Book.

(d) S^ee Art. 7, *ante*, p. 441.
(e) These numbers must correspond.

This part is to be retained by the Collector.

Terrier of Lands and Tenements belonging to the Parish of ——— in the ——— Union (a).

Name of the Estate.	Tenure of the Estate.	Name of the Parish or Place where situate.	Name of Tenant or Occupier.	Yearly Rent.	Present Application of Rents.	Date of Original Gift or Conveyance, and Trusts thereof.	Incumbrances on the Estate.	Remarks.	Signature of Overseers and Date of Signing.

Inventory of Stock, Moneys, and Effects, belonging to the Parish of ——— in the ——— Union (a).

Amount of principal Fund.	Nature of Security in which invested.	Amount of Yearly Income.	Present Application of Income.	Date of Original Gift or Assignment, and Trust thereof.	Trustees in whose Names now standing.	Remarks.	Signature of Overseers and Date of Signing.

(a) See Art. 5, ante, p. 440.

Sched. A.—Parochial Accounts.—Collector of Parish.

The Collecting and Deposit Book (b).

_____ UNION.   Parish of _____
                  _____ Collector.

RECEIPTS.						DEPOSITS.			
From Rates.			From other Sources.						
Date of Receipt.	Date of the Rate and that of the Arrear, if any.	No. of Receipt in full or of Instalment.	Amount.	Date.	On what Account, and from whom received.	Amount.	Total.*	Date.	Initial of the Overseer with whom deposited.	With whom deposited, or to whom paid.	Amount.
			£. s. d.			£. s. d.	£. s. d.				£. s. d.

* When the Collector deposits or pays any sum, he shall carry out the Total in this Column against the entry of the sum in the Deposits; and when he deposits money with the Overseer he shall request him to insert his initials in the proper column.

(b) See Art. 10, *ante*, p. 442.

The Collector's Monthly Statement (a).

UNION.

Parish of _____   Month of _____ 186 .

Drs.	The Ratepayers in account with the Collector.					Amount of Rates collected since last Month's Statement ... Ditto legally excused ... Ditto irrecoverable ... Ditto recoverable ...	Crs.		
		£	s.	d.			£	s.	d.
Recoverable Arrears, as per last Month's Statement ...									
on the ____ day of ____									
Amount of Rate allowed									
	Total					Total			

Dr.	The Collector in account with the Overseers.				Initials of the Overseer.	Amount deposited with the Overseers Or their Banker ... Ditto paid to the Treasurer by direction of the Overseers ... Ditto paid to any other authority with the like direction Balance (if any) in the Collector's hands	Cr.		
		£	s.	d.			£	s.	d.
Balance (if any) in the Collector's hands at the end of last month									
Amount of Rates collected since ...									
Other sums than Rates collected since (viz.) ...									
	Total					Total			

Moneys due in aid of the Poor-rates, but not yet collected.

	£	s.	d.

Received the ____ day of ____ 186 .

_____ Collector.

or

_____ 18 . _____ Overseer (as the case may be).

_____ Clerk to the Guardians.

The statements received by the Overseers are to be preserved by them, and those received by the Guardians are to be preserved by the Clerk, and all are to be laid before the Auditor.
* Place for the Initials of the Overseer who, having received the money, receives this statement from the Collector.
(a) See Art. 11, *ante*, p. 443.

Sched. A.—*Parochial Accounts.*—*Collector of Parish.*

The Collector's Unpaid Rates Statement (a).

_____Union.

Parish of _____

Showing the Number of Rates made during the Half-year last ended, with Dates of their Allowance, and the Names of the Parties rated to the Relief of the Poor who are in arrear in respect of the under-mentioned Rates made previous to and during the Half-year ended (Lady *or* Michaelmas) Day immediately before that in course of Collection on that day.

The Number of Poor Rates allowed during the Half-year ended at_____ last _____[ ].

Dates of the Allowances_____.

NAMES OF PERSONS IN ARREAR.

Date of the Rate.	Number in Rate Book.	Name of the Person Assessed.	Amount of Rates.	Reason why not paid.
			£. *s.* *d.*	

Dated_____ 186. _____*Collector.*

Shown to me this_____ day of_____ 186 .

_____{ One of the Overseers of the Parish aforesaid.

And to me this _____ day of_____ 186.

_____. *Auditor.*

If the Collector should be provided with a list of persons legally excused by a written order of the Justices, and whose names have been duly struck out of the rate by such Justices, in conformity with the Statute 54 G. 3. c. 170, § 11, with the numbers placed in the Rate Books against their names, it will be sufficient for him to fill up the last four columns of this Form, by inserting the total amount excused from each rate, and the total amount of the corresponding rateable value; and it will not be necessary to insert the numbers or the names of the persons so excused.

(a) See Art. 1-, *ante*, p. 444.

SCHEDULE (B.)

Containing the General Accounts of the Union, to be kept by the Clerk to the Board of Guardians.

The General Ledger (a).

Fo. ——— UNION. ———

Dr.						CONTRA.				Cr. UNION. Fo. ———
Date.	Folio of Minute Book.	Folio of corresponding Credit.	Corresponding *Credit* and Items.		Totals. (1)	Date.	Folio of Minute Book.	Folio of corresponding Debit.	Corresponding *Debit* and Items.	Totals. (2)
			To		£. s. d.				By	£. s. d.

(1) When to any account any sum is debited, part of which is credited to one account, and the remainder to another or others, the several sums so credited are to be written in this column, and their total in the next column. The several accounts to which such parts are credited to be written against them respectively, together with the requisite explanation in the column for "Corresponding Credit and Items."
(2) When to any account any sum is credited, part of which is debited to one account, and the remainder to another or others, the several sums so debited are to be written in this column, and their total in the next column. The several accounts to which such parts are debited to be written against them respectively, together with the requisite explanation in the column for "Corresponding Debit and Items."

(a) See Art. 10, note b. (1).

Schedule B.—Clerk's Books. 497

Parochial Ledger Account (a).

_____ Union. Parish of _____ Half-year ended _____ 180 .

Dr. Cr. Fo. _____

Fo. _____

Date.	Folio of Minute Book.	Folio of corresponding Credit.		Totals.
				£. s. d.
			To Balance against the Parish brought forward	
			Contribution to the Common Fund apportioned on the day of _____ *	
			Instalment of Workhouse Loan	
			Interest	
			County Rate	
			Other separate Charges stated in detail, as follows:—	
			Balance in favour of the Parish . .	

Date.	Folio of Minute Book.	Folio of Corresponding Debit.		Totals.
				£. s. d. £. s. d.
			By Balance in favour of the Parish brought forward .	
			Payment to the Treasurer of the Union	
			" "	
			" "	
			Payment on Auditor's Certificate ordered to be credited to the Parish .	
			Income from Parish Property, viz.—.	
			Other Receipts or Credits stated in detail, as follows:—	
			Balance against the Parish	

* This should be the date of the distribution at the end of the half-year.

(*a*) See Art. 16, *ante*, p. 448.

The Relief Order Book (a).

_____ UNION.

Quarter ending _____ 186 .

No. in the Application and Report Book (if any).	Name of Applicant.	Name of Relief District.	Where resident.	Relief ordered or allowed by the Board of Guardians.				For what Time ordered or allowed.	Other Orders of the Board (if any).
				Amount in Money.	In Kind.				
					Quantity and Description.	Value.			
				s. d.		*s. d.*			

Dated this _____ Day of _____ 190 , } _____ *Clerk.*
being for the _____ Week of the Quarter.

(a) See Art. 16, *ante*, p. 448. Every pauper admitted provisionally into the Workhouse under Article 84 of the Consolidated Order, *ante*, p. 68, will remain there until the Board of Guardians give further directions. Consequently a pauper so admitted will be reported to the Guardians at their next meeting after his admission, and if the Guardians order him to continue in the Workhouse, or order him to be discharged, their order in that respect will appear in the last column of the Relief Order Book, and also in the Relieving Officers' Application and Report Book. If the admission of the pauper took place on his order, so also any order which the Guardians may make under Article 90 (*ante*, p. 65) as to the continuance of any pauper in the Workhouse should be entered in the Relief Order Book.

Schedule B.—Clerk's Books. 499

The Order Check Book (b).

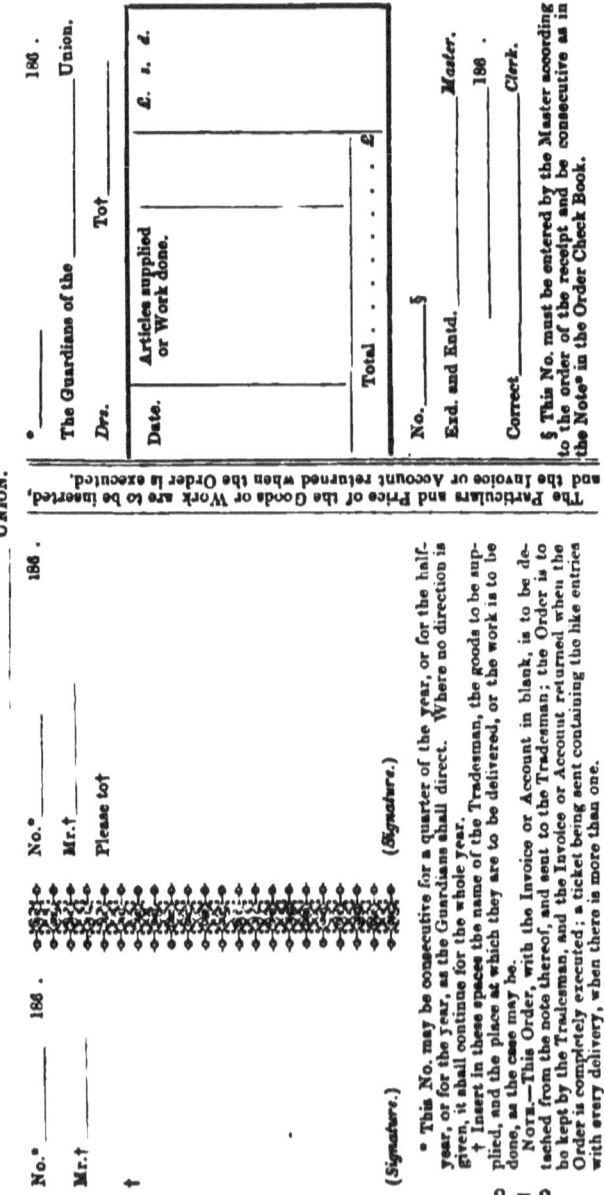

* This No. may be consecutive for a quarter of the year, or for the half-year, or for the year, as the Guardians shall direct. Where no direction is given, it shall continue for the whole year.

† Insert in these spaces the name of the Tradesman, the goods to be supplied, and the place at which they are to be delivered, or the work is to be done, as the case may be.

NOTE.—This Order, with the Invoice or Account in blank, is to be detached from the note thereof, and sent to the Tradesman; the Order is to be kept by the Tradesman, and the Invoice or Account returned when the Order is completely executed; a ticket being sent containing the like entries with every delivery, when there is more than one.

(b) See Art. 16, *ante*, p. 449.

§ This No. must be entered by the Master according to the order of the receipt and be consecutive as in the Note* in the Order Check Book.

2 K 2

The Parochial List and Statement of Account (a).

UNION.

Parish of _____

List of Paupers who were admitted into the Workhouse from this Parish, or who resided in it while relieved, together with a Statement of the Amounts respectively credited and debited to the Parish, in the Union Accounts for the Half-year ending _____ 186 .

IN-DOOR POOR.					OUT-DOOR POOR.							
										Relief given to each Pauper during the Half-year.		
										In Money.	In Kind.	Medical Relief only.
No. in List (if any).	Names of the Paupers.	No. of days' Maintenance.			No. in List (if any).	Names of the Paupers.	Where resident.	Cause of requiring Relief.	£. s. d.	£. s. d.	£. s. d.

Master.   *Relieving Officer.*

Dr.   Cr.

	£. s. d.		£. s. d.
[To ...] the Parish, brought forward		Balance in favour of the Parish, brought forward	
[...] Out-door Fund, apportioned		Contributions and other Moneys paid to the Treasurer of the Union upon Orders of the Guardians	
		Payments upon Disallowances or Surcharges made by the Auditor and directed by the Guardians to be applied to the credit of the Parish	

14 Wives.   Families of Soldiers, Sailors, and Marines relieved.

501

the Half-year ended _____ 186 .

OUT-DOOR.														
the Workhouse (not including						Lunatics, Insane Persons, and Idiots.		Summary of the preceding Columns of Out-door Paupers.						
				Not Able-bodied.										
								Adults.						
	Families of Soldiers, Sailors, and Marines relieved.		Resident Families of other non-resident Males relieved.			Children under 16 relieved with Parents.	Orphans or other children under 16, relieved without Parents						Vagrants relieved out of the Workhouse.	Total relieved out of the Workhouse.	Gross Total, being the Sum of Columns A and B.
Wives.	Children.	Wives.	Children.	Males.	Females.			Males.	Females.	Children under 16.	Males.	Females.	Children under 16.	Total.			
14	15	16	17	18	19	20	21	22	23	24					A	B	C
																	$

. . . .

mes appear both in the In-door and Out-door Relief ⎫
in the Relief Lists originally, but whose Relief ⎬ ¶
the Non-settled Poor Account . . . . . ⎭
otal of Paupers relieved in the Half-year . . . . ,

bers to be deducted on account of entries in both the In-door and
 Order.
 from the Relief List to the Account of Non-settled Poor, the Clerk
ve him information of any such cases which appear in his Relief List

*Paupers relieved in the Half-year ended _____ 186 .

OUT-DOOR.																				
the Workhouse (not including Classes 22, died.						Not Able-bodied.				Lunatics, Insane Persons, and Idiots.			Summary of the Preceding Columns of Out-door Paupers.							
													Adults.							
Families relieved on account of Parent being in Gaol, etc.		Families of Soldiers, Sailors, and Marines relieved.		Resident Families of other non-resident Males relieved.		Males.	Females.	Children under 16 relieved with Parents.	Orphans, or other Children under 16, relieved without Parents.	Males.	Females.	Children under 16.	Males.	Females.	Children under 16.	Total.	Vagrants relieved out of the Workhouse.	Total relieved out of the Workhouse.	Gross Total, being the sum of Columns A and B	Deduct Persons relieved, both In-door and Out-door, and included twice in Column C; also Persons whose Relief has been transferred to the Non-settled Poor Accounts.	Net Total of Persons relieved
Wives.	Children	Wives.	Children	Wives.	Children																
12	13	14	15	16	17	18	19	20	21	22	23	24					B	C.		

erent Cases attended by the Medical Officers in each District and in the Workhouse in the Half-year.

Medical Officer.	District or Workhouse.	Number of Cases
	Total	

_____ day of _____ 186 .   _____ Clerk.
_____ day of _____ 186 .   _____ Auditor.

ent is to be made up from the 'Pauper Classification Book,' and must show the number ed in the half-year both in and out of the Workhouse, including those who have received nly. Lunatics, Paupers in Hospitals, Children in Authorized Schools, and Non-resident e ascertained from the Minute Book, or the accounts in the Ledger relating thereto, if e Relieving Officer's Accounts.
must contain the names of the Parishes from which the Paupers have been admitted into or in which the Paupers were residing when they first received relief during the half-year. is to contain the total numbers to be deducted from the gross total for each Parish. n is to contain the net total for each Parish.
0, *ante*, p. 467.

...nd Liabilities for the Half-year ended _____ _____ 186_ (a).

PARTICULARS OF COMMON CHARGES.		Outstanding Liabilities of the Guardians at the End of the Half-year.		
		Creditor's Name or Description.	Description of the Claim.†	£. s. d.
...aintenance ....Relief (including Non-resident Re- ...r)........ ...ers in Hospitals and Schools ....ties in Asylums, Registered Hos- ...als, or Licensed Houses ....inal Lunatics ....ies or other Remuneration of Officers ...ers' Rations ....rannuation Allowances ....d Medical Fees ....ration ....ination ....stration ....l Expenses ....r Charges, viz. :—‡	£. s. d.			
Con... ce...				
Total				
Exp... sp... ye...		Liabilities at the End of the corresponding half of last year		
As c... wit... dit... cor... ing las...		As compared with the Liabilities at the End of the corresponding half of last year	Increase Decrease	

...e Principal and the Interest, if any be due, should be entered separately.

...erk. _____ day of _ 18 .
...ditor. _____ day of _____ 18 .

SCHEDULE (C.)

Containing the Book to be kept by the *Collector of the Guardians* (b).

Form of Collector's Book.

_____ UNION.

		Receipts.			Payments to the Treasurers.		
Date.	No. of Receipt.	From whom received.	On what account.	Amount.	Date.	On what account.	Amount.
				£. s. d.			£. s. d.

Form of Collector's Receipt (b).

This part to be retained by the Collector.

No. _____

_____ Union.

____ day of _____ 186 .

_____

For _____

£ _____

_____ Union.

____ day of _____ 186 .

Received of _____

the Sum of _____

on behalf of the above-named Union

in respect of _____

£ _____

(Signed) _____
        Collector for the said Union.

(b) See Art. 17, *ante*, p. 450.

SCHEDULE (D).

Containing the Form of the Treasurer's Book (a).

_____ UNION.

Account of Receipts and Payments on behalf of the Guardians of the Union for the Half-year ended _____ day of _____ 186 .

_____ Treasurer.

RECEIPTS.				PAYMENTS.			
Date.	From whom.	On what Account.	Amount.	Date of Payment.	Date of Order.	Name of Payee.	Amount.
			£. s. d.				£. s. d.

Signed this _____ day of _____ .

_____ Treasurer.

Note.—This account is to be balanced at the end of every quarter, and the balance signed by the Treasurer.

(a) See Art. 18, *ante*, p. 451.

SCHEDULE (E).

Containing the Forms of the Workhouse Accounts to be kept by the *Master of the Workhouse.*

The Inventory Book (b).

UNION _____ Master _____

Date of Entry.	Fixtures.	Furniture.	Utensils.	Bedding.†	House Linen.†	Other Effects.	Articles transferred, condemned, or disposed of.		
							Date.	Notes of Articles transferred to other Parts of the House.	Notes of Articles condemned, or disposed of.

(*) (*)

* A separate page is to be devoted to each office, room, or apartment, and in this space is to be inserted the name of the office, room, or apartment to which the page is appropriated.

† Under the head "Bedding" are to be entered mattresses, beds, blankets, sheets, and rugs; and under "House Linen," are to be entered tablecloths and towels.

A blank space should be left at the end of the account for each apartment or division for the insertion of new articles. Notes of articles transferred to other parts of the house, condemned, or disposed of, should be made as soon as the same takes place, and the new purchases should be punctually entered so as to represent the exact state of the house in reference to the articles to be entered in this book at all times.

(b) See Art. 19 (1), *ante*, p. 451.

Admission and Discharge Book (a).

UNION _____

Master of the Workhouse at _____

ADMITTED.																			DISCHARGED.											
Day of the Month.	Day of the Week.	Next Meal after Admission.	Name.	Calling, if any.	Religious Persuasion.	When born.	Class for Diet.*								Number allotted to the Pauper's Clothes.	Parish from which admitted.†	By whose Order admitted.	Date of the Order of Admission.	If born in the House, Name of Parent.	Observations on Condition at the time of Admission, and any other General Remarks.	Date.	Day of the Week.	Last Meal before Discharge.	Name.	Class for Diet.*								How Discharged; and if by Order, by whose Order.	In case of Death, say "Dead."	Observations on General Character and Behaviour in the Workhouse.
							1	2	3	4	5	6	7	8											1	2	3	4	5	6	7	8			

* When a Pauper is admitted before breakfast, the Master is to enter in the column for "next meal after admission" the letter B; when before dinner, the letter D; and when before supper the letter S. And when a Pauper is discharged after breakfast, the Master is to enter in the column for "last meal before discharge" the letter B; when after dinner, the letter D; and when after supper, the letter S.

* The columns "Class for Diet" are to be filled up by the figure 1. The Classes should correspond with the Classes of the Diet Table in use in the Workhouse. The columns 4a and 6a are for the Children.

† Unless the Guardians require the Vagrants to be entered in another book, the word "Vagrant" must be entered in this column against every person admitted as a Vagrant instead of the name of the Parish.

(a) See Art. 10 (3), ante, p. 458.

Schedule E.—In-door Relief.—Master's Books.

Admission and Discharge Book for Vagrants (b).

_____ UNION. _____ Master of the Workhouse at _____

ADMITTED.						DISCHARGED.					Whether searched on Admission, and if so, what, if anything, found.†
Day of the Month.	Day of the Week.	Hour of Admission.	Names of Vagrant, wife, and family.	Age.	Calling or Occupation.	Where he Slept last night.	At what hour of the next day discharged.*	Whether set to work.	If not, why?	What work done.	To what place going.

* *Note.*—When a Vagrant has remained in the Vagrant Ward for 24 hours and is not then discharged, or when he is sooner removed into the ordinary wards of the Workhouse, he should be forthwith duly entered in the Workhouse Admission and Discharge Book.
† See the Provision in the Statute 11 & 12 Vict. c. 110, s. 10.

In Unions within the Metropolis, columns must be added for *the nature and quantity of food given and the cost.*

(b) See Art. 19 (2), *ante*, p. 452.

General Order for Accounts.

UNION.

Admission and Discharge Book (a).

Master of the Workhouse at _____

ADMITTED.

Day of the Month.	Day of the Week.	Next Meal after Admission.	Name.	Calling, if any.	Religious Persuasion.	When born.	Class for Diet.*										Number admitted to the Pauper's Clothes.	Parish from which admitted.	By whose Order admitted.	Date of the Order of Admission.	If born in the House, Name of Parent.	Observations on Condition at the time of Admission, and any other General Remarks.
							1	2	3	4	5	6	7	8	8a	9					

DISCHARGED.

Date.	Day of the Week.	Last Meal before Discharge.	Name.	Class for Diet.*									How Discharged; and if by Order, by whose Order.	In case of Death, say "Dead."	Observations on general Character and Behaviour in the Workhouse.
				1	2	3	4	5	6, 7	8	8a	9			

When a Pauper is admitted before breakfast, the Master is to enter in the column for "next meal after admission" the letter B; when before dinner, the letter D; and when before supper the letter S. And when a Pauper is discharged after breakfast, the Master is to enter in the column for "last meal before discharge," the letter B; when after dinner, the letter D; and when after supper, the letter S.

The Columns "Class for Diet." are to be filled up by the figure 1. The Classes should correspond with the Classes of the Diet Table in use in the Workhouse, and are to apply to Vagrants as well as to the able-bodied, and 7 are for the Children.

The words "Vagrant" or "Vagrants" (if more than one) must be entered in another book, the word "Vagrant" must be entered in this column against every Vagrant instead of the name of the Parish.

(a) See Art. 10 (3), ante, p. 468.

Schedule E.—In-door Relief.—Master's Books.

Admission and Discharge Book for Vagrants (b).

Union. _____ Master of the Workhouse at _____

ADMITTED.						DISCHARGED.				
Day of the Month.	Day of the Week.	Hour of Admission.	Names of Vagrant, wife, and family.	Age.	Calling or Occupation.	Where he slept last night.	At what hour of the next day discharged.	Whether set to work.	If not, why?	What work done.	To what place going.	Whether searched on Admission, and if so, what, if anything, found.†

* *Note.*—When a Vagrant has remained in the Vagrant Ward for 24 hours and is not then discharged, or when he is sooner removed into the ordinary wards of the Workhouse, he should be forthwith duly entered in the Workhouse Admission and Discharge Book.
† See the Provision in the Statute 11 & 12 Vict. c. 110, s. 10.

In Unions within the Metropolis, columns must be added for *the nature and quantity of food given and the cost.*

(b) See Art. 19 (2), *ante*, p. 452.

In-door Relief List for the _____ UNION. Half-year ending _____ 186 .

Able-bodied and their Families (exclusive of Vagrants).					Not Able-bodied and their Families (exclusive of Vagrants).							Lunatics, Insane Persons, and Idiots.					
Adults.			Children under 16 of Able-bodied Inmates.		Adults.				Children under 16.						Calling of Pauper.	When born.	Of what religious persuasion.
Married Couples.					Married Couples.					Of Parents (not Able-bodied) being Inmates.		Orphans or other children relieved without their Parents.					
Males.	Females.	Other Males.	Other Females.	Illegitimate Children.	Other Children.	Males.	Females.	Other Males.	Other Females.	Illegitimate.	Other Children.		Males.	Females.	Children under 16.			
1	2	3	4	5	6	7	8	9	10	11	12	13	14	15	16			

1. The columns for the classification of the Paupers are to be filled by inserting the figure 1 in the proper column opposite each name, and leaving all the rest blank.

2. Whenever, in this Relief List, two or more persons of the same name occur, the Master of the Workhouse shall annex to the name of each of such persons a number in brackets, to distinguish him from other persons of the same name.

(a) See Art. 19 (3), *ante*, p. 452, and the General Order of the

Schedule E.—In-door Relief.—Master's Books.

Parish of*_____ (a).

_____ Master of the Workhouse at _____

Name of Pauper.	Number of Days in the House in each Week.																											Totals for the Half-year.
	1st Week.	2nd Week.	3rd Week.	4th Week.	5th Week.	6th Week.	7th Week.	8th Week.	9th Week.	10th Week.	11th Week.	12th Week.	13th Week.	14th Week.	15th Week.	16th Week.	17th Week.	18th Week.	19th Week.	20th Week.	21st Week.	22nd Week.	23rd Week.	24th Week.	25th Week.	26th Week.	27th Week.
Total days for each Week.																												

3. The number of each class of paupers actually relieved on the *first of January* and on the *first of July* respectively, in each year, is to be shown at the beginning of this book, a portion of the book being set apart and ruled for this purpose.

* This should be the Parish from which the Pauper, or in case of a child born in the Workhouse from which its mother, was admitted.

Poor Law Board, dated 23rd August, 1859, *ante*, p. 299.

Abstract of the In-door Relief Lists for the Half-year ending ———— 186 (a).

UNION ————

Master of the Workhouse at ————

Folio of the In-door Relief Lists.	Parishes.	Number of Days in each Week.																										Total Days for the Half-year.
		1st Week.	2nd Week.	3rd Week.	4th Week.	5th Week.	6th Week.	7th Week.	8th Week.	9th Week.	10th Week.	11th Week.	12th Week.	13th Week.	14th Week.	15th Week.	16th Week.	17th Week.	18th Week.	19th Week.	20th Week.	21st Week.	22nd Week.	23rd Week.	24th Week.	25th Week.	26th Week.	27th Week.	
	Vagrants																												
	Total Days for each Week																												

The aggregate number of days in each week passed in the Workhouse by the total number of Paupers from each Parish must be taken from the columns of total days for the several weeks in the In-door Relief Lists. Paupers admitted as Vagrants who remain in the Workhouse are to be enumerated among the Paupers admitted from the Parish where the Workhouse is situated.

A few sheets of this Abstract (according to the extent of the Union) are to be bound up at the end of the Book containing the In-door Relief Lists.

(a) See Art. 19 (4), ante, p. 465.

Schedule E.—In-door Relief.—Master's Books.

The Master's Day Book (b).

UNION ————————

Master of the Workhouse at ————————

Date.	No. of Order.	No. of Invoice, or Bill.	Name.	Trade.	INVOICES.							
					Provisions.	Clothing.	Furniture and Property.	Necessaries.	Repairs.			
					£. s. d.	£. s. d.	£. s. d.	£. s. d.	£. s. d.	£. s. d.	£. s. d.	£. s. d.
				Total . .								

The money columns should be added up weekly.

(b) See Art. 19 (5), *ante*, p. 453.

Summary of the Master's Day Book for the Quarter ending ———— 186 (a).

———— UNION.

———— Master of the Workhouse at ————

No. of the Week.	NAMES or TRADE.						Total.	ACCOUNT CHARGED.				
								Provisions.	Clothing.	Furniture and Property.	Necessaries.	Repairs.
	£ s. d.	£ s. d.	£ s. d.	£ s. d.	£ s. d.	£ s. d.	£ s. d.	£ s. d.	£ s. d.	£ s. d.	£ s. d.	£ s. d.
1												
2												
3												
4												
5												
etc.												
13												

(a) See Art. 1V (7), ante, p. 457.

Schedule E.—In-door Relief.—Master's Books.

The Master's Book of Receipts and Payments (b).

_____ Union. _____ Master of the Workhouse at _____

RECEIPTS.		PAYMENTS.	
Date.	Name and Particulars.	Date.	Name and Particulars.

Balanced this ____ day of _____.   (Signed) _____ Master.

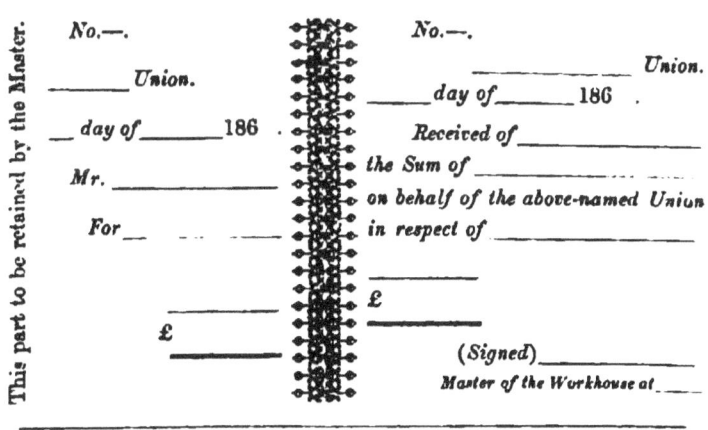

Master's Receipt Check Book (b).

(b) See Art. 19 (6), *ante*, p. 453.

Daily Provisions Consumption Account for _____ UNION.

Class	Total Numbers	Deduct. Sick.*	Deduct. Absent	Net Numbers	Prepared Provisions. (1) oz. each	lb. oz.	Pints each	each	Class	Total Numbers	Deduct. Sick.*	Deduct. Absent	Net Number
1									1				
2									2				
3									3				
4									4				
4a									4a				
5									5				
†—									—				
6									6				
7									7				
8									8				
8a									8a				
9									9				
Vagrants													
Totals (2)									Totals				
Quantities of the several principal Articles in their unprepared state taken from the Stores to supply the above Meals (3).													
Waste (if any) . . .													

(1) The names of the articles prescribed in the Dietary are to be inserted.
(2) The total quantities on this line represent the quantities of the several articles
(3) The quantities of the several principal articles in their unprepared state, entered under the quantities of prepared provisions for each meal, and carried to the allowance which he claims for waste, arising out of the preparation or distribution
* Those only of the Sick who have not the ordinary diet are to be deducted.
† On this line are to be placed such of Class 5 as have larger allowances than the work, or such paupers as receive peculiar allowances under the Medical Officer's advice

(a) See Art. 19 (S),

Schedule E.—In-door Relief—Master's Books.

the _____ day of _____ 186 . (a).

_____ Master of the Workhouse at _____

DINNER.				SUPPER.								
Prepared Provisions.						Deduct.			Prepared Provisions.			
oz. each.	lb. oz.	each.	each.	Class.	Total Numbers.	Sick.*	Absent.	Net Numbers.	oz. each.	lb. oz.	each.	each.
				1								
				2								
				3								
				4								
				4a								
				5								
				6								
				7								
				8								
				8a								
				9								
				Totals								

of prepared provisions required for each meal.
necessary to supply the quantities of prepared provisions so required, are to be "Weekly Provisions Consumption Account." Here also the Master may enter the of the provisions; and in the case of meat, out of the weight of bone.

Diet Table gives, on account of their being employed as nurses or in the household without being entered on the Sick List.

ante, p. 454.

518 General Order for Accounts.

Weekly Provisions Consumption Account. The _____ Week of the Quarter ending _____ 186_ . (a)

UNION. _____

Master of the Workhouse at _____

Date.	Day of the Week.	Meal.	Consumed by the Paupers.		Taken from the Stores for the Officers and Servants of the Workhouse (1).	Number of Paupers in the House during the day.	Number of Members of the Establishment.
			lb. oz.	lb. oz.			
		Breakfast					
		Dinner					
		Supper					
		Breakfast					
		Dinner					
		Supper					
		Breakfast					
		Dinner					
		Supper					
		Breakfast					
		Dinner					
		Supper					
		Breakfast					
		Dinner					
		Supper					
		Breakfast					
		Dinner					
		Supper					
						(?)	

(1) This total should agree with the total number of days in the Abstract of the In-door Relief List for the corresponding week.

(a) See Art. 19 (b), ante, p. 464.

Schedule E.—In-door Relief—Master's Books.

Provisions Receipt and Consumption Account for the _____ Week of the Quarter ending _____ 186 . (b).

_____ UNION. Master of the Workhouse at _____

ARTICLES.	Stock brought forward.	New Stock.	No. of Invoice.	Totals of Stock brought forward, and new Stock.	Consumed.		Remaining in Store.	Totals consumed and remaining in Store.	Required for next Week.
					By the Paupers.	By the Officers and Servants of the Workhouse.			

The "New Stock" of the several Articles, and the quantities "Consumed," "by the Paupers," and "by the Officers and Servants of the Workhouse," respectively, are to be carried to the "Summary of Provisions Received and Provisions Consumed."

(b) See Art. 19 (10), ante, p. 455.

Summary of Provisions Received and Provisions Consumed in the Quarter ending _____ 186 . (a)

_____ UNION.   _____ Master of the Workhouse at _____

	*	lb. oz.	lb. oz.									
Received 1st week												
,, 2nd												
,, 3rd												
,, 4th												
,, 5th												
,, 6th												
,, 7th												
,, 8th												
,, 9th												
,, 10th												
,, 11th												
,, 12th												
,, 13th												
Totals received												
Consumed by the Paupers { 1st week												
2nd												
3rd												
4th												
5th												
6th												
7th												
8th												
9th												
10th												
11th												
12th												
13th												
Totals consumed by the Paupers.												
Consumed by the Officers and Servants of the Workhouse { 1st week												
2nd												
3rd												
4th												
5th												
6th												
7th												
8th												
9th												
10th												
11th												
12th												
13th												
Totals consumed by the Officers and Servants of the Workhouse.												

* The names of the Articles are to be placed at the head of the The "Totals received," the "Totals consumed by the Paupers, consumed by the Officers and Servants of the Workhouse," "Balance of the Provisions Account for the Quarter."

(a) See Art. 19 (11), ante, p. ___.

Schedule E.—In-door Relief—Master's Books.

Balance of the Provisions Account for the Quarter ending _____ 186 . (b)

_____ UNION. Master of the Workhouse at _____

Articles.	Stock brought forward.	Price.	New Block. Cost of Stock brought forward.	New Block. Price.	Cost of New Stock.	Total Cost of New Stock, and Stock brought forward.	Consumed. By the Paupers. Quantities.	Cost.	By the Officers and Servants of the Workhouse. Quantities.	Cost.	Stock remaining in Store. Quantities.	Cost of Stock remaining in Store.	Total Cost of Articles Consumed and in Store.
		s. d.	£. s. d.	s. d.	£. s. d.	£. s. d.		£. s. d.		£. s. d.		£. s. d.	£. s. d.

Submitted to _____ Member of the Visiting Committee this _____ day of _____ 186 , and found to be correct.

(Signed) {

(a) See Art. 19 (12), *ante*, p. 465.

Clothing Materials Receipt

_____ UNION.

(*)			
RECEIVED.			
Date.	Of whom.	No. of Invoice.	Quantity.

Submitted to _____ Member of the Visiting Committee this _____ day of _____ 186 .

* A separate Account is to be kept of each article, and the name of the article is
The entries are to be made in the true order of time according as the articles are
year.
Sheets, bedding, and house linen are to be entered in the Inventory.
The articles of clothing into which the materials are converted are to be carried

Clothing Receipt and

_____ UNION.

		Men's and Boys' Clothing.						Women's and Girls' Clothing.							
Date.	From whom or whence received, and No. of the Invoice.	Coats and Jackets.	Waistcoats.	Trousers.	Shirts.	Shoes.	Stockings.	Hats.	Handkerchiefs.	Gowns and Frocks.	Under Petticoats.	Upper Petticoats.	Shifts.	Aprons.	Handkerchiefs.	Shoes.	Stockings.	Caps.	Bonnets.

Submitted to ____ Member of the Visiting Committee this _____ day of _____ 186 .

In the several Columns is to be entered, according to the circumstances of the
The entries are to be made in the true order of time, according as the articles are
(a) See Art. 19 (13), ante, p. 456.

Schedule E.—In-door Relief—Master's Books.

and Conversion Account (a).

Master of the Workhouse at _____

	CONVERTED.		Folio of Clothing Receipt and Expenditure Book or of Inventory Book.
Date.	Into what.	Quantity used.	

and found to be correct. (Signed) { _____

to be entered at the head of the page.
received and converted; and the account is to be made up and balanced every half-
to the Clothing Receipt and Expenditure Account in their proper columns.

Expenditure Account (b).

Master of the Workhouse at _____

	GIVEN OUT.																		
	Men's and Boys' Clothing.									Women's and Girls' Clothing.									
Date.	Number of the Suit.	Size.	Coats and Jackets.	Waistcoats.	Trousers.	Shirts.	Shoes.	Stockings.	Hats.	Handkerchiefs.	Date.	Number of the Suit.	Size.	Gowns and Frocks.	Under Petticoats.	Upper Petticoats.	Shifts.	Aprons.	Handkerchiefs.	Shoes.	Stockings.	Caps.	Bonnets.

and found to be correct. (Signed) { _____

case, the number of the articles received and given out.
received and converted, and the Account is to be made up and balanced every Half-year.
(b) See Art. 19 (14), ante, p. 456.

Clothing Register Book (a).

UNION ———— Master of the Workhouse at ————

MALES.								FEMALES.							
No.*	Date of Admission.	Names.	[Size .]	Date of Discharge.	No.	Date of Admission.	Names.	[Size .]	Date of Discharge.	No.	Date of Admission.	Names.	[Size .]	Date of Discharge.	

* By the No. here is intended the Number given by the Master to each suit. The odd numbers shall be assigned to the Males, and the even to the Females.

(a) See Art. 19 (16), *ante*, p. 467.

Schedule E.—*In-door Relief—Master's Books.*

Necessaries and Miscellaneous Account for the _____ Week of the Quarter ending _____ 186_. (b).

_____ UNION.   *Master of the Workhouse at* _____

Articles.	Stock brought forward.	New Stock.	No. of Invoice.	Totals of Stock brought forward and New Stock.	Consumed.			Remaining in Store.	Totals Consumed and remaining in Store.	Observations.
					By the Paupers.	By the Officers and Servants of the Workhouse.	On the Workhouse.			

(b) See Art. 19 (17), *ante*, p. 458.

Quarterly Summary of the Necessaries and Miscellaneous
_____ UNION.

Week.*																			
Received.	1st 2nd 3rd 4th 5th 6th 7th 8th 9th 10th 11th 12th 13th ,,																		
Totals																			
Consumed by the Paupers.	1st 2nd 3rd 4th 5th 6th 7th 8th 9th 10th 11th 12th 13th ,,																		
Totals																			
Consumed by the Officers and Servants, and on the Workhouse.	1st 2nd 3rd 4th 5th 6th 7th 8th 9th 10th 11th 12th 13th ,,																		
Totals																			

* The names of the several articles are to be
(a) See Art. 19 (1b).

Schedule E.—In-door Relief—Master's Books.

Account for the quarter ending _____ 186 . (a).

_____ Master of the Workhouse at _____

	Week.
	1st
	2nd
	3rd
	4th
	5th
	6th
	7th
	8th
	9th
	10th
	11th
	12th
	13th
	,,
	Totals
	1st
	2nd
	3rd
	4th
	5th
	6th
	7th
	8th
	9th
	10th
	11th
	12th
	13th
	,,
	Totals
	1st
	2nd
	3rd
	4th
	5th
	6th
	7th
	8th
	9th
	10th
	11th
	12th
	13th
	,,
	Totals

placed at the head of the several columns.
ante, p. 458.

Balance of the Necessaries and Miscellaneous Account for the Quarter ending .... 186 . (a).

UNION. _____ Master of the Workhouse at _____

Articles.	Stock brought forward.	Price.	Cost of Stock brought forward.	New Stock. Price.	Cost of New Stock.	Total Cost of New Stock and Stock brought forward.	Consumed. By the Paupers.		Consumed. By the Officers and Servants of the Workhouse.		Consumed. On the Workhouse.		Stock remaining in Store.	Cost of Stock remaining in Store.	Total Cost of Articles consumed and in Store.
		s. d.	£. s. d.	s. d.	£. s. d.	£. s. d.	Quantities.	Cost. £. s. d.	Quantities.	Cost. £. s. d.	Quantities.	Cost. £. s. d.	Quantities.	£. s. d.	£. s. d.
TOTALS .															

Examined &c.

Report &c. kept by Relieving Officer.

Quantity and Description of Relief in Kind.	Required by Overseers.	Given by Relieving Officer.

kept by *the Relieving Officer.*

186 (a).

Relieving Officer of the _____ District.

Quantity and Description of Relief in Kind.				Relief ordered by Guardians.			Other Orders of the Board of Guardians.	Date when Order made.	Initials of Chairman or Clerk.	Observations.
Reported as given by Overseers.	Given by Relieving Officer.	Value.	Date when given.	In Kind.		For what Time allowed, or Nature of the Order made.				
				Quantity and Description.	Value.					
		s. d.		s. d.		s. d.				

...on is made where there is no such Residence.

Report Book.

...nquire closely into the causes of the applications for relief, and to insert

...s of the applications for relief by able-bodied labourers, where the ap-...oss of work, name the particular sort of work.

...s of the applications for relief of children who become chargeable from ...eir parents to provide for them, specify the nature of the inability or ...insanity;" "Father's inability to obtain work;" "Father absent from ..."

... arising from infirmity of mind or body, designate the nature and extent ..., " or "Idiot," or "Deaf and Dumb," or "Crippled in the hand or ..."

...hould be a fresh entry of the case under the date of the renewed application.

_____ UNION.

Parish of _____. H_____

STATIS___

Able-bodied, or the Families of Abl___

Adult Males (married or single) relieved in Cases of sudden and urgent necessity.	Adult Males (married or single) relieved in Cases of their own Sickness, Accident, or Infirmity.	Adult Males relieved on account of Sickness, Accident, or Infirmity of any of the Family, or of a Funeral.	Adult Males (married or single) relieved on account of want of Work, or other Causes.	Families of Adult Males, in Columns 1, 2, 3, and 4, resident with the Father.		Widows.	Children under 16, dependent on Widows.	Single Women without Children.
				Wife.	Children under 16.			
1	2	3	4	5	6	7	8	9

1. If an able-bodied man, being head of the family, is sick or tempo___ out of work, in column 4; and in either case the whole family depend ___ columns 5 and 6.
2. If the relief is given on account of the sickness of a wife or child only, and the head of the family, are to be inserted in the list; the ma___ any other case in column 4, the wife or child in column 5 or 6. If the ___ member of a family, the surviving head of the family only is to be ente___ viving head of the family, then the person buried must be considered a ___ children dependent on them is to be entered in the proper columns in th___
3. Non-resident paupers, when paid through the Relieving Officer, ar___ which they are settled, but non-settled paupers residing in the Union, w___ to be entered under the name of the Parish where they reside. Vagrant___ where the application was made to the Relieving Officer, where the Out___ where it is kept, the total number of vagrants and the amount of relief a___

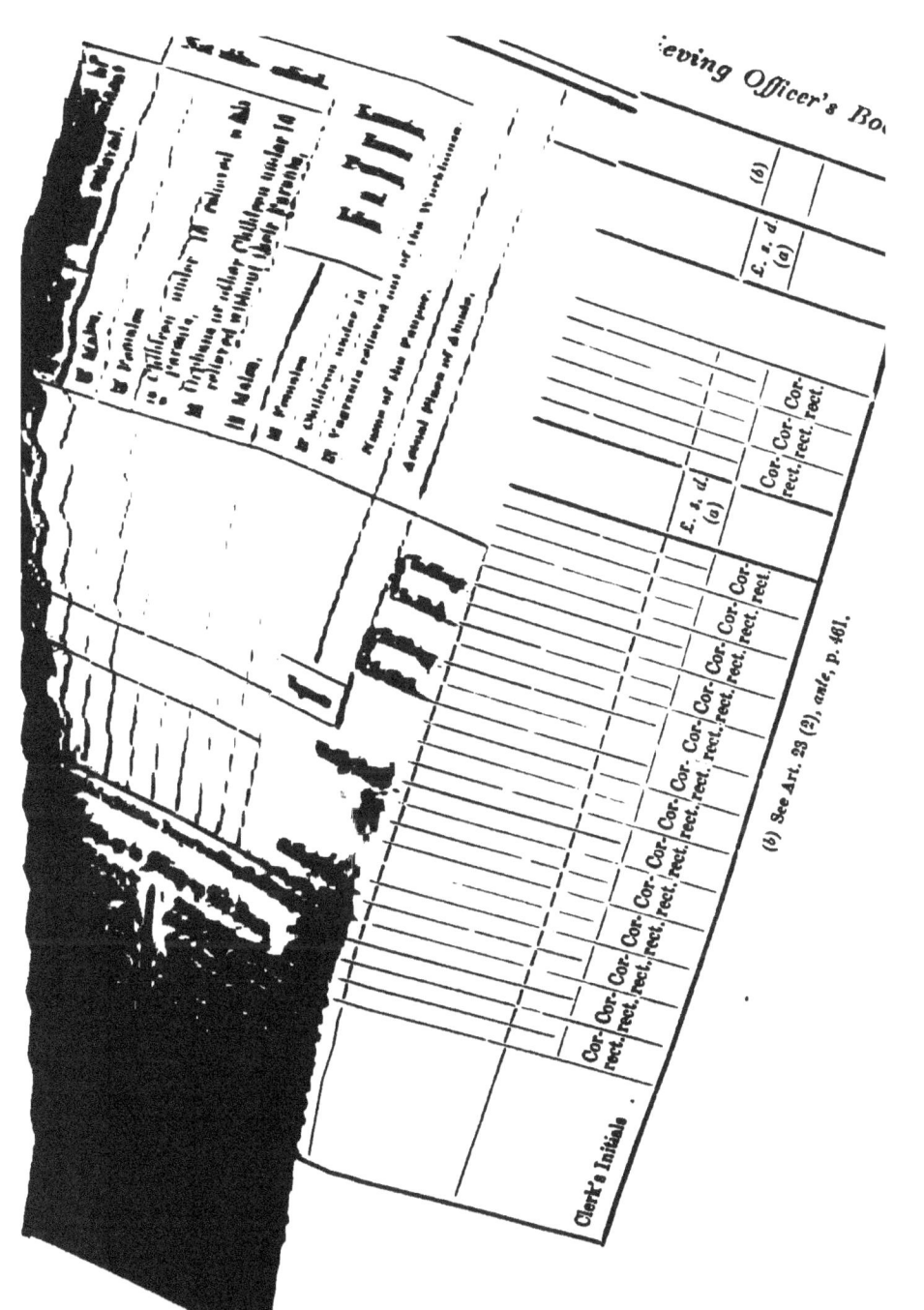

530

Par{Relieving Officer of the _____ District.

Adult Males (married or single) relieved in Cases of sudden and urgent necessity.	MONEY PORTION.									
	1st Week, ending	(c)	13th Week, ending	Totals for the First Quarter.		1st Week, ending	(c)	13th Week, ending	Totals for the Second Quarter.		Totals for the Half-year.
				In Money.	In Kind.				In Money.	In Kind.	
	s. d.	s. d.	s. d.	s. d.	s. d.	s. d.	s. d.	s. d.	s. d.	s. d.	£. s. d.
											(b)
				£. s. d. (a)					£. s. d. (a)		
....		Crt.	Crt.	Crt.	Correct.	Crt.	Crt.	Crt.	Crt.	Correct.	Correct.

1. If be entered twice in the half-year, either in the money or statistical portion of out of alteration in the circumstances of the case.
column Pauper," the name of the head of the family alone is to be inserted.
2. If actually relieved on the *first of January* and on the *first of July* is to be shown only, a list, a portion of the List being set apart and ruled for that purpose. By perany otcular days is meant not only persons to whom relief is actually given on either members is for any period which includes either of these days.
viving rterly totals of the relief in money and kind, will answer to the cross-castings childre." The final total marked (b) will be the amount of the two quarterly totals;
3. Ng obtained by cross-casting for each pauper the quarterly totals in money and which t
to be e through the medium of Tickets upon Tradesmen, all relief out of the cash in where money or articles of necessity, is to be entered as money. Relief given from where i is in kind.
ch consecutive week.

Sch. F.—*Out-door Relief—Relieving Officer's Books.* 531

Out-door Relief List.—Alternative Form for the Money Portion (*l*).

Parish of _____   Union _____   Half-year ending _____ 186 .   District _____
Relieving Officer of the _____

Name of the Pauper.	1st Week, ending		2nd Week, ending		3rd Week, ending		4th Week, ending		5th Week, ending		6th Week, ending		7th Week, ending		8th Week, ending		9th Week, ending		10th Week, ending		11th Week, ending		12th Week, ending		13th Week, ending		Totals for the First Quarter.	1st Week, ending		2nd Week, ending		3rd Week, ending		Totals for the Second Quarter.	Totals for the Half-Year.
	In Money.	In Kind.	In Money.	In Kind.	In Money.	In Kind.	In Money.	In Kind.	In Money.	In Kind.	In Money.	In Kind.	In Money.	In Kind.	In Money.	In Kind.	In Money.	In Kind.	In Money.	In Kind.	In Money.	In Kind.	In Money.	In Kind.	In Money.	In Kind.	£. *s. d.*	In Money.	In Kind.	In Money.	In Kind.	In Money.	In Kind.	£. *s. d.* (*a*)	£. *s. d.*
Clerk's Initials .	Cor-rect.		Cor-rect.		Cor-rect.		Cor-rect.		Cor-rect.		Cor-rect.		Cor-rect.		Cor-rect.		Cor-rect.		Cor-rect.		Cor-rect.		Cor-rect.		Cor-rect.			Cor-rect.		Cor-rect.		Cor-rect.		£. *s. d.* (*a*)	(*b*)

(*b*) See Art. 23 (2), *ante*, p. 481.

Out-door Relief List for Vagrants (a).

Week ending _____ UNION. _____ Relieving Officer of the _____ District. _____

Date.	Name of Vagrant, Wife, and Children.	Ages.	Ordinary Occupation or Trade.	Place of Birth of Vagrant, if known.	Where come from this day.	Where going to.	Parish where the Application is made.	Nature of Relief.	Cost.	Observations.
									s. d.	

Summary for the Week ending as above:— Men _____ ; Women _____ ; Boys _____ ; Girls _____ . Total _____

(Signed) _____
Relieving or Assistant Relieving Officer.

(a) See Art. 89 (4), ante, p. 383

Sch. F.—Out-door Relief—Relieving Officer's Books.

Abstract of the Out-door Relief Lists (b).

UNION _____ . Relieving Officer of the _____ District.

Names of Parishes.	1st Week.	2nd Week.	3rd Week.	4th Week.	5th Week.	6th Week.	7th Week.	8th Week.	9th Week.	10th Week.	11th Week.	12th Week.	13th Week.	14th Week.	15th Week.	16th Week.	17th Week.	18th Week.	19th Week.	20th Week.	21st Week.	22nd Week.	23rd Week.	24th Week.	25th Week.	26th Week.	Total.
Totals . .																											
Clerk's Initials																											

(b) See Art. 23 (3), ante, p. 462.

The Relieving Officer's Receipt and Expenditure Book (a).

UNION. DISTRICT. Week of the Quarter ending 184 .

Relieving Officer in account with the Board of Guardians of the Union.

Dr. Date.	Money received, and Tickets issued.	£. s. d.	£. s. d.

Cr.	To be charged to the Common Fund of the Union, or to some other Union or Parish.	£. s. d.	£. s. d.

(a) See Art. 23 (3), ante, p. 468.

Sch. F. Out-door Relief.—Relieving Officer's Books.

Summary of Receipts and Expenditure for the Quarter ended _____ 186 . (a).

_____ UNION. _____ District.

Relieving Officer of the _____

(To be entered immediately after the Account for the last Week of every Quarter in the Relieving Officer's Receipt and Expenditure Book.)

Dr.	Money. £ s. d.	Kind. £ s. d.
Balance brought forward		
As per Receipt and Expenditure Book, 1st week		
,, ,, 2nd week		
,, ,, 3rd week		
,, ,, 4th week		
,, ,, 5th week		
,, ,, 6th week		
,, ,, 7th week		
,, ,, 8th week		
,, ,, 9th week		
,, ,, 10th week		
,, ,, 11th week		
,, ,, 12th week		
,, ,, 13th week		
	(A)	(B)

Cr.	Money. £ s. d.	Kind. £ s. d.
Parishes* in Relieving Officer's District, as per Out-Relief List, viz.—		
,,		
,,		
,,		
Totals (1)		
Unions and Parishes charged with Relief to Non-settled Poor, as per Out-Relief List, viz.—		
,,		
,,		
Totals (2)		
Sums of Totals (1) and (2) respectively		
Balance in hand at the end of the Quarter		
	(A)	(B)

The totals marked (A) and (B) respectively must correspond. The totals of the expenditure in money in respect of the relief of the settled and non-settled Poor, with the balance in hand (if any), will give the total marked (A), and those of the relief in kind will give the total marked (B), on the credit side of this account.

* The *Parishes* here mean the Parishes of the Union in which the Paupers reside, or have received their Relief, and the amount expended in each Parish is to be shown.

(a) See Art. 23 (4), *ante*, p. 463.

2 M

SCHEDULE (G).

_____ *Audit District.*

A Statement of the Auditor,

In reference to the Books of the _____ Union, for the Half-year ended 186 .

As to the Books required to be kept by the CLERK,

Mr. _____

By the TREASURER,

Mr.

By the COLLECTOR OF THE GUARDIANS.

Mr. _____

OBSERVATIONS.

	CLERK.
Minute Book.	
General Ledger.	
Non-settled Poor Ledger.	
Parochial Ledger.	
Relief Order Book.	
Order Check Book.	
Pauper Classification Book.	
Petty Cash Book.	
	TREASURER.
The Treasurer's Book.	
	COLLECTOR OF THE GUARDIANS.
The Collector's Book.	
The Audit of the above Books was concluded the	*day of* 186 .

_____ *Auditor.*

Date _____ 186 .

Against the name of any Book contained in this Statement which is not kept at all, or is imperfectly kept, the Auditor is to write in the former case "not kept," and in the latter "imperfectly." In case of any Book being imperfectly kept, the general nature of the imperfection to be set forth *on the other side*, together with such observations as the Auditor considers requisite.

(*a*) See Arts. 50 and 51, *ante*, p. 479.

Schedule G.—Auditing of Accounts.

_____ Audit District.

A Statement of the Auditor,

In reference to the Books of the _____ UNION, for the Half-year ended 186 .

As to the Books required to be kept by the MASTER OF THE WORKHOUSE.

Mr. ___

Inventory.	
Admission and Discharge Book.	
In-door Relief List.	
Abstract of In-door Relief List.	
Master's Day-book.	
His Receipt and Payment Book.	
Quarterly Summary of Day Book.	
Master's portion of Workhouse Medical Relief List.	
Daily Provisions Consumption Account.	
Weekly Provisions Consumption Account.	
Provisions Receipt and Consumption Account.	
Quarterly Summary of Provisions Received and Consumed.	
Quarterly Balance of Provisions Account.	
Clothing Materials Receipt and Conversion Account.	
Clothing Receipt and Expenditure Account.	
Clothing Register Book.	
Necessaries and Miscellaneous Account.	
Quarterly Summary of the Necessaries and Miscellaneous Account.	
Quarterly Balance of the Necessaries and Miscellaneous account.	
The Audit of the above Books was concluded the	day of 186 .

_____ Auditor.

Date _____ 186 .

Against the name of any Book contained in this Statement which is not kept at all, or is imperfectly kept, the Auditor is to write in the former case "not kept," and in the latter "imperfectly." In case of any Book being imperfectly kept, the general nature of the imperfection to be set forth on *the other side*, together with such observations as the Auditor considers requisite.

_____ *Audit District.*

A Statement of the Auditor.

In reference to the Books of the Officers of the _____ UNION, for the Half-year ended   186 .

As to the Books required to be kept by the RELIEVING OFFICER.

Mr. _____

OBSERVATIONS.

Application and Report Book.	
Out-door Relief List.	
Out-door Relief List for Vagrants.	
Abstract of Out-Relief List.	
Receipt and Expenditure Book.	
Quarterly Summary of Receipts and Expenditure.	
The Audit of the above Accounts was concluded the day of 186 .	

_____ *Auditor.*

*Date*_____ 186 .

Against the name of any Book contained in this Statement which is not kept at all, or is imperfectly kept, the Auditor is to write in the former case "not kept," and in the latter "imperfectly." In case of any Book being imperfectly kept, the general nature of the imperfection to be set forth *on the other side*, together with such observations as the Auditor considers requisite.

Schedule G.—*Auditing of Accounts.* 539

_____*Audit District.*

A Statement of the Auditor,

In reference to the Books of the PARISH of _____
in the _____ UNION, for the Half-year ended 186 .

As to the Books required to be kept by the Overseers, Assistant Overseer, or Collector,*

Mr. _____

_____ (*Address*).

Appointed under the authority of _____ †

OBSERVATIONS.

Rate Book.	
Receipt and Payment Book.	
Rate Receipt Check Book.	
Collecting and Deposit Book.	
Monthly Statements.	
Unpaid Rates Statement.	
The Audit of the above Books was concluded the day of 186 .	

_____*Auditor.*

Date _____ 186 .

---

* Retain one of these Names, as the case may be.

† Insert whether under an Order of the Poor Law Commissioners or Poor Law Board (and if so, the date), or under the Statute 59 Geo. III. c. 12, or other Statute.

Against the name of any Book contained in this Statement which is not kept at all, or is imperfectly kept, the Auditor is to write in the former case "not kept," and in the latter "imperfectly." In case of any Book being imperfectly kept, the general nature of the imperfection to be set forth on *the other side*, together with such observations as the Auditor considers requisite. He is also to report whether any paid officer has in any respect disobeyed, neglected, or departed from any of the regulations of this Order applicable to his office.

_____ Audit District.
___ Union.

To the Poor Law Board.

I CERTIFY that I have Audited the Accounts of the Guardians of the _____ Union, and of their several Officers, and of the Overseers and Officers of the several Parishes therein, and have carefully examined all the Books required by the Orders of the Poor Law Board to be kept, and find no defect in the Books required to be kept by the following Paid Officers:—

Office.	Name.	Office.	Name.
Audit completed this	day of		186 .

_____ Auditor.
Date _____ 186 .

_____ _____ Audit District.

Statement in reference to the Officer's Securities required to be produced at the Audit next after the 25th day of March, 186 , *in the* _____ *Union.*

Name of the Union and Parishes.*	Names of every Officer required to give Security.†	Under what Authority appointed.	Office.	Whether the Security was produced.	Whether any Certificate or Proof was produced that each Surety is living, and is not Bankrupt or Insolvent, or that the Security was otherwise in force.	Observations.

Dated _____ 186 . _____ _____ Auditor.

* The Officers of the Union should be placed first in order.
† This term applies to every Officer so required to give security whose salary has been allowed or entered in any account at this Audit, whether of the Union or any Parish therein.

SCHEDULE (H).

Containing the Names of the Unions to which the foregoing Order refers.

[The Unions named in the Schedule are those in the Schedule to the General Consolidated Order, *ante*, p. 206, and the Unions mentioned, *ante*, page 211, with the exception of the Norwich, Westminster, and Woolwich Unions.]

Given under our hands and Seal of Office, this Fourteenth day of January, in the year One thousand eight hundred and sixty-seven

L. S.

GATHORNE HARDY, *President.*
S. H. WALPOLE.
B. DISRAELI.

RALPH A. EARLE, *Secretary.*

A separate Order of Accounts was issued to the Forehoe Incorporation on the 20th May, 1867; and as regards the East and West Flegg, Mutford and Lothingland, and Tunstead and Happing Incorporations, the General Order for Accounts, dated the 17th March, 1847, still remains in force. That Order will be found in the fifth edition of this work, page 342.

Orders for Accounts have been issued to the following single Parishes and Townships under Boards of Guardians, and places under local Acts, on the dates undermentioned:—

1. *Single Parishes and Places under Boards of Guardians.*

Alston-with-Garrigill . . . . . . 15th December, 1854.
Bermondsey . . . . 2nd March, 1836.
East Stonehouse . . . . 7th August, 1851.

Great Yarmouth	8th March, 1850 (*a*).
Holbeck	11th November, 1862.
Hunslet	31st October, 1862.
Leeds	26th August, 1857 (*b*).
Manchester	10th March, 1851.
Mile End Old Town	27th January, 1858.
St. George-the-Martyr, Southwark	19th November, 1857.
St. Giles, Camberwell	12th March, 1856.
St. Luke, Chelsea	4th September, 1850 (*c*).
St. Mary, Lambeth	30th August, 1860. (altered 18th May, 1861).
St. Mary, Rotherhithe	7th March, 1860.
St. Marylebone	11th May, 1868.
St. Pancras	29th August, 1867.
Saddleworth	23rd June, 1853.
Saddleworth (Collector's Order)	22nd August, 1857.
Stoke-upon-Trent	7th March, 1854.
Toxteth Park	17th February, 1858.
Whittlesea, St. Mary and St. Andrew	21st June, 1852.

2. *Places under Local Acts.*

Alverstoke	29th July, 1852.
Birmingham	23rd February, 1850 (*d*).
Bristol	17th February, 1857 (*e*).
Bury St. Edmund's	4th December, 1857.
Canterbury	12th June, 1852 (*e*).
Chester	18th September, 1851 (*f*).
Chichester	21st February, 1853 (*e*).

(*a*) In the Parish of Great Yarmouth the General Order of 18th November, 1850, prescribing the form of Poor Rate is still in force.

(*b*) Rescinded as regards duties of Collectors 14th June, 1858.

(*c*) The provisions of this Order relating to the books and duties of the Collector of Poor-rates have been rescinded, and further provisions made in that behalf by an Order dated 21st March, 1854.

(*d*) The provisions of this Order applicable to the office of Storekeeper were rescinded, and further provisions made in that behalf, by an Order dated 11th December, 1851. Further alteration, as regards the books of the Relieving Officer, was made in it by an Order dated 24th May, 1855.

(*e*) These Orders apply only to the Accounts of the Guardians and their Officers.

(*f*) Article 8 of this Order, as to the payment of money by Collectors of Poor-rates, was rescinded by an Order dated 9th July, 1858.

Exeter	9th May, 1857 (e).
Kingston-upon-Hull	3rd May, 1850 (e).
Oswestry	26th April, 1851.
(Collector's Order)	4th July, 1856.
Oxford	10th June, 1853.
Plymouth	6th August, 1853 (e).
St. Chad, Shrewsbury	8th June, 1861 (g).
Meole Brace, Shrewsbury	8th May, 1862 (g).
St. Mary, Shrewsbury	8th May, 1862 (y).
St. Alkmond, Shrewsbury	8th May, 1862 (g).
St. Julian, Shrewsbury	8th May, 1862 (g).
Holy Cross and St. Giles, Shrewsbury	8th May, 1862 (g).
Shrewsbury	5th August, 1850 (h).
Salisbury	10th March, 1859.
Southampton	16th March, 1850 (e).
Stoke Damerel	31st January, 1855.

Inasmuch as the provisions of the Orders above-mentioned differ in some instances from those contained in the General Order for Accounts of the 17th March, 1847, the Officers, in acting upon the Order in force in their particular Union or Parish, should refer to the original Order in the possession of the Guardians, and note the variances between that Order and the General Order.

(g) These Orders apply only to the Accounts of the Overseers, Collectors, and Relieving Officers.

(h) This Order only applies to the Accounts of the Master of the Workhouse.

ACCOUNTS.—SUSPENSORY ORDER.

(17*th January*, 1868.)

To the Auditors *of the several* **Audit Districts** *named in the Schedule hereunto annexed ;* —

To the Guardians of the Poor of the several Unions comprised in such Districts ;

To all others whom it may concern.

WHEREAS by a General Order of the Poor Law Board, bearing date the 14th day of January, 1867, addressed to the Guardians of the Poor of the several Unions named in the Schedule (II.) thereunto annexed, the Poor Law Board made certain regulations as to the keeping of accounts, and the accounting of the persons therein mentioned to the Auditor, and the Poor Law Board required that such regulations should apply to every case in which the Poor Law Board should not assent to a departure from any of the regulations contained in the said Order.

And whereas in Article 50 of the said recited Order (*a*), it is required that the Auditor shall, at the close of each audit of the accounts of the Union, transmit to the Poor Law Board a certain statement as to the Books directed by that Order to be kept, and shall deliver copies thereof to the Board of Guardians.

And whereas it appears to the Poor Law Board to be expedient to allow a departure from this regulation, as hereinafter set forth.

I am therefore directed to state that the Poor Law Board authorize the Auditors of the districts comprising such Unions, and named in the Schedule hereunto annexed, to

---

(*a*) *Ante,* p. 479.

withhold the transmission of the copies of the statements aforesaid to the Boards of Guardians, until further directions in that behalf shall be given by the Poor Law Board.

SCHEDULE above referred to.

Names of the several Audit Districts.

Bedfordshire and Hertfordshire.
Berkshire and Hampshire.
Buckinghamshire and Northamptonshire.
Cambridgeshire and Huntingdonshire.
Cheshire and Denbighshire.
Cornwall and Devonshire.
Cumberland, East, and Westmoreland.
Cumberland, West.
Devonshire, Central (*a*).
Devonshire, North.
Devonshire, South-East.
Durham and Northumberland.
Durham and Yorkshire.
Essex.
Gloucestershire and Monmouthshire.
Hampshire and Wiltshire.
Herefordshire.
Kent, East.
Kent, West.
Lancashire, South, and Cheshire.
Lancashire, West and North.
Leicestershire and Nottinghamshire.
Lincolnshire and Rutlandshire.
London.
Metropolitan, North-East.
Metropolitan, North-West.
Metropolitan South-East.
Metropolitan, South-West.
Norfolk, East.
Norfolk, West.
Oxfordshire and Warwickshire.
Shropshire and Montgomeryshire.
Somersetshire and Wiltshire.
Somersetshire, West.
Staffordshire and Worcestershire (*b*).
Suffolk, East.
Suffolk, West.
Sussex, East, and Surrey.
Wales, North.
Wales, South.
Wiltshire and Gloucestershire.
Yorkshire, North-East.
Yorkshire, South.
Yorkshire, West.

Dated this Seventeenth day of January, in the year One thousand eight hundred and sixty-eight.

G. SCLATER-BOOTH, *Secretary to the Poor Law Board.*

(*a*) The Unions in this district have since been added to the South-East Devonshire District.

(*b*) The Unions in this district, on the death of the late Auditor were added to the Oxfordshire and Warwickshire, and Shropshire and Montgomeryshire Districts.

LIST OF MR. GLEN'S WORKS,

1846 to 1868.

The South Wales Turnpike Road Acts (7 & 8 Vict. c. 91, 8 & 9 Vict. c. 61) ; with Introduction, Notes, and Cases 1846

Practical Instructions for the Making of Wills, agreeably to the Statute 1 Vict. c. 26 1847

The General Consolidated Order and other General Orders of the Poor Law Commissioners; with Explanatory Notes, etc.
First Edition 1847
——— *Second Edition* 1850
——— *Third Edition* 1855
——— *Fourth Edition* 1859
——— *Fifth Edition* 1864
——— *Sixth Edition* 1868

The Nuisances Removal and Diseases Prevention Acts; with Notes, etc. *First Edition* 1848
——— *Second Edition* 1848
——— *Third Edition* 1849
——— *Fourth Edition* 1853

The Small Tenements Rating Act, and the Parish Vestries and Vestry Clerks Act; with Introduction, Notes, etc. *First Edition* 1850
——— *Second Edition* 1851
——— *Third Edition* 1855
——— *Fourth Edition* 1866

The Poor Law Board Act (12 & 13 Vict. c. 103); with Notes . 1849

The Metropolitan Interments Act, 1850; with Introduction, Notes, etc. 1850

The Acts relating to the Relief of the Poor passed in the Session 1851; with Notes, etc. 1851

The Poor Law Statutes, 1852, together with the County Rates Act, 15 & 16 Vict. c. 81 1852

Justice of the Peace, and County Borough Poor Law Union and Parish Law Recorder. *Joint Editor*, volumes 16 to 22 inclusive .... 1852 to 1858

List of Mr. Glen's Works, continued.

The Act to Extend and make Compulsory the Practice of Vaccination, and the Poor Law Acts Session 1853; with Notes, etc.	1854
Archbold's Parish Officer. *Second Edition*	1855
The Poor Law Guardian, his Powers and Duties in the right execution of his Office. *First Edition*	1855
——— *Second Edition*	1857
The Duties of Vestrymen, Members and Officers under the Metropolis Local Management Act and the Metropolitan Building Act	1856
The Acts Regulating the Duties of Justices of the Peace out of Sessions known as Jervis's Acts; with Notes and Cases. *First Edition*	1857
——— *Second Edition*	1861
——— *Third Edition*	1868
The Statutes in force relating to the Poor Parochial Unions and Parishes collated with each other, and with references to the Cases upon each Statute, and an extensive Index (43 Eliz. c. 2 to 19 & 20 Vict. c. 112). Vol. I.	1857
——— (20 Vict. c. 19 to 29 & 30 Vict. c. 118). Vol. II.	1864 and 1866
The Burial Board Acts of England and Wales; with Introduction, Notes, etc. *First Edition*	1858
——— *Second Edition*	In the Press.
The Law relating to the Removal of Nuisances Injurious to Health	1858–1860
The Law in relation to the Legal Liabilities of Engineers, Architects, Contractors, Builders, etc.	1860
The Law relating to Public Health and Local Government in relation to Sanitary and other matters, with the Public Health Act, 1848, the Local Government Act, 1858, the Incorporated and Amending Acts. *First Edition*	1858
——— *Second Edition*	1862
——— *Third Edition*	1865
——— *Fourth Edition*	1866
——— *Fifth Edition*	In the Press, 1868
The Public Works (Manufacturing Districts) Act, 1863, and the Relief in Aid Acts, 1862, 1863, and the other Acts of the Session 1863 relating to Local Authorities	1863
The Law relating to the Registration of Births, Deaths, and Marriages, and the Marriage of Dissenters in England; with Notes and Cases	1860
A Treatise on the Law of Highways. *First Edition*	1860
——— *Second Edition*	1865
The Law relating to the Licensing of Refreshment and Wine Houses, and the Wine Licences and Refreshment Houses Act	1860
The Law relating to the Removal of Scotch and Irish Poor from England	1861
Poor Law Legislation, Sessions	1861 to 1867

The Acts for the Better Management of Highways in England, 1862, 1864; with Introduction and Notes. *First Edition* . 1862
———— *Second Edition* 1863
———— *Third Edition* 1864
———— *A New Edition* :—By Alexander Glen, of Christ's College, Cambridge, and the Middle Temple 1868
Snowden's Police Officers', Constables' Guide, and Magistrates' Assistant. *Fifth Edition* 1862
———— *Sixth Edition* 1866
The Prison Act, 1865, and the Acts relating to Gaols and Prisons 1865
The Union Chargeability Act, 1865; with an Introduction and Commentary; also the Practice of Poor Removals adapted to the Removal of Union Poor. *First Edition* 1865
———— *Second Edition* 1866
The Cattle Diseases Prevention Acts, 1866 (Great Britain and Ireland) 1866
The Metropolitan Poor Act, 1867; with Notes and Appendix of Incorporated Statutes 1867
The Representation of the People Act, 1867; with Introduction and Notes. *First Edition* 1867
———— *Second Edition* 1868
———— *Third Edition* 1868
The Parliamentary Registration Manual, being a Practical Guide to the Duties of the several Officers in respect of the Registration of County, City, and Borough Voters, and the Revision Courts. *First Edition* 1868
———— *Second Edition* 1868
The Fourth Edition of Shelford's Law of Railways, bringing the whole of the law on the subject down to the present time. By W. C. Glen, Barrister at Law. In the Press 1868

INDEX.

₊ *The letters before the figures refer to the Notes.*

ABLE-BODIED, meaning of term, *a*, 359; Guardians must decide questions of, *a*, 359; paupers in Workhouse, employment of, on task of work, *e*, 85; in what cases their families may be detained in, *b*, 88; persons in employment, prohibition of relief to, 386.
Able-bodied pauper, apprenticeship of child of, *a*, 40.
Able-bodied poor, prohibition of out-door relief to, 358; relieved out of Workhouse to be set to work, 387.
Absconding from Workhouse, when punishable, *b*, 90; with Workhouse clothing, 105.
Absence of Relieving Officer from District, *a*, 182.
Abstract of in-door relief list, 452; form of it, 512; of out-relief list, 462, form of it, 533.
Accident, payment for medical or other assistance rendered necessary by, *a*, 128; relief in cases of, 359, 385, 387; duty of Relieving Officer in cases of, 184: non-resident relief in cases of, 365.
Accidental death in Workhouse, to be reported to Poor Law Board by Medical Officer, 341.
Accouchement fees, 129–131, *a*, 130.
Account of Treasurer to be kept and balanced half-yearly, 148; of relief to non-settled poor, how to be kept by Relieving Officer, 191.
Accounts, examination of, by Guardians, 32; for non-resident relief, 54; of officer who has been removed or suspended, to be audited before payment of salary, 125; relating to non-settled and non-resident poor, 145; of Union Treasurer, audit of, 119; duty of Relieving Officer as to submitting, for audit, 191.
Accounts, of Overseers, 435; of Collector of Parish, 440; of Clerk to Guardians, 445; of Collector of the Guardians, 450; of Treasurer, 451; of Master of the Workhouse, 451; when binding on Matron, 460; of Relieving Officer, 460; examination and closing of, 464, 465; day of week on which to be closed, *e*, 465; to be open to inspection at audit, 473; duty of auditor in regard to, 474, 475: illegal for Parish Officers to alter after made up for audit, *e*, 437.
Accounts to be opened in Union Ledger, 446.
Accounts of Union, to be deposited for inspection of ratepayers, 469.

Accounts, objection to, by ratepayers, 476; auditor to hear and decide, 476.
Accounts of Parish, to be made up and balanced half-yearly, 465; to be deposited for inspection of ratepayers, 465.
Accounting Officer, death of, auditor's certificate cannot be enforced, *a*, 480.
Accumulation of books and documents, steps to be taken by Guardians, *b*, 481.
Actions at law, duty of Clerk as to conducting, 272.
Adding up columns of Rate Book, 436.
Adjourned audit, notice of, to be given by Clerk, 469.
Adjournment of meetings of Guardians, 23; of audit, 469; duty of Clerk in such case, 469.
Administration of relief, fundamental principles of, *b*, 28; to non-settled poor, 51, *a*, 52; when to be weekly or oftener, 383.
Administration of religious consolation to sick paupers by Chaplain, 176.
Admission to Workhouse, order of Guardians for, of pauper, 33; in what manner paupers shall be admitted, 58, 59, *a*, 59; duty of Master of Workhouse as to, 162; of Matron, 172; under an order of removal, 59, *b*, 63; on Sundays, *b*, 61; of part of family only, *b*, 62; of persons labouring under infectious diseases, *b*, 63; how when money is found on them, *b*, 63; of chronic lunatics, *b*, 64; duty of Medical Officer, 158.
Admission to Workhouse, limitation of hours for, in the case of vagrants, *b*, 74.
Admission and Discharge Book, 452; form of it, 508; for vagrants, 452; form of it, 509.
Adoption of children from Workhouse, *b*, 89.
Adult pauper, relief cannot be given for education of, *b*, 29.
Advertisements in newspapers, 37, *a*, 37; of appointments of officers, 114, *b*, 114.
Advertising audits, *a*, 473; cost of, how defrayed, *a*, 473.
Africa, relief to natives of, 373.
Age of binding pauper apprentice, 40; of nurture, relief to children under, 363; what is, *c*, 363.
Aged married couples living together in Workhouses, 71, *c*, 72.
Aged paupers, medical relief to, 50.
Aged person, relief to, under order of Justices, 402.
Agency charges, are within meaning of disbursements incurred by Clerk to Guardians, *a*, 274.
Agent of candidate for Guardian, may accompany Deliverer or Collector of Voting Papers, 233.
Agreements with cemetery companies for burial of paupers, *c*, 167.
Agreements, by whom to be prepared, 144.
Allocation of charges, entries thereof to be made in Guardians' minutes, 445.
Allowance of food in Workhouse, when paupers may require to be weighed, 84; of indentures of apprenticeship, *a*, 43; of bills by Guardians, 57; to Clerk of the Peace for taxation of bills of costs, 431.
Allowances to Officers by tradesmen prohibited, 193.
Allowances to paupers, payment of, 188.

Index. 551

Alteration of resolution of Guardians, how to be effected, 26.
Alterations to Workhouse, 108; duty of Master as to, 172; of relief districts, 115; of accounts after having been made up for audit, illegal, *e*, 437.
Amended Dietary Table, form of it, 289.
Amputation, fees for, 126; what certificate required previous to performing, 128.
Anatomical examination of bodies of paupers dying in Workhouse, *c*, 168.
Annual scrutiny of register of owners and proxies, *b*, 5.
Answering letters, duty of Clerk as to, *a*, 142.
Applications for relief, decisions of Guardians on, how to be recorded, 461.
Applications for relief, duty of Relieving Officer as to, 182.
Application of money found on pauper dying in Workhouse, *c*, 169; of property of paupers, *e*, 372.
Application and Report Book, 460; form of it, 529; Proceedings of Relief Committees to be entered in, 258; of District Relief Committees, 262.
Application of certified balances, *a*, 271.
Applications to Guardians of paupers in Workhouse, duty of Master as to, 171.
Appointment—of Committees of Guardians, 27; of Workhouse Visiting Committee, 106; time when to be appointed, *d*, 106; of Medical Officers in cases of emergency, 332; in case of vacancy, 332; of Officers, 109; what Officers, 109; of assistants to Officers, 109; mode of, 113; to be reported to Poor Law Board, 114; what previous notice shall be given, 114; by advertisement, 114; of temporary substitute during sickness, etc., of Officer, 136; in the case of vacancies, 137; of successors to Medical Officers, 137; of their substitutes, 136; of paid Workhouse Visitor, *d*, 106; of Medical Officers, duration of, 329, 330, 331; of Superintendent of pauper labour, 109; of Pay-clerk of the poor, 319; of proxy, form of it, *b*, 17; of Collector of poor-rates, 408; of Collector of the Guardians, 304; of more than one, 312.
Appointment of Officers, Guardians may specify limit of age for candidates, *c*, 117; Guardians may pay travelling expenses of any candidate, 316.
Apprenticeship of pauper children, 40; what children, *a*, 40; a species of relief, *a*, 40; no child to be apprenticed more than forty miles from parish to which child belongs, *b*, 42; certificate of Medical Officer, 150; duty of Relieving Officer as to, 187; of child of able-bodied pauper, *a*, 40; mode of charging cost of clothing given to, *b*, 41; to the sea service, *b*, 49, *b*, 50; order relating to, issued to places not in Union, 418; list of places to which issued, 427, 428.
Approval of Poor Law Board to departure from Prohibitory Order, how it is expressed, *b*, 371.
Area of Medical Districts, 115.
Arithmetical accuracy of accounts, Auditor to ascertain, 475.
Arrear of Rates, lists of person in, to be made by Collector, 444.
Arrears of Rates, how to be entered in new rate, 435.
Asia, relief to natives of, 373.
Assessment Committee, to be appointed by Guardians at their first

2 N

meeting, *c*, 21; how in case of omission, *c*, 21; right of individual Guardians to be present at, *c*, 21; Minute Book of, how to be kept, *f*, 140.
Assessment to poor-rate, form of it, 484; in the case of owners, 436.
Assignment of indenture of Apprenticeship, 49.
Assistant of Medical Officer, duties cannot be delegated to, *b*, 138; but may be appointed substitute, *c*, 138.
Assistant nurses, should be paid officers, *c*, 179.
Assistant Overseer, signature of, to poor-rate, 484; bonds, *b*, 57; power of, to give an order for admission of a pauper to Workhouse, *b*, 62; disqualified for being Guardian, *b*, 117; prohibited from receiving money for relief of non-settled pauper, 194; to assist Overseers in making out and serving notices of arrears of rates, 415; increase of remuneration to, 413; bound to obey majority of Overseers, *b*, 444.
Assistant to Matron, employment of paupers as, 72.
Assistant Officers, employment of, 109; appointment of, need not be reported to Poor Law Board, 315; how in Metropolitan Unions and Parishes, *d*, 315; where salaries are wholly, or in part, repaid from Consolidated Fund the appointments must be reported, *d*, 315.
Assistants to Medical Officers, employment of unqualified, *c*, 156.
Asylum districts in metropolis, formation of, 218.
Attachment of wages to pay for medical relief or loan, *c*, 153; in repayment of relief, *c*, 371.
Attendance of Clerk at audit, *f*, 141; of Overseers, 403.
Attendance—of Collector on Board of Guardians, 409; of contractors on Guardians, 39; of Medical Officer at Workhouse, 157; returns to Guardians as to, 160; at meetings of Guardians, 150; to distinguish in his books when paupers have been attended by others, 152; of pauper apprentice at divine worship, 47; of Dissenting Ministers at Workhouse, 93, *a*, 93; of inmates at parish church, 96; of Dissenters, 97; of Roman Catholics, *b*, 97; of Relieving Officers at meeting of Guardians, 182; of Union and Parish Officers at audit, 473.
Attorney, Guardian may act as, for Union or for parishes therein, *b*, 35.
Audit, notice of time and place of, to be given, 473; form of, *a*, 472; duty of Vestry Clerk to attend, *d*, 435; of Overseers, 473; of Collectors, 440; notice of, by Clerk, 468; by Auditor, 471; publication of, *a*, 473; adjournment of, 469; extraordinary audit, 471; attendance of officers at, 473; bonds of Officers to be produced at, 57; of accounts of Officers renewed or suspended before payment of salary to, *b*, 124, 125; production of accounts to, by Clerk, 141; his attendance thereat, *f*, 141; of accounts of Union Treasurer, 149; duty of Relieving Officer as to submitting his accounts for, 191; of accounts, duty of Overseers as to, 403; of the accounts of an Officer who has resigned, 480.
Auditing of accounts, 471; to be half-yearly, 471.
Auditor, duty of, to see that columns of Rate Book are correctly cast, *a*, 436; statements of, as to books of Officers and securities, 479; forms of, 536, 537, 538, 539, 540; statistical and financial statements to be submitted to, 467; his duty thereupon, 467; salary, how paid, *a*, 473; duty of, as to audit of accounts, 471, *a*, 472, 474, 475, 476; his certificate in Union ledger, 478; his report on books of Officers, 479; forms of his reports, 536, 540; vote of Vice-

Chairman when there are two at election of, *a*, 22; should not give advice to Officers as to legality of particular expenditure, *a*, 472; report to Guardians on books of Officers, suspensions of, 545.
Authentication of Relieving Officer's accounts by Clerk, 191.
Authenticity of testimonials to character, importance of ascertaining, *e*, 112.
Authorities granting qualifications for Medical Officer, *a*, 336.
Average waste in the consumption of certain provisions, table of, *c*, 477.

Bad character, sub-classification of paupers of, in Workhouse, 71, *b*, 71.
Balance of account, Auditor to certify, 476.
Balance-sheet of receipts and payments to be made out by Overseers, 438; form of it, 488; to be signed by Overseers and presented to Auditor for signature, 438; a copy to be delivered to Guardians, 438, 476; a copy to be produced by Overseers at next Vestry Meeting, 438, *c*, 438; to be preserved with other parochial documents, 438; to be certified by Auditor, 476.
Balances, application of, when paid to Treasurer of Union, *a*, 271; of Treasurer's account to be ascertained by Clerk, 145.
Balancing Collecting and Deposit Book, 443; Treasurer's account half-yearly, 148.
Ballot, Guardians voting by, *b*, 26.
Banker's Pass Book of Overseers, production of to Auditor, *a*, 474.
Banking firm should not be appointed as Treasurers of Union, *e*, 111; security to be given by, when appointed, *b*, 133.
Bank of England acting as Treasurer of Guardians, duties of Treasurer not to apply to, 150.
Bankruptcy of Officer, does not vacate the office, *d*, 134; not a legal disqualification for office, *d*, 134.
Bankruptcy of Treasurer not to vacate his office, *d*, 136.
Baptism of children in Workhouse, *b*, 96, *a*, 175.
Bed, duty of Master to see that Paupers are in, 165; of Matron, 173; time at which paupers in Workhouse shall go to, 80.
Bedding, relief for purchase of, 384; to be supplied to paupers undergoing punishment by confinement, 102; at Workhouse, inventory of, 451.
Beds, number of paupers to occupy each, 85; duty of Matron to see that they are kept clean and wholesome, 173.
Behaviour of women and children, duty of Matron as to, 173.
Beyond the seas, relief to wife of persons, 369; meaning of the term, *b*, 369.
Bills, examination of, by Guardians, 57, *a*, 57; production of, by Relieving Officers, with vouchers, 192.
Bills of costs, taxation of, 430; of contractor's contracts, to stipulate that they shall be sent in, 39; of parcels for provisions, examination of, by Master, 170.
Binding pauper children apprentices, preliminaries to, 43, 44, 45.
Births in Workhouse, registration of, 165; of still-born children, *g*, 165; form of register of, 276.
Bishop of diocese to consent to appointment of Chaplain, 122; fees in such case, *a*, 122; no power to remove Chaplain from office, *d*, 131.
Blankets, washing of, to be superintended by Matron of Workhouse, 173.
Blind pauper, maintenance of, in institutions, *b*, 31; payment of costs incurred in conveyance to, *b*, 31.

Board-room, suspension of copies of rules in, 105.
Bodily infirmity, relief in cases of, 359, 385, 387; non-resident, relief in cases of, 365, 385, 387.
Bonds, custody of, 57; production of, at audit, 57; the Clerk's bond, *b*, 57; of Assistant Overseers and Collectors, *b*, 57; of Officers generally, 131; release of sureties, *c*, 132; Guardians entitled to possession of, on resignation of Officer, *c*, 132; by whom to be prepared, *a*, 144; statement of Auditor as to, 479.
Bone-dust, paupers not to be employed in preparing, 86.
Bones to be accounted for by Master of Workhouse, *b*, 122.
Books, examination of, by Guardians, *a*, 33; for Workhouse inmates, *c*, 91; of account, by whom to be supplied, *f*, 142, 481; custody of, *a*, 143, 481; purchase of, 481; report of Auditor on, 479; submission of, by Relieving Officer for audit, 191; required to be produced to Auditor by Overseers, *a*, 473.
Borrowing money, when Guardians can and cannot, *a*, 270.
Boxes, to be provided for collection of voting paper, 233; voter may deposit his own paper in, 233.
Boys in Workhouse, when they may be classed with men, 73; education of, 86.
Bread-baking, average results in Unions, *c*, 477.
Burial club, fee to Medical Officer for certificate of death of child insured in, *c*, 151.
Burial-ground for paupers, consecration of, *c*, 167.
Burial of paupers, when the Guardians may reimburse themselves the cost of, *b*, 65, *c*, 169; of paupers dying in Workhouse, 166; place of burial, *c*, 167; fees payable, *c*, 167; of persons dying in hospitals, *c*, 169; relief for the purposes of, 360, 388; burial, as to the liability attaching to parents, *b*, 360, *c*, 372.
Business of Guardians, not advisable to send notice to Guardians of what is proposed to be transacted at ordinary meeting, *b*, 27; order in which it is to be transacted, 27, *d*, 27.
Business, relief not to be granted for the purpose of establishing persons in, *b*, 29, 384.
Bye-law as to appointment of Officers, *b*, 114.

Calls of Guardians upon Overseers for contributions to Union funds cannot be made retrospectively, *e*, 267.
Cancelling indentures of apprenticeship, *a*, 46, 49.
Cancer in the breast, fee not payable for removing, *a*, 127.
Candidates for Election as Guardian, may be present at casting-up of votes, *e*, 13, 234.
Candidates for office of Guardian, publication of their names, *b*, 10.
Candidates for Office, Guardians may pay travelling expenses of any, 316.
Card for medical or other extras to be affixed at head of bed of patient in Workhouse, 341.
Cards in Workhouse, prohibition of, 92.
Carriage for conveyance of paupers to or from Workhouses, not exempt from duty, *d*, 186.
Casting up columns of Rate Book, 436; votes at election of Guardians 13.
Casting-vote of presiding Chairman, *b*, 24.

Casual poor, when regulations for admission of paupers to Workhouse are not to apply to, 68; treatment and diet of, 74; in the Metropolis, dietary for, 293; out-door relief to, 365, 385.

Catechizing Workhouse children by Chaplain, 175.

Cattle diseases expenses, amount must be stated in Contribution Order, *a*, 270.

Cemetery companies, agreements with, for burial of paupers, *c*, 167.

Certificate of Auditors of balance due on an account, 475; of balance-sheet in Union ledger, 478; form of, 478.

Certificates of election of Guardians, cost of, how to be defrayed, 220; of Guardians elected, when there is no contest, 10; when number of candidates reduced by refusals to serve, 11; of election after a contest, 14; form of it, 198; of Justices in the case of pauper apprenticeship, *a*, 43; as to capacity of child, 43; Medical Officer to give certificate in such case, 150; of sickness of pauper, 150; in regard to lunatic paupers, *c*, 151; of Schoolmasters and Schoolmistresses, *b*, 176.

Certificate—required previous to amputations, 128; Medical man must be registered, *a*, 129; of Medical Officer in respect of death of child insured in burial club, *c*, 151; of vaccination, persons authorized to grant, 355.

Certified balance, application of, when paid to Treasurer of Union, *a*, 271.

Certified industrial schools or establishments, as to admission of children and paupers into, *d*, 368.

Chairman, election of, 20; definition of term, 483; duration of office, 20; how if he refuses to act, or becomes incapable, 22; at commencement of first meeting of Guardians, *c*, 20; to preside at meetings, 24; may move resolutions, etc., *a*, 24; is bound to fill the chair if present at a meeting, *a*, 24; his second or casting-vote, *b*, 24; how he should record his vote, *b*, 25; not bound to submit illegal motions, *b*, 26; to sign minutes, 28, *a*, 28.

Change in extent of medical districts, 331; of meetings of Guardians, 20; notice of, 23; of diet of paupers in Workhouse, 82.

Chaplain, appointment of, 109; qualification required, 122; his duties, powers of Incumbent of parish as to, *c*, 110, *a*, 122; cannot delegate his duties to his Curate, *a*, 136; to be sent for in case of dangerous illness of paupers, 166; duties of, 174; removal of from office, *d*. 134.

Chaplain's Report Book, should be kept in custody of Workhouse Master, *a*, 176.

Charge of Workhouse linen, etc., confided to Matron, 173.

Charges, entries of allocation of, to be made in minutes of Guardians, 445.

Charging borrowed money on poor-rates, *a*, 270.

Chelsea pensioners, repayment of relief to, *b*, 362, *c*, 372.

Cheque upon Treasurer of Guardians, form of it, 279; Clerk prohibited from using, 193; duty of, as to transmission of, 193.

Childbirth, fees for attendance on, 129, *a*, 130; a sickness within, exception to Prohibitory Order, *a*, 360.

Children, admission of, in Workhouse by order of Justices, under Industrial Schools Act, *b*, 69; classification of, in Workhouses, 69–73; their parents to have interviews with them, 73; education of them,

86, 177; in schools of their own religious persuasion, *b*, 29; examination, etc., of, by Chaplain. 175; of out-door children, *a*, 86; control of Guardians over, when orphans, *b*, 87; females under age of sixteen cannot discharge themselves from Workhouse without consent of parent, *b*, 88; adoption of, from Workhouse, *b*, 89; granting leave of absence from Workhouse, to, *b*, 89; for purposes of recreation, 90; baptism of, *b*, 96, *a*, 175; of lunatic parent need not be included in quarterly list, *c*, 156; punishment of them in Workhouse, 102, 103, duty of Medical Officer as to their diet and treatment, 160; as to their vaccination, 160; registration of births of, 165; duty of Schoolmaster and Schoolmistress as to, 177; relief of, when neglected or ill-used by parents, *d*, 187.

Children, education of, in receipt of out-door relief, *a*, 86, *d*, 368.

Children in Workhouse or establishment out of Union, relief to, 367, 386.

Children in Workhouse, duty of Matron as to, 173; cleanliness of, *b*, 178; duty of Matron, *b*, 178; of Schoolmistress, *b*, 178.

Children in Workhouse, education of, in religion of parent, *c*, 95; fit for service, report of, to be made to Guardians, 170; when they need not accompany their parents to Workhouse, *a*, 359.

Children of Master and Matron living in Workhouse, *e*, 111.

Children of persons not residing in Union, relief to, 362.

Children, maintenance of, in schools or institutions for deaf, dumb, blind, lame, or idiotic, *b*, 29.

Children within the age of nurture, the mother cannot consent to the separation of her children from her, *e*, 363.

Christian religion, instruction of Workhouse children in, 86.

Christmas Day, diet of paupers in Workhouse on, 82; no work to be done on, 95.

Chronic lunatics, reception and treatment in Workhouse, *b*, 64; arrangements for removal of, to Workhouses, *b*, 64.

Churching women after childbirth in Workhouse, *b*, 96, *a*, 175.

Churchwarden should not be appointed an officer of a Union, *b*, 117.

Circulation of papers of an improper tendency in Workhouses, 91.

Claims of owners and proxies, annual scrutiny of registers of, *b*, 5; duty of Overseers as to, 404.

Classification of paupers in Workhouse, 68, *b*, 69; how, when labouring under disease, 71, *b*, 70; of children, 69, 73; duty of Medical Officer as to sick paupers, 158.

Clean linen, etc., for paupers in Workhouse, duty of Matron as to, 173.

Cleansing paupers on admission to Workhouse, 67, 163, 172; wards of Workhouse, 164, 173; responsibility of Master as to, 171.

Clerk to Guardians, his appointment, 109; desirable that he should be a professional man, *e*, 111; qualification required, 117; to give security, 131; cannot be suspended from office by Guardians, *d*, 135; his personal attendance to his duties, *a*, 136; Vice-Chairman, discharge of duties of office of Clerk by, 137; exempt from serving office of Parish Constable, *e*, 139; to make return of salaries for purposes of income tax, *a*, 142; should bring under notice of Guardians neglect of any officer, *d*, 147; duties under Union Assessment Committee Act, *e*, 139; cannot delegate his duty of attending meetings of Guardians, *f*, 139; in regard to keeping and examining accounts, 141; and their production to Auditor, 141; his attendance thereat, *a*, 141; duty of, as to correspondence of Union, 142; production of Union books by, on *subpœna*, *a*, 143; duty of, as to contracts and bonds, 144; as to calling extraordinary meeting of Guardians, 144; to countersign Guardians' orders upon Overseers and Treasurer, 144; not when illegal, *c*, 144; to ascertain Treasurer's balance, 145; as to non-settled poor account, 145; as to communicating instructions to the other officers, 146; as to conducting legal business of the Guardians, 272; if an attorney, may be employed by Overseers as such, *a*, 274; as to preparation of returns, etc., 146; as to election of Guardians, 146; time for sending lunatic returns, *b*, 146; as to attending committees of Guardians, *d*, 147; production of Relieving Officer's accounts to, for inspection and authentication, 191; duty as to strayed children and insane persons, 297; his accounts, 445; examination of accounts by, 464, 470; to prepare statistical and financial statements half-yearly, 467; and transmit them to Poor Law Board, 468; duty of, as to parochial lists and accounts, 470.

Clerk to Guardians to conduct elections of Guardians, 4; to have assistants appointed, 4; Relieving Officers to assist, 191; duty of, to publish notice of election of Guardians, 5; duty of, in regard to nomination papers, 8; his certificate when there is no contest, 10; how when there is a contest, 10; in what cases voting-papers may be filled up and delivered to him in person, 12, *c*, 13; examination and casting up of votes, 13, *e*, 13; his certificate of election when there has been a contest, 14; his notification of election to successful candidates, 14; to make out a list of candidates and deliver the same to the Guardians, together with the nomination and voting-papers, 14; copies of list to be sent to Overseers by, 15; course of proceeding in case of his decease or absence, 16; his remuneration, *c*, 125, 219, 222; to make out list of persons nominated as Guardians, 232; to make out list of candidates for election, 232; to make arrangements to allow agent of candidate to accompany collector or deliverer of voting-papers, 233; to allow candidate or his agent to be present at casting up of votes, 234; to give notice of change of meetings, and of extraordinary meetings, 23; to sign order for admission of pauper to Workhouse, 33; duty of, as to orders for contributions, 266; has no authority to stay proceedings taken against Overseers for non-payment of contribution order, *a*, 270; bond of, to be deposited with Treasurer, *b*, 57; to report excess of paupers in Workhouse to Poor Law Board, 76; to report appointments of Officers to Poor Law Board, 114; prohibited from using Guardians' cheques, 193; duty of, as to transmission to persons in whose favour they are drawn, 193; attendance of, as a witness, *d*, 192; right of to charge for conducting settlement and removal cases, *a*, 266; must conduct proceedings when Guardians are the local authority for removal of nuisances, *a*, 274.

Clerk to Guardians being a solicitor, Guardians cannot employ another solicitor to conduct their legal business, *a*, 273.

Clerks of the peace, taxation of bills of costs by, 430.

Closing of Union Accounts, 465; day of week for, *c*, 465; table showing days for, *c*, 466.

Clothes of paupers in Workhouse, 67, *d*, 67, 165; dying in Workhouse, inventory of, to be delivered to Guardians, 169.

Clothes given to destitute pauper, how to be charged, c, 457.
Clothing (Workhouse) accounts, 456; forms of them, 522; numbering suits, c, 457.
Clothing given to pauper apprentices, mode of charging, b, 41.
Clothing, contracts for supply of, 36; for pauper apprentice, 47; of paupers in Workhouse, materials of, 84; stamping, b, 84; duty of Master to see to repair of, 165; of Matron, 173; numbering of, 173; relief for purchase of, 384; when out-door relief shall be given partly in, 383, 393.
Clothing materials receipt and conversion account, 456; form of it, 522.
Clothing materials receipt and conversion account to be balanced half-yearly, 457.
Clothing receipt and expenditure account, 456; form of it, 522; to be balanced half-yearly, 457.
Clothing register book, 457; form of it, 524.
Coast-guardsmen, travelling allowances to widows and children, b, 190.
Cod-liver oil, supply of, c, 195.
Collecting and Deposit Book, 442; form of it, 493; when to be balanced, 443.
Collection of voting papers, 12; boxes or bags to be provided for, 233.
Collector of the Guardians, appointment of, 304; qualification, 304; duties, 305; remuneration, 306; security, 307; continuance in office, 308; suspension of, 308; supply of vacancy in office of, 308; form of Collector's Book, 309; form of Receipt Book, 310.
Collector of the Guardians Book, 450; form of it, 505; form of receipt to be given by, 505.
Collector of the Parish, duties in respect of valuation list, 440; to assist Overseers in preparation of Rate Book, 440; to attend with Overseers before Auditor, 440; to prepare receipts for poor-rate, 441; when to pay over money collected by, 442; to keep Collecting and Deposit Book, 442; form of it, 493.
Collector of Poor-rates, bond of, b, 57; to give security, 131; prohibited from receiving money for relief of non-settled pauper, 194; construction of word in Accounts Order, 482; accounts of, 440; attendance of, on Board of Guardians, 409; salary or poundage of, charging of, in accounts, 410; monthly statements to be made by, 443; form of them, 494; to prepare unpaid rates statements, 444; form of them, 495; payment of money by, 442; when to balance Collecting and Deposit Book, 443; bound to obey majority of Overseers, b, 444; his appointment, 408; his qualification, 408; his duties, 408; his remuneration, 410; to give security, 411; continuance, etc., in office, 411; definition of, 482.
Collectors of the Guardians, appointment of, 312; duties do not interfere with those of Collectors of the Poor-rate, a, 306.
Collectors of Poor-rates, order relating to increase of remuneration in certain cases, 413; to assist Overseers in making out and serving notices of arrears of rates, 415.
Collectors of voting-papers, agents of candidates accompanying, a, 12.
Combustibles to be taken from paupers in Workhouse, 92.
Commissioners, mode in which they can vote at election of Guardians, c, 3.
Commissioners in Lunacy, visitation of Workhouses by, b, 79; their powers in this respect, b, 79.

Committee of Guardians, appointment of, 27; for visiting Workhouse, 105; their duties, 106, *d*, 105; duty of Clerk as to attending, *d*, 147; relief committees, 257; district committees, 261; for relief, how formed, 258.
Common fund, expenses attending election of Guardians to be defrayed out of, 220, 221.
Communion in Workhouse, *b*, 96, *a*, 175.
Compensation to Clerk for Election of Guardians in Wards, *a*, 221.
Compensation for pauper labour not allowed, *a*, 85; to Officers for extraordinary services, 124.
Complaints of Workhouse Inmates, attention to, *a*, 84; book for, *a*, 84.
Compound fracture defined, *a*, 127; fee for treatment of, 126.
Compulsory examination of persons of paupers admitted to Workhouse, *b*, 67.
Compulsory vaccination, *a*, 160.
Condition to be inserted in Vaccination Contract, form of, *a*, 348.
Confinement of paupers in Workhouse for refractory conduct, 101; period of confinement, *b*, 100, *c*, 101; supply of bedding, etc., in such case, 102.
Confirmation of minutes of Guardians, 28, *a*, 28.
Consecration of burial-ground for paupers, *c*, 167.
Consent on binding pauper apprentice, 41, *a*, 42; of Bishop of diocese to appointment of Chaplain, 122.
Constructive situation of Workhouse, *c*, 167.
Contagious diseases in Workhouses, *b*, 63, *b*, 67, *b*, 70; duty of Relieving Officer as to, *c*, 185.
Contagious disorder, detention in Workhouse of person suffering from, *b*, 87.
Contested election of Guardians, remuneration to Clerk for conducting, 221.
Continuance in Office of Guardians for a second year, *b*, 19; of Board of Guardians till 15th April, *c*, 20; of Officers generally, 133; of Medical Officers, 135, *c*, 135, 137, *d*, 137; of Superintendent of pauper labour, 395.
Contracts of Guardians, 34; tenders to be required in the first instance, 36; for works or repairs at Workhouse, 37; when not under seal, *a*, 36; notice as to, 37; how to be entered into, 37, *a*, 38; acceptance of tender not binding upon contractor, *a*, 38; sureties to, 39; exemption of, from stamp duty, *a*, 38; when voidable, *a*, 38; when they may be entered into without previous tenders, 38; to provide for delivery of contractors' bill, 39; for reception of children of other Unions in Workhouse, *a*, 86; by whom to be repaired 144; for vaccination, form of, 346.
Contractor, attendance of, on Guardians, 39, *b*, 39.
Contribution Orders, 55, 266; how to be made, 266; validity of, *c*, 268; form of them, 275; not retrospective, *c*, 267; how to be addressed, *a*, 269; how to be enforced, *a*, 270; how to be signed, 275; service of, on Overseers, *c*, 55; how to be served, *a*, 269; as to receipt by Treasurer of portion of amount of contribution order, or instalment, *c*, 147; when to be made, 268, *a*, 269; may be made payable by instalments, *a*, 269; basis upon which calculation is to be made, *a*, 269; duty of Overseers in regard to 403.

Control of Guardians over orphan children, *b*, 87.
Conveyance of paupers to Workhouse, *d*, 185.
Conveyance of poor persons from Parish, prohibition as to, *b*, 189, 55*a*.
Copies of accounts, when they may be taken, 469.
Copies of minutes, individual Guardians not entitled to take, *f*, 141; of Prohibitory Order to be hung up in Workhouse, *a*, 256.
Coroner's inquests, holding of, in Workhouses, *e*, 168.
Corporal punishment of female children prohibited, 103; how in the case of male children, 103.
Corporations, mode in which they can vote at election of Guardians, *c*, 8.
Corpses, admission of, into Workhouse, *e*, 168.
Correction of accounts by Auditor, 475.
Correspondence of Union Clerk's duty as to, 142, *a*, 142.
Cost of forms for election of Guardians, how to be defrayed, *e*, 125; of proceedings for vagrancy, *a*, 273.
Costs, right to, between two Unions in a Court of law, conducted by respective Clerks, *a*, 274.
Counterfeit characters, indictment for having uttered, *e*, 112.
Counting votes of Guardians, *b*, 25.
County-rate, a separate expenditure, 266.
Cow, relief cannot be given for purchase of, *b*, 29.
Credit not to be taken by Relieving Officer for money not paid, 192.
Cubic space required for paupers in Workhouse, *a*, 76; report of Committee on, *d*, 76.
Curate, delegation of duties of Chaplain to, *a*, 136.
Custody, relief to persons in, *a*, 362; to wives of such persons, 369.
Custody of books and papers, 481; of nomination and voting-papers after election of Guardians, 14; of bonds, 57, *b*, 57; of Parish documents, *a*, 438, *f*, 142; Workhouse not an improper repository for, *d*, 438; of Union books, *a*, 143.
Cutting hair of paupers in Workhouse, *e*, 68.

Daily muster of paupers in Workhouse, 81.
Daily Provisions Consumption Account, 454; form of it, 516.
Damage to property of Guardians, when punishable, *b*, 90.
Dangerous illness of paupers in Workhouse, Chaplain, relatives or friends to sent for, 166; relief in case of, by Overseers, 401, 402.
Dangerous lunatics in Workhouse, when detention of, unlawful, 71, 77, *b*, 77.
Dangerous Structures, admission to Workhouse of persons removed from, *b*, 59.
Dark room, no child shall be confined in, as a punishment, 102.
Day Book of Master, 453; form of it, 513; summary form of, 514.
Day of week on which Union Accounts are to be closed, *c*, 465.
Deaf and dumb child, apprenticeship of, 40, 46.
Deaf and dumb pauper, maintenance of, in institution, *b*, 31; payment of cost incurred in conveyance to, *b*, 31.
Death, of Clerk during election of Guardians, course of proceeding in such case, 16; pauper in Workhouse at the approach of, not to be left unattended, 166; notices to be given in the case of,

166; registration of. 169; entry of, to be made by Medical Officer in Medical Relief Book, 161; inventory of clothes and property of, to be delivered to Guardians, 169; form of register of death, 277.
Debts incurred by Guardians, when to be paid, b, 39; Poor Law Board may extend time, a, 32.
Debts, limit of time within which they may be paid, b, 39.
Deceased Officer, liability of personal representatives of, to account to Auditor, 480.
Deceased pauper, effects of, b, 65.
Decision of Guardians on application for relief, how to be recorded, 461.
Declaration of Overseers as to poor-rate, 435; as to amount of rate, 435.
Defects, in diet, drainage, ventilation, etc., at Workhouse to be reported by Medical Officer to Guardians, 160, 341; in Workhouse infirmary, 160; in qualification of or election of Guardians not to invalidate proceedings, a, 15.
Deficiency of funds in Treasurer's hands, report of, to be made to Poor Law Board, 148.
Delivery of medicines to paupers, c, 154; of voting-papers at election of Guardians, 10.
Departures from Prohibitory Orders to be reported to Poor Law Board, 370, 388, 394.
Deposit Book, when to be balanced, 443.
Deposit of accounts for inspection before audit, 465; time of, b, 465.
Deputy Officer, when not allowed, 137.
Destitute pauper, supply of clothes to, how to be charged, c, 457.
Detention—of paupers in receiving-ward of Workhouse, 67; of dangerous lunatics, 77, b, 77; person in Workhouse on the ground that he is a lunatic, b, 78; of children, b, 87; of mothers of bastard children, b, 87; of persons having infectious or contagious diseases, b, 87; or mental disease, b, 87; how, when under order of removal, b, 89; of family of able-bodied man, b, 88.
Determination—of indenture of pauper apprentice, a, 46; of office of Master or Matron, on removal of either, 134; of Medical Officer, 262.
Dice to be taken from paupers in Workhouse, 92.
Diet of casual poor in Workhouses, 74; of paupers generally, 80; to be according to dietary table, 82; of infants, 83; for sick, d, 83; of Workhouse Officers, b, 123; of sick paupers in Workhouse, duty of Medical Officer as to, 158; of children and women suckling, 160.
Dietaries in Workhouses, orders as to, 284–289; for sick paupers in Workhouse, 161; form of them, 202; report on, b, 82.
Dietary for, casual poor, in the Metropolis, 293; for children in Workhouses, 291.
Dining-hall, meals to be taken in, c, 81; suspension of copies of rules in, 105.
Disallowance of items in accounts by Auditor, 474, 476; Auditor to state his reasons for making, 475.
Disallow and strike out, definition of, 475.
Discharge Book of paupers from Workhouse, 452.

Discharge of paupers from Workhouse—on Sundays, *b*, 61; power of Master and Relieving Officer as to, *b*, 61; of Guardians, *a*, 66; after notice from pauper, 86; of children and persons of weak intellect, *b*, 87; of persons who are liable to punishment, *b*, 88; of wife without husband, *b*, 88; on temporary leave of absence, *b*, 89; of duties of Officers in person, 137.
Discipline of Workhouse, directions of Guardians as to, 32; of paupers therein, 80; how it should be maintained by the Master, *c*, 162.
Dislocations, fees for treatment of, 126.
Dismissal of Officers by Guardians, 134.
Dismissed Officers disqualified for being Guardians, *b*, 117; payment of salary of, 125; not to remain on Workhouse premises, 135.
Disorderly conduct of paupers in Workhouse, what offences shall amount to, 99; punishment for, 100, 101; proceedings by Master, *c*, 163.
Dispenser at Workhouse, account of, 459.
Disqualified, Guardian, should at once cease to act, *b*, 20; no resignation necessary, *b*, 20.
Dissenters in Workhouses, religious assistance and instruction to, 93; attendance of, at public worship, 97.
Dissolute women in Workhouses, how to be dealt with, *b*, 70.
Distance, measure of, in the case of the place of service of a pauper apprentice, *b*, 42.
Distribution of food in Workhouse, duty of Master as to, 165.
District Auditor, vote of Vice-Chairman, when there are two, at election of, *a*, 22.
District Medical Officer, appointment of, 109; duration of it, 329; salary not to include certain operations, 126; duties of, 152.
District of Medical Officers, change in extent of, 331.
District Medical Relief Book, form of, 276; inspection of, by Relieving Officer, 467; Relief Committee's order for, 261.
District school, relief to children sent to, from Union not in district, *d*, 368.
Districts, metropolitan asylum, formation of, 218; names of those formed, 218.
Divine service, attendance of pauper apprentice at, 47; discharge of paupers from Workhouse during, *b*, 87; performance of, 96.
Division of Parishes into wards for election of Guardians, 248; of Boards of Guardians into relief committees, 257; of poor-rate, 436; of Unions into general and medical relief districts, 115.
Domiciliary visits of Medical Officer to sick paupers, *c*, 152.
Doors of Workhouse, duty of Porter as to locking, 181.
Drainage of Workhouse, 108; defects in, to be reported to Guardians by Medical Officer, 160.
Dropsy, fee not payable for tapping for, *a*, 127.
Drugs, repayment of half the cost of, *b*, 123.
Drunken persons, admission of, to Workhouse, *b*, 60.
Drying clothes in Workhouse, 173.
Duly qualified medical practitioner defined, *a*, 129.
Dumb child, apprenticeship of, 40, 46.
Duration of medical appointments, 135, 329, 330.
Duties of Collector of poor-rates, 408; of Pay-clerk of the poor, 320; of the Collector of the Guardians, 305.

Duties of Master of pauper apprentice, 46 ; of Officers to be discharged in person, 137.

Duties to be discharged by Officers, 112 ; by Clerk, 139 ; by Treasurer, 147 ; by Medical Officer, 150 ; by District Medical Officer, 152 ; by Workhouse Medical Officer, 157 ; by Master of Workhouse, 161 ; by Matron, 172 ; by Chaplain, 174 ; by Schoolmaster and Schoolmistress, 176 ; by Nurse, 179 ; by Porter, 180 ; by Relieving Officer, 182 ; by Superintendent of Out-door Labour, 192 ; by Auditor, 471–479 ; by Overseers, 401.

Education of adults, relief for, not lawful, *b*, 29 ; of out-door children, *b*, 29, *a*, 86 ; of children in Workhouse, 86 ; in industrial schools, *a*, 86, *d*, 368, 385 ; relief to defray costs of, *d*, 368.

Educational, Vaccinating stations, list of, 355.

Effects in Workhouse, inventory of, 451 ; of deceased paupers, disposal of them, *b*, 65.

Egress of persons from Workhouse, to be entered in Porter's Book, 180.

Elbow joint, fee for treatment of fracture of, *a*, 127.

Election of Chairman, 20 ; notice of unnecessary, *b*, 22 ; of Vice-Chairman, 20 ; duration of their office, 20 ; how if either refuse or become incapable to act, 22.

Election expenses, remuneration to Clerk for conducting, *e*, 125, 220, 221 ; orders for, 219, 222 ; Unions to which issued, 222 ; Parishes, 224–226.

Election of Guardians, ratepayers qualified to vote at, to be distinguished in Rate Books, 2 ; qualification of voters at, *c*, 2 ; mode in which public companies can vote at, *e*, 3 ; minors cannot vote at, *c*, 3 ; Returning office shall be concluded by entries in register, *b*, 5 ; to be conducted by Clerk of Union, 4 ; how, when no Clerk, or during his illness, 4 ; scale of voting at, *e*, 4 ; his Assistants, 4 ; duty of Relieving Officer as to, 191 ; Overseers to produce Rate Books and register of owners to Clerk when required, 5 ; notice as to, 5 ; form of it, 241 ; publishing of notice, 7 ; nomination of candidates, 7 ; publication of the names of the Candidates and their nominators, *b*, 10 ; how to be signed and delivered, and when, 8 ; certificate of Guardians elected, when there is no contest, 10 ; how, when there is a contest, 10 ; notice of election to be given, 14 ; refusal of candidate to serve, 10 ; certificate of election in such case, 11 ; voting-papers, how to be filled up, 11 ; when invalid, 12 ; collection of them, 12 ; how, in case of omission, 12, 13, *c*, 13 ; examination and casting up of votes, 13 ; certificate of election after a contest, 14 ; notice to be given to candidates duly elected, 14 ; list of candidates to be made out by Clerk and delivered to Guardians, together with nomination- and voting-papers, 14 ; copies of list to be sent to Overseers, 15 ; course of proceedings in case of decease or absence of Clerk, 16 ; within what time validity of the election may be called in question, *a*, 15 ; defects in, not to invalidate proceedings, *a*, 15 ; *quo warranto* will lie to try title of Guardians, *a*, 15 ; time within which delivery of nomination-papers must be made, 232 ; Clerk to make out list of persons nominated, 232 ; how to be published, 232 ; Clerk to make out list of candidates for, 232 ; right of voter to inspect, 233 ; agent of candidate may accompany deliverer or collector of voting-papers, 233 ;

boxes or bags to be provided for collecting voting-papers, 233; candidate or his agent may be present at casting up of votes, 254; nomination- and voting-papers open to inspection of nominator or candidate, 234; time within which they may be inspected, 234; validity of election may be inquired into by Poor Law Board, *a*, 15; order for a fresh election, 254; Parishes divided into wards for, 248; duties of Overseers in regard to, 402; table showing days for proceedings connected with, 9; in wards, nominator must be qualified to vote in ward for which he nominates, *c*, 8; scale of voting in wards, *e*, 11; mode of voting, *e*, 12.

Embezzlement, surcharge by Auditor on account of, 478.

Emergency, appointment of Medical Officer in cases of, 332; meetings of Guardians in cases of, 24.

Emoluments, when account should be sent in, 471; payment of, 471.

Employment—of female paupers in Workhouse, 172; of able-bodied males in receipt of out-door relief, 387, 394; places for, to be reported to Poor Law Board, 388, 394; of Medical Officer, when not duly qualified, 330; of Midwife, to attend pauper women in their confinement, *c*, 152; of paupers in household work and sick wards in Workhouses, *a*, 72; generally, 85, 163; at factories, *d*, 85; not in pounding bones, 86.

Enforcement of regulations by Master of Workhouse, 163.

Equality of votes of Guardians on a division, *b*, 25.

Estimate preparatory to making orders on Overseers for contributions, 266; of provisions for Workhouse to be submitted to Guardians by Master, 170.

European Assurance Association, guarantee of, accepted by Poor Law Board, *a*, 133.

Examination of parcels brought to Workhouse, 181; taken out by paupers, 181; by Relieving Officers, of applicants for relief, 182; by Auditor, 474.

Examination—of books of Officers by Clerk. 141, 464; and closing of accounts, 464; by the Auditor, 475; of receipts for poor-rates before collection of rate, 442; (anatomical) of bodies of paupers dying in Workhouse, *c*, 168; (*post-mortem*) of the bodies of paupers after death, *a*, 161; of votes at election of Guardians, 13; of books and accounts by Guardians, 32; of Treasurer's account, 33; how to be made by Guardians, *a*, 33; of pauper child previous to being apprenticed, 44; of bills by Guardians, 57, *a*, 57; of pauper on admission to Workhouse, 66; duty of Medical Officer, 158, 163; of person not compulsory, *b*, 67; of Workhouse children by Chaplain, 176.

Examination of lunatic, course recommended by Poor Law Board, *a*, 159.

Excess of paupers in Workhouse to be reported to Poor Law Board, 76.

Execution of contracts and bonds, 144, *a*, 144.

Exemption—of contracts from stamp duty, *a*, 38; of orders of Guardians for payment of money, *e*, 56; of bonds, *b*, 57; of receipts of Union Treasurer for money paid to him by Overseers on contribution orders, *e*, 149.

Exercise, children in Workhouse when they may leave for purposes of, 90.

Expenditure Book of Relieving Officer, 463.

Expenses of Auditor, how to be paid, *a*, 473; of election of Guardians, *e*, 125; order for, 219; Unions to which issued, 222; Parishes, 224, 226.

Expenses incurred by Guardians in attending meetings cannot be repaid, *c*, 23.

Expensive medicines, supply of, *e*, 195; recommendation of Committee of House of Commons thereon, *e*, 195.

Extinguishment of fires and lights in Workhouse, 165, 173.

Extra charges not permitted to be made by Officers, *b*, 122; relief, authority of Medical Officer to order, *c*, 155; remuneration to Officers, 122; to Medical Officers, 126.

Extra fees, when account of, should be sent in, 471; payment of, 471.

Extraordinary meetings of Guardians, 23; requisition for, 144; form of it, 199; audit, how held, 471; effect of it, 471.

Extra-parochial places constituted Parishes, *b*, 194.

Extracts from minutes, individual Guardians not entitled to, *f*, 141.

Factories, employment of Workhouse inmates at, *d*, 84.

False characters of candidates for office, indictment for having uttered, *e*, 112.

Family to be discharged from Workhouse at same time as pauper, 87, *b*, 88.

Family of Master and Matron living in Workhouse, *e*, 111, *b*, 122.

Farm Account, when to be kept, 459.

Farmers, employment of Workhouse inmates by, *d*, 85.

Fast-days, no work to be done by paupers in Workhouse on, *a*, 95.

Fees, to Bishop's Secretary for consent to appointment of Chaplain, *a*, 122; on burial of paupers, *c*, 167; to District Medical Officers for surgical operations, etc., 126; not payable to other medical men, *a*, 127; payable in respect of all classes of paupers, *a*, 127; how, when the patient does not survive more than thirty-six hours, 129; cumulative fees, 129; special cases, 129; to Medical Officers in midwifery cases, 129–130; under Friendly Societies Act, in respect of death of child insured in burial club, *e*, 151; for quarterly visits to pauper lunatics, *c*, 156.

Felony, person convicted of, ineligible to be appointed as a paid Officer, *e*, 112.

Female child, corporal punishment of, prohibited, 103.

Females in Workhouse, their moral conduct and behaviour, duty of Matron as to, 173; searching of, 172; employment of, 172.

Fermented liquors in Workhouse, when not to be allowed, 83, *e*, 85; punishment of paupers for introducing, 104, *b*, 105; Porter to prevent admission of, 181.

Fever cases in Workhouses, *a*, 71; duty of Relieving Officer to visit, *c*, 185.

Financial Statement, 467; to be submitted to Auditor, 467; his duty thereupon, 467; form of, 503.

Fires in Workhouse, extinguishment of, 165, 173.

Fistula, fee not payable for operation for, *a*, 127.

Fixtures at Workhouse, contracts for, 37; repair of, 108; inventory of, 451.

Flogging children in Workhouse, prohibition as to, 103.

Food, duty of Master as to distribution of, in Workhouse, 165; as to

weighing allowances to paupers, 84; not to be taken out of dining-hall by paupers, *c*, 81; of infants in Workhouse, 83; when out-door relief shall be given partly in, 383, 393.
Forfeiture in the event of resigning office without previous notice, 118.
Forged testimonials to character, indictment for having, *c*, 112.
Forms for election of Guardians, cost of, how to be defrayed, *c*, 125, 220.
Form, of Collector, of the Guardians' Book, 309; of Receipt Book, 310.
Form, of voting-paper, 236; of notices of election for Unions, 241; for Parishes and Townships, 244.
Form, of poor-rate, 484; of order for contributions, 275.
Fractures (simple), fees for treatment of, 126.
Fraud, person convicted of, ineligible to be appointed paid Officer, *c*, 112.
Fraud, meaning of the word, *a*, 14.
Fresh election of Guardians, order for, 254.
Friendly Societies Act, fees to Medical Officer under, *c*, 151; subscriptions cannot be paid out of poor-rates, *b*, 30.
Friends of paupers in Workhouse to be sent for in case of their dangerous illness, 166.
Fry, Mr. Danby, reference to his work on Lunacy Acts, *b*, 80.
Fuel, contracts for supply of, 36; when out-door relief shall be given partly in, 383.
Funds, orders of Guardians upon Overseers to provide, 33.
Funeral expenses, relief on account of, *b*, 360.
Furniture of Workhouse, provision of, by Guardians, 32; contracts for supply of, 36; repair of, 108; responsibility of Master as to, 171; inventory of, 451; relief cannot be given to replace, *b*, 29.

Games of chance, prohibition of, 92, *a*, 92.
Gaol, relief to families of persons in, 362, 387.
Gate of Workhouse to be kept by Porter, 180.
General accounts of the Union, mode of keeping, 445; Ledger to be kept by Clerk, 445; form of it, 496; Receipt Cheque Book, 439.
Girls in Workhouses, when they may be classed with women, 73; education of, 86.
Good Friday, in the case of election of Guardians acts to be done the following day, 7; no work to be done on, in Workhouse, 95.
Goods for Workhouse, limitation on purchase of, by Master, 172.
Goods seized for rent or destroyed by fire, relief cannot be given to replace, *b*, 29, *a*, 66; penalty on Guardians when concerned in the supply of, for poor for profit, *b*, 35; does not extend to Guardian who is a member of a Joint Stock Company who supply, *b*, 35; contracts for supply of, 36.
Goods, ordering of, by Guardians, *c*, 449; laxity in respect of ordering, *a*, 32.
Government of the Workhouse, 58; admission of paupers, 58; classification of paupers, 68; discipline and diet of paupers, 80; to be exercised by the Guardians, 108; of Workhouse Schools, regulations for, 217.
Grace to be said before and after meals in Workhouse, 165.
Gratuities to Officers, 124; prohibited, 193.
Greenwich pensioners, repayment of relief to, *b*, 362, *c*, 372.

Index. 567

Guarantee Society, security of, for Officers, when it may be taken, 133, *a*, 133.

Guardian, becoming disqualified, should at once cease to act as, 20; qualification of, 241.

Guardians, election of, when to appoint substitute for Clerk at election of Guardians, 4; to appoint assistants at the election, 4; qualification for office of, *e*, 6; nomination of, 7; certificate of election when there is no contest, 10; how when there is a contest, 10; notice of election to be given, 14; custody of nomination- and voting-papers after election, 14; *quo warranto* will lie to try title of, *a*, 15; but may be inquired into by Poor Law Board, *a*, 15; resignation of, *b*, 19; continuance of, in office for a second year, *b*, 19; Officers disqualified for election as, *b*, 117; remuneration to Clerk for conducting, *e*, 125; election expenses, order for, 219, 222; order for a fresh election, 254.

Guardians, their meetings, 20; change of meetings, 20; continuance in office, *b*, 19, *c*, 20; at first meeting to elect Chairman, and Vice-Chairman, 20; may elect at any time two Vice-Chairmen, 22; to appoint Assessment Committee at first meeting, *c*, 21; right of individual Guardians to be present at meetings of the Assessment Committee, *c*, 21; notice of change of meeting, 23; how if three be not present, 23; adjournment of meeting, 23; extraordinary meetings, 23; meetings of emergency, 24; power to act at meetings of the Board only, *c*, 23; payment of, out of rates, illegal, *c*, 23; their proceedings, 24; questions to be decided by a majority of votes, 24; cannot act by deputy, *b*, 26; or vote by proxy, *b*, 26.

Guardians, how their votes should be taken, *b*, 25; how a resolution of, may be rescinded, 26; may appoint Committees to consider any subject, 27, *c*, 27; order of business to be conducted by, 27, *d*, 27; cost of refreshments to, cannot be defrayed out of poor-rates, *a*, 31; provender for their horses, *a*, 32; their contracts, 34; penalty on, for supplying goods for poor, *b*, 35; how as to the purchase of old stores of Union by Guardians, *b*, 35; may act as attorney for the Guardians or for any Parish in the Union, *b*, 35; their orders for contributions, 268; for payment of money, 55, *e*, 56; order of, for admission to Workhouse, 59; duty of, when pauper admitted otherwise, 65; power to discharge paupers, 66, *a*, 66; visitation of lunatic asylums by, *b*, 80; contracts of, for reception of children of other Unions in Workhouse, *a*, 86; in industrial schools, *a*, 86; duty of, as to punishment of paupers in Workhouse, 104; government of the Workhouse by, 108; to appoint Officers, 109; what duties they may require their Officers to perform, 112; what a majority of, *b*, 113; empowered to pay for medical assistance in cases of accident, *a*, 128; who are medical men should not give certificates for pauper amputations, *a*, 129; what Officers they may dismiss, 134; appointed as paid substitutes for Officers must cease to act as Guardian during his tenure of office, *b*, 137; suspension of Officers by, 135; duty of Relieving Officers as to executing their orders, 191; Relief Committees of, 257; definition of, 317.

Guardians, power to pay travelling expenses of any candidate for a Poor Law appointment, 316.

Guardians, cannot be repaid expenses incurred in attending meetings of, *c*, 23.

2 o

Hair of paupers in Workhouse, cutting of, *c*, 68.
Hearing of personal applications for relief, *a*, 32.
Hernia (strangulated), fee for operation for, 126, *a*, 127.
Highway Precept, rate in £ required for, should be stated in Rate Receipt Cheque Book, 490.
Hire, prohibition of relief to able-bodied persons employed for, 386.
Hog-wash to be accounted for by Master of Workhouse, *b*, 123.
Holidays, admission and discharge of paupers on, into and from Workhouse, *b*, 61.
Holy Communion, administration of, to Workhouse inmates, *b*, 96, *a*, 175.
Horse, relief cannot be given for purchase of, *b*, 29.
Horses of Guardians, supply of provender to, *a*, 32.
Hospitals, burial of persons dying in, *c*, 169; expense of conveying paupers to, 384.
Hospital, as to maintenance of pauper in, *d*, 366.
Hours for admission of vagrants to Workhouse, limitation of, *b*, 74; for meals, 81.
House of Commons, practice of, as to voting, *b*, 25.
Household work, employment of paupers at, in Workhouses, 72; extra allowances of food to, 83.
Housekeeper, person taking pauper apprentice must be one, 41.
Houseless Poor in Metropolis, relief to, *b*, 61.
House linen at Workhouse, inventory of, 451.
House property, relief of persons possessed of, *b*, 30.
Husband and wife living together in Workhouse, *c*, 72; discharge of wife from, without husband's consent, *b*, 88.

Illegal motions submitted at meetings of Guardians, *b*, 26.
Illegal orders of Guardians for payment of money, Clerk not bound to countersign, *c*, 144; removal of poor persons, *b*, 189.
Illegitimate children, treatment of mothers of, in Workhouses, *b*, 69; training of, as nurses, *b*, 70; relief to widows having, 361.
Illness of paupers in Workhouse, duty of Master in case of, 165.
Illness, dangerous, relief in cases of, 401.
Immoral character, subclassification of paupers of, in Workhouses, 71.
Imperfectly kept books, report of Auditor on, 479.
Implements of trade, relief cannot be given to purchase, *b*, 29, 384; or to redeem from pawn, 384.
Income Tax, Clerk to the Guardians is the proper Officer to make return of Officers' salaries for, *a*, 142.
Incumbent of Parish, his consent to the appointment of Chaplain not necessary, *c*, 110.
Indenture of apprenticeship, allowance of, *a*, 43; execution of, 46; cancelling of, *a*, 46; how to be executed, 46.
In-door Relief List, 452; form of it, 510; abstract of 452; form of it, 512; inspection of, by Relieving Officer, 467.
Industrial Schools, maintenance, etc., of children in, *a*, 86, 367, *d*, 368; what children may be sent to *b*, 59; admission of children into Workhouse, preparatory to their being sent to, *b*, 59; refractory children in Workhouse to be sent to, *a*, 86.
Industrial instructors, repayment of portion of salary, *b*, 177; scale of, *b*, 177; number to be employed, *b*, 177.
Industrial training of children in Workhouse, 178.
Infant, cannot be appointed to an office of pecuniary trust, *c*, 117.

Index. 569

Infant Poor in Workhouse or establishment out of Union, relief to, 367.
Infants in Workhouse, their diet, 83.
Infectious diseases, admission to Workhouse of persons labouring under, *b*, 63, *b*, 66; separation of, from other inmates, *b*, 70; persons labouring under, can be detained in Workhouse, *b*, 87; penalty for publicly exposing themselves, *b*, 88; duty of Relieving Officer as to, *c*, 185.
Infirm paupers, medical relief to, 50; duty of Overseers in regard to relief of, on order of Justices, 402.
Infirmary of Workhouse, defects in, to be reported to Guardians by Medical Officer, 160.
Infirmary, expense of conveying paupers to, 384.
Ingress of persons to Workhouse to be entered in Porter's Book, 180.
In-maintenance, definition of, 483.
Inmates of Workhouse, number of, to be reported to Guardians at their meetings, 171; cubic space required for, *a*, 76.
Inquests, holding of, in Workhouse, *c*, 168.
Inquiry by Relieving Officer into cases of applicants for relief, 183.
Inquiry as to settlement, relief must not be withheld pending, *b*, 31.
Irremovable poor, relief to, 365, *b*, 365.
Insane paupers in Workhouse, duty of Master, 165; discharge of, from Workhouse, *b*, 88; Master to report when restraint or compulsion is exercised on, 171.
Insane persons found straying, order relating to, 296; notice as to, 298.
Insolvency of master of pauper apprentice, how in the case of, 49.
Inspection of paupers in Workhouses, 81, 164, 172.
Inspection—of Relieving Officer's and Master's Books by Clerk, 464; of Union accounts by ratepayers, 469; at audit, 473; of nomination- and voting-papers after election of Guardians, *a*, 14; of Minute Book or Union papers by individual Guardians, *f*, 141, *a*, 143; by strangers, *f*, 141, *a*, 143; of accounts by Clerk, 141; duty of Relieving Officer to produce accounts for, 191.
Instalments, contribution order may be made payable by, *a*, 269; poor-rate paid by, 439.
Instalment Rate Receipt Cheque Book, 441; to be kept by Collector of Parish, 441; form of it, 491; when receipt is to be given, 441.
Instruction of children in Workhouse, 86; in principles of religion, 93; generally, 175.
Instructions to Officers to be communicated by Clerk, 146.
Interest cannot be paid by Guardians to Treasurer on overdrawn accounts, *c*, 125.
Interment of body of pauper dying in Workhouse, duty of Master to provide for, 166.
Interviews—between parents and their children in Workhouses, 73; of members of family in different Workhouses, 73; with paupers in Workhouses, 90.
Introduction of spiritous or fermented liquors into Workhouse, 105, *b*, 105.
Inventory of clothes, etc., of paupers dying in Workhouse, to be delivered to Guardians, 169.
Inventory of stock, moneys, etc., to be made out by Overseers, 440; form of it, 492; of Workhouse goods, etc., 451; form of it, 507.
Invoices for provisions, examination of, by Master of Workhouse, 170.

2 O 2

Joint-Stock Company, mode in which they can vote at election of Guardians, *c*, 3.
Journeymen cannot take a pauper apprentice, 41.
Justices of the Peace, allowance of indentures of apprenticeship by, *a*, 43; certificate, *a*, 43; consent to cancelling indenture, *a*, 46; before whom Overseers should be summoned for non-payment of contribution order, *a*, 270; order of, for admission to Workhouse, *b*, 60; appointment of, to a Union office, *b*, 117; Medical Officer not bound to attend before, to prove permanent disability of pauper, *c*, 151; proceedings before, for punishment of disorderly paupers in Workhouse, *c*, 164.

Keys of Workhouse to be received by Master from Porter every night, 165; duty of Porter as to, 181.
Kind, administration of out-door relief, when to be partly in, 383, 393.
Kitchen, responsibility of Master as to cleanliness of, 171.
Kitchen-stuff to be accounted for by Master of Workhouse, *b*, 122.

Labour test for able-bodied paupers, 393.
Labourers, grant of midwifery orders for wives of, *a*, 184.
Lascars, relief to, 373.
Law bills, taxation of, 430.
Leave of absence to paupers in Workhouse, 89, *b*, 89; to Officers, *a*, 136.
Legal business of the Guardians, to be conducted by Clerk, 272, *a*, 272, 273.
Legal Expenses, what within the scope of Clerk's duty, 272; exceptions, 272; bill for, must be taxed before paid, 274.
Legally qualified Medical Practitioner, defined, *a*, 129.
Letters acknowledging receipt of money exempt from stamp duty, *a*, 55; duty of Clerk, as to answering, *a*, 142; of paupers in Workhouse, *b*, 65, *c*, 91, *b*, 163, *d*, 181.
Liability of persons to obtain relief for those of their household, *a*, 32; of Guardians to repay non-resident relief, *a*, 54; of sureties of Union Treasurer in respect of cheques, *c*, 132; of sureties generally, *c*, 132; of Overseers for medical relief illegally ordered, *c*, 154; of persons voluntarily undertaking office, 480.
Liabilities of the Guardians, to be inserted in financial statement, *a*, 467.
Library for Workhouse, establishment of, *b*, 91.
Licensed Ministers, for what purposes they may visit Workhouses, 92; construction of term, *c*, 93.
Lights in Workhouse, extinguishment of, 165, 173.
Lime-washing Workhouse, 108.
Limitation as to order of Guardians for admission to Workhouse, 65, *a*, 65; of hours of admission of vagrants, *b*, 74; of numbers to be admitted into Workhouse, 76.
Linen for paupers in Workhouse, supply of, 173; charge of, confided to Matron, 173; washing, drying, and getting up, to be superintended by Matron, 173.
List of Guardians elected to be made out by Clerk, 14; and sent to Overseers, 15; to be affixed by them to church doors, etc., 16; of paupers having permanent medical relief, 50.
List of In-door Poor, when to be made out by Master, 469.
Lithotomy, fee not payable for operation, *a*, 127.

Lithotrity, fee not payable for operation, *a*, 127.
Litigation arising out of settlement and removal cases, right of Clerk to charge for, *a*, 266.
Loan, when Guardians can and cannot raise, *a*, 270; relief by way of, 371, 388; collection of and recovery, *c*, 372; when medical relief may be given by way of, *a*, 184.
Locking up Workhouse, duty of Porter as to, 181.
Lodging for pauper apprentice, 47.
Lodging, provision of, in cases of sudden and urgent necessity, 370.
Lunatic, attendance of Justice at residence of, to examine, *a*, 159.
Lunatics in Workhouse, duty of Medical Officer as to, 153; Master to report restraint or compulsion used upon, 171, 174.
Lunatic asylums, etc., visitation of, by Guardians, *b*, 80; duty of Relieving Officer to convey to, *a*, 159; expense of conveying paupers to, 384; relief to wife of person in, 369.
Lunatics, return of, time within which to be made, *b*, 146; discharged from asylum upon trial, duty of Medical Officer to give certificate in such case, *c*, 151; Medical Officer's quarterly visits to, *c*, 156; apprentice of child of, 42, *a*, 42; pauper in Workhouse, detention of, when dangerous, 77, *b*, 77; detention of persons in Workhouse, on ground of being, *b*, 77; treatment of, *b*, 80; visitation of, by Commissioners in Lunacy, *b*, 78; discharge of, from Workhouse, *b*, 88; duty of Master in case of pauper becoming, 165.
Lunatics, expenses incurred in removing to asylums, how to be charged, *c*, 461; to be entered in Relieving Officer's Receipt and Expenditure Book. 463.
Lunatic soldiers, relief to, *d*, 187.
Lunatics, chronic, reception and treatment in Workhouse, *b*, 64.

Maintenance of children of Master and Matron in Workhouse, *c*, 111, *b*, 122.
Maintenance, charge of pauper under order of removal, statement of charges to be delivered at Workhouse. *b*, 64.
Majority of Guardians required for appointment of Officers, 113; what a majority, *b*, 113.
Majority of votes of Guardians, questions to be determined by, 24.
Male children, corporal punishment of, in Workhouse, 103.
Management of Workhouse, directions of Guardians as to, 32.
Marine, relief to family of, 362.
Mark of voter at election of Guardians, 12.
Marking Workhouse clothing, 173, 456.
Married couples in Workhouse living together when aged, 71, *b*, 71.
Married woman cannot take a pauper apprentice, 41.
Married women, relief to, *b*, 362.
Masters not bound to provide medical aid for servants in sickness, *c*, 371.
Master of pauper apprentice, his duties, 46; how if he become insolvent, 49.
Master of Workhouse, appointment of, 109; and Matron should be man and wife, *e*, 111; their children, *e*, 111; qualification required, 117; to give security, 131; duties of, 161; general responsibility of, *c*, 161; duty as to admitting poor brought to Workhouse by police, *b*, 60; can refuse admission of pauper with order of Overseer, *b*, 62; should accompany visiting committee

round Workhouse. *d*, 106; exempt from serving office of Parish Constable, *c*, 162; as to admission of paupers, 163; to cause paupers to be searched, 163; to read prayers, 164; to inspect and call over paupers, 164; authority of, as to letters addressed to paupers, *b*, 163; as to their receiving presents of money, *b*, 163; to decide the class to which a pauper belongs, *b*, 163; as to taking proceedings before Justices for punishment of disorderly paupers, *c*, 164; to provide employment for inmates, 164; to visit sleeping wards of male paupers, 164; to say, or cause to be said, grace before meals, 165; to visit all male wards to see that lights are out, 165; duty of, when pauper is at the approach of death, 166; to receive keys from Porter, 165; to cause birth of every child born in Workhouse to be registered, 165; duty of, on death of pauper, 166; to provide for interment of body, 166; to cause deaths to be registered, 169; to deliver inventory of clothes, etc., of deceased pauper to Guardians, 169; duty as to strayed children and insane persons, 296.

Master of Workhouse, power of, to admit paupers, 59, *b*, 60; to discharge them, *b*, 61; duty of, when persons are brought to Workhouse without an order, *b*, 60; when they are labouring under infectious diseases, *b*, 63; duty of, when he finds money in possession of pauper, *b*, 63; to muster paupers daily, 81; when to fix hours for rising and going to bed of certain classes of paupers, 82; to weigh food of paupers when required, 84; to account for refuse, etc., *b*, 122, *b*, 170; how if he should vacate his office by death or otherwise, 134; always to sleep in the Workhouse, *a*, 136; books to be kept by, 451; account of receipts and payments, 453; form of it, 515; Receipt Cheque Book, 453; form of it, 515; should take charge of Chaplain's Report Book, *a*, 176; to make out Parochial List and Statement of Account, 469; form of it, 500; or List of In-door Poor, 469; should not act as Removing Officer, *b*, 190; procure Minister for the purpose of affording religious instruction to orphan children, 301.

Matches to be taken from paupers in Workhouse, 92.

Materials for clothing paupers in Workhouse, 84.

Materials, etc., for setting the poor on work, may be provided by Guardians and charged to Common Fund, *a*, 394.

Matron of Workhouse, appointment of, 109; to give security, 131; power of, to admit paupers to Workhouse, 59; employment of paupers as assistants to, 72; to muster female paupers daily, 81; to weigh food of paupers when required, 84; duties of, 172; to assist the Master in general management of Workhouse, 174; should accompany Visiting Committee round Workhouse, *d*, 106; duty as regards cleanliness of children, *b*, 178; when order for accounts is binding on, 460.

Meals in Workhouse, times for, 81; where to be taken, 81; discharge of pauper during, *b*, 87; duty of Master as to, 164; grace to be said before and after, 165.

Measure of distance in the case of the place of service of a pauper apprentice, *b*, 42.

Medical assistance in cases of accidents, payments for, by Guardians, *a*, 128.

Medical attendance on paupers defined, 195, duty of Relieving Officer as to, 184; tenders for, prohibited, 115; on pauper apprentice, 49; on Workhouse Officers, *b*, 123.

Index. 573

Medical certificate, when it is to be required previous to punishment of pauper in Workhouse, 102; in the case of amputations, 128; to be given by registered medical man, *a*, 129; as to sickness of pauper, *c*, 151.

Medical districts, division of Union into, 115; area and population of, 115; change of extent of, 331.

Medical extras, evils of incautious administration of, *c*, 155; authority of Medical Officer to order, *c*, 155.

Medical Officer defined, 196; qualification of, 120, 334; to be registered under Medical Act, *b*, 119, 335; not required to attend Workhouse Officers in sickness, *b*, 123; fees to, in midwifery cases, 130, 131; duration of office, 135.

Medical Officer, examination of pauper child previous to being apprenticed, 43; be deemed to have knowledge that a pauper in his district is a lunatic, *b*, 78; duties of, 150; to give information as to paupers under his care to Guardians when required, 150; his report as to prevalence of sickness among paupers, 150; to attend meetings of Guardians when required, 150; to give certificates as to pauper apprenticeship, 150; of sickness of pauper, 151; in respect of lunatic pauper, *c*, 151; not bound to attend before Justices to prove permanent disability of pauper unless summoned, *c*, 151; duty of, under Friendly Societies Act, *c*, 151.

Medical Officers to make a report to Relieving Officer of poor persons on whom they attend without an order, 157; duty of, as to Weekly Medical Relief List, 157; determination of office of, 332; temporary appointment of, 332; in case of a vacancy, 332; employment by, of unqualified assistants, *c*, 156.

Medical Officer, terms to be used by, in keeping his books, 151; to distinguish in his books when attendances are given by others than himself, 151; duty of, as to attendance on persons he considers not to be destitute, *c*, 153; how in the case of members of sick clubs, *c*, 153; responsibility of, if he attends pauper without an order, *c*, 154; authority to order medical extras, *c*, 155; how, if pauper refuses to submit to medical treatment, *c*, 156; quarterly visits of, to lunatics, *c*, 156.

Medical Officer for a district, appointment of, 109; duration of appointment of, 329; qualification of, 120; salary not to include certain operations, etc., 126-130; duration of office, 135; personal discharge of duties by, 138; his substitute, 138; duties of, 152; as to domiciliary visits to paupers, *c*, 152.

Medical Officer may act as the substitute for another Medical Officer, *c*, 138; objection of Guardians to substitute, nominated by, *c*, 138; transfer of, from one district to another does not vacate appointments, *d*, 115.

Medical Officer for Workhouse, appointment of, 109; continuance in Office or appointment of successor, 137, 329; personal discharge of duties by, 138; his substitute, 138; authority to order tobacco and snuff for paupers, *b*, 92; his duties, 157; attendance of, at Workhouse, 157; examination of state of paupers on admission, 158; duty of, as to lunatic paupers, *a*, 158; duty of, as to diet, classification, and treatment of sick paupers and lunatics, 158; to make quarterly returns of lunatics in Workhouse, *a*, 160; as to vaccination, 160; as to drainage, etc., 160; as to Infirmary, and nurses

neglecting their duty, 160; as to returns to Guardians of attendance, 160; of death of pauper, 161; not authorized to make *post mortem* examinations, *a*, 161; duty of, as to dietaries for sick paupers, 161.
Medical Officer of Workhouse to keep Report Book, 341; what to be reported, 341; to deliver the Book to Guardians, 341; to enter on card extras necessary for patient, 341; to report to Poor Law Board every sudden or accidental death in Workhouse, and cause thereof, 342; to report to Poor Law Board half-yearly on state of Workhouse, 342; list of inquiries to be reported on, 342.
Medical Officer of Workhouse, his certificate as to fitness of a pauper child to be apprenticed, 43; to examine paupers on admission to Workhouse, 66; his authority as to diet of paupers in Workhouse, 82; as to surgical operations, *d*, 157.
Medical Officer's salary, repayment of portion of, by Government, *b*, 123.
Medical practitioner defined, *a*, 129.
Medical relief, principles on which it should be administered, *a*, 51; to permanent paupers, 50, *c*, 153; in cases of dangerous illness, 401; on loan, *c*, 371; entry of, in Application and Report Book, 460.
Medical relief to parents does not pauperize the children, *c*, 156.
Medical Relief List, duty of Medical Officer as to, 157; of Workhouse Medical Officer, 160.
Medical Relief Book, 160; form of it, 202, 203; of Workhouse, duty of Master in respect of, 170.
Medical Relief Order Cheque Book, form of it, 205.
Medical relief defined, 195; to members of sick clubs, *c*, 153; to servants, *c*, 153; authority of Overseers to order, *c*, 154; duty of Relieving Officer as to, 184; when it should be given by way of loan, *a*, 184.
Medical terms to be used by Medical Officers, 151.
Medical treatment, refusal of pauper to submit to, *c*, 156, *d*, 157.
Medicines defined, 195; tenders for supply of, prohibited, 115; supply by Medical Officer of district, 152; in what state they should be supplied, *c*, 154; delivery of, to paupers, 157; administration of, to Workhouse paupers, 157; supply of, when expensive, *c*, 195; recommendation of Committee of House of Commons thereon, 195; repayment from Parliamentary Grant of half the cost of, *b*, 123.
Medicines and medical appliances, account of, 459; how entered, 460.
Meetings of Guardians, 20; how, if three Guardians be not present, 22; adjournment of them, 23; extraordinary meetings, 23; Guardians to act at a meeting, except in certain cases, *c*, 23; notice of change of, to be given, 23; how, in cases of emergency, 24; presence of strangers at, *d*, 27; Clerk cannot delegate his duty of attending, *f*, 139; presence of Clerk at, *f*, 141; attendance of Medical Officers at, 150, *b*, 150; Relieving Officer to attend, 182.
Members of sick clubs, medical relief to, *c*, 153.
Memorandum to be inserted by Overseers in their Receipt and Payment Book, 437.
Mental infirmity, relief in cases of, 360, 385; non-resident relief in cases of, 365.
Methylated spirit, objection to use of, in medical tinctures, *b*, 152.
Metropolitan Police, inspection of casual wards by, *b*, 61.
Metropolitan asylum district, 218.
Midwife, employment of, to attend pauper women in their confinement, *c*, 152.

Midwifery orders, principles on which they should be given, *c*, 153, *a*, 184; fees to Medical Officers, 129, 130.
Military, relief to, when lunatic, *d*, 187.
Ministers, for what purposes they may visit Workhouses, 93, *e*, 93.
Minors cannot vote at election of Guardians, *c*, 3.
Minutes of Guardians to be signed by presiding Chairman, *a*, 24–27; reading of, 28; confirmation of, *a*, 28; how to be kept, 139, *f*, 140; individual Guardians not entitled to take copies of them, *f*, 141; entry of Medical Officers' Report therein, 364.
Minute Book of Assessment Committee, how to be kept, *f*, 140; right of ratepayer to inspect, *f*, 140.
Minutes of Guardians, motion made and seconded should be entered in, *f*, 140.
Misbehaviour of paupers in Workhouse, punishment for, 97.
Misconduct of Workhouse Officers to be reported to Guardians by Master, 171; by Matron to Master, 174.
Money sent to paupers in Workhouse, *b*, 163; how, if found on pauper by Porter, *d*, 181; found on pauper dying in Workhouse, application of, *c*, 179; for non-resident relief, transmission of, 52, *b*, 53; found in possession of pauper admitted to Workhouse, *b*, 63; in their letters, *b*, 65; arising from sale of Parish property, application of, *e*, 149; Relieving Officer not to take credit for, unless actually paid, 192; receipt and payment of, by Officers, 193.
Monthly statements to be made by Collector, 443; form of them, 494; to be delivered to Guardians and Overseers, 443.
Moral conduct of females and children, duty of Matron as to, 173; of children generally, 174; report on, by Chaplain, 175.
Mothers of illegitimate children, treatment of, in Workhouses, *b*, 70; training of, as nurses, *b*, 70; cannot be prevented from discharging themselves from Workhouse, *b*, 88; but must take their children with them, *b*, 88.
Muster of paupers in Workhouse, 81, 164, 172.

Necessaries and Miscellaneous Account, 458; form of it, 525; quarterly summary of, 458; form of it, 526; quarterly balance of, 459; form of it, 528.
Neglect of children by parents, relief in such case, *d*, 187.
Negligence of Workhouse Officers to be reported by Master to Guardians, 171; by Matron to Master, 174.
Newspapers, no authority to advertise notice of election of Guardians in, *d*, 7; notice as to contracts to be advertised in, 37; what newspapers, *a*, 37.
Night, discharge of paupers from Workhouse in the, *b*, 87.
Nomination of candidates at election of Guardians, 7; form of it, 198; cannot be withdrawn, *e*, 7; how to be signed and delivered, and when, 8; order in which to be inserted in voting-papers, 10; how when unqualified person is nominated, 10; how when person nominated tenders his refusal to serve, 10; if more than one nomination of the same person, the names of all nominations should appear, *b*, 10.
Nomination-papers, a place for their reception need not be appointed in each Parish, *a*, 6; to be delivered to Guardians after election, and preserved, 14.

Nomination-papers, time within which they must be delivered, 232; if by post, 232; to be open to inspection of candidates or nominators, 234.

Nominator must be qualified to vote in particular ward for which he nominates a Guardian, *e*, 8.

Non-resident poor defined, 196; relief to, 51; how, through private channels, *a*, 52; transmission of money for, *b*, 52; counts for, how and when to be discharged, 54; liability of Guardians for, *a*, 54; duty of Clerk as to accounts relating to, *a*, 54, 145; relief to families of, 365, 387.

Non-resident relief, prohibition of, 365, *b*, 365, 385.

Non-settled Poor Ledger, 448; as to keeping separate book for, *c*, 448.

Non-settled poor defined, 196; relief to, 51; duty of Clerk as to accounts relating to, 145; duty of Relieving Officer as to, 190; Officers prohibited from receiving money for relief of, 194.

Non-settled relief, acknowledgments of money for, exempt from Stamp duty *a*, 55.

Notice of audit to be given by Clerk, 468; form of, 468; of adjourned audit, 469; by auditor, form of, *a*, 472.

Notice of election of Guardians, 5; form of it, 229, 241; for Parishes and Townships, 244; publishing of, 7; to be given to candidates duly elected, 14; cost of, how to be defrayed, 220; of change of meetings of Guardians, and of extraordinary meetings, to be given, 23; to rescind resolution of Guardians, 26; as to contracts of Guardians, 37; to be given by pauper on leaving Workhouse, 86; of appointment of Officers to be given, 114; what, required of certain Officers previous to resignation, 118; to Guardians, to be signed by Clerk, 144.

Notice to be given to Guardians when elected, form of it, 229; of change of period, time, and place of meeting, form of it, 199; of adjourned meeting, 200; of extraordinary meeting, 200; as to determining office of Medical Officer, 331.

Notices of arrears of rates, Collectors and Assistant Overseers to assist Overseers in making out and serving, 415.

Notices to be given in the case of death of pauper in Workhouse, 166.

Nottingham, election of Guardians in, *a*, 2.

Nourishment to sick poor, remarks on supply of extra to, *c*, 155.

Number of paupers to be admitted into Workhouse, limitation as to, 76; of inmates to be reported to Guardians at their meetings, 171.

Numbering clothing of paupers in Workhouse, 456; duty of Matron as to, 173.

Nurse at Workhouse, appointment of, 109; qualification required, 118; dismissal of, by Guardians, 134; duties of, 179.

Nurses, training as, of mothers of illegitimate children in Workhouses, *b*, 70; employment of paupers in Workhouse as, 72; extra allowances of food to, 83; neglect of, to be reported to Guardians by Medical Officer, 160; circular of Poor Law Board as to duties of, *c*, 179; remuneration of, *c*, 179; assistants to should be paid Officers, *c*, 179.

Nurture, relief to children under age of, 363; what is the age of nurture, *c*, 363.

Objections to accounts, 378, 476.

Index. 577

Offences in Workhouses, 97.
Offenders in custody of police, how, when application made for their admission to Workhouse, *b*, 62.
Officers, their duties, 139; are bound to learn them, *d*, 139; prohibited from acting as relief agents for other Unions, *b*, 53; receipt and payment of money by, 193.
Officers, appointment of, 109; what Officers, 109; duties to be discharged by, 112; by what Officers, 113; how to be appointed, 113; notice of, 114; by advertisement, 114; qualifications of, 117; disqualified for being Guardians, *b*, 117; qualifications required for medical appointments, 120, 334; their remuneration, 122; up to what day their salaries are payable, 124; how, when suspended from office, 125, *d*, 125; security to be given by, 131; continuance and suspension of, 133-137; supply of vacancies, 133-137; appointment of temporary substitute during sickness, etc., 136, *a*, 136; leave of absence to, *a*, 136; how, when vacancy arises by death or otherwise, 137; personal discharge of duties by, 137; of Workhouse, manner in which they ought to discharge their duties, *c*, 162; opinions of Poor Law Commissioners as to the choice of Officers, *c*, 162.
Officers, appointment of assistant, 315; not to be reported to Poor Law Board for approval, 315; except in certain cases, *d*, 315; Annual List of must continue to be made, *d*, 315; Guardians may pay travelling expenses of any candidate, 316; superannuation allowances to, *b*, 123; not to exceed two-thirds of salary, *b*, 123.
Officers of Workhouse, smoking in, Workhouse or yards, *b*, 92.
Official correspondence, how to be conducted, *a*, 142.
Operations (surgical), fees to District Medical Officers for, 126; how, if pauper refuses to undergo, *d*, 157.
Order, Cheque Book, 449; form of it, 499.
Order for contributions and payments, 266-268; form of it, 275; how to be addressed, *a*, 269; how to be enforced, *a*, 270; form of it, 275; service of, upon Overseers, *c*, 55; duty of Overseers in regard to, 403; to be countersigned by Clerk, 144, *c*, 144.
Order of removal, admission of paupers to Workhouse under, 59, *b*, 64; pauper under, cannot be detained in Workhouse, *b*, 89.
Order of Relieving Officer for admission to Workhouse, 59; of Overseer, 59.
Order upon Treasurer of Guardians for payment of money, 279.
Orphan children, control of Guardians over, *b*, 87.
Orphans, education of, in certified schools of their religion, *b*, 29.
Out-door children, relief for their education, *a*, 86.
Out-door labour test for paupers, 393.
Out-door relief, ticket for, 34; form of it, 201; prohibition of, to able-bodied poor, 358; regulation of, 383; to casual poor, 365.
Out-door Relief List, 461; form of it, 530; alternative form for, 531; abstract of, 462; form of it, 533; to remain in the custody of the Clerk, 462.
Out-door Relief List for Vagrants, 462; form of it, 532.
Out-relief, definition of term, 483.
Overdrawn account of Treasurer, interest on, cannot be paid by Guardians, *c*, 125, *e*, 149.
Overseer, defined, 194, 482.
Overseers, authority of, to order medical relief, *c*, 154, legal liability to

Medical Officer, a Div., not empowered to grant non-resident relief, s. 267.
Overseers, to be summoned in Easter Week persons qualified to vote at election of Guardians, 1; to attend the Clerk with Rate Books and registers of voters, when required, 3; lists of Guardians elected to be sent to, and affixed to church doors, 19; order of, for admission of paupers to Workhouse, 79, n. 81; visitation of lunatics in asylums, etc., by s. 79; Accounting Officer to report cases relieved by, 266; their duties generally, 401; as to the audit of their accounts, 403; duty of, in preparing copies of parochial lists and statements, 457; payment to Guardians even to provide funds, 268; duty of, in respect of Statements of Receipts and Payments, 439; to make out return of lands and tenements belonging to Parish, 440; to make out inventory of stock of moneys belonging to Parish, 440; form of return, 442; form of inventory, 442; to check Rate Receipt Cheque Book, etc., should obtain receipt of Treasurer for payment of contributions, etc., 443; may object to names being entered on Register of voters, s. 46, n. 479; to give public notice of such objection, s. 46; may make fresh register of voters, s. 464; declaration to be made re as to amount in Rate, 457; notice of audit to be given 10, s. 471; books required to be produced to Auditor by, s. 473; penalty on, for neglecting to provide funds for relief of the poor, s. 270; duty of, as to payment of contributions, 403; duty of, in regard to election of Guardians, 462; in regard to making poor rates, 402.
Overseers' Banker's Pass Book, s. 474.
Overseers' Accounts to be made up and balanced half-yearly, 465; to be inspected for inspection of ratepayers, 465.
Overseers' Receipt and Payment Book, entries to be made therein, 437; form of it, 438; memorandum to be made by Overseers in, 437; only actual receipts should be entered in, s. 437.
Owners assessed to poor-rate, how the Overseers may proceed in such case, s. 437; scale of votes at election of Guardians, s. 4; statement of, to be produced by Overseers to Clerk at election of Guardians, 5; form of the s. 16; law relating to votes of, A. 18; register of, s. 19; claims to vote at election of Guardians, duty of Overseers as to, 404.

Pacific Ocean Islands, relief to natives of, 373.
Paid Officers disqualified for being Guardians, A. 112.
Paid Visitor to Workhouse, appointment of, s. 106.
Papers of an improper tendency, circulation of, in Workhouses prohibited, 91.
Parcels brought to Workhouse, examination of, 181; taken out by paupers, 181.
Parents in Workhouses to have interviews with their children, 73.
Parish, definition of, A. 194, 241, 317.
Parish Constable, Clerk to Guardians exempt from serving as, s. 139 Relieving Officer exempt from serving as, s. 162; Master of Workhouse exempt from serving as, s. 162.
Parish church, attendance of inmates of Workhouse at, 96.
Parish documents, custody of, s. 142.
Parish Officer, liability of person appointed though refusing to exercise the office, s. 271.

Index. 579

Parish property, application of money arising from sale of, *e*, 149.
Parliamentary business, duty of Clerk as to conducting, 272.
Parochial Accounts to be made up and balanced half-yearly, 465; to be deposited for the inspection of ratepayers, 465; mode of keeping, 435.
Parochial List and Statement of Account, 469; form of it, 500.
Parochial Ledger, 448; form of it, 497; as to keeping a separate book for, *c*, 448; entries to be made in, *b*, 448.
Partners in a firm, votes of, at election of Guardians, *c*, 4.
Partners cannot be appointed joint Medical Officers, *c*, 119.
Partner of Medical Officer may be his substitute, *c*, 138; of Clerk transacting legal business for Guardians, *a*, 274.
Pass Book, as to the production by Treasurer to Guardians, *d*, 149.
Pauper apprenticeship, 40; duties of Master, 46; certificate of Medical Officer, 150; duty of Relieving Officer as to, 187.
Pauper admitted to Workhouse by Master, cannot be afterwards discharged by him, *a*, 163.
Pauper Classification Book, 449; form of it, 501.
Pauper, discharge of, from Workhouse, *b*, 61, *a*, 66, 86, *b*, 37, *b*, 89; visits of strangers to, 90.
Pauper dying in Workhouse, inventory of clothes and property of, to be delivered to Guardians, 169.
Pauper labour, compensation for, in Workhouse, not allowed, 85; task of work, *b*, 75, *e*, 85.
Pauper lunatics, Medical Officer's quarterly visits to, *c*, 156.
Pauper servants, employment of, in Workhouses, *a*, 72, *e*, 85.
Paupers in Workhouse desirous of making complaints, etc., to be brought before Guardians, 171.
Pawns, relief to redeem, prohibited, 384.
Pay-Clerk of the poor, appointment of, 319.
Payment of debts, circular relating to, *a*, 32.
Payments by Guardians of sums under £5, *c*, 56; of salaries, 124; of money by Treasurer of Union, 148; of relief to paupers by Relieving Officers, 188; by Officers of Union, 193; of paupers' rents prohibited, 369, 385.
Pay of pauper apprentice, 47.
Pecuniary compensation for pauper labour prohibited, 85, *e*, 85.
Penal dress for Workhouse inmates not permitted, *b*, 84.
Penalty on Guardians and others supplying goods for poor, *b*, 35; on Overseers neglecting to provide funds for relief of the poor, *a*, 270.
Pensions, how they may be made available in repayment of relief, *b*, 362, *c*, 372.
Pensioners, mode of claiming repayment of relief, *c*, 371.
Period for which relief should be ordered, *b*, 31.
Period within which nomination- and voting-papers may be inspected, 234.
Perjury, person convicted of, ineligible to be appointed paid Officer, *e*, 112.
Permanent paupers, medical relief to, 59, 156; form of ticket for, 201.
Perquisites not permitted to Officers, *b*, 122.
Personal discharge of duties by Officers, 137; by Medical Officers, 138.
Personal representatives of Officers, their duty as to accounting to Auditor, 480.

Persons voluntarily undertaking office, liability of, 480.
Persons of paupers, examination of, not compulsory, *b*, 67.
Petty Cash Book to be kept by Clerk, 450; entries to be made therein, *b*, 450.
Places appointed for employment of out-door paupers to be reported to Poor Law Board, 388, 394.
Place of audit, notice of, to be given, 473; of burial of pauper dying in Workhouse, *c*, 167; of service of pauper apprentice, 42, 48.
Pledge, relief cannot be given to redeem, *b*, 29.
Police, admission to Workhouse of destitute persons taken to by, *b*, 60, *b*, 62; duty of Master to relieve poor brought to Workhouse by, *a*, 163; inspection of casual wards by, *b*, 61.
Poor Law Board, may inquire into validity of election of Guardians, *a*, 15; to issue order for new election when previous election declared null, *a*, 15; may accept resignation of Guardians, *b*, 19; their consent to change of meetings of Guardians, 20; to issue orders directing Guardians to appoint Assessment Committee on Guardians' failure to do so at first meeting, *c*, 21; approval of, to departure from Prohibitory Order, how expressed, *b*, 371; departures from Prohibitory Order to be reported to, 370; may extend time for the payment of debts contracted by Guardians, *a*, 32.
Poor-rate, declaration to be made by Overseers, 435; division of, 436; may be made in more books than one, *b*, 436; tender of, in copper money illegal, *c*, 439; payment of, by country notes or by cheques not a legal tender, *c*, 439; duty of Overseers in regard to, 402; how to be signed by Parish Officer, 484.
Poor Removal and Settlement Committee, appointment of, *c*, 27.
Population of medical districts, 115.
Porter to Workhouse, appointment of, 109; recommended by Poor Law Commissioners, *c*, 162; his duty, 180; dismissal of, by Guardians, 134.
Porter's Book, entry therein of names of persons resorting to Register Office, *a*, 180.
Post mortem examination of the bodies of paupers, *a*, 161.
Powers of Guardians to be exercised at a meeting of the Board, *c*, 23.
Prayers, reading of, in Workhouse, 95, 164; by Chaplain, 174, *a*, 174.
Precedence of Vice-Chairmen, 22.
Pregnant pauper in Workhouse, punishment of, when disorderly or refractory, 102.
Premium on pauper apprenticeship, 41.
Preparation of Assistant Overseers' and Collectors' bonds, *b*, 58; of contracts and bonds, 144.
Presiding Chairman, when to be elected at meetings of Guardians, 24.
Principles on which relief should be administered, *b*, 28; medical relief, *a*, 51.
Printed papers, when circulation of, in Workhouses prohibited, 91, *c*, 91.
Prison, pauper committed to, for offences in Workhouse cannot be re-admitted to Workhouse without fresh order, *b*, 62.
Prisoners, relief to families of, 362, 388; to wives of, 369.
Privileged communication, what is a, *b*, 150.
Proceedings of Guardians, when not to be invalidated, *a*, 15; how, at their meetings, 24.

Production of pauper apprentice before Guardians, 48; of accounts to Auditor by Clerk, 141; of Union accounts and papers on subpœna, *a*, 143.
Prohibited articles found on paupers on admission to Workhouse, 68; what are, *e*, 68; Porter to prevent admission of, 181.
Prohibition of out-door relief to able-bodied poor, 358; of relief to able-bodied persons employed for hire, 386.
Prohibitory Order, copies of, should be hung up in Workhouse, *a*, 356; administration of relief under, 358.
Property, relief of persons possessed of, *b*, 30, *b*, 63; of pauper dying in Workhouse, inventory of, to be delivered to Guardians, 169; application of, *c*, 372.
Protestant Dissenters in Workhouse, religious assistance and instruction to, 93, *e*, 93-95.
Protests of individual Guardians not entered on minutes, *f*, 140.
Provender to horses of Guardians, *b*, 32.
Provisional Order for admission to Workhouse, 59.
Provision Account, Daily, 454; form of it, 516; Weekly, 454; form of it, 518; Receipt and Consumption, 455; form of it, 519; Quarterly Summary, 455; form of it, 520; Balance of, 455; form of it, 521.
Provisions, definition of term, 482.
Provisions for Workhouse, estimates for, to be submitted to Guardians by Master, 170; storing of, by Master, 170; issue of, 170; of Workhouse Officers, *b*, 123.
Proxies, claims to vote at elections of Guardians, *e*, 3; duty of Overseers as to, 404.
Proxy, votes of, at election of Guardians, *e*, 3; form of appointment of, *b*, 17; form of statement of, *b*, 17; law relating to votes of, *b*, 18; register of, *b*, 18; Guardians cannot vote by, at meeting of Board, *b*, 26.
Public exposure of persons labouring under infectious diseases, *b*, 88.
Public Worship, attendance of Workhouse inmates at Parish Church, 96; of Dissenters, 97.
Publishing notice of election of Guardians, 7.
Puerperal malady, fee for Medical Officer's attendance on, 131.
Punishment Book, to be kept by Master of Workhouse, 103; and laid before Guardians, 104.
Punishment of pauper for refusing to perform task of work in Workhouse, *b*, 75; destroying his clothes or property of Guardians, *b*, 75; for misbehaviour in Workhouse, 97; of children in Workhouse, 103; for introducing spirituous or fermented liquors into Workhouse, 104, *b*, 105.
Purchase of goods by tender, 36; by Master of Workhouse, restraint as to, 172.

Qualification of Officers, 117; of Medical Officers, 120, 334; by registration under Medical Act, *c*, 119, 335; of Chaplain, 122; of Collector of poor-rates, 408; of voters at election of Guardians, *c*, 2; of elected Guardians, *e*, 5; within what time the validity of, for Guardians may be called in question, *a*, 15; defects in, not to invalidate proceedings of Guardians, *a*, 15.
Qualification of a Guardian, to be determined upon annual rateable value of the property, 241.

Quarterly Summary, of Master's Day Book, 453 ; form of it, 514 ; of Provisions received and consumed, 455 ; form of it, 520 ; Balance of the Provisions Account, 455 ; form of it, 521.

Quarterly returns of lunatics in Workhouse to be made by Medical Officer, *a*, 160.

Quarterly visits of Medical Officer to lunatic paupers, *c*, 156.

Queries, answers to, to be inserted in Workhouse Visitors' Book, 106.

Quinine, supply of, *e*, 195.

Quo Warranto will lie to try the title of a Guardian, *a*, 15.

Quorum, appointment of, in the case of Workhouse Visiting Committee, *d*, 106.

Rate Book, persons qualified to vote at election of Guardians to be distinguished in, 2 ; to be produced to Clerk when required, 5 ; duty of Overseers in regard to, 402 ; how to be kept, 435 ; form of, 484 ; when closed to be kept by Vestry Clerk, *d*, 435.

Rate Receipt Cheque Book, 438 ; form of it, 490 ; demand note to be left with ratepayer, 439 ; when rate is paid by instalments, 439 ; when receipt is to be given, 439 ; Collector of Parish to fill up and use, 441.

Ratepayers, scale of votes of, at election of Guardians, *c*, 4 ; not entitled to copies or extracts from Minutes of Guardians, *f*, 141.

Rations of Workhouse Officers, *b*, 123.

Reading prayers in Workhouse, 95, 164 ; by Chaplain, 174.

Reappointment of Medical Officer, 332.

Receipt and Payment Book of Overseers, how to be kept, 437 ; form of it, 486.

Receipt and payment of money by Officers, 193.

Receipts, exemption of, from Stamp duty, *a*, 38, *e*, 149.

Receiving-ward of Workhouse, paupers on admission to be placed in, 66 ; detention of paupers in, 67.

Redeeming goods in pledge, relief cannot be given for, *b*, 29, 384.

Refractory conduct of paupers, what offences shall amount to, 99 ; punishment for, 100, 101.

Refractory children in Workhouse, power to send to industrial schools, *b*, 59, *a*, 86.

Refreshments to Guardians, cost of, cannot be defrayed out of poor-rates, *a*, 31.

Refusal of paupers to submit to medical treatment, *c*, 156 ; to accept relief in Workhouse, course of proceeding in such case, *d*, 187.

Refusal to serve, of candidate nominated for office of Guardian, 11, *d*, 11 ; to continue to act as Guardian for second year, form of, *b*, 19.

Refuse at Workhouse to be accounted for, *b*, 122, *b*, 170.

Register of births in Workhouse, form of it, 204, 276 ; of deaths, 204, 277 ; of owners' claims to vote at election of Guardians to be produced by Overseers to Clerk, 5 ; scrutiny of, *b*, 5 ; how to be prepared, *b*, 18 ; of attendances of Medical Officer is not receivable in evidence for the party making it as a public official book, *a*, 161.

Register Office in Workhouse, entry in Porter's Book of names of persons going to, *a*, 180.

Register of owners, Overseers may object to name inserted in, *a*, 404 ; may cause new register to be made, *a*, 404.

Registrar-General, statistical nosology of, 151.

Registration of Medical Officers, *c*, 119, 335 ; of births in Workhouses, 165 ; of stillborn children, *g*, 165 ; of deaths in Workhouse, 169.
Regulations, enforcement of, by Master of Workhouse, 163.
Relatives of paupers in Workhouse to be sent for in case of their dangerous illness, 166.
Release of sureties to Officer's bond, *c*, 132.
Relief, applications for, when to be disposed of by Guardians, 28-31 ; principles on which it should be administered, *b*, 28 ; to persons in receipt of charitable contributions, *b*, 29 ; for the education of out-door children, *b*, 29 ; of persons having unavailable property, *b*, 30 ; education and maintenance of children who are blind, deaf, dumb, lame, or idiotic, *b*, 29 ; to pay subscriptions to Friendly Societies illegal, *b*, 30 ; for what time relief should be ordered, *b*, 31 ; must not be withheld during inquiry as to settlement, *b*, 31 ; temporary, to applicants waiting at Board-room, *a*, 31 ; liability of persons to obtain, for those of their household, *a*, 32 ; ticket for out-door, to be given to applicant, 33 ; to non-settled and non-resident poor, 51 ; of vagrants, *b*, 74 ; to sick paupers, 359 ; duty of Relieving Officer, 182 ; in cases of sudden or urgent necessity, 185, 359 ; payment of, by Relieving Officers, 188 ; to non-settled poor, 190 ; Guardians to determine chargeability of, *b*, 189 ; in extraparochial places, *b*, 183, *b*, 194 ; to persons in custody of the law, *b*, 183 ; to lunatic soldiers, *d*, 187 ; relief to boys and girls in employment should not be given, *a*, 359 ; to children in Workhouse or establishment out of Union, 367 ; to families of soldiers, sailors, or marines, 362 ; granted contrary to Prohibitory Order to be reported to Poor Law Board, 370 ; to persons in employment prohibited, 386 ; to persons in custody of the law, *a*, 362 ; to their families, 362, 369 ; to wife of person beyond the seas, 369 ; by way of loan, 371, 388 ; to set persons up in trade or business prohibited, 384 ; to redeem pawns prohibited, 384 ; or purchase tools, etc., 384 ; for the purposes of burial, 360, 387 ; to widows, 361, 385 ; to families of prisoners, 362, 369 ; of families of persons out of the Union, 362, 369 ; to children under the age of nurture, 363 ; to non-resident widows, 366, 385 ; to defray cost of education, *d*, 368 ; to resident family of non-resident man, 368 ; in payment of rent prohibited, 369 ; to servants when sick, *c*, 371 ; to Lascars and natives of Asia, Africa, or Islands of South Sea or Pacific Ocean, 373 ; when to be administered partly in kind, 383 ; periods for which to be given, 383 ; for purchase of clothing or bedding, 384.
Relief Order Book, 448 ; form of it, 498 ; entries to be made therein, *d*, 449.
Relieving Officer, appointment of, 109 ; qualification required, 117 ; to devote his whole time to his duties, 117 ; to give security, 131 ; his duties, 182 ; duty of, as regards In-door Relief List, 467 ; District Medical Relief Books, 467 ; as to distinguishing paupers in Out-door Relief List, 470 ; to deliver copy of such Lists to Overseers of each Parish, 470 ; as regards the burial of paupers, *d*, 187 ; responsibility of, with regard to giving out-door relief to ablebodied, *b*, 189 ; as to giving money to casual poor for travelling expenses, *b*, 189 ; to submit his accounts for audit, 191 ; to assist the Clerk in conducting election of Guardians, 191 ; to observe all lawful orders of the Guardians, 191 ; not to take credit for or enter

2 P

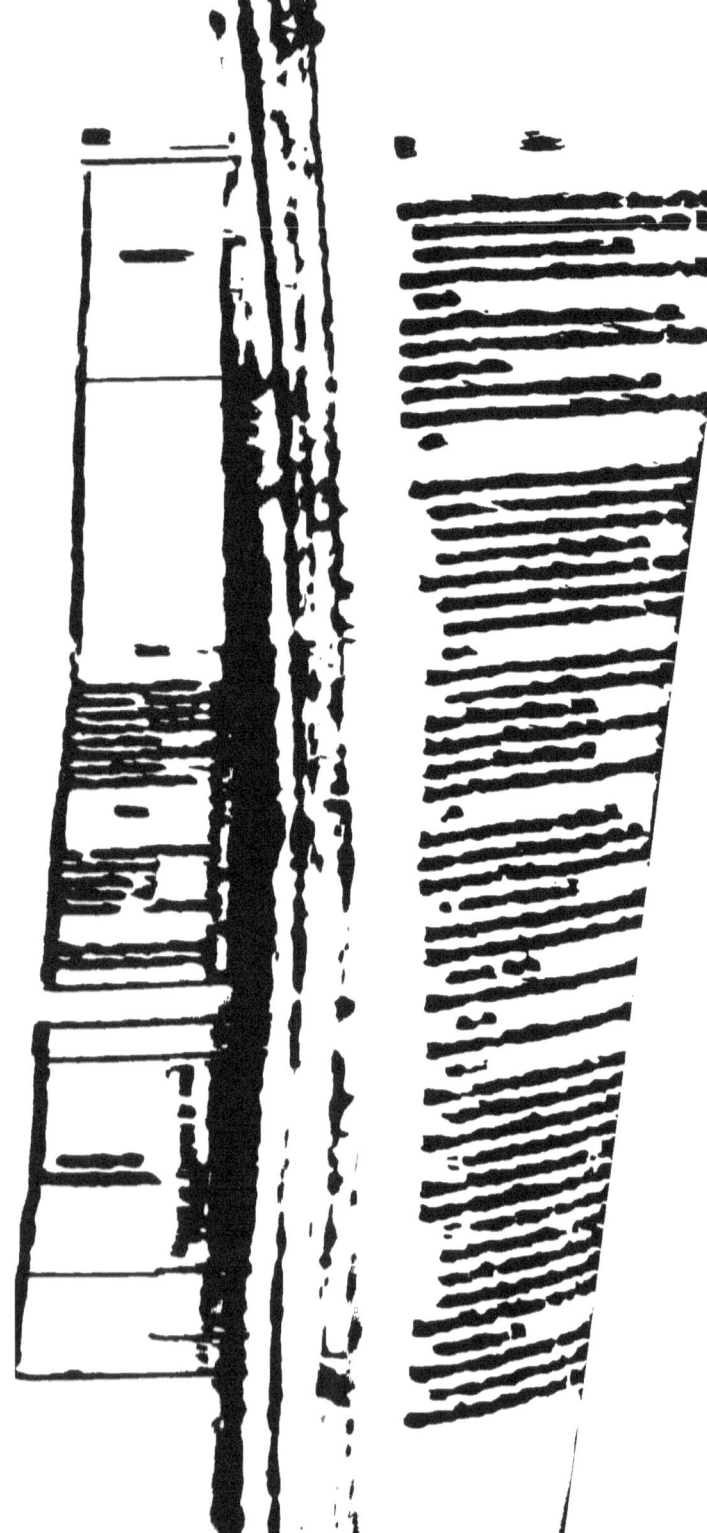

335; of births in Workhouses, of deaths in Workhouses, 169. f Workhouse, 163. sent for in case of their dan-

2.

osed of by Guardians, 28-31; inistered, *b*, 28; to persons in *b*, 29; for the education of having unavailable property, children who are blind, deaf, ay subscriptions to Friendly ime relief should be ordered, inquiry as to settlement, *b*, 31; Board-room, *a*, 31; liability ir household, *a*, 32; ticket for 3; to non-settled and non-re- to sick paupers, 359; duty of dden or urgent necessity, 185, ers, 188; to non-settled poor, eability of, *b*, 189; in extra- ersons in custody of the law, lief to boys and girls in em- 9; to children in Workhouse to families of soldiers, sailors, Prohibitory Order to be re- persons in employment pro- of the law, *a*, 362; to their beyond the seas, 369; by way up in trade or business pro- ibited, 384; or purchase tools, , 360, 387; to widows, 361, 69; of families of persons out under the age of nurture, 363; to defray cost of education, *d*, ent man, 368; in payment of en sick, *c*, 371; to Lascars and f South Sea or Pacific Ocean, tly in kind, 383; periods for se of clothing or bedding, 384. ; entries to be made therein,

qualification required, 117; to es, 117; to give security, 131; In-door Relief List, 467; Di- as to distinguishing paupers in ver copy of such Lists to Over- ds the burial of paupers, *d*, 187; giving out-door relief to ey to casual poor for trav counts for audit, 191; to f Guardians, 191; to o 1; not to take credit for

2 P

money not paid, 192; to produce to Guardians bills and vouchers for payments, 192; attendance of, as witness before Justices, *d*, 191; not to receive money for relief of non-settled pauper, 194; duty of, with respect to District Relief Committee, 262; pauper apprenticeship, 44; order for admission of pauper to Workhouse, 59, *b*, 59; powers as to their discharge, *b*, 61; paupers labouring under infectious diseases admitted to Workhouse, *b*, 63; duty of, in regard to lunatic pauper, *b*, 79; attendance of, as a witness, *a*, 118; on the removal of paupers, *a*, 143; claim for compensation in such case, *a*, 143; forwarding medicines to sick paupers, *c*, 154; supply of extra relief on the certificate of Medical Officer, *c*, 155; duty as regards lunatic paupers, *a*, 158, 159; to attend meetings of Guardians, 182; to receive applications for relief, examine and report thereon, 182; in cases of sickness or accident, 184, 185; cases of sudden or urgent necessity, 185; discretion in granting relief in sudden and urgent cases, *d*, 186; to report to Guardians cases relieved by Overseers, 186; pauper apprentices, 187; when to assist other Relieving Officers, 188; paying relief to paupers, 188; to non-settled poor, 190; to produce his accounts to Clerk for inspection and authentication, 191; absence of, from district, *a*, 182; not to determine chargeability of relief, *b*, 189; duty of, as regards renewed applications for relief, *b*, 183; duty of, as regards visits to fever cases, *c*, 185; as to conveyance of paupers to Workhouse, *d*, 185; accounts of, 460; examination of, by Clerk, 464; not expedient for him to accompany lunatic to distant asylum, *a*, 159; exempt from serving as Parish Constable, *a*, 182; may refer child to Public Vaccinator for vaccination, *b*, 184; transfer of, from one district to another does not vacate appointment, *d*, 115; should not act as Removing Officer, *b*, 190.

Relieving Officer's Receipt and Expenditure Book, 463; form of it, 534; summary of, 463; form of it, 535; expenses incurred in removing lunatics to be entered in, *c*, 463.

Religion of parent, children to be educated in, *c*, 95.

Religious consolation by Chaplain to sick paupers, 176.

Religious instruction of Workhouse children, 86; Order relating to, 299; of adults and children not of the Established Church, 92, *c*, 92; by Chaplain, 175.

Religious state of Workhouse inmates, report of, by Chaplain, 176.

Removal of paupers, Union Officers not bound to attend before Magistrates as witnesses unless summoned, *a*, 143; of Scotch or Irish paupers proceeding to effect removal of all within scope of Clerk's duties, 273; of poor persons contrary to law, *b*, 189; by consent of Guardians, *b*, 190; Master or Relieving Officer should not be employed as Removing Officer, *b*, 190.

Removal of suspension from Officer, 136, *d*, 136.

Remuneration—of Collector of Poor-rates, 410; increase of, 413; of pauper apprentice, 47; of Officers, 122; of Treasurer, 125.

Rent, relief cannot be given to purchase goods seized for, *b*, 29; or to pay, 369, 385.

Repairs—at Workhouse contracts for, 36; generally, 108; laxity in respect of ordering, *a*, 32; of pauper's clothing at Workhouse, 165; duty of Master as to, 170.

Repayment of salaries, by Treasury, scale of, *b*, 176.

Report of Auditor, as to books of Officers and their bonds, 479; of ap-

pointment of Officers to be made to Poor Law Board, 114; of general and medical relief districts, 115; of Medical Officer to Guardians of sickness amongst paupers under his care, 150.
Report of Auditor to Guardians on Books of Officers, suspension of, 544.
Report Book of Master of Workhouse to be kept, 171.
Report Book of Medical Officer of Workhouse to be produced to Visiting Committee, 341; to Poor Law Inspector, 341.
Report of children in Workhouse fit for service to be made to Guardians, 170; of number of inmates to be made to Guardians, 171.
Report to Poor Law Board of deficiency of funds in hands of Treasurer, 148; of departures from Prohibitory Order, 370, 389, 394.
Report of Relieving Officer on applications for relief, 183; on paupers receiving relief, 183; of cases relieved by Overseers, 186.
Reports on Workhouse, reading of, by Guardians, 32.
Reports to be made by Medical Officer of Workhouse to Guardians, 341; to Poor Law Board, 342.
Requisition for extraordinary meeting of Guardians, 23, 144; form of it, 199.
Rescinding resolutions of Guardians, 26, *a*, 26.
Residence, not the duty of Guardians to find, for paupers discharged from Workhouse, *a*, 66.
Residence of Relieving Officer, 117.
Resignation of Officers, 133, 137; what notice is required, 118; appointment of successors, 137; how Officers are to account on, 480.
Resignation of Guardians, how to be tendered to Poor Law Board, *b*, 19.
Resolutions of Guardians, may be moved by Chairman, *a*, 24; how to be rescinded, 26.
Responsibility of Officers for discharge of duties, *d*, 139.
Restraint of paupers in Workhouse of unsound mind, 171, *b*, 78.
Retrospective rates cannot be made, *c*, 267; nor contribution orders on Overseers, *c*, 267.
Return of Guardians elected, 14; need not be sent to all Parishes for a special election, *a*, 16.
Returning Officer at election of Guardians shall be concluded by entries in register, *b*, 5.
Returns, duty of Clerk as to preparing, 146, *b*, 150; District Medical Officers, 157; Workhouse Medical Officers, 160.
Revision of register of owners and proxies, *b*, 19.
Roman Catholic Children, education of, in schools of their own religion, *b*, 29.
Roman Catholics, arrangement for Priest to visit inmates of Workhouse, *c*, 94; attendance of, at public worship, *b*, 97.
Rules, copies of, to be suspended in Workhouse, 105.

Sacrament, administration of, in Workhouse, *b*, 96, *a*, 175.
Sailor, relief to family of, 362.
Salaries of Officers, 122, *b*, 122; when to be paid, 470; payment may be deferred until accounts are audited, 470; how in the case of extra fees or emoluments, 471; of Treasurer, 125; repayment of certain, by Government, *b*, 123; up to what day they are payable, 124; regulation of Treasury as to number of days in each quarter, and as to payment for a broken period, *b*, 124; of Officers who are

2 P 2

suspended from office, 125, *e*, 125; of District Medical Officers, not to include certain operations, etc., 126; payment of, by Guardians before audit, 470; of Auditors, how paid, *a*, 473.

Salaries of Industrial Instructors, repayment of from Parliamentary Grant, *b*, 177.

Sale of rations of Workhouse Officers, *b*, 123; of Parish property, application of proceeds, *e*, 149.

Scale of voting at election of Guardians, *c*, 4; of certificate to Schoolmaster and Schoolmistress, *b*, 176.

School, attendance of pauper apprentice at, 47.

School districts, time for election of Managers for, *c*, 22.

Schoolmaster, appointment of, 109; should not be conjoined with any other office, *e*, 111; his duties, 176.

Schoolmistress, appointment of, 109; should not be conjoined with any other office, *e*, 111; her duties, 176; duty as regards cleanliness of children, *b*, 178.

Scrutiny of registers and owners claiming to vote at election of Guardians, *b*, 5; of votes of Guardians, at a meeting of the Board, *b*, 25.

Sea-bathing Infirmary, maintenance of paupers in, *d*, 366.

Sea service, apprenticeship to, 49; forms for, 50; expenses of conveying boys to place where they are to be bound may be paid out of poor-rate, *b*, 384.

Seal, contracts of Guardians not under, *a*, 36.

Searching paupers on admission to Workhouse, 67, *e*, 67, 163; female paupers by Matron, 172; by Porter, 181.

Security of Officers, 131; of Guarantee Society, 133, *a*, 133; how, in the case of a banking firm, 133, *b*, 133; of Collector of Poor-rates, 410; report of Auditor on, 479; of Collector of the Guardians, 307.

Sermons, when to be preached in Workhouse by Chaplain, 174.

Servants, employment of paupers as, in Workhouses, 72, *a*, 72, *e*, 85; medical relief to, *c*, 153, *c*, 371.

Service of contribution orders upon Overseers, *c*, 55, *a*, 146.

Service of pauper apprentice, place of, 42, 48.

Service, report of children in Workhouse fit for, to be made to Guardians, 170.

Settlement and Poor Removal Committee, appointment of, *c*, 27.

Settlement, relief not to be withheld during inquiry as to, *b*, 31.

Shelter, provision of, in cases of sudden and urgent necessity, 370.

Show of hands, votes of Guardians to be taken by, *b*, 25.

Sick Asylum Districts in Metropolis, list of, 218.

Sick clubs, medical relief to members of, *e*, 153.

Sick dietaries in Workhouses, *d*, 83, 161.

Sick paupers in Workhouse, duty of Matron as to, 173; out-door paupers, duty of Relieving Officer, *d*, 187; conveyance of, to infirmaries, *b*, 190.

Sick paupers, information as to, to be supplied to Guardians by Medical Officer, when required, 150; his certificate of sickness, 150; visitation of, by Chaplain, 176; duties of nurse, 179; duty of Relieving Officer as to, 184; relief to, 359, 365, 387.

Sick poor, remarks on supply of extra nourishment to, *c*, 155.

Sick ward of Workhouse, paupers on admission to be placed in, if sick, 66; employment of paupers in, 72; to be lighted at night, 179.

Sickness, relief in cases of, 359; childbirth is, within meaning of Prohibitory Order, *a*, 360; non-resident relief in cases of, 365, 385.
Signature of Parish Officers to poor-rate, 484.
Signature of Auditor may be impressed with a stamp, *c*, 478.
Simple fractures or dislocations, fees for treatment of, 126.
Sleeping apartments for aged married couples in Workhouses, 71; paupers in Workhouses, not to remain in during the day, 81; visitation of, by Master, 164; by Matron, 172.
Smallpox cases, duty of Relieving Officer as to, *c*, 185.
Smoking in Workhouses prohibited, 92; Officers may be prohibited from, *a*, 92.
Snuff, supply of, to paupers in Workhouse, *b*, 92, *a*, 161.
Soldier, relief to, when lunatic, *d*, 187; to family of, 362.
South Sea Islands, relief to natives of, 373.
Space required for paupers in Workhouse, 76, *a*, 76.
Special election of Guardians, remuneration to Clerk for conducting, *a*, 220; Order for, 254.
Spirituous liquors, not to be allowed to inmates of Workhouse, 83; and when to be allowed, *d*, 84; punishment of paupers for introducing into Workhouse, *b*, 105; Porter to prevent admission of, 181.
Stamp duty, exemption of contracts from, *a*, 38; of receipts for payment of money, *a*, 38; letters acknowledging receipt of money, *a*, 55; orders of Guardians for payment of money, are, *c*, 56; how, when orders are for sums less than 20*s*. and under £5, *c*, 56; Collectors' and Assistant-Overseers' bonds not liable to, *b*, 57; so also bonds of other Officers, *c*, 131.
Stamp duty, receipts of Union Treasurer for money paid by Overseers on Contribution Orders not liable to, *e*, 149; receipts for payment of, non-settled relief exempt from, *a*, 55.
Stamping Workhouse clothing, *b*, 84, 173.
Statement of Auditor as to books of Officers, 479; form of them, 536–540; as to securities, 479; form of it, 540.
Statement of owners and proxies to be given to Overseers, *c*, 3; to be produced to Clerk at election of Guardians by Overseers, 5; form of them, *a*, 16, *a*, 17.
Statements of Union and Parish Accounts, right of owner or ratepayer to inspect at any time, 481.
Statistical nosology of Registrar-General, 151.
Statistical statement, to be prepared by Clerk, half-yearly, 467; to be submitted to Auditor, 467; his duty thereupon, 467; form of it, 502.
Stillborn children in Workhouse, registration of, *g*, 165.
Stipulation to be inserted in Vaccination Contract, form of, *a*, 348.
Stockings for paupers in Workhouse, supply of, 173; charge of, confided to Matron, 173.
Stores for Workhouse, provision of, by Guardians, 32.
Stores, when unserviceable, application of, *b*, 170.
Storing provisions in Workhouse, duty of Master, 170.
Strangers, presence of, at meetings of Guardians, *c*, 27; inspection of books of Union by, *f*, 141.
Strangulated hernia, fee for, 127.
Strayed children, order relating to, 296; notices as to, 297.
Subclassification of paupers in Workhouses, 71.

Substitute for Officer, appointment of, 136; Guardian appointed for an Officer, liability of, *b*, 137; of Medical Officer, 138, *c*, 138; any Medical Officer of Union may act as, *c*, 138; power of Guardians object to appointment, *c*, 138.

Successor to Medical Officer, appointment of, 332.

Sudden illness, medical relief by Overseer in case of, 401.

Sudden or urgent necessity, what constitutes, *b*, 359; admission of cases of, to Workhouse, 59, 163; medical relief in cases of, on order of Overseer, *c*, 154; duty of Relieving Officer, 185; relief in cases of, 359, 387; lodging in cases of, 370, 385.

Sudden death in Workhouse, to be reported to Poor Law Board by Medical Officer, 341.

Suits in Equity, duty of Clerk as to conducting, 272.

Sunday, acts falling to be done upon, in election of Guardians, to be done following day, *a*, 7, *a*, 8; admission and discharge of paupers to Workhouse on, *b*, 61; no work to be done on, 95.

Sunday School, attendance of pauper apprentice at, 47.

Superannuation, allowances to Officers, *b*, 123; age at which they are entitled, *b*, 123; period of service required, *b*, 123.

Superintendent of out-door labour, appointment of, 109; duties of, 192; suspension of, from office, 395.

Superintending paupers at work, arrangements for, to be reported to Poor Law Board, 388.

Supply of Medical attendance and medicines, 152, *c*, 154.

Supply of vacancy in Office, 133.

Surcharge made by Auditor, notice of must previously be given, *b*, 474; reasons to be stated for making, 475.

Surety to contracts with Guardians, 38; to bonds of Officers, 131, *c*, 131; release of, *c*, 132.

Surgical appliances, what are within the meaning of, *e*, 196; repayment of half the cost of from Parliamentary Grant, *b*, 123.

Surgical fees, payable to District Medical Officers, 127.

Surgical operation, refusal of pauper to submit to, *d*, 157.

Suspension of rules in Workhouse, 105; of Officers, 133–137; removal of, by Poor Law Board, 136; of Collector, 411; of Superintendent of pauper labour, 395.

Table showing days for proceedings connected with election of Guardians, 9.

Task of work for vagrants in Workhouse, *b*, 74; punishment for refusing to perform, *b*, 75; other paupers in Workhouse may be employed on, *e*, 85; enforcement of, *b*, 164.

Taxation of bills of costs, 430; of Clerk's bill for legal business, 274.

Temperature of sick wards in Workhouses, *a*, 77.

Temporary appointment of Medical Officer, 332.

Temporary lodging in cases of sudden and urgent necessity, 370, 385.

Temporary relief to applicants waiting at Board room, *a*, 31; change of diet of paupers in Workhouse, 83; leave of absence of pauper from Workhouse, 89.

Temporary substitute for Officer, appointment of, 136.

Tender of refusal to serve office of Guardian, 10; of resignation of Guardian to Poor Law Board, *b*, 19.

Tenders for supply of goods for Union, 36; when to be opened, 37; when they may be dispensed with, 38; for supply of medicines or medical attendance prohibited, 115; of resignation of office, *b*, 118; acceptance thereof not a binding contract, *a*, 38.
Term of pauper apprenticeship, 41.
Terms (medical) to be used by Medical Officers in keeping their books, 151.
Terrier of lands, etc., to be made out by Overseers, 440; form of it, 492.
Testimonials to character, candidate indicted for having forged, *e*, 112.
Ticket for out-door relief, 34; form of it, 200; for permanent medical relief, 51, 156; form of it, 201.
Times within which delivery of nomination-papers must be made, 232.
Times for meals, etc., in Workhouses, 81.
Tobacco, supply of, to paupers in Workhouse, *b*, 92, *a*, 161.
Tools, relief cannot be given to purchase, *b*, 29, *a*, 66; or to redeem from pawn, 384.
Trade, relief cannot be given for the purpose of setting persons up in, *b*, 29, 384; or for teaching one to an adult, *b*, 25; Relieving Officer not to follow any, 118, *a*, 118.
Tradesmen, attendance of, on Guardians, 39.
Training youths in Workhouses, 164; children, 172, 178.
Transfer of Medical or Relieving Officer from one district to another, does not vacate appointment, *d*, 115.
Transfer of money in hands of Treasurer from Parish to Union Account, *e*, 149.
Transmission of money for non-resident relief, 52; of cheques drawn by Guardians, 193.
Travelling expenses of candidates, Guardians may pay, 316.
Travelling expenses of paupers, when they may be defrayed and when not, *b*, 190.
Treasurer, account of, examination of, by Guardians, 33; books of examination by Guardians, *a*, 33; to be balanced half-yearly, 148; certified balances paid to, application of, *a*, 271; orders of Guardians on, are exempt from Stamp duty, *e*, 56; as to liability for paying forged cheques, *e*, 56; balance of, to be ascertained by Clerk, 145; to report deficiency of funds to Poor Law Board, 148, *a*, 271; to submit his accounts for audit, 148; appointment of, 109, how in the case of a firm, *e*, 111; qualification required, 117; his remuneration, 125; Guardians cannot pay interest to, on overdrawn account, *e*, 125; to give security, 131; how in the case of a banking firm, *b*, 133; cannot be suspended from office by Guardians, *d*, 135; bankruptcy of, does not vacate his office, *d*, 135; his duties, 147; as to receipt of portion of amount of contribution order or instalment, *e*, 147; to receive money certified by District Auditor to be due, *e*, 148; form of cheque to be drawn upon Guardians, 279; duty of Officers to pay money into the hands of, 193; can only keep one general account with the Guardians, *d*, 451.
Treasurer's Book, 451; form of it, 506.
Treasury regulations as to payment of salaries for a broken period of a quarter, *b*, 124.
Treatment of lunatics in Workhouse, *b*, 77; of sick paupers in Workhouse, duty of Medical Officer as to, 158; of children and women suckling, 160; of vagrants, *b*, 74.

Trinkets found on paupers by Porter, *d*, 181.
Tumours, fee not payable for removing, *a*, 127.
Unclaimed bodies of paupers, anatomical examination of, *c*, 168.
Union accounts, closing of, 465; day of week for closing of, *c*, 465, 466; Tables showing days for, *c*, 466; to be deposited for inspection of ratepayers, 469.
Union books, custody of, *a*, 143.
Union, division of, into general and medical relief districts, 115; definition of, 316.
Unlawful introduction of spirituous or fermented liquors into Workhouse, 104.
Unpaid Rates Statement, 444; form of it, 495.
Unqualified Assistants, employment by Medical Officers of, *c*, 156.
Unserviceable stores, application of, *b*, 170.
Unsound mind, detention in Workhouse of paupers of, when dangerous, 77; Master to report restraint or compulsion exercised upon, 171, 174.
Unused rate receipts, how to be disposed of, 442,
Urgent necessity, admission of cases of, to Workhouse, 59, 163; duty of Relieving Officer as to, 185; relief in, 359, 385; lodging in cases of, 370, 385, 401.
Union Assessment Committee Act, Clerk's duties under, *c*, 139.
Utensils for setting poor to work to be charged to common fund, *a*, 394.

Vacancy in office, supply of, 133, 137, 332.
Vaccination, order regulating form of contract, 345; regulations of Privy Council relating to, 351, 353.
Vaccination in Workhouse, duty of Medical Officer to undertake, 160; fee for, *a*, 160.
Vagrants, searching on admission to Workhouse, 68, *e*, 68; relief and treatment of them, *b*, 74; task of work for, *b*, 75; enforcement of, *b*, 164; prosecution of, duty of Guardians as to, *a*, 273.
Vagrants, Admission and Discharge Book for, 452; form of, 509; Outdoor Relief List for, 462; form of it, 532; relief given to, in Workhouse, to be entered by Master in his books, *a*, 462; how, when given by Overseers, *a*, 462.
Validity of election of Guardians, within what time it may be called in question, *a*, 15; *quo warranto* will issue; *b*, 15; Poor Law Board may inquire into, *b*, 15; of Contribution Order, *c*, 268.
Valuation Lists, Collectors of Parish to assist Overseers in preparing, 440.
Ventilation of Workhouses, *a*, 77, 106; defects in, to be reported to Guardians by Medical Officer, 160; duty of Master as to, 164; of Matron, 173.
Vestry, parochial lists and statements to be laid before, 438.
Vestry Clerk, duty of, in regard to Parish accounts, *d*, 435, *d*, 441, *a*, 442; duty of Auditor to report on his bond, 479; to attend audit, *d*, 435.
Vice-Chairman, election of, 20; duration of office, 20; two may be elected, 22; their precedence, 22; how if he refuses to act or becomes incapable, 22; voting of, at election of District Auditor, *a*, 22; when to preside at meetings, 24; discharge of duties of Clerk by, 137.

Visitation of wards of Workhouse by Master, 164; by Matron, 173.
Visitation of Workhouses by Commissioners in Lunacy, *b*, 79; of lunatic asylums, etc., by Guardians, etc., *b*, 80; of sick paupers by Chaplain, 176.
Visiting Committee of Workhouse to enter in a book observations as to lunatics in Workhouse, *b*, 80; appointment of, 105; their duties, 106; right of members of, to visit the Workhouse singly, *d*, 105; how, if the Guardians do not appoint a committee, *d*, 106; paupers desirous of making complaints to be brought before, 171.
Visiting Committee to certify as to quarterly balance of the Treasurer's and Miscellaneous Account, 459.
Visiting Committee, Master and Matron duly to accompany, *d*, 106.
Visitor of Workhouse, appointment of paid, *d*, 106.
Visitors' Book at Workhouse, entries to be made in, 106.
Visits to paupers in Workhouse, 90; by licensed Ministers, 92, *c*, 92; by Medical Officers, 138; out-door paupers by district Medical Officers, *c*, 152; pauper lunatics, *c*, 156; of Relieving Officers to paupers receiving relief, 182, 185; to non-settled poor, 190; to fever and contagious diseases cases, *c*, 185.
Voluntarily undertaking office, liability of persons, 480.
Voter at election of Guardians, qualification of, *c*, 2; how to vote, 11; marksmen, 12.
Votes at election of Guardians, scale of, *c*, 4; candidates may be present at casting up of, 234; law in relation to votes of owners and proxies, *c*, 3; partners in a firm, *c*, 4.
Votes of Guardians, questions to be determined by a majority of, 24; how, in the case of an equality of votes, 24, *b*, 24; how to be taken, *b*, 25; scrutiny of, *b*, 25; how Chairman should record his vote, *b*, 24; by ballot, *b*, 26; what a majority, *b*, 113.
Voting-papers at election of Guardians, how to be prepared, 10; form of, 236; distribution of them, 10; to distinguish persons not duly qualified for Guardian, 10; how to be filled up by voters, 11; when invalid, 12; collection of them, 12, *a* 12; how in case of omission, *b*, 6, 12, 13, *c*, 13; examination and casting up of votes, 13; to be delivered to Guardians after election, and preserved, 14; no one has a right to inspect, *a*, 14; cost of, how to be defrayed, 220.
Voting-papers, agents of candidates may accompany collectors of, *a*, 12; 233.
Voting-papers, boxes or bags to be provided for, 233; voter may deposit his own paper in, 233,
Vouchers for payments, production of, by Relieving Officers, 192.

Wards for election of Guardians, nominator of Guardian for, must be qualified to vote in particular ward for which he nominates, *e*, 8; scale of voting in, *e*, 11; mode of voting in, *e*, 12; compensation to Clerk for election of Guardians in, *a*, 221; how to be computed, *a*, 221.
Wages for pauper apprentice, 47.
Wages, prohibition of relief to persons earning, 386, 394; relief should not be given so as to interfere with, *d*, 361; attachment of, in repayment of relief, *c*, 387.
Wales, medical districts in, 116.

Wards, division of Parishes into, for election of Guardians, 2, 248.
Wards of Workhouse, visitation of, by Master, 165; by Matron, 173.
Warmth of Workhouse, defects as to, to be reported to Guardians, 160.
Washing Workhouse linen, etc., duty of Matron as to, 173.
Waste, Table of average, in the consumption of certain provisions, *c*, 477; in distribution of provisions, allowance to be made for, *a*, 454, *c*, 477.
Wayfarers, searching of, on admission to Workhouse, *e*, 67; when regulations as to admission of paupers are not to apply to, 68; treatment and diet of, 74.
Week, day on which it should terminate, *c*, 465.
Weekly administration of relief, 383.
Weekly allowances to paupers, payment of, 188.
Weekly examination of accounts by Clerk, how to be made, *a*, 465.
Weekly Provisions Consumption Account, 454; form of it, 518.
Weighing allowances of food to paupers in Workhouse, 84.
Widows, relief to, 361; non-resident, 367, *c*, 367, 385.
Widows, as to irremovability of, for twelve months, *c*, 367, *b*, 366.
Wife, discharge of, from Workhouse without her husband, *b*, 88; relief to, when separated from husband, *c*, 363, 368, 386, 388; cannot be compelled to enter Workhouse with her husband, *b*, 88.
Witness, duty of Relieving Officer to attend as, *a*, 118, *a*, 143; of Clerk, *a*, 143, *d*, 192; pauper in Workhouse subpœnaed as, *b*, 89.
Wives of labourers, grant of midwifery orders for, *a*, 184.
Women of bad character in Workhouses, how to be dealt with, *b*, 69.
Women, relief to, when separated from their husbands, *c*, 363, 368, 386, 388.
Women suckling children in Workhouse, duty of Medical Officer as to their diet and treatment, 160; of Matron, 173.
Work, task of, for vagrants in Workhouse, *b*, 75; for other paupers, *e*, 85.
Workhouse, where now to be constructively situated, *c*, 167.
Workhouse Chapel, cannot be consecrated, *a*, 175; may be licensed by Bishop of the Diocese, *a*, 175.
Workhouse, principle, enunciation of, *a*, 58; directions of Guardians as to management of, 32; reports on, reading of, by Guardians, 32; provision of furniture and stores for, 32; Guardians' orders for admission of paupers to, 33; contracts for works or repairs at, 37, admission of paupers, 58; Guardians cannot give an order for, to pauper who is not resident in the Union, *b*, 60; under an order of removal, 59,*b*, 64; classification of paupers, 68; limitation of number of paupers to be admitted into, 76; cubic space required for paupers in, *a*, 76; ventilation of, *a*, 77; visitation of, by Commissioners in Lunacy, *b*, 79; discipline and diet of the paupers in Workhouse, 80; materials for clothing of, 84; number of paupers to occupy each bed, 85; employment of paupers, 85; penal dress for inmates prohibited, *b*, 84; education of children in, 86; contracts for reception of children in, *a*, 86; discharge of paupers from, *b*, 61, *a*, 66, 86, *b*, 87; *subpœna* of pauper in, as a witness, *b*, 89; visits to paupers in, 90; prohibition of certain papers in, 91; gaming in, prohibited, 91; smoking not to be allowed, 92; reading prayers in, 95; divine service in, 95; punishment of paupers for misbehaviour in, 97; defects as to diet, drainage, ventilation, etc., to be

Index. 593

reported to Guardians by Medical Officer, 160; admission of corpse into, *c*, 168; holding coroner's inquests in, *c*, 168; anatomical examination of the bodies of paupers dying in, *c*, 168; constructive situation of, *c*, 167; conveyance of paupers to, duty of Relieving Officer, *d*, 186; copies of Prohibitory Order should be hung up in, *a*, 356; dietaries, orders as to, 284, 287; ingress and egress of persons to be entered in Porter's Book, 180; refusal to accept relief in, course of proceeding in such case, *d*, 186; repairs and alterations, 108; lime-washing, 108; in respect of drainage, warmth, or ventilation, 109; government of, by Guardians, 108; reports as to state of, to be made to Guardians by Master, 171.

Workhouse, admission to, of child preparatory to being sent to Industrial School, *b*, 59; of persons removed from dangerous structures, *b*, 59.

Workhouse dress, paupers on admission to be clothed in, 67.

Workhouse inmates, attention to complaints of, *a*, 84.

Workhouse, defects in, to be reported to Guardians by Medical Officer, 341; to Poor Law Board, 342.

Workhouse, arrangements for reception of chronic lunatics in, *b*, 64; cubic space required in, *a*, 76; report of Committee, *a*, 76; ventilation of, *a*, 77.

Workhouse, definition of, 317.

Workhouse library, establishment of, *c*, 91.

Workhouse, not an improper repository for documents of a Parish, *d*, 438.

Workhouse, Master's accounts, 451.

Workhouse Master, appointment of, 109; his duties, 161; Matron, appointment of, 109; her duties, 172; Chaplain, appointment of, 109; his duties, 174; Schoolmaster, appointment of, 109; his duties, 176; Schoolmistress, appointment of, 109; her duties, 176; Porter, appointment of, 109; his duties, 180; Nurse, appointment of, 109; duties of, 179.

Workhouse Medical Officer, appointment of, 109; his duties, 157; reports to be made by, to Guardians, 341; to Poor Law Board, 342; to enter on card medical or other extras required for patient, 341; what defects in Workhouse to report, 341.

Workhouse medical return, 160; Relief Book, duty of Master in respect of, 170.

Workhouse Officers, after dismissal not to remain on the premises, 135; cannot require Medical Officer of Workhouse to attend on them in sickness, *b*, 123; manner in which they ought to discharge their duties, *c*, 162; negligence or misconduct of, to be reported by Master to Guardians, 171.

Workhouse Punishment Book, form of it, 201; Medical Relief Book, form of it, 202.

Workhouse Visiting Committee, appointment of, 105; their duties, 106; paid visitor, *d*, 106.

PRINTED BY
J. E. TAYLOR AND CO., LITTLE QUEEN STREET,
LINCOLN'S INN FIELDS.

CATALOGUE

OF

𝕷𝖆𝖜 𝖂𝖔𝖗𝖐𝖘

PUBLISHED BY

MESSRS. BUTTERWORTH,

LAW BOOKSELLERS AND PUBLISHERS

TO THE QUEEN'S MOST EXCELLENT MAJESTY,

AND TO

H. R. H. THE PRINCE OF WALES.

"*Now for the Laws of England (if I shall speak my opinion of them without partiality either to my profession or country), for the matter and nature of them, I hold them wise, just and moderate laws: they give to God, they give to Cæsar, they give to the subject what appertaineth. It is true they are as mixt as our language, compounded of British, Saxon, Danish, Norman customs. And surely as our language is thereby so much the richer, so our laws are likewise by that mixture the more complete.*"—LORD BACON.

LONDON:

7, FLEET STREET, E. C.

1868.

INDEX TO CATALOGUE.

	Page
Abridgment.	
Petersdorff	22
Accounts,	
Law of. Pulling	32
Actions at Law.	
Browne	34
Kerr	14
Williams	27
Acts,	
Index of. Archer	32
Admiralty,	
Practice.	
Coote	30
Reports.	
Browning & Lushington	38
Robinson	38
Swabey	38
Lushington	38
Articled Clerk.	
Francillon	35
Attachment,	
Foreign, Brandon	20
Australia.	
Torrens	31
Banking.	
Grant	9
Keyser	32
Bankruptcy,	
In County Courts.	
Davis	11
Bar.	
Law Students' Guide	36
Smith	20
Pearce	33
Barbados.	
Law of	33
Belligerents.	
Hamel	31
Bills of Exchange.	
Grant	9
Blackstone.	
Stephen's	6
Blockade.	
Deane	35
Boundaries.	
Hunt	4
Brokers.	
Keyser	32
Carriers,	
Inland. Powell	21
Railway. Shelford	22
Catalogue,	
General	37
Chamber Practice.	
Com. Law. Parkinson	28

	Page
Chancery Practice.	
O'Dowd	34
Hunter	18
Goldsmith	14
Drafting. Lewis	7
Charitable Trusts.	
Tudor	23
Church Building.	
Trower	15
Collieries.	
Bainbridge	16
Colonial Law.	
Barbados	33
Torrens	31
Commentaries.	
Stephen's Blackstone's	6
Common Law,	
Practice.	
Dixon	9
Lush	8
Kerr	14
Quain & Holroyd	34
Companies.	
Grant	32
Shelford	22
Compensation,	
Law of.	
Ingram	25
Shelford	22
Consolidation Acts.	
Shelford	22
Constitution.	
May	18
Stephen	6
Contraband of War.	
Moseley	20
Deane	35
Contracts,	
Specific Performance.	
Fry	30
Conveyancing,	
Introduction.	
Lewis	7
Practice.	
Barry	12
Smith	21
Tudor	13
Forms.	
Crabb	16
Christie	16
Shelford	16
Rouse	19
Convictions,	
Synopsis of. Oke	24
Forms. Oke	24
Copyholds,	
Enfranchisement.	
Rouse	5
Law of. Scriven	25

	Page
Coroner.	
Baker	33
Corporations in General.	
Grant	32
Costs,	
Law of. Gray	31
County Courts.	
Davis	11
Practice in Equity.	
Davis	11
Crimes.	
Davis	20
Criminal Law.	
Davis	20
Oke	24, 32
Customs.	
Hamel	33
Deeds.	
Tudor	13
Descents.	
Fearne	37
Divorce.	
Brandt	34
Swabey & Tristram	38
Browning	17
Drainage.	
Woolrych	21
Wilson	36
Ecclesiastical.	
Badeley	37
Practice.	
Coote	32
Pamphlet.	
Bayford	37
Judgment.	
Burder v. Heath	36
Long v. Cape Town	37
Election,	
Law.	
Lewis	36
Warren	35
Committees.	
Warren	35
Sharkey	36
England,	
Laws of.	
Blackstone	6
Stephen	6
Francillon	35
English Bar.	
Pearce	33
Smith	21
Equity,	
County Courts. Davis	11
Draftsman. Lewis	7
Pleader. Drewry	27
Suit in. Hunter	18
See Chancery.	

INDEX TO CATALOGUE.

Evidence,
  County Court. Davis 11
  Law of. Powell 23
  Wills. Wigram 30
  Circumstantial.
    Wills 25

Examinations.
  Benham's (Preliminary) Guide 6
  Halliday's Reporter 28
  Mosely's (Intermediate and Final) Guide 6

Fences.
  Hunt 4

Fisheries.
  Oke 26

Forms,
  Conveyancing.
    Crabb 16
    Rouse 39
  Magisterial. Oke 24
  Pleading. Greening 34
  Probate. Chadwick 17

Game Laws.
  Oke 26

Highways.
  Glen 29

Hindu Law.
  Cutler 31

House of Lords,
  Reports. Clark 38
  Practice. May 18

International Law.
  Deane 35
  Hamel 32
  Phillimore 35

Jamaica Riot.
  Williams 37

Joint Stock Companies.
  Shelford 39
  Accounts. Pulling 32

Jurisprudence.
  Law Magazine 40

Justice of Peace.
  Oke 26

Lands Clauses Acts.
  Ingram 25
  Shelford 22

Law Magazine 40

Law Studies.
  Smith 20

Leading Cases,
  Real Property. Tudor 13

Leases.
  Crabb 16
  Rouse 19

Legacy Duties.
  Shelford 19

Local Government.
  Glen 29

Lord Mayor's Court.
  Brandon 20

Lunacy.
  Phillips 28

Magisterial Law.
  Oke 24
  Forms. Oke 24

Maritime Warfare.
  Deane 35
  Hamel 31

Masters and Servants.
  Davis 10

Masters and Workmen.
  Lovesy 24

Maxims,
  Equity. Higgins 39

Merchant Shipping.
  O'Dowd 23

Militia Laws.
  Dwyer 36

Mines and Minerals.
  Bainbridge 31

Mortgages.
  Fisher 39
  Rouse 19

Pamphlets 37

Parliamentary.
  May 18
  Warren 35

Partnership.
  Dixon 9
  Tudor's Pothier 35

Patents.
  Norman 35

Petty Sessions.
  Oke 24

Pleading,
  Common Law.
    Greening 34
    Williams 27
  Equity. Drewry 27

Poor Law,
  Orders. Glen 29

Precedents,
  Conveyancing.
    Crabb 16
    Rouse 19
  Pleading.
    Chitty, Jun. 15

Priority.
  Fisher 39

Private Bills.
  May 18

Prize Law.
  Lushington 23

Probate,
  Practice. Coote 4
  Forms. Chadwick 17
  Duties. Shelford 19
  Reports.
    Swabey & Tristram 38

Railways.
  Shelford 22
  Compensation.
    Ingram 25

Real Property.
  Tudor 13
  Chart. Fearne 36

Registration.
  Warren 35

Religious,
  Confessions. Badeley 37
  Doctrine.
    Burder v. Heath 36
  Discipline.
    Long v. Cape Town 37
  Supremacy of Crown 36

Ritual.
  Bayford 37
  Hamel 36

Roman Law.
  Cutler 33
  Tomkins 27

Sewers.
  Woolrych 21

Sheriff.
  Sewell 36

Sheriff's Court.
  Davis 10

Specific Performance.
  Fry 30

Stock Exchange.
  Keyser 32

Succession Duty.
  Shelford 22

Suit in Equity.
  Hunter 15

Summary Convictions.
  Oke 24

Tolls.
  Gunning 34

Treaties.
  Hertslet 35

Trusts, Charitable.
  Tudor 23

Turnpike Laws.
  Oke 26

Wills.
  Crabb 16
  Tudor 13
  Wigram 30

Winding-up.
  Shelford 39

Window Lights.
  Latham 16

Wreck.
  O'Dowd 39

Law Works published by Messrs. Butterworth.

COOTE'S & TRISTRAM'S PROBATE PRACTICE.—5th Edit.

THE PRACTICE of the COURT of PROBATE in Common Form Business. By HENRY CHARLES COOTE, F.S.A., Proctor in Doctors' Commons, &c., &c. Also a Treatise on the Practice of the Court in Contentious Business, by THOMAS H. TRISTRAM, D.C L., Advocate in Doctors' Commons, and of the Inner Temple. Fifth Edition, with great Additions, and including all the Statutes, Rules, Orders, &c., to the present time; together with a Collection of Original Forms and Bills of Costs. 8vo. 24s. cloth.

"A fifth edition in so short a time is a success that few law books can boast, and it is well deserved. Mr. Coote as a proctor possesses that intimate acquaintance with the minutiæ of practice which experience only can supply, and Dr. Tristram's education as an advocate enables him to treat of the jurisdiction of the Probate Court, the law which it administers, and the principles established for the administration of that law, with a mastery of his subject that has made this production of the united labours of two such competent men the accepted text book of the Probate Court. Having noticed its successive editions as they appeared, it remains only to say that it brings down the statutes and cases to the present time."—*Law Times on the 5th Edition.*

"The profession will be glad to welcome the publication of this most valuable work. When the monopoly which the proctors and advocates enjoyed in Doctors Commons was abolished, and the practice in probates and letters of administration was thrown open to the general profession, the uninitiated derived greater benefit and instruction from this book than from any other which was published for their guidance. It has become an acknowledged necessity in the library of every practitioner. Since the publication of the last edition new rules have been promulgated for the Court of Probate, other regulations have been made by acts of parliament and an order in council, and the practice of the Court has in some respects been altered and settled. These changes have been attended to. A more useful book than this we do not know, and we need not say more than that in this edition the authors have done all in their power to increase its utility and secure its completeness."—*Law Magazine and Review.*

"We must not omit to praise the complete character of the Appendix, which, occupying more than half the whole work, presents us with the statutes, the orders in council, rules and fees, tables of costs and forms, and leaves nothing to be desired by the proctor or solicitor either in the routine of common form or in the stages of suits."—*Law Journal on the 5th Edition.*

HUNT ON BOUNDARIES AND FENCES.

THE LAW RELATING TO BOUNDARIES AND FENCES. By ARTHUR JOSEPH HUNT, of the Inner Temple, Esq., Barrister at Law. Post 8vo. 9s. cloth.

"Among other matters discussed are the rights of property on the sea shore; navigable and private rivers; the duties of mine owners with regard to boundaries; the rights and liabilities of landlords and tenants as to fences, hedges and ditches, and the liability to make and repair the same; the duty to fence land adjoining roads; the law relating to trees and hedges on the boundaries of property, &c. The second chapter of Mr. Hunt's work, which relates to fences generally, is especially worthy of perusal, as cases are repeatedly arising between adjoining proprietors. Too much praise cannot be given to the modesty of an author, who, following the example of early text writers, con-

Hunt on Boundaries and Fences—*continued.*

structs his work on the so called utterances of the Judges, and does not, like some writers, place too much reliance upon his own *ipse dixit*. With these remarks we take leave of Mr. Hunt's book, recommending it as a work containing a great deal of information in a small compass, and one on which no small amount of time, labour and research must necessarily have been bestowed."—*Law Times.*

" Mr. Hunt has done good service by collecting and arranging, in a clear and convenient manner, a large amount of information which lies scattered through the old text books, the reports and the statutes, and to which there has hitherto been no clue. Mr. Hunt appears to have ransacked the American as well as the English treatises and reports: but his work is not a mere compilation: he has investigated for himself and stated the results concisely and clearly."—*Jurist.*

"The law of boundaries and fences, is, in the work before us, treated with great ability, and as the language is clear, and, as far as may be, free from technicalities, it will be found useful beyond the limits of the legal profession."—*Athenæum.*

"This is a very useful work as a common place book on the subject of which it treats."—*Law Magazine.*

"This is a concise and well-written book on a small but not unimportant subject, and displays considerable care both in arrangement and detail. It will be seen that the author very carefully and completely dissects his subject, and then very succinctly treats of the parts."—*Solicitors' Journal.*

ROUSE'S COPYHOLD ENFRANCHISEMENT MANUAL.—Third Edition.

The COPYHOLD ENFRANCHISEMENT MANUAL; enlarged, and treating the subject in the Legal, Practical and Mathematical Points of View; giving numerous Forms, Rules, Tables and Instructions for Calculating the Values of the Lord's Rights; Suggestions to Lords' Stewards, and Copyholders, protective of their several Interests, and to Valuers in performance of their Duties; and including the Act of 1858, and Proceedings in Enfranchisement under it. By ROLLA ROUSE, Esq., of the Middle Temple, Barrister at Law. Third Edition, much enlarged. 12mo. 10s. 6d. cloth.

"This new edition follows the plan of its predecessor, adopting a fivefold division:—1. The Law. 2. The Practice, with Practical Suggestions to Lords, Stewards and Copyholders. 3. The Mathematical consideration of the Subject in all its Details, with Rules, Tables and Examples. 4. Forms. 5. The Statutes, with Notes. Of these, we can only repeat what we have said before, that they exhaust the subject; they give to the practitioner all the materials required by him to conduct the enfranchisement of a copyhold, whether voluntary or compulsory."—*Law Times.*

"When we consider what favor Mr. Rouse's Practical Man and Practical Conveyancer have found with the profession, we feel sure the legal world will greet with pleasure a new and improved edition of his copyhold manual. The third edition of that work is before us. It is a work of great practical value, suitable to lawyers and laymen. We can freely and heartily recommend this volume to the practitioner, the steward and the copyholder "—*Law Magazine.*

" Now, however, that copyhold tenures are being frequently converted into freeholds, Mr. Rouse's treatise will doubtless be productive of very extensive benefit; for it seems to us to have been very carefully prepared, exceedingly well composed and written, and to indicate much experience in copyhold law on the part of the author."—*Solicitors' Journal.*

STEPHEN'S COMMENTARIES.—Sixth Edition.

NEW COMMENTARIES ON THE LAWS OF ENGLAND, partly founded on Blackstone. By HENRY JOHN STEPHEN, Serjeant-at-Law. The Sixth Edition, prepared for the press by JAMES STEPHEN, LL.D., of the Middle Temple, Barrister-at-Law, late Recorder of Poole, and Professor of English Law at King's College, London. 4 vols. 8vo. (*In active preparation.*)

BENHAM'S STUDENT'S EXAMINATION GUIDE.

The STUDENT'S GUIDE to the PRELIMINARY EXAMINATION for ATTORNEYS and SOLICITORS, and the Oxford and Cambridge Local Examinations and the College of Preceptors, to which are added numerous Suggestions and Examination Questions selected from those asked at the Law Institution. By JAMES ERLE BENHAM, of King's College, London. 12mo. 3s. cloth.

"The book is artistically arranged. It will become a useful guide and instructor, not only to Law Students, but to every Student who is preparing for a preliminary examination."—*Law Journal.*

"This book is intended for the use of those who are about to undergo the preliminary examinations for attorneys and solicitors and for the Oxford and Cambridge local examinations. The student may learn from Mr. Benham what he has to do and the way to do it. We have no doubt that 'Benham's Student's Examination Guide' will be largely patronised in this examining age."—*Standard.*

"The author of this treatise has written the present most serviceable work, by aid of which the examinations should be passed without difficulty"—*Sunday Times.*

"A useful little treatise by Mr. James Erle Benham, intended to supply to Students, about to encounter the examination which precedes entering into articles of clerkship, the necessary information as to subjects of Study,"—*Star.*

"He has succeeded in producing a book which will doubtless prove useful to those Students who desire to prepare themselves for examination without the assistance of a tutor."—*Irish Law Times.*

"It is certainly a useful guide to that curious *olla podrida* expected from the candidate. It may be well to have a systematised mode of "cram," suggested in a distinct and accurate manner."—*London Review.*

MOSELY'S HANDY BOOK FOR ARTICLED CLERKS.

A PRACTICAL HANDY BOOK of ELEMENTARY LAW designed for the use of ARTICLED CLERKS, with a course of Study, and Hints on Reading for the Intermediate and Final Examinations. By M. S. MOSELY, Solicitor, Clifford's Inn Prizeman, M. T. 1867. 12mo. cloth.

MESSRS. BUTTERWORTH, 7, FLEET STREET, E.C.

LEWIS ON EQUITY DRAFTING.

PRINCIPLES of EQUITY DRAFTING, with an APPENDIX of FORMS. By HUBERT LEWIS, B.A., of the Middle Temple, Barrister-at-Law, Author of "Principles of Conveyancing explained and Illustrated." Post 8vo. 12s. cloth.

"Practically the rules that apply to the drafting and reading of bills will apply to the composition of the County Court document that will be substituted for the bill. Mr. Lewis's work is therefore likely to have a much wider circle of readers than he could have anticipated when he commenced it, for almost every page will be applicable to County Court Practice, should the bill, in any shape or under any title be retained in the new jurisdiction,— without it we fear that equity in the County Courts will be a mass of uncertainty,— with it every practitioner must learn the art of equity drafting, and he will find no better teacher than Mr. Lewis."—*Law Times.*

"We have little doubt that this work will soon gain a very favourable place in the estimation of the Profession. It is written in a clear and attractive style, and is plainly the result of much thoughtful and conscientious labour."—*Law Magazine and Review.*

LEWIS'S INTRODUCTION TO CONVEYANCING.

PRINCIPLES of CONVEYANCING EXPLAINED and ILLUSTRATED by CONCISE PRECEDENTS. With an Appendix on the Effect of the Transfer of Land Act in Modifying and Shortening Conveyances. By HUBERT LEWIS, B.A., late Scholar of Emman. Coll. Cambridge, and of the Middle Temple, Barrister-at-Law. 8vo. 18s. cloth.

"The preface arrested our attention, and the examination we have made of the whole treatise has given us (what may be called a new sensation) pleasure in the perusal of a work on Conveyancing. We have, indeed, read it with pleasure and profit, and we may say at once that Mr. Lewis is entitled to the credit of having produced a very useful, and, at the same time, original work. This will appear from a mere outline of his plan, which is very ably worked out. The manner in which his dissertations elucidate his subject is clear and practical, and his expositions, with the help of his precedents, have the best of all qualities in such a treatise, being eminently judicious and substantial. Mr. Lewis's work is conceived in the right spirit. Although a learned and goodly volume, it may yet, with perfect propriety, be called a 'handy book.' It is besides a courageous attempt at legal improvement; and it is, perhaps, by works of such a character that law reform may be best accomplished."—*Law Magazine and Review.*

"It is clear that no labour has been spared to achieve its object; every page contains ample evidence of thoroughness and conscientiousness in the execution of the task undertaken. By the diligent and painstaking student who has duly mastered the law of property, this work will undoubtedly be hailed as a very comprehensive exponent of the Principles of Conveyancing."—*Legalcian, or Articled Clerks' Magazine.*

"The perusal of the work has given us much pleasure. It shows a thorough knowledge of the various subjects treated of, and is clearly and intelligibly written. Students will now not only be able to become proficient draftsmen, but, by carefully studying Mr. Lewis's dissertations, may obtain an insight into the hitherto neglected Principles of Conveyancing."—*Legal Examiner.*

"On the whole, we consider that the work is deserving of high praise, both for design and execution. It is wholly free from the vice of bookmaking, and indicates considerable reflection and learning. Mr. Lewis has at all events succeeded in producing a work to meet an acknowledged want, and we have no doubt he will find many grateful readers amongst more advanced, not less than among younger students."—*Solicitors' Journal and Reporter.*

"Mr. Lewis has contributed a valuable aid to the law student. He has condensed the Practice of Conveyancing into a shape that will facilitate its retention on the memory, and his Precedents are usefully arranged as a series of progressive lessons, which may be either used as illustrations or exercises."—*Law Times.*

LUSH'S COMMON LAW PRACTICE. By DIXON.
Third Edition.

LUSH'S PRACTICE of the SUPERIOR COURTS of COMMON LAW at WESTMINSTER, in Actions and Proceedings over which they have a common Jurisdiction: with Introductory Treatises respecting Parties to Actions; Attornies and Town Agents, their Qualifications, Rights, Duties, Privileges and Disabilities; the Mode of Suing, whether in Person or by Attorney, in Formâ Pauperis, &c. &c. &c.; and an Appendix, containing the authorised Tables of Costs and Fees, Forms of Proceedings and Writs of Execution. Third Edition. By JOSEPH DIXON, of Lincoln's Inn, Esq., Barrister-at-Law. 2 vols. 8vo. 46s. cloth.

"Lush's Practice is what Tidd's Practice was in our days of clerkship, and what Archbold's Practice was in our early professional days—the practice in general use, and the received authority on the subject. It was written by Mr. Lush when he was only a junior rising into fortune and fame. His practical knowledge, his clearness and industry, were even then acknowledged, and his name secured for his work an immediate popularity which experience has confirmed and extended. But the book was in its turn productive of considerable advantage to the author; it largely increased the number of his clients. When new editions were called for, Mr. Lush was too occupied with briefs to find time for the preparation of books; and hence the association of his name with that of Mr. Dixon as editor, and by whom the new edition has been produced. Mr. Dixon reminds us, that twenty-five years have passed since Mr. Lush made his appearance as an author, and vast indeed have been the changes the law has since witnessed. So numerous are they, that the editor has found it the most convenient course to ignore, as it were, the second edition, to take the text of the original work as it came fresh from Mr. Lush's pen, and to mould that to the present practice. He is thus enabled to assure the reader that for every alteration in, or addition to, the text, he alone is responsible. The index is very copious and complete. Under Mr. Dixon's care, Lush's Practice will not merely maintain, it will largely extend, its reputation."—*Law Times.*

"This is an excellent edition of an excellent work. We think that Mr. Dixon has been wise in basing his work on the original edition of the Practice, and not upon the second edition published in the year 1856. As Mr. Lush's heavy professional engagements made it impossible for him to remodel his book himself, the best course was, that it should be re-edited at first hand, and not indirectly. Literary patchwork is always objectionable. To edit an author is a task requiring great skill; but to edit an author's Editor is still more difficult. We congratulate Mr. Dixon on the judgment he has displayed in selecting the former alternative. He has effected a most successful 'restoration.' As far as the great changes in the law permit, he has re-produced the original work. He has adopted Mr. Lush's arrangement, and only made those alterations and additions which recent legislature has rendered indispensable. The whole work, which contains altogether 1,183 pages, concludes with a copious index entirely re-written and very considerably enlarged. Altogether, both in what he has omitted and what he has added, Mr. Dixon has been guided by sound discretion. We trust that the great and conscientious labours he has undergone will be rewarded. He has striven to make his work 'thorough,' and because he has done so, we take pleasure in heartily recommending it to every member of both branches of the profession."—*Solicitors' Journal.*

"The profession cannot but welcome with the greatest cordiality and pleasure a third edition of their old and much valued friend 'Lush's Practice of the Superior Courts of Law.' Mr. Dixon, in preparing this edition, has gone back to the original work of Mr. Justice Lush, and, as far as the legislative changes and decisions of the last twenty-five years would allow, reproduced it. This adds greatly to the value of this edition, and at the same time speaks volumes for Mr. Dixon's conscientious labour."—*Law Journal.*

MESSRS. BUTTERWORTH, 7, FLEET STREET, E.C. 9

DIXON'S LAW OF PARTNERSHIP.

A TREATISE on the LAW OF PARTNERSHIP. By JOSEPH DIXON, of Lincoln's Inn, Esq., Barrister at Law, Editor of "Lush's Common Law Practice." 1 vol. 8vo. 22s. cloth.

"Mr. Dixon's manual on the law of partnership will be an acceptable addition to the shelves of our law libraries, whilst from its portable size it will be equally useful as a companion in Court. He has evidently bestowed upon this book the same conscientious labour and painstaking industry for which we had to compliment him some months since when reviewing his edition of 'Lush's Practice of the Superior Courts of Law,' and, as a result, he has produced a clearly written and well-arranged manual upon one of the most important branches of our mercantile law."—*Law Journal.*

"Mr. Dixon has done his work well. The book is carefully and usefully prepared."—*Solicitors' Journal.*

"Mr. Dixon enters into all the conditions of partnerships at common law, and defines the rights of partners among themselves; the rights of the partnership against third persons; the rights of third persons against the partnership; and the rights and liabilities of individuals, not actually partners, but liable to be treated by third persons as partners."—*Times.*

"We heartily recommend to practitioners and students Mr. Dixon's treatise as the best exposition of the law we have read, for the arrangement is not only artistic, but conciseness has been studied without sacrifice of clearness. He sets forth the principles upon which the law is based as well as the cases by which its application is shown. Hence it is something more than a digest, which too many law books are not; it is really an essay."—*Law Times.*

"The appearance of this volume at the present time is very opportune. Mr. Dixon has done wisely in limiting his work to private partnerships. The law of public companies is now a distinct matter, and each subject has attained a magnitude which renders its separate treatment desirable. The law of partnerships at common law, as it is established by the latest decisions, will be found concisely stated in these pages. The matter is well arranged and the work is carefully executed."—*Athenæum.*

"It is with considerable gratification that we find the subject treated by a writer of Mr. Dixon's reputation for learning, accuracy and painstaking. Mr. Lindley's view of the subject is that of a philosophical lawyer. Mr. Dixon's is purely and exclusively practical from beginning to end. We imagine that very few questions are likely to come before the practitioner which Mr. Dixon's book will not be found to solve. Having already passed our opinion on the way in which the work is carried out, we have only to add, that the value of the book is very materially increased by an excellent marginal summary and a very copious index."—*Law Magazine and Review.*

GRANT'S LAW OF BANKING.—Second Edition by Fisher.

GRANT'S LAW of BANKERS and BANKING and BANKS of ISSUE, Limited and Chartered, and Winding-up; Directors, Managers and Officers; and the Law as to Cheques, Circular Notes or Letters of Credit, Bank Notes, Exchequer Bills, Coupons, Deposits, &c. (Appendix contains the Bank Notes Issue Bill, and Reasons for Bill, and Official Bank Returns). Second Edition. By R. A. FISHER, Esq., of the Middle Temple, Barrister at Law. 8vo. 21s. cloth.

"The present editor has very much increased the value of the original work, a work whose sterling merits had already raised it to the rank of a standard text-book."—*Law Magazine.*

"No man in the profession was more competent to treat the subject of Banking than Mr. Grant. This volume appears opportunely. To all engaged in the litigations, as well as to all legal advisers of bankers, Mr. Grant's work will be an invaluable assistant. It is a clear and careful treatise on a subject not already exhausted, and it must become *the* text-book upon it."—*Law Times.*

"A Second Edition of Mr. Grant's well-known treatise on this branch of the law has been called for and very ably supplied by Mr. Fisher."—*Law Times, Second Notice.*

"The learning and industry which were so conspicuous in Mr. Grant's former work are equally apparent in this. The book supplies a real want, which has long been felt both by the profession and by the public at large."—*Jurist.*

"We commend this work to our readers. This treatise is at once practical and intelligible, and is of use alike to the unprofessional as well as the professional reader. No bank, whether a private concern or a joint-stock company, should be without it."—*Money Market Review.*

DAVIS'S LAW OF MASTER AND SERVANT.

THE MASTER AND SERVANT ACT, 1867: with an Introduction, Notes and Forms, Tables of Offences, and an Index. By JAMES EDWARD DAVIS, Esq., Barrister at Law, Stipendiary Magistrate for Stoke-upon-Trent. 12mo. 6s. cloth.

"We are glad to see that the question has been treated so ably and carefully as it is in the present volume. Mr. Davis was one of the commissioners whose recommendations led to the passing of the act of last session, so that he is well fitted to point out the scope and general intentions of the statute, while his experience as stipendiary magistrate of Stoke-upon-Trent render his suggestions as to the practice and procedure to be employed in working out its provisions peculiarly valuable."—*Solicitors' Journal.*

"The task that Mr. Davis undertook in editing this new Master and Servant Act has been well performed, and indeed in a manner that probably no one, who did not enjoy the exceptional advantages for the purpose that Mr. Davis does, could have executed so satisfactorily."—*Irish Law Times.*

"With such a manual before them as that of Mr. Davis, magistrates and practitioners will have little difficulty in fully comprehending the law and knowing how to apply it. We therefore recommend this edition to them."—*Gloucester Journal.*

"The edition of the act which Mr. Davis, the stipendiary magistrate at Stoke-upon-Trent, has just published, will prove of great use as a clue to this legislative labyrinth. In this little work so much of the statutes referred to as is required to make the new law intelligible is quoted at full length; and Mr. Davis has also added sundry tables of matters and things within the jurisdiction of justices under the Master and Servant Act which remedy as far as possible the omissions of the measure itself."—*Saturday Review.*

"This will be found a useful little work for all who have occasion to inquire into master and servant laws as affected by the statute of last session. This book is calculated to be especially serviceable to magistrates and justices of the peace, and they undoubtedly will find it very useful. It is written by one of themselves and is therefore likely to be particularly adapted to their wants."—*Law Journal.*

"He has been enabled to present in this volume a lucid interpretation of the recent act; an interpretation, the necessity for which will be appreciated from the fact that the act of 1867 has been based on a number of statutes to which it refers merely in a schedule. This book summarises the state of the law before the passing of the act and points out the changes which have been effected thereby."—*Observer.*

DAVIS'S COUNTY COURTS ACT, 1867.

THE COUNTY COURTS ACT, 1867; and the Provisions of the Common Law Procedure Act, 1854, relating to Discovery, Attachment of Debts and Equitable Defences applied by Order in Council to the County Courts. Edited, with Notes and Introduction and a Chapter on Costs, together with all the New County Court Rules, by JAMES EDWARD DAVIS, Esq., Barrister at Law. Royal 12mo. 12s. cloth.

"This volume contains a preface, an introductory chapter, the act itself, annotated, a chapter on costs, the order in council, all the new rules, forms and orders, &c., and a full index. The principal feature which attracted our attention is the chapter on costs, no other treatise on the act which has yet appeared having dealt with this important subject specifically. It would be unfair to extract, even in an abridged form, this valuable addition to the law literature of the County Courts, and we would recommend our readers to obtain Mr. Davis's volume, even though they already possess any of the treatises published on the new act. The whole work is done in Mr. Davis's usually thorough and efficient manner, and the book is got up in Messrs. Butterworths' best style."—*Law Times.*

"Mr. Davis has good title to come before the public with a book on the new County Courts Act, inasmuch as he has already occupied the ground by his Manual on the Practice and Evidence and other Proceedings in the County Courts, and might feel himself called upon to complete his former treatise by adding what was rendered necessary by the changes of the law; as he justly says, the best way to acquire a thorough knowledge and comprehension of the jurisdiction and practice of the County Courts is, to treat the new law as supplemental to the former law. We may add, that this treatise is arranged very clearly, and the practitioner can in a moment find the information which he may require. The book is admirably printed and there is a good index to the whole volume."—*Law Journal.*

*** *This edition may be used either as an Appendix to the Third Edition of Davis's Practice and Evidence in the County Courts, or as an independent Work.*

DAVIS'S COUNTY COURTS EQUITABLE JURISDICTION.

THE ACT to CONFER on the COUNTY COURTS a LIMITED JURISDICTION in EQUITY, 28 & 29 Vict. cap. 99, with the New Rules, and the Forms and Costs of Proceedings; also Introductory Chapters, copious Notes and a full Index. By JAMES EDWARD DAVIS, Esq., of the Middle Temple, Barrister at Law. Royal 12mo 5s. cloth.

DAVIS'S COUNTY COURTS PRACTICE AND EVIDENCE.—Third Edition.

A MANUAL of the PRACTICE and EVIDENCE in ACTIONS and other PROCEEDINGS in the COUNTY COURTS, including the PRACTICE IN BANKRUPTCY, with an Appendix of Statutes and Rules. By JAMES EDWARD DAVIS, of the Middle Temple, Esq., Barrister at Law. Third Edition, considerably enlarged. One thick volume. Royal 12mo. 28s. cloth.

*** *This is the only Work on the County Courts which gives Forms of Plaints and treats fully of the Law and Evidence in Actions and other Proceedings in these Courts.*

"Mr. Davis succeeded in easily establishing his work as *the* Practice of the County Courts, and in maintaining the position he had won. All who have used it speak well of it. They say they can readily find what they want, and, better still, it contains the information they want, which cannot be said of all books of practice, whose error it often is, that the writers assume too much knowledge on the part of their readers, and omit instructions in common things. This has been Mr. Davis's design in his *Practice of the County Courts*, and three editions prove with what success he has accomplished that design. There is another feature of this work. Besides the practice, it contains a complete treatise on evidence in the County Courts, after the manner of Selwyn's Nisi Prius. Each of the subjects of litigation ordinarily brought before the courts is separately treated, and the law minutely stated, with the evidence required to sustain or to defend the action. Thus, all that can be wanted in court is contained under one cover, greatly to the saving of time and temper in laborious search.

"It is undoubtedly the best book on the Practice of the County Courts, and the appearance of a third edition proves that such is the opinion of the Profession."—*Law Times*.

"This is the third edition of a text-book which is well known in both branches of the Legal Profession. From a small beginning it has gradually grown into a bulky volume of 829 pages, and now contains an inexhaustive exposition of the Law and Practice relating to the County Courts. The second part of this manual contains a valuable digest of the Law of Evidence, as applicable to the Procedure of the County Courts. In this particular it certainly excels all the other text-books on the subject. The importance of this part of the work cannot be too highly estimated. The chapters on the County Court Practice in Bankruptcy display the usual care and ability of the author, and give a completeness to a work which has hitherto been deservedly popular in the Profession."—*Law Magazine*.

"This is a greatly enlarged edition of Davis's County Court Practice, a work well enough known to need no introduction to the legal public, or at any rate to that portion thereof which is concerned with proceedings in the County Courts. The edition before us follows in its main features the second edition of the book, but it is to that second edition as the full-blown rose to the bud, not merely in quantity but in quality. We can safely and heartily recommend the book for the perusal of all intending practitioners in any County Court."—*Solicitors' Journal*.

BARRY'S PRACTICE OF CONVEYANCING.

A TREATISE on the PRACTICE of CONVEYANCING. By W. WHITTAKER BARRY, Esq., of Lincoln's Inn, Barrister-at-Law, late holder of the Studentship of the Inns of Court, and Author of "The Statutory Jurisdiction of the Court of Chancery." 8vo. 18s. cloth.

CONTENTS.

CHAP. 1. Abstracts of Title.—CHAP. 2. Agreements.—CHAP. 3. Particulars and Conditions of Sale.—CHAP. 4. Copyholds.—CHAP. 5. Covenants—CHAP. 6. Creditors' Deeds and Arrangements.—CHAP. 7. Preparation of Deeds.—CHAP. 8. On Evidence.—CHAP. 9. Leases.—CHAP. 10. Mortgages.—CHAP. 11. Partnership Deeds and Arrangements.—CHAP. 12. Sales and Purchases.—CHAP. 13. Settlements.—CHAP. 14. Wills.—CHAP. 15. The Land Registry Act, 25 & 26 Vict. c. 53.—CHAP. 16. The Act for obtaining a Declaration of Title, 25 & 26 Vict. c. 67.—INDEX.

"This treatise supplies a want which has long been felt. There has been no treatise on the practice of conveyancing issued for a long time past that is adequate for the present requirements. Mr. Barry's work is essentially what it professes to be, a treatise on the practice of conveyancing, in which the theoretical rules of real property law are referred to only for the purpose of elucidating the practice. The opening chapter on abstracts is a very good one, and goes at once in medias res, discussing the very centre of practical difficulties, the preparation of abstracts. The solicitor will find in this chapter a very excellent collection of useful suggestions. The chapter on particulars and conditions of sale is written in Mr. Barry's happiest tone. His observations on copyholds are very judicious and useful. The chapter on leases abounds with excellent suggestions, which are the more valuable as good precedents for leases are as rare as good precedents for agreements. After treating of partnership deeds and arrangements, and sales and purchases, Mr. Barry gives an excellent chapter on settlements. Mr. Barry appears to have a very accurate insight into the practice in every department of our real property system. Although we cannot boast, like Duval, of having ever read abstracts of title with pleasure, we have certainly read Mr. Barry's chapter on abstracts, and numerous other parts of his work, with very considerable satisfaction, on account of the learning, great familiarity with practice, and power of exposition of its author. The treatise, although capable of compression, is the production of a person of great merit and still greater promise."—*Solicitors' Journal.*

"The author of this valuable treatise on conveyancing has most wisely devoted a considerable part of his work to the practical illustration of the working of the recent Statutes on Registration of Title, and for this as well as for other reasons we feel bound to strongly recommend it to the practitioner as well as the student. The author has proved himself to be a master of the subject, for he not only gives a most valuable supply of practical suggestions, but criticises them with much ability, and we have no doubt that his criticism will meet with general approval."—*Law Magazine.*

"Readers who recal the instruction they gathered from this treatise when published week by week in the pages of the 'Law Times' will be pleased to learn that it has been re-produced in a handsome volume, which will be a welcome addition to the law library. It will be remembered that the papers so contributed by Mr. Barry were remarkable for the precision with which the law was stated. A work, the substance of which is so well known to our readers, needs no recommendation from us, for its merits are patent to all, from personal acquaintance with them. The information that the treatise so much admired may now be had in the more convenient form of a book will suffice of itself to secure a large and eager demand for it."—*Law Times.*

"The work is clearly and agreeably written, and ably elucidates the subject in hand."—*Justice of the Peace.*

"We must content ourselves with the

Barry's Practice of Conveyancing—*continued.*

statement that the present is a work of very great ability. There is no modern work which deals with precisely the same subject, and we have no doubt whatever that this will prove a book of very great value both to the practitioner and to the student at law."—*Athenæum.*

"The reader will not be in doubt in Mr. Barry's work. He has given the student an introduction to the practice of conveyancing, such as Mr. Joshua Williams has written with reference to the principles of the law of real property. Of course he travels in great part over the same ground as the more elaborate treatises on the law of vendors and purchasers, and we think he discriminates between leading cases and the refinements upon them very happily. His book is not a mere book of reference, but can be read profitably as a treatise."—*Spectator.*

TUDOR'S LEADING CASES ON REAL PROPERTY.
Second Edition.

A SELECTION of LEADING CASES on the LAW relating to REAL PROPERTY, CONVEYANCING, and the CONSTRUCTION of WILLS and DEEDS; with Notes. By OWEN DAVIES TUDOR, Esq., of the Middle Temple, Barrister at Law, Author of "Leading Cases in Equity." Second Edition. One thick vol., royal 8vo., 42s. cloth.

"The Second Edition is now before us, and we are able to say that the same extensive knowledge and the same laborious industry as have been exhibited by Mr. Tudor on former occasions characterize this later production of his legal authorship; and it is enough at this moment to reiterate an opinion that Mr. Tudor has well maintained the high legal reputation which his standard works have achieved in all countries where the English language is spoken, and the decisions of our Courts are quoted."—*Law Magazine and Review.*

"The work before us comprises a digest of decisions which, if not exhaustive of all the principles of our real property code, will at least be found to leave nothing untouched or unelaborated under the numerous legal doctrines to which the cases severally relate. To Mr. Tudor's treatment of all these subjects, so complicated and so varied, we accord our entire commendation. There are no omissions of any important cases relative to the various branches of the law comprised in the work, nor are there any omissions or defects in his statement of the law itself applicable to the cases discussed by him. We cordially recommend the work to the practitioner and student alike, but especially to the former."—*Solicitors' Journal and Reporter.*

"In this new edition, Mr. Tudor has carefully revised his notes in accordance with subsequent decisions that have modified or extended the law as previously expounded. This and the other volumes of Mr. Tudor are almost a law library in themselves, and we are satisfied that the student would learn more law from the careful reading of them, than he would acquire from double the time given to the elaborate treatises which learned professors recommend the student to peruse, with entire forgetfulness that time and brains are limited, and that to do what they advise would be the work of a life."—*Law Times.*

"This well-known work needs no recommendation. Justice, however, to Mr. Tudor requires us to say that familiarity with its pages from its first appearance have convinced us of its value, not only as a repertory of cases, but a judicious summary of the law on the subjects it treats of. So far as we can see, the author has brought down the cases to the latest period, and altogether there have been added about 170 pages of notes in the present edition. As a guide to the present law the book will now be of great value to the lawyer, and it will be especially useful to him when away from a large library."—*Jurist.*

GOLDSMITH'S EQUITY.—Fifth Edition.

THE DOCTRINE and PRACTICE of EQUITY: or, a Concise Outline of Proceedings in the High Court of Chancery. Designed principally for the Use of Students. By GEORGE GOLDSMITH, Esq., M.A., Barrister-at-Law. Fifth Edition, including all the alterations made in pursuance of the late Acts, and the Orders thereon to the present time. Post 8vo. 16s. cloth.

"This book has been written expressly for the use of students. For the ordinary pass examination candidates for the bar have usually been examined by the reader on equity upon Smith's 'Manual of Equity Jurisprudence,' and the 'Elementary View of the Proceedings in a Suit in Equity' by Mr. Hunter. Both are useful text books; the one containing a compendious statement of principles and the other a general outline of practice. The excellences of each appear to be successfully combined in Mr. Goldsmith's treatise. Though professedly an elementary work, its merits are greater than its pretensions. Professing to accomplish a limited task, that task has been well done. We cordially recommend Mr. Goldsmith's treatise to those for whom it was designed."—*Law Magazine and Review.*

"A volume designed for the law student. But when we say this, we do not mean that it is fitted for law students only; we purpose only thus to distinguish it from a 'Practice.' Every lawyer knows that he needs for reading a very different sort of book from that required in practice. But it does not follow that the former class of books should be thrown aside the moment the student becomes a lawyer. In the first place, it is not probable that, during his studentship, he will have mastered the entire science of law, or even learned all its principles; and he should never cease to read treatises until he has acquired them. Even if his industry and capacity have been so great as to enable him to master so much, he will find frequent need to refresh his memory. His law will soon grow rusty if he does not sometimes rub it up by reference to the books that teach it systematically. Hence such a volume as Mr. Goldsmith has published is a perennial, and while addressed principally to the student, it may be profitably read by the practitioner. Five editions attest the approval of those who have experienced the benefit of its instructions. It has grown in bulk with each successive appearance, as Mr. Goldsmith discovered what were the wants of his readers; and a continued succession of new topics has been added. It is now an extremely comprehensive sketch of the history, jurisdiction and practice of our Courts of Equity—a summary of what could be obtained only by hard reading of Reeve and Spence and Ayckbourn and Drewry. It commences with an historical outline; then it states the principles of equity jurisprudence; then it shows their application to the various subject-matters that fall within its jurisdictions; and, finally, it presents a clear and very instructive sketch of the procedure by which those jurisdictions are enforced."—*Law Times.*

"It contains a great deal of miscellaneous information, and if a student were confined to the selection of one book on equity, both for its doctrine and practice, he could hardly do better than choose the one before us."—*Solicitors' Journal.*

KERR'S ACTION AT LAW.—Third Edition.

An ACTION at LAW: being an outline of the JURISDICTION of the SUPERIOR COURTS of COMMON LAW, with an Elementary View of the Proceedings in Actions therein. By ROBERT MALCOLM KERR, LL.D., Barrister at Law; now Judge of the Sheriff's Court of the City of London. The Third Edition. 12mo. 13s. cloth.

"There is considerable merit in both works (John William Smith's and Malcolm Kerr's); but the second (Kerr by Bassett Smith) has rather the advantage, in being more recent, and published since the Common Law Procedure Act, 1860.'—*Jurist.*

"Mr. Kerr's book is more full and detailed than that of Mr. John William Smith, and is therefore better adapted for those who desire to obtain not merely a general notion but also a practical acquaintance with Common Law Procedure."—*Solicitors' Journal.*

"This is just the book to put into a Student's hand when he enters the legal profession. We have had occasion more than once to recommend it to the notice of our junior brethren."—*Legulcian.*

"Mr. Bassett Smith has proved himself very competent for the office. As a third edition the volume needs no description and permits no criticism. Enough to say that its present appearance will amply sustain the reputation it had already acquired."—*Law Times.*

MESSRS. BUTTERWORTH, 7, FLEET STREET, E.C. 15

TROWER'S CHURCH BUILDING LAWS.

THE LAW of the BUILDING of CHURCHES, PARSONAGES, and SCHOOLS, and of the Division of Parishes and Places. By CHARLES FRANCIS TROWER, M.A., of the Inner Temple, Esq., Barrister at Law, late Fellow of Exeter College, Oxford, and late Secretary of Presentations to Lord Chancellor Westbury. Post 8vo. 8s. cloth.

"A good book on this subject is calculated to be of considerable service both to lawyers, clerics and laymen; and on the whole, after taking a survey of the work before us, we may pronounce it a useful work. It contains a great mass of information of essential import to those who as parishioners, legal advisers or clergymen are concerned with glebes, endowments, district chapelries, parishes, ecclesiastical commissions and such like matters, about which the public and notably the clerical public seem to know but little, but which it is needless to say are matters of much importance."—*Solicitors' Journal.*

"The questions discussed make the work a most valuable legal guide to the clergy. Mr. Trower proposes by this volume to assist the clergy and the lawyers in their dealing with these subjects. His book is just the one we could wish every clergyman to possess, for if it was in the hands of our readers they would be saved the trouble of asking us very many questions."—*Clerical Journal.*

"Mr. Trower brings his professional research to the rescue. In a well arranged volume this gentleman points out concisely and intelligibly how the difficulties which usually beset parties in such matters may be avoided."—*Oxford University Herald.*

"The learned author of this lucid volume has done his best to summarise the several Acts of Parliament that bear upon Ecclesiastical Structures and to explain their meaning. On all the topics germane to its title this volume will be found a handy-book of ecclesiastical law, and should on that account be made widely known among the clergy. The production is worthy of its author, and will we hope shortly establish itself in the good esteem of the clerical and general public."—*Church Mail.*

"Mr. Trower aims very successfully at giving a complete account of the present state of the law, and rendering it as nearly as possible intelligible, and we hope that it may prove useful to all church building clergy and laity. It is a compact and handy treatise, very clearly written, well arranged, easy of reference, and besides a good table of contents it has an elaborate index. It is a book we are glad to have and to recommend."—*Literary Churchman.*

CHITTY, JUN., PRECEDENTS IN PLEADING.—3rd Edition.

CHITTY, JUN., PRECEDENTS in PLEADING; with copious Notes on Practice, Pleading and Evidence, by the late JOSEPH CHITTY, Jun., Esq. Third Edition. By the late TOMPSON CHITTY, Esq., and by LEOFRIC TEMPLE and R. G. WILLIAMS, Esqrs., Barristers at Law. Part I. Royal 8vo. 20s. cloth. (*Part II. is in Preparation.*)

"To enter into detailed criticism and praise of this standard work would be quite out of place. In the present instance the matter has fallen into competent hands, who have spared no pains. This valuable and useful work is brought done to the present time, altered in accordance with the cases and statutes now in force. Great care has been expended by the competent editors, and its usefulness, as heretofore, will be found not to be confined to the chambers of the special pleader, but to be of a more extended character. To those who knew the work of old no recommendation is wanted, to those younger members of the profession who have not that privilege we would suggest that they should at once make its acquaintance."—*Law Journal.*

"A book almost as well known to the profession as 'Tidd' was has been republished, we might almost say rewritten, and adapted to the requirements of modern pleading. Few there are for whom assistance will not be found by reference to these pages, which serve yet another useful purpose, by helping the lawyer to pick holes in his adversary's pleadings, as well as properly to frame his own. Nor is the volume useful in the superior courts only; practitioners in the county courts will find it a valuable adviser in the preparation of pleadings, such as they are."—*Law Times.*

"The value of this practical work has greatly increased in the practical hands of the editors. It is framed solely with the view of being a safe and ready guide for the practitioner in the art of pleading. The notes are concise and suggestive, and almost every precedent is accompanied by a list of the cases supporting it. The precedents themselves give abundant proof of the learning and care that have been devoted to them. We hope that the remainder will soon be published. When it is finished the work will, without doubt, be the best and most complete work on pleading in our libraries."—*Law Magazine.*

CHRISTIE'S CRABB'S CONVEYANCING.—Fifth Edition, by Shelford.

CRABB'S COMPLETE SERIES of PRECEDENTS in CONVEYANCING and of COMMON and COMMERCIAL FORMS in Alphabetical Order, adapted to the Present State of the Law and the Practice of Conveyancing; with copious Prefaces, Observations and Notes on the several Deeds. By J. T. CHRISTIE, Esq., Barrister-at-Law. The Fifth Edition, with numerous Corrections and Additions, by LEONARD SHELFORD, Esq., of the Middle Temple, Barrister-at-Law. Two vols. royal 8vo, 3*l*. cloth.

"In carefulness we have in him a second Crabb, in erudition Crabb's superior; and the result is a work of which the original author would have been proud, could it have appeared under his own auspices. It is not a book to be quoted, nor indeed could its merits be exhibited by quotation. It is essentially a book of practice, which can only be described in rude outline and dismissed with applause, and a recommendation of it to the notice of those for whose service it has been so laboriously compiled."—*Law Times.*

"Mr. Shelford has proved himself in this task to be not unworthy of his former reputation. To those familiar with his other works it will be a sufficient recommendation of this work that Mr. Shelford's name appears on the title-page; if there be any who are not well acquainted with them, we venture to recommend to such the work before us, as the most generally useful and convenient collection of precedents in conveyancing, and of commercial forms for ordinary use, which are to be had in the English language."—*Solicitors' Journal and Reporter.*

"Those who have been in the habit of using Crabb's work will allow that his 'Prefaces' contain practical observations of considerable utility to the professional man. The flow of time carrying with it many changes, and some reforms in the law relative to conveyancing, have imposed the obligation upon Mr. Shelford of carefully revising all, and in many instances has rendered it expedient for him to re-write not a small portion of some of these Prefaces. Mr. Shelford has also had to exercise, and we doubt not with correct judgment has exercised, his discretion as to where he should reject Forms which he deemed it advisable to omit, and where he should revise them or introduce new ones, to meet the modern exigencies and characteristics of conveyancing. To this important part of his duty—the remodelling and perfecting of the Forms—even with the examination which we have already been able to afford this work, we are able to affirm, that the learned editor has been eminently successful and effected valuable improvements."—*Law Magazine and Review.*

"It possesses one distinctive feature in devoting more attention than usual in such works to forms of a commercial nature. We are satisfied from an examination of the present with the immediately preceding edition that Mr. Shelford has very considerably improved the character of the work, both in the prefaces and in the forms. The two volumes contain several hundred pages of additional matter, and both the latest cases and decisions appear to be noticed in the prefaces. Indeed it is evident that Mr. Shelford has modernised the whole work, and thus given it an additional value. On the whole the two volumes of Crabb's Precedents, as edited by Mr. Leonard Shelford, will be found extremely useful in a solicitor's office, presenting a large amount of real property learning, with very numerous precedents: indeed we know of no book so justly entitled to the appellation of 'handy' as the fifth edition of Mr. Crabb's Precedents."—*Law Chronicle.*

LATHAM ON THE LAW OF WINDOW LIGHTS.

A TREATISE on the LAW of WINDOW LIGHTS. By FRANCIS LAW LATHAM, of the Inner Temple, Esq., Barrister at Law. Post 8vo. 10s. cloth.

"This is not merely a valuable addition to the law library of the practitioner, it is a book that every law student will read with profit. It exhausts the subject of which it treats."—*Law Times.*

"His arrangement is logical and he discusses fully each point of his subject. The work in our opinion is both perspicuous and able, and we cannot be complimentary to the author on it"—*Law Journal.*

"A treatise on this subject was wanted, and Mr. Latham has succeeded in meeting that want."—*Athenæum.*

BROWNING'S DIVORCE AND MATRIMONIAL PRACTICE.

THE PRACTICE and PROCEDURE of the COURT for DIVORCE AND MATRIMONIAL CAUSES, including the Acts, Rules, Orders, Copious Notes of Cases and Forms of Practical Proceedings, with Tables of Costs. By W. ERNST BROWNING, Esq., of the Inner Temple, Barrister-at-law. Post 8vo. 8s. cloth.

"Mr. Browning's little volume will doubtless become *the* practice of the Divorce Court."—*Law Times*.

"The time has come for a matrimonial Chitty's Archbold. Whether Mr. Browning has taken the great guide to practice in the common law courts for his model, or not, we cannot say; but, if he is an imitator, he has copied with success. Clearness of arrangement and statement, and brevity, are the most apparent merits of his book. It is therefore easy to consult and bears throughout a thoroughly practical air. If the future editions are edited with the same care and ability that have been bestowed upon this, it will probably take its place as *the* Practice of the Divorce Court."—*Jurist*.

"Mr. Browning confines himself almost wholly to the practice and procedure, although his book contains a good deal of information on the *law* of divorce. He appears to have diligently collated the reported cases, which he states with precision and clearness. This little work is therefore calculated to be useful to those who practise before Sir C. Cresswell. The appendix of forms will be particularly serviceable to the inexperienced; and, since we have alluded to the appendix, we ought not to omit noticing the very useful precedents of bills of costs which it contains. These alone are sufficient to obtain a good circulation for this manual."—*Solicitors' Journal*.

"A work of very considerable merit and great practical utility, and we have in this work what the lawyer and the practitioner require. We have the principles of law clearly and perspicuously enunciated and most copiously verified. The various subjects are methodically distributed, and the style is polished and agreeable. All the forms now in use, and taxed bills of costs, are also appended to the work. After careful study of this work, we unhesitatingly recommend it as well to the student as to the legal practitioner."—*Law Magazine and Review*.

"The author has set to work to supply a want in a proper spirit—and tells us simply what the practice of the court now is, without inquiring what it should be. The forms in the Appendix, we are assured, have been used in practice. The arrangement is good, and the whole work has an unpretending business-like air about it which will recommend it to the profession."—*Athenæum*.

CHADWICK'S PROBATE COURT MANUAL.

EXAMPLES of ADMINISTRATION BONDS for the COURT of PROBATE; exhibiting the principle of various Grants of Administration, and the correct mode of preparing the Bonds in respect thereof; also Directions for preparing the Oaths; arranged for practical utility. With Extracts from Statutes; also various Forms of Affirmation prescribed by Acts of Parliament, and a Supplemental Notice, bringing the Work down to 1865. By SAMUEL CHADWICK, of Her Majesty's Court of Probate. Royal 8vo. 12s. cloth.

"We undertake to say that the possession of this volume by practitioners will prevent many a hitch and awkward delay, provoking to the lawyer himself and difficult to be satisfactorily explained to the clients."—*Law Magazine and Review*.

"The work is principally designed to save the profession the necessity of obtaining at the registries information as to the preparing or filling up of bonds, and to prevent grants of administration and administration with the will annexed being delayed on account of the defective filling up of such instruments."—*Solicitors' Journal*.

"Mr. Chadwick's volume will be a necessary part of the law library of the practitioner, for he has collected precedents that are in constant requirement. This is purely a book of practice, but therefore the more valuable. It tells the reader what *to do*, and that is the information most required after a lawyer begins to practise."—*Law Times*.

HUNTER'S SUIT IN EQUITY.—Fourth Edition.

AN ELEMENTARY VIEW of the PROCEEDINGS IN A SUIT IN EQUITY. With an Appendix of Forms. By SYLVESTER J. HUNTER, B.A., of Lincoln's Inn, Barrister at Law. Fourth Edition, by G. W. LAWRANCE, M.A., of Lincoln's Inn, Barrister at Law. Post 8vo. 10s. cloth.

"It is now ten years since Mr. Hunter's modest and unpretending volume first saw the light, and few we imagine have been the students of equity practice during those years who have not been indebted to its pages for their first initiation into the mysteries of the Court of Chancery. Within the compass of three hundred pages the reader (as far as is possible without the result of practical experience) may obtain an accurate idea of the various incidental proceedings leading up to and following the decree, while the several stages of the suit are all carefully illustrated by forms referred to in the text and collected together in an appendix at the end of the volume. We will only add that we are glad to find this little work is in such good hands, and while it continues to receive from time to time Mr. Lawrance's careful revision, we venture to predict for it a long-lived success and many future editions."—*Law Journal.*

"An outline, after this fashion, of a suit in equity is contained in Mr. Hunter's little volume, and that it has been found to perform its promise is proved by its arrival at a fourth edition. Mr. Lawrance has added a chapter on the equitable jurisdiction of the county courts."—*Law Times.*

"This book has now maintained for so long a time the position of a standard manual for the use of law students that there is little for us to say respecting its general scope. The work is intended for beginners, and the design is excellently carried out. Everything is there which ought to be placed before the learner, and yet the book is not encumbered with references and details which would serve merely to embarrass him; the arrangement is also very clear. Since the issue of the first edition in 1858, two successive editions besides the present have been prepared by Mr. Lawrance. the present editor, a sufficient guarantee that the book has answered the purpose for which it was intended."—*Solicitors' Journal.*

"A fourth edition attests the confidence of the Profession, especially the junior branch of it, in Mr. Hunter's Suit in Equity. As a rule a work to pass into further editions must have real merit. This merit Mr. Hunter's work contains. The style in which it is written is singularly clear and attractive for a book of practice, which is no doubt the cause of its acquiring and retaining the pre-eminence it possesses amongst books of its class."—*Law Examination Reporter.*

SIR T. E. MAY'S PARLIAMENTARY PRACTICE.—6th Edit.

A PRACTICAL TREATISE on the LAW, PRIVILEGES, PROCEEDINGS and USAGE of PARLIAMENT. By Sir THOMAS ERSKINE MAY, K.C.B., of the Middle Temple, Barrister at Law, Clerk Assistant of the House of Commons. Sixth Edition, Revised and Enlarged. One very thick vol. 8vo.

(*In active preparation.*)

CONTENTS:—Book I. Constitution, Powers and Privileges of Parliament.—Book II. Practice and Proceedings in Parliament.—Book III. The Manner of passing Private Bills, with the Standing Orders in both Houses, and the most recent Precedents.

ROUSE'S PRACTICAL CONVEYANCER.

Third Edition.

The PRACTICAL CONVEYANCER, giving, in a mode combining facility of reference with general utility, upwards of Four Hundred Precedents of Conveyances, Mortgages and Leases, Settlements, and Miscellaneous Forms, with (not in previous Editions) the Law and numerous Outline Forms and Clauses of WILLS and Abstracts of Statutes affecting Real Property, Conveyancing Memoranda, &c. By ROLLA ROUSE, Esq, of the Middle Temple, Barrister at Law, Author of "The Practical Man," &c. Third Edition, greatly enlarged. Two vols. 8vo. 30s. cloth.

"The best test of the value of a book written professedly for practical men is the practical one of the number of editions through which it passes. The fact that this well-known work has now reached its third shows that it is considered by those for whose convenience it was written to fulfill its purpose well."—*Law Magazine*.

"This is the third edition in ten years, a proof that practitioners have used and approved the precedents collected by Mr. Rouse. In this edition, which is greatly enlarged, he has for the first time introduced Precedents of Wills, extending to no less than 116 pages. We can accord unmingled praise to the conveyancing memoranda showing the practical effect of the various statutory provisions in the different parts of a deed. If the two preceding editions have been so well received, the welcome given to this one by the profession will be heartier still."—*Law Times*.

"So far as a careful perusal of Mr. Rouse's book enables us to judge of its merits, we think that as a collection of precedents of general utility in cases of common occurrence it will be found satisfactorily to stand the application of the test. The draftsman will find in the Practical Conveyancer precedents appropriate to all instruments of common occurrence, and the collection appears to be especially well supplied with those which relate to copyhold estates. In order to avoid useless repetition and also to make the precedents as simple as possible, Mr. Rouse has sketched out a number of outline drafts so as to present to the reader a sort of bird's-eye view of each instrument and show him its form at a glance. Each paragraph in these outline forms refers, by distinguishing letters and numbers, to the clauses in full required to be inserted in the respective parts of the instrument, and which are given in a subsequent part of the work, and thus every precedent in outline is made of itself an index to the clauses which are necessary to complete the draft. In order still further to simplify the arrangement of the work, the author has adopted a plan (which seems to us fully to answer its purpose) of giving the variations which may occur in any instrument according to the natural order of its different parts."—*Law Journal*.

"That the work has found favor is proved by the fact of our now having to review a third edition. This method of skeleton precedents appears to us to be attended with important advantages. Space is of course saved, but besides this there is the still more important consideration that the draftsman is materially assisted to a bird's-eye view of his draft. Everyone who has done much conveyancing work knows how thoroughly important, nay, how essential to success, is the formation of a clear idea of the scope and framework of the instrument to be produced. To clerks and other young hands a course of conveyancing under Mr. Rouse's auspices is, we think, calculated to prove very instructive. To the solicitor, especially the country practitioner, who has often to set his clerks to work upon drafts of no particular difficulty to the experienced practitioner, but upon which they the said clerks are not to be quite trusted alone, we think to such gentlemen Mr. Rouse's collection of Precedents is calculated to prove extremely serviceable. We repeat, in conclusion, that solicitors, especially those practising in the country, will find this a useful work."—*Solicitors' Journal*.

BRANDON'S PRACTICE OF THE MAYOR'S COURT.

NOTES of PRACTICE of the MAYOR'S COURT of the CITY of LONDON in ORDINARY ACTIONS: with the Mayor's Court Procedure Act, and the Sections of the several Acts of Parliament applied by the Queen in Council to that Court. By WOODTHORPE BRANDON, Esq., of the Middle Temple, Barrister at Law. 8vo. 9s. cloth.

BRANDON'S LAW OF FOREIGN ATTACHMENT.

A TREATISE upon the CUSTOMARY LAW of FOREIGN ATTACHMENT, and the PRACTICE of the MAYOR'S COURT of the CITY OF LONDON therein. With Forms of Procedure By WOODTHORPE BRANDON, Esq., of the Middle Temple, Barrister-at-Law. 8vo. 14s. cloth.

MOSELEY ON CONTRABAND OF WAR.

WHAT IS CONTRABAND OF WAR AND WHAT IS NOT. A Treatise comprising all the American and English Authorities on the Subject. By JOSEPH MOSELEY, Esq., B.C.L., Barrister at Law. Post 8vo. 5s. cloth.

"This manual will be found to be of considerable practical value, inasmuch as it seems to be sufficiently exhaustive of the branch of the maritime public law of which it treats. We think this manual, which contains a good table of contents, will be found to possess practical merit, and seldom to necessitate a reference to the more learned authorities."—*Law Magazine and Review.*

SMITH'S BAR EDUCATION.

A HISTORY of EDUCATION for the ENGLISH BAR, with SUGGESTIONS as to SUBJECTS and METHODS of STUDY. By PHILIP ANSTIE SMITH, Esq., M.A., LL.B., Barrister at Law. 8vo., 9s. cloth.

"This work is one of great interest in the present day. It evidently emanates from the pen of a thoughtful man."—*Law Magazine.*

DAVIS'S CRIMINAL LAW CONSOLIDATION ACTS.

THE CRIMINAL LAW CONSOLIDATION ACTS, 1861; with an Introduction and practical Notes, illustrated by a copious reference to Cases decided by the Court of Criminal Appeal. Together with alphabetical Tables of Offences, as well those punishable upon Summary Conviction as upon Indictment, and including the Offences under the New Bankruptcy Act, so arranged as to present at one view the particular Offence, the Old or New Statute upon which it is founded, and the Limits of Punishment; and a full Index. By JAMES EDWARD DAVIS, Esq., Barrister-at-Law. 12mo. 10s. cloth.

MESSRS. BUTTERWORTH, 7, FLEET STREET, E.C.

POWELL'S LAW OF INLAND CARRIERS.—Second Edition.

THE LAW OF INLAND CARRIERS, especially as regulated by the Railway and Canal Traffic Act, 1854. By EDMUND POWELL, Esq., of Lincoln College, Oxon, M.A., and of the Western Circuit, Barrister at Law. Author of " Principles and Practice of the Law of Evidence." Second Edition, almost re-written. 8vo. 14s. cloth.

" The treatise before us states the law of which it treats ably and clearly, and contains a good index."—*Solicitors' Journal.*
" Mr. Powell's writing is singularly precise and condensed, without being at all dry, as those who have read his admirable book of Evidence will attest. It will be seen, from our outline of the contents, how exhaustively the subject has been treated, and that it is entitled to be that which it aspires to become, the text book on the law of Carriers."—*Law Times.*
" The subject of this treatise is not indeed a large one, but it has been got up by Mr. Powell with considerable care, and contains ample notice of the most recent cases and authorities."—*Jurist.*
" The two chapters on the Railway and Canal Traffic Act, 1854, are quite new, and the recent cases under the provisions of that statute are analyzed in lucid language."—*Law Magazine.*

WOOLRYCH ON SEWERS.—Third Edition.

A TREATISE on the LAW OF SEWERS, including the Drainage Acts. By HUMPHRY W. WOOLRYCH, Serjeant at Law. Third Edition, with considerable Additions and Alterations. 8vo. 12s. cloth.

" Two editions of it have been speedily exhausted, and a third called for. The author is an accepted authority on all subjects of this class."—*Law Times.*
" This is a third and greatly enlarged edition of a book which has already obtained an established reputation as the most complete discussion of the subject adapted to modern times. Since the treatise of Mr. Serjeant Callis in the early part of the 17th century, no work filling the same place has been added to the literature of the profession. It is a work of no slight labour to digest and arrange this mass of legislation—this task, however, Mr. Serjeant Woolrych has undertaken, and an examination of his book will, we think, convince the most exacting that he has fully succeeded. No one should attempt to meddle with the Law of Sewers without its help."—*Solicitors' Journal.*

SMITH'S PRACTICE OF CONVEYANCING.

An ELEMENTARY VIEW of the PRACTICE of CONVEYANCING in SOLICITORS' OFFICES, with an Outline of the Proceedings under the Transfer of Land and Declaration of Title Acts, 1862, for the use of Articled Clerks. By EDMUND SMITH, B.A., late of Pembroke Coll. Cambridge, Attorney and Solicitor. Post 8vo 6s. cloth.

" This little work will be found very useful to beginners in Conveyancing. The writer has the moral courage to commence at the very beginning, and to avoid a parade of learning which would be entirely useless to articled clerks in their noviciate. The account given by him of the proceedings in solicitors' offices, in purchases, sales, mortgages, leases, settlements and wills, is very simple and intelligible, while at the same time it is so accurate and complete that even old practitioners may read it with advantage. It is on the whole a highly creditable performance for a country solicitor."—*Solicitors' Journal and Reporter.*

PETERSDORFF'S ABRIDGMENT OF THE COMMON LAW.
New Edition.
Now complete in 6 vols.   Royal 8vo. 7*l.* 7*s.* cloth.

A CONCISE PRACTICAL ABRIDGMENT of the COMMON AND STATUTE LAW, as at present administered in the Common Law, Probate, Divorce and Admiralty Courts, excluding all that is obsolete, overruled or superseded : comprising a Series of Condensed Treatises on the different Branches of the Law, with detailed Directions, Forms and Precedents; an Alphabetical Dictionary of Technical Law Terms and Maxims, and a Collection of Words that have received a Special Judicial Construction ; the whole illustrated by References to the principal Cases in Equity, and in the Scotch, American and Irish Reports, and the most eminent text writers.   By CHARLES PETERSDORFF, Serjeant-at-Law, assisted by CHARLES W. WOOD, Esq., and WALKER MARSHALL, Esq., Barristers-at-Law.

" Mr. Serjeant Petersdorff has brought to a close his labours upon this great and useful work. It is a complete dictionary of the law as it exists at the present day, and is also an index to every law library. We noticed the plan and object of this work at some length on the completion of the first volume. Now that the sixth has been published, we have nothing to add except that the execution seems to be in the best style of this laborious jurist and professional writer."—*Times.*

SHELFORD'S SUCCESSION DUTIES.—Second Edition.

THE LAW relating to the PROBATE, LEGACY and SUCCESSION DUTIES in ENGLAND, IRELAND and SCOTLAND, including all the Statutes and the Decisions on those Subjects: with Forms and Official Regulations. By LEONARD SHELFORD, Esq., of the Middle Temple, Barrister at Law. The Second Edition, with many Alterations and Additions. 12mo. 16*s.* cloth.

"The treatise before us, one of the most useful and popular of his productions, being now the text book on the subject, nothing remains but to make known its appearance to our readers. Its merits have been already tested by most of them."—*Law Times.*
" Mr. Shelford's book appears to us to be the best and most complete work on this extremely intricate subject."—*Law Magazine.*

SHELFORD ON THE LAW OF RAILWAYS.—Third Edition.

THE LAW of RAILWAYS, including the Three General Consolidation Acts, 1845, and the other General Acts for regulating Railways in England and Ireland, with copious Notes of Decided Cases on their Construction, including the Rights and Liabilities of Shareholders, Allottees of Shares, and Provisional Committee-men, with Forms, &c. By LEONARD SHELFORD, Esq., of the Middle Temple, Barrister at Law. Third Edition. Royal 12mo. 30*s.* cloth.

POWELL ON EVIDENCE.—Third Edition by Cutler and Griffin.

THE PRINCIPLES and PRACTICE of the LAW of EVIDENCE. By EDMUND POWELL, M.A., Barrister-at-Law. Third Edition, by JOHN CUTLER, B.A., of Lincoln's Inn, Barrister-at Law, Professor of English Law and Jurisprudence, and Professor of Indian Jurisprudence at King's College, London, and EDMUND FULLER GRIFFIN, B.A., of Lincoln's Inn, Barrister-at-Law. 12mo. 15s. cloth.

TUDOR'S CHARITABLE TRUSTS.—Second Edition.

THE LAW of CHARITABLE TRUSTS; with the Statutes, including those of 1862, the Orders, Regulations and Instructions issued pursuant thereto, and a Selection of Schemes, with Notes. By OWEN DAVIES TUDOR, Esq., of the Middle Temple, Barrister-at-Law, Author of 'Leading Cases in Equity.' Second Edition, containing all the recent Statutes and Decisions. Post 8vo. 18s. cloth.

" Mr. Tudor in the present edition of his work has struck out beyond his original intention, and has made it a complete compendium of the law of charities. In carrying out this intention his object appears to have been to produce a practical and concise summary of this branch of the law. No living writer is more capable than Mr. Tudor of producing such a work: his Leading Cases in Equity, and also on the Law of Real Property, have deservedly earned for him the highest reputation as a learned, careful and judicious text-writer. The main feature of the work is the manner in which Mr. Tudor has dealt with all the recent statutes relating to this subject: we have only to add that the index is very carefully compiled."—*Solicitors' Journal.*

" Mr. Tudor's excellent little book on Charitable Trusts. It is indeed no longer a little book but a bulky one of some 650 pages. Mr. Tudor however is a singularly painstaking author; his books, as the profession well knows, are models of industry and care, and hence their popularity. This second edition has collected the cases decided since the issue of the first, and their number is surprising—upwards of one thousand. Mr. Tudor has made his work complete by the introduction of several schemes for the settlement of charities, so that it is in all respects the text-book for the lawyer as well as a hand book for reference by trustees and others engaged in the management of charities."—*Law Times.*

" The account of the Law of Mortmain and the statutes respecting charitable bequests in their bearing on the different religious orders is full and definite, and the duties of trustees are explained in a clear and straightforward way. Altogether this work must be exceedingly useful, not to say indispensable, to all persons who are connected with charitable trusts, whether as founders, managers or trustees."—*English Churchman.*

" To this second edition large additions are made, and it is now a complete compendium of the Law of Charities."—*Clerical Journal.*

O'DOWD'S MERCHANT SHIPPING ACT.

THE MERCHANT SHIPPING AMENDMENT ACT, 1862; with an Introductory Analysis; an Appendix containing the Statute and incorporated Provisions of antecedent Acts; a Digest of Cases of Salvage and Collision, with reference to the newly-extended Jurisdiction; Practical Forms and a copious Index. By JAMES O'DOWD, Esq., of the Middle Temple, Barrister-at-Law, and Assistant Solicitor for the Merchant Shipping Department of Her Majesty's Customs. 12mo. 7s. 6d. cloth.

LUSHINGTON'S NAVAL PRIZE LAW.

A MANUAL of NAVAL PRIZE LAW. By GODFREY LUSHINGTON, of the Inner Temple, Esq., Barrister at Law. Royal 8vo. 10s. 6d. cloth.

OKE'S MAGISTERIAL SYNOPSIS.—10th Edition.

The MAGISTERIAL SYNOPSIS: a Practical Guide for Magistrates, their Clerks, Attornies, and Constables, Summary Convictions and Indictable Offences, with their Penalties, Punishments, Procedure, &c.; being Alphabetically and Tabularly arranged. By GEORGE C. OKE, Chief Clerk to the Lord Mayor of London. Tenth Edition. 1 very thick vol. 8vo. (*In the Press.*)

OKE'S MAGISTERIAL FORMULIST.—Fourth Edition.

The MAGISTERIAL FORMULIST: being a complete collection of Forms and Precedents for practical use in all Cases out of Quarter Sessions, and in Parochial Matters, by Magistrates, their Clerks, Attornies and Constables. By GEORGE C. OKE, Chief Clerk to the Lord Mayor of London, Author of "The Magisterial Synopsis." Fourth Edition. 8vo. 38s. cloth.

*** *This New Edition is brought down to the close of the last Session of Parliament, 1867, is much enlarged and improved, and contains the Forms under the New Master and Servant Act, 1867, and the Magisterial Legislation of the last six years.*

LOVESY'S LAW OF MASTERS AND WORKMEN.
(*Dedicated, by permission, to Lord St. Leonards.*)

The LAW of ARBITRATION between MASTERS and WORKMEN, as founded upon the Councils of Conciliation Act of 1867 (30 & 31 Vict. c. 105), the Master and Workmen Act (5 Geo. 4, c. 96), and other Acts, with an Introduction and Notes. By C. W. LOVESY, Esq., of the Middle Temple, Barrister at Law. 12mo. 4s. cloth.

"Where the adoption of this act is contemplated a better handbook could not be provided for the guidance of masters and men than this edition of the act, which has been carefully and intelligently noted by Mr. Lovesy, as being printed in a convenient form for use and provided with an excellent index."—*Law Times.*

"The professed object of the author has been to give the substance of the two statutes in a popular form, and in that endeavour he seems to have succeeded."—*Law Journal.*

"We think the duty has been well performed by Mr. Lovesy; he has given us a clear and concise statement of the effect of the five statutes aforesaid, and we think his little book will be found extremely useful."—*Solicitors' Journal.*

"I think you have bestowed much attention upon the later statute and added some useful notes."—*Lord St. Leonards.*

"The notes which he has introduced will considerably facilitate the attainment of his object. The book is not exclusively addressed to the legal world, all those who come within the comprehensive terms of employers and employed may refer to it with advantage, and we sincerely trust that the publication of this useful work wi'l be the means of decreasing some of the existing difficulties."—*Justice of the Peace.*

SCRIVEN ON COPYHOLDS.—Fifth Edition by Stalman.

A TREATISE ON COPYHOLD, CUSTOMARY FREEHOLD, and ANCIENT DEMESNE TENURE, with the Jurisdiction of Courts Baron and Courts Leet. By JOHN SCRIVEN, Serjeant at Law. The Fifth Edition, containing references to Cases and Acts of Parliament to the present time. By HENRY STALMAN, Esq., of the Inner Temple, Barrister-at-Law. Abridged in 1 vol. royal 8vo. 30s. cloth.

"No lawyer can see or hear the word 'copyhold' without associating with it the name of Scriven, whose book has been always esteemed not merely the best but the only one of any worth. Until a commutation of the tenure for a fixed rent-charge, after the manner of a tithe commutation, is compelled by the legislature, this treatise will lose none of its usefulness to the solicitors in the country."—*Law Times.*

"It would be wholly superfluous to offer one word of comment on the general body of the work. Scriven on Copyholds has for exactly half a century been not only a standard work but one of unimpeachable authority, and in its pages the present generation has learned all that is known of copyhold and customary tenures. All that is necessary to say is, that in the present edition of Scriven on Copyholds Mr. Stalman has omitted what was useless to retain, and inserted what it was necessary to add. Until copyholds have disappeared utterly, it is at least certain that Scriven on Copyholds by Stalman will hold undisputed sway in the profession."—*Law Journal.*

INGRAM ON COMPENSATION FOR LANDS, &c.

COMPENSATION TO LAND AND HOUSE OWNERS: being a Treatise on the Law of the Compensation for Interests in Lands, &c. payable by Railway and other Public Companies; with an Appendix of Forms and Statutes. By THOMAS DUNBAR INGRAM, of Lincoln's Inn, Esq., Barrister at Law. Post 8vo. 10s. cloth.

"Whether for companies taking land or holding it, Mr. Ingram's volume will be a welcome guide. With this in his hand the legal adviser of a company, or of an owner and occupier whose property is taken, and who demands compensation for it, cannot fail to perform his duty rightly."—*Law Times.*

"We can safely recommend this small volume of Mr. Ingram's as a safe reliable mentor on every subject connected with railway compensation."—*News of the World.*

"It is lucid, painstaking, and complete, and will be found a work of great practical value."—*Morning Advertiser.*

"The result is before us in a condensed and perspicuous form, and Mr. Ingram, in producing this very useful book at this particular time, has performed a service which will, we doubt not, be appreciated alike by the public and the legal profession."—*Standard.*

"The task which Mr. Ingram has had to perform must have involved the expenditure of much time, labour and research. He has brought to it the requisite ability, a knowledge of his subject, and copious command of materials, and the result is a work of genuine utility to the public and to the legal profession."—*Shipping and Mercantile Gazette.*

"His explanations are clear and accurate, and he constantly endeavours not only to state the effect of the law which he is enunciating, but also to show the principle upon which it rests."—*Athenæum.*

WILLS ON EVIDENCE.—Fourth Edition.

AN ESSAY on the PRINCIPLES of CIRCUMSTANTIAL EVIDENCE. Illustrated by numerous Cases. By the late WILLIAM WILLS, Esq. Fourth Edition. Edited by his Son, ALFRED WILLS, Esq., Barrister at Law. 8vo. 10s. cloth.

OKE'S TURNPIKE LAWS.—Second Edition.

The LAWS of TURNPIKE ROADS: comprising the whole of the General Acts; the Acts as to the Union of Trusts, for facilitating Arrangements with their Creditors; the interference of Railways and other Public Works with Roads; their Non-repair, and enforcing Contributions from Parishes, (including also the Acts as to South Wales Turnpike Roads,) &c. &c.; practically arranged, with Cases, Notes, Forms, &c. &c. By GEORGE C. OKE, Author of "The Magisterial Synopsis" and "The Magisterial Formulist," &c. Second Edition. 12mo., 18s. cloth.

"In the 'Synopsis' Mr. Oke is unique; the plan was perfectly original, and he has no competitor. In the Turnpike Law he is himself a competitor with others, who had previously possession of the field. Nevertheless, so well has he executed his design that his volume has fairly taken precedence in the esteem of the profession, because he has written it with the same industrious research and painstaking correction which distinguished the 'Synopsis.'"—*Law Times.*

"All Mr. Oke's works are well done, and his 'Turnpike Laws' is an admirable specimen of the class of books required for the guidance of magistrates and legal practitioners in country districts."—*Solicitors' Journal.*

OKE'S GAME AND FISHERY LAWS.—Second Edition.

A HANDY BOOK of the GAME and FISHERY LAWS; containing the whole Law as to Game, Licences and Certificates, Poaching Prevention, Trespass, Rabbits, Deer, Dogs, Birds and Poisoned Grain throughout the United Kingdom, and Private and Salmon Fisheries in England. Systematically arranged, with the Acts, Decisions, Notes, Forms, Suggestions, &c. &c. By GEORGE C. OKE, Author of "*The Magisterial Synopsis,*" &c. &c. Second Edition. 12mo. 10s. 6d. cloth.

∗⁎∗ This Edition includes Chapters on the Scotch and Irish Game Laws, Property in Game, Suggestions for Amendment of the Laws, the Poaching Prevention Act, 1862, the Poisoned Grain Prohibition Act, 1863, &c. &c.

"The work is carefully composed, and contains a full index."—*Solicitors' Journal.*

"Care and industry are all that can be shown in such productions, and these qualities are generally shown in the present works. Mr. Oke's book takes a somewhat larger range than Mr. Paterson's, as it embraces the late statute relating to the Salmon Fisheries."—*Athenæum.*

"The plan of Mr. Oke's Handy Book is a very plain and useful one. * * It will be a most acceptable addition to the country gentleman's library, and presents a most intelligible guide to the existing English laws on game and fish, brought down to the present time."—*The Field.*

"To sportsmen, as well as to those magistrates and professional gentlemen who are concerned in the administration of the Game Laws, Mr. Oke's digest and interpretation of the various statutes will prove of great assistance."—*Stamford Mercury.*

"Mr. Oke makes the laws easily comprehended in all their bearings, so that the person requiring information will find it at once, and that in a condensed form. * * It is a work that every sportsman would find useful, now that the season is before him and he is anxious to know how the law stands under the recent acts of parliament."—*Bell's New Messenger.*

"We recommend justices, landlords, and others whom it behoves to be well acquainted with the Game Laws, to supply themselves with a copy of this work; they will find every requisite information in a small space and in an intelligible form."—*Cambridge Chronicle.*

TOMKINS' INSTITUTES OF ROMAN LAW.

THE INSTITUTES of ROMAN LAW. Part I., containing the Sources of the Roman Law and its External History till the Decline of the Eastern and Western Empires. By FREDERICK TOMKINS, M.A., D.C.L., Barrister at Law, of Lincoln's Inn. Part I., royal 8vo. 12s. cloth. (To be completed in Three Parts.)

"This work promises to be an important and valuable contribution to the Study of the Roman Law."—*Law Magazine*.

"This work is pronounced by its author to be strictly elementary. But in regard to the labour bestowed, the research exercised, and the materials brought together, it seems to deserve a more ambitious title than that of an elementary treatise. The chapter on Legal Instruction, detailing the systems of legal education pursued in the various epochs of Rome, reflects great credit on the author, and, so far as we know, is purely original, in the sense that no preceding English writer has collated the matter therein contained."—*Law Journal*.

"Dr. Tomkins has chosen his subject wisely in at least one respect, there can be no doubt that a good introductory treatise on the Roman Law is sorely needed at present. The present part is only an instalment. But the present part is unquestionably both valuable in itself and of good promise for the future. We know of no other book in which anything like the same amount of information can be acquired with the same ease. We shall look with great interest for the publication of the remainder of this treatise. If the second part is as well executed as the first, and bears a due proportion to it, we think the work bids fair to become the standard text-book for English students."—*Solicitors' Journal*.

"Of all the works on the Roman Law we believe this will be the best suited to law students. Mr. Tomkins gives us a simple English history of Roman Law, arranged most lucidly with marginal notes and printed in a form calculated for easy reading and retention in the memory. We welcome the book of Mr. Tomkins. It is calculated to promote the study of Roman Law, and both at the universities and in the Inns of Court it is a work which may safely and beneficially be employed as a text-book."—*Law Times*.

DREWRY'S EQUITY PLEADER.

A CONCISE TREATISE on the Principles of EQUITY PLEADING, with Precedents. By C. STEWART DREWRY, Esq., of the Inner Temple, Barrister at Law. 12mo., 6s. boards.

CONTENTS:—What Persons are entitled to sue in Equity, and in what manner to sue.—Of the Modes of instituting a Suit in Equity.—Of the Defence of Suits.—Of Pleas.—Of Answers.—Of Amended Bills.—Of Revivor and Supplemental Bills.—Of Interlocutory Applications —Of the Proceedings on going into Evidence.—Of Appeals.—Conclusion.—Appendix of Precedents.

"Mr. Drewry will be remembered by many as the author of the very popular and excellent treatise on the Practice in Equity. He has now contributed to the library of the lawyer another work of equal value, written for younger members of the profession and for students, in which he describes the principles and general rules of Equity Pleading. It will be found of great utility, as introductory to the more elaborate treatises, or to refresh the memory after the study of the larger books."—*Law Times*.

WILLIAMS ON PLEADING AND PRACTICE.

An INTRODUCTION to the PRINCIPLES and PRACTICE of PLEADING in the SUPERIOR COURTS of LAW, embracing an outline of the whole Proceedings in an Action at Law, on Motion, and at Judges' Chambers; together with the Rules of Pleading and Practice, and Forms of all the principal Proceedings. By WATKIN WILLIAMS, of the Inner Temple, Esq., Barrister at Law. 8vo. 12s. cloth.

Mr. Williams has undertaken a work requiring great care in its treatment; but we have no hesitation in saying that he has brought to bear on his task powers of arrangement and clearness of expression of no ordinary character, and has produced a work creditable to himself and useful to the Profession. For the Student especially the book has features of peculiar value, it is at the same time scientific and practical, and throughout the work there is a judicious union of general principles with a practical treatment of the subject, illustrated by forms and examples of the main proceedings."—*Jurist*.

LAW EXAMINATION REPORTER.

THE LAW EXAMINATION REPORTER, edited by RICHARD HALLILAY, Esq., containing all the Questions and Answers at the Examinations of Law Students at the Incorporated Law Society. Published in numbers at 6d., by post 7d., every Term on the Morning of the Second Day after the Examination.

CONTENTS.

No. I. HIL. TERM, 1866.—Notice to Readers; How to Study; The Examiners; Examination Questions and Answers.
No. II. EAST. TERM, 1866.—Notice to Readers; What to Study for Pass or Honours; The Examiners; Examination Questions and Answers.
No. III. TRIN. TERM, 1866.—My first Criminal Client; Important Bills in Parliament; The Examiners; Examination Questions and Answers.
No. IV. MICH. TERM, 1866.—On Memory, its Abuse and Aids; Result of the past, Intermediate and final Examinations; The Examiners; Examination Questions and Answers.
No. V. HIL. TERM, 1867.—Sketches at a Police Court; Reviews of New Books; Observations on the Michaelmas Term's Questions; The Examiners; Examination Questions and Answers, &c.
No. VI. EAST. TERM, 1867.—Notice to Readers; The Preliminary Examinations and the Judges' Dispensations; Observations on the Hilary Term's Equity Questions; Correspondence; The Examiners; Examination Questions and Answers, &c.
No. VII. TRIN. TERM, 1867.—Notice to Readers; The Rejected and the Reason; Examination and Legal News; The Examiners; Intermediate Examination Questions: Final Examination Questions and Answers.
No. VIII. MICH. TERM, 1867.—New Statutes; Result of Past Examinations; New Prizes; Law Societies; Reviews of Books; The Examiners; The Intermediate Questions; All the Michaelmas Terms Examination Questions and Answers.
No. IX. HIL. TERM, 1868.—Proposed Amalgamation of the Bar and the Attornies; New Statutes and Rules; Reviews of New Books; Moot Points; Intermediate Examination Questions; The Examiners; All the Hilary final Questions and Answers.

PHILLIPS'S LAW OF LUNACY.

THE LAW CONCERNING LUNATICS, IDIOTS, and PERSONS of UNSOUND MIND. By CHARLES P. PHILLIPS, M.A., of Lincoln's Inn, Esq., Barrister at Law, and Secretary to the Commissioners of Lunacy. Post 8vo., 18s. cloth.

"Mr. Phillips has, in his very complete, elaborate and useful volume, presented us with an excellent view of the present law, as well as the practice, relating to lunacy."—*Law Magazine and Review.*

PARKINSON'S COMMON LAW CHAMBER PRACTICE.

A HANDY BOOK FOR THE COMMON LAW JUDGES' CHAMBERS. By GEO. H. PARKINSON, Chamber Clerk to the Hon. Mr. Justice Byles. 12mo. 7s. cloth.

"For this task Mr. Parkinson is eminently qualified."—*Jurist.*

"It is extremely well calculated for the purpose for which it is intended. So much work is now done in Common Law Chambers by junior clerks that such a little treatise is much wanted. Mr. Parkinson has performed his task skilfully and with care."—*Solicitors' Journal.*

"The practice in Chambers has become sufficiently important to call for a treatise devoted to it, nor could a more competent man for the task have presented himself than Mr. Parkinson, whose great experience as well as intelligence have long placed him in the position of an authority on all matters appertaining to this peculiar but very extensive branch of Common Law Practice."—*Law Times.*

"There is much that would prove very useful to the practitioner in Mr. Parkinson's compilation, and which, so far as we are aware, is not to be found in any other book collected with equal conciseness."—*Law Magazine and Review.*

BUTTERWORTH, 7, FLEET STREET, E.C. 29

GLEN'S LAW OF HIGHWAYS.—Second Edition.

LAW of HIGHWAYS: comprising the Highway Acts, 1862 and 1864: the South Wales Highway Act: the Leading Decisions of the Courts on the subject of Highways, Ferries, &c., including the Duties of Highway Boards, Surveyors of Highways, the Law of Highways in Local Board of Health Districts, Highways affected by Railways, and Locomotives on Highways; with an Appendix of Statutes in force relating to Highways. By W. CUNNINGHAM GLEN, Esq., Barrister-at-Law. Second Edition. 20s. cloth.

"... have need of information it is, could not resort to a better adviser than this Work. It is conveniently arranged, because copiously indexed."

"... undertook a Work that was required not only by the profession but by a class of persons interested in highways, and Mr. Glen's reputation has no doubt qualified him to discharge such a task with ability. Mr. Glen has succeeded in what he proposes, and his Treatise is invaluable to all practitioners in the Law of Highways."—*Solicitor.*

"... we may confidently venture the statement in the preface, that nearly claim to be recognised as an authority on the law of highways who are engaged officially in the administration of that branch of law. It is so, as we from personal knowledge can affirm, and, we may add, is received by them as a trustworthy guide in the discharge of their duties."—*Law Times (on 2nd Edit.)*

"The present edition of Mr. Glen's work contains a great deal of valuable matter entirely new. To those interested in the law of highways this manual as it now appears will be found a safe and efficient guide."—*Law Magazine (on 2nd Edition).*

"Glen has an established reputation in the legal profession as a careful and laborious writer, and this new edition of his new work on highway law will convince those who refer to it that he has neglected no topic likely to be useful to those whose duties require them to have a knowledge of this particular branch of the law. This work aspires above others which profess merely to be annotated reprints of acts of parliament. It will be found to contain much information which might be looked for elsewhere in vain. The general law upon the subject is set forth with a care and lucidity deserving of great praise, and a good index facilitates reference, and renders this work the most complete on this important subject which has yet been published."—*Justice of the Peace.*

"Mr. Glen may well say that an entire revision of the first edition was necessitated by the recent statutes, and his second edition is a bulky volume of 800 pages. His work may be read with satisfaction by the general student as well as referred to with confidence by the practitioner. We need say nothing further of this second edition than that we think it likely to maintain fully the reputation obtained by its predecessor. It has the advantages, by no means unworthy of consideration, of being well printed and well indexed, as well as well arranged, and a copious index of statutes renders it a perfect compendium of the authorities bearing in any way on the law of highways."—*Solicitors' Journal on the Second Edition.*

GLEN'S POOR LAW BOARD ORDERS.—Fifth Edition.

The General CONSOLIDATED and other ORDERS of the POOR LAW COMMISSIONERS and of the POOR LAW BOARD, together with the General Orders relating to Poor Law of Accounts, the Statutes relating to the Audit of Accounts, Appeals and the Payment of Debts, with Explanatory Notes elucidating the Orders, Tables of Statutes, Cases and Index. By W. CUNNINGHAM GLEN, Esq., of the Middle Temple, Barrister at Law, and of the Poor Law Board. Fifth Edition. 12mo. 12s. cloth.

WIGRAM ON WILLS.—Fourth Edition.

An EXAMINATION of the RULES of LAW respecting the Admission of EXTRINSIC EVIDENCE in Aid of the INTERPRETATION of WILLS. By the Right Hon. Sir JAMES WIGRAM, Knt. The Fourth Edition prepared for the press, with the sanction of the learned Author, by W. KNOX WIGRAM, M.A., of Lincoln's Inn, Esq., Barrister at Law. 8vo. 11s. cloth.

"In the celebrated treatise of Sir James Wigram, the rules of law are stated, discussed and explained in a manner which has excited the admiration of every judge who has had to consult it."—*Lord Kingsdown, in a Privy Council Judgment, July 8/4, 1858.*

"There can be no doubt that the notes of Mr. Knox Wigram have enhanced the value of the work, as affording a ready reference to recent cases on the subjects embraced or arising out of Sir James Wigram's propositions, and which frequently give additional support, and in some instances an extension to the original text."—*Law Chronicle.*

"Understood as general guides, the propositions established by Sir James Wigram's book are of the highest value. But whatever view may be entertained, the book is one which will always be highly prized, and is now presented in a very satisfactory shape, thanks to the industry and intelligence displayed in the notes by the present editor."—*Solicitors' Journal and Reporter.*

FRY'S SPECIFIC PERFORMANCE OF CONTRACTS.

A TREATISE on the SPECIFIC PERFORMANCE of CONTRACTS, including those of Public Companies. By EDWARD FRY, B.A., of Lincoln's Inn, Esq., Barrister at Law. 8vo. 16s. cloth.

"Mr. Fry's work presents in a reasonable compass a large quantity of modern learning on the subject of contracts, with reference to the common remedy by specific performance, and will thus be acceptable to the profession generally."—*Law Chronicle.*

"There is a closeness and clearness in its style, and a latent fulness in the exposition, which not only argue a knowledge of the law, but of those varying circumstances in human society to which the law has to be applied."—*Spectator.*

"Mr. Fry's elaborate essay appears to exhaust the subject, on which he has cited and brought to bear, with great diligence, some 1,500 cases, which include those of the latest reports."—*Law Magazine and Review.*

COOTE'S NEW ADMIRALTY PRACTICE.

The NEW PRACTICE of the HIGH COURT of ADMIRALTY of ENGLAND; with the Rules of 1859, and a Collection of Original Forms, and Bills of Costs, &c. By HENRY CHARLES COOTE, F.S.A., one of the Examiners of the High Court of Admiralty of England, Author of "The Practice of the New Court of Probate," "The Practice of the Ecclesiastical Courts," &c. 8vo. 12s. cloth.

"Mr. Coote has promptly entered the new field thus opened to him, and laid the first modern book on the subject before the new comers. He has the great advantage of experience, as he has been long a practitioner in the Court as a proctor."—*Law Times.*

"It is a very excellent and complete production."—*Law Chronicle.*

"The work before us is characterised by lucid arrangement of the subject-matter, as well as by a constant appreciation of what suits the convenience of practitioners."—*Solicitors' Journal.*

MESSRS. BUTTERWORTH, 7, FLEET STREET, E.C.   31

BAINBRIDGE ON MINES.—Third Edition.

A TREATISE on the LAW of MINES and MINERALS. By WILLIAM BAINBRIDGE, Esq., F.G.S., of the Inner Temple, Barrister at Law. Third Edition, carefully revised, and much enlarged by additional matter relating to Rights of Way and Water and other Mining Easements, the Construction of Leases, Cost Book and General Partnerships, Injuries from Undermining and Inundations, Barriers and Working out of Bounds and Disputes with Workmen. With an Appendix of Forms and Customs, and a Glossary of English Mining Terms. 8vo. 30s. cloth.

"After an interval of eleven years we have to welcome a new edition of Mr. Bainbridge's work on Mines and Minerals. It would be entirely superfluous to attempt a general review of a work which has for so long a period occupied the position of the standard work on this important subject. Those only who, by the nature of their practice, have learned to lean upon Mr. Bainbridge as on a solid staff, can appreciate the deep research, the admirable method, and the graceful style of this model treatise. Therefore we are merely reduced to the enquiry, whether the law has, by force of statutes and of judicial decisions, undergone such development, modification or change since the year 1856 as to justify a new edition? That question may be readily answered in the affirmative; and the additions and corrections made in the volume before us furnish ample evidence of the fact. It may be also stated that this book, being priced at 30s., has the exceptional character of being a cheap law publication."—*Law Journal.*

"Mr. Bainbridge was, we believe, the first to collect and publish, in a separate treatise, the Law of Mines and Minerals, and the work was so well done that his volume at once took its place in the law library as the text book on the subject to which it was devoted. This work must be already familiar to all readers whose practice brings them in any manner in connection with mines or mining, and they well know its value. We can only say of this new edition that it is in all respects worthy of its predecessors."—*Law Times.*

Gray's Treatise on the Law of Costs in Actions and other PROCEEDINGS in the Courts of Common Law at Westminster. By JOHN GRAY, Esq., of the Middle Temple, Barrister at Law. 8vo. 21s. cloth.

*** This work embraces the whole modern Law and Practice of Costs, including the important provisions of the Common Law Procedure Act and Rules, 1852, and the recent Statutes affecting the Jurisdiction of the County Courts.

The South Australian System of Conveyancing by Registration of TITLE; with Instructions for the Guidance of Parties Dealing, illustrated by Copies of the Books and Forms in use in the Land Titles Office. By ROBERT R. TORRENS. To which is added the South Australian Real Property Act, as Amended in the Sessions of 1858. With a copious Index. By HENRY GAWLER, Esq, Barrister, Solicitor to the Land Titles Commissioners. 8vo. 4s. half cloth.

Grant's Law of Corporations in General. A Practical TREATISE on the LAW of CORPORATIONS in GENERAL, as well Aggregate as Sole; including Municipal Corporations, Railway, Banking, Canal and other Joint-Stock and Trading Bodies, Dean and Chapters, Universities, Colleges, Schools, Hospitals, with *quasi* Corporations aggregate, as Guardians of the Poor, Churchwardens, Churchwardens and Overseers, &c., and also Corporations sole, as Bishops, Deans, Canons, Archdeacons, Parsons, &c. By JAMES GRANT, Esq., of the Middle Temple, Barrister at Law. Royal 8vo. 26s. boards.

Pulling's Practical Compendium of the Law and Usage of MERCANTILE ACCOUNTS; describing the various Rules of Law affecting them, the ordinary Mode in which they are entered in Account Books, and the various Forms of Proceeding, and Rules of Pleading, and Evidence for their Investigation, at Common Law, in Equity, Bankruptcy and Insolvency, or by Arbitration. With a SUPPLEMENT, containing the Law of Joint Stock Companies' Accounts, under the Winding-up Acts of 1848 and 1849. By ALEXANDER PULLING, Esq. of the Inner Temple, Barrister at Law. 12mo. 9s. boards.

Coote's Practice of the Ecclesiastical Courts, with Forms and Tables of Costs. By HENRY CHARLES COOTE, Proctor in Doctors' Commons, &c. One thick Vol. 8vo. 28s. boards.

Hamel's International Law.—International Law in connexion with Municipal Statutes relating to the Commerce, Rights and Liabilities of the Subjects of Neutral States pending Foreign War; considered with reference to the Case of the "Alexandra," seized under the provisions of the Foreign Enlistment Act. By FELIX HARGRAVE HAMEL, of the Inner Temple, Barrister at Law. Post 8vo. 3s. sewed.

Oke's New Criminal Acts, 1861, with the Offences, Punishments and Procedure: whether Punishable Summarily or on Indictment; Alphabetically and Tabularly arranged. By GEORGE C. OKE, Author of the "Magisterial Synopsis." 8vo. 6s. cloth.

Keyser on the Law relating to Transactions on the STOCK EXCHANGE. By HENRY KEYSER, Esq., of the Middle Temple, Barrister at Law. 12mo. 8s. cloth.

Cutler's Legal Systems—English, Roman, Hindu and MAHOMMEDAN. On the STUDY of the ENGLISH, ROMAN, HINDU and MAHOMMEDAN LEGAL SYSTEMS, with especial regard to their salient points of Agreement and Difference: being a Lecture delivered at King's College, London. By JOHN CUTLER, B.A., of Lincoln's Inn, Barrister at Law, Professor of English Law and Jurisprudence, and Professor of Indian Jurisprudence, at King's College, London. 8vo. 1s. sewed.

Blayney's Practical Treatise on Life Assurance. Second Edition. By FREDERIC BLAYNEY, Esq. 12mo. 7s. boards.

The Laws of Barbados. (By Authority.) Royal 8vo. 21s. cloth.

Pearce's Guide to the Bar and Inns of Court.—A Guide to the Inns of Court and Chancery; with Notices of their Ancient Discipline, Rules, Orders and Customs, Readings, Moots, Masques, Revels and Entertainments, including an account of the Eminent Men of the Honorable Societies of Lincoln's Inn, the Inner Temple, the Middle Temple and Gray's Inn, &c.; together with the Regulations of the Four Inns of Court as to the Admission of Students, Keeping Terms, Lectures, Examination, Call to the Bar, &c. &c. &c. By ROBERT R. PEARCE, Esq., of Gray's Inn, Barrister at Law. 8vo. 8s. cloth.

Baker's Practical Compendium of the Recent Statutes, CASES, and DECISIONS affecting the OFFICE of CORONER, with Precedents of Inquisitions, and Practical Forms. By WILLIAM BAKER, Esq., one of the Coroners for Middlesex. 12mo. 7s. cloth.

Hamel's Laws of the Customs, consolidated by direction of the Lords Commissioners of her Majesty's Treasury (16 & 17 Vict. caps. 106 & 107); with a Commentary containing Practical Forms, Notes of Decisions in Leading Customs Cases, Appendix of Acts; also a Supplement for 1854, containing a Commentary on the three Acts (17 & 18 Vict. caps. 28, 29 and 122), and a Summary of the existing Duties and a copious Index. By FELIX JOHN HAMEL, Esq., Solicitor for her Majesty's Customs. 1 vol. royal 8vo. 16s. cloth.

Greening's Forms of Declarations, Pleadings and other
PROCEEDINGS in the Superior Courts of Common Law, with the
Common Law Procedure Act, and other Statutes; Table of Officers'
Fees; and the New Rules of Practice and Pleading, with Notes. By
HENRY GREENING, Esq., Special Pleader. Second Edition. 12mo.
10s. 6d. boards.

Brandt's Treatise on the Law, Practice and Procedure
of DIVORCE and MATRIMONIAL CAUSES under the Act 20 &
21 Vict. c. 85; containing the Act, also the Rules, Orders, and Forms
issued thereunder; together with Precedents. By WILLIAM BRANDT,
of the Inner Temple, Barrister at Law. 12mo. 7s. 6d. boards.

Browne's Practical Treatise on Actions at Law, embracing
the subjects of Notice of Action; Limitation of Actions;
necessary Parties to and proper Forms of Actions, the Consequence
of Mistake therein; and the Law of Costs with reference to Damages.
By ROWLAND JAY BROWNE, Esq., of Lincoln's Inn, Special
Pleader. 8vo. 16s. boards.

Gunning's Practical Treatise on the Law of Tolls; and
therein of Tolls Thorough and Traverse; Fair and Market Tolls;
Canal, Ferry, Port and Harbour Tolls; Turnpike Tolls; Rateability
of Tolls; Exemption from Tolls; Remedies and Evidence in Actions
for Tolls. By FREDERICK GUNNING, Esq., of Lincoln's Inn, Barrister
at Law. 8vo. 9s. boards.

Quain and Holroyd's New System of Common Law Pro-
CEDURE according to the COMMON LAW PROCEDURE ACT,
1852. By J. R. QUAIN, of the Middle Temple, Barrister at Law,
and H. HOLROYD, of the Middle Temple, Special Pleader. 12mo.
7s. 6d. cloth.

O'Dowd's New Practice of the Court of Chancery, as
regulated by the Acts and Orders for the Improvement of the Jurisdiction
of Equity, 15 & 16 Vict. c. 86; for Abolishing the Office of
Master, 15 & 16 Vict. c. 80; and for Relief of the Suitors, 15 & 16
Vict. c. 87; with Introduction, Notes, the Acts, the Orders, and a
copious Index. By JAMES O'DOWD, Esq., Barrister at Law. Second
Edition, corrected, greatly improved, and with the decisions. 12mo.
7s. 6d. boards.

MESSRS. BUTTERWORTH, 7, FLEET STREET, E.C. 35

Phillimore's Commentaries on International Law. By
The Right Hon. Sir ROBERT PHILLIMORE, Knt., now Judge of the
High Court of Admiralty of England. 4 vols. 8vo. 5*l*. cloth.

*Extract from Pamphlet on "American Neutrality," by GEORGE BEMIS (Boston).—
"Sir Robert Phillimore, the present Queen's Advocate, and author of the most
comprehensive and systematic 'Commentaries on International Law' that England
has produced."*

*** Vol. 2, price 22*s*., Vol. 3, price 32*s*., Vol. 4, price 30*s*., may be
had separately to complete sets.

Deane's Law of Blockade, as contained in the Judgments
of Dr. Lushington and the Cases on Blockade decided during 1854.
By J. P. DEANE, D.C.L., Advocate in Doctors' Commons. 8vo.
10*s*. cloth.

Pothier's Treatise on the Contract of Partnership.
Translated from the French, with Notes, by O. D. TUDOR, Esq., Barrister at Law. 8vo. 5*s*. cloth.

Hertslet's Complete Collection of the Treaties and Con-
ventions, and Reciprocal Regulations, at present subsisting between
Great Britain and Foreign Powers, and of the Laws, Decrees, and
Orders in Council concerning the same, so far as they relate to Commerce and Navigation, Slave Trade, Post Office Communications, Copyright, &c., and to the Privileges and Interests of the Subjects of the
High Contracting Parties; compiled from Authentic Documents. By
LEWIS HERTSLET, Esq., Librarian and Keeper of the Papers, Foreign
Office. Vols. 1 to 11, 8vo. 12*l*. 15*s*. boards.

Norman's Treatise on the Law and Practice relating to
LETTERS-PATENT for INVENTIONS. By JOHN PAXTON
NORMAN, M.A., of the Inner Temple, Barrister at Law. Post 8vo.
7*s*. 6*d*. cloth.

Francillon's Law Lectures. Second Series. Lectures,
ELEMENTARY and FAMILIAR, on ENGLISH LAW. By
JAMES FRANCILLON, Esq., County Court Judge. First and Second
Series. 8vo., 8*s*. each, cloth.

Warren's Manual of the Parliamentary Election Law of
the UNITED KINGDOM, with reference to the Conduct of Elections, and the Registration Court; with a copious Index, and all the
Statutes and Decisions down to 1857. By SAMUEL WARREN, D.C.L.,
Q.C. One thick volume, royal 12mo. 25*s*. cloth.

Warren's Manual of the Law and Practice of Election
COMMITTEES, being the concluding portion of a "*Manual of
Parliamentary Election Law.*" By SAMUEL WARREN, D.C.L., Q.C.
Royal 12mo. 15*s*. cloth.

Lewis's Election Manual for England and Wales: being a Plain and Practical Key to the existing Laws affecting Returning Officers, Electors, Candidates and Election Agents, with the Text of the Principal Statutes, including the Corrupt Practices Acts; with Forms, Explanatory Notes and Precedents. By CHARLES EDWARD LEWIS, Solicitor. Third Edition. 12mo. 5s. boards.

The Law Student's Guide; containing an Historical Treatise on each of the Inns of Court, with their Rules and Customs respecting Admission, Keeping Terms, Call to the Bar, Chambers, &c., Remarks on the Jurisdiction of the Benchers, Observations on the Study of the Law, and other useful Information. By P. B. LEIGH, Esq., of Gray's Inn, Barrister at Law. 12mo. 6s. boards.

A Treatise on the Law of Sheriff, with Practical Forms and Precedents. By RICHARD CLARKE SEWELL, Esq., D.C.L., Barrister at Law, Fellow of Magdalen College, Oxford. 8vo. 1l. 1s.

Dwyer's Militia Laws and Regulations. A Compendium of the PRINCIPAL LAWS and REGULATIONS relating to the MILITIA of GREAT BRITAIN and IRELAND. By EDWARD DWYER, B.A., of Lincoln's Inn, Esq., Barrister at Law. 12mo. 5s. 6d.

Drainage of Land: How to procure Outfalls by New Drains, or the Improvement of Existing Drains, in the Lands of an Adjoining Owner, under the Powers contained in Part III. of the Act 24 & 25 Vict., cap. 133, 1861; with Explanations of the Provisions, and Suggestions for the Guidance of Landowners, Occupiers, Land Agents and Surveyors. By J. WM. WILSON, Solicitor.

Sharkey's Hand-Book of the Practice of Election Committees; with an Appendix of Forms and Precedents. By P. BURROWES SHARKEY, Solicitor and Parliamentary Agent. Second Edition. 12mo. 10s. 6d. cloth.

Fearne's Chart, Historical and Legigraphical, of Landed Property in England, from the time of the Saxons to the present Æra, displaying at one view the Tenures, Modes of Descent and Power of Alienation of Lands in England at all times during that period. On a sheet, colored, 6s.; on a roller, 8s.

Burder v. Heath. Judgment delivered on November 2, 1861, by the Right Honorable STEPHEN LUSHINGTON, D.C.L., Dean of the Arches. Folio, 1s. sewed.

The Law relating to Ritualism in the United Church of England and Ireland. By F. H. HAMEL, Esq., Barrister at Law. 12mo. 1s. sewed.

Archdeacon Hale's Enquiry into the Legal History of the Supremacy of the Crown in Matters of Religion; with especial reference to the Church in the Colonies. With an Appendix. By W. H. HALE, M.A., Archdeacon of London. Royal 8vo. 4s. cloth.

MESSRS. BUTTERWORTH, 7, FLEET STREET, E.C. 37

The Judgment of the Right. Hon. Dr. Lushington, D.C.L., &c. &c., delivered in the Consistory Court of the Bishop of London, in the cases of Westerton against Liddell (clerk) and Horne and others, and Beale against Liddell (clerk) and Parke and Evans, on December 5th, 1855. Edited by A. F. BAYFORD, D.C.L. Royal 8vo., 2s. 6d. sewed.

The Judgment of the Dean of the Arches, also the Judgment of the PRIVY COUNCIL, in Liddell (clerk) and Horne and others against Westerton, and Liddell (clerk) and Park and Evans against Beal. Edited by A. F. BAYFORD, LL.D.: and with an elaborate analytical Index to the whole of the Judgments in these Cases. Royal 8vo., 3s. 6d. sewed.

The Case of Long v. Bishop of Cape Town, embracing the opinions of the Judges of Colonial Court hitherto unpublished, together with the decision of the Privy Council, and Preliminary Observations by the Editor. Royal 8vo., 6s. sewed.

A General Catalogue of all Modern Law Works now on Sale by Messrs. BUTTERWORTH, with a Chronological List of all the Reports from the earliest Period to the present Time, and an Index of Subjects for convenience of reference: intended as a Guide to Purchasers. 8vo. 1s. sewed. (*Gratis to Purchasers.*)

Law Pamphlets.

Observations on the County Courts and Local Municipal Courts, as Courts for the Recovery of Small Debts. By WOODTHORPE BRANDON, Esq., Barrister at Law. 8vo., 6d. sewed.

Jamaica Riot.—The Case of George William Gordon; with Preliminary Observations on the Jamaica Riot of Oct. 11, 1865, and a Preface. By B. T. WILLIAMS, Esq., M. A., Barrister at Law. 8vo. 2s. sewed.

The Privilege of Religious Confession in English Courts of Law, considered in a Letter to a Friend. By EDWARD BADELEY, Esq., M.A., Barrister at Law. 8vo. 2s.

Our Judicial System. A Speech in the House of Commons, February 22nd, 1867. By SIR ROUNDELL PALMER, Q.C., M.P. 8vo., 1s. sewed.

On the Necessity for Additional Common Law Judges. A Paper read before the Metropolitan and Provincial Law Association, October, 1866. By J. ANDERSON ROSE. 8vo., 1s. sewed.

More Judges: Are they wanted? By T. W. Wheeler, B.A., Barrister at Law. 8vo., 1s. sewed.

A Plan for the Formal Amendment of the Law of England. By THOMAS ERSKINE HOLLAND, M.A., Barrister at Law. 8vo., 1s. sewed.

A Digest of the Law: How attainable? By R. Malcolm KERR, LL.D., Advocate and Barrister at Law. 8vo., 1s. sewed.

CLARK'S HOUSE OF LORDS REPORTS.

The HOUSE of LORDS CASES on Appeals, Writs of Error and Claims of Peerage. By CHARLES CLARK, Esq., of the Middle Temple, Barrister at Law, Reporter by appointment to the House of Lords.

Complete in Eleven Vols., and containing all the Cases decided from 1847 to 1866.

SWABEY AND TRISTRAM'S PROBATE AND DIVORCE REPORTS.

REPORTS of CASES decided in the COURT of PROBATE and in the COURT for DIVORCE and MATRIMONIAL CAUSES. By Dr. SWABEY, D.C.L., Advocate, and Barrister at Law of Gray's Inn, and Dr. TRISTRAM, D.C.L., Advocate in Doctors' Commons, and of the Inner Temple. Vols. I., II. and III., and Vol. IV. Part I., containing all the Cases at present decided, from 1858 to the present time. Price 7l. 11s. 6d. sewed.

DR. ROBINSON'S NEW ADMIRALTY REPORTS.

REPORTS of CASES in the COURT of ADMIRALTY, commencing with the Judgments of the Right Honourable Stephen Lushington, D.C.L. By WILLIAM ROBINSON, D.C.L. Advocate.

Three Vols. containing Cases decided from 1833 to 1850. 4l. 7s. 6d. sewed.

SWABEY'S ADMIRALTY REPORTS.

REPORTS of CASES in the COURT of ADMIRALTY, from 1855 to 1859. By M. C. MERTTINS SWABEY, D.C.L., of Doctors' Commons, and of Gray's Inn, Barrister at Law. Complete in 1 Vol. containing 3 Parts. Price 34s. sewed.

VERNON LUSHINGTON'S ADMIRALTY REPORTS.

REPORTS of CASES in the COURT of ADMIRALTY, and on APPEAL to the PRIVY COUNCIL. By VERNON LUSHINGTON, Esq., Barrister at Law. Complete in 1 volume, containing cases from 1859 to 1863. Price 2l. 10s. sewed.

BROWNING and LUSHINGTON'S ADMIRALTY REPORTS.

REPORTS of CASES in the COURT of ADMIRALTY, and on APPEAL to the PRIVY COUNCIL, 1863—1865. By ERNST BROWNING and VERNON LUSHINGTON, Esqrs., of the Inner Temple, Barristers at Law. Parts I and II. Price 26s.

(*These Reports are in continuation of those by* MR. LUSHINGTON, *and will comprise the Cases to the end of Trinity Term,* 1865.)

PREPARING FOR PUBLICATION.

Sir T. Erskine May's Parliamentary Practice. The Sixth Edition. In one thick volume. 8vo.

Mr. Serjeant Stephen's New Commentaries on the Laws of England. Partly founded on Blackstone. The Sixth Edition. By JAMES STEPHEN, LL.D., of the Middle Temple, Barrister at Law. In 4 vols. 8vo.

Stephen's Questions for Law Students on the Sixth Edition of Mr. Serjeant Stephen's New Commentaries on the Laws of England. In 1 vol. 8vo.

The Commentaries of Gaius on the Roman Law, with an English Translation and Annotations. By FREDERICK TOMKINS, Esq., M.A., D.C.L., and WILLIAM GEORGE LEMON, Esq., LL.B., Barristers at Law, of Lincoln's Inn. In 8vo.

The Institutes of Roman Law. Part II. By FREDERICK TOMKINS, Esq., M.A., D.C.L., Barrister at Law, of Lincoln's Inn. To be complete in 3 parts, royal 8vo.

A Digested Index to all the Reports in the House of Lords, from the commencement of the Series by Dow in 1814 to the present time, intended as a Supplementary Volume to Clark's House of Lord's Cases. By CHARLES CLARK, Esq., Barrister at Law. In 1 Vol. Royal 8vo.

Oke's Magisterial Synopsis.—The Tenth Edition. In 8vo.

Fisher on the General Law of Mortgage and other Securities upon Property, including the subject of Priority. Second Edition. In Two vols. Royal 8vo.

A Collection of Mortgage Precedents and Decrees; intended as a Companion Work to the General Law of Mortgage. By W. R. FISHER, Esq., of Lincoln's Inn, Barrister at Law. In 1 vol. Royal 8vo.

Shelford's Law of Joint Stock Companies.—Second Edition. By F. L. LATHAM, of the Inner Temple, Esq., Barrister at Law. In 12mo.

Shelford's Law of Railways.—Fourth Edition, containing the whole of the Consolidation and other General Acts for Regulating Railways in England, Scotland and Ireland to the present time, and including the Companies Act, 1862; Lord Campbell's Act; the Law of Rating Railways to Local Taxes, with Notes of decided Cases on their Construction and Forms, &c.; the whole brought down to the latest period by W. CUNNINGHAM GLEN and C. W. LOVESY, Esquires, of the Middle Temple, Barristers at Law. In 2 vols. Royal 8vo.

Chitty's (Jun.) Precedents in Pleading.—Third Edition. By the late TOMPSON CHITTY, LEOFRIC TEMPLE, and R. G. WILLIAMS, Esqrs., Barristers at Law. Part II. (completing the work). In royal 8vo.

Browning and Lushington's Admiralty Reports.—Vol. I. Part III.

Swabey and Tristram's Probate and Divorce Reports.—Vol. IV. Part II. (Completing the Series.)

Law Magazine and Review for May.—No. 49, United New Series.

Hallilay's Law Examination Reporter.—No. 10, for Easter Term, 1868.

THE LAW MAGAZINE AND LAW REVIEW.
(NEW SERIES.)

Published Quarterly in FEBRUARY, MAY, AUGUST & NOVEMBER, *at 5s.*

THE two QUARTERLY ORGANS of the Legal Public, and of those concerned in the administration and enactment of the Laws of the United Kingdom, have, since May, 1856, with great advantage, been amalgamated under one management—that of the Editor of the LAW MAGAZINE. From that time to the present, it has been the endeavour of the publishers to redeem the pledge then given, that this periodical should be rendered worthy of the support of the practising lawyer—whether barrister or solicitor—of the jurist, the legislator, and the magistrate.

No. 48, *of the United New Series, published in* FEBRUARY, *contains :*—

1. Corruption and Cost of Elections. The Corrupt Practices at Elections Bill. By W. D. Christie, late Minister at Brazil.—2. Remarks on the Court of Appeal in Chancery.—3. Law of Evidence: Incompetency on the Ground of Interest. By F. R. Falkiner, Q.C., of the Irish Bar.—4. Parliamentary Government in England.—5. Administration of the Poor Law.—6. Law Reform and the County Courts.—7. Oaths; their Utility Questioned. By Edward Gardner, LL.D.—8. Legal Ethics of the Fenian State Trials.—9. The late Edward James, Q.C., M.P.—10. Maritime Law. Events of the Quarter. Reviews of Books, &c.

₀ *An Annual Subscription of* 20s. *if paid in advance to the Publishers,* MESSRS. BUTTERWORTH, 7, *Fleet Street, London, E.C., will ensure the* LAW MAGAZINE AND LAW REVIEW *being sent postage free to any part of the Kingdom for the period of one year, or it may be ordered of any Bookseller.*

Communications for the Editor *may be addressed to the care of the Publishers, to whom also* Advertisements intended for insertion *should be sent.*

Imprinted at London,

nvmber Seuen in Flete strete within Temple barre,
whylom the signe of the Hande and starre,
and the Hovse where liued Richard Tottel,
printer by Special patents of the bokes of the Common lawe
in the seueral reigns of
Kng Edw. VI. and of the qvenes Marye and Elizabeth.

www.ingramcontent.com/pod-product-compliance
Lightning Source LLC
Chambersburg PA
CBHW021220300426
44111CB00007B/379